Oral Interpretation

ELEVENTH EDITION

Timothy Gura

PROFESSOR AND CHAIR,
DEPARTMENT OF SPEECH COMMUNICATION ARTS AND SCIENCES,
BROOKLYN COLLEGE OF THE CITY UNIVERSITY OF NEW YORK

Charlotte I. Lee

LATE OF NORTHWESTERN UNIVERSITY

Houghton Mifflin Company   Boston   New York

Publisher: Patricia A. Coryell
Executive Editor: Suzanne Phelps Weir
Sponsoring Editor: Mary Finch
Development Manager: Sarah Helyar Smith
Development Editor: Julia Casson
Senior Project Editor: Tracy Patruno
Manufacturing Coordinator: Carrie Wagner
Marketing Manager: Elinor Gregory

Cover photo: Rainer Binder/Getty Images

Credits appear on page 539, which is hereby considered an extension of the copyright page.

Printed in the U.S.A.

Library of Congress Control Number: 2002109471

ISBN: 0-618-30817-2

23456789-MP-08 07 06 05

CONTENTS

To the Student   xv
To the Instructor   xvii

PART ONE

Basic Principles   1

CHAPTER ONE   **A Beginning and an End**   **3**

Expect This!   **3**
Interpretation Requires Communicating   **4**
Interpretation Engages an Audience   **6**
    Ethical Responsibilities   7
    Technical Responsibilities   7
Interpretation Involves a Literary Work in
    Its Intellectual and Emotional Entirety   **8**
    Analysis: Content   9
    Analysis: Structure   9
Interpretation Celebrates a Literary Work in
    Its Aesthetic Entirety   **10**
Important Early Questions: Why Perform?
    Is this Acting?   **10**
Sources of Material   **13**
Intertextuality   **14**
Choosing Your Selection: Three Touchstones   **15**
    Universality   15
    Individuality   16
    Suggestion   16
    Applying the Touchstones   16
    The Sense of Death, Helen Hoyt   17
    I Felt a Funeral, Emily Dickinson   17
    Dulce, Deborah Sherman   18
Preliminary Analysis: Hoyt's Poem   **20**
    Universality   20
    Individuality   21
    Suggestion   21

Preliminary Analysis: Dickinson's Poem   22
Preliminary Analysis: Sherman's Story   23
Remember This!   25
Bibliography   26

CHAPTER TWO   **Analyzing the Selection**   **29**

Expect This!   29
Preparing the First Performance   30
Major Structural Components   31
   Denotative and Connotative Meanings   31
   Persona   32
   Locus   33
   Placing Action Out Front   35
   Climax   37
   New Words, Maury Yeston   38
Major Aesthetic Components   39
   Unity and Harmony   40
   Variety and Contrast   40
   Balance and Proportion   41
   Rhythm   43
Using the Tools   43
   Sample Analysis of a Story   44
   The Story of an Hour, Kate Chopin   44
   Sample Analysis of a Poem   49
   I Felt a Funeral, Emily Dickinson   49
Synthesis   55
   Rehearsing the Selection   56
   Excerpts and Introductions   57
Analyzing the Rehearsal and the
Performance   59
Remember This!   60
Selections for Analysis and Oral
Interpretation   61
   When I Heard the Learn'd Astronomer,
     Walt Whitman   61
   Sonnet, John Keats   62
   The Starlight Night, Gerard
     Manley Hopkins   62
   Desert Places, Robert Frost   63
   from *A Christmas Memory*, Truman Capote   64
   Ringing the Bells, Anne Sexton   65
   Dreaming, Amanda McBroom   66
   Homework, Peter Cameron   68

*Upon Learning That a Junior High School
Acquaintance Has Been Nominated for an
Academy Award,* Joanne Gilbert   74
How to Watch Your Brother Die,
  Michael Lassell   75
from *Harry Potter and the Sorcerer's
Stone,* J. K. Rowling   78
Bibliography   **81**

CHAPTER THREE   **Voice Development for
Oral Interpretation**   **85**

Expect This!   **85**
Relaxation Technique   **87**
Breath Control   **88**
  The Physiology of Breathing   88
  Breathing Exercises   89
Volume and Projection   **93**
  Control of Projection   93
  Focus of Projection   94
Pitch and Quality   **96**
  The Wild Honeysuckle, Philip Freneau   96
  from *I Hear America Singing,*
    Walt Whitman   97
Rate and Pause   **97**
Intelligibility of Speech   **99**
Dialect   **100**
Remember This!   **102**
**Selections for Analysis and Oral
  Interpretation**   **102**
  A Night at the Opera, William Matthews   103
  from *A Very Rigid Search,* Jonathan
    Safran Foer   104
  Confess, Early and Often, Jane Smiley   106
  Jabberwocky, Lewis Carroll   109
  from *The Little Girls,* Elizabeth Bowen   110
  Dover Beach, Matthew Arnold   114
  Back at the Ranch, Jay Allison   115
  Her Story, Naomi Long Madgett   118
  The Lesson, Toni Cade Bambara   119
  from *The Night Chant,* Navajo Ceremonial
  Chant, Translated by Washington
  Matthews   126

from *Blue Highways,* William Least
Heat Moon   126
The Voice You Hear When You Read Silently,
Thomas Lux   129
Bibliography   **130**

CHAPTER FOUR

Use of the Body in Oral Interpretation   133

Expect This!   **133**
Technique   **134**
Posture   **136**
Kinesics   **136**
Gesture   137
Muscle Tone   138
Performance Anxiety   139
Sense Imagery   **140**
Empathy   **143**
Using Your Body in Rehearsal   **145**
Eye Contact   **147**
**Analyzing the Rehearsal and the
Performance**   **148**
Remember This!   **150**
**Selections for Analysis and Oral
Interpretation**   **151**
The Second Coming, William Butler Yeats   151
Flying Finish, Bill Hayes   152
Ulysses, Alfred, Lord Tennyson   154
*Autumn Begins in Martins Ferry,
Ohio,* James Wright   156
from *Friday Night Lights,* H. G. Bissinger   157
The .38, Ted Joans   159
Still Life, Diane Ackerman   160
Girl, Jamaica Kincaid   161
Affirmative Action, Lucille Clifton   162
The Race, Sharon Olds   163
The Negro Speaks of Rivers, Langston
Hughes   165
Old Lady's Winter Words,
Theodore Roethke   166
from *Jarheads,* Anthony Swofford   168
from *As You Like It,* William Shakespeare   170
Admission of Failure, Phyllis Koestenbaum   171
Bibliography   **171**

PART TWO

Interpretation of Prose 173

CHAPTER FIVE

Style and Types in Fiction and Nonfiction 175

Expect This! 175
Style 177
  Paragraphs 178
  Sentences 179
  Speech Phrases 182
  Balancing Sentences 183
  Diction: The Choice of Words 185
  Tone Color: The Sounds of Words 186
  Rhythm in Prose 187
  Description 187
Types of Prose 189
  Factual Prose 189
  Personal Essays 190
  Journals, Diaries, and Letters 191
  Oral Histories 193
  Family Storytelling: The Tales of Everyday Life 194
  Folktales 195
  Short Stories and Novels 197
Remember This! 198
Selections for Analysis and Oral Interpretation 198
  from *June Recital,* Eudora Welty 198
  from *The Joy Luck Club,* Amy Tan 200
  from *The Revolution Remembered,* John C. Dann, Editor 203
  from *Everything We Had,* Al Santoli, Editor 205
  from *The Seacoast of Despair,* Joan Didion 207
  from *I Know Why the Caged Bird Sings,* Maya Angelou 211
  from *Women's Diaries of the Westward Journey,* Lillian Schlissel, Editor 213
  The Makeup Artist, Dana Tierney 217
  To Austin Dickinson, Emily Dickinson 219
  from *Working,* Studs Terkel 221

KEEP OUT! (*A Boy's Bedroom*),
   Lynda Barry   224
Bibliography   227

CHAPTER SIX   **Narration**   **231**

Expect This!   231
Who Is Telling the Story? Point of View   233
  First-Person Narrators   234
  Second-Person Narrators   236
  Third-Person Narrators   238
What Is Going on Here? Action and Plot   241
What Sort of People Live in This Story?
  Character   242
What Are They Saying to Each Other?
  Dialogue   243
Creating Character   245
Where Is All This Taking Place? Setting   247
Cutting and Excerpting   248
Analyzing the Rehearsal and the
  Performance   250
Remember This!   253
Selections for Analysis and Oral
  Interpretation   253
  The Prison, Bernard Malamud   254
  A & P, John Updike   259
  Snow, Ann Beattie   265
  from *Sula,* Toni Morrison   267
  from *The Lost Language of Cranes,*
    David Leavitt   269
  Popular Mechanics, Raymond Carver   272
  Jacob's Chicken, Miloš Macourek   273
  The Key to My Father, Harlan Coben   275
  from *The Conversion of the Jews,*
    Philip Roth   280
Bibliography   285

PART THREE

Interpretation of Drama   287

CHAPTER SEVEN   **Solo Performance of Drama**   **289**

Expect This!   289
The Nature of Drama   290

Why Perform Drama? 291
What Is the Difference Between Acting
  and Interpretation? 292
Structural Elements of a Play 294
Analyzing a Scene 295
Working a Scene 299
Rhythm 306
Style 307
Scenography 308
Putting It Together 309
Remember This! 310
Selections for Analysis and Oral
  Interpretation 311
  from *Fifth of July*, Lanford Wilson 311
  from *Fires in the Mirror*, Anna
    Deavere Smith 313
  from *Othello*, William Shakespeare 320
  from *She Stoops to Conquer*,
    Oliver Goldsmith 323
  from *Flyin' West*, Pearl Cleage 327
Bibliography 331

CHAPTER EIGHT **Technique in Drama** **335**

Expect This! 335
Technique in Interpretation 337
  Control 338
  Memorizing Lines 339
  Setting the Scene 340
Properties 341
Embodying Characters 343
Coordinating Bodies and Voices of
  Characters 344
  Gender Roles 344
  Clothes and Voice 345
  Special Situations 346
Physical Contact 347
Interplay of Characters 348
  Picking Up Cues 349
Physical Focus 350
  Methods of Focus 351
  Angle of Placement 352
The Reading Stand 355
Cutting and Excerpting 356

Analyzing the Rehearsal and the
  Performance 357
Remember This! 359
Selections for Analysis and
  Oral Interpretation 360
    from *Sunday in the Park with*
      George, Stephen Sondheim 360
    from *Curse of the Starving Class,*
      Sam Shepard 362
    from *Romeo and Juliet,*
      William Shakespeare 365
    from *Betrayal, Scene Five,*
      Harold Pinter 367
    from *Death and the King's Horseman,*
      Wole Soyinka 373
Bibliography 378

PART FOUR

Interpretation of Poetry 379

CHAPTER NINE **Language of Poetry** 381

Expect This! 381
Poetic Content 383
Classification of Poetry 385
  Narrative Poetry 385
  Lyric Poetry 387
  Dramatic Poetry 389
  Music and Dramatic Poetry 391
Figurative Language 392
  Allusions 393
  Figures of Speech 394
  Sensory Appeals 396
  To Autumn, John Keats 396
Poetic Syntax 398
Tone Color 400
Titles 402
Analysis and Poems 403
Remember This! 404
Selections for Analysis and Oral
  Interpretation 404
    Power, Corrine Hales 404
    The Windhover, Gerard Manley Hopkins 406
    The Toast, Susan Minot 407

Wild Grapes, Robert Frost   407
Spring is like a perhaps hand,
  e. e. cummings   410
The House Was Quiet and the World Was
  Calm, Wallace Stevens   411
Nikki-Rosa, Nikki Giovanni   411
Saving Memory, Mary Stewart Hammond   413
Mid-Term Break, Seamus Heaney   414
On Sleeping Together, Barbara Howes   415
Talking in Bed, Philip Larkin   416
The Hospital Window, James Dickey   416
Most Like an Arch This Marriage,
  John Ciardi   418
First Grade, William Stafford   418
Preface to a Twenty Volume Suicide Note,
  Imamu Amiri Baraka   419
Bibliography   **420**

CHAPTER TEN   **Structure of Poetry**   **423**

Expect This!   **423**
Why Study Prosody?   **425**
Kinds of Verse   **426**
The Stanza   **429**
The Line   **430**
  Foot Prosody   430
  Scanning the Poem   431
  Stress Prosody   433
  Syllabic Prosody   433
  Open the Gates, Stanley Kunitz   433
  Interpreter's Use of Line Lengths   435
Cadences   **437**
Rhyme   **440**
Intention and Performance   **442**
Analyzing the Rehearsal and the
  Performance   **443**
Remember This!   **444**
Selections for Analysis and Oral
  Interpretation   **444**
  One Art, Elizabeth Bishop   445
  The Waking, Theodore Roethke   445
  Do Not Go Gentle into That Good Night,
    Dylan Thomas   446
  Journey of the Magi, T. S. Eliot   447
  The Magi, Louise Glück   448

A Blessing, James Wright   449
Heartbeats, Melvin Dixon   450
*Who Among You Knows the Essence of
     Garlic?* Garrett Kaoru Hongo   451
My Last Duchess, Robert Browning   453
*The Kilgore Rangerette Whose Life Was
     Ruined,* Cynthia MacDonald   455
from *Fatal Interview,* Edna St. Vincent
     Millay   457
Cinderella, Anne Sexton   457
Cinderella's Story, Mona van Duyn   460
Today Is a Day of Great Joy, Victor
     Hernandez Cruz   463
from *Horses Make a Landscape Look More
     Beautiful,* Alice Walker   464
Bibliography   **465**

PART FIVE

Group Performance   469

CHAPTER ELEVEN   **Group Performance of Literature**   **471**

Expect This!   **471**
Readers Theater   **473**
     Differences from Familiar Theatrical
          Conventions   474
     Technical Cautions   476
Chamber Theater   **478**
     A Sample Chamber Theater Script   479
Group Performance of Compiled Scripts   **485**
Other Kinds of Literature   **488**
     Concrete Poetry   488
     Film Scripts   489
**Directing the Group Performance of
     Literature**   **489**
Some Concluding Cautions   **492**
**Analyzing the Rehearsal and the
     Performance**   **493**
Remember This!   **495**
**Selections for Analysis and Oral
     Interpretation**   **495**
     from *The Metamorphoses,* Ovid   496
     from *The Caucasian Chalk Circle,
          Section III,* Bertolt Brecht   500

40-Love, Roger McGough   503
Forsythia, Mary Ellen Solt   504
Apfel, Reinhard Döhl   505
from *Oedipus the King,* Sophocles   506
Unforgiven, David Ray   510
After the Overdose, Robin Robertson   513
from *Sunday Bloody Sunday,*
  Penelope Gilliatt   514
Bibliography   **517**

APPENDIX A   **Building and Presenting a Program**   **519**

Selecting Material   **519**
Unifying the Program:
  A Traditional Method   **520**
Using Multiple Readers, Different
  Types of Literature, and Multimedia   **521**
Staging the *New York Times*   *522*
Other Options   **524**
Adapting to the Audience   **525**
Timing   **526**

APPENDIX B   **A Brief History of Theories of Interpretation**   **528**

Bibliography   *536*

Acknowledgments   538
Subject Index   545
Author and Selection Index   550

TO THE STUDENT

IN THE PAGES THAT FOLLOW WE INVITE YOU TO DO UNFAMILIAR THINGS. You will be embodying and evoking stories, poems, and plays. You will attempt to communicate the world you discover in those works to the world of your audience. In fact, you engage in such activities all the time and have been performing since before you began to speak. You have already accumulated a great deal of useful experience with audiences. So, all of the real-life part of you will be enormously useful in this study. In the process, if you undertake the exercise with conviction, you will learn not only about the texts you perform and the texts others perform, but about yourself as well.

Of course, this book can teach you many ways to embrace literature and give life to its performance. In Part I we describe a method of detailed analysis that helps you develop your own responses to literature and provides the foundation on which you can build your performance. We guide you through each step of your first performance. In Part II we look at prose and narration. Drama is the focus in Part III, where we suggest approaches to character and scene analysis and offer helpful tips about creating characters and scenes vividly in the minds of your audience. Part IV deals with poetry. Group performance is discussed last—in Part V—because the success of any group depends on the preparation and technical skill of every individual involved in it.

If you are already a performer, you will find that the method we encourage increases your flexibility in handling various kinds of material. If you are new to performing—or if you have spent time studying literature by other methods—you will find that performance before an intelligent audience is a valuable test of the thoroughness and accuracy of your study. You will also discover why others find performing so challenging and enjoyable. Whatever your previous experience in performance, this book asks questions. Sometimes the answers will lead you to other questions. In Chapters 2, 4, 6, 8, 10, and 11 we ask a series of questions to help you analyze your own rehearsal and performance and the performances of your classmates. These questions are not rules or recipes; they are ways to help you think carefully and precisely about all the choices that made your performance uniquely yours. Additionally, each of the selections is followed by one or two questions that ask you to consider a central performance problem in that text. We offer practical suggestions for solving specific problems and a wide choice of literary selections at various levels of sophistication and degrees of difficulty.

One final word about the selections at the ends of the chapters: Each is substantial and challenging. Each contains clear clues to help you perform. Some may even "remind you of something you did not know you knew," as Robert Frost has written. But if one selection seems difficult, don't give up on it right away; walk around a bit in its shoes before dismissing it. You may be surprised at how much you discover about yourself as you reach out to understand the literature. In that respect (as in many others), what you derive from *Oral Interpretation* will depend on how much of yourself you are willing to invest. Let us know how you make out.

TO THE INSTRUCTOR

IF, AS THE GREEKS TAUGHT US, THE ONLY CONSTANT IS CHANGE, THEN *Oral Interpretation* has become "something of great constancy." So markedly does the world we inhabit today differ from the world Charlotte Lee knew when, at midcentury, she began the journey, that she surely never envisioned most of the changes we now take for granted. Like the world that is its home, *Oral Interpretation* has changed, but Charlotte Lee would greet this edition like the old friend it is—updated, to be sure, and vigorously lively, but resting comfortably on the foundations she constructed more than half a century ago. And perhaps the most heartening development of the twenty-first century for Charlotte would be the explosion of interest in the performance of literature—from traditional theatrical events to innovations such as poetry "slams," autobiographical performances, stagings of nonfiction—because most make use of principles consistently at the heart of this book.

One thing that hasn't changed is the title: *Oral Interpretation.* Such consistency does not divorce the study detailed here from the broad scope of the field. On the contrary, it reiterates an abiding commitment to the firmest possible foundation for students beginning to study performance. Only through careful analysis and appreciation of a literary work of art can a student begin to fulfill the requirements and responsibilities of a performing art. Thus, as in earlier editions, art continues to unify the concerns of this book. True, literary works of art are always in part the result of the social and political forces that shape them, but they are not simply sociological, political, or anthropological tracts. Although these pages often refer to the various ways in which the texts— and even the nature of the "text" itself—can be viewed, the methods and materials in this edition remain focused on the student whose early experience with the performance of literature will prepare him or her for the wonders open to all who read and perform literature.

This edition maintains the principles on which all its predecessors rested. Thus, analysis guides appreciation and, more immediately, serves as the indispensable first step in any rehearsal. The process of analysis described here emphasizes the writer's relationship with the reader, the reader's response to the writer, and the resulting position that the interpreter takes in re-creating the experience, regardless of the form the writer has chosen. In addition to an awareness of the work's complexities, performance demands a voice and body flexible enough to suggest all the subtleties that close analysis reveals. And the only reliable yardstick to measure the success of the performance remains the text itself. Like all the earlier editions, this edition insists that the destination of all interpreters and critics—regardless of how or where they perform—must remain that which they begin with: the literature.

Readers familiar with the recent editions will recognize the format. For example, the six sections called "Analyzing the Rehearsal and the Performance," which appear in Chapters 2, 4, 6, 8, 10, and 11, still contain practical hints for describing and evaluating student performances and conclude with several general questions that guide students to analyze their performances and those of classmates. These suggestions probe the concerns raised in the surrounding pages. Similarly, the headnotes to each selection and the specific questions that follow address the kinds of problems beginning performers are likely to confront. Moreover, they point to the most important postperformance question: How fully did *this* performer communicate *this* text to *this* audience?

Even veteran users of the book will discover pervasive innovations in this new edition. For example, each chapter now begins with a brief set of behavioral objectives ("Expect This!") to alert the reader to the kinds of knowledge, comprehension, application, analysis, synthesis, or evaluation that the chapter expects. In addition, each chapter concludes with "Remember This!"—a brief review of the principal issues explored in detail. Chapter 1 ("A Beginning and an End") has been extensively revised to accommodate students with little performance or literature background. We first define the oral interpretation of literature (to understand *what* we are undertaking) and then explore the rationale (to understand *why* we analyze and perform). Confronted by many new responsibilities, often beginning students understandably conflate interpretation and acting, and this issue is discussed (but it will never be settled). Chapter 2 ("Analyzing the Selection") walks a student through the process of preparing and presenting the first performance. The theoretical and analytical issues (locus, persona, the intrinsic factors) and the practical performance issues (placing action out front, some characteristics and types of introductions) are explored. Moreover, sample analyses of stories and poems put into practice the theories introduced earlier.

Throughout the book other changes expand coverage on vocal production and physical activity and gesture in performance—each with a number of practical exercises for students to explore both in class and in rehearsal. And, consistently, the Eleventh Edition continues the tradition of placing the oral interpretation of literature within the broader communication and performance studies community. Thus, with a reliable foundation based on analysis and a careful, step-by-step introduction to the first performance, with useful guides to developing voice and body, students explore the chapters on prose—Chapters 5 and 6—which draw attention to the kinds of stories we tell in life, to the experiences we have already polished in countless settings, and to the issues raised when a performer "appropriates" another's words. Chapters 7 and 8 explore the dynamics of drama by examining classic plays as well as more recent innovations in theater performance, all the while retaining a strong focus on how the solo interpreter can create believable characters and meaningful interactions. The chapters on poetry—Chapters 9 and 10—continue to stress the structural foundations of even the most contemporary experiments. And the final discussion of the ways in which groups perform texts—Chapter 11—includes attention to compiled and media-influenced performances while retaining the essential elements of Readers Theater and Chamber Theater. Building individual programs occupies Appendix A, and the history of the field—the foundations on which current trends rest—fills Appendix B.

The Eleventh Edition—about the same size as its predecessors—offers much more material than can be covered comfortably in a single term. However, an instructor can assemble a rigorous course by selecting from among the options offered. If students begin with the introductory material in Part I, they will acquire the fundamental principles of analysis, selection, and evaluation of literature; with the book in hand, students then apply these principles to a story and a poem. Students especially in need of work in voice and movement can consult the chapters that deal with each of these concerns. These early chapters establish principles common to all kinds of literature and complement modal, rhetorical, or dramatistic approaches. Note that some topics are discussed in more than one chapter. For example, dialogue is essential to performing narration and therefore is introduced in Chapter 2 and discussed in Chapters 5 and 6, but it is also crucial to performing drama, and therefore dialogue is more elaborately handled in Chapter 8. The same can be said of characterization. We indicate where concepts overlap and direct students to examine other chapters for further elaboration. Thus, what may seem like redundancy in some chapters in fact permits flexible use of this edition.

The continuing value of intertextuality still informs the way new selections have been added. Frequently this edition asks students to focus on the dialogue between one text and another; to probe the ways in which the interpretation of one text relates to other, often quite different, texts; and to examine how the performance process useful in one case may (or may not) inform the performance process necessary in others. Particularly in the discussions of group performances and of planning programs, this edition asks students to encourage the broad "conversation" that occurs when one work of art confronts another.

Just as new people enliven the conversations we have, you and your students will encounter for the first time in this edition literature by J. K. Rowling, Jonathan Safran Foer, Anthony Swofford, Susan Minot, and Harlan Coben. Philip Roth's "The Conversion of the Jews" returns in response to popular demand. Works by familiar authors debut in this edition: an engaging poem by Robert Frost and a charming letter Emily Dickinson wrote to her brother. None of these new works is simple, but all challenge and reward conscientious students. When you use the selections, your students will be able to consult the work *after*—never during—the performance, and the text itself guides the discussion. When only the performer knows the text, the audience can neither measure achievement nor provide useful suggestions. Ambitious students have access to thoroughly revised bibliographies, incorporating the most current theory and practice, all deftly annotated by Matthew Spangler, University of North Carolina at Chapel Hill.

No book lasts more than two days unless it touches its readers directly. Textbooks, perhaps, have a longer lease on life (if more tenuous grasp!) than most novels or essays, but *Oral Interpretation* has survived more than half a century chiefly because of two essential intangibles for which its authors have never been responsible: the interest and enthusiasm of gifted students confronting works of literature that move them deeply, and the spark that only a dedicated teacher can give any body of knowledge. This edition seeks to guide, encourage, and challenge its users in the hope that if our suggestions seem inadequate, students and teachers together will devise a newer, fuller, more expressive response.

Colleagues across the years and from throughout the country have substantially improved this edition, and some of their contributions merit special mention. John Anderson's innovative and imaginative reading and performing improves the discussion of theory and selections. The sensible and affectionate questions and suggestions of Beverly Whitaker Long, Mary Frances HopKins, Mary Susan Strine, and Judith Espinola (to name four out of many) refined theories and practices that inform this book. Frank Galati's fecund imagination never withers, never stales. Rose Ortiz, Eileen Hendrickson, and Michael Powell brought inquiries and suggestions directly from their classes.

This Eleventh Edition also benefits from the wise counsel of

E. Teresa Choate, *Kean University*

Diane DeFranco-Kling, *Sterling College*

Denise Elmer, M.S., *Angelo State University*

Dr. Myra G. Gutin, *Rider University*

Julia Lenardon, *Michigan State University*

E. M. Lewis IV, *Winona State University*

David M. Lucas, Ph.D., *Ohio State University*

Heather McMahon, *Indiana University*

Theresa Mitchell, *Emporia State University*

No one who writes about performances writes alone. From the moment Charlotte Lee conceived this book until the moment you read it, one abiding community of scholars has generously, unfailingly, inspiringly contributed to the theory and the practices it describes. The National Communication Association (NCA), as it is now known, is the professional home of the most innovative and rigorous collaboration of scholarship and practice any writer could desire. In particular, its journal *Text and Performance Quarterly* and the members of the Performance Studies Division, through their annual convention presentations, have shaped, refined, developed, and encouraged most of this edition in countless unrecognized ways. Here, now—and with deep gratitude—we acknowledge their great-hearted advice and exemplary leadership.

PART ONE

Basic Principles

The sense of danger must not disappear:
The way is certainly both short and steep,
However gradual it looks from here;
Look if you like, but you will have to leap.

W. H. Auden

"Leap Before You Look"

CHAPTER ONE

A Beginning and an End

By the end of this chapter, you should be able to:

- Explain the relationship between art and communication.
- Cite several different kinds of performance you encounter in daily life.
- Assess the means by which interpreters communicate with audiences.
- Define the intellectual, emotional, and aesthetic components of a literary work.
- Provide at least two reasons for performing literature.
- Describe three touchstones for selecting literature to perform.
- Show how universality, individuality, and suggestion operate (or fail to operate) in a poem or a story.
- Undertake the first of your analysis-and-rehearsal sessions.

Interpretation is the art of communicating to an audience a work of literary art in its intellectual, emotional, and aesthetic entirety.

Selections Discussed in This Chapter

In explaining some topics, we mention texts that are reprinted either within the chapter itself or at the end of a chapter. Use the guide below for quick reference to acquaint yourself with selections you may not fully recall.

Author	Title	Location
Helen Hoyt	"The Sense of Death"	Chapter 1, page 17
Emily Dickinson	"I Felt a Funeral"	Chapter 1, page 17
Deborah Sherman	"Dulce"	Chapter 1, page 18
Anne Sexton	"Cinderella"	Chapter 10, page 457
Mona van Duyn	"Cinderella's Story"	Chapter 10, page 460

Interpretation Requires Communicating

Interpretation is the *art of communicating* to an *audience* a work of *literary art* in its *intellectual, emotional,* and *aesthetic entirety.* This chapter explains each of the highlighted terms in this definition, and helps you prepare for your first performance. Art implies skill in performance. No sooner have we used the word *performance*—and suggested the study of it—than a constellation of allied concerns and interlocking interests emerges. *Performance* means different but related things in different contexts. Actors and actresses and singers give performances, of course. We speak of how we performed on a test, how a car performs after a tune-up, and how well a friend performs under pressure. In class you take notes, raise your hand to ask a question, sit quietly while a bore drones on and on, turn in papers on the due date: in short, you *perform* as a student. When you and your romantic partner are together in front of the fire on a snowy evening, you practice a different set of performance behaviors (we suspect). When you're at work, your performance comprises still other actions, language, gestures, and manners.

In fact, all of us perform every day: as student, parent, child, spouse, roommate, short-order cook, waitress, or swimmer. The vast array of performance behaviors you have already mastered will help you in this course. In fact, you'll find yourself reexecuting familiar performances and discovering and inventing new ones when confronting a work of literature.

In this book we spend most of our time on the performance of literature. We don't suggest that this is the only performance useful or desirable for study. On the contrary, we refer often to other kinds of performances—performance art, performance as argument, political performance, ethnographic performance, and storytelling—as we discuss the skills you'll need and will acquire for the performance of literature. With the help of anthropologists, social scientists, and communications specialists, we can view performance from a number of different perspectives. We can observe how other cultures value and exploit performance in important rituals. We can watch how our families enact their own unique rituals (Thanksgiving dinner, say, or important birthdays and anniversaries) with the care of a performance. We can analyze the performance of everyday conversation and note how carefully we pause to search for a word when we want to avoid offending a significant other. These studies of performance hone our observational skills and make us more aware of the strategies authors use to make their texts "like life" (or they show how far other texts oppose accepted patterns). From just such opportunities the entire field of *performance studies* emerged, and we encourage you to consider pursuing those avenues if you find this path congenial.

Performing *literature* alerts us in new and vital ways to the kinds of performance that surround our daily lives. We also think it enriches the way we study all kinds of performance. After all, you watch the U.S. Open differently if you've tried to play tennis; you taste food differently if you've also tried cooking; and you probably see an object differently when you've seriously tried to sketch, draw, or paint it. We perform literature because it changes the literature for us, and it changes us in the process.

Every art requires discipline and training in the use of the appropriate tools. The writer of a literary selection is a creative artist who orders ideas, words, sounds, and rhythms into a particular form, putting them into written symbols. The interpreter, in turn, brings personal experience and insight to bear on the printed symbols and assumes the responsibility of re-creating this written text into a new "text": the performance. This process demands thorough analysis, painstaking rehearsal, and strict discipline in the use of voice and body.

You may have been puzzled for a moment when we referred to the performance as a "text." For many scholars today, *text* does not simply refer to words or symbols printed on a page, but rather to any "site of meaning," or to anything that conveys meaning to a viewer or a reader. Thus, songs are texts; paintings are texts; a billboard, some graffiti, a dance—each conveys meaning and thus each is a text. Most often *text* refers to words ordered and printed on a page, and we use *text* when we want to convey the larger relationship between words and other signs and symbols of meaning.

The writer (indeed, the maker of any "text") is a creative artist. You, the interpreter, are also a creative artist. You select and respond to a meaningful example of literary art to share with your audience. From the moment you appear in front of your audience, through whatever you evoke and embody, you create a *new* artistic product. It obviously owes much to the author, but in fact it exists because of your creative act as the interpreter. That's why some compare the oral interpreter's art to the art of the musician playing the work of a composer.

The truest and finest art can be disarming in its seeming simplicity. The audience sees only the result, not the means to obtain the result. Technical display is not art. We may be exhilarated by the technical proficiency of a pianist who presents the notes of the music with awesome facility and accuracy. However, just as music is more than a sequence of notes, literature is more than a string of words. Art requires the systematic application of knowledge and skill to achieve a desired result. The desired result in interpretation is in part precisely the same as that in any other phase of speech: communication. In your case, communication includes communion, the *sharing* of an *experience*, first with the work performed and then with an audience.

If an audience says "What a beautiful voice!" or "What graceful gestures!" the interpreter has failed. When the audience's attention is held by the impact of the material presented, the interpreter has succeeded. But this unobtrusiveness on the part of the interpreter does not result from casual preparation or from a feeling that because the literature is the important thing, you need do no more than face the audience, open the book, and open your mouth. On the contrary, your effectiveness is the result of a preparation so thorough and a technique so perfectly coordinated that the audience cannot see the wheels go around. Great art only *looks* simple.

Interpretation Engages an Audience

... *communicating to an audience* ... Perhaps you have already completed other courses in other aspects of communications: public speaking, interpersonal communications, small-group or family communications. What you learned in those courses about conveying messages to audiences will help you here. And the presentational skills you honed in those courses—sufficient volume, clarity of diction, control of pitch and rate, for example—will be used in every class of this course. And if you have studied how the medium affects the message, you will already recognize that the interpreter *transforms* texts in the act of performance. Doubtless, as your study progresses, you will find many other similarities to the communication studies you have already completed, and you will be able to compare your responsibilities in, say, a public-speaking assignment with your responsibilities as an interpreter.

Given today's technology, an audience may consist of one person or several million. No matter what the size or nature of the audience, your responsibilities as an interpreter are the same. You should communicate as skillfully as possible what is on the printed page and your response to it, making intelligent use of every detail to achieve the organic whole. The listeners' understanding, their mental and emotional responses to the content and to the form in which it is presented, depend to a large degree on your ability to discover these elements and project them satisfactorily in their proper relationship.

How do you communicate these elements to the audience? By vocal and physical suggestion. You use voice and body, in conjunction with an alert and informed mind. Interpreters train their voices and bodies to respond to the particular requirements of a work of literature. They strive to eliminate anything that may distract the audience from experiencing the text. They are aware of the effect of posture, muscle tone, and general platform presence, and they try to devise physical action that aids communication without calling attention to itself. Interpreters work with their voices during practice periods so that they may be heard and understood. They need flexibility in range, force, stress, and volume if they are to bring out whatever strength and beauty that author has achieved through the sounds and relationships of the words. Their concentration on communicating, on sharing, the material at hand must be strong and continuous. During early rehearsals, interpreters stop to work on difficult segments, as pianists repeatedly finger complicated passages or dancers work through a complicated series of steps in slow motion or basketball players practice free throws. In later rehearsals, when the selection is thoroughly in mind and has indeed become a part of them, interpreters turn their attention outward to an imagined audience.

We need to mention here two very different issues, both of which we'll explore more fully later. Like all other communicators, interpreters presenting texts to audiences need to remember their *ethical responsibilities* and their *technical responsibilities.*

Ethical Responsibilities

What does it mean to appropriate, or become, another's "voice"? Anthropologists reporting fieldwork observations have explored this question for some time, but it applies equally well to performers of more traditional texts. Interpreters represent the words of others in a manner that respects the life of the source. Interpreters carefully embody and evoke the "other"—that is, a text written or spoken by someone else—because that respect enables the audience to come closer to the authentic experience. We all recognize that several paragraphs from a story won't encompass all of the story's scope, but we endeavor to be sure those paragraphs are consistent with the story's shape and reach. Similarly, if we perform the words of another human being—a letter, say, or a memoir, or a recollection—we take care that those words are presented with the respect we hope greets our own words.

Technical Responsibilities

On the technical side it's likely that beginning performers in particular will confront performance anxiety (or communication apprehension, stage fright, "butterflies"). Every performer knows the experience— and it doesn't happen simply in front of a class. (Remember getting tongue-tied when you tried to ask someone special out on a date? Or that nightmare job interview when *everything* went wrong?) The tension of performance can never be totally eliminated, but it can be usefully channeled into your performance. It takes time and effort, but you *can* master it.

The most common remedies for performance anxiety are rehearsal, concentration, and memorization during preparation, and relaxation prior to performance. Sometimes an interpreter chooses to memorize selections completely; other times, not. Whatever you choose, you must concentrate on embodying and sharing literature rather than on the act of remembering the words. If you choose not to memorize completely, you must be free enough of the physical text to concentrate on communicating with the audience rather than on reading the words. If you have analyzed the material in detail, *put it back together again,* and practiced conscientiously, you will likely have your selection so firmly in mind that you'll need to glance at the page only occasionally—and will probably have fewer (or less troubling) encounters with stage fright. And, before beginning your performance, focus your mind and your breathing on a steady, regular pace. Relax your muscles. Exhale. Begin. (Stage fright and relaxation techniques are discussed at greater length in Chapters 2 and 4.)

Interpretation Involves a Literary Work in Its Intellectual and Emotional Entirety

. . . a work of literary art in its intellectual, emotional, . . . Your concern is to communicate the total effect of the literary work of art. This does not mean that you should present only complete works or that you cannot use excerpts. Neither does it mean that the listeners will always receive the full impact of a complex poem. How fully they respond depends in part on their backgrounds and their familiarity with the work.

Listening is a wholly time-bound activity. In rehearsal you are able to go back and reread certain passages to clarify their relationship with the whole. You know where the entire selection is going and how it gets there. Your audience, however, has only a fraction of a second to hear words, to translate them into ideas, and to add associations and responses, which are guided by your skillful vocal and physical suggestions. Thus, if you understand only half of what you hope to share with the members of your audience, their chances of comprehension and response become minimal. All the various qualities that contribute to the total effect of a selection must be held in their proper relation to the whole.

For purposes of analysis, it is convenient to break a work down into its parts. We may conveniently speak of content and structure, of logical meaning, and of emotive quality. Separating literature into these elements, however, is useful *only* as a way of getting at full understanding. Content and structure do not exist as separate entities; they work together to form one organic whole. Examine them in relation to each other. Then, always put the material back together after each step in your analysis of it.

Analysis is one of the most difficult aspects of interpretation, but also one of the most rewarding. We refer to it frequently in the chapters that follow. As soon as you have discovered one or more clues given by the author, reread the entire selection *aloud*, seeing how what you have just discovered works within the whole. Rehearse aloud even before you are ready to pay particular attention to vocal techniques.

Analysis: Content

Although it is difficult to isolate and to discuss separately certain aspects of a work of art, a full appreciation of the whole is enhanced by careful analysis of the particulars. To begin, distinguish the content from the structure of a piece of literature. In the broadest sense, *content* has to do with what is being said, *structure* with the way it is said. Content has two aspects. The first is the *intellectual*, or *logical*, aspect, which is simply what the material says. Analysis of content involves an intellectual understanding of the meanings of the words and the relationships between words and groups of words. The other aspect of content is its *emotive* quality, the capacity of both meaning and sound to arouse pleasure or pain, to stimulate the reader and listeners to activity or repose through association. Words seldom have meaning independent of association, or emotion-arousing qualities without meaning. Consequently, *for all purposes except analysis,* the logical and emotive qualities of a work of art can never be divorced. Understanding takes place simultaneously on the intellectual and emotional levels, so you must find out exactly what the author is saying, experience emotionally what is said, and communicate the total response—intellectual and emotional—to the audience.

Analysis: Structure

Structure involves the way a writer has organized the expression of ideas, his or her choice of words, and the relationships of the parts to each other and to the whole. Structure is concerned with the manner of expression, ranging from simple lucidity to the most complex ornamentations of language. The structure of prose, for instance, includes the patterns of phrases and individual sentences, as well as the effect created by several sentences in combination. The structure of drama involves the rhythm of the characters' speeches, their choice of words, the structure of the sentences, and the interrelationship of the speeches, scenes, and acts of the entire play. The structure of poetry includes all the patterns, the sounds of words in combination, stanzaic structure, scansion, rhyme, and length of line. These elements are examined in more detail as these types of writing are discussed in later chapters.

Interpretation Celebrates a Literary Work in Its Aesthetic Entirety

. . . aesthetic entirety . . . The phrase "aesthetic entirety" embraces all the qualities that must be considered to appreciate a piece of writing as a successful work of literary art. These elements should always be evaluated in relation to each other and to the whole.

Aesthetics deals with the theory of the fine arts and the individual's response to the arts. Although the field of aesthetics includes all areas of art—and in this book we talk about painting, music, and film—our primary concern is literary art. As a study, aesthetics concerns itself with the ordering of the parts of a work of art, as well as with the response of the beholder. In our case, you the interpreter and your audience are the beholders. The interpreter is also, obviously, a creator. At the moment, we need to be aware only that there are aesthetic standards for the way that parts work together to create a literary whole. It is this whole, with all its elements intact and correlated, that we are sharing with the audience.

Important Early Questions: Why Perform? Is This Acting?

Students beginning a course in oral interpretation often aren't quite sure what to expect and may be entering the course inexperienced in what it will demand. Typically, these students ask, "What is the point of this course? What are the benefits of performing literature? What's in it for me?" There are as many answers to these questions as there are interpreters, but most responses are some combination of these ideas:

- Oral interpretation asks you to do something *with* literature beyond analyzing it.

- Oral interpretation asks you to polish your voice and body and to develop your presentational skills.

- Oral interpretation asks you to share with others some experiences that are important to you.

- Oral interpretation helps you to understand yourself.

At first, this book and the course of study it proposes may strike you as strange. After all, for most of our lives we have been taught to read silently, not to move our lips, and to get through the material as rapidly as possible. You have probably been asked to look at poems and stories and plays much as you examine rocks in the geology lab or dissect frogs in biology. You have likely been encouraged to point out metaphors, tragic flaws, or third-person narrators, as if literature were simply a bunching together of all these elements. Too often, looking at literature this way leads to study *around* the work and ignores much of the excitement or delight you may have felt when you were reading.

In contrast, interpretation starts out by asking you to speak up. We ask you to experience what the characters are undergoing. Not only can you put to use all those "facts" you learned in other literature courses, but you can engage yourself at the same time. You select literature you respond to, and in the process of carefully analyzing it and rehearsing it, you come to understand how it lives and how (and often why) it moves you. You can then communicate what you have discovered to the audience, and the audience is doubly enriched because it sees and hears a performance that is not simply the words of the poet and not simply the interpretation of the informed performer, but a rich blending of the two.

To communicate in this way, you use your body and your voice—and in the rehearsal process you develop the flexibility of both of those instruments. The moment we refer to using your body and voice to create the literature in the audience's mind, and mention rehearsals, some students respond, "Oh, now I understand—you want me to act it out!" Other students look puzzled because, as they say, "I thought all we had to do was read the story out loud." Between these two approaches, however, you will find the real pleasure and enlightenment of this course. Oral interpretation asks that you embody fully the literature you have chosen, using vocal and physical techniques that actors and actresses also use.

"Acting it out" suggests dramatizing every tiny gesture, restricting or eliminating the narrative posture, and miming crucial events. This kind of presentation can remove audience members from participating in the literature because the performer leaves no room for them to occupy the story or the poem. Similarly, if you "read the story out loud," you are not likely to be much concerned about the audience, either. You won't establish the crucial placement of the literature out in front of the audience. Merely "reading out loud" may leave you tied to the printed text, droning on in unvaried cadence regardless of the speaking character, and depriving audience members of the clues in body and voice they need to flesh out character, attitude, or emotional state. This kind of performance leaves no room for an audience because it closes them out of the text. (We examine the acting versus interpretation debate much more extensively at the beginning of Chapter 7.)

Happily, the ground between these two choices is wide and accessible. Performing literature asks you to share your excitement about a text with your audience. If you were lucky enough to be read to when you were a child, you probably remember how transporting that experience was. It's good to keep that image in mind now, many years later. Often, you were seated on, say, your parent's lap, the book itself in front of you, held in place by the very arms that held you secure. You heard the sounds aurally, of course, but you felt them, too—in the breathing of the reader. You saw the illustrations and imagined how they reflected the real life you knew. You entered the story in part because the "story" surrounded you. Even today those "surrounding" performances are the most compelling because they allow performer, text, and audience each to contribute fully to the encounter, each to draw life from the others, each to emerge more richly satisfied because of the encounter. The more you perform in class, the more you watch other students perform, the more readily will you be able to recognize how performer, text, and audience collaborate to establish the impact of the event.

What use can all this be to you? We think this course can change your life, because we have seen it happen for many students over many years. Doubtless, you will respond that we are anything but objective judges in this matter. Although that is true, most people find their deepest fulfillment in hours away from work: with their families, with their significant others they discover (and come to crave) something that enhances their sense of being human. Literature has always responded to this craving; it was thriving long before any formal study of it. We think interpretation is the fullest way to enjoy stories, poems, and plays, because it allows us to share our experiences and our pleasures with others, and it allows others to join us in creating that experience.

Some performers work on a large, expansive scale—just as some painters prefer to work in acrylics on yards of canvas. Other performers, with different resources, may choose to work on a smaller scale, just as some artists prefer to work in watercolors on small sheets of paper. In the case of painters and sculptors, size does not signify achievement, and the same is true of performers. A quadriplegic performer is no less capable than a dancer of embodying a poem; the richness of the achievement is geared to your reach, not your grasp, and the ability you have to use fully all the skills and possibilities at your disposal. All performers confront rocky patches when they rehearse, but not all performers face the same pitfalls. You discover and expand your unique potential in rehearsal because that, in part, is what the audience wants to see and hear.

Happily, the rewards don't stop there. When we perform a poem, story, or play, a part of us becomes a part of the literature. We move out of ourselves and try to look at life from the perspectives of the people in the story, try to see the world through another's eyes. When we go back to being ourselves, a little bit of us will have changed in that encounter. For a few moments, we will have lived in someone else's skin. Our world desperately needs more people who try to understand how others feel and think. We believe peacemakers have always been encouraged by precisely that motive. That is why, in the largest sense, the outcome of any performance course is not merely a series of performances, although they are indispensable to our knowing ourselves and others. The final goal of such a course—and, we think, the best reason to pursue oral interpretation—is the most annealing act of which humans are capable: understanding.

Sources of Material

Today, interpreters choose from an almost unlimited range of material. They may use traditional literary forms such as prose, poetry, or drama in epic, lyric, or dramatic modes. Alternatively, they may choose to perform works that do not fit into traditional classifications: autobiography, letters,diaries, oral history, interviews, personal narrative, ethnographic research, concrete poetry, and even conversation. This freedom of choice is a distinct advantage for an experienced interpreter, but it may present the beginning student with a problem. From the wealth of available material, where do you begin to select something?

The first question, obviously, is where to look. The selections at the ends of chapters in this book offer a wide variety of material and should be helpful. However, part of your assignment may be to find your own material, and literary anthologies are a good place to begin your search.

Anthologies are especially valuable to the beginning student of interpretation because they offer a wide selection in a single volume. You will find collections of all types of prose: essays, short stories, humorous and satirical pieces, biographies, letters, diaries, and even novels. You will find poetry classified by kind (such as lyric, narrative, humorous, or didactic), by period or nation (such as Elizabethan, Russian, or contemporary American), and by subject or spirit (such as poems about nature, love, religion, protest, or patriotism). If you decide to try drama, you will find many volumes that include either entire plays, both one-act and full-length, or selected scenes. Other anthologies cut across these classifications, presenting, for example, chronological surveys of a particular type of literature or examples of regional writing. Of course, there are volumes of selected works by individual authors. Dozens of useful anthologies are available in inexpensive editions in any bookstore or in hardback editions in any library.

After your first few assignments, you will have a better idea of the kind of material that appeals to you and where to look for it. You might begin by asking yourself, "What am I most interested in?" Is it the city or the country? Is it some exotic part of the world or your own home state? Perhaps you are much more interested in people than in places. What kind of people? In what circumstances?

Intertextuality

You probably recall the story of Cinderella, the beautiful young girl who is abused by her wicked stepmother and nasty stepsisters but nevertheless manages to win the prince's hand. The story is everywhere: in children's books, in poems, in plays, in musicals, in films, on television. As we described the story just now, you probably conjured up associations of your own experiences with the story. If, in a completely unrelated tale, you find a character referring to the plight of another as "a real Cinderella story," some of your earlier associations would doubtless color your response to this new reference. Such interaction between tales (we like to call it a "conversation") enriches our responses and has come to be known as *intertextuality*.

Contemporary literary theorists find that such conversations between texts occur commonly. When one poem "talks" with another poem, both poems profit because each resonates differently when in the company of the other. Just as two paintings hanging next to each other on a wall can clash or blend, so can two stories when they are compared. Remember, the stories don't relinquish their individual integrity, but when they are perceived together, the range of impressions and experiences expands. Such expansion also, obviously, informs the rehearsal and performance process.

Postmodern theorists revel in such rich potential in part because resonating texts (and their performers) expand our awareness and consciousness of the interdependence of art and life. You need not subscribe to this notion to enjoy the ways in which poems talk with stories: most of the selections you'll find throughout this book can be displayed profitably next to another text (in the same chapter or elsewhere in the book). Try your own responses to two poems about Cinderella, Anne Sexton's "Cinderella" and Mona van Duyn's "Cinderella's Story," both works that take a decidedly contemporary look at events that, for some of us, seem locked in a fairy-tale past. (The poems can be found at the end of Chapter 10.)

Choosing Your Selection: Three Touchstones

To choose material because of its interesting subject matter does not imply that you should make no effort to evaluate its literary worth. On the contrary, throughout this book the evaluation of material through analysis is a constant concern.

Most of us are attracted first to a piece of writing by what it says—its content. As we become more sophisticated, we appreciate more fully the complex relationship between meaning and structure. Knowing what you like is not as important as establishing criteria for evaluating a literary work's success or failure. Understanding why you do or do not want to study a certain selection is important. You don't have to like it, but you may learn to respect its qualities as good literature.

Let us assume that you have made a tentative choice of material or have narrowed down the possibilities to two or three selections whose content is equally appealing. Before making a final decision, consider three factors as touchstones: *universality, individuality*, and *suggestion*.

Universality

Universality does not mean that the material will immediately appeal to all persons regardless of their intellectual or cultural backgrounds. It means, rather, that the idea expressed touches on a common experience. The emotional response it evokes is one that most readers (and listeners) have felt at one time or another: love or hate, hope or fear, joy or despair, confronting death or reclaiming life—what William Faulkner called "the human heart in conflict with itself."

Literature draws its material from life, but literature is not exactly life. A writer selects motivations, imposes order on the flux of human existence, and gives us clues that direct us in relating our own experiences to the order he or she has chosen. Even deliberately distorted events can have relevance to our existence. When writing has universality, you will respond to it, using your background and experience. When you communicate all the levels of meaning to those in the audience, they in turn will have a basis for identification with their own experiences.

However, you need not have undergone an event to test your own experience against that recorded by the author. Even without an identical experience, you certainly have known, to at least some degree, joy or sorrow, fear or yearning, hope or love—emotions that the recorded experience calls forth. Although your own reaction to the specific situation might not be the same as the author's, strive to open yourself. Adapt your own remembered event to make your response relevant to, and respectful of, what the author has recorded.

Individuality

The second touchstone of good writing is *individuality*—the writer's own fresh approach to a universal subject. This quality is revealed in choice of words, images, and method of organization. You cannot decide whether the author has handled the subject with individuality unless you have some acquaintance with a wide variety of literature. After some time and experience, you will be able to recognize that individuality results in large part from the author's selectivity and control and is reflected in both content and structure. We take a closer look at the element of individuality when we compare three works later in this chapter.

Suggestion

The subtlest and most rewarding writing is characterized by *suggestion.* The readers are left with something to do, with room to inhabit the work. This does not mean that the writing is obscure. It means, rather, that the author has chosen references and words that allow the readers to enrich the subject matter from their own backgrounds. There must be, however, enough clear signals for the readers' imaginations to follow. Frequently, considerable analysis is necessary to find and use these signals properly. Once the possibilities for relevant association are realized, however, the writing continues to grow in meaning and in emotional impact for both the interpreter and the audience. We touch on this aspect, too, in our later comparison.

Applying the Touchstones

The three touchstones—universality, individuality, and suggestion—are closely related. They enhance and balance each other in effective writing. The author's idea has been drawn from an experience that all people are able to share. The method of expressing that idea is different from the method used by other authors. The associated ideas and responses point the way for the reader's imagination to follow and allow for continuing enrichment through the various levels of meaning. Sometimes these three qualities are not present in equal force in a selection, nor is it necessary for them to be. If any one quality is totally absent or patently weak, however, you will do well to look elsewhere for material that interests and moves your audience.

To illustrate, let us look at two brief poems, one by Helen Hoyt and one by Emily Dickinson, and a short story by Deborah Sherman. Each work contains an intensely personal experience with death and is written in the first person.

The Sense of Death
HELEN HOYT

Since I have felt the sense of death,
Since I have borne its dread, its fear—
Oh, how my life has grown more dear
Since I have felt the sense of death!
Sorrows are good, and cares are small,
Since I have known the loss of all.

Since I have felt the sense of death,
And death forever at my side—
Oh, how the world has opened wide
Since I have felt the sense of death!
My hours are jewels that I spend,
For I have seen the hours end.

Since I have felt the sense of death,
Since I have looked on that black night—
My inmost brain is fierce with light
Since I have felt the sense of death.
O dark, that made my eyes to see!
O death, that gave my life to me!

Before we look at the second poem, a word of explanation may be in order. Emily Dickinson did not usually give her poems titles and in fact never readied them for publication in our current sense of giving a final version to a printer or publisher for public consumption. Consequently, some of her poems have several versions, each differing in punctuation and even in word choice. Dickinson's use of capital letters and dashes is unique. She frequently capitalizes all the nouns and sometimes uses dashes instead of commas. The dashes seem compatible with interrupted or suspended thought units.

I Felt a Funeral
EMILY DICKINSON

I felt a Funeral, in my Brain,
And Mourners to and fro
Kept treading—treading—till it seemed
That Sense was breaking through—

And when they all were seated,
A Service, like a Drum—
Kept beating—beating—till I thought
My Mind was going numb—

And then I heard them lift a Box
And creak across my Soul
With those same Boots of Lead, again,
Then Space—began to toll,

As all the Heavens were a Bell,
And Being, but an Ear,
And I, and Silence, some strange Race
Wrecked, solitary, here—

And then a Plank in Reason, broke,
And I dropped down, and down—
And hit a World, at every Crash,
And Got through knowing—then—[1]

The three touchstones we have been discussing do not occur solely in poetry. Many obvious differences distinguish those two poems from the story that follows: length of sentences or, indeed, of the selection itself; arrangement by stanza or by paragraph; very different word choice. More telling are the similarities the works share. This story—as concerned with death and its impact as are Hoyt's and Dickinson's poems—is tightly controlled by its first-person narrator. There is no doubt that the story demonstrates a sense of death, no doubt that its narrator feels a funeral quite keenly. Can you decide why the author chose such a simple title?

Dulce

DEBORAH SHERMAN

I can still hear the pick hitting the caliche, Lambert breathing hard, sweat at the edge of his gray hair. I knew that the difficulty in breathing wasn't just from the steady swinging of the heavy pick, nor was it because of his age. He said later that he couldn't cry and yet his eyes were red and I could see the tears.

When I saw Dulce lying there, the blood still wet, a small pool on the pavement, I couldn't touch her or move her. I ran to get Lambert, the one person who Dulce would never leave. "Damn it," he said. "Son of a bitches." Slowly, with Paula Sue at his side, bowlegged and tired, he walked down to the highway. I didn't have to watch him to know that he touched every part of Dulce to make sure that it was really true. He came so quietly up the driveway, carrying Dulce the way one carries a butchered lamb, holding the front paws in one hand and the back in the other, her head hanging by his legs. Gently, caressing her, he laid her on the grass by the ditch where he had buried Trixie a few years ago, then he went to put

---

1. Dickinson's manuscript shows an earlier version in which the last line reads "And Finished knowing—then—."

on his boots and get the pick and shovel. When he came back he looked at me. "Do you think that animals do things like this because they don't want to live?"

"No, Lambert," I said, "it was just an accident, a stupid accident."

"Maybe they're unhappy and don't want to live."

"No, Lambert."

"When Barbara and I first lived here, the house was right over there, and this tree was our tree." He kept digging. "When I put Trixie here I told Trixie this is your tree now. Now it's Duls' too." He got on his hands and knees, loosening a big rock. "Do you think this is wide enough? Enough room for her feet?"

"Ya, I think so, Lambert."

But he widened it anyway.

"Do you think this is deep enough? I made it deeper than this for Trixie."

"Ya, I think so, Lambert."

But he made it deeper anyway.

"Paula Sue," he said, "go get the hoe, the little one, in the shed."

His breathing was becoming labored, strained. Dulce was lying beside him. It was almost as if she were asleep, out in the pasture keeping him within view at all times even if she dozed off, waiting for him to finish whatever little chore he was occupied with. He looked down at her. "Do you think those who are supposed to die suffer later for being kept alive past their time?" The pick stopped. "When it's your time it's your time."

"I don't know, Lambert," I said, watching him climb slowly out of the hole.

When Paula Sue came back with the hoe he got in the hole again and carefully scraped the earth from the corners, making the surface flat and smooth. "Go ask Barbara for some rags, I know she has some," he said quietly, so slowly, so gently.

Paula Sue walked up with an old blanket. "It has pee on it though."

I looked at the blanket. "That's okay."

"No, that's not good for Duls. Barbara has other ones. Go ask her."

"It's okay, Lambert," I said. But Paula Sue had already dropped the blanket and was walking toward the house.

This time when Paula Sue came back, she brought the old patchwork quilt that used to be her bedspread. Lambert put down his hoe and looked at the quilt. A neighbor had made it. "It's too good."

"No," said Paula Sue, "it's got lots of tears in it."

I smiled, watching her pointing out each tear. "It's okay, Lambert."

He took the quilt and laid it in the hole, smoothing out each wrinkle. And then he went to Dulce, his hand petting her, automatically. He picked her up gently, as if afraid of disturbing her, and lowered her onto the blanket. "Let's clean up your nose, Duls," he said, as he took his glove and wiped the blood from her face. He wrapped her in the blanket.

"Are you ready, Lambert?" I said. He just nodded, and I started shoveling the dirt over her as fast as I could. Ma had come out to see her lowered into the hole and as the colors disappeared she said that it was only right that Dulce have that quilt.

Lambert bent down and laid his hand on the earth, "Bye Duls, bye Duls." He picked up his worn tools and, dragging the old blanket that Canoncito had peed on, he walked back up to the house.

When I came around the corner, he was on the portal, sitting on the bench, his head bent down, his hands holding Dulce's white bowl. He just sat there, not moving. All the other dogs were at his feet, as if they knew that something had happened.

"Just a few minutes ago. We were in the shop and Duls was lying there on the chair, the old chair from Denver. We shared a cheese, what do you call it, a cheese ball. We ate together, Duls and me. Just a few minutes ago."

None of these works denies the fact or the effect of death, but they present this universal experience in markedly different ways. In her poem Hoyt talks about the aftermath of having sensed death, probably physical death. Dickinson is talking about the period of the *sensing*. She probably is also talking about despair, a kind of spiritual death so numbing and soul shattering that it became a "funeral" in her brain (although some others think she is talking about the transitions of spiritual life). Sherman partakes of and observes the impact of death on a family. All three women use straightforward language and sentences. Hoyt draws definite, even moralistic, conclusions; Dickinson merely describes the experience and draws no conclusions. Sherman recounts events and lets us create the impact.

Preliminary Analysis: Hoyt's Poem

Hoyt obviously wishes to place death in sharp contrast to a resulting acute appreciation of life. Half of the lines are concerned with death and half with life, and this comfortable balance belies the distinct impression that this poem is more about death than life.

Universality

"Since" for Hoyt means "after," as well as "because." She repeats her title in six of the eighteen lines of the poem and approximates it by parallel construction in three more. Such repetition could be most effective in creating a driving, insistent impact. The phrase "felt the sense of death," however, does not cut into our consciousness with much force. The word "sense" implies recognition or perception. It is quite possible to "feel" a "perception," and Hoyt's perception of death is characterized by "dread," "fear," "forever at my side," "the hours end," "black night," and "O dark." Each of these references has been used in the same connection for so many centuries that it has become trite. And Hoyt gives us no time or incentive to establish an individual identification with what the "sense" of death was for her, or indeed might be for us.

Individuality

Admittedly, Hoyt tells us that the experience of sensing death led her to a new value of life. Unfortunately, her references to life are equally vague and familiar. Life is referred to in "grown more dear," "Sorrows are good," "cares are small," "world has opened wide," "hours are jewels that I spend," "inmost brain is fierce with light," "eyes to see," and "gave my life to me." "Sorrows" is so general and inclusive and allows for such a weight of personal association that we cannot fix on the paradox of sorrows being "good" before we are whisked on to "cares" that are "small." Presumably, this line is intended to set up a balance, but it is not entirely successful, partly because of the inclusiveness of "sorrows" and "cares," and partly because even small cares are not "good," as she asks us to believe sorrows have become. Even the singular form of "sorrow" and "care" would at least have allowed us to accept these terms in a more abstract sense and hence to identify more easily with the emotional implication. There is, too, a disturbingly familiar ring in the phrase "hours are jewels" and in the verb "spend." One does not "spend" jewels: the association here is strained. The phrase "inmost brain is fierce with light" is probably the strongest line of the poem, particularly since the poet has set it carefully against "black night." But, again, it only goes back to the already quite familiar refrain.

Suggestion

With little individuality in either the selection of details or the way they are expressed, *suggestion* is also poorly established beyond the poem's basic premise. After one comes close to death, life becomes more precious. You probably knew that before you read the poem. The words and figures of speech lack the force, and freshness, that would make us think about something important in an entirely new way. We aren't even permitted much room to enter her world.

Hoyt's poem permits, even encourages, consideration of the touchstones in a discrete, almost unrelated, manner. Because the poem's components seem more like lists than cohesive units, it is easy to separate its parts for analysis. Effective literature, in contrast, rarely affords you such an easy path; just like life itself, literature proves that there is a clear and discernible difference between simple and simple-minded.

To watch the touchstones masterfully coalesce provides another lesson in why great poetry transcends the commonplace. Consider Dickinson's poem.

Preliminary Analysis: Dickinson's Poem

Dickinson also begins her poem with "I felt," but the clear positioning of the event in past time and its implied completion put it firmly in perspective. She introduces the extended metaphor of a funeral service, but the impressions she creates densely refuse to be simplified. In this respect—and in many others—what makes Dickinson's poems universal is what makes them individual, and what details she provides suggest the complex characterizations she creates. For example, that funeral service carries a complex weight of values and images. We are bombarded by associations of grief, dignity, ritual, the presence of the body, and a grim formal finality. To "feel" a funeral goes beyond merely attending one, and a funeral "in my Brain" goes still further. We immediately encounter, then, a *universal* subject, death, approached in a new and *individual* way, and the details described *suggest* a spiritual death that destroys the life of the senses, crushes hope, and even denies the power of the soul.

Now consider how carefully Dickinson weaves these characteristics together.

We are given time to develop associations. Our focus is sharpened by the mourners going to and fro and by the sound they make "treading—treading." We then are returned to sensation in the last line of the first stanza. Consider two superficially contradictory interpretations. On one level, "Sense" may be taken to mean the mind bending under the strain of the "treading." This interpretation is strongly suggested by the word "Brain" in the opening line. But Dickinson may also mean that awareness—"Sense"—had become so acute that the sensation was unbearable. These two interpretations are not mutually exclusive, and both can operate well here in a deliberate, disturbing, but highly functional ambiguity.

The balancing of the funeral service with the sensation felt in the brain continues to the last line of the third stanza. It is held together and kept vivid by a strict chronological progression, as well as by constant references to sound, already prepared for by "treading—treading." Sound reaches an almost unbearable intensity as "Space—began to toll," and it becomes overwhelming in the opening lines of the next stanza. Our attention is snatched from this climax of sound by "and Silence," which by its very contrast is equally deafening.

At the same time, the mourners and the pallbearers disappear abruptly, leaving the senses "solitary." The experience does not stop there, however. In a swift downward pattern, suggesting a lowering into the grave and much more, the breaking "Plank in Reason" suggests a wealth of associations and adds still another dimension to the horror of the drop "down, and down—," which culminates in the highly graphic "hit" and "Crash" in the next-to-last line. The repeating "and" involves us in this swift and helpless dropping.

The last line, like several of the others, offers the reader room to think and moves on more than one level. "Got through" may mean "finished" with a mortal type of knowledge. It also may imply having "broken through" into a superhuman, mystical type of knowledge that is possible only after death or a great spiritual crisis. The "—then—" also functions on more than one level. It completes the chronological progression; it terminates the immediate recorded experience; it teases us with a hint that there was more. A skilled performer can convey this multiplicity of meanings to the audience.

During the discussion of Dickinson's poem, we refer to a "deliberate . . . ambiguity." *Ambiguity* is sometimes confused with lack of clarity, but here the term means "having more than one possible meaning, all of which are relevant and congruent within the organic whole of the piece of writing." Ambiguity may result in some obscurity, but it also affords the reader access to the several levels of the work. The kind of ambiguity we have been discussing is one of the richest sources of suggestion.

Hoyt uses outworn references to suggest the terror of death and the glory of life. Dickinson's images stir the senses. At the same time, she engages our minds by juxtaposing unexpected and strongly suggestive words. Almost any line serves as an example, but two of the most striking are the opening line and the reference to "a Plank in Reason." Much more can be said about Dickinson's poem—and we say some of it in the next chapter. At its best, then, suggestion takes us beyond the poem without taking us out of the poem. *Suggestion* and *individuality* go hand in hand to help establish *universality*.

Preliminary Analysis: Sherman's Story

Deborah Sherman's short tale is small without being little. In raw, unembroidered language—no jewel-like hours here—she explores the ways four people are affected by the death of a pet. Elaborate language is not needed to elevate this event for its participants. In coming to understand the relationship of the narrator, Lambert, Paula Sue, and Ma, we understand not only how much Dulce affected their lives but how much they rely on one another. The decisions each person makes are made with the help of the others, and all decisions are directed not to the dead animal but to the world they shared when Dulce was alive, when even something as insignificant as a "cheese ball" could be meaningful because of its being shared. This short story phrases big questions in small ways.

One need not have lost a dog to recognize the *universality* of this tale. Lambert has difficulty phrasing his fears, but it is clear that his questions are on the minds of all the family. Similarly, they all search for the best way to remember their dead. This effort to survive Dulce's death suggests some of the ways that they will undertake life after Dulce. This sentiment seems to fill their little community, for by the end of the story, "All the other dogs were at his feet, as if they knew that something had happened." Communities joining to bury their dead and beginning to live again is, sadly but splendidly, one of the oldest stories told, a story told as often to mark a group's having "Got through knowing" as to survive a present moment of pain. *Universal* is a small word to describe the tale.

Yet this is a striking family group, and their lives are probably not like yours. A farm in the Southwest might seem unfamiliar to urban dwellers or coastal residents. That setting establishes the *individuality* of the family. Note the images of Lambert in the fields with Dulce "out in the pasture keeping him within view at all times even if she dozed off" and Lambert's carrying the dead body "the way one carries a butchered lamb." Deaths commonly occur on this ranch, but this death is different. What would suffice will not do: Lambert makes the grave wider, though it need not be, and deeper, though it is big enough. He dedicates the tree to Dulce, as he dedicated it to a predecessor, Trixie. In each event, in detail after detail, Sherman shows us how this death uniquely affects these lives—and, in its small way, us.

This simple story can, in its decidedly simple way, raise complicated and complex questions, so that what unfolds before us *suggests* echoes and shadows much larger than a dead dog on a ranch. As they did for Dickinson, sounds provide potent images for Sherman. The tale begins with the sounds of the pick hitting the caliche, which is hard clay earth—that hard, striking sound with a rhythm like a heartbeat. That sound echoes Lambert's breath and tantalizingly contrasts with Dulce's silence. What do we learn about the relationship between master and pet when Lambert picks the dead Dulce up, "his hand petting her, automatically"? Or watch his hands, again, "holding Dulce's white bowl" and remembering the simple sharing moments before her death. These glimpses of the fleeting moments of life—what Hoyt describes so broadly as "Sorrows are good, and cares are small" (although Lambert and Paula Sue are not likely to consider this loss either good or small)— help us understand the ways in which death interrupts, startles, and isolates those who live on.

In our discussion of these three works, we have not even touched on rhythm, sound patterns, the structural complexities of verse, and narrative strategies. We explore these matters in succeeding chapters when we focus on analysis. Our intention here was to illustrate how the three touchstones—universality, individuality, and suggestion—can operate (or fail to operate) within a text and to sketch the kind of useful analysis that begins the process of performing.

REMEMBER THIS!

At this point, if you have followed all of our discussions about performing literature, you are likely to be eager to try it for yourself, and the next chapter is designed to help you, step by step, to experience the process, from earliest analysis to preliminary voicings to advanced rehearsals, culminating in you performing for your classmates. Although it may seem that all the important work lies ahead, it is crucial that you keep the key elements from this chapter in mind:

- Performance naturally occurs all the time in daily life. Be on guard to spot it when you encounter it, because watching others perform tells us a lot about performing ourselves.

- Watch carefully to see how voice and gesture affect audiences in real life. What is it about the salesclerk's nasal whine that so annoys you? When the sanitation man wipes his forehead, what is it that makes you know how tired he is?

- Scrutinize very carefully the literature you consider performing, and choose a challenging poem or story over one that you think will be easy.

- Remember to select literature that provides a place your audience can inhabit, a distinctive perspective on the world, and an opportunity for diverse experiences to share common ground.

Now, let's begin!

Bibliography

The following brief list of resources can assist students and instructors. The websites provide practical resources for students in search of material. The books are theoretical in nature, providing direct and indirect connections to the theory and practice of oral interpretation today.

For the Student

Searching for material to perform always challenges students. Needless to say, we recommend the selections at the end of the chapters in this book. Here are two online sources students have found useful:

www.bibliomania.com
> *More than two thousand literary works available for perusal and downloading.*

www.gutenberg.net
> *More than sixty-two hundred complete electronic books available for perusal and downloading.*

For the Instructor

Aristotle. "The Poetics." In *The Basic Works of Aristotle,* edited by Richard McKeon, 1455–87. New York: Random House, 1941.
> *One of the cornerstones of aesthetic theory. In this essay Aristotle sets out definitions of representation, character, and identification in performance.*

Butler, Judith. *Excitable Speech: A Politics of the Performative.* New York: Routledge, 1997.
> *Through an analysis of hate speech, Butler shows how performance can resignify language with new meanings and thereby open up possibilities for agency and identity.*

Carlson, Marvin. *Performance: A Critical Introduction.* New York: Routledge, 1996.
> *A detailed and accessible overview of performance as it applies to the social sciences, history, and contemporary history.*

Geiger, Don. *The Sound, Sense, and Performance of Literature.* Glenview, IL: Scott, Foresman, 1963.
> *The performer of literature is the focal point of this slender book, which is built on the premise that oral interpretation is itself an act of criticism.*

Goffman, Erving. *The Presentation of Self in Everyday Life.* New York: Doubleday, 1959.
> *A foundational text in viewing everyday life as performance.*

Ong, Walter. *Orality and Literacy: The Technologizing of the Word.* New York: Routledge, 1982.

A detailed, structural account of the relationship between oral and written language.

Schechner, Richard, and Willa Appel, eds. *By Means of Performance: Intercultural Studies of Theatre and Ritual.* Cambridge: Cambridge University Press, 1990.

A diverse collection of essays from top scholars in the field theorizing about performance.

Turner, Victor. *From Ritual to Theatre: The Human Seriousness of Play.* New York: PAJ Publications, 1982.

Turner describes key concepts, such as "social drama," "liminality," and "communitas," useful for an understanding of performance as social reflection and intervention.

Winn, James A. *The Pale of Words: Reflections on the Humanities and Performance.* New Haven, CT: Yale University Press, 1998.

A stimulating proposal for humanists and performance scholars to join forces.

It may be the case that you expected what you are hearing now. But even in that case you expected something different.

Peter Handke
"Offending the Audience"

CHAPTER TWO

Analyzing the Selection

EXPECT THIS!

This chapter describes a step-by-step process to help you prepare your first performance. By the end of this chapter you should be able to:

- Differentiate between denotative and connotative meanings in the text you have chosen to perform.

- Describe the persona in your chosen text.

- Characterize the major aspects of locus operating in the text.

- Show how the climax functions in the text.

- Explain the effects of the intrinsic factors (unity and harmony, variety and contrast, balance and proportion, rhythm) in your chosen text.

- Use the sample analyses (of a story and of a poem) to plan your own analysis of the text.

- Select and employ appropriate rehearsal strategies tailored to the text you have chosen to perform *and* to your performance experience.

- Plan an appropriate introduction for the text.

You cannot perform what you do not know, and you cannot shape your rehearsal until you understand the shape of what you are rehearsing.

Selections Discussed in This Chapter

In explaining some topics, we mention texts that are reprinted either within the chapter itself or at the end of a chapter. Use the guide below for quick reference to acquaint yourself with selections you may not fully recall.

Author	Title	Location
Deborah Sherman	"Dulce"	Chapter 1, page 18
Maury Yeston	"New Words"	Chapter 2, page 38
		(continued)

Author	Title	Location
Kate Chopin	"The Story of an Hour"	Chapter 2, page 44
Emily Dickinson	"I Felt a Funeral"	Chapter 2, page 49
Walt Whitman	"When I Heard the Learn'd Astronomer"	Chapter 2, page 61
Anne Sexton	"Ringing the Bells"	Chapter 2, page 65
Amanda McBroom	"Dreaming"	Chapter 2, page 66
Peter Cameron	"Homework"	Chapter 2, page 68
Joanne Gilbert	"Upon Learning That a Junior High School . . ."	Chapter 2, page 74
Michael Lassell	"How to Watch Your Brother Die"	Chapter 2, page 75
Stephen Sondheim	"Finishing the Hat," from *Sunday in the Park with George*	Chapter 8, page 360

IN CHAPTER 1 WE USED THREE TOUCHSTONES — UNIVERSALITY, individuality, and suggestion—to examine two short poems and a story that appear on their surfaces to be about the same thing. Our discussion revealed many differences among the selections. It also presents a starting point for interpreters to learn to choose a selection.

Preparing the First Performance

You cannot perform what you do not know, and you cannot shape your rehearsal until you understand the shape of what you are rehearsing. This chapter will help you as you prepare your first performance. First, we explore the major structural components of a work of literary art: the denotative and connotative meanings of the words, the ways in which the words are put together to achieve their central purpose, the agents of speaking, and the relationship between the speaker and the world of the work. Next, we look at how the major aesthetic components of a work of literature operate together to enrich the experience of the performer and the audience. To help you through this segment, we explore a story you may not know and a poem we examined briefly in Chapter 1. Your selection will probably have many different features, but when you choose a selection, you'll have the experience of knowing what to look for and where to find it. Finally, we apply all we have discovered by carefully rehearsing the selection. Synthesis sometimes seems more difficult than analysis, but the real challenge is to embody and evoke all that you have discovered, and to be open and ready for discovery during the rehearsal process itself.

Major Structural Components

Once you've selected the text that most interests you, thoroughly investigate everything within that particular piece of literature. You should know precisely what the author has given you. Accept responsibility for discovering and making proper use of the author's organization and method of presentation. Only when you fully understand the author's achievement can you decide how to use your own technique to create the experience for the audience.

Denotative and Connotative Meanings

First, of course, find out precisely what the literature is saying. You may easily understand the general meaning of a selection and yet find some specific lines or phrases that are not entirely clear. If so, look up the unfamiliar words and references. The word or allusion is there because, for the author, it is not *almost* the right word, it is *precisely* the right word. Consequently, you cannot hope to comprehend the author's full purpose with only a vague idea of the definitions or connotations of the words. In fact, an idea may be distorted if you mistake the full meaning of a word or phrase.

The dictionary is, of course, the first source to consult. The dictionary gives primarily *denotative* meanings—what a word means *explicitly*. For example, it defines *funeral* as "the ceremonies held in connection with the burial or cremation of the dead." But, of course, we all know perfectly well what the denotative meaning of *funeral* is. As we look at the word in Emily Dickinson's poem in Chapter 1, however, a cluster of associations grows out of our experience with *funeral*. Gradually, the word begins to mean more than its bare dictionary definition. That "more" is the *connotative* meaning: suggestions of associations and overtones that go beyond the explicit, or denotative, meaning.

These associations are a crucial part of what *we* bring to the text, and they represent our relationship (and experience) with the concept. In New Orleans, African American funerals are often marked by loud processions with boisterous music to send the deceased on a unique journey.[1] In contrast, you may have experienced funerals as somber,

---

1. See the vivid *Rejoice When You Die: The New Orleans Jazz Funeral* by Leo Tuchet and Vernel Bagneris (Baton Rouge: Louisiana State University Press, 1998) for a lively discussion and photographs.

moist-eyed affairs. Successful writers provide enough clues to the way the word should be taken that the connotative meaning is "negotiated" between you and the author. But remember that connotation requires "in *addition* to," not "instead of."

Moreover, connotation is essential to both the emotive part and the logical part of content. When the narrator in "Dulce" (the short story in Chapter 1) says that Lambert carried Dulce "the way one carries a butchered lamb," we recognize that "butchered" is associated with meat prepared to be eaten. When the word is coupled with "lamb" (with all its implications of gentle innocence), we respond viscerally to this image of the dead dog. Sherman chose those words precisely because they presented the image she wanted her narrator to convey, colored in language sympathetic to the narrator's stance.

Closely allied with connotative meanings is the function of *allusions*, or references to persons, places, or events (real or mythological) that call up relevant associations. Lambs, for instance, have complex reverberations in the Judeo-Christian tradition, and thus, the narrator's description of Dulce also conjures up other slain lambs we may have encountered, not simply in literature but in the Scriptures (the paschal lamb) and in music ("Worthy is the Lamb that was slain") or film (*The Silence of the Lambs*). Allusions, then, also unlock the intertextuality of the works that engage us.

Once you have made sure of the full meaning of the words, the interpreter must then examine the organization of ideas. Most material divides rather easily into three parts: the introduction, or lead-in portion; the body of the material; and the conclusion, or tying-up unit.

Usually, the body of the material contains the author's main point. Within each unit, however, there are key sentences or phrases on which the logical and emotional progression depends. They may contain a new idea or another aspect of an idea introduced previously. The interpreter should know the position and function of each key so that it can be clearly established in the minds of the audience in its proper relationship to all the other phrases and sentences and to the whole unit.

Persona

One good way to understand the shape of a work is to discover who narrates it. *Persona* (plural form, *personae*) refers to the speaker, the one who relates the experience in a text, whether the text is fictional or true, poetry or prose, dramatic or nondramatic. It would be convenient to say that the *persona* and the author are the same, but this isn't the case. True, the speaker may closely resemble the author in thought and attitude (as is often the case in lyric poetry, such as the Dickinson poem), but more often the persona will differ significantly from the author.

Authors, as creative artists, do not simply repeat the world they inhabit; rather, they use the world they know to create a new world that in important ways may resemble the world we inhabit, but in more important ways follows only its own rules.

This is not so different from what we do in the everyday performance of our lives. We have numerous personae: student, child, parent, lover. These personae share some characteristics, but at different times we highlight some elements and soft-pedal others (or, at least, we hope we do: consider a lover who acts like a parent).

In drama, obviously, there may be many speakers, and although all are under the control of the author, the speaking character's motivation and reactions will arise from the dramatic situation and from his or her relationships with other characters. In some cases one or more characters may seem to speak directly for the playwright, indicating a particular attitude toward the world, human nature, or the events of the play. Such a character may even resemble the playwright in biographical details or may share an immediate concern or a general interest with the playwright. For example, Stephen Sondheim is a composer and lyricist, not a painter, but he, too, must "finish the hat"—because it's what all artists do (see the end of Chapter 8). Amanda McBroom dreams, but she need not have the same dreams as the speaker of her "Dreaming" (see the end of this chapter).

Whether in poetry or prose, the narrator's voice is clearly the controlling voice, telling us what we need to know about background and plot progression. The narrator may even be a character in the story and involved directly in the events; in this case he or she speaks in his or her own persona as that character, as in Deborah Sherman's "Dulce" or in Peter Cameron's "Homework" (at the end of this chapter).

In lyric poetry the persona is often the poet speaking. Of course, poets change their minds and their moods. They may create a thinly veiled mouthpiece to express their ideas or reactions. Indeed, this capacity contributes to what makes a poet's voice distinctive and inimitable. But we cannot simply say, however tempting it may be, that a poem represents a poet's point of view. Most good poets are a lot more complex than even their richest poems, just as there is a lot more to you than what you do in one performance.

Locus

Once you know *who* is speaking, determine from what vantage points the persona speaks. *Locus* refers to the physical and psychological positions from which the speaker relates the events to the audience. The persona may be inside the events—like Michael Pechetti in Cameron's "Homework." The persona may be watching the events from the side, pointing out important factors we might otherwise overlook or explaining important background to us—like the narrator in Sherman's "Dulce." The persona may be far enough away from the events (in time, geography, or distance) to reflect on the long-term impact of the events—like the narrator in Kate Chopin's "The Story of an Hour" (later in this chapter). Therefore, understanding a persona will always be—in part!—a matter of understanding the physical vantage point, or physical place, from which the speaker views the actions and addresses the audience. First, determine as much as you can about that *physical* place—for example, you were standing on the southwest corner of Main and Hudson when the truck collided with the bus. Then try to describe the *psychological* place the persona occupied—you were thinking about buying a lottery ticket and didn't look up until you heard the crunch of steel. The two aspects of locus provide the foundation on which you can create the persona's speaking, and they are the essential guides to understanding the speaker's relationship to the audience.

Locus encompasses both time and space. You already know its related words: *location, locale,* and *locate.* When directors shoot films "on location," they are concerned with locus. In its most basic sense, then, the locus of the work is the place where the action occurs. In "Dulce," we saw the locus sharply focused at the grave during most of the story; in Anne Sexton's "Ringing the Bells" (at the end of this chapter), the locus is clearly the music room in the institution in which the speaker is confined.

Locus also involves the relationship between the speaker of a given line and the world that speaker inhabits—not just the rooms or streets or buildings in the story but the audience to whom the speaker addresses that line and the relationship the speaker enjoys with that audience. For example, you tell the story of an accident you witnessed on Main and Hudson differently if your audience is your spouse, or your four-year-old son, or the police sergeant interviewing eyewitnesses, or the judge and jury listening to testimony in a damages trial. Each time the locus changes because each time the relationship between speaker and audience changes. In Cameron's "Homework" (at the end of this chapter) the persona, Michael, speaks differently to his guidance counselor, Mrs. Dietrich, than he does to his sister. The way the performer presents the persona must reflect that difference in locus.

Examine the relationship between the persona and the audience. Is the audience overhearing what is being said (as in Maury Yeston's "New Words" later in this chapter), or is the character addressing the audience directly (as in Sexton's "Ringing the Bells")? Is a character speaking directly to an audience *in* the story, and is that audience one person or several people? How will you demonstrate your answers to these questions to the audience who sees and hears the performance you are preparing? All these questions about the relationship between the speaker and his or her surroundings are questions of locus.

Placing Action Out Front

One distinctive element of oral interpretation is the performer's *place-ment of action.* The persona focuses on different points, depending on the locus of a given line. Suppose one character addresses another char-acter in the text you have chosen to perform. As interpreter, you envi-sion the character to whom you are speaking as slightly above and slightly beyond the heads of your audience. Thus, when the narrator in "Dulce" speaks to Lambert, the performer imagines Lambert out front, just a tad above and beyond the heads of the audience watching the performance (as in Figure 2.1); when Lambert responds, the performer locates another point slightly to the side of the "Lambert" location to represent the narrator whom Lambert is questioning (as in Figure 2.2). This placement of the action out front continues similarly, to establish a unique placement for all the speaking characters in a given selection.

Not all texts are dialogue, of course. Sometimes a narrator de-scribes a scene, summarizes some past events, or even reflects on what has happened. Then the placement differs slightly. The performer still fo-cuses out front in the audience areas—without, of course, singling out any specific audience member as the object of the words (as in Figure 2.3). In this situation, the speaker is frankly admitting the presence of the audience. For example, the storyteller is telling the story to the au-dience and wants to help the audience imagine the ranch, the ground,

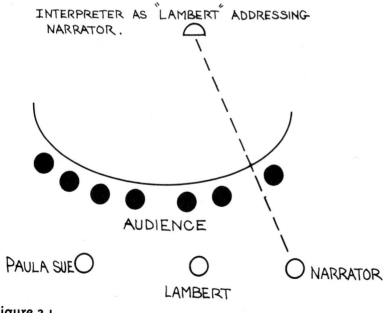

Figure 2.1

INTERPRETER AS NARRATOR IN THE
ACTION ADDRESSING "LAMBERT."

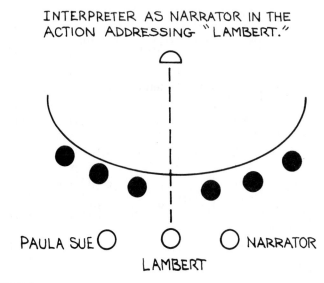

PAULA SUE ○   ○   ○ NARRATOR
LAMBERT

Figure 2.2

INTERPRETER AS NARRATOR ADDRESSING
AUDIENCE

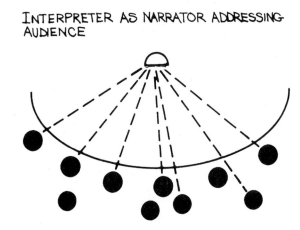

Figure 2.3

the way Lambert holds the dead Dulce, so the performer paints the picture to include the audience in the locale. Rather than focusing attention on a given point beyond the audience, the interpreter may be establishing eye contact with the audience. The narrator in "Dulce" describes how Lambert carried the dog to the ditch, how he leveled the ground for the grave—and describes these scenes so as to include the audience. Then, when Lambert addresses the narrator, or the narrator speaks to Paula Sue, the interpreter focuses again on the character locations so carefully established earlier.

At first, placing action out front will seem difficult, but work very slowly and keep two rules in mind:

1. Characters talk to characters. When you speak as a character, focus your eyes on whomever or whatever the persona is addressing, and be sure that point is slightly above and slightly beyond the heads of your audience. Some interpreters call this a "closed" situation, in that the audience is not visibly recognized by the performer.

2. Narrators often speak directly to the audience, to explain something that happened or to describe a scene. Then the interpreter establishes with the audience the same kinds of eye contact you would encounter in delivering a public speech. Some interpreters call this an "open" situation because the persona frankly admits and exploits the presence of the audience.

The text you have chosen to perform is likely to feature many variations of these two aspects of placing action, but keeping the fundamental principles in mind will help you devise performance choices that respond to the unique intricacies of your text.

For some interpreters locus has an even larger scope. A poem (or a story or play) evokes an attitude toward the events it recounts. This attitude is not simply the same perspective as the point of view of the narrator, although the narrator's position is obviously a part of it. In Joanne Gilbert's "Upon Learning That a Junior High School Acquaintance Has Been Nominated for an Academy Award" (at the end of this chapter), we may be amused by the enraged response of the speaker to the nominee, but humor was certainly far from the speaker's fierce thoughts. In this poem, locus, in its fullest sense, includes the relationship between the entire tale and the world the tale inhabits or describes.

Climax

You've defined the persona, and you understand where the speaker is speaking. You have discovered that some parts are more important than others. Sometimes a detail becomes important only later in the development of the plot or action. More often, however, a key detail indicates a high point of logical development or emotional impact and thus may be considered a *climax*. Sometimes several minor climaxes can lead up to (or follow) the major climax. Consider Yeston's "New Words."

New Words

MAURY YESTON

Look up there, high above us, in a sky of blackest silk.
See how round like a cookie, see how white as white as milk.
Call it the moon, my son; say "moon."
Sounds like your spoon, my son; can you say it?
New word today, say "moon."

Near the moon, brightly turning, see the shining sparks of light.
Each one new, each one burning, through the darkness of the
    night.
We call them "stars," my son; say "stars."
That one is "Mars," my son; can you say it?
New word today, say "stars."

As they blink all around us, playing starryeyed games,
Who would think it astounds us, simply naming their names?

Turn your eyes from the skies now, turn around and look at me.
There's a light in my eyes now, and a word for what you see.
We call it "love," my son; say "love."
So hard to say, my son; it gets harder.
New words today we'll learn to say:
Learn "moon," learn "stars," learn "love."

Each of the new words functions as a climax for the stanza that explains it, and the persona helps the boy pronounce it, but two of the new words ("moon" and "star") clearly lead up to the most important new word ("love").

A climax may be the culmination of the logical content, the high point of the emotional impact, or a combination of the two. What kind do you think is Yeston's major climax? Even though we speak of *logical climax* and *emotional climax*, this splitting of the term is done only for the purpose of convenient analysis. Ultimately, we reunite the two parts because that's the way they operate in the work being performed.

In a play or story the *logical climax* is often called the *crisis*. The *crisis* is the point at which the conflict becomes so intense that a resolution must occur and after which only one outcome is possible. In an essay the logical climax occurs when the writer makes the main point with such clarity that the conclusion is inevitable. In a poem it is the point at which the author completes the logical development on which the emotional content is based.

The *emotional climax* is the moment of highest emotional impact and involvement for the reader. If this seems to be a completely subjective matter, remember that the writer gives us clues to follow. If your analysis is careful and you let the author lead the way, you generally are moved most strongly at the point of emotional climax.

Sometimes the highest emotional intensity coincides with the logical climax. Often, however, this is not the case. The logical climax may precede and prepare for the emotional high point. This happens when the emotional climax depends on a character's or speaker's response to a completed cycle of events. On the other hand, if the outcome of events depends on an emotional reaction, the emotional climax precedes the logical climax, as it does in Dickinson's poem in Chapter 1. Here the impact of space, silence, and solitude precedes the completion of the fall. In "Dulce" the logical climax occurs when Lambert places the dog in the grave he so carefully prepared, but the emotional climax occurs later as he sits contemplating her white bowl.

You may find this dual aspect of climax difficult to convey, but understanding and experience will help you cope with the problem. The logical climax, for instance, probably needs a particularly high degree of definition on the part of the interpreter. If you drive too hard at your listeners with this concept, however, the impact of the emotional climax may be decreased. The audience will receive the full emotional impact only if you respond personally while reading. This does not mean that you should pull out all the stops and burst into tears or shake your fists in fury. You should, however, train yourself to respond in such a way that your nonverbal communication (or body signals) harmonize with what the words are saying.

Major Aesthetic Components

At this point you are well on your way to your first performance. (You will survive!) Now you can see more clearly how your selection depends on denotative and connotative meanings in the words, the personae who speak the words, the locus, and the emotional and logical climaxes. Your selection, however, also depends on many more subtle components to sustain its life as a work of art. These factors, which we call *intrinsic factors*, are found in varying degrees in all successful writing. The intrinsic factors are *unity and harmony, variety and contrast, balance and proportion*, and *rhythm*. We call them intrinsic because they are clearly discernible *within* the printed selection and because all reasonably qualified readers recognize them.

The intrinsic factors are not separate entities. They have bearing on and are affected by the arrangement and organization of the material and also by its logical meaning and emotive quality. No one factor can be completely separated from the others. They overlap and affect one another. Many elements in the writing may contribute to more than one of these factors within a single selection. Yet each makes its own subtle contribution to the whole. We discuss the intrinsic factors briefly and then identify and examine them in both a story and a poem.

Unity and Harmony

Unity is the combining and ordering of all the parts that make up the whole. It consists of those elements of content and form that hold the writing together and keep the readers' and listeners' minds focused on the total effect.

Unity may be achieved in any number of ways. The persona is a strong unifying factor, as is locus. The setting and time may change within a piece of narrative, but the locus—the physical and psychological relationship of the persona to the events that control the persona's point of view—usually remains constant. Sometimes the persona or the characters go through a clear and unmistakable process of development that in its progression unifies the material. As you look at a selection, observe all of the details that help accomplish this unification. Connectives such as *and, then, next, a few hours later,* and *after this* are important. Approach each selection as a new problem and analyze it carefully to find everything that holds the material together.

Harmony is the appropriate adjustment of parts to one another to form a satisfying whole, the concord between the idea and the way that idea is expressed. Harmony is achieved in part through the author's choice of words, the sentence structure, and the relationship of phrases and clauses within the sentences. Obviously, then, it depends to a large extent on elements of style. In poetry, rhythmic elements serve to enhance harmony.

Another important source of harmony is the selection of details that set up associations in the readers' minds. Thus, harmony is paired with unity. Although these two factors have different definitions, they are clearly interdependent and must function together if the writing is to achieve its intended effect. Recall, for example, how all of the action in "Dulce" is unified around the *time* just after the body was discovered and around the *place* where Dulce is to be buried. Each character responds to Dulce's death, but none share precisely the same response: the harmony they evoke in speaking of Dulce (or acting on her memory) intensifies our response to the tale.

Variety and Contrast

A picture painted in only one color or a musical composition with only one repeated melody is generally dull and uninteresting. In the same way, literature that lacks variety and contrast is not likely to hold a reader's attention for long.

Variety is provided when two things of the same general kind differ from each other in one or more details. For example, several characters of the same age, sex, and social background essentially may agree but express themselves differently. Or one character, at two or more points of his or her development, may retain unifying qualities but may demonstrate reactions in varying ways.

Contrast is concerned with the opposition or differences between associated things. Two characters may be set against each other by their opposing responses to a situation, or by different actions and motivations. Characters may be contrasted in appearance, age, wisdom, emotion, or any number of other attributes. One place or time may be contrasted with another. Quiet may be set against noise, dark against light, hope against despair, positive elements against negative ones.

Variety and contrast function together to change the emphasis or to heighten an effect. In Walt Whitman's "When I Heard the Learn'd Astronomer" (at the end of this chapter), the first four lines begin in similar ways ("When I heard," "When the proofs," "When I was shown," "When I sitting heard"), but their *variety* suggests the growing impatience of the speaker. All the acts others did to the speaker nicely contrast with the act the speaker himself completes by looking "up in perfect silence at the stars." Moreover, the first four lines are *about* the stars, but the poem resolves itself only when the speaker *engages* the stars directly. You will find that variety and contrast provide invaluable clues for vocal and physical vividness, but watch that you do not exceed the bounds of unity and harmony by overemphasizing variety and contrast.

Balance and Proportion

Balance and *proportion* are difficult to evaluate. The test you will need to apply is how well they implement the other factors and contribute to the effect of the whole.

Because proportion provides balance, the two factors should be considered together. A seesaw balances when the fulcrum is exactly the same distance from each end of the board. When equal weights are placed at each end, that balance is retained. When a heavier weight is placed on one end of the board, the balance is destroyed. Balance can be restored by an adjustment of proportions, either by moving the fulcrum toward the end on which the heavier weight rests or by moving the heavier object closer to the fulcrum.

When equal weights or quantities lie at equal distances from a central point (or fulcrum), the balance is said to be symmetrical. For example, identical candlesticks placed equidistant from the center of a mantelpiece provide a symmetrical balance. Perfect balance is satisfying to the senses, but sometimes the asymmetrical or unequal balance achieved by an adjustment of distance, weights, and masses may be more interesting and effective. Instead of the candlesticks on the mantel, there may be a tall plant at one end and a low, bright-colored bowl at the other. These two objects do not agree in size and shape, but the bulk, height, or weight of the one somehow balances the intensity of color in the other.

Within a piece of literature, balance is brought about by the intensity or the proportion of content on either side of the point at which the entire selection seems to pivot and change direction. This point of balance occurs at the crisis in a story or a play. In a poem, as on a seesaw, it is called the *fulcrum*. The fulcrum, or point of balance, may or may not coincide with either the logical or the emotional climax.

Point of balance is more important in the consideration of brief, compact selections than of longer units, and you will find it particularly helpful when you analyze poetry. As we mention in Chapter 1, in the twelfth line of Dickinson's "I Felt a Funeral," attention shifts from the funeral and things of the earth to "Space." This, then, indicates the fulcrum of the poem.

Some selections seem to balance almost exactly in the middle: about the same amount of material leads up to and away from the fulcrum. This is clearly the case with Kate Chopin's "The Story of an Hour" (analyzed later in this chapter). Such symmetrical balance requires the interpreter to build to the proper point and not to allow the audience's interest to wane thereafter.

Frequently in contemporary writing, however, the balance is off-center, with the result that proportion is maintained not so much within the work itself as in the *interaction* of the work with the audience, as though some space was left in the work for the audience to do its part in completing, or fulfilling, the balance. Look at Michael Lassell's "How to Watch Your Brother Die" (at the end of this chapter). The poem describes a series of events experienced by the persona, each of which occupies approximately the same amount of space in the text, thus maintaining the *proportion* of the poem while balancing the speaker's growing realizations. Yet the greater proportion of the total material precedes the fulcrum ("Stroke / your split eyebrow with a finger / and think of your brother alive."), and the few remaining words simply leave us to confront what the persona has learned about himself, and about the different cultural experiences of straights and gays, and what we have discovered about ourselves.

Such asymmetrical balance is effective when the author has been careful to weight the briefer component with enough vividness or emotional intensity to enable it to hold its own against the greater number of words and images it must balance. Be sure in your rehearsal that you allow time for those in the audience to do the work of "finishing" the performance.

Rhythm

In literature *rhythm* is usually thought of as an element of poetic structure, such as the relationship between stressed and unstressed syllables. Rhythm, however, is an important aspect of content as well. *Rhythm of content* evolves from the interaction of logical and emotional content. We discuss structural rhythm in the later chapters on prose style (Chapter 5) and poetic structure (Chapter 10).

Rhythm of content may be established in many ways in both prose and poetry, and it will begin to emerge as you study details of organization and style. For example, in Dickinson's "I Felt a Funeral," there is a steady alternation between references to the speaker in the poem and to "them." The briefer a selection is, the more important rhythm of content is likely to be.

A rhythm of content can be set up by the recurrent shift of attention from one character to another or from one place or time to another, or by the alternation of description and narration or dialogue and exposition as occurs in "Dulce." The rhythm of emotional quality can be measured by the increased and decreased intensity of the reader's response, and it becomes evident as the minor climaxes are discovered. As you analyze, you will discover many more ways of identifying and expressing this factor.

Rhythm of content is important to an interpreter because most people are able to concentrate fully and exclusively on an idea for only a brief time. The skillful writer permits the reader to relax from time to time. By understanding and conveying this rhythm of concentration, you can do the same for your audience.

Furthermore, listeners cannot be held at a high emotional pitch for long periods of time. In spite of themselves and in spite of the interpreter's best efforts, they experience a sense of relaxation after high points of emotional response. The informed interpreter will welcome this relaxation so that the emotional climaxes may be more effective, especially if these climaxes depend on accumulation of feeling. Be careful, however, not to break your own concentration. As we have seen, rhythm is also an excellent device for keeping variety and contrast in control within the essential frame of unity.

Using the Tools

We've covered a lot of ground thus far in describing a process. Now let's see it work with two different texts—a story that may be new to you and a poem with which you have become familiar. The devices of analysis are really only tools to help you understand both what the author wrote and how it is written. *Do not allow yourself to pass by the analysis stage, however.* You wouldn't begin a long car journey to a place you've never been without carefully consulting a reliable map. Literary analysis, as we have said, is not an end in itself for interpreters; analysis is the way interpreters map an informed and rich rehearsal period that alone can guarantee the fullest possible performance. Analysis makes performance choices clearer and less capricious.

The analyses of a story and of a poem that follow differ in several respects, in part, obviously, because poems and stories differ. These works are *examples*. You may discover aspects of the literature we have not mentioned, or you may emphasize something we have only touched on. Remember: Informed discussion requires information. Look carefully, and gauge cautiously. An exciting journey is about to begin.

Sample Analysis of a Story

"The Story of an Hour" was written around the end of the nineteenth century by the American author Kate Chopin. Read it carefully once or twice before reading the analysis. (The paragraphs are numbered for easy reference.)

The Story of an Hour
KATE CHOPIN

Knowing that Mrs. Mallard was afflicted with a heart trouble, great care was taken to break to her as gently as possible the news of her husband's death.   1

It was her sister Josephine who told her, in broken sentences, veiled hints that revealed in half concealing. Her husband's friend Richards was there, too, near her. It was he who had been in the newspaper office when intelligence of the railroad disaster was received, with Brently Mallard's name leading the list of "killed." He had only taken the time to assure himself of its truth by a second telegram, and had hastened to forestall any less careful, less tender friend in bearing the sad message.   2

She did not hear the story as many women have heard the same, with a paralyzed inability to accept its significance. She wept at once, with sudden, wild abandonment, in her sister's arms. When the storm of grief had spent itself she went away to her room alone. She would have no one follow her.   3

There stood, facing the open window, a comfortable, roomy armchair. Into this she sank, pressed down by a physical exhaustion that haunted her body and seemed to reach into her soul.   4

She could see in the open square before her house the tops of trees that were all aquiver with the new spring life. The delicious breath of rain was in the air. In the street below a peddler was crying his wares. The notes of a distant song which some one was singing reached her faintly, and countless sparrows were twittering in the eaves.   5

There were patches of blue sky showing here and there through the clouds that had met and piled one above the other in the west facing her window. 6

She sat with her head thrown back upon the cushion of the chair quite motionless, except when a sob came up into her throat and shook her, as a child who has cried itself to sleep continues to sob in its dreams. 7

She was young, with a fair, calm face, whose lines bespoke repression and even a certain strength. But now there was a dull stare in her eyes, whose gaze was fixed away off yonder on one of those patches of blue sky. It was not a glance of reflection, but rather indicated a suspension of intelligent thought. 8

There was something coming to her and she was waiting for it, fearfully. What was it? She did not know; it was too subtle and elusive to name. But she felt it, creeping out of the sky, reaching toward her through the sounds, the scents, the color that filled the air. 9

Now her bosom rose and fell tumultuously. She was beginning to recognize this thing that was approaching to possess her, and she was striving to beat it back with her will—as powerless as her two white slender hands would have been. 10

When she abandoned herself, a little whispered word escaped her slightly parted lips. She said it over and over under her breath: "Free, free, free!" The vacant stare and the look of terror that had followed it went from her eyes. They stayed keen and bright. Her pulses beat fast, and the coursing blood warmed and relaxed every inch of her body. 11

She did not stop to ask if it were not a monstrous joy that held her. A clear and exalted perception enabled her to dismiss the suggestion as trivial. 12

She knew that she would weep again when she saw the kind, tender hands folded in death; the face that had never looked save with love upon her, fixed and gray and dead. But she saw beyond that bitter moment a long procession of years to come that would belong to her absolutely. And she opened and spread her arms out to them in welcome. 13

There would be no one to live for during those coming years; she would live for herself. There would be no powerful will bending her in that blind persistence with which men and women believe they have a right to impose a private will upon a fellow-creature. A kind intention or a cruel intention made the act seem no less a crime as she looked upon it in that brief moment of illumination. 14

And yet she had loved him—sometimes. Often she had not. What did it matter! What could love, the unsolved mystery, count for in face of this possession of self-assertion which she suddenly recognized as the strongest impulse of her being. 15

"Free! Body and soul free!" she kept whispering. 16

Josephine was kneeling before the closed door with her lips to the keyhole, imploring for admission. "Louise, open the door! I beg; open the door—you will make yourself ill. What are you doing, Louise? For heaven's sake open the door." 17

"Go away. I am not making myself ill." No; she was drinking in the   18
very elixir of life through that open window.

Her fancy was running riot along those days ahead of her. Spring   19
days, and summer days, and all sorts of days that would be her own.
She breathed a quick prayer that life might be long. It was only yesterday she had thought with a shudder that life might be long.

She arose at length and opened the door to her sister's importuni-   20
ties. There was a feverish triumph in her eyes, and she carried herself
unwittingly like a goddess of Victory. She clasped her sister's waist,
and together they descended the stairs. Richards stood waiting for
them at the bottom.

Some one was opening the front door with a latchkey. It was   21
Brently Mallard who entered, a little travel-stained, composedly carrying his grip-sack and umbrella. He had been far from the scene of accident, and did not even know there had been one. He stood amazed at
Josephine's piercing cry; at Richards' quick motion to screen him from
the view of his wife.

But Richards was too late.   22

When the doctors came they said she had died of heart disease—of   23
joy that kills.

You already know the most important questions an interpreter confronts: "Who is telling this story?" and "What is happening during the
story?" All of the devices of structure we have mentioned, all of the intrinsic factors, all of the author's skill, give clues to help you discover
the answer to these questions. "The Story of an Hour" provides a rich
opportunity to examine the ways an author creates a storyteller and a
story to tell.

First, of course, we have to be sure we understand the dictionary
meanings of all of the words. Are you sure that "elixir" (paragraph 18)
refers to a cure-all? Are Josephine's "importunities" (paragraph 20) requests or demands or both? Have you ever seen a picture of a "goddess
of Victory"? There are several famous sculptures based on this theme.
How does Mrs. Mallard carry herself to look like such a figure? Once
these questions are answered, we can investigate the story in more depth.

In the space of this hour (although performing the entire story
takes about ten minutes), Mrs. Mallard undergoes an extraordinary
change. On one hand, the *variety* of characters in the story see only a
woman distraught with grief who appears to die from joy at the appearance of the husband she thought dead. *Balancing* that view, we
know that within this hour Mrs. Mallard begins to live another, richer
life of independence, a life of her own. When her old life returns (in the
person of her husband), she knows that the rich new life she had em-
braced will never be possible, and she dies from a "joy that kills." The
narrator wants us to imagine what pained disappointment goes through
her mind when she sees her husband again. But just as we did not share
her thoughts when she learned of her husband's death, we do not share

her thoughts when she sees he lives. Yet because we were with her only for the time she began to live, we know Mrs. Mallard better than any of her family or friends.

"Who is telling the story?" The unnamed storyteller clearly knows all the people in the tale. For all of them—storyteller and characters—Mrs. Mallard unites the tale, from the first paragraph to the last. The other characters—Josephine, Richards, and Brently—exist only as agents in her life, and their words sometimes *harmonize* with our feelings, sometimes *contrast* with our responses. The narrator describes Mrs. Mallard's grief over her husband's presumed death, notes carefully her fears and concerns, and dwells at length on the impending changes his death carries. In so brief a story, her victory is scrupulously described. Clearly, the narrator has a close, sensitive relationship with Mrs. Mallard and thus the *locus* of the tale is intimate.

We understand this relationship more fully when the narrator tells us of Mrs. Mallard's change. After having expended "the storm of grief," Mrs. Mallard "went away to her room alone. She would have no one follow her" (paragraph 3). But *we* follow her closely, guided by the narrator, who describes for us the furnishings of this room barred to everyone else (paragraph 4), the view only Mrs. Mallard can see (paragraphs 5 and 6), Mrs. Mallard's very private behavior (paragraph 7), and her physical features as she is experiencing the change (paragraph 8). Because of the narrator's special access to Mrs. Mallard, we are privileged to know her in complex ways others cannot. And our view gets richer. We move from the world outside Mrs. Mallard to the world inside her. In contrast to what others hear through the doors, we observe a woman confronting independence.

As Mrs. Mallard begins to consider life without her husband, the narrator carefully describes the internal turmoil Mrs. Mallard experiences—how she feels, what she thinks, how her body throbs with anxiety and fear (paragraphs 9 and 10)—and permits us to hear her whispered cries (paragraph 11). The narrator shows us how Mrs. Mallard starts to live without a husband (paragraphs 12–14). Her new status both dismays and exhilarates her. It seems to have rushed in on her after the stately opening paragraphs, but there is something splendid about it all the same. She continues to repeat the exhilarating word "Free!" (paragraph 16). This is certainly an important *emotional climax*.

To *balance* this internal view, at this point the narrator returns us to the world outside the bedroom. Josephine's concern about Mrs. Mallard and her fear that she will make herself ill *contrast* sharply with what we know about how exciting these glimpses of freedom have been. Given just these few moments of freedom, Mrs. Mallard now eagerly anticipates what her own life might become, and remembers how little she had to look forward to only yesterday (paragraph 19). With this realization of her future, she rises to confront at last the old world she inhabited. Triumphing over her past, she now sees the future she had never even been able to hope for (paragraph 20). Just as at the beginning of the story, she again receives news about her husband.

The final scene moves quickly. Note that, although the narrator obviously knows who is there, we are told that "some one" opens the front door (paragraph 21). In suspense, we rejoin the world of the story for a moment, not knowing who will appear. All in the hall turn to see who is intruding on this scene of grief (or, in Mrs. Mallard's case, joy), only to discover Brently's return. Richards again tries to help but is too late (just as earlier he had been too hasty). The doctors diagnose Mrs. Mallard's death of a heart overjoyed. We know better.

The language the narrator chooses describes both Mrs. Mallard and the narrator. The opening paragraphs of the story contain formal, rather stilted grammar and vocabulary: the passive voice ("was afflicted," "was taken") and the legalistic "It was" introducing the summarized action of the story. Such forms tend to remove action from immediate experience, making it seem something that happened to someone else. The *rhythm* is stately and gradual. The Mrs. Mallard of the opening paragraphs differs from the rejuvenated woman who emerges ready to face a new life. In paragraphs 9 and 10, colorful language conveys the terror of her acceptance. "Powerful will bending" and "blind persistence" describe the relationship between men and women (paragraph 14). The forces of life seem to rush in on her. Love is characterized as an "unsolved mystery" that pales in front of the "possession of self-assertion," which becomes "the strongest impulse of her being," an "elixir" transforming her into a "goddess of Victory" over the past she has known (paragraphs 15–20). As the story concludes, the language returns to its placid depiction of the opening, and the tempo resumes its slow, stately progress. The events again seem to happen to someone we do not know. Brently Mallard's appearance and the subsequent events are narrated from afar. He "stood amazed" at the cry of his sister-in-law and at his partner's attempt to "screen him from the view of his wife" (a tantalizing phrase). All the narrator tells us about Mrs. Mallard's death is in one paragraph of six syllables. Only afterward does the word "died" appear, placed in the mouths of the doctors who, like everyone else in Mrs. Mallard's world, misunderstood her life.

Several other clues inform us about this narrator. He or she is sensitive to the natural world as the appropriate order of things, relies on the good sense and the justness of personal integrity, is sympathetic, and clearly understands what living in the world requires. Josephine and Richards are compassionate characters who care deeply about Mrs. Mallard. Her husband is kindly and enjoys his wife's affection. But this narrator knows that none of them understand who *she* is. Ironically, her family's loving concern simply reinforces her sense of living the trapped, airless life. With her discovery that she can—and must—live her own life, she also sees how she could no longer live any other way. And she doesn't.

Finally, of course, this narrator is supremely interested in life's ironies. Little ironies abound. The sad message of Brently Mallard's death actually brings a kind of joy to his wife. Richards's haste at the beginning to protect Mrs. Mallard and his tardiness at the end eventually contribute to her death. The doctors' diagnosis is true, but not at all in the way they mean or everyone else believes. Mrs. Mallard begins to live after years of marriage have been violently ended. In the springtime of the year she, too, comes to a new life, but she dies just as she is beginning to know what her new life is like.

Variety and *contrast* in tempo and character, *balance* and *proportion* in narrative and scene, *unity* and *harmony* of theme and incident, rendered with delicate but clear changes of *rhythm* that seem almost effortless: these elements have characterized successful storytelling for centuries. This story, then, is built in a classic form: a summarized opening scene initiates the rising action leading to the carefully described scene at the emotional fulcrum of the story. The moment of self-discovery leads inevitably to the emotional and thematic climax of the story in the last two paragraphs. By using suspense, surprise, understatement, and irony, the storyteller captures in a brief moment a story to resonate beyond an hour.

Sample Analysis of a Poem

In Chapter 1 we evaluated Dickinson's poem with regard to the touchstones of universality, individuality, and suggestion. Let us look again at Dickinson's "I Felt a Funeral" to discover how the details of the intrinsic factors work together as well. Since the poem is brief, it is repeated here, and the lines are numbered for easy reference.

I Felt a Funeral
EMILY DICKINSON

I felt a Funeral, in my Brain,	1
And Mourners to and fro	2
Kept treading—treading—till it seemed	3
That Sense was breaking through—	4
And when they all were seated,	5
A Service, like a Drum—	6
Kept beating—beating—till I thought	7
My Mind was going numb—	8
And then I heard them lift a Box	9
And creak across my Soul	10

With those same Boots of Lead, again,	11
Then Space—began to toll,	12
As all the Heavens were a Bell,	13
And Being, but an Ear,	14
And I, and Silence, some strange Race	15
Wrecked, solitary, here—	16
And then a Plank in Reason, broke,	17
And I dropped down, and down—	18
And hit a World, at every Crash,	19
And Got through knowing—then—	20

You probably don't need to look up any words from this poem in the dictionary, but if you check "treading," "race," and "boots," you will discover the subtle scope of Dickinson's meaning. In our earlier discussion, we touched briefly on the connotation of some of the words. We come back to this matter later, for it is impossible to avoid it in a selection so filled with suggestion. For the moment let us move on to *organization*.

Organization of the Poem

The first line gives the complete opening situation. We know that she "felt" rather than saw a funeral, and that she felt it in her brain. Immediately the possibility opens up that this poem is not about an actual funeral but about a sensation and thus is, in a highly poetic way, an analogy. It may be about the sense of death, or despair, or both. In any case it is about *sensation* within the rational part of one's body. That is a paradox in itself. To establish this essential paradox, Dickinson uses two stanzas, which we may consider as the introduction. The third and fourth stanzas take us from the tightly enclosed earthly place to "Space" and the almost intolerable tolling followed by silence. In the opening line of the final stanza, we begin the descent and the conclusion of the experience. Thus, the organization is really very simple and unified. The *logical climax* is located in the last line, where the experience reaches its only possible outcome.

Although each stanza has its own emotional buildup, the major *emotional climax* coincides with the *fulcrum*, where heaviness is suddenly replaced by space and sound swells to sudden silence. In the final line of the middle stanza, the poem turns from earth and people, in a sense, to space and solitude. After the weight of the box, the "creak across my Soul"—which strongly suggests a creak across a floor—and the "Boots of Lead," we are suddenly confronted, in a sharp *contrast*, with a vast and empty expanse of space, which is, as we have said, the fulcrum. It is approximately in the center of the poem and causes no trouble as far as *balance* and *proportion* of stanzas are concerned.

The poem gives us a sense of continuing development, yet without real speed except for lines 19 and 20, where the drop occurs. This is achieved in part by the structure. The effect of steady continuation first suggested in "to and fro" is strengthened by the connectives "and," "till," "and when," and "and then." It is interesting that the use of the word "and" increases sharply in the last stanza so that the drop picks up speed, and the experience is terminated with the final "then."

The verb forms also help create this effect. Although the entire poem is in the past tense, there is a subtle variation within it. The repetition in "Kept treading—treading," "Kept beating—beating," and "down, and down," combined with the subjunctive or progressive tense of "was breaking," and "was going," gives a feeling of action continuing over a period of time. It is interesting to notice, however, that at the fulcrum there is a shift into the infinitive with "began to toll," followed immediately by a subjunctive form throughout the entire fourth stanza ("As" in line 13 implies "as if"). We use the subjunctive to speak of a condition contrary to fact. The final stanza returns to the simple past with "broke," "dropped," "hit," and "Got through"—about as completed a past as one can have!

Nature of the Persona

We have already mentioned the use of "I felt" in the opening line. Taking the first person singular *I*, we find that the poem moves from "I felt" to "I thought," "I heard," "And I, and Silence" to "I dropped," "[I] hit," and "[I] Got through." Although the first four *Is* are evenly spaced one to a stanza, the last three occur in quick succession in the last three lines. Our attention is focused on the *I* at the opening of the poem, and then we are quickly introduced to the mourners. The *rhythm* of attention alternates, although not with perfect regularity, until line 12, when "Space" is introduced. We have no references to the mourners or to the funeral after that, and the next reference to *I* is "I, and Silence." A look at the funeral references reveals that they continue at least by implication through line 13 with "toll" and "Bell," but it is really "Space" that begins to toll and "the Heavens" that are a bell.

Here we must mention Dickinson's skillful use of motifs. A specific set of references that a writer returns to often is called a *motif*. A motif in music, design, or literature is any detail repeated often enough to become important. In music it may be a phrase of melody or a set of chords. In design it may be a leaf, a flower, or any particular element used in a pattern. In literature the repeated reference need not be an *exact* repetition of images or ideas. It may present recurring references to a concept such as the elements: storms, clouds, or sunshine. It may refer repeatedly to things related to each other, such as colors, nature, or animals.

The first line of Dickinson's poem refers to "my Brain," and this reference is strengthened and at the same time is made more specific three lines later by "Sense," which we discussed in Chapter 1 when we talked about suggestion. Thus, we move from "my Brain" to "it seemed," "Sense," "I thought," and "My Mind." This mental motif does not reappear until the final stanza, which opens with a reference to "Reason" and closes with "knowing." We are very carefully returned to the persona with "I" in line 15; "Reason" and "knowing" are in identical positions with "Brain" and "Sense" in the opening stanza. Although psychologists might disagree, "heard" in line 9 appears to be more physical than emotional. The next reference is to "Soul," then to "Being," and then to "Race," a large, general, abstract category rather than a specific personal reference. Moreover, the race is "strange," "Wrecked," and, most important, "solitary." Even more subtle is the use of "Ear" with "Being." Thus, lines 9 through 16 form a unit that differs from the rest of the poem in motif. As we have remarked, there is also a shift in verb form, and this is the only place in the poem where a sentence continues past the stanza break without being broken by a dash.

Charting the Details

A simple listing by line, as in the table on page 53, makes this discussion more graphic. Remember, however, that a list is not a poem or a performance. It is useful only as a step in analysis. (In the interest of clarity, we do not follow Dickinson's use of capital letters.) For us, the analysis is useful only insofar as it makes for a more productive rehearsal, which will lead to the fullest possible performance. If you have carefully analyzed your text, you will know how each word or phrase subtly echoes another later in the work, and you can use your voice to prepare your audience subtly to respond to that similarity. For example, "treading" in line 3 can be voiced in a manner that prepares your audience for "breaking" and "beating" later in the poem. Perhaps you will focus your gaze in a specific location when the persona describes what she hears. Take care not simply to repeat that gesture from one line to another, but retain unity in the range of contrasts you demonstrate. A conscientious performer—with a flexible and responsive voice and body—can devise a wide range of subtly connected behaviors, but *only* if he or she knows what to connect and where.

Applying the Intrinsic Factors in Rehearsal

Remember that the intrinsic factors are closely related; any single detail may contribute to more than one of them. Let us now see how what we have found relates to unity and harmony, variety and contrast, balance and proportion, and rhythm, and how that can inform our rehearsal.

Line	Persons	Mental and Physical Motifs	Connectives	Verb Forms	Funeral Motifs	Sound and Silence
1	I	I felt		I felt	funeral	
	my	my brain				
2	mourners		and		mourners	
3	they (implied)	it seemed	till	kept treading treading it seemed was breaking		treading treading
4	my (implied)	sense				
5	they (mourners)		and when	were seated		
6					service drum	drum
7	I	I thought	till	kept beating beating I thought was going		beating beating
8	my	my mind				
9	I	I heard	and then	I heard lift	box	heard them
	them (mourners)					
10	them (implied) my	my soul	and	creak		creak across
11	their (implied)				lead	boots of lead
12		space	then	began to toll	toll	toll FULCRUM
13		heavens		as [if] . . . were	bell	bell
14		being ear	and	as [if] . . . were (implied)		ear
15	I and silence	race	and . . . and	as [if] . . . were (implied)		silence
16				as [if] . . . were (implied)		solitary
17		reason	and then	broke		plank broke
18	I		and . . . and	dropped		
19	I (implied)		and	hit		crash
20	I (implied)	knowing	and then	got through		

The use of "I" and "my" helps to *unify* the poem. It recurs frequently in the first ten lines and reappears in the final stanza, both explicitly and implicitly. But something changes within the speaker between those uses: the opening "I" who "felt a Funeral" undergoes telltale experiences that alter the way the voice sounds and the body stands by the time "I dropped down, and down." Connectives hold the poem together, and the simple progression of events records the speaker's progress, but the performer's voice and body have to reflect the impact of these events. We can glimpse some of the impact from the psychological motifs that open and close the poem, but the performer has to select what vocal and physical behavior can help the audience understand the impact. The sound motif—heavy in the beginning, peaking at the fulcrum, ironically strengthened by the sudden silence, and returning with force in the final stanza—needs to find vocal and physical life in the performance choices you make. Just as the intrinsic factors reflect the *poem's* achievement, they inform the various ways you "try out" the poem during rehearsal. Unity and harmony pervade performance choices, just as variety and contrast, balance and proportion, and rhythm affect the performance choices you consider, and then reject or adapt, during rehearsal.

We cannot fully appreciate harmony until we have examined poetic structure, but certainly the heaviness just referred to and the continuing, unbroken downward progression are harmonious with the sensation that Dickinson describes. "Drum" suggests funeral drums; a tolling bell, also associated with funerals, prolongs the mood. Can your voice sound accordingly? "Wrecked," "broke," and "Crash" help suggest the destruction following the tolling of "Space." Careful examination reveals a remarkable harmony between what is being said and the connotations and sounds of the words that say it. Don't waste any sounds!

Within the unity of this brief poem, we find enough variety and contrast to hold our interest. Just look at the funeral motif and the sound motif to see how Dickinson used very subtle variety indeed. Too much variety within so brief a poem would seriously threaten unity, especially since contrast is so sharp. The poet's isolation is contrasted with the multiplicity of people in "Mourners" and "they all," until the isolation reaches its culmination in "I, and Silence . . . solitary." Their actions are contrasted with her immobility and numbing sensations. Space and the heavens are set off against weight and the tangible things of earth. Silence is set against a crescendo of sound. It is, in fact, because of these contrasts that the fulcrum operates so successfully.

Balance and proportion are obvious in the poem, since there are almost an equal number of lines and an equal amount of emotional weight on either side of the fulcrum. The buildup to the fulcrum is steady. Immediately after the point of balance is reached, the action ceases momentarily. How does that knowledge shape your rehearsal? How can your performance "freeze" for just a moment? Although the emotional and logical climaxes fall in the second portion of the poem, they do not overbalance the heaviness and familiarity of the funeral motif in the first section. Moreover, the emotional climax is controlled by abstractions: "the Heavens," "Being," and "strange Race." After the emotional climax, the speed picks up (watch your rate!), and the repeated use of "and" tightens the progression to the conclusion. How will you show that to your audience?

Rhythm of content is strongest in the shifts from the poet to the mourners that we mentioned earlier and in the focus on their actions and then on her responses. Again, there is not enough room for an elaborate pattern of rhythm of content in twenty short lines. As we continue to look at the poem, however, we are aware that both the variety and the contrast make a rhythmic contribution, as do some of the elements in unity.

Innumerable small details also contribute to the intrinsic factors. We cannot resist calling attention to the remarkable spacing of "treading," "creak across," and "Plank," all of which suggest floor boards. These words are placed with mathematical precision in lines 3, 10, and 17. The use of the already familiar "I" with "heard" controls the unity, and "heard" prepares us for "toll," "Bell," "Ear," "Silence," "Plank . . . broke," and finally "Crash."

By this point, you have learned a lot about the poem. What can you do with this information to inform your rehearsal? Now that you know how Dickinson put the poem together, you can begin to plan your performance to mirror her structure. Your rehearsal will be a search for the "sounding" that communicates most fully your understanding of the poem. Did Dickinson know you were going to do this analysis and plan all these details? Of course not. But they are still there, awaiting your voice and body to find their life. Now we begin putting it together.

Synthesis

The difficult task of synthesis comes next. Synthesis takes time—time to grow, correct, adjust, and grow again. In this process the interpreter begins to work as an artist. Slowly, step by step, all the parts are reassembled so that the selection is once more an ordered work of literary art and not a mere list of details. Don't expect to do it all at once. Putting a literary selection back together after analysis is as complex as reassembling a delicate watch, a complicated stereo system, or the engine of a car. Every piece must go where it belongs to function properly with every other piece. The process may seem like a juggling act the first few times you try it, but synthesis will get easier and more interesting each time. You may not be entirely satisfied with your first few attempts, but that is because now you know much more and no longer need to rely on good luck or slick tricks that you hope will work.

Rehearsing the Selection

It is impossible to set up a system that will work for every interpreter with every selection: each piece of literature presents its own problems and opportunities, and every performer has different strengths. However, the following procedure may give you a general working outline:

- Some performers like either to enlarge a copy of their chosen text photographically or to reproduce the text in a large, legible typeface. A fresh copy, easy to consult during performance, can be highlighted with distinctive markings to remind you to increase volume or rate, control character differentiation, or maintain cohesion in a long passage. Because this "script" is for you only, you can mark it in any way you wish.

- Read the selection aloud. What images can you see? If you were going to make a movie of this selection, what would the audience see *at each moment*? Pay attention, as you read it again, to what it means and "how" it goes about achieving meaning. Read it aloud again.

- As you are reading, note carefully what your voice is doing and how your body is responding. You haven't made performance choices yet, but if emotions and gestures are coming through in these early readings, remember where and why and what you are doing. You may not end up with that specific gesture or inflection pattern, but you will know that an audience is likely to want special attention paid at that point.

- Give some attention to the method of organization. Key words, phrases, and sentences come into play here, as do the denotations and connotations of words. Locate the climax or the fulcrum, and determine how the author brings the material to a close so that your audience will know where the selection is going and when it gets there.

- Look at all the elements that contribute to unity and harmony. What holds the selection together and keeps it moving? How is the unity and movement reinforced throughout the selection?

- Examine the imagery in the selection; allow yourself to respond fully with your mind and emotions. How does the imagery contribute to unity and harmony, and how and where does it provide variety and contrast? Don't forget the importance of connotation here. Let your body and voice succumb to the imagery. What do you see? What do you hear?

- Who is speaking in the selection? Is this persona thinking aloud for us to overhear, or addressing another person specifically? How would he or she respond to the connotation and imagery you have identified? What is the locus—the physical, psychological, and temporal position—of the persona in relation to the experience being shared? Is it a memory of the past, is it the present, or is it the future?

- How does the author balance the two parts on either side of the fulcrum? Is there a strong rhythm of content in the emotional buildups and drops, in the alternation of attention to activity and passivity, past and present, or in any other aspect? How can your body and voice convey this rhythm to your audience?

- Keep reading the selection aloud as you fit these pieces together. Start several days ahead so you have time to allow the parts to meld. Be sure your voice reveals all the things you have discovered. Reflect the imagery and connotations in your voice quality, pace, and volume. Give every word its full value of sound.

Remember that audience members do not want to hear your analysis; they want the literature. If the analysis has been thorough and the preparation sound, trust the author and yourself. But until you know what and how the author has written, you cannot possibly perform the work to its full potential.

Excerpts and Introductions

Some of the selections in this book may be too long to be practical for a class assignment, but most of them offer units that may be used as excerpts. Feel free to use only a portion of a selection when time constrains you, but be careful not to damage the work in the process of selecting the words that will fill your requirements.

When you excerpt a play or a story, be sure to select a unit with at least a minor climax, so that your audience will get a clear sense that something is happening. You need to be aware of the key sentences or phrases in earlier sections that your audience must know about to understand and respond to the climax. For example, Peter Cameron's "Homework" contains many briefer scenes that build throughout the story, and each responds vividly to the pressure of performance. However, if you start your performance after the story begins, you will have to brief your audience on the pertinent events you have skipped. For that reason (and others), many interpreters prefer to excerpt from the beginning of the work, rather than after a great deal has happened that needs to be rehashed in your introduction. Obviously, if you can perform a complete work, you will not face this challenge, but remember that reluctance to face challenges ought *not* be a reason to disqualify any text from performance.

If you excerpt, why not use the author's own words to introduce your performance. Suppose you have chosen to perform that last half of Peter Cameron's "Homework." You could introduce yourself as Michael Pechetti and brief your audience on what's been happening to you recently. The introduction might go something like this:

> Hi! My name is Michael Pechetti. I haven't been going to class for the last week. My dog, Ked, was sitting outside of the A & P last Thursday when he got smashed by some kid pushing a shopping cart. This morning I sat at the table writing the note excusing me for my absence. I am eighteen, an adult, and thus able to excuse myself from school.

You could then join the text with the line beginning "In Spanish class we are seeing a film on flamenco dancers."

Notice that that introduction does not mention either the title of the story or the author. If your audience is already familiar with the work, mentioning them may not be necessary.

Alternatively, for your introduction you could select a sentence that features a key phrase, make brief additional comments in your own words, and proceed directly to the performance. Sometimes your audience will need to be prepared for something that occurs during your segment, and it will be smoother to explain that in the introduction. Audiences who are unfamiliar with the work you have selected are entitled to know the author and, if it's relevant, the title.

Don't tell the audience what they are about to hear; prepare them to listen and watch intelligently. For example, perhaps a literature class is reading American women's fiction, and you volunteer to perform Kate Chopin's story. Your introduction might go something like this:

> Sometimes we think not much can happen to us in the space of an hour, but Kate Chopin tells the story of a woman who in even less time came to understand what her life *could* be. Writing at the end of the nineteenth century, Chopin's subtle, economical stories distinguished her among the women writing at the time. This is Kate Chopin's "The Story of an Hour."

In short, tailor your introduction to the work you have selected to perform, as well as to the audience that has assembled to experience your performance.

Keep your introduction as brief as possible: you don't want the porch to be larger than the house! Introductions should help you establish the mood you want to create. Address your comments directly to the audience without using written notes. That way audience members can more easily believe that this is a special performance just for them. Introductions—and transitions, if they are necessary—should appear to be spontaneous. They are an important part of your performance, but they are not what your audience wants to hear. Before working on the porch, be sure the house is sturdy.

After you have completed your analysis, strive with each rehearsal for the finished polish of a performance. The more you rehearse, the closer you come to the goal you imagine. Many performers find irresistible texts that they perform for several years, certain that some performances get qualities that others miss, but equally sure that they have not incorporated in *one* performance all they know about the work. We list below some questions to ask yourself after each rehearsal or performance. If you have a classmate, you can use these questions to appraise each other's performance.

Analyzing the Rehearsal and the Performance

Whether it is a rehearsal or a performance, wait a few minutes before undertaking analysis. In fact, it may not be until some hours later that you get a clear image of your achievements—and your shortcomings. Students often say things happen in performance that never happened in rehearsal, and things didn't happen in performance that were carefully planned in rehearsal. Try not to lose your perspective. When the adrenalin of performance subsides (and rehearsal should always aim for the engagement and commitment of performance!), ask yourself some questions:

- Did you keep your concentration steady? If not, what caused the break? Where did it occur? Why there?

- Did you control and preserve the unity so that there was an effective beginning, middle, and conclusion?

- Did your introduction tell those in the audience what they needed for background, especially if you used an excerpt? Did it set the proper mood for the selection? Was it too long?

- Were variety and contrast allowed to work effectively while remaining well within the essential unity and harmony? Did you allow for the rhythm of content while keeping the thread of unity firm and clear?

- Did the audience respond as you expected? Did any of your performance mannerisms distract the audience from what they were hearing?

Part of your responsibility—and pleasure—in an interpretation class is to be a good audience. Put your own worries aside for a time and really *listen* and react to the readings of others. Often you learn as much or more from someone else's performance as from your own. Your instructor's comments may seem vague or theoretical until you see or hear someone else's performance. Then suddenly you see how what someone else did helped communicate the selection or detracted from it.

You will probably be asked to comment about others' readings. In your comments about these performances, try to describe to the performer exactly what you saw and heard. Avoid such comments as "I liked it" or "It was nice." Of course, the reader will be pleased that you liked it, but without more specific comments on why you liked it, he or she will not know how to improve. Mention instead a specific moment in the performance. A comment like "The way you held your head made Mrs. Mallard seem very stern and cold at the end of the story" or "Your voice at the opening of 'I Felt a Funeral' was very high-pitched and sounded as if you were about to scream" will help the performer focus specifically on exactly what happened during the performance. Only in this way can the performer learn what he or she successfully communicated to you. Together you and the reader can examine the selection to see if it calls for the actions or mannerisms you describe. And you can compare your responses with those of other audience members to be sure that the performance was equally effective for others in the audience. Finally, we have found that performers are more likely to listen carefully if they think you enjoyed some aspect of the reading. Why not begin by mentioning something specific that succeeded in the performance and then move on to the elements that still need work?

REMEMBER THIS!

We've covered a great deal of ground in this chapter, but preparing for your first performance takes time, and new responsibilities do not always come easily. The next chapter offers extensive advice about using your voice in performance, and to benefit thoroughly from that training, you will need to remember:

- How to grasp denotative and connotative meanings.

- How to define and embody the persona.

- How locus operates on different levels to create impact and effect.

- How climax is prepared and presented.

- How the intrinsic factors (unity and harmony, variety and contrast, balance and proportion, rhythm) collaborate.

- How thorough analysis helps to shape your rehearsal plan.

- How your performance choices emerge from your rehearsal discoveries *and* from your performance experience.

- How to shape an appropriate introduction.

Now, we offer some challenging possibilities.

Selections for Analysis and Oral Interpretation

Each of these selections must be analyzed thoroughly. Do not try to make each one follow the pattern of Chopin's story or Dickinson's poem, however, because every piece of writing is unique. Look for all the details that we have discussed. Then decide which ones contribute to unity and harmony, and see where variety and contrast exist within the unity and harmony. Find the fulcrum and climaxes, and consider balance and proportion. Look carefully for rhythm of content. Remember that details may contribute to more than one of the intrinsic factors.

Begin with the whole selection and let it work on you until you feel comfortable with it. Then move into an objective analysis. After each step, go back to the complete selection and see how the pieces fit together. Remember that your audience wants the total effect, not the separate pieces. Each selection is followed by one or two questions to assist your rehearsal or to begin class discussion.

Although these three poems all have stars as their main motif, they vary considerably in the ways they treat this theme. Each poem shows strong marks of individuality. In each case the locus is here on earth. The poems make an interesting comparison. In the first poem, by Walt Whitman, repetition creates both frustration and relief. The exquisite delay that culminates in the last syllable of the last line must never become sluggish.

When I Heard the Learn'd Astronomer

WALT WHITMAN

When I heard the learn'd astronomer,
When the proofs, the figures, were ranged in columns before me,
When I was shown the charts and diagrams, to add, divide, and
    measure them,
When I sitting heard the astronomer where he lectured with much
    applause in the lecture-room,
How soon unaccountable I became tired and sick,
Till rising and gliding out I wander'd off by myself,
In the mystical moist night-air, and from time to time,
Look'd up in perfect silence at the stars.

- ◆ How can you demonstrate the persona's growing dismay?

- ◆ At what word did your persona first see the stars?

Sonnet

JOHN KEATS

Bright star! would I were as steadfast as thou art—	1
Not in lone splendor hung aloft the night	2
And watching, with eternal lids apart,	3
Like nature's patient, sleepless Eremite,	4
The moving waters at their priest-like task	5
Of pure ablution round earth's human shores,	6
Or gazing on the new soft fallen mask	7
Of snow upon the mountains and the moors—	8
No—yet still steadfast, still unchangeable,	9
Pillow'd upon my fair love's ripening breast,	10
To feel for ever its soft fall and swell,	11
Awake for ever in a sweet unrest,	12
Still, still to hear her tender-taken breath,	13
And so live ever—or else swoon to death.	14

- How did your performance of the *still*s in line 9 differ from the *still*s in line 13? Why?

The Starlight Night

GERARD MANLEY HOPKINS

Look at the stars! look, look up at the skies!	1
O look at all the fire-folk sitting in the air!	2
The bright boroughs, the circle-citadels there!	3
Down in dim woods the diamond delves! the elves'-eyes!	4
The grey lawns cold where gold, where quickgold lies!	5
Wind-beat whitebeam! airy abeles set on a flare!	6
Flake doves sent floating forth at a farmyard scare!	7
Ah well! it is all a purchase, all is a prize.	8
Buy then! bid then—What?—Prayer, patience, alms, vows.	9
Look, look: a May-mess, like on orchard boughs!	10
Look! March-bloom, like on mealed-with-yellow sallows!	11
These are indeed the barn; withindoors house	12
The shocks. This piece-bright paling shuts the spouse	13
Christ home, Christ and his mother and all his hallows.	14

- Did you see each manifestation of stars before moving on to the next?

- How did you show your audience the auction that begins in line 9?

Stars do not exhilarate every poet. One critic claimed that "Desert Places" ranked among the most terrifying poems in the English language. Frost's characteristic accessibility has never been more alluring—or more dangerous. Be sure to take all the time your audience needs to establish the locus of the first two stanzas, and then track very carefully how the vision outward changes direction.

Desert Places

ROBERT FROST

Snow falling and night falling fast oh fast
In a field I looked into going past,
And the ground almost covered smooth in snow,
But a few weeds and stubble showing last.

The woods around it have it—it is theirs.
All animals are smothered in their lairs.
I am too absent-spirited to count;
The loneliness includes me unawares.

And lonely as it is that loneliness
Will be more lonely ere it will be less—
A blanker whiteness of benighted snow
With no expression, nothing to express.

They cannot scare me with their empty spaces
Between stars—on stars where no human race is.
I have it in me so much nearer home
To scare myself with my own desert places.

◆ How did your body and voice mark the fulcrum?

◆ A shift in rate in the last stanza reveals the speaker's fear. What prepared your audience for the revelation before then?

The narrator in this excerpt is clearly a grown man remembering a special time in his childhood. Although the characters vary considerably in age, their attitudes are perfectly attuned. All the speeches are given to the woman. Her short sentences have the excitement and vitality of immediacy, which gives nice contrast to the quieter but warm and happy memory of the narrator, thus providing an essential rhythm.

from **A Christmas Memory**

TRUMAN CAPOTE

Imagine a morning in late November. A coming of winter morning more than twenty years ago. Consider the kitchen of a spreading old house in a country town. A great black stove is its main feature; but there is also a big round table and a fireplace with two rocking chairs placed in front of it. Just today the fireplace commenced its seasonal roar.

A woman with shorn white hair is standing at the kitchen window. She is wearing tennis shoes and a shapeless gray sweater over a summery calico dress. She is small and sprightly, like a bantam hen; but, due to a long youthful illness, her shoulders are pitifully hunched. Her face is remarkable—not unlike Lincoln's, craggy like that, and tinted by sun and wind; but it is delicate too, finely boned, and her eyes are sherry-colored and timid. "Oh my," she exclaims, her breath smoking the windowpane, "it's fruitcake weather!"

The person to whom she is speaking is myself. I am seven; she is sixty-something. We are cousins, very distant ones, and we have lived together—well, as long as I can remember. Other people inhabit the house, relatives; and though they have power over us, and frequently make us cry, we are not, on the whole, too much aware of them. We are each other's best friend. She calls me Buddy, in memory of a boy who was formerly her best friend. The other Buddy died in the 1880's, when she was still a child. She is still a child.

"I knew it before I got out of bed," she says, turning away from the window with a purposeful excitement in her eyes. "The courthouse bell sounded so cold and clear. And there were no birds singing; they've gone to warmer country, yes indeed. Oh, Buddy, stop stuffing biscuit and fetch our buggy. Help me find my hat. We've thirty cakes to bake."

It's always the same: a morning arrives in November, and my friend, as though officially inaugurating the Christmas time of year that exhilarates her imagination and fuels the blaze of her heart, announces: "It's fruitcake weather! Fetch our buggy. Help me find my hat."

The hat is found, a straw cartwheel corsaged with velvet roses out-of-doors has faded: it once belonged to a more fashionable relative. Together, we guide our buggy, a dilapidated baby carriage, out to the garden and into a grove of pecan trees. The buggy is mine, that is, it was bought for me when I was born. It is made of wicker, rather unraveled, and the wheels wobble like a drunkard's legs. But it is a faithful object; springtimes, we take it to the woods and fill it with flowers, herbs, wild fern for our porch pots; in the summer, we pile it with picnic paraphernalia and sugar-cane fishing poles and roll it down to the edge of a creek; it has its winter uses, too: as a truck for hauling firewood from the yard to the kitchen, as a warm bed for Queenie, our tough little orange and white rat terrier, who has survived distemper and two rattlesnake bites. Queenie is trotting beside it now.

Three hours later we are back in the kitchen hulling a heaping buggy-load of windfall pecans. Our backs hurt from gathering them: how hard they were to find (the main crop having been shaken off the trees and sold by the orchard's owners, who are not us) among the concealing leaves, the frosted deceiving grass. Caarackle! A cheery crunch, scraps of miniature thunder sound as the shells collapse and the golden mound of sweet oily ivory meat mounts in the milk-glass bowl. Queenie begs to taste, and now and again my friend sneaks her a mite, though insisting we deprive ourselves. "We musn't, Buddy: If we start, we won't stop. And there's scarcely enough as there is. For thirty cakes." The kitchen is growing dark. Dusk turns the window into a mirror: our reflections mingle with the rising moon as we work by the fireside in the firelight. At last, when the moon is quite high, we toss the final hull into the fire and with joined sighs, watch it catch flame. The buggy is empty, the bowl is brimful.

- Did your audience see, hear, touch, smell, and taste all of the elements described?

- Did you allow time for each image to sink in?

Anne Sexton is often spoken of as a poet of the "confessional" school. This poem is an outgrowth of her actual experience in an institution, but her skill takes it beyond fact. The long sentence with its nursery rhyme construction of clauses must be used as a connected unit. The last sentence is an important contrast. The speaker's mental disturbance must not be overplayed. She is perfectly, but detachedly, in control of her logic. Locus is obviously of great importance here.

⑥ Ringing the Bells

ANNE SEXTON

And this is the way they ring
the bells in Bedlam
and this is the bell-lady
who comes each Tuesday morning
to give us a music lesson

and because the attendants make you go
and because we mind by instinct,
like bees caught in the wrong hive,
we are the circle of crazy ladies
who sit in the lounge of the mental house
and smile at the smiling woman
who passes us each a bell,
who points at my hand
that holds my bell, E flat,
and this is the gray dress next to me
who grumbles as if it were special
to be old, to be old,
and this is the small hunched squirrel girl
on the other side of me
who picks at the hairs over her lip,
who picks at the hairs over her lip all day
and this is how the bells really sound,
as untroubled and clean
as a workable kitchen,
and this is always my bell responding
to my hand that responds to the lady
who points at me, E flat;
and although we are no better for it,
they tell you to go. And you do.

◆ How did you show your audience everyone else in "the circle of crazy ladies"?

One of the most distinctive of the current composer-lyricist-performers, Amanda McBroom is probably best known for "The Rose." You do not need to know the country-flavored melody she devised for the following lyrics to glimpse the ferocity of the speaker's intentions.

 Dreaming

AMANDA McBROOM

I'm twenty-one and I'm five-foot-nine
Got a face and a body to change your mind;
I'm a picture so fine to see,
Whenever I walk the streets of town
The men and boys they all fall down,
Calling, "Darling, come home with me;
Oh pretty darling, please come home with me!"

My daddy, he's a business man,
Got a big old castle in Switzerland
And a mansion by the sea.
He spends his time with queens and kings,
And he fills his pockets with diamond rings,
And he brings them home to me.
Oh yes, he brings them all home to me.

Dreaming helps you make it through the day,
Dreaming when there's nothing left to say.
Dreaming helps to take the pain away.
Me, I live in dreams.

My husband, he's a movie star
Comes home every night in a brand new car,
And he calls me the perfect wife.
We got a big old house with a hundred rooms,
And a fine rose garden that always blooms.
It's a very happy life;
Oh, yes, a very happy life.

Dreaming, it's a way to pass the time;
Dreaming everything will turn out fine.
Dreaming, it's the only thing that's mine.
Me, I live in dreams.

With the dishes done and the kids all gone,
I stand and stare at the old brown lawn,
Close my eyes now I'm free.
Down my walk comes a handsome man,
He takes me by my rough, red hand
And he heals it with a kiss,
Says, "Let me take you away from all of this."

Dreaming, no it's not the same as lies.
Dreaming, it's the easiest disguise.
Dreaming that there's love still in your eyes,
Me, I live in dreams;
Me, I live in dreams.

- ◆ How did your audience know where you placed the fulcrum?

- ◆ Is the "you" implied in the last stanza present from the first line?
  How did you show that to your audience?

Compare this story about the death of a pet with Deborah Sherman's "Dulce," but don't miss the distinctive differences. The present tense here increases the immediacy of the tale as it moves Michael (the storyteller) closer to us. Try to determine precisely what Keds's death means to him. This story also affords many opportunities to excerpt.

Homework

PETER CAMERON

My dog, Keds, was sitting outside of the A. & P. last Thursday when he got smashed by some kid pushing a shopping cart. At first we thought he just had a broken leg, but later we found out he was bleeding inside. Every time he opened his mouth, blood would seep out like dull red words in a bad silent dream.

Every night before my sister goes to her job she washes her hair in the kitchen sink with beer and mayonnaise and eggs. Sometimes I sit at the table and watch the mixture dribble down her white back. She boils a pot of water on the stove at the same time; when she is finished with her hair, she steams her face. She wants so badly to be beautiful.

I am trying to solve complicated algebraic problems I have set for myself. Since I started cutting school last Friday, the one thing I miss is homework. Find the value for n. Will it be a whole number? It is never a whole number. It is always a fraction.

"Will you get me a towel?" my sister asks. She turns her face toward me and clutches her hair to the top of her head. The sprayer hose slithers into its hole next to the faucet.

I hand her a dish towel. "No," she says. "A bath towel. Don't be stupid."

In the bathroom, my mother is watering her plants. She has arranged them in the tub and turned the shower on. She sits on the toilet lid and watches. It smells like outdoors in the bathroom.

I hand my sister the towel and watch her wrap it round her head. She takes the cover off the pot of boiling water and drops lemon slices in. Then she lowers her face into the steam.

This is the problem I have set for myself:

$$\frac{245(n + 17)}{34} = 396(n - 45)$$

$$n =$$

Wednesday, I stand outside the high-school gym doors. Inside, students are lined up doing calisthenics. It's snowing, and prematurely dark, and I can watch without being seen.

"Well," my father says when I get home. He is standing in the garage testing the automatic door. Every time a plane flies overhead, the door opens or closes, so my father is trying to fix it. "Have you changed your mind about school?" he asks me.

I lock my bicycle to a pole. This infuriates my father, who doesn't believe in locking things up in his own house. He pretends not to notice. I wipe a thin stripe of snow off the fenders with my middle finger. It is hard to ride a bike in the snow. This afternoon on my way home from the high school I fell off, and I lay in the snowy road with my bike on top of me. It felt warm.

"We're going to get another dog," my father says.

"It's not that," I say. I wish everyone would stop talking about dogs. I can't tell how sad I really am about Keds versus how sad I am in general. If I don't keep these things separate, I feel as if I'm betraying Keds.

"Then what is it?" my father says.

"It's nothing," I say.

My father nods. He is very good about bringing things up and then letting them drop. A lot gets dropped. He presses the button on the automatic control. The door slides down its oiled tracks and falls shut. It's dark in the garage. My father presses the button again and the door opens, and we both look outside at the snow falling in the driveway, as if in those few seconds the world might have changed.

My mother has forgotten to call me for dinner, and when I confront her with this she tells me that she did, but that I was sleeping. She is loading the dishwasher. My sister is standing at the counter, listening, and separating eggs for her shampoo.

"What can I get you?" my mother asks. "Would you like a meatloaf sandwich?"

"No," I say. I open the refrigerator and survey its illuminated contents. "Could I have some scrambled eggs?"

"O.K.," says my mother. She comes and stands beside me and puts her hand on top of mine on the door handle. There are no eggs in the refrigerator. "Oh," my mother says; then, "Julie?"

"Did you take the last eggs?"

"I guess so," my sister says. "I don't know."

"Forget it," I say, "I won't have eggs."

"No," my mother says. "Julie doesn't need them in her shampoo. That's not what I bought them for."

"I do," my sister says. "It's a formula. It doesn't work without the eggs. I need the protein."

"I don't want eggs," I say. "I don't want anything." I go into my bedroom.

My mother comes in and stands looking out the window. The snow has turned to rain. "You're not the only one who is unhappy about this," she says.

"About what?" I say. I am sitting on my unmade bed. If I pick up my room, my mother will make my bed: that's the deal. I didn't pick up my room this morning.

"About Keds," she says. "I'm unhappy too. But it doesn't stop me from going to school."

"You don't go to school," I say.

"You know what I mean," my mother says. She turns around and looks at my room, and begins to pick things off the floor.

"Don't do that," I say. "Stop."

My mother drops the dirty clothes in an exaggerated gesture of defeat. She almost—almost—throws them on the floor. The way she holds her hands accentuates their emptiness. "If you're not going to go to school," she says, "the least you can do is clean your room."

In the algebra word problems, a boat sails down a river while a jeep drives along the bank. Which will reach the capital first? If a plane flies at a certain speed from Boulder to Oklahoma City and then at a different speed from Oklahoma City to Detroit, how many cups of coffee can the stewardess serve, assuming she is unable to serve during the first and last ten minutes of each flight? How many times can a man ride the elevator to the top of the Empire State Building while his wife climbs the stairs, given that the woman travels one stair slower each flight? And if the man jumps up while the elevator is going down, which is moving—the man, the woman, the elevator, or the snow falling outside?

The next Monday I get up and make preparations for going to school. I can tell at the breakfast table that my mother is afraid to acknowledge them for fear it won't be true. I haven't gotten up before ten o'clock in a week. My mother makes me French toast. I sit at the table and write the note excusing me for my absence. I am eighteen, an adult, and thus able to excuse myself from school. This is what my note says:

> DEAR MR. KELLY [my homeroom teacher]:
>   Please excuse my absence February 17–24. I was unhappy and did not feel able to attend school.
>
> > Sincerely,
> > MICHAEL PECHETTI

This is the exact format my mother used when she wrote my notes, only she always said, "Michael was home with a sore throat," or "Michael was home with a bad cold." The colds that prevented me from going to school were always bad colds.

My mother watches me write the note but doesn't ask to see it. I leave it on the kitchen table when I go to the bathroom, and when I come back to get it I know she has read it. She is washing the bowl she dipped the French toast into. Before, she would let Keds lick it clean. He liked eggs.

In Spanish class we are seeing a film on flamenco dancers. The screen wouldn't pull down, so it is being projected on the blackboard, which is green and cloudy with erased chalk. It looks a little as if the women are sick, and dancing in Heaven. Suddenly the little phone on the wall buzzes.

Mrs. Smitts, the teacher, gets up to answer it, and then walks over to me. She puts her hand on my shoulder and leans her face close to mine. It is dark in the room. "Miguel," Mrs. Smitts whispers, "*Tienes que ir a la oficina de* guidance."

"What?" I say.

She leans closer, and her hair blocks the dancers. Despite the clicking castanets and the roomful of students, there is something intimate about this moment "*Tienes que ir a la oficina de* guidance," she repeats slowly. Then, "You must go to the guidance office. Now. *Vaya.*"

My guidance counsellor, Mrs. Dietrich, used to be a history teacher, but she couldn't take it anymore, so she was moved into guidance. On her immaculate desk is a calendar blotter with "LUNCH" written across the middle of every box, including Saturday and Sunday. The only other things on the desk are an empty photo cube and my letter to Mr. Kelly. I sit down, and she shows me the letter as if I haven't yet read it. I reread it.

"Did you write this?" she asks.

I nod affirmatively. I can tell Mrs. Dietrich is especially nervous about this interview. Our meetings are always charged with tension. At the last one, when I was selecting my second-semester courses, she started to laugh hysterically when I said I wanted to take Boys' Home Ec. Now every time I see her in the halls she stops me and asks me how I'm doing in Boys' Home Ec. It's the only course of mine she remembers.

I hand the note back to her and say, "I wrote it this morning," as if this clarified things.

"This morning?"

"At breakfast," I say.

"Do you think this is an acceptable excuse?" Mrs. Dietrich asks. "For missing more than a week of school?"

"I'm sure it isn't," I say.

"Then why did you write it?"

Because it is the truth, I start to say. But somehow I know that saying this will make me more unhappy. It might make me cry. "I've been doing algebra at home," I say.

"That's fine," Mrs. Dietrich says, "but it's not the point. The point is, to graduate you have to attend school for a hundred and eighty days, or have legitimate excuses for the days you've missed. That's the point. Do you want to graduate?"

"Yes," I say.

"Of course you do," Mrs. Dietrich says.

She crumples my note and tries to throw it into the wastepaper basket but misses. We both look for a second at the note lying on the floor, and then I get up and throw it away. The only other thing in her wastepaper basket is a banana peel. I can picture her eating a banana in her tiny office. This, too, makes me sad.

"Sit down," Mrs. Dietrich says.

I sit down.

"I understand your dog died. Do you want to talk about that?"

"No," I say.

"Is that what you're so unhappy about?" she says. "Or is there something else?"

I almost mention the banana peel in her wastebasket, but I don't. "No," I say. "It's just my dog."

Mrs. Dietrich thinks for a moment. I can tell she is embarrassed to be talking about a dead dog. She would be more comfortable if it were a parent or a sibling.

"I don't want to talk about it," I repeat.

She opens her desk drawer and takes out a pad of hall passes. She begins to write one out for me. She has beautiful handwriting. I think of her learning to write beautifully as a child and then growing up to be a guidance counsellor, and this makes me unhappy.

"Mr. Neuman is willing to overlook this matter," she says. Mr. Neuman is the principal. "Of course, you will have to make up all the work you've missed. Can you do that?"

"Yes," I say.

Mrs. Dietrich tears the pass from the pad and hands it to me. Our hands touch. "You'll get over this," she says. "Believe me, you will."

My sister works until midnight at the Photo-Matica. It's a tiny booth in the middle of the A. & P. parking lot. People drive up and leave their film and come back the next day for the pictures. My sister wears a uniform that makes her look like a counterperson in a fast-food restaurant. Sometimes at night when I'm sick of being at home I walk downtown and sit in the booth with her.

There's a machine in the booth that looks like a printing press, only snapshots ride down a conveyor belt and fall into a bin and then disappear. The machine gives the illusion that your photographs are being developed on the spot. It's a fake. The same fifty photographs roll through over and over, and my sister says nobody notices, because everyone in town is taking the same pictures. She opens up the envelopes and looks at them.

Before I go into the booth, I buy cigarettes in the A. & P. It is open twenty-four hours a day, and I love it late at night. It is big and bright and empty. The checkout girl sits on her counter swinging her legs. The Muzak plays "If Ever I Would Leave You." Before I buy the cigarettes, I walk up and down the aisles. Everything looks good to eat, and the things that aren't edible look good in their own way. The detergent aisle is colorful and clean-smelling.

My sister is listening to the radio and polishing her nails when I get to the booth. It is almost time to close.

"I hear you went to school today," she says.

"Yeah."

"How was it?" she asks. She looks at her nails, which are so long it's frightening.

"It was O.K.," I say. "We made chili dogs in Home Ec."

"So are you over it all?"

I look at the pictures riding down the conveyor belt. I know the order practically by heart: graduation, graduation, birthday, mountains, baby, baby, new car, bride, bride and groom, house . . . "I guess so," I say.

"Good," says my sister. "It was getting to be a little much." She puts her tiny brush back in the bottle, capping it. She shows me her nails. They're an odd brown shade. "Cinnamon," she says. "It's an earth color." She looks out at the parking lot. A boy is collecting the abandoned shopping carts, forming a long silver train, which he noses back toward the store. I can tell he is singing by the way his mouth moves.

"That's where we found Keds," my sister says, pointing to the Salvation Army bin.

When I went out to buy cigarettes, Keds would follow me. I hung out down here at night before he died. I was unhappy then, too. That's what no one understands. I named him Keds because he was all white with big black feet and it looked as if he had high-top sneakers on. My mother wanted to name him Bootie. Bootie is a cat's name. It's a dumb name for a dog.

"It's a good thing you weren't here when we found him," my sister says. "You would have gone crazy."

I'm not really listening. It's all nonsense. I'm working on a new problem: Find the value for n such that n plus everything else in your life makes you feel all right. What would n equal? Solve for n.

- How did you help your audience understand why Michael tells us this story?

This poem rewards performance in part because audiences respond so posi-
tively, and in part because we so fully understand the speaker's dilemma. Trust
the line length completely; you will not be disappointed.

Upon Learning That a Junior High School Acquaintance Has Been Nominated for an Academy Award

JOANNE GILBERT

Ungainly in candy-striped pajamas as a Who
from whom the Grinch stole Christmas
temporarily—
she wasn't that memorable.
Tonight, same frizz of hair,
same awkward gait,
with much of the world watching,
she apparently is.

When I first started to see her in movies,
I wanted to
clench   the   screen,
tear
        great
            gobs
from her face, shouting,
"It's not fair!
It should be me!"
Cool rationality turned
my sour grapes to
sour wine and
I plotted her public embarrassment:
I would send our Junior High Yearbook to *The National Enquirer*
(anonymously, of course)
so the world could feast its eyes on her
chubby, orthodontic countenance.
Meanwhile, I worried I'd run into her at her films,
remaining invisible,
glowering
as she misremembered me.

Tonight she wears outrageous earrings and floats among the
    privileged,
eyes the golden statuette,
smiles benignly,
never once recalling
I live.

Chatting with heroes, this Amazon has no idea I know her battle
    scar;
a cyst on her egg sac—the whole untimely ripped at her ripening—
front cover material
most definitely.

The envelope please . . .
es me because it
does   not   grant
her wish.
An eye for an eye;
I am satisfied.
I was teased more than she, after all.
Justice as the camera—still trained on her—reveals nothing.
It is right; she was only a Who—
I was the narrator.

 ◆ How did you embody the speaker's wide range of physical and vocal responses?

*This powerful poem features a second-person narrator who comes to under-
stand his brother and himself in ways he hadn't expected. The shape of the lines
trace the thoughts that race through his mind and describe the change that
occurs by the end. Lassell's poem is among the earliest—and finest—of the
works of art that speak about the holocaust of AIDS.*

How to Watch Your Brother Die

MICHAEL LASSELL

When the call comes, be calm.
Say to your wife, "My brother is dying. I have to fly
to California."
Try not to be shocked that he already looks like
a cadaver.
Say to the young man sitting by your brother's side,
"I'm his brother."
Try not to be shocked when the young man says,
"I'm his lover. Thanks for coming."
Listen to the doctor with a steel face on.
Sign the necessary forms.
Tell the doctor you will take care of everything.
Wonder why doctors are so remote.

Watch the lover's eyes as they stare into
your brother's eyes as they stare into

space.
Wonder what they see there.
Remember the time he was jealous and
opened your eyebrow with a sharp stick.
Forgive him out loud
even if he can't understand you.
Realize the scar will be
all that's left of him.

Over coffee in the hospital cafeteria
say to the lover, "You're an extremely good-looking
young man."
Hear him say,
"I never thought I was good enough looking to
deserve your brother."
Watch the tears well up in his eyes. Say,
"I'm sorry. I don't know what it means to be
the lover of another man."
Hear him say,
"It's just like a wife, only the commitment is
deeper because the odds against you are so much
greater."
Say nothing, but
take his hand like a brother's.

Drive to Mexico for unproven drugs that might
help him live longer.
Explain what they are to the border guard.
Fill with rage when he informs you,
"You can't bring those across."
Begin to grow loud.
Feel the lover's hand on your arm,
restraining you. See in the guard's eye
how much a man can hate another man.
Say to the lover, "How can you stand it?"
Hear him say, "You get used to it."
Think of one of your children getting used to
another man's hatred.

Call your wife on the telephone. Tell her,
"He hasn't much time.
I'll be home soon." Before you hang up say,
"How could anyone's commitment be deeper than
a husband and wife?" Hear her say,
"Please, I don't want to know the details."

When he slips into an irrevocable coma
hold his lover in your arms while he sobs,
no longer strong. Wonder how much longer
you will be able to be strong.
Feel how it feels to hold a man in your arms
whose arms are used to holding men.
Offer God anything to bring your brother back.
Know you have nothing God could possibly want.
Curse God, but do not
abandon Him.

Stare at the face of the funeral director
when he tells you he will not
embalm the body for fear of
contamination. Let him see in your eyes
how much a man can hate another man.
Stand beside a casket covered in flowers,
white flowers. Say,
"Thank you for coming" to each of several hundred men
who file past in tears, some of them
holding hands. Know that your brother's life
was not what you imagined. Overhear two mourners say,
"I wonder who'll be next."

Arrange to take an early flight home.
His lover will drive you to the airport.
When your flight is announced say,
awkwardly, "If I can do anything, please
let me know." Do not flinch when he says,
"Forgive yourself for not wanting to know him
after he told you. He did."
Stop and let it soak in. Say,
"He forgave me, or he knew himself?"
"Both," the lover will say, not knowing what else
to do. Hold him like a brother while he
kisses you on the cheek. Think that
you haven't been kissed by a man since
your father died. Think,
"This is no moment not to be strong." Fly
first class and drink scotch. Stroke
your split eyebrow with a finger
and think of your brother alive. Smile
at the memory and think
how your children will feel in your arms,
warm and friendly and without challenge.

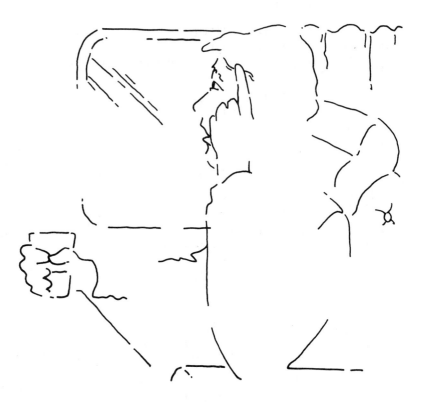

- How did you demonstrate the wide range of physical responses in the speaker?

- Where, specifically, in the speaker's world does his brother exist?

Harry Potter was a typically unhappy, abused orphan until he discovered—on his eleventh birthday—that he was a wizard and, come September, would begin to study at Hogwart's School of Witchcraft and Wizardry. To outfit Harry for his new school, Rubeus Hagrid (the school's enormous gamekeeper) has taken him to shop for books, gowns, potion ingredients, and an owl. Now the only thing that Harry still needs is a wand. And the only place for wands is Ollivanders.

FROM **Harry Potter and the Sorcerer's Stone**

J. K. ROWLING

A magic wand . . . this was what Harry had been really looking forward to.

The last shop was narrow and shabby. Peeling gold letters over the door read Ollivanders: Makers of Fine Wands since 382 B.C. A single wand lay on a faded purple cushion in the dusty window.

A tinkling bell rang somewhere in the depths of the shop as they stepped inside. It was a tiny place, empty except for a single, spindly chair that Hagrid sat on to wait. Harry felt strangely as though he had entered a very strict library; he swallowed a lot of new questions that had just occurred to him and looked instead at the thousands of narrow boxes piled neatly right up to the ceiling. For some reason, the back of his neck prickled. The very dust and silence in here seemed to tingle with some secret magic.

"Good afternoon," said a soft voice. Harry jumped. Hagrid must have jumped, too, because there was a loud crunching noise and he got quickly off the spindly chair.

An old man was standing before them, his wide, pale eyes shining like moons through the gloom of the shop.

"Hello," said Harry awkwardly.

"Ah yes," said the man. "Yes, yes. I thought I'd be seeing you soon. Harry Potter." It wasn't a question. "You have your mother's eyes. It seems only yesterday she was in here herself, buying her first wand. Ten and a quarter inches long, swishy, made of willow. Nice wand for charm work."

Mr. Ollivander moved closer to Harry. Harry wished he would blink. Those silvery eyes were a bit creepy.

"Your father, on the other hand, favored a mahogany wand. Eleven inches. Pliable. A little more power and excellent for trans-figuration. Well, I say your father favored it—it's really the wand that chooses the wizard, of course."

Mr. Ollivander had come so close that he and Harry were almost nose to nose. Harry could see himself reflected in those misty eyes.

"And that's where . . ."

Mr. Ollivander touched the lightning scar on Harry's forehead with a long, white finger.

"I'm sorry to say I sold the wand that did it," he said softly. "Thirteen-and-a-half inches. Yew. Powerful wand, very powerful, and in the wrong hands . . . well, if I'd known what that wand was going out into the world to do. . . ."

He shook his head and then, to Harry's relief, spotted Hagrid.

"Rubeus! Rubeus Hagrid! How nice to see you again. . . . Oak, sixteen inches, rather bendy, wasn't it?"

"It was, sir, yes," said Hagrid.

"Good wand, that one. But I suppose they snapped it in half when you got expelled?" said Mr. Ollivander, suddenly stern.

"Er—yes, they did, yes," said Hagrid, shuffling his feet. "I've still got the pieces, though," he added brightly.

"But you don't *use* them?" said Mr. Ollivander sharply.

"Oh, no, sir," said Hagrid quickly. Harry noticed he gripped his pink umbrella very tightly as he spoke.

"Hmmm," said Mr. Ollivander, giving Hagrid a piercing look. "Well, now—Mr. Potter. Let me see." He pulled a long tape measure with silver markings out of his pocket. "Which is your wand arm?"

"Er—well, I'm right-handed," said Harry.

"Hold out your arm. That's it." He measured Harry from shoulder to finger, then wrist to elbow, shoulder to floor, knee to armpit and round his head. As he measured, he said, "Every Ollivander wand has a core of a powerful magical substance, Mr. Potter. We use unicorn hairs, phoenix tail feathers, and the heartstrings of dragons. No two Ollivander wands are the same, just as no two unicorns, dragons, or phoenixes are quite the same. And of course, you will never get such good results with another wizard's wand."

Harry suddenly realized that the tape measure, which was measuring between his nostrils, was doing this on its own. Mr. Ollivander was flitting around the shelves, taking down boxes.

"That will do," he said, and the tape measure crumpled into a heap on the floor. "Right then, Mr. Potter. Try this one. Beechwood and dragon heartstring. Nine inches. Nice and flexible. Just take it and give it a wave."

Harry took the wand and (feeling foolish) waved it around a bit, but Mr. Ollivander snatched it out of his hand almost at once.

"Maple and phoenix feather. Seven inches. Quite whippy. Try—"

Harry tried—but he had hardly raised the wand when it, too, was snatched back by Mr. Ollivander.

"No, no—here, ebony and unicorn hair, eight and a half inches, springy. Go on, go on, try it out."

Harry tried. And tried. He had no idea what Mr. Ollivander was waiting for. The pile of tried wands was mounting higher and higher on the spindly chair, but the more wands Mr. Ollivander pulled from the shelves, the happier he seemed to become.

"Tricky customer, eh? Not to worry, we'll find the perfect match here somewhere—I wonder, now—yes, why not—unusual combination—holly and phoenix feather, eleven inches, nice and supple."

Harry took the wand. He felt a sudden warmth in his fingers. He raised the wand above his head, brought it swishing down through the dusty air and a stream of red and gold sparks shot from the end like a firework, throwing dancing spots of light on to the walls. Hagrid whooped and clapped and Mr. Ollivander cried, "Oh, bravo! Yes, indeed, oh, very good. Well, well, well . . . how curious . . . how very curious . . ."

He put Harry's wand back into its box and wrapped it in brown paper, still muttering, "Curious . . . curious . . ."

"Sorry," said Harry, "but *what's* curious?"

Mr. Ollivander fixed Harry with his pale stare.

"I remember every wand I've ever sold, Mr. Potter. Every single wand. It so happens that the phoenix whose tail feather is in your wand, gave another feather—just one other. It is very curious indeed that you should be destined for this wand when its brother—why, its brother gave you that scar."

Harry swallowed.

"Yes, thirteen-and-a-half inches. Yew. Curious indeed how these things happen. The wand chooses the wizard, remember. . . . I think we must expect great things from you, Mr. Potter. . . . After all, He-Who-Must-Not-Be-Named did great things—terrible, yes, but great."

Harry shivered. He wasn't sure he liked Mr. Ollivander too much. He paid seven gold Galleons for his wand, and Mr. Ollivander bowed them from his shop.

- ◆ All that is magical is new and amazing to Harry but quite commonplace to the other characters. How did you establish their different attitudes?

- ◆ When he finally gets the right wand, Harry changes. How did you show the change?

Bibliography

What follows is not intended to exhaust writings in the vast field of literary analysis and criticism. Rather, we direct you to selected works that have proved useful for students and instructors.

Bacon, Wallace, and Thomas Sloane, eds. "Criticism Since the 1970s," *Text and Performance Quarterly* 11, no. 3 (1991).
Leaders in the interpretation/performance studies fields address the use and usefulness of contemporary literary theory.

Bakhtin, M. M. *The Dialogic Imagination.* Edited by Michael Holquist. Translated by Caryl Emerson and Michael Holquist. Austin: University of Texas Press, 1981.
An influential collection of writings on the relationship between narrators and characters in fiction.

Burke, Kenneth. *Counterstatement.* Berkeley: University of California Press, 1931.

Burke, Kenneth. *Philosophy of Literary Form.* Baton Rouge: Louisiana State University Press, 1941.

In these works Burke makes a powerful argument for literature as "symbolic action" and an agent of change.

Eagleton, Terry. *Literary Theory: An Introduction.* Minneapolis: University of Minnesota Press, 1983.

A handbook covering the major trends in twentieth-century literary criticism from an author who is a respected literary critic.

Loomba, Ania. *Colonialism/PostColonialism.* New York: Routledge, 1998.

A lucid and detailed account of the key issues that frame postcolonial studies.

Pollack, Della, et al. "Reading Robert Scholes: A Symposium of Essays in Textual Power." *Text and Performance Quarterly* 12, no. 1 (1992): 64–77.

Several insightful responses to Scholes's discussion of literary theory by scholars of performance.

Said, Edward. *Orientalism.* New York: Pantheon Books, 1978.

A foundational work in postcolonial studies, Said's book explores how the knowledge produced about "the Orient" in European literary texts served the ideology of colonial power.

Scholes, Robert. *Protocols of Reading.* New Haven, CT: Yale University Press, 1989.

Considering a wide range of literary theory, Scholes expands upon and demonstrates Jacques Derrida's assertion that "all the world's a text."

. . . human voices vary even more. Each one possesses
more notes than the richest instrument of music. And the
combinations in which the voice groups these notes are as
inexhaustible as the infinite variety of personalities.

Marcel Proust
Within a Budding Grove

CHAPTER THREE

Voice Development for Oral Interpretation

EXPECT THIS!

Voice and body are inseparable in performance, and effective management of one depends on economic use of the other. Separating our study does not mean that voice and body are unrelated (any more than an analysis of form is not affected by content, and vice versa). In this chapter, our central focus is voice, and by the end of the chapter you should be able to:

- Understand and demonstrate effective relaxation exercises.
- Clarify the need for, and uses of, effective breath control, and illustrate proper breathing techniques.
- Model appropriate control of volume.
- Exemplify effective control of projection.
- Efficiently vary vocal pitch and vocal quality.
- Manifest appropriate control of rate and pause.
- Illustrate effective use of appropriate pronunciation and articulation.
- Recognize and employ appropriate dialect variation.

Body and voice together become an instrument you must learn to control and coordinate.

Selections Discussed in This Chapter

In explaining some topics, we mention texts that are reprinted either within the chapter itself or at the end of a chapter. Use the guide below for quick reference to acquaint yourself with selections you may not fully recall.

Author	Title	Location
William Shakespeare	from *Julius Caesar*	Chapter 3, page 95
William Shakespeare	from *The Merchant of Venice*	Chapter 3, page 95

(continued)

Author	Title	Location
Philip Freneau	"The Wild Honeysuckle"	Chapter 3, page 96
Walt Whitman	from "I Hear America Singing"	Chapter 3, page 97
Edmond Rostand	from *Cyrano de Bergerac*	Chapter 3, page 98
Toni Cade Bambara	"The Lesson"	Chapter 3, page 119
Jamaica Kincaid	"Girl"	Chapter 4, page 161

BODY AND VOICE TOGETHER BECOME AN INSTRUMENT YOU MUST learn to control and coordinate. You need to know first of all just how your voice functions. With practice, you can provide a wider range in pitch, greater flexibility in volume and stress, richer variations in quality, and finer degrees of subtlety in duration and rate. Once you understand these factors, develop your voice as deliberately as a singer does. As your voice control improves, you will be increasingly able to meet, with intelligence and sensitivity, the demands of the various kinds of literary material.

Students who have had voice training may find the following discussion useful only as a review. Some of the principles of voice training apply to specific problems facing interpreters. A few minutes spent on the exercises will be most valuable during rehearsal periods when you are working on a particularly demanding selection.

People with musculoskeletal or neurological disabilities, or people with neurogenic speech disorders, may find some of the exercises we propose either inadequate or unsuitable for their needs and abilities. When we speak of good posture, suppleness, free movement, and body and voice responsiveness, we do not seek to exclude people whose disabilities may limit their responsiveness in these areas. In our experience these students have been signally successful in adapting the exercises to their unique needs and, moreover, in devising new and intriguing ways to expand their expressiveness on their own scale. Indeed, all performers adapt exercises to extend their unique capacities. Don't despair if one or another suggestion doesn't immediately apply to you; look, rather, at the goal to be achieved and the principles involved, and ask yourself how the body and voice you know best—your own—can achieve the goal with the means at your disposal. Adapt these exercises and those that follow in Chapter 4 to your unique needs. Your instructor will be able to assist you to do so.

Relaxation Technique

When the body is tense, the voice that emerges is tense. You know that because the sounds that come from you when you are frightened do not resemble the sounds you make when you are relaxed. Moreover, the volume, rate, and pitch you typically use when discussing dinner plans with your partner are not likely to be useful when you are performing. Even when you speak up in class, tensions might emerge that constrict the body or the breath. Wherever in the body the physical tensions strike, they will always imprison the voice.

Therefore, effective use of the voice depends on being able to control the tensions and anxieties that affect performance. Everyone responds differently to the anxieties of performing. Some of your fellow students may seem unfazed by standing in front of an audience; others will suffer locked knees, blurred vision, palpitating heart, dry mouth, loss of vocal control, and worse. Relaxation enables control, but relaxation techniques need to be practiced (and adapted to your performance behavior). We offer several different ways to go about relaxing prior to rehearsal and performance, and the list of possibilities is easily as long as the list of performers. Learn to note what works for you, and adapt the less efficient methods so that they can help your specific symptoms.

Here's one exercise that often works with students. The tasks require simple, physical awareness—so don't move on to the next step until you feel comfortable and *aware* in the position you are holding:

1. Stand easily with your feet parallel and not much farther apart than your hips.

2. Very gently raise yourself up on the balls of your feet; then return to the starting position. Repeat three or four times, slightly energizing your feet.

3. Guard to be sure your knees don't lock, and guard to be sure they aren't too bent: you aren't skiing.

4. Check your spine: keep it straight but not ramrod or rigid.

5. You've probably started to tense your shoulders. If you have, release them.

6. Drop your head onto your chest; take the time to feel its weight there.

7. Let the weight of your head g-r-a-d-u-a-l-l-y increase so that it takes your upper body with it and you slowly flop forward from the waist.

8. When you are bent in half, shake your shoulders out. At this point guard against the two most common challenges: be sure that your

knees are neither locked nor squishy, and be sure that the back of your neck is free.

9. Slowly (almost vertebra by vertebra, if you can), starting at the base of your spine, raise yourself up, being sure that your arms and your shoulders aren't doing the work.

10. When you have fully risen, let your shoulders fall easily and naturally into place. Don't arrange them or present them, and be sure that your head is still on your chest.

11. The last thing to come up should be your head. Let it rise slowly into its comfortable place, breathing regularly, jaw free.

You may want to repeat this sequence or have a classmate monitor your progress. Note carefully which steps give you problems and which steps reward your effort. If you are like most students who perform it conscientiously, you will find yourself both relaxed and "centered"—aware of how your body is working, and ready to develop breath control.

Breath Control

The first concern of anyone interested in voice improvement should be breath control; it is impossible to produce good vocal tone without it.

In *inhalation*—intake of air—the major concern is amount; in *exhalation*—letting out of air—the major concern is control. The whole process of breathing rests on a basic physiological and physical principle: the balance of tension and relaxation in opposing sets of muscles serves to control the creation of a vacuum.

The Physiology of Breathing

When we inhale and pull a quantity of air into the body, the diaphragm—the large dome-shaped muscle at the floor of the chest—lowers and pushes downward against the *relaxed* abdominal muscles; thus, the lengthwise dimension of the chest is increased. As this action is taking place, the muscles between the outer surfaces of the ribs lift and extend the rib cage, and the side-to-side and front-to-back expansion of the chest is accomplished. This increase in size creates a vacuum inside the chest cavity. Atmospheric pressures force air into the vacuum, so that the pressure inside the body becomes equal to the pressure outside the body. The air is forced down through the windpipe (trachea) and through the bronchial tubes and finally enters the flexible air sacs in the lungs in which the bronchioli terminate. The air sacs in the lungs inflate as the air enters, and when the lungs are thus extended, the process of inhalation is complete. Obviously, breathing is an active muscular process.

When it is time for soundless exhalation to take place (following the exchange of oxygen and carbon dioxide in the blood), the muscles in the diaphragm relax, and the diaphragm rises into the dome-shaped position again. The muscles on the outside of the rib cage relax as the ones between the ribs on the inside contract. This action pulls the extended rib cage inward. All of this pressure upward and inward acts on the elastic lung tissue containing the air that was forced in during inhalation. The elastic tissue begins to collapse, and the air is forced out of the lungs, up through the bronchial tubes and windpipe, and finally out of the nose or mouth. Thus, one cycle of respiration is completed.

Breathing Exercises

Although you have been breathing all your life—and speaking for a good part of it—you may not be aware of how breathing works with your voice. Now that you have a relaxation exercise, consider this exercise to introduce sound into the body and to train your breathing to improve your speech:

1. Begin by doing two minutes of jumping jacks, rotating your arms in their sockets (this helps to loosen the rib cage and frees the diaphragm).

2. Immediately lie on the floor with this book under your head (to acquire proper spinal alignment).

3. Simply breathe, noting carefully how your body functions during breathing. What parts are moving when you breathe? What parts are still? Can you detect any tension not needed for breathing?

4. When your breathing has slowed down, raise your knees so your feet are flat on the floor: this allows the spine and lower back to lengthen.

5. Breathe in through your nose, and breathe out as if you were blowing out a candle (position your lips as though you were about to use a straw, but *don't inhale*). The narrower opening results in airflow resistance, which can strengthen the expiration muscles we will use in a later exercise.

6. Voice a sustained /s/ sound while on your back. Don't worry about achieving full volume; concentrate instead on maintaining the steadiness of air stream. With each repetition, try to prolong the sound.

7. Get off the floor. There's another exercise waiting.

As you just learned, in exhaling for speech, a speaker takes another action besides the relaxing of the diaphragm in the lower chest area. This action is the firm contraction of the abdominal muscles that are relaxed for inhalation. As they contract for exhalation, they support the action accomplished by the relaxing of the diaphragm and in this way help control the outflow of air. This process, known as *forced exhalation,* is simply the continuation of the action that takes place in the process of exhalation during silent breathing.

You may want these muscular processes to function effectively to give smooth interpretation to long flowing lines of poetry. You may want to force a swift exhalation for command or expression of emotion in dramatic dialogue. Here's a way to develop greater breath capacity and better control over exhalation.

Proper breathing is possible only when your posture is good. If each muscle is to perform its assigned function, your body should be in a state of controlled relaxation—that is, in a state of nicely balanced relaxation and essential tension just as you felt concluding the previous exercise. Wrongly induced tension inhibits the flexibility of muscles that control the intake and the outward flow of air. One of the most frequent errors in breathing practice is forcing the muscles of the rib cage and the abdomen into a rigid position. These muscles must be firm, but they cannot function if they are locked.

Let's prepare for an exercise. Can you see how it repeats some things we did in the relaxation exercise? Check off the following steps or ask a classmate to monitor your compliance:

1. Stand at ease, hands at your sides.

2. Support your weight evenly and comfortably.

3. Have your spinal column erect but not ramrod stiff.

4. Keep your shoulders level and your neck free from tension. (If you are unintentionally tightening up, let your head fall forward and then slowly rotate it to relax the tension.)

5. *Don't* lift your shoulders—you will be putting tension precisely where you don't want it!

6. Check your form carefully.

Now we can begin the exercise. In four simple steps you can discover the proper balance between tension and relaxation. Better still, you can feel *where* the concentration of energy should be—at the belt line rather than in your throat. If you work out regularly—and follow the instructions for proper form—you may recognize some of these techniques. Or try lying on your back with this book placed on your stomach. As you watch the book rise and fall, you can see the easy, relaxing, in-and-out movements of the muscles at the base of your ribs and below them.

1. Take a deep, comfortable breath and hold it. Contract your abdominal muscles *sharply,* and force the air out of your chest on a single vocalization, such as "Ah—h—h," as if audibly sighing. Hold the contraction of these muscles an instant, and then *suddenly* release the tension. Notice that air rushes into the chest and fills the lower portion of the lungs (or perhaps more) when you release the tension. Exhale by forcing air out of your chest with the gradual contraction of your abdominal muscles as your diaphragm relaxes and returns to its dome-shaped position.

2. Stand easily and repeat the process described in step 1. As the air rushes in on the release of tension in the abdominal muscles, make a conscious effort to lift your upper rib cage slightly. (Be careful *not* to lift your shoulders!) More space will be created in your upper chest, and your whole chest will be well extended and able to accommodate a large intake of air. The upper portion of your lungs, as well as the lower, should be filled now. Exhale, pushing the air out with the relaxing of your diaphragm and the gradual contracting of your abdominal muscles and lowering of your rib cage. (Don't collapse and let your shoulders sag!)

3. Still standing, place your hands, palm in, on the lower portion of your rib cage so that your fingers are touching. Begin to inhale slowly. As you inhale, your ribs should push your hands apart. When the lower part of your breath cavity is full and you have allowed your chest to lift *slightly* until it, too, is full, you should have a full breath. Hold it for a second or two and let it out in a *whoosh!*

4. Repeat step 3, and when you have a full breath, tuck in your abdominal muscles slightly and hold your breath for a second until you feel in complete control. Now, as you start to exhale the full breath, begin to count aloud. As you begin to run out of breath for vocalizing, gradually contract your abdominal muscles (*not* the upper chest ones) as you continue counting. When you can no longer force air out of your chest by the strong but comfortable contraction of your abdominal muscles, stop the vocalized counting. Don't sacrifice a good quality of tone in the effort to "squeeze out" more sound. This will result only in undue tension in your upper chest and throat muscles—the very thing you want to avoid.

Many instructions say "Breathe in" and *then* "Breathe out." This exercise suggests breathing out first, to empty your chest of air at the beginning of the exercise. In this way, you avoid "stuffing" the chest. Then comes the breathing in, followed by the controlled breathing out. This is the inevitable order, whether or not you are "exercising," for you cannot hold your breath forever. Don't try.

Don't continue to work steadily at this or any other exercise when you begin to feel tired. It should become increasingly clear that the sooner you can make this method automatic, the easier the whole breathing process will be. As with any exercise, be sure to maintain proper form.

As you become able to take in larger amounts of air with ease and to continue exhalation to support the tone, you should be able to count more numbers on one breath. With each exercise period, try to say a few more, always being careful not to strain your throat, force the tone, or sacrifice quality. You should count at what seems an easy volume and a pleasing level of pitch.

When you perform, phrasal units need to be separated by pauses of varying lengths. During these pauses you have an opportunity to re-plenish your supply of breath. Take care not to let the pauses break the continuity of thought. The position and duration of the pauses should always grow out of the relationship of the phrases to each other, and to the complete thought being expressed. Learn to breathe where you must pause, not pause in order to breathe. It is usually impossible to get a full breath except in the major pauses that complete the units of thought. Therefore, the final step in breath control is to *learn to inhale quickly and unobtrusively while still using the proper muscles.*

Frequently a speaker inhales properly and uses the full capacity for breath but still cannot sustain a long flow of sound. The problem here—inadequate control of exhalation, not an insufficient supply of air—is one of the major causes of dropping final words or syllables so that they do not carry to the last row of your audience. It also contributes to the impulse to rush through those final syllables. Here's another simple exercise to determine whether the control muscles collapse instead of exerting steady pressure as they relax. Start by repeating the preparations described earlier. Then follow these steps:

1. Inhale a full, comfortable breath. (Remember, your shoulders are relaxed, not around your earlobes!)

2. Hold a lighted match directly in front of your lips as close as your profile will allow.

3. Start to count aloud in a full voice. You should be able to continue counting until the match burns out. If you blow out the flame before then, check the control level of the muscles in and around your rib cage. Most of us exhale more than we need to on certain sounds, such as "*two*" or "*three*" or "*four.*"

4. Light another match. Take another deep breath (keeping your shoulders relaxed!) and try the exercise again.

5. Speak very softly this time, consciously controlling the rate of relaxation of the muscles involved. You won't explode. You will become aware of *where* the control must be exercised.

6. Gradually increase your volume to normal. You will find that the flame flickers but that you will not extinguish it by a sudden, uncontrolled spurt of air.

Volume and Projection

The words *volume* and *projection* are sometimes used interchangeably. Indeed, they are both part of your ability to be heard and understood. For this discussion, we consider *volume* to be the degree of loudness, and *projection* to be the act of directing the voice to a specific target.

You should be able to make your voice fill the room in which the audience is gathered. You should learn to control the volume of your voice to fill a large space easily without distorting your voice and without blasting down the back wall if space is limited. With practice, you will learn how much volume is required and how you can achieve the greatest possible flexibility within that requirement.

Control of Projection

Being understood also depends to a degree on the speaker's control of projection. The first requirement of adequate projection is to have enough volume and support so that the tone will carry as far as the material and situation demand. The second requirement is to have the proper mental attitude. Good communication is a product not only of breath control but also of your constant awareness of the listeners. This awareness is often spoken of in the theater as *audience sense.* Although this sense is difficult to explain, it has its base in the speaker's attitude of reaching out toward an audience with every line. Performers with a fine sense of audience participation have a psychological set that helps their voices reach out to the audience regardless of the energy of the ideas or emotions being expressed. As you perform, keep the back row of listeners in mind and be sure that your words include them.

This mental attitude toward communication has a direct and observable effect on the physiological control of projection. By thinking *to* your listeners as well as *of* them, wanting to be sure that they hear and share the full effect of the literature, you will tend to hold a posture that keeps your throat free from tension. If you do not maintain in your mind their need to hear and be understood, they will abandon you.

Focus of Projection

It is sometimes helpful to think of your voice as a tangible thing—an object to be aimed and thrown at a target. This trick of *throwing the voice* may smack of ventriloquism, yet it is a practice everyone uses at times. A child calling to attract the attention of playmates down the street sends his voice to where they are. Football fans shouting advice to the players on the field direct their voices without conscious thought. When carrying on a conversation in a room full of people, one person may project across the room to answer a remark or add to a discussion. When people wish to be confidential, they let their voices drop, and their circle of mental focus narrows to fill only the desired area.

The following exercises for focus of projection can be practiced most effectively in a large room. They each involve imagining yourself in a concrete situation. By thinking specifically of what to do and by using any words that come to mind, the interpreter can concentrate on the suggested volume and focus.

1. You are seated at a desk in the center front of the room. You see a friend at the door; you call an easy greeting. She waves and goes on. You think of something that you ought to tell her. You call her name quickly, but she apparently doesn't hear, for she keeps on going. Without leaving your place, call again. Have a good full breath as you start to call, and direct the sound at her quickly disappearing back. Do the same thing again with more volume and longer sounds supported by forced exhalation. Catch her this time!

2. You are giving directions to a group of people about how to decorate the room for an event. The room is large, and everyone must hear. Direct your remarks to various places, thinking of certain people who might be there. After you have given instructions and the group starts to work, a person in the front of the group asks a question. You shift your focus of projection, reduce your volume, and answer the person who asked the question. Then you decide that others might need that special information, too. You raise your volume and expand your area of projection to attract everyone's attention; then you repeat to the group what you said to the individual. As you do this, take care to direct your voice to the various parts of the room so that everyone will hear.

When you have made some progress in projection through these exercises, move on to practice with literary material.

Here's an interesting problem in projection found in Shakespeare's *Julius Caesar*. As Brutus goes up into the pulpit to make his famous speech to the crowd, he addresses a single remark to those near him. In the opening sentence, try to get the feeling of first speaking to those who stand around you, and then of including the several hundred citizens who are milling around the forum. It is necessary to quiet the crowd during the early part of the speech.

> BRUTUS: Be patient till the last. Romans, countrymen, and lovers! hear me for my cause, and be silent, that you may hear; believe me for mine honor, and have respect to mine honor, that you may believe; censure me in your wisdom, and awake your senses, that you may the better judge. If there be any in this assembly, any dear friend of Caesar's, to him I say, that Brutus' love to Caesar was no less than his. If then that friend demand why Brutus rose against Caesar, this is my answer: Not that I lov'd Caesar less, but that I lov'd Rome more.

In the following lines from the famous trial scene of Shakespeare's *The Merchant of Venice*, two characters are speaking. Our primary concern here is not with the difference in their voices or mental attitudes, but rather with the changes in focus and consequent projection in their speeches. (The parenthetical stage directions are inserted for this specific exercise and do not appear in the text of the play.) The Duke speaks to Portia at close range on his greeting and first question and on the opening line of his second speech. After "take your place," it is assumed that she moves away from him; thus, his question "Are you acquainted with the difference / That holds this present question in the court?" must carry over a greater distance than his first remarks but should still be addressed directly to Portia. His order to Antonio and Shylock to "stand forth" may be thought of as carrying even farther, since they are probably among a group of people outside the judge's area. Practice the Duke's speeches until you can place them where you want them, and then follow the same procedure in Portia's speeches.

> DUKE: Give me your hand. Came you from old Bellario?
> PORTIA: *(To Duke as she gives him her hand)* I did, my lord.
> DUKE: You are welcome; take your place. *(She moves away from him.)*
>   Are you acquainted with the difference
>   That holds this present question in the court?
> PORTIA: *(From her place a few feet away from the Duke)* I am informed thoroughly of the cause.
>   *(To the assemblage)* Which is the merchant here, and which the Jew?
> DUKE: Antonio and old Shylock, both stand forth.
> PORTIA: *(To Shylock after he has stepped forward from the crowd)* Is your name Shylock?

In working to develop volume and projection, you are concentrating on one of the basic requirements of all speech: that it reach its audience. Volume depends largely on adequate breath supply and proper support in exhalation. Projection combines these physical aspects with the psychological aspect of mental directness. We discuss this concept of physical and mental focus in later chapters. For the moment it is enough to recognize the relationship.

Pitch and Quality

Although pitch and quality are different attributes of sound, they are so closely related in origin and control in the human voice that they may be considered together. The way the vocal bands vibrate basically determines both the pitch and the quality of the vocal tone: the pitch is formed by the rate of vibration, and the quality by the complexity of the vibration.

The *pitch* of a sound is its place on the musical scale. In terms of the scale range, pitch is high, medium, or low. It is important for interpreters to become skillful in using pitch to suggest shades of meaning and to build to climaxes. Changes in pitch give variety and contrast to the material being read and help hold the audience's attention. Because a change of pitch produces *inflection,* a speaker's *inflection range* is the entire pitch span between the highest and lowest tones that he or she is capable of making comfortably.

Any pattern in the variation of levels of pitch results in *melody.* When there are no discernible changes of pitch, the result is a *monotone.* Although melody is an asset to the interpreter, it can also become a problem. Most people have in their daily speech a characteristic pattern of inflections, which is part of their own personalities. Some of that pattern will be carried over into their work before an audience. Often, however, a reader's pattern is so marked that it calls attention to itself and thus gets in the way of re-creation of the material. For example, one of the most common and annoying vocal patterns in reading poetry permits each line or each new thought to start on a high pitch and drift to a low tone at the close. The following lines are an example of poetic structure in which this problem must be controlled.

The Wild Honeysuckle
PHILIP FRENEAU

Fair flower, that dost so comely grow,
Hid in this silent, dull retreat,
Untouched thy honied blossoms blow,
Unseen thy little branches greet:
    No roving foot shall crush thee here,
    No busy hand provoke a tear.

And again, in less conventional poetry:

FROM I Hear America Singing

WALT WHITMAN

I hear America singing, the varied carols I hear,
Those of mechanics, each one singing his as it should be blithe
   and strong,
The carpenter singing his as he measures his plank or beam,
The mason singing his as he makes ready for work, or leaves off
   work . . .

Quality, more difficult to define distinctively, is best described as the characteristic of a tone that distinguishes it from all other tones of the same pitch and intensity. This characteristic is sometimes called *timbre* or, to use the German word, *Klang,* meaning the "ring" of the tone. In describing quality, one frequently uses words that suggest color—a *golden* tone, a *silver-voiced* orator, a *blue* note.

Quality of tone is perhaps most closely associated with mood and feeling. Connotation and emotional response have a strong effect on quality, and empathy (which we discuss more fully in the next chapter) plays its part in the degree of tension or relaxation it imposes on the vocal mechanism. Vocal quality is influenced by your empathic response to whatever elements of emotion, strength, and beauty are inherent in the material.

Rate and Pause

The *rate* at which people speak is often habitual, a part of their personalities and their entire backgrounds. Your customary rate probably serves you very well for ordinary conversation, but you may need to adjust this habitual rate to accommodate an author's style and purpose. *Audiences cannot listen as rapidly as a performer can speak.* Interpreters must learn to hear themselves in rehearsal and in conversation. There is no magic formula for slowing a too-rapid pace; to do this requires constant attention. It is helpful to select material that by its style and connotation encourages a slow pace of delivery. Frequently the mere physical process of forming a sequence of sounds affects the rate at which a sentence can be read intelligibly and effectively. In addition, by changing the rate, you can express subtle variety in a selection. Emotion, connotation, suggestion, and the combination of vowels and consonants all provide clues for knowing when to speed up your speaking pace and when to slow it down. You cannot convey a text's unique richness without taking the time to display it.

Rate is determined not only by the speed with which sounds are uttered in sequence, but also by the length and frequency of pauses that separate the sequences of sounds. You must recognize *phrasal pauses,* which clarify the relationships of words in phrases to convey units of thought. The pause may also become one of your most effective tools for building suspense and climaxes and for reinforcing a selection's emotional content.

Beginning interpreters are often afraid to pause. A pause motivated by real understanding may be sustained for a much longer time and with greater effect than you might realize. You need only be sure that during the pause something relevant to the material is going on in your own mind and consequently in the minds of your listeners. You should work not only to use pauses in the most effective places but also to vary and sustain the lengths of the pauses as the material demands.

Unfortunately, punctuation is an unreliable guide to pausing. Punctuation is used on the printed page to signal the eyes. It guides the reader in establishing the relationship of words and phrases and their division into sentences. Remember that rules and fashions change in punctuation. Your full understanding of and response to your material, and your sense of responsibility to your audience, are the final determining factors in your use of pauses.

In the following scene from Edmond Rostand's *Cyrano de Bergerac,* Cyrano is speaking of his monstrous nose and its effect on his entire being. You can make exquisite use of pause here. As you work on the interpretation, you will realize that the tempo of the scene changes with "Oh, not that ever!" You will see how this change to a faster, more smoothly flowing rate is effected. You also will realize that the change goes hand in hand with Cyrano's struggle to turn from his romantic self-disclosure to his customary half-comic acceptance of his nose.

> CYRANO: My old friend—look at me,
> And tell me how much hope remains for me
> With this protuberance! Oh I have no more
> Illusions! Now and then—bah! I may grow
> Tender, walking alone in the blue cool
> Of evening, through some garden fresh with flowers
> After the benediction of the rain;
> My poor big devil of a nose inhales
> April . . . and so I follow with my eyes
> Where some boy, with a girl upon his arm,
> Passes a patch of silver . . . and I feel
> Somehow, I wish I had a woman too,
> Walking with little steps under the moon,
> And holding my arm so, and smiling. Then
> I dream—and I forget . . .
>   And then I see
> The shadow of my profile on the wall!
> LEBRET: My friend! . . .
> CYRANO: My friend, I have my bitter days,

Knowing myself so ugly, so alone.
Sometimes—
LEBRET: You weep?
CYRANO: (Quickly) Oh, not that ever! No,
That would be too grotesque—the tears trickling down
All the long way along this nose of mine?
I will not so profane the dignity
Of sorrow. Never any tears for me!

Notice how Cyrano's earlier, gradually slower rate permits the audience to feel his well-hidden revelation almost before he speaks, and how he quickly covers his heartsickness with wit.

To develop additional skill in your use of rate of speaking, try to work on selections that demand basically different rate patterns. As you read the material aloud with feeling, you will realize that to be effective you must observe the *quantity*, or length, of the individual vowel and consonant sounds, as well as the length of pauses between sounds. In a prevailing rapid rate, the sounds as well as the pauses are often short; in a slower rate, they are long.

Intelligibility of Speech

To be fully intelligible, speech should be not only audible but also distinct and accurate. You need to be heard in order to be understood. Listeners cannot keep their attention on the material if they must constantly "translate" unclear speech sounds or mispronunciations. Therefore, all speech sounds should be correct as well as distinct and pleasing. Few things are more irritating to the listener than a speaker's self-conscious, overly careful mouthing of consonants. This conveys affectation and insincerity. Moreover, it draws attention to the speaker's technique and away from the material. On the other hand, a speaker who cannot be understood certainly cannot communicate. Consequently, you should learn to pronounce and articulate words with such clarity and accuracy that any audience is able to understand you.

A distinction between pronunciation and articulation may be helpful. *Pronunciation* refers to the *correctness* of sounds and accents in spoken words. *Articulation* refers to the *shaping* of the sounds by the speaker's lips, teeth, tongue, and hard and soft palates.

Pronunciation is considered to be acceptable when all the sounds of a word are uttered correctly in their proper order and with accent (stress) on the proper syllable. Stress carries meaning in English. There is a big difference, for instance, between *refúse* and *réfuse*. Current good usage is the guide to correct pronunciation. A standard dictionary or a good pronouncing dictionary is the final authority. Unfamiliar polysyllabic words are not always the ones that trip up readers. Because you may distrust your pronunciation of such words, you probably will look them up in the dictionary. The real pitfalls are the common, everyday words that you may have fallen into the habit of pronouncing incorrectly. Mispronunciation can distract listeners so much that they momentarily lose the thought that you are trying to communicate.

Most of us have ingrained in our speech patterns certain regional or ethnic influences. These are usually slight deviations (from so-called standard speech) in some individual sounds, the melody pattern, or both. For instance, one need only consider the difference in pronunciation of /r/ as one travels from New England through the Midwest and into the South to be aware that Standard American Speech is "standard" for very few of us. Further, audiences associate accents or dialects with certain stereotypes. Therefore, some effort should be made to develop Standard American Speech, if only to use it "on special occasions," when material and audiences are better served by the elimination of any regionalisms or obtrusive vocal mannerisms.

Dialect

Dialect, or accent, is basically a matter of the way separate sounds are formed and, far more important, the use of a melodic or rhythmic flow as the sounds go together. An author who wants dialect to provide a part of the character may indicate this through spelling, syntax, word choice, or all three (look at Toni Cade Bambara's "The Lesson" at the end of this chapter or, in a different dialect, in the excerpt from Jonathan Safran Foer's *A Very Rigid Search*," also this chapter). Because a writer is black or Hispanic or British or from New England does not mean that the interpreter should mimic such regional speech. If the author wrote in dialect, you should read it as well as you can. If not, make your own speech sufficiently flexible to conform to the total demand of the selection you have chosen. When an interpreter's own dialect seems incongruous for the speaker in the selection, the contradiction can distract the listeners, particularly if the audience doesn't share the regional dialect.

Expansive immigration has led many people to acquire English in addition to their native languages, and your class may include many who are bilingual or even trilingual. Performers who are fluent in languages in addition to English often substitute into English settings sounds from their native languages that may not correspond completely with English-language sounds. Conversely, some sounds in English do not occur in other languages, so very common words that present little challenge to native speakers can snag non-native speakers. For example, *cat, caught, curt, cut, could, brother, bird* and *sheep/ship* may present pronunciation problems. Diphthongs, too, cause non-native speakers real problems. If your native language is not English, try to sound out troublesome words for a native speaker, and listen carefully to the sound you produce and the correction your friend offers.

Even native speakers of English confront problems when audience members are accustomed to a regional dialect or a speech pattern other than the performer's. Audiences want to be able to understand what they hear; it is infinitely better to understand and enjoy a performance than to sit wondering what everyone else is responding to. If the way your audience "hears" spoken English is significantly different from the way you speak it, give listeners enough time to process what they hear. You need to help them understand you, and taking time to do so during your presentation—and being sure you strive for standard speech—will help.

Finally, dialect can also raise issues of ethical responsibilities. Particularly for those who choose to perform works from a culture other than their home culture (we *vigorously* encourage such experiments for many reasons), appropriating the other's voice can be a daunting undertaking. Take courage. You do not have to have lived life in a small southern town to attempt a story by Eudora Welty or Flannery O'Connor; you need not be an African American to perform Nikki Giovanni. What you need is respect for the other, a willingness to listen and (even) challenge the other's voice, and an appreciation of maintaining the difference between your own speech and another's speech. Vocally, this means that you respect the melody of another's speech as much as the richness of its metaphor; the precision of another's accent as much as the power of its impact. If you perform an oral history or prepare an ethnographic performance, you may have access to records of how the original speakers pronounced their words, and thus you'll need to listen carefully for the clues these records offer. On the other hand, if you select a segment of a novel in which the characters live in a culture different from your own, your respect for the work's integrity is enough to encourage you to find out how the people in that novel sound by comparing their words to tapes, videos, films, or recordings representative of that culture's speech. For example, the demanding speaker of Jamaica Kincaid's "Girl" (at the end of Chapter 4) has a distinct West Indian speech pattern that is reproduced in the rhythm integral to the selection. Similarly, you may be unfamiliar with a religious service in which the congregation participates as vigorously as does Sister Monroe in Maya Angelou's *I Know Why the Caged Bird Sings* (at the end of Chapter 5). If you select Angelou's memoir, though, be sure the action occurs in *her* church, not in yours.

All speech contributes to social stratification. We judge people by *how* they say whatever they say. Dialect contributes hugely to position and influence in society, and we would be naive not to recognize the potent authority of speech. We recognize the way dialect affects social status in our home culture but may be less aware of how it operates in other cultures. Again, respectful inquiry is the key. Don't be deterred from asking legitimate questions of a speaker from another culture or language. Honest inquiry is the foundation of understanding.

Selections for Analysis and Oral Interpretation

In analyzing these selections, pay particular attention to the vocal problems each one presents. Almost all of the selections require more than a normal supply of breath because they either contain long, flowing sentences or demand an unusual amount of volume or force. Some pieces present interesting problems in projection. They all require you to work with a maximum flexibility of range to communicate the richness of sounds effectively. They also demand an awareness of your bodily responses.

There's something comic and something exultant in this poem that catches the human voice in one of its most glorious artistic achievements: singing. At the same time, the poem suggests some of the extravagant powers the voice possesses, even as it poses disturbing questions for audience members and performers alike. What kinds of knowledge do you need to perform this poem?

A Night at the Opera

WILLIAM MATTHEWS

"The tenor's too fat," the beautiful young
woman complains, "and the soprano
dowdy and old." But what if Otello's
not black, if Rigoletto's hump lists,
if airy Gilda and her entourage
of flesh outweigh the cello section?

In fairy tales, the prince has a good heart,
and so as an outward and visible
sign of an inward, invisible grace,
his face is not creased, nor are his limbs gnarled.
Our tenor holds in his liver-spotted
hands the soprano's broad, burgeoning face.

Their combined age is ninety-seven; there's
spittle in both pinches of her mouth;
a vein in his temple twitches like a worm.
Their faces are a foot apart. His eyes
widen with fear as he climbs to the high
B-flat he'll have to hit and hold for five

dire seconds. And then they'll stay in their stalled
hug for as long as we applaud. Franco
Corelli once bit Birgit Nilsson's ear
in just such a command embrace because
he felt she'd upstaged him. Their costumes weigh
fifteen pounds apiece; they're poached in sweat

and smell like fermenting pigs; their voices rise
and twine not from beauty, nor from the lack
of it, but from the hope for accuracy
and passion, both. They have to hit the note
and the emotion, both, with the one poor
arrow of the voice. Beauty's for amateurs.

- How did you employ variety in pitch, quality, and rate in this poem?

- Is this poem also about gospel singers, rap singers, dancers, trumpeters, actors, interpreters? Why?

Not everybody who talks knows what they are saying. Take Alex, a 25-year-old native of Odessa, Russia, who has learned English in part by reading too many thesauruses. The result: Alex often chooses the "wrong" word and ends up revealing something about himself—and about us. With his aged grandfather serving as driver (and accompanied by his grandfather's dog named, believe it or not, Sammy Davis, Jr., Jr.), Alex acts as a translator/guide for an American tourist and the novel's "hero," Jonathan. He is searching for a vanished town named Trachimbrod and for a young woman named Augustine who rescued his grandfather from death during a Nazi raid in World War II. The only record that Jonathan—and Alex—have to help them is an old photograph of Jonathan's grandfather as a young man, standing with a young girl and her family. On the back his grandfather wrote, "This is me with Augustine, 1942." Now, at the end of a very long day filled with failure and rebuffs, their car stops one more time. Work carefully to be sure that your voice reveals distinctive— and different—changes with each character and each speech.

FROM **A Very Rigid Search**

JONATHAN SAFRAN FOER

"There," my grandfather said, as darkness was verging, and pointed his finger at a person roosting on the steps of a very diminutive house. It was the first person that we had viewed in many minutes. He arrested the car. "Go." Because I did not know what else to say, I said, "O.K." I said to the hero, "Come!" There was no rejoinder. "Come," I said, and rotated. The hero was manufacturing Zs, and so was Sammy Davis, Jr., Jr. There is no necessity for me to move them from repose, I said to my brain. I took with me the photograph of Augustine, and was very circumspect not to disturb them as I closed the car's door.

The house was white wood that was falling off of itself. As I walked more proximal, I could perceive that it was a woman roosting on the steps. She was very aged, and peeling the skin off of corn. "Leniency," I said, while I was still a petite amount distant. I said this so that I would not make her a terrified person. "I have a query for you." She was donning a white shirt and a white dress, but they were covered with dirt and places where liquids had dried. I could perceive that she was a very poor woman. All of the people in the small towns are very poor, but she was more poor. This was clear-cut because of how svelte she was, and how broken all of her belongings were.

She smiled as I became proximal to her, and I could see that she did not have any teeth. Her hairs were white, her skin had brown marks, and her eyes were blue. She was not so much of a woman, and what I signify here is that she was very petite, and appeared as if she could be obliterated with one finger. "Leniency," I said, "I do not want to pester you—" "How could anything pester me on such a beautiful evening?" "Yes, it is beautiful." "Where are you from?" she asked. This shamed me. I rotated over in my head what to manufacture. "Odessa." She put down one piece of corn and picked up another. "I have never been to Odessa," she said, and moved hairs that were in front of her face to behind her ear. It was not until this moment that I perceived how her hairs were as long as her. "You must go there," I said. "I know. I know I must. I am sure there are many things that I must do." "And many things that you must not do also." I was trying to make her a sedate person, and I accomplished. She laughed. "You are a sweet boy." "Have you ever heard of a town dubbed Trachimbrod?" I inquired. "I was informed that someone proximal to here would know of it." She put her corn on her lap. "What?" "I do not want to pester you, but have you ever heard of a town dubbed Trachimbrod?" "No," she said, picking up her corn and removing its skin. "I have never heard of that." "I am sorry to have confiscated your time," I said. "Have a good day." She presented me with a sad smile.

I commenced to perambulate away, but I felt so awful. What would I inform the hero when he was no longer manufacturing Zs? What would I inform my grandfather? For how long could we fail until we surrendered? Darkness was near, and I felt as if all the weight was residing on me. There are only so many times that you can utter "It does not hurt" before that begins to hurt even more than the hurt. Not-truths hung in front of me like fruit. Which could I pick for the hero? Which could I pick for my grandfather? Which for myself? Then I remembered that I had the photograph of Augustine, and, although I do not know what it was that coerced me to do it, I rotated back around and exhibited the photograph to the woman. "Have you ever witnessed anyone in this photograph?"

She examined it for several moments. "No."

I do not know why, but I inquired again. "Have you ever witnessed anyone in this photograph?"

"No," she said again, although this second no did not seem like a parrot, but like a different variety of "no."

"Have you ever witnessed anyone in this photograph?" I inquired, and this time I held it very proximal to her face.

"No," she said again, and this seemed like a third variety of "no."

I put the photograph in her hands. "Have you ever witnessed anyone in the photograph?"

"No," she said, but in her "no" I was certain that I could hear, Please persevere. Inquire me again.

So I did. "Have you ever witnessed anyone in the photograph?"

She moved her thumbs over the faces, as if she were attempting to erase them. "No."

"Have you ever witnessed anyone in the photograph?"

"No," she said, and she put the photograph on her lap.

"Have you ever witnessed anyone in the photograph?" I inquired.

"No," she said, still examining it, but only from the angles of her eyes.

"Have you ever witnessed anyone in the photograph?"

"No."

"Have you ever witnessed anyone in the photograph?"

"No," she said. "No."

I saw a tear descend to her white dress.

"Have you ever witnessed anyone in the photograph?" I inquired, and I felt cruel, I felt like an awful person, but I was certain that I was performing the right thing.

"No," she said, "I have not. They all look like strangers."

Darkness was amid us. I perilled everything. "Has anyone in this photograph ever witnessed you?"

"I have been waiting for you for so long."

I pointed to the car. "We are searching for Trachimbrod."

"Oh," she said, and she released a river of tears. "You are here. I am it."

- ◆ Members of your audience are likely to need a little time to understand what Alex means. What characteristics of their responses told you it was all right to continue?

- ◆ The two central characters are opposites: young and old, male and female, seeking and withholding information. Distinguish their differences, but be sure we see how they are similar. How did you make each "No" into a kind of question?

Most of us can probably point to a decisive moment in our maturing, when the child we were suddenly realizes that taking responsibility is part of growing up. Jane Smiley's conversational voice here may mislead you into thinking this recollection insignificant, but don't fall for it. Rather, ask yourself why this narrator must use such a relaxed voice for such a telling experience.

⊚ Confess, Early and Often

JANE SMILEY

The term my grandmother used for my grandfather was "impatient." What I and the other grandchildren knew was that even

though our grandfather indulged us with candy bars, teased us by grabbing our legs under the table and exclaiming, "Snakes! Snakes!" and taught us everything from diving to poker playing, he was quick to anger and a little unpredictable. It was therefore with horror that I watched my 9-year-old friend Susan Clayton rip one of the bridge cards while we were playing a forbidden game of slapjack. The point of the game was to slap one's hand down on the pile whenever a jack was turned over, and thereby claim the pile. The game was forbidden because we'd torn a card before. I had, in fact, climbed on a chair, and then the dining-room table, in order to get the cards down from the dish rail near the ceiling where my grandfather had put them. Now another card, from the deck bought to replace the damaged one, was torn. My grandfather believed in corporal punishment, and my grandmother, too. I was not too old to be switched, at 9. I had recently been switched for leaving my glasses in the mailbox, where they were broken by a heavy package. I gathered up the cards, including the torn one, and stuffed them back in their case beside the second, similar deck that was also ruined, then I climbed the chair and the table, and set them on the dish rail, exactly in the spot and the position where I'd found them. It was the middle of the afternoon, late summer. My friends and I went outside to find something else to do.

I entered upon a prolonged season of dread. I felt those cards above my head every time I walked through the dining room. The point, I well knew, was not the torn card but the defiance compounded by the secrecy. Secrecy, a form of lying, was a variety of interest that compounded daily. My grandfather hated secrets, hated dishonesty of any sort. His greatest compliment to my mother was that she was incapable of dishonesty. That meant his rearing of her had been a success. Clearly I now fell humiliatingly short of that standard. Humiliating for me, but also for him and for her.

The days clicked by, each given distinction by my fear that my grandfather would sit back one night at the dinner table and say, "How about a couple of rubbers of bridge?" The diabolical element of this scenario was that since my grandmother didn't play cards, the suggestion of bridge only arose if there happened to be company. For my grandfather to discover a torn card in his new deck, the card that would reveal everything about my personal corruption, in front of relatives, our only kind of company, would only be an added humiliation for him. When bridge players came to dinner, I could hardly keep myself from staring in blank dread at the glowing damaged cards above his head. Twice in the autumn when he suggested cards, I had to distract him without manifesting panic. I don't remember what I said or did. I only remember staring sincerely into his eyes with the intensity that comes from desperate lying. One morning toward Thanksgiving, when I was alone in the house, I climbed up and looked into the card case. The torn jack was still there, still torn.

My grandfather continued to express the friendliest and most affectionate interest in me. He drove me wherever I wanted to go. He told me jokes in the car. He said things like, "Keep your feet, you'll get a draw out of it" and "Longer than a Mormon clothesline," expressions that I didn't understand but represented some larger, more colorful way of looking at the world that I knew he exemplified. He sang "Streets of Laredo," "Lorena," "Oh, Shenandoah." He told stories about the ranch and the tannery and his boyhood and my grandmother, about my mother and my aunts and uncles. I wondered how far he would withdraw once he knew; the torn card had disappeared, a tiny seed in a field of silent lies.

I took the coward's way out, and told my mother one night in the spring, after overhearing my family planning bridge that weekend with Uncle Berger and Aunt Elizabeth. She tried to be shocked and briskly disappointed, but she couldn't work up much outrage. She helped me buy another double deck of bridge cards at the drugstore. They cost 3 dollars and 75 cents and had pictures of Whirlaway and Determine on their backs. I presented my grandfather with the new cards and the news of the torn jack at the same time, the next night at dinner. He couldn't work up much anger, either, not even for show. But then, he wasn't an authoritarian, only, as my grandmother said, "impatient."

I never again played slapjack. I learned to confess early and often, because the scariest thing after all was not what they might find out, but that they didn't know.

- ◆ How did your voice reflect the persona's growing fear of grandfather's discovery? Did your voice suggest "the coward's way out"? How?

In addition to being richly rewarding to speak, Lewis Carroll's poem broke new ground in shaping sounds into sense and set the stage for James Joyce's Finnegans Wake *and other efforts that multiply the carrying capacity of words.*

Jabberwocky

LEWIS CARROLL

'Twas brillig, and the slithy toves
   Did gyre and gimble in the wabe:
All mimsy were the borogoves,
   And the mome raths outgrabe.

"Beware the Jabberwock, my son!
   The jaws that bite, the claws that catch!
Beware the Jubjub bird, and shun
   The frumious Bandersnatch!"

He took his vorpal sword in hand;
   Long time the manxome foe he sought—
So rested he by the Tumtum tree,
   And stood awhile in thought.

And, as in uffish thought he stood,
   The Jabberwock, with eyes of flame,

Came whiffling through the tulgey wood,
    And burbled as it came!

One, two! One, two! And through and through
    The vorpal blade went snicker-snack!
He left it dead, and with its head
    He went galumphing back.

"And hast thou slain the Jabberwock?
    Come to my arms, my beamish boy!
O frabjous day! Callooh, Callay!"
    He chortled in his joy.

'Twas brillig, and the slithy toves
    Did gyre and gimble in the wabe:
All mimsy were the borogoves,
    And the mome raths outgrabe.

- ◆ There is nothing silly for the personae in this tale. How did your voice distinguish among the speakers?

There is great opportunity for vocal variety here. Let the young "interpreters" in the story enjoy the elocutionary aspects of their selections. Note carefully the narrator's descriptions of each of the girls' antics. Don't caricature these young women—each is a character in herself.

 FROM **The Little Girls**

ELIZABETH BOWEN

Thick cream glazed blinds were pulled most of the way down. Failing to keep out the marine sunshine, they flopped lazily over the open windows in the hot June breath rather than breeze haunting the garden. St. Agatha's had been a house, IV-A Classroom probably the morningroom. The blinds were lace-bordered. There was a garlanded wallpaper—called to order by having on it a bald, pontifical clock, only a size or two smaller than a station one, a baize board clustered with lists and warnings, and sepia reproductions of inspiring pictures, among them "Hope," framed in oak. Of oak were the desks, to which were clamped high-backed seats. An aroma of Plasticine came from the models along the chimneypiece, and from jars of botanical specimens near a window whiffs of water slimy with rotting greenery were fanned in—the girl in charge of the specimens being absent with one of her summer colds. Chalk in the neighbourhood of the blackboard and ink thickening in china wells in the desks were the only other educational smells.

A dozen or so girls, most of them aged eleven, some ten, some twelve, sat at the desks. All wore their summer tunics of butcher-blue. By turning their heads, left, they could have seen strips of garden, parching away, between restless lace and stolid white window sills. Politely, however, most of them faced their teacher; this they could do for Miss Kinmate, if little else. This was the first lesson after mid-morning break with its milk and biscuits—even the slight feast had thrown IV-A into a gorged condition. But this also was the Tuesday poetry hour, to which Miss Kinmate attached hopes. Each girl (the idea was) chose for herself the short poem or portion of a longer one which, got by heart, she was to recite.

One more of them had just taken the stand.

"There *was* a time when meadow, grove and stream,
The earth and—"

"Stop!" cried Miss Kinmate. "Before we begin, not *too* much expression. Wordsworth was not as regretful as all that."

"I thought he was. Like some old, fat person saying, 'There *was* a time when I could jump over a ten-foot wall.'"

"That would be silly."

"Well, this is silly, in a way."

"Your old, fat man would not be speaking the truth. Have you any idea how high a ten-foot wall is?"

"Yes."

"I wonder whether you have. Because, even a Greek athlete could probably not jump over that." (From a back desk, a hand shot up.)

"*Yes*, Olive?"

"How high could a Greek athlete probably jump?"

"That would depend."

The child Clare, during this intermission, stood stonily contemplating her audience—hands behind her, back to the blackboard, feet planted apart, tongue exploring a cavity in a lower molar. At a moody sign from Miss Kinmate, she went on:

"—and every common sight,
To *me* did seem
Apparell'd in celestial *light*,
The glory and freshness of a dream.
It is *not* now as it has been of yore;—
Turn whereso'er I may,
By night *or* day,
The things which—"

"Stop! Oh dear, what are we to do?"

"I thought—"

"Well, don't—*try!* Otherwise, go and sit down. Ruining that beautiful poem!"

"Yes, Miss Kinmate."

"And don't make eyes at the others. Next time, choose a poem you understand."

"I do know another. Shall I try that?"

Miss Kinmate looked at the clock. The whole class (but for Sheila Beaker, who couldn't be bothered, and Muriel Borthwick, who having picked at a good big scab on her arm now dabbed blotting-paper at the resultant blood) did likewise, in an awed, considering way. "Very well," Miss Kinmate conceded. "Go on, Clare—though remember, there are others to come."

The child, having drawn a breath twice her size, launched with passion into her second choice:

> "Last night among his fellow roughs
> He jested, quaff'd and swore:
> A drunken private of the Buffs,
> Who never look'd before.
> Today, beneath the foeman's frown,
> He stands in Elgin's place,
> Ambassador from Britain's crown,
> And type of all her race.
>
> Poor, reckless, rude, low-born, untaught,
> Bewilder'd and alone,
> A heart, with English instinct fraught,
> He yet can call his own.
> *Ay! tear* his body limb from limb,
> Bring *cord,* or *axe,* or *flame!*—
> He only knows, that not through him
> Shall England come to shame.
>
> Fair Kentish hopfields round him seemed
> Like dreams to come and go;
> Bright leagues of cherry blossom—"

"Stop! Time's up, I'm afraid. A pity, because you were doing better." Miss Kinmate's eye roved round. "Diana, try and not sit with your mouth open—wake up! What is the name of the poem Clare's just recited?"

"'The Drunken Private of the Buffs.'"

"Not exactly.—Well, who and whose poem next? Muriel: you!"

"I think I'm bleeding too much."

"What, cut yourself?"

"Not exactly."

"Better go and find Matron."

Gory Muriel left. Miss Kinmate had to cast round all over again. *"Sheila,* then. Sheila, we'll hear you now."

Southstone's wonder, the child exhibition dancer, rose, tossed back her silver-gold plaits, and habituatedly stepped forward into the limelight. An ornate volume, open at the required page and gildedly looking like a school prize (which it was, though not awarded to her), was bestowed by her upon Miss Kinmate, with what was less a bow than a flowerlike inclination of the head. She then half-turned, with a minor swirl of the tunic, and, facing the footlights, glided three steps sideways into the place of doom left vacant by Clare. Here reality struck the prodigy amidships. Bewitched, since she rose from her desk, by her own performance, she had lost sight for that minute or two of her entrance's true and hideous purpose. She was to be called upon not to spring about but to give tongue. A badgered hatred of literature filled her features. She did deliver her poem, though in the manner of one voicing, with wonderful moderation, a long-nursed and justifiable complaint:

"Up the airy mountain,
Down the rushing glen,
We daren't *go* a-hunting
For fear of little *men;*
Wee folk, good folk,
Trooping all together;
Green jacket, red cap,
And white owl's feather!

Down on the rocky *shore*
Some make their home;
They *live* on crispy pancakes
Of yellow tide-foam;
Some, in the reeds
Of the black mountain-lake,
With frogs for *their* watch-dogs,
All night awake.
High on the hill-top
The old *King* sits.
He is now so old and grey
He's nigh lost . . . ?
. . . his bridge of white wits?
. . . his mist of white wits?
. . . *his* bridge?
. . . *his wits* . . . ?"

She ran down, ticked over uncertainly, gave right out, and turned on Miss Kinmate a look as much as to say: "Well, there you are. What else would you expect?"

"Never mind," Miss Kinmate hastened to say. "It went nicely so far. Though a little mournful—fairies are gay things, aren't they?"

Sheila had no idea.

"And one word wrong in your second line. It should be 'rushy,' not 'rushing.' How could a glen rush?"

"I thought it meant they were all rushing about," said Sheila Beaker, still more deeply aggrieved.

"Sheila chose a delightful poem, at any rate," Miss Kinmate informed the class—who knew to a girl whose the choice had been: Mrs. Beaker's.

♦ How did you demonstrate Miss Kinmate's growing dismay?

Although this poem was written during the nineteenth century, it certainly is relevant to the world today. The poem's strength lies in the quality of mind and attitude that it reflects. The final sentence should be carefully controlled vocally to keep the last part of the stanza from overbalancing the important plea for fidelity.

 ## Dover Beach

MATTHEW ARNOLD

The sea is calm tonight.
The tide is full, the moon lies fair
Upon the straits;—on the French coast the light
Gleams and is gone; the cliffs of England stand
Glimmering and vast, out in the tranquil bay.
Come to the window, sweet is the night-air!
Only, from the long line of spray
Where the sea meets the moon-blanched land,
Listen! you hear the grating roar
Of pebbles which the waves draw back, and fling,
At their return, up the high strand,
Begin, and cease, and then again begin,
With tremulous cadence slow, and bring
The eternal note of sadness in.

Sophocles long ago
Heard it on the Aegean, and it brought
Into his mind the turbid ebb and flow
Of human misery; we
Find also in the sound a thought,
Hearing it by this distant northern sea.

The Sea of Faith
Was once, too, at the full, and round earth's shore
Lay like the folds of a bright girdle furled.
But now I only hear
Its melancholy, long, withdrawing roar,
Retreating, to the breath
Of the night-wind, down the vast edges drear
And naked shingles of the world.

Ah, love, let us be true
To one another! for the world, which seems
To lie before us like a land of dreams,
So various, so beautiful, so new,
Hath really neither joy, nor love, nor light,
Nor certitude, nor peace, nor help for pain;
And we are here as on a darkling plain
Swept with confused alarms of struggle and flight,
Where ignorant armies clash by night.

◆ How did you indicate vocally the several shifts in locus?

Here is an essay about a very personal memory that tellingly describes a moment we have all encountered. Be sure that you portray the young Allison as clearly as you portray the man he has become.

 ## Back at the Ranch

JAY ALLISON

A young boy molts. Tender skin falls off, or gets scraped off, and is replaced by a tougher, more permanent crust. The transition happens in moments, in events. All of a sudden, something is gone and something else is in its place. I made a change like that standing in the back of a pickup truck when I was 15.

It was 1967 and I had a summer job at a camp in Wyoming. It was beautiful there, high-pasture country with a postcard view of the Tetons. As an apprentice counselor I straddled the worlds of boys and men, breathing the high air, watching over kids, hanging out with cowboys. The cowboys wrangled the horses for the camp and were mostly an itinerant group, living in summer cabins below the barn, and they tolerated my loitering down there. I hitched up my jeans just like them, braided my lasso like them, smoked and cursed and slouched like them.

On the day it happened, I was standing with a group of cowboys by the ranch office. We heard the sound of a big engine

coming in the long driveway, and after a while a red Corvette Sting Ray convertible, of all things, motored up in front of us. Conversation stopped. In the driver's seat was a hippie. His hair fell straight down his back and a bandanna was tied around his head. His style may have been standard for somewhere, but not for Jackson, Wyo.

The guy was decked out with beads and earrings and dressed in fantastic colors, and next to him his girlfriend, just as exotic, with perfect blond hair, looked up at us over little square glasses with a distracted, angelic expression. All in a red Corvette.

I was fascinated, mesmerized. I looked around me with a big grin and realized that I was alone in this feeling. The cowboys all had hard stares, cold eyes. I adjusted, a traitor to myself, and blanked out my expression in kind.

The hippie opened up a big smile, and said: "I went to camp here when I was a kid . . . came by to say hi. Is Weenie around?"

In that moment, Weenie, the owner of the place, having heard the throb of the engine, appeared in the ranch office door and walked toward us with a bowlegged stride, his big belt buckle coming first. He walked right up to the driver and looked down on him.

"Get out." Weenie didn't say hi. "Get out of here now."

"What? Wait a minute. I came to say hi. I went to camp here. I just came to say hi."

"Get the hell off this ranch. *Now*." And staring at the hippie, Weenie kicked some dust up on the side of the Corvette.

"What's wrong with you, man?"

"You're what's wrong with me, son."

I noticed the cowboys were nodding. I nodded. Weenie's right. The guy should leave. He doesn't belong here.

"But you sent me a Christmas card!" By this time, the hippie had choked up a little. "I don't believe it. You sent me a goddamn Christmas card!"

The group of us closed in a little around the car. We-don't-like-that-kind-of-talk-from-a-hippie was the feeling I was getting. Thumbs came out of belt-loops. Jaws began to work.

"Looks like the little girlie's cryin'," said one of the cowboys, a tough one named Hondu. He spoke with his lips turned down on one side as if he was mouthing a cigarette. "Maybe the little girlie needs a haircut."

"Maybe so," said another, with mock consideration.

The notion rested in the air peacefully for a moment, then, in a sudden whipping motion, Hondu's jackknife was out, open and raised. With his other hand, he reached down and grabbed a fat bunch of the hippie's hair and pulled it toward him. Smiling grimly, he hacked it off and held it up for us to see.

During this, I looked down at the hippie's face, which was lifted up and sideways in such a way that he was looking right at me. Involuntarily, my head tilted just like his and we froze like that for a second.

"There now, that's better, ain't it?" asked Hondu.

The hippie, stunned, turned to his girlfriend, whose eyes and mouth had been wide open as long as he had been sitting there. Then he turned back to us, his face contorted, helpless. And then he went wild. He threw open his door and tried to jump up from the seat, but forgot that his seat belt was fastened and it held him in place. He struggled against it, screaming, swinging his arms like a bar fighter trying to shrug off his buddies restraining him. It was funny. Like a cartoon.

I looked around. We were all laughing. Our group closed up a little more, and came toward the car. The air bristled. He was the one who started the trouble. Well, he would get what he was looking for, all right.

The hippie stopped struggling, threw the Vette into gear, and fish-tailed in the dust. We all jumped out of the way, but the open door of the car bumped into Weenie's favorite dog, a Rhodesian Ridgeback, an inside-out-looking animal that gave a wild yelp and ran straight into a willow thicket. We could hear his yips over the sound of the big engine as the hippie gunned it and took off.

That settled it. The hippie hit the dog.

Without hesitation, we jumped into one of the trucks. Rifles were drawn from the rack in the cab. Other weapons were thrown up into the bed of the pickup. I was standing there and caught one.

We took off, and because the rough road slowed down the Corvette, we were gaining. I was filled with a terrible, frightening righteousness. I was holding a rifle, chasing a man and a woman with a rifle in my hand. I looked around at my partners in the truck, and the air came out of me. We meant harm. We didn't care. I wondered who I was exactly. I needed to know. And in that moment, it happened: I switched sides and never said a word about it.

We hit the asphalt road and floored it, but we couldn't catch the Corvette. No way. The smoke from its exhaust settled around us like fog in the valley.

Still, 23 years later, I can see the two of us clearly, chosen by the same moment. Memory cuts back and forth between our faces. The wind pulls tears from the hippie's eyes; his long hair waves behind him in his fiery convertible rocketing down Route 191 under the Tetons. I with my short hair stand in the back of a pickup truck watching after him, chasing after him, following, facing the same wind.

- ◆ How did you demonstrate the fulcrum?

- ◆ What did you do with your body and voice to suggest Allison's body?

The poem following is devastating in the cold simplicity of its literary style. The attitude of the persona is underscored by the word choice, the stark syntax, and the stanza division counting off the three "places." Keep the quotations within the unity of this attitude.

Her Story

NAOMI LONG MADGETT

They gave me the wrong name, in the first place.
They named me Grace and waited for a light and agile dancer.
But some trick of the genes mixed me up
And instead I turned out big and black and burly.

In the second place, I fashioned the wrong dreams.
I wanted to dress like Juliet and act
Before applauding audiences on Broadway.
I learned more about Shakespeare than he knew about himself.
But of course, all that was impossible.
"Talent, yes," they would tell me,
"But an actress has to look the part."
So I ended up waiting on tables in Harlem
And hearing uncouth men yell at me:

"Hey momma, you can cancel that hamburger
And come on up to 102."

In the third place, I tried the wrong solution.
The stuff I drank made me deathly sick
And someone called a doctor.
Next time I'll try a gun.

- How did you demonstrate the internal state of the speaker prior to
  the first line?

The fierce resilience of this narrator is only partly a result of environment. The coarse language and rough behavior only disguise the crucial vulnerability of the speaker. The audience needs to see all the levels in performance, of course, but not all at once. Keep all the characters full, involved in the tale.

The Lesson

TONI CADE BAMBARA

Back in the days when everyone was old and stupid or young and foolish and me and Sugar were the only ones just right, this lady moved on our block with nappy hair and proper speech and no makeup. And quite naturally we laughed at her, laughed the way we did at the junk man who went about his business like he was some big-time president and his sorry-ass horse his secretary. And we kinda hated her too, hated the way we did the winos who cluttered up our parks and pissed on our handball walls and stank up our hallways and stairs so you couldn't halfway play hide-and-seek without a goddamn gas mask. Miss Moore was her name. The only woman on the block with no first name. And she was black as hell, cept for her feet, which were fish-white and spooky. And she was always planning these boring-ass things for us to do, us being my cousin, mostly, who lived on the block cause we all moved North the same time and to the same apartment then spread out gradual to breathe. And our parents would yank our heads into some kinda shape and crisp up our clothes so we'd be presentable for travel with Miss Moore, who always looked like she was going to church, though she never did. Which is just one of the things the grownups talked about when they talked behind her back like a dog. But when she came calling with some sachet she'd sewed up or some gingerbread she'd made or some book, why then they'd all be too embarrassed to turn her down and we'd get handed over all spruced up. She'd been to college and said it was only right that she should take responsibility for the young ones' education, and she not even related by marriage or blood. So they'd go for it. Specially Aunt Gretchen. She was the main gofer in the family. You got some ole dumb shit foolishness you want somebody to go for, you send for Aunt Gretchen. She been screwed into the go-along for so long, it's a blood-deep natural thing with her. Which is how she got saddled with me and Sugar and Junior in the first place while our mothers were in a la-de-da apartment up the block having a good ole time.

So this one day Miss Moore rounds us all up at the mailbox and it's puredee hot and she's knockin herself out about arithmetic. And school suppose to let up in summer I heard, but she don't never let up. And the starch in my pinafore scratching the shit outta me and I'm really hating this nappy-head bitch and her goddamn college degree. I'd much rather go to the pool or to the show where it's cool. So me and Sugar leaning on the mailbox being surly, which is a Miss Moore word. And Flyboy checking out what everybody brought for lunch. And Fat Butt already wasting his peanut-butter-and-jelly sandwich like the pig he is. And Junebug punchin on Q.T.'s arm for potato chips. And Rosie Giraffe shifting from one hip to the other waiting for somebody to step on her foot or ask her if she from Georgia so she can kick ass, preferably Mercedes'. And Miss Moore asking us do we know what money is, like we a bunch of retards. I mean real money, she say, like it's only poker chips or monopoly papers we lay on the grocer. So right away I'm tired of this and say so. And would much rather snatch Sugar and go to the Sunset and terrorize the West Indian kids and take their hair ribbons and their money too. And Miss Moore files that remark away for next week's lesson on brotherhood, I can tell. And finally I say we oughta get to the subway cause it's cooler and besides we might meet some cute boys. Sugar done swiped her mama's lipstick, so we ready.

So we heading down the street and she's boring us silly about what things cost and what our parents make and how much goes for rent and how money ain't divided up right in this country. And then she gets to the part about we all poor and live in the slums, which I don't feature. And I'm ready to speak on that, but she steps out in the street and hails two cabs just like that. Then she hustles half the crew in with her and hands me a five-dollar bill and tells me to calculate 10 percent tip for the driver. And we're off. Me and Sugar and Junebug and Flyboy hangin out the window and hollering to everybody, putting lipstick on each other cause Flyboy a faggot anyway, and making farts with our sweaty armpits. But I'm mostly trying to figure how to spend this money. But they all fascinated with the meter ticking and Junebug starts laying bets as to how much it'll read when Flyboy can't hold his breath no more. Then Sugar lays bets as to how much it'll be when we get there. So

I'm stuck. Don't nobody want to go for my plan, which is to jump out at the next light and run off to the first bar-b-que we can find. Then the driver tells us to get the hell out cause we there already. And the meter reads eighty-five cents. And I'm stalling to figure out the tip and Sugar say give him a dime. And I decide he don't need it bad as I do, so later for him. But then he tries to take off with Junebug foot still in the door so we talk about his mama something ferocious. Then we check out that we on Fifth Avenue and everybody dressed up in stockings. One lady in a fur coat, hot as it is. White folks crazy.

"This is the place," Miss Moore say, presenting it to us in the voice she uses at the museum. "Let's look in the windows before we go in."

"Can we steal?" Sugar asks very serious like she's getting the ground rules squared away before she plays. "I beg your pardon," say Miss Moore, and we fall out. So she leads us around the windows of the toy store and me and Sugar screamin, "This is mine, that's mine, I gotta have that, that was made for me, I was born for that," till Big Butt drowns us out.

"Hey, I'm goin to buy that there."

"That there? You don't even know what it is, stupid."

"I do so," he say punchin on Rosie Giraffe. "It's a microscope."

"Whatcha gonna do with a microscope, fool?"

"Look at things."

"Like what, Ronald?" ask Miss Moore. And Big Butt ain't got the first notion. So here go Miss Moore gabbing about the thousands of bacteria in a drop of water and the somethinorother in a speck of blood and the million and one living things in the air around us is invisible to the naked eye. And what she say that for? Junebug go to town on that "naked" and we rolling. Then Miss Moore ask what it cost. So we all jam into the window smudgin it up and the price tag say $300. So then she ask how long'd take for Big Butt and Junebug to save up their allowances. "Too long," I say. "Yeh," adds Sugar, "outgrown it by that time." And Miss Moore say no, you never outgrow learning instruments. "Why, even medical students and interns and," blah, blah, blah. And we ready to choke Big Butt for bringing it up in the first damn place.

"This here costs four hundred eighty dollars," say Rosie Giraffe. So we pile up all over her to see what she pointin out. My eyes tell me it's a chunk of glass cracked with something heavy, and different-color inks dripped into the splits, then the whole thing put into a oven or something. But for $480 it don't make sense.

"That's a paperweight made of semi-precious stones fused together under tremendous pressure," she explains slowly, with her hands doing the mining and all the factory work.

"So what's a paperweight?" asks Rosie Giraffe.

"To weigh paper with, dumbbell," say Flyboy, the wise man from the East.

"Not exactly," say Miss Moore, which is what she say when you warm or way off too. "It's to weigh paper down so it won't scatter and make your desk untidy." So right away me and Sugar curtsy to each other and then to Mercedes who is more the tidy type.

"We don't keep paper on top of the desk in my class," say Junebug, figuring Miss Moore crazy or lyin one.

"At home, then," she say. "Don't you have a calendar and a pencil case and a blotter and a letter-opener on your desk at home where you do your homework?" And she know damn well what our homes look like cause she nosys around in them every chance she gets.

"I don't even have a desk," say Junebug. "Do we?"

"No. And I don't get no homework neither," says Big Butt.

"And I don't even have a home," say Flyboy like he do at school to keep the white folks off his back and sorry for him. Send this poor kid to camp posters, is his specialty.

"I do," says Mercedes. "I have a box of stationery on my desk and a picture of my cat. My godmother bought the stationery and the desk. There's a big rose on each sheet and the envelopes smell like roses."

"Who wants to know about your smelly-ass stationery," say Rosie Giraffe fore I can get my two cents in.

"It's important to have a work area all your own so that . . ."

"Will you look at this sailboat, please," say Flyboy, cuttin her off and pointin to the thing like it was his. So once again we tumble all over each other to gaze at this magnificent thing in the toy store which is just big enough to maybe sail two kittens across the pond if you strap them to the posts tight. We all start reciting the price tag like we in assembly. "Handcrafted sailboat of fiberglass at one thousand one hundred ninety-five dollars."

"Unbelievable," I hear myself say and am really stunned. I read it again for myself just in case the group recitation put me in a trance. Same thing. For some reason this pisses me off. We look at Miss Moore and she lookin at us, waiting for I dunno what.

"Who'd pay all that when you can buy a sailboat set for a quarter at Pop's, a tube of glue for a dime, and a ball of string for eight cents? It must have a motor and a whole lot else besides," I say. "My sailboat cost me about fifty cents."

"But will it take water?" say Mercedes with her smart ass.

"Took mine to Alley Pond Park once," say Flyboy. "String broke. Lost it. Pity."

"Sailed mine in Central Park and it keeled over and sank. Had to ask my father for another dollar."

"And you got the strap," laugh Big Butt. "The jerk didn't even have a string on it. My old man wailed on his behind."

Little Q.T. was staring hard at the sailboat and you could see he wanted it bad. But he too little and somebody'd just take it from him. So what the hell. "This boat for kids, Miss Moore?"

"Parents silly to buy something like that just to get all broke up," say Rosie Giraffe.

"That much money it should last forever," I figure.

"My father'd buy it for me if I wanted it."

"Your father, my ass," say Rosie Giraffe getting a chance to finally push Mercedes.

"Must be rich people shop here," say Q.T.

"You are a very bright boy," say Flyboy. "What was your first clue?" And he rap him on the head with the back of his knuckles, since Q.T. the only one he could get away with. Though Q.T. liable to come up behind you years later and get his licks in when you half expect it.

"What I want to know is," I says to Miss Moore though I never talk to her, I wouldn't give the bitch that satisfaction, "is how much a real boat costs? I figure a thousand'd get you a yacht any day."

"Why don't you check that out," she says, "and report back to the group?" Which really pains my ass. If you gonna mess up a perfectly good swim day least you could do is have some answers. "Let's go in," she say like she got something up her sleeve. Only she don't lead the way. So me and Sugar turn the corner to where the entrance is, but when we get there I kinda hang back. Not that I'm scared, what's there to be afraid of, just a toy store. But I feel funny, shame. But what I got to be shamed about? Got as much right to go in as anybody. But somehow I can't seem to get hold of the door, so I step away from Sugar to lead. But she hangs back too. And I look at her and she looks at me and this is ridiculous. I mean, damn, I have never ever been shy about doing nothing or going nowhere. But then Mercedes steps up and then Rosie Giraffe and Big Butt crowd in behind and shove, and next thing we all stuffed into the doorway with only Mercedes squeezing past us, smoothing out her jumper and walking right down the aisle. Then the rest of us tumble in like a glued-together jigsaw done all wrong. And people lookin at us. And it's like the time me and Sugar crashed into the Catholic church on a dare. But once we got in there and everything so hushed and holy and the candles and the bowin and the handkerchiefs on all the drooping heads, I just couldn't go through with the plan. Which was for me to run up to the altar and do a tap dance while Sugar played the nose flute and messed around in the holy water. And Sugar kept givin me the elbow. Then later teased me so bad I tied her up in the shower and turned it on and locked her in. And she'd be there till this day if Aunt Gretchen hadn't finally figured I was lyin about the boarder takin a shower.

Same thing in the store. We all walkin on tiptoe and hardly touchin the games and puzzles and things. And I watched Miss Moore who is steady watchin us like she waitin for a sign. Like Mama Drewery watches the sky and sniffs the air and takes note of just how much slant is in the bird formation. Then me and Sugar bump smack into each other, so busy gazing at the toys, 'specially the sailboat. But we don't laugh and go into our fat-lady bump-stomach routine. We just stare at that price tag. Then Sugar run a finger over the whole boat. And I'm jealous and want to hit her. Maybe not her, but I sure want to punch somebody in the mouth.

"Watcha bring us here for, Miss Moore?"

"You sound angry, Sylvia. Are you mad about something?" Givin me one of them grins like she tellin a grown-up joke that never turns out to be funny. And she's lookin very closely at me like maybe she plannin to do my portrait from memory. I'm mad, but I won't give her that satisfaction. So I slouch around the store being very bored and say, "Let's go."

Me and Sugar at the back of the train watchin the tracks whizzin by large then small then gettin gobbled up in the dark. I'm thinkin about this tricky toy I saw in the store. A clown that somersaults on a bar then does chin-ups just cause you yank lightly at his leg. Cost $35. I could see me askin my mother for a $35 birthday clown. "You wanna who that costs what?" she'd say, cocking her head to the side to get a better view of the hole in my head. Thirty-five dollars could buy new bunk beds for Junior and Gretchen's boy. Thirty-five dollars and the whole household could go visit Granddaddy Nelson in the country. Thirty-five dollars would pay for the rent and the piano bill too. Who are these people that spend that much for performing clowns and $1000 for toy sailboats? What kinda work they do and how they live and how come we ain't in on it? Where we are is who we are, Miss Moore always pointin out. But it don't necessarily have to be that way, she always adds then waits for somebody to say that poor people have to wake up and demand their share of the pie and don't none of us know what kind of pie she talking about in the first damn place. But she ain't so smart cause I still got her four dollars from the taxi and she sure ain't gettin it. Messin up my day with this shit. Sugar nudges me in my pocket and winks.

Miss Moore lines us up in front of the mailbox where we started from, seem like years ago, and I got a headache for thinkin so hard. And we lean all over each other so we can hold up under the draggy ass lecture she always finishes us off with at the end before we thank her for borin us to tears. But she just looks at us like she readin tea leaves. Finally she say, "Well, what did you think of F.A.O. Schwarz?"

Rosie Giraffe mumbles, "White folks crazy."

"I'd like to go there again when I get my birthday money," says Mercedes, and we shove her out the pack so she has to lean on the mailbox by herself.

"I'd like a shower. Tiring day," say Flyboy.

Then Sugar surprises me by sayin, "You know, Miss Moore, I don't think all of us here put together eat in a year what that sailboat costs." And Miss Moore lights up like somebody goosed her. "And?" she say, urging Sugar on. Only I'm standin on her foot so she don't continue.

"Imagine for a minute what kind of society it is in which some people can spend on a toy what it would cost to feed a family of six or seven. What do you think?"

"I think," say Sugar pushing me off her feet like she never done before, cause I whip her ass in a minute, "that this is not much of a democracy if you ask me. Equal chance to pursue happiness means an equal crack at the dough, don't it?" Miss Moore is besides herself and I am disgusted with Sugar's treachery. So I stand on her foot one more time to see if she'll shove me. She shuts up, and Miss Moore looks at me, sorrowfully I'm thinkin. And somethin weird is goin on, I can feel it in my chest.

"Anybody else learn anything today?" lookin dead at me. I walk away and Sugar has to run to catch up and don't even seem to notice when I shrug her arm off my shoulder.

"Well, we got four dollars anyway," she says.

"Uh hunh."

"We could go to Hascombs and get half a chocolate layer and then go to the Sunset and still have plenty money for potato chips and ice cream sodas."

"Uh hunh."

"Race you to Hascombs," she say.

We start down the block and she gets ahead which is O.K. by me cause I'm going to the West End and then over to the Drive to think this day through. She can run if she want to and even run faster. But ain't nobody gonna beat me at nuthin.

- ◆ How did you distinguish between the narrator's participation in the scene she describes and her activity in telling?

- ◆ If you chose to perform only an excerpt from the story, how did you make the "lesson" of your segment clear to your audience?

This small fragment of a Navajo ceremonial chant presents a real challenge to the interpreter. The repetition and the end-stopped lines are important for the quality of ritual and chant, but they should not be allowed to become monotonous. There is no need to attempt a musical accompaniment or tone, because the writing itself is so rich. Pay particular attention to the variety found in the middle of the lines where there are subtle word shifts. It will help to think of the first lines as a cohesive unit, the "beauty" lines as a unit, and the last four lines as another phase of this prayer of purification. Remember the Native Americans' mystical kinship with the earth on which they walk.

 ### FROM The Night Chant

NAVAJO CEREMONIAL CHANT, TRANSLATED BY WASHINGTON MATTHEWS

In beauty may I walk.
All day long may I walk.
Through the returning seasons may I walk.
On the trail marked with pollen may I walk.
With grasshoppers about my feet may I walk.
With dew about my feet may I walk.
With beauty may I walk.
With beauty before me, may I walk.
With beauty behind me, may I walk.
With beauty above me, may I walk.
With beauty below me, may I walk.
With beauty all around me, may I walk.
In old age wandering on a trail of beauty, lively, may I walk.
In old age wandering on a trail of beauty, living again, may I walk.
It is finished in beauty.
It is finished in beauty.

- Did your voice mark the differences in the repeated words?

- How did you avoid monotony?

William Least Heat Moon set out on back roads and byways to discover something about himself and about America. His itinerary arose almost entirely by whim, but he often found unique people and learned subtle lessons, as in this segment from Blue Highways.

 ### FROM Blue Highways

WILLIAM LEAST HEAT MOON

Had it not been raining hard that morning on the Livingston square, I never would have learned of Nameless, Tennessee. Waiting for the rain to ease, I lay on my bunk and read the atlas to pass time rather than to see where I might go. In Kentucky were towns with fine names like Boreing, Bear Wallow, Decoy, Subtle, Mud Lick, Mummie, Neon; Belcher was just down the road from Mouthcard, and Minnie only ten miles from Mousie.

I looked at Tennessee. Turtletown eight miles from Ducktown. And also: Peavine, Wheel, Milky Way, Love Joy, Dull, Weakly, Fly, Spot, Miser Station, Only, McBurg, Peeled Chestnut, Clouds, Topsy, Isoline. And the best of all, Nameless. The logic! I was heading east, and Nameless lay forty-five miles west. I decided to go anyway.

The rain stopped, but things looked saturated, even bricks. In Gainesboro, a hill town with a square of businesses around the Jackson County Courthouse, I stopped for directions and breakfast. There is one almost infallible way to find honest food at just prices in blue-highway America: count the wall calendars in a cafe.

> No calendar: Same as an interstate pit stop.
> One calendar: Preprocessed food assembled in New Jersey.
> Two calendars: Only if fish trophies present.
> Three calendars: Can't miss on the farm-boy breakfasts.
> Four calendars: Try the ho-made pie too.
> Five calendars: Keep it under your hat, or they'll franchise.

One time I found a six-calendar cafe in the Ozarks, which served fried chicken, peach pie, and chocolate malts, that left me searching for another ever since. I've never seen a seven-calendar place. But old-time travelers—road men in a day when cars had running boards and lunchroom windows said AIR COOLED in blue letters with icicles dripping from the tops—those travelers have told me the golden legends of seven-calendar cafes.

To the rider of back roads, nothing shows the tone, the voice of a small town more quickly than the breakfast grill or the five-thirty tavern. Much of what the people do and believe and share is evident then. The City Cafe in Gainesboro had three calendars that I could see from the walk. Inside were no interstate refugees with full bladders and empty tanks, no wild-eyed children just released from the glassy cell of a stationwagon backseat, no longhaul truckers talking in CB numbers. There were only townspeople wearing overalls, or catalog-order suits with five-and-dime ties, or uniforms. That is, here were farmers and mill hands, bank clerks, the dry goods merchant, a policeman, and a chiropractor's receptionist. Because it was Saturday, there were also mothers and children.

I ordered my standard on-the-road breakfast: two eggs up, hashbrowns, tomato juice. The waitress, whose pale, almost translucent skin shifted hue in the gray light like a thin slice of mother of pearl, brought the food. Next to the eggs was a biscuit with a little yellow Smiley button stuck in it. She said, "You from the North?"

"I guess I am." A Missourian gets used to Southerners thinking him a Yankee, Northerners considering him a cracker, a Westerner sneering at his effete Easternness, and the Easterner taking him for a cowhand.

"So whata you doin' in the mountains?"

"Talking to people. Taking some pictures. Looking mostly."

"Lookin' for what?"

"A three-calendar cafe that serves Smiley buttons on the biscuits."

"You needed a smile. Tell me really."

"I don't know. Actually, I'm looking for some jam to put on this biscuit now that you've brought one."

She came back with grape jelly. In a land of quince jelly, apple butter, apricot jam, blueberry preserves, pear conserves, and lemon marmalade, you always get grape jelly.

"Whata you lookin' for?"

Like anyone else, I'm embarrassed to eat in front of a watcher, particularly if I'm getting interviewed. "Why don't you have a cup of coffee?"

"Cain't right now. You gonna tell me?"

"I don't know how to describe it to you. Call it harmony."

She waited for something more. "Is that it?" Someone called her to the kitchen. I had managed almost to finish by the time she came back. She sat on the edge of the booth. "I started out in life not likin' anything, but then it grew on me. Maybe that'll happen to you." She watched me spread the jelly. "Saw your van." She watched me eat the biscuit. "You sleep in there?" I told her I did. "I'd love to do that, but I'd be scared spitless."

"I don't mind being scared spitless. Sometimes."

"I'd love to take off cross country. I like to look at different license plates. But I'd take a dog. You carry a dog?"

"No dogs, no cats, no budgie birds. It's a one-man campaign to show Americans a person can travel alone without a pet."

"Cain't travel without a dog!"

"I like to do things the hard way."

"Shoot! I'd take me a dog to talk to. And for protection."

"It isn't traveling to cross the country and talk to your pug instead of people along the way. Besides, being alone on the road makes you ready to meet someone when you stop. You get sociable traveling alone."

She looked out toward the van again. "Time I get the nerve to take a trip, gas'll cost five dollars a gallon."

"Could be. My rig might go the way of the steamboat." I remembered why I'd come to Gainesboro. "You know the way to Nameless?"

"Nameless? I've heard of Nameless. Better ask the amlance driver in the corner booth." She pinned the Smiley on my jacket. "Maybe I'll see you on the road somewhere. His name's Bob, by the way."

"The ambulance driver?"

"The Smiley. I always name my Smileys—otherwise they all look alike. I'd talk to him before you go."

"The Smiley?"

"The amlance driver."

And so I went looking for Nameless, Tennessee, with a Smiley button named Bob.

- ♦ What did you do in your performance to suggest the sincerity of the narrator's interest in the people in the City Cafe?

That you have been reading aloud for longer than you have been in this course is something we mentioned early in the first chapter. Here the poet directs us to attend closely the voice we know best and, by listening carefully, to hear what it tells us about ourselves.

The Voice You Hear When You Read Silently

THOMAS LUX

is not silent, it is a speaking-
out-loud voice in your head: it is *spoken*,
a voice is *saying* it
as you read. It's the writer's words,
of course, in a literary sense
his or her "voice" but the sound
of that voice is the sound of *your* voice.
Not the sound your friends know
or the sound of a tape played back
but your voice
caught in the dark cathedral
of your skull, your voice heard
by an internal ear informed by internal abstracts
and what you know by feeling,
having felt. It is your voice
saying, for example, the word "barn"
that the writer wrote

but the "barn" you say
is a barn you know or knew. The voice
in your head, speaking as you read,
never says anything neutrally—some people
hated the barn they knew,
some people love the barn they know
so you hear the word loaded
and a sensory constellation
is lit: horse-gnawed stalls,
hayloft, black heat tape wrapping
a water pipe, a slippery
spilled *chirrr* of oats from a split sack,
the bony, filthy haunches of cows . . .
And "barn" is only a noun—no verb
or subject has entered into the sentence yet!
The voice you hear when you read to yourself
is the clearest voice: you speak it
speaking to you.

- ◆ What vocal elements did you employ each time you spoke "barn"?

- ◆ For some students of performance, "uttering" is "outering"—making audible what is internal. Would Lux agree? Do you?

Bibliography

The following works provide practical advice for the care and development of the voice, and they suggest ways in which the concept of "voice" figures in the study of performance.

Berry, Cicely. *Text in Action.* London: Virgin, 2001.
  Practical voice exercises from a voice director of the Royal Shakespeare Company.

Crannell, Kenneth. *Voice and Articulation: Developing Career Speech.* 3rd ed. Belmont, CA: Wadsworth, 1999.
  Numerous useful exercises and an audio recording of important examples enrich this broad examination of the ways voice can suggest character.

Kenley, Joan. *Voice Power.* New York: Henry Holt, 1988.
  A well-written practical guide to vocal production, with useful exercises for control and sustenance.

Madison, D. Soyini. "That Was My Occupation: Oral Narrative, Performance, and Black Feminist Thought." In *Exceptional Spaces: Essays in Performance and History,* edited by Della Pollock. Chapel Hill: University of North Carolina Press, 1998.

This essay illustrates the power of orality for the empowerment and survival of a former sharecropper and black woman from Mississippi.

Mayer, Lyle. *Fundamentals of Voice and Diction.* 13th ed. New York: McGraw-Hill, 2004.

One of the enduring classics about developing vocal skill.

Rodenburg, Patsy. *The Actor Speaks: Voice and the Performer.* New York: St. Martin's Press, 2000.

Practical advice from the current head of the voice department at the Royal National Theater.

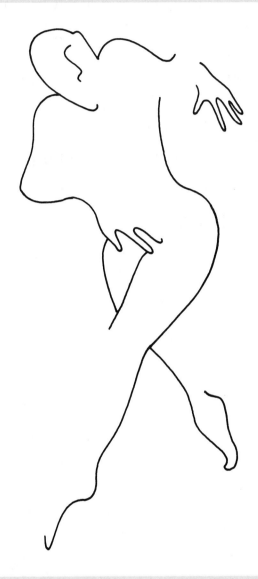

O body swayed to music, O brightening glance.
How can we know the dancer from the dance?

W. B. Yeats

"Among School Children"

CHAPTER FOUR

Use of the Body in Oral Interpretation

EXPECT THIS!

Your experience working on voice mirrors the kinds of activities you will encounter when learning to use the body in oral interpretation. Here you will need to develop effective relaxation techniques, too, but you will also note carefully how your body responds to the stimuli of your text, and you will develop the skills necessary to convey that physical sensation to the audience. By the end of this chapter, you should be able to:

- Define technique and explain its function in interpretation.

- Recognize the role that good posture plays in performance.

- Explain and illustrate the roles that kinesics (especially as applied to gesture and muscle tone) plays in rehearsal and performance.

- Point to examples of each kind of sense imagery, and suggest ways in which they inform rehearsal and performance.

- Describe the three steps in which empathy works for the interpreter.

- Develop a series of physical activities appropriate to each new selection you rehearse and perform.

An interpreter, who is both instrument and instrumentalist, must devote attention to technique.

Selections Discussed in This Chapter

In explaining some topics, we mention texts that are reprinted either within the chapter itself or at the end of a chapter. Use the guide below for quick reference to acquaint yourself with selections you may not fully recall.

Author	Title	Location
Deborah Sherman	"Dulce"	Chapter 1, page 18
Kate Chopin	"The Story of an Hour"	Chapter 2, page 44
		(continued)

Author	Title	Location
Charles Dickens	from *A Tale of Two Cities*	Chapter 4, page 141
Thomas Wolfe	from "The Golden World" in *Look Homeward, Angel*	Chapter 4, page 142
Bill Hayes	"Flying Finish"	Chapter 4, page 152
James Wright	"Autumn Begins in Martins Ferry, Ohio"	Chapter 4, page 156
Ted Joans	"The .38"	Chapter 4, page 159
Diane Ackerman	"Still Life"	Chapter 4, page 160
Jamaica Kincaid	"Girl"	Chapter 4, page 161
Sharon Olds	"The Race"	Chapter 4, page 163
Theodore Roethke	"Old Lady's Winter Words"	Chapter 4, page 166

YOU HAVE DECIDED ON A TEXT THAT INTERESTS YOU AND IS worth preparing for performance. Your next responsibility is to work on understanding its elements—its logical meaning, its emotive overtones, and its qualities of literary craftsmanship. If you respond fully to all of the clues you find, the experience expressed in the writing will become part of you. At this point control of the twofold instrument of body and voice becomes important. Just as a musician cannot give a satisfactory performance without having perfected the handling of his or her musical instrument, so an interpreter, who is both instrument and instrumentalist, must devote attention to technique.

Technique

The term *technique* does not imply artificiality in the use of body and voice. In fact, the finer the technique is, the less apparent it should be to the audience. *Technique* may be defined as style of performance. In the art of interpretation the interpreter wants the audience to focus on the material, so overt attention to technique belongs in the rehearsal period. Display of vocal ability or physical virtuosity as an end in itself is interesting only to the degree that an exhibition of calisthenics or an observation of free-throw practice would be interesting. The interpreter develops and uses technique as a means of communicating the text; the text is not used as a vehicle for displaying technique.

You develop vocal and bodily technique by practicing, so that your muscles will respond to the demands made on them without apparent prompting or effort. During a performance you concentrate on the material and on the response of the audience to that material. If you are adequately prepared, and you sustain your concentration, your vocal mechanism and body will respond according to the habits you set up in rehearsal. As your skill increases through experience, this habitual response will become more dependable. You will also be able to undertake new challenges.

Oral interpretation obviously involves the use of the voice, but don't underestimate the very significant role of the body in oral interpretation. As a matter of fact, the body begins the process of communication even before the voice is heard. From the moment the audience becomes aware of your physical presence, you arouse a response, establishing in your listeners what psychologists call a "set," or condition of mental readiness, toward what they are about to hear. It is true that you may not begin to communicate the *specific* material until you speak, but your bodily actions suggest a particular mental attitude toward yourself, the audience, and the material. Thus, in one sense, your performance begins the moment you leave your seat.

Bodily action may be defined as any movement of the muscles of the body. This movement may be an elaborate gesture or merely a relaxing or tensing of the small muscles around the eyes or mouth, across the shoulders and back, or in the legs. It may be a combination of any or all of these movements.

Although we touch briefly on separate areas of bodily action, such as posture, gesture, muscle tone, and empathy, remember that no bodily movement exists in isolation. Moreover, for a movement to be significant, it must be considered within a specific context. Sometimes what the body is communicating deliberately contradicts the words being uttered. This incongruity can be a useful technique for certain kinds of comedy if that is the text's clear intention embodied by the performer. Unless it is evident in the writer's style, however, incongruity can interfere with what an unwary interpreter is trying to accomplish. When what we see contradicts what we hear, we believe the visual. Thus, when what we see underscores and reinforces what we hear, the impact of the material is sharpened considerably.

All aspects of the bodily action speak to an audience, whether the performer intends them or not. One common problem occurs when the *performer's* gestures or bodily habits override a *character's* habits. We recognize that bodily action—like voice—is one part of creating character. The performer must take care that the audience sees the bodily action intended for the character, not some habitual (and easily overlooked) habit of the performer. For example, a performer may have a nervous habit of brushing hair off his forehead. This bodily action might be useful in creating a character, but if all the characters brush hair off their foreheads, and if the narrator brushes hair off her forehead, too, the audience is likely to focus on the gesture rather than on the language. In life, you have seen people relate events that they *said* happened to them but that are not believable to you because they contradict what you heard. What holds true for life often holds true for literature: the way a body moves can reveal as much as or more than words. If you want proof, recall the last time you watched someone you thought was "quite fine" walk down the street.

Posture

The basis of effective bodily action is good *posture,* which is primarily a matter of comfortable positional relations among the various parts of the body. Good posture is the arrangement of the bones and muscles so that each unit does its job of supporting and controlling the bodily structure without unnecessary tension or strain.

For many, good posture requires standing easy from the ankle to the crown of the head, so that the skeletal structure falls into alignment. For those with musculoskeletal or neurological disabilities, some of the exercises we propose will be inappropriate—but the responsibility to respond fully remains precisely the same. Every performer needs to expand the customary repertoire of behaviors; every performer needs to achieve flexibility with the instrument. Performers present widely different capacities—for movement, for voice, for appreciation of text, for ability to engage an audience. You need to work specifically with *your* body and *your* behavior to be sure that you operate at optimum capacity. That you cannot tap-dance does not excuse you from responding fully; that you run two miles daily is no substitute for careful, specific, responsive embodiment of your selection.

Test your own posture by repeating the relaxation exercise on page 87 in Chapter 3.

Kinesics

Kinesics offers a way to look at the interaction between what the voice is saying and what the body is saying. *Kinesics* is the study of fine and gross bodily movement, gesture, posture, and locomotion. You probably have encountered elements of kinesics in the popular field known as body language. If you examine the popular literature on body language, you can pick up some useful suggestions about creating characters. You are also likely to touch on a much more rigorous area of research: *nonverbal communication.* This discipline examines physical activity, of course, but also includes scrutiny of physical characteristics, paralanguage, tactile communication, proxemics, artifacts, and environmental and cultural factors. Kinesics is one subpart of nonverbal communication. Each of these areas rewards a performer's careful study, because each suggests ways in which what we *do* conveys meaning about who we *are*—and that knowledge is essential to anyone charged with the task of bringing character to life in performance. We focus here on gesture and on muscle tone, and, later, on "Performance Anxiety," but these three large areas in no way exhaust the topic.

Gesture

A *gesture* may be defined as any movement that helps express or emphasize an idea or emotional response. Gesture includes both clearly discernible bodily movement and subtle changes in posture and muscle tone. Many people still think of gesture in its narrowest sense—as an overt action of the hands and arms and occasionally the head and shoulders. These parts of the body do not function as separate entities, however. Rather, they involve a "follow-through" that both affects and is affected by the degree of muscular tension in every other part of the body.

An effective gesture amplifies or enriches the meaning of the text; it does not simply repeat the denotative information of the words. If a character says, "I'd love a doughnut right now," and the performer rubs his or her stomach in a circular motion, the gesture isn't telling us anything more than the words tell us, and thus it is a *mimetic* gesture. If, on the other hand, at the conclusion of the line the performer pretends to make gagging sounds, we know that the behavior sharpens the sense of the line, and thus the gesture enriches the performance. Whatever does not amplify the text for the audience confuses them. Performers give audiences what they need and protect them from what they don't need.

Your use of gesture normally depends on two considerations. The first, as we have said, is your material. You should use whatever bodily action is necessary to make the meaning clear to your audience and to convey the emotional quality effectively. The second consideration is the personality and capacity of the interpreter. Some of us find it easier than others do to respond physically. If you are among the former, you will need to guard against superfluous gestures that obstruct the audience's ability to engage the material. On the other hand, if you shy away from physical display, don't let gesture become an issue when you are before an audience. The minute your concentration slips from the material to "what do I do with my hands?" your audience will quickly sense your anxiety. We have all seen "stiff" speakers try to inject "liveliness" in their speeches—and cringed at the results.

Nevertheless, responsiveness is such an important factor in the total process of communication that you would do well to work on gestures conscientiously during rehearsal periods. In the early phases of rehearsal, using large, exaggerated actions or moving freely about the room, responding consciously and overtly to all the empathic cues and muscle imagery in the selection is often helpful. This overt response during preparation forms the basis of *muscle memory*, in which the muscles "remember" the big action, and muscle tone reflects this remembering even after you discard or modify specific overt gesture.

If, on the other hand, you have a tendency to "talk with your hands," you should use whatever movements make you feel at ease and help communicate your material. It is important, however, to remember both facets of this advice: "make you feel at ease" and "help communicate." Be sure that what makes you feel at ease doesn't distract your audience and thus actually block communication.

Perhaps you have developed certain repetitious movements, such as constantly raising and lowering one hand, tilting your head, shrugging your shoulders, or swaying back and forth. Such personal mannerisms, called *autistic gestures* because they grow out of your own personality, divert attention away from what you are saying and to you and prevent the audience from concentrating on your material. Moreover, they can seriously interfere with the creation of a character or the persona in the literature. Occasionally checking yourself before a large mirror or videotaping a rehearsal will help call this fault to your attention. Remember: These habitual gestures won't be easy to detect because they are part of your everyday equipment. Look carefully.

Muscle Tone

Muscle tone refers to the degree of tension or relaxation present in the entire body. When you perform, remember that an audience responds more strongly to what it sees than to what it hears.

Muscle tone occurs as a result of muscle memory, complete response to the material, and the interpreter's concentration on sharing that material with the audience. It is vital to the fulcrum and climax of "Dulce" (Chapter 1), for example, or to "The Story of an Hour" (Chapter 2). Usually we are not aware of muscle tone as a separate aspect of bodily action and need only to be reminded occasionally that it must not distract from or negate the other aspects of performance.

When one's body is in a state of controlled relaxation, with no undue muscular strain or tension, it moves responsively. Don't confuse controlled relaxation with apathy or lack of physical energy. The interpreter who looks tired, depressed, or bored communicates an unfortunate impression to the audience and draws an undesirable response because the listeners reflect in their own muscle tone this sense of weariness, depression, or boredom. Relaxation is an easing of tension; it is not total disintegration. The degree of relaxation is controlled in the interest of dignity and poise, and it is dictated by the requirements of the material being presented.

Performance Anxiety

Muscle tone is also affected by the performer's mental and emotional state. A performer's emotional state can vary from obvious, overpowering tension (weak knees, trembling hands, voice out of control, panicked expression) to an appearance of assured, confident relaxation. Your emotional and mental state varies in direct proportion to your own self-confidence, your confidence in the value and appeal of the material you have chosen to perform, and your certainty that the audience can profit from what you have prepared. Any successful performance carries with it excitement—if it's not exciting, why watch? Often beginning performers transform that excitement into tensions that can seriously obstruct all the work they have invested. The key is to channel the tension into the performance so that it becomes an asset and not a hazard. No performer worth watching is free of fear—regardless of how long he or she has been working; but when the tension is performance-directed, it becomes energizing, a surge of intense living. If you dance, run, engage in strenuous physical exercise, you know the adrenalin "high" that comes when everything works as planned.

Performance anxiety ("butterflies in the stomach") can seem crippling to a beginning performer. Unless the problem is pathologic, you can turn the tension into a vital, stimulating performance. Tension is *not* stage fright, which immediately sets up a fear pattern-and-response in your muscles, your breathing, your voice. Try the following process during rehearsal; the memory can help you just before performance:

1. Relax. (Use the exercise we provide on page 87, or one you have devised for yourself.)

2. Think carefully about the first sentence you will utter in the selection you will perform. What occupies that speaker's mind? What is that speaker *doing*? What just occurred which prompts that speaker to speak?

3. Think about that speaker's body—posture, costume, attitude toward the characters and activities in the selection. Is the speaker eager to speak to us? How does this eagerness (or lack thereof) show in the speaker's legs? chest? head? eyes?

4. Try to match your body with speaker's body in *at least three ways:* Hold your head the way you see speaker's head. Stand (or sit or slouch) with your spine as you see speaker's spine. Decide on one telltale gesture the speaker could make (pushing up her glasses, pulling his earlobe with his thumb and index finger, grimacing at a

painful memory about to be revealed). Duplicate each physical act with your body.

5. Exhale. Concentrate completely on what happens inmmediately before the speaker speaks the first words of your selection.

6. Move to the performance space and begin.

As you do with every other exercise we offer, you will refine and adapt these suggestions to your own performance habits and mannerisms. You have invested a great deal of time and effort selecting worthy material, analyzing carefully how its components operate, and deciding on the performance choices to embody and evoke all you have learned. The time immediately before your performance needs to be focused on what you have decided and achieved, not on what you didn't do or couldn't do or didn't think of. Focus your attention on your work, and your audience will respond to your professional engagement and involvement, without which no performance can ever succeed.

Sense Imagery

Literature rich in universality and suggestion depends for much of its effectiveness on the skillful use of sense imagery. Images that appeal predominantly to the sense of sight are called *visual;* to the sense of hearing, *auditory;* to the sense of taste, *gustatory;* and to the sense of smell, *olfactory.* The sense of touch is appealed to in *tactual* (or *tactile*) imagery, which involves a sensation of physical contact, pressure, or texture, and in *thermal* imagery, which refers to the feelings of heat and cold.

Two additional types of imagery appeal directly to the muscles or motor sense. The first is *kinetic imagery,* which refers to large, overt actions of the muscles: running, jumping, sitting down, walking away. The second type is *kinesthetic imagery,* which refers to muscle tension and relaxation. Kinesthetic imagery is closely related to muscle memory and resultant muscle tone; it is likely to be present in any particularly rich sense appeal. Clearly, from what we know of muscle tone, and, indeed, the whole area of kinesics, these actions are invariably accompanied by tension or relaxation. Rarely in literature do you find a kinetic action or motor image that does not clearly indicate how and why someone ran or jumped or sat or walked. What is the difference between "I was terrified and I ran" and "I ran for the sheer joy of being young in summer"?

A kinesthetic image reveals *how* an action is performed—the degree of bodily tension or relaxation that goes along with the kinetic, overt action. The kinesthetic aspect is governed by the emotional state of the person performing the action and helps communicate that emotional state to the audience. You should identify fully with the *how* and the *why* of the actions performed by the personae or characters in a selection. A kinesthetic response is also involved in our reactions to height and distance. It operates very strongly in all the poems about stars in Chapter 2, for instance, and, very differently, in "The .38" (at the end of this chapter).

Let's try an experiment. Let your whole body respond completely to these two contrasting phrases: "Right above my head there was a huge bumblebee" and "Far off on the horizon I could see a single gull flying high and then swooping low over the expanse of water." Your responses are kinesthetic as well as visual. There need be no overt action involving the persona. But the emotional states differ, just as they do between "She sat primly waiting" and "She sat dozing in the sun." A kinesthetic image, unlike a kinetic one, can often stand alone.

Sense imagery helps create distinct and individual personalities. See how brilliantly Theodore Roethke uses it in "Old Lady's Winter Words," on page 166. Or consider the narrator in Bill Hayes's "Flying Finish" (page 152) as he and his lover watch the aerialists and acrobats whirling above them. How do their bodies tense and relax in response to what they see? to what they know about their futures?

Rarely does an image appeal to only one sense. In literature that is rich in suggestion, images carry complex appeals. Look at the wealth of images James Wright packs into the twelve brief lines of "Autumn Begins in Martins Ferry, Ohio" (page 156). It is chiefly through imagery that Ted Joans achieves such power with "The .38" (page 159) or Diane Ackerman vivifies a fatal encounter in the splendidly titled "Still Life" (page 160). In all of these selections—and in countless others—imagery contributes strongly to the effectiveness of the intrinsic factors.

Sometimes, though, imagery confines itself to a single type of primary appeal, such as the auditory impulse in "The .38." Other times it displays very little unity of type but is held together by restrictions limited to locale. Look at all the vivid visual images in Jamaica Kincaid's "Girl" (page 161). Watch how they deepen and enrich the olfactory images, until we can see and smell the world created. Imagery may be slanted toward one person or object (as in "The Race" by Sharon Olds, page 163), or it may focus on the parts of a series of details that relate to one object, place, or person. Charles Dickens uses this cumulative technique to describe a battle in *A Tale of Two Cities:*

> With a roar that sounded as if all the breath in France had been shaped into the detested word, the living sea rose, wave on wave, depth on depth, and overflowed the city to that point. Alarm-bells ringing, drums beating, the sea raging and thundering on its new beach, the attack began. . . .
>
> Cannon, muskets, fire and smoke . . . Flashing weapons, blazing torches, smoking wagon-loads of wet straw, hard work at neighboring barricades in

all directions, shrieks, volleys, execrations, bravery without stint, boom, smash and rattle, and the furious sounding of the living sea . . .[1]

Dickens begins with the auditory appeal, to which he adds complexity that reaches its height in "cannon, muskets, fire and smoke." Then he shifts to the visual and kinetic imagery of "flashing weapons," returning almost at once to the auditory appeal in "shrieks, volleys," which comes to a climax in "boom, smash and rattle." Finally, he blends this into "the furious sounding of the living sea."

In "The Golden World," a chapter in his novel *Look Homeward, Angel*, Thomas Wolfe gives the interpreter a complex problem in unity through imagery. The following sentence illustrates his use of cumulative technique:

> He knew the good male smell of his father's sitting room; of the smooth worn leather sofa, with the gaping horse-hair rent; of the blistered varnished wood upon the hearth; of the heated calf-skin bindings; of the flat moist plug of apple tobacco, stuck with a red flag; of wood-smoke and burnt leaves in October; of the brown tired autumn earth; of honey-suckle at night; of warm nasturtiums; of a clean ruddy farmer who comes weekly with printed butter, eggs and milk; of fat limp underdone bacon and of coffee; of a bakery-oven in the wind; of large deep-hued string beans smoking-hot and seasoned well with salt and butter; of a room of old pine boards in which books and carpets have been stored, long closed; of Concord grapes in their long white baskets.[2]

In this single sentence the imagery is predominantly olfactory, but within this unity of appeal there is a variety of place. The progression from interior to exterior and back to interior may prove troublesome unless the interpreter is careful to group the objects that appeal to the senses. The excerpt opens in the sitting room, where it remains through mention of the visual detail of "a red flag." Without warning or apparent motivation, the scene shifts to the outdoors, but the olfactory motif remains strong, and there is unity of appeal in the focus of attention on the earth and its produce. This speaker is following his nose. The "ruddy farmer" with his "butter, eggs and milk" sets up the train of thought that centers on the smell of food and calls up the rest of the images within the sentence. Included in these images is the "room of old pine boards in which books and carpets have been stored," an image that for the author belongs with these others, but to the interpreter may seem like an interpolation among the many references to food. The unifying factor here might be best classified as the author's presentation through a "stream of consciousness." To keep the transitions clear and acceptable, you should be careful to group the images by association of

1. Charles Dickens, *A Tale of Two Cities.*
2. Thomas Wolfe, *Look Homeward, Angel.*

place or type of appeal, keeping in mind the importance of the primary olfactory appeal and the fact that the memories cluster around a single house. Do not forget, or allow your listeners to forget, that the sentence begins with "He knew the . . . smell of. . . ."

Obviously, the type and vividness of the imagery should be in harmony with the total intention of the piece of literature: harmonious with the character and setting in a narrative and with the tastes and experiences of the intended audience in didactic writing and essays. Even the adjectives used to give the objects added richness should be highly appropriate: "heated calf-skin bindings" and "burnt leaves," for example, in the excerpt from *Look Homeward, Angel.* Books bound in watered silk would certainly not be harmonious with the "good male smell."

A skillful author is acutely aware, consciously or subconsciously, of the speed with which the senses tire. Thus, as Thomas Wolfe does with his "red flag," an author suddenly will vary the appeal to allow readers to shift their response to another sense. The interpreter must not allow the variety to overshadow or violate the essential unity but rather use this variety to fulfill its purpose of relief, in a sense to reinforce the unity.

Usually an author provides help with this problem. On close observation, you will discover that the author has not really abandoned the primary appeal but has only allowed it to shift momentarily to a secondary position. There may also be a fairly consistent relationship between two types of imagery.

In the matter of balance and proportion, imagery is often used to weight a unit so that with this added vividness the section is comparable to a more detailed unit. In this case, imagery is usually combined with other factors as well—especially to heighten a climax or to sharpen a contrast.

In some literary selections imagery provides an interesting rhythm between logical content and emotional quality. Kinesthetic response is so much a part of emotional response that it cannot be ignored or underestimated; it is also basic to the implementation of empathy.

Empathy

One of the interpreter's most powerful tools is the control and use of empathy. Although the roots of the word are Greek, *empathy* is a term borrowed from modern psychology. It means literally a "feeling into," and it results from the ability and willingness to project yourself intellectually and emotionally into a piece of literature or any other type of art. This emotional association enables you to embody the mental and the emotional states of the speaker and characters in the selection. Such identification results in a corresponding physical response. The *interaction* of these emotional and physical responses, as they intensify each other, is the basis of empathy as it concerns the interpreter.

Every writer who deals with emotions uses words and phrases in such a way as to cause some mental disturbance, which may take the form of pleasure or pain, activity or repose. As an interpreter, you respond fully to these words and phrases. If you have not experienced precisely what the author is describing or creating, recall some parallel or approximate situation that has evoked a comparable response in you. As you react emotionally to the written material, your muscles tighten or relax, usually without a conscious effort on your part. This tightening or relaxing of muscles affects the tone of your entire body. Try the following simple experiment to experience how this interaction actually works:

1. Divorce your mind from your immediate surroundings, and recall some occasion or experience that made you feel happy and exhilarated. It does not matter in the least what the experience was, as long as it made you feel particularly pleased with yourself and with your world. Spend as long as you wish recapturing the circumstances and the accompanying response.

2. Turn your thoughts to a set of circumstances that once made you violently angry. Concentrate on every detail and allow yourself to become thoroughly resentful. This is your chance to say all the things you thought of after it was too late.

3. Go back to the pleasant situation. Recapture the experience as completely as you can. As you allow your mood to change and the happy memory to take over, notice what is happening to your muscles.

4. Keeping your muscle tone exactly as it is, go back to the anger you felt before. Don't let a muscle tighten or change. It is clearly impossible to be as thoroughly angry as you were when your muscles were responding freely, though unconsciously.

Empathy works for the interpreter in three distinct steps: from the literature to the interpreter, from the interpreter to the audience, and from the audience back to the interpreter.

As we read a piece of literature, we relate to it actively. We all have had the experience of coming out of a concert, movie, or play or of finishing a book and being physically exhausted and, often, exhilarated. We are worn out not because we have been uncomfortable but because we have participated so thoroughly that our muscles are tired. This participation, which combines intellect, emotions, and body, is the first step in empathy. It is partly what makes us choose a selection to read in the first place. (You may lose this empathic response in the middle phases of rehearsal while you are trying to determine climaxes, the fulcrum, the intrinsic factors, and all of the other elements involved in analysis. But when you get the material back together again and look forward to sharing it with an audience, the empathic response comes back, strengthened by your newly developed mastery over the parts that make up the whole.) Thus, the first step in empathy is your own response to the stimulus provided by the literature. Without this response the second step is impossible. If you don't respond, choose another selection!

The second step in empathy has to do with the audience's response to the interpreter's material. When you respond empathically to the selection, you give physical cues to the listeners. Thus, we return to the whole concept of nonverbal communication. The audience responds to your muscle tone, usually unconsciously; this physical activity intensifies or inhibits their emotional involvement, just as your muscle tone intensified or inhibited your own emotional response in the exercise just described. Have you ever noticed that simply because someone else is frowning, smiling, or yawning, you tend to frown and feel depressed or irritated, or to smile and feel happy, or to yawn and feel tired or bored?

Successful interpreters are aware of the value of empathy, even in the way they approach the platform. During your introduction you can use this element to help establish an emotional readiness in the audience. When the selection is brief and intense, you will find that listeners move with you much more surely if you make full use of empathy. Their own mental and emotional states of readiness affect the tone of all their muscles. The members of the audience, by unconscious imitation of what they see, will adopt the physical tone that you project. By imitating your physical tone, listeners put themselves into psychic readiness for the response you wish to get from them.

The third step in empathy is the interpreter's ultimate reward: the audience sends back an empathic response through its concentration and its alternating tension and relaxation. You will feel listeners respond, see them lean forward, hear them laugh. Thus, the cycle is complete: from the printed page to the interpreter, out to the audience, and back to the interpreter.

Using Your Body in Rehearsal

Using your body effectively in performance requires careful rehearsal. Because you create impressions of the physical life of texts by exploiting your own physical life, you need to be conscious of what you do every day. You may be blithely unaware of the physical impression you make. Do you squirm when you watch yourself on a video, certain that you never twisted your neck just that way or did that odd thing with your left knee? The same behaviors you use to express yourself in everyday life are, in fact, performances—that is, selected from an arsenal of behaviors. You can watch yourself in life and attune yourself to the ways you habitually use your body. Aerobics, dancing, or any substantive repeated physical activity heightens your awareness of how you use your body, if only because you're sore in strange places the next morning! Awareness is the first step in selection, because you can't choose appropriate behaviors intelligently until you know the full range of choices.

Keep one caution in mind, however. Using your own repertoire of behaviors does not mean that you reconstruct the text in your own image. You may like to feel that you are the center of your own universe, but interpretation asks you to try to imagine how the *text* moves and responds. You may, luckily enough, find that it moves just as you do; more often, however, careful scrutiny shows that it moves *its* way, and you will need to adapt your own behavior to fit its dance. Indeed, the richness of these experiences arises precisely because performance allows you to *try* to see what it's like to live in another's skin, to sing in another's voice.

On a more technical level, a study of mime is valuable to interpreters because it makes them acutely aware of how each separate muscle contributes to an overall impression. It demands subtle control and flexibility of the entire body working as a fluid unit. Similarly, any dance or physical exercise reminds us of how we move, and how we see others move.

So-called sensitivity sessions or awareness exercises are as valuable to interpreters as they are to actors. They involve the conscious recall of sensuous experience. Because interpreters should always consider all of the stimuli received from the senses, strong concentration and a responsive body are indispensable during your preparation and rehearsal periods. By making yourself more open to the experience of the literature you are reading, you will enrich both your own and your audience's pleasure. Therefore, such exercises are helpful in achieving the first step in empathy. The wider you cast your net, the richer the options.

A word of warning: For most of us the muscular response is in itself a result of mental activity. The outward, physical signs are an indication of that inner activity, never a substitute for it. If the mental and emotional responses come first, the muscular response should follow. It doesn't work nearly so fully the other way around.

Rich responses, however, are not enough. You must be able to channel and direct that response to your audience. A good rehearsal technique to help achieve this second step in empathy is to work occasionally with other people and attempt to create a mood in them without words—a sort of silent game of charades. You will develop an awareness of the way in which a response can be turned out to include other people, and you will sharpen and refine both your muscle memory and posture control.

After you have developed your own capacity to respond and have learned the all-important method of directing that response out for an audience to share, return to the text. Carefully and *objectively* evaluate how relevant your response is to the experience the author has written about. Then eliminate the areas of your own subjectivity that conflict with the writing. This can be the most challenging—and rewarding— part of rehearsal. It requires you to give up a gesture that is not needed or to recognize that either the first or second half is enough—but not both. You can do it.

Eye Contact

Beginning interpreters are often puzzled by the intricate range of possibilities they must manage with just their eyes and faces. "Where do I look?" "What are my eyes doing?" "What should my facial expression be?" We have often heard these questions from students. The text you selected provides the *specific* answers, but some general observations can help. In this chapter we have explored the ways you can respond to an important injunction: allow your *body* to speak the literature, just as your voice does. To do this, you must *visualize* whatever the speaker sees. If, as performer, you see it before you describe it, your audience will see it with you; in a sense, the audience sees it "reflected" in your eyes. Focus your attention on the character who is being addressed or on the audience—your analysis has helped you to determine the focus of any given line. (It becomes apparent how useful *locus* can be in directing you to the most appropriate choice.)

Recall our discussion about the placement of action (see page 35). If you are addressing your audience as, say, the narrator of *Friday Night Lights* would do (at the end of this chapter), let your eyes contact each member of the audience in the way that an effective public speaker makes each listener feel that he or she is being individually addressed. If, on the other hand, you are addressing another character as, say, Tam Hollingshead or Mike Belew does at the very beginning of *Friday Night Lights,* start your rehearsal by imagining the person slightly above and slightly beyond the heads of the audience. The character you are addressing may move during the selection but will never leave that world just beyond the audience because, by placing your focus out front, you put your audience in the exciting middle of the action.

Your facial expressions should reflect what the literature demands: is your speaker desperately in love? on the verge of a fine rage? trying to excite the football team to make an impressive debut? fondly reminiscing? plotting revenge? Your face should reflect the speaker's mood (or moods) at the same time it encourages your audience to create their worlds with you. If you rehearse conscientiously, what seems artificial and clumsy will slowly become natural and fluent. Better still, you will have polished the physical clues your listeners need to engage themselves in your work.

Analyzing the Rehearsal and the Performance

Before you begin to examine your degree of success in making your voice and body work together to give your audience the selection you chose in its *aesthetic entirety,* go back and recheck the questions in the "Analyzing the Rehearsal and the Performance" section in Chapter 2 (page 59). During this performance you may have focused your attention on some of the problems that occurred in your earlier performances. Did you achieve the improvement you were seeking? Don't be discouraged if you are still encountering the same problems. Slight progress is still progress. Take some heart from what you have achieved rather than becoming discouraged with what you haven't yet achieved. However slight your improvement, remember that the fullest performance is the result of slow and continuing self-monitoring, careful attention to the responses of the audience, and hard work.

Don't try to solve every problem in every rehearsal. Instead, concentrate on the trickiest or most difficult problem. Work on it at every rehearsal until a solution begins to jell. For example, if you are reading a story, be sure that you are absolutely clear about what the narrator sounds like and looks like before you get too involved in the characters in the story. Have you chosen a lyric poem? Make sure your voice and your body accurately reflect the structure of the poem. Are you giving each line the weight it needs to carry the fullest possible meaning, or are you rushing through the piece just to be sure that you get all the words in? Solving the major problems will give you the luxury of working on the minor difficulties. As you seem to be making progress with the larger dilemmas, gradually add others—but don't forget that the foundation is getting better and better.

Each selection demands a fresh start and perhaps a different point of attack from the last one. Don't allow yourself to perform only one kind of literature just because you are most comfortable with it. Instead, experiment with many different kinds of selections. If you respect the literature and yourself as a performer, your audience will find something of value to see and hear.

The walk to the front of the room gives you a good opportunity to collect your thoughts for your introduction. Take the time to get a good, satisfying (but inaudible) breath and to become comfortable. Get your body focused on exactly what the persona is thinking immediately prior to the first words in your selection. When you are ready—and your audience is ready—begin.

Although the following questions relate directly to the chapters on voice development and the use of the body, they also apply to any performance you give. Why not ask a classmate to compare answers with you?

- Could you be heard? Could you be understood? (These are not always the same thing. Why?)

- Was your breath control satisfactory and comfortable? Did you find yourself running out of breath at places you previously had under control? What happened in the lines just preceding these new problem areas?

- Were you able to control and vary the pace to support the demands of your selection? Remember, audiences listen at a much slower rate than you can speak. Give them time to understand.

- Were you careful to use pauses effectively, being sure that you did not break the unity or destroy the harmony but made use of variety and contrast to achieve balance and proportion, to bring out the climaxes, and to suggest the fulcrum? Was your concentration steady during the pauses?

- Was there a regional dialect or melody pattern in your selection—or in your performance—that interfered with the audience's full enjoyment of the personae? Was monotone a problem?

- Was your body communicating what your voice was communicating? Did your body and your voice complement each other? Did you remember that your performance begins the instant you leave your seat and continues until you return to it?

- Did your body respond to the imagery honestly, without ignoring the intrinsic factors?

- Did you notice any physical mannerisms that inhibited what you were trying to communicate?

These questions are also helpful in analyzing the performances of other readers. Remember to be descriptive: (1) Select one striking moment in another's performance and see if you can describe *precisely* what the performer did to achieve such distinction. Take the time to sketch verbally exactly what the performer's body was doing and exactly how the performer's voice behaved at that moment. (2) Compare your responses with those of your classmates. (3) Now, together, compare all of these descriptions with the actual text of the selection. Did the performance coincide with the selection? How? Did it veer away from what the author intended? Where? How? Why?

Finally, ask yourself, Where in the performance (whether your own or another's) did literature and the reader correlate most closely? Why? Before you begin your next performance, try to remember what you did to achieve such a richly rewarding blend. But above all, begin to work on your next performance. There is no time to rest on easy victories, nothing to learn without valiant effort.

REMEMBER THIS!

Like its predecessor on voice, this chapter on using the body has been intentionally technical. We offered you a number of exercises and wanted you to be "up and doing" as much as possible. Both chapters are also intentionally open-ended: performers never stop working on the expressiveness of their bodies any more than they stop working on their voices. No football receiver has ever told his coach that he's "caught enough passes" (and lived to tell about it!). As you progress, you will find many opportunities to recall:

- The role of technique in rehearsal and performance.

- The need for proper posture in rehearsal and performance.

- Ways to exploit gesture and muscle tone in analysis, rehearsal, and performance.

- The variety of possible sense images and their functions during rehearsal and performance.

- The rewards of using empathy during rehearsal and performance.

- Techniques for controlling performance anxiety (stage fright) and focusing energy into the selection and the audience.

- Specific rehearsal strategies that target your body and whatever "performer gestures" can obscure your work.

Now you are equipped to explore varieties of literature, starting with prose in Chapter 5.

Selections for Analysis and Oral Interpretation

All of the following selections have a strong suggestion of physical action. In preparing them for oral interpretation, let your muscles respond completely; in some cases you may want to take time to work out a specific action (which you may or may not use in performance) to help you achieve the proper empathy. Because your voice and body must work together, many of the selections at the end of Chapter 3 also provide opportunities for bodily action, although they were chosen primarily because of their vocal demands.

Remember that each selection must be analyzed for organization, attitude, the elements of literary art, and suggested bodily action.

Be sure you understand all the allusions in this first selection. The action described is not that of the speaker, but kinesthetic imagery is very strong.

The Second Coming

WILLIAM BUTLER YEATS

Turning and turning in the widening gyre
The falcon cannot hear the falconer;
Things fall apart; the centre cannot hold;
Mere anarchy is loosed upon the world,
The blood-dimmed tide is loosed, and everywhere
The ceremony of innocence is drowned;
The best lack all conviction, while the worst
Are full of passionate intensity.
Surely some revelation is at hand;
Surely the Second Coming is at hand.
The Second Coming! Hardly are those words out
When a vast image out of *Spiritus Mundi*
Troubles my sight: somewhere in sands of the desert
A shape with lion body and the head of a man,
A gaze blank and pitiless as the sun,
Is moving its slow thighs, while all about it
Reel shadows of the indignant desert birds.
The darkness drops again; but now I know
That twenty centuries of stony sleep
Were vexed to nightmare by a rocking cradle,
And what rough beast, its hour come round at last,
Slouches towards Bethlehem to be born?

- What physical behavior did you use to demonstrate the speaker's increasing desperation? What happened to your body just before the words "but now I know"?

This essay explores different kinds of bodies: the vibrantly alive acrobats defying gravity and the slowly dying partner now trapped "in the land of AIDS." The gulf that separates the H.I.V.-negative from the H.I.V.-positive can never be totally bridged, but the leap of faith between them illumines every life. The experiences of these two San Franciscans are only superficially site-specific.

 Flying Finish

BILL HAYES

Here we are, in this car, at this moment, at this place we hoped never to be. I don't know which of us seems more lost and defeated. His seat belt buckled, Steve stares out the window. I think to myself wearily, we haven't even gotten home yet and we've already moved to a new place. We are itinerants, our old lives wiped out, the future stretching no more than a few miles. We have new identities, new language, new names. He is planning for the next stop. I am in charge of driving.

I cannot help retracing our steps, frantically searching for something of intense personal value, lost within the space of a few minutes, a few city blocks. We walked from the parking garage, through the heavy office doors and into the waiting room, where we stopped for a moment. A nurse brought us into a tiny, overheated room, and we waited anxiously, as if stuck in a broken-down elevator, for the door to open.

We had led our lives this way for four years: on a grim treasure hunt across his body, following the natural history of H.I.V. disease, with one clue leading to another. From AZT to ddC to 3TC. T-cell count to T-cell count. From the symptom-free period to early signs of complete immune-system breakdown. All the while, treading in the safety zone of the not-yet-sick and dodging an actual AIDS diagnosis. Now, the hunt was over. We knew time was probably up.

The doctor appeared and began leafing through Steve's file nonchalantly, as if she were looking for a telephone number. He peeked over her shoulder. "So, am I in the land of AIDS?" He said it playfully, covering for fear, as if he were guessing at a riddle.

With a childlike sense of denial that seemed rational at the time, I furiously prayed to my dead friend Carol to stop time and magically switch around the T-cell numbers. My daydream was interrupted by the doctor. She was speaking very, very slowly. "You are . . . in the land . . . of AIDS. . . ."

Although perfectly aware that Steve could cross over into AIDS some day, for years I found strength and pride in pronouncing, "He is H.I.V.-positive—asymptomatic." H.I.V. sounded clinical, yet survivable. It rolled fluidly off my tongue. AIDS, though, is like a mouthful of plaster—a death sentence stuck in the sympathetic bailiff's throat. I cannot bear to say it to his face. On Castro Street, I run into a friend, Glen, whom I haven't seen in over a year. He dropped out of sight, he explains, when he fell in love with a man who was H.I.V.-positive. Glen, a survivor of dozens of friends' AIDS deaths, was H.I.V.-negative, like me. But he determined to give it up for his lover: his sacrifice would symbolize the purest romantic commitment and insure that he would follow him to the grave. Glen tried to get infected through unprotected sex, he admits, but it didn't work. He remained H.I.V.-negative. The boyfriend, meanwhile, fell in love with someone else. And Glen, in a more traditional response to his problems, took an overdose of pills. He called 911 before passing out.

I don't know if I am more stunned by his story or by my response to it—completely unfazed. I intimately understand the mad logic that drives someone to such extremes. The powerlessness I feel against the virus can be so frustrating I sometimes think I would try anything, as Glen did, to stop it. But, become H.I.V.-infected? I am certain that it would do nothing but make me sick. It's not simply that we have made a promise to each other, with the healthy partner pledging to help the ill one. But that the separation between H.I.V.-negative and H.I.V.-positive is the separation between two people heightened to an extraordinary intensity. We can never be truly united. We can never fully understand one another— even in love, even in illness, even in death.

I very much doubt, in any event, that there is a person with AIDS who would wish the disease on someone he loved. Healthy lovers, friends and family represent, for many, the future they may not have. Steve isn't joking when he insists that I drive our car. In case there's an accident, I will have the air bag and the best chance of surviving. My future is very important to him, he states. By this, he means not only that I will share my life with him, but that his legacy will live with me. In my long and healthy life, there is hope for him. . . .

Here we are, in the last aisle, at the end of the row, at this place we do not really wish to be. We had bought circus tickets weeks before. Exhausted and uninterested, we had nevertheless been unable to think of a good reason not to use them. Huddled together for warmth, we hold hands beneath our crossed legs. Ushers close the canvas door flaps, music comes up, a spotlight snaps on. The show begins.

A corps of acrobats emerges from the darkness dressed in sparkling green leotards and head caps. Like caterpillars nibbling at a leaf, they gently pull away pieces of the green flooring. Trampolines are stretched seamlessly underneath. The acrobats line up, sprint, and the moment they hit the trampolines, fly into space. One after another, they are transformed into birds, twisting, spinning, defying gravity as they climb higher and higher. Sometimes their leaps are so high, they have ages to dive in a thrilling, slow-motion free fall. It seems as if I have a lifetime to watch. But each finishes in a flash, replaced in midair by another. As the act reaches its climax, two acrobats vault at once from opposite sides, their bodies dangerously—and flawlessly—interweaving.

I watch the gorgeous birds flying. It is so beautiful—painfully beautiful, like looking into the sun—I have to shut my eyes. In their elegant leaps into space and falls to earth, time is infinite in the moment. I can see everything, ineffably, at once.

I turn to Steve, perched uncomfortably on the hard wooden bench: his future clipped, the years spinning by, his exquisite body falling. And his life strikes me not simply as tragic, but—like the acrobat's leap—as sublime, breathtaking: speeded up, a series of complex twists and turns of beauty and pain, courage and fear, skill and daring, over in a moment. I realize I cannot save Steve. Nor can I only watch. But I can throw my body into midair with his, gracefully flying.

- ◆ How did your persona's body differ in the various locales of this piece?
- ◆ The acrobats are vibrantly active. How did you show the impact of their vitality on the speaker's body and voice?

Muscle tone and posture help suggest the power and strength of the Greek hero in the next selection. These qualities are more important than his age. His memories of past actions and his hope for future ones are strongly kinesthetic as he considers them, and they set up a clear rhythm of content.

 Ulysses

ALFRED, LORD TENNYSON

It little profits that an idle king,
By this still hearth, among these barren crags,
Matched with an aged wife, I mete and dole
Unequal laws unto a savage race,
That hoard, and sleep, and feed, and know not me.

I cannot rest from travel; I will drink
Life to the lees. All times I have enjoyed
Greatly, have suffered greatly, both with those
That loved me, and alone; on shore, and when
Through scudding drifts the rainy Hyades
Vexed the dim sea. I am become a name;
For always roaming with a hungry heart
Much have I seen and known—cities of men,
And manners, climates, councils, governments,
Myself not least, but honored of them all,—
And drunk delight of battle with my peers,
Far on the ringing plains of windy Troy.
I am a part of all that I have met;
Yet all experience is an arch wherethrough
Gleams that untraveled world, whose margin fades
Forever and forever when I move.
How dull it is to pause, to make an end,
To rust unburnished, not to shine in use!
As though to breathe were life! Life piled on life
Were all too little, and of one to me
Little remains: but every hour is saved
From that eternal silence, something more,
A bringer of new things; and vile it were
For some three suns to store and hoard myself,
And this gray spirit yearning in desire
To follow knowledge, like a sinking star,
Beyond the utmost bound of human thought.
    This is my son, my own Telemachus,
To whom I leave the sceptre and the isle,—
Well-loved of me, discerning to fulfil
This labor, by slow prudence to make mild
A rugged people, and through soft degrees
Subdue them to the useful and the good.
Most blameless is he, centred in the sphere
Of common duties, decent not to fail
In offices of tenderness, and pay
Meet adoration to my household gods,
When I am gone. He works his work, I mine.
    There lies the port; the vessel puffs her sail;
There gloom the dark broad seas. My mariners,
Souls that have toiled, and wrought, and thought with me,—
That ever with a frolic welcome took
The thunder and the sunshine, and opposed
Free hearts, free foreheads,—you and I are old;
Old age hath yet his honor and his toil.

Death closes all; but something ere the end,
Some work of noble note, may yet be done,
Not unbecoming men that strove with Gods.
The lights begin to twinkle from the rocks;
The long day wanes; the slow moon climbs; the deep
Moans round with many voices. Come, my friends,
'Tis not too late to seek a newer world,
Push off, and sitting well in order smite
The sounding furrows; for my purpose holds
To sail beyond the sunset, and the baths
Of all the western stars, until I die.
It may be that the gulfs will wash us down;
It may be we shall touch the Happy Isles,
And see the great Achilles, whom we knew.
Though much is taken, much abides; and though
We are not now that strength which in old days
Moved earth and heaven, that which we are, we are;
One equal temper of heroic hearts,
Made weak by time and fate, but strong in will
To strive, to seek, to find, and not to yield.

- ◆ Your audience should feel themselves a part of Ulysses' audience.
  What did you do physically to demonstrate locus and character?

Here are two works about that uniquely American obsession, high school football. Let Wright's images appear clear and vivid; don't miss a syllable.

Autumn Begins in Martins Ferry, Ohio

JAMES WRIGHT

In the Shreve High football stadium,
I think of Polacks nursing long beers in Tiltonsville,
And gray faces of Negroes in the blast furnace at Benwood,
And the ruptured night watchman of Wheeling Steel,
Dreaming of heroes.

All the proud fathers are ashamed to go home.
Their women cluck like starved pullets,
Dying for love.

Therefore,
Their sons grow suicidally beautiful
At the beginning of October,
And gallop terribly against each other's bodies.

- What happens to the speaker between "Dying for love" and "Therefore"?

- How did you create the world that gives rise to the game?

H. G. Bissinger's account of one season of the Odessa, Texas, Permian High School Panthers explores the impact of high school football on a town, a school, and the people who play and watch it. In this excerpt he cannily captures the excitement, tension, and thrill of an opening game. Let your body show us the power of these descriptions and memories.

FROM **Friday Night Lights**

H. G. BISSINGER

"Some of you haven't played before, been in the spotlight," said assistant coach Tam Hollingshead in those waning hours before Permian would take the field against El Paso Austin. He knew what the jitters of the season opener could do, how the most talented kid could come unglued in the sea of all those lights and those thousands of fans. He offered some succinct advice.

"Have some fun, hustle your ass, and stick the hell out of 'em."

"It's not a party we're goin' to, it's a business trip," Mike Belew told the running backs. "If you get hurt, that's fine, you're hurt. But if you get a lick, and you're gonna lay there and whine about it, you don't belong on the field anyway."

The team left the field house and made its way to the stadium in a caravan of yellow school buses. They went through their pre-game warmups with methodical, meticulous determination. Then they went to the dressing room and sat in silence before Gaines called the team to huddle around him. He didn't say much. He didn't have to.

Everyone knew what was at stake, that if all went without a hitch, this game would be the beginning of a glorious stretch that would not end until the afternoon of December 17 with a state championship trophy. It would be a sixteen-game season, longer than that of any college team in America and as long as most of the pro teams' seasons. Three and a half months of pure devotion to football where nothing else mattered, nothing else made a difference.

"That 1988 season is four and a half minutes away," Gaines said quietly with a little smile still on his lips. "Let's have a great one."

At the very sight of the team at the edge of the stadium, hundreds of elementary school kids started squealing in delight. They wore imitation cheerleading costumes and sweatshirts that said PERMIAN PANTHERS #1. They began yelling the war cry of "*MO-JO!*

MO-JO! MO-JO!" in frantic unison, rocking their arms back and forth. A little girl in glasses put her hand to her mouth, as if she had seen something incredible, and it made her momentarily speechless between screams. As the black wave of the Permian players moved out into the middle of the field, eight thousand other souls who had filled the home side rose to give a standing ovation. This moment, and not January first, was New Year's day.

Brian Johnson opened the season with a fifteen-yard run off the right side through a gaping hole to the Permian 47, lurching forward for every possible extra inch. Two quick passes from Winchell to split end Lloyd Hill gave Permian a first down at the El Paso Austin ten. Winchell looked good, setting up with poise in the pocket, throwing nicely, no rushed throws skittering off the hand.

Then Don Billingsley, the starting tailback for the Permian Panthers, got the ball on a pitch. He was a senior, and it was his debut as a starter.

The roars of the crowd got louder and louder as Don took the ball and headed for the goal line. A touchdown on the first drive of the season seemed destined, to the delight of the thousands who were there. And no one wanted it more, no one felt it more, than Charlie Billingsley.

It was his son Don down there on that field with the ball. But it was more than the natural swell of parental pride that stirred inside him.

Twenty years earlier, Charlie Billingsley himself had worn the black and white of Permian, not as some two-bit supporter but as a star, a legend. He still had powerful memories of those days, and as he sat in the stands on this balmy and beautiful night where the last wisps of clouds ran across the sky like a residue of ash from a once-brilliant fire, it seemed impossible not to look down on the field and see his own reflection.

- ◆ How did you suggest the attitudes of the many people who inhabit this excerpt?
- ◆ Did you follow Bissinger's sentence length carefully?

This poem performs brilliantly, but be sure that you know exactly what the relationship is between the speaker and the events. And don't throttle the end—it will take care of itself.

The .38

TED JOANS

I hear the man downstairs slapping the hell out of his stupid wife
   again
I hear him push and shove her around the overcrowded room
I hear his wife scream and beg for mercy
I hear him tell her there is no mercy
I hear the blows as they land on her beautiful body
I hear glasses and pots and pans falling
I hear her fleeing from the room
I hear them running up the stairs
I hear her outside my door
I hear him coming toward her outside my door
I hear her banging on my door
I hear him bang her head on my door
I hear him trying to drag her away from my door
I hear her hands desperate on my doorknob
I hear the blows of her head against my door
I hear him drag her down the stairs
I hear her head bounce from step to step
I hear them again in their room
I hear a loud smack across her face (I guess)
I hear her groan—then
I hear the eerie silence
I hear him open the top drawer of his bureau (the .38 lives there)
I hear the fast beat of my heart
I hear the drops of perspiration fall from my brow
I hear him yell I warned you
I hear him say damn you I warned you and now it's too late
I hear the loud report of the thirty eight caliber revolver then
I hear it again and again the Smith and Wesson
I hear the bang bang bang of four death dealing bullets
I hear my heart beat faster and louder—then again
I hear the eerie silence
I hear him walk out of their overcrowded room
I hear him walk up the steps
I hear him come toward my door
I hear his hand on the doorknob
I hear the doorknob click
I hear the door slowly open
I hear him step into my room
I hear the click of the thirty eight before the firing pin hits the bullet
I hear the loud blast of the powder exploding in the chamber of
   the .38

I hear the heavy lead nose of the bullet swiftly cutting its way
    through the barrel of the .38
I hear it emerge into space from the .38
I hear the bullet of death flying toward my head the .38
I hear it coming faster than sound the .38
I hear it coming closer to my sweaty forehead the .38
I hear its weird whistle the .38
I hear it give off a steamlike noise when it cuts through my sweat
    the .38
I hear it singe my skin as it enters my head the .38 and
I hear death saying, *Hello, I'm here!*

- At what line did terror finally fill the speaker? What was your body doing?

Consider a poem that may prove Wallace Stevens's opinion that poetry can kill a man. Time operates here in a special way and permits the speaker to check all the body's responses to invasions. Don't miss any of the opportunities for kinesthetic response.

 ### Still Life

DIANE ACKERMAN

The bullet has almost entered the brain:
I can feel it sprint down the gunbarrel
rolling each bevel around like a hoop
on a pigslide of calibrated steel and oil.
Now it whistles free and aloft
in that ice-cold millimeter of air,
then boils as the first layer of skin
shales off like ragged leaves of soap.
The trigger's omnipresent click
makes triggers all over the body fire
to the sound of Japanese shutters closing
one by one a skein of threads.
Now it tunnels through palisades,
veins, arteries, white corpuscles
red and battered as swollen ghosts,
cuts the struts on a glacial bone
jutting out like the leg of a single flamingo,
feints and draws in close for the kill
egged on by a mousegray parliament of cells.

- Where was your speaker's focus? Why?

This world may seem foreign to you, but the speaker clearly knows every inch of it in her bones. And she is not reluctant to offer very specific instructions to her restive pupil. Your challenge here is to keep this enormous sentence together while suggesting place, time, and action. What a marvelous opportunity for an ambitious performer!

Girl

JAMAICA KINCAID

Wash the white clothes on Monday and put them on the stone heap; wash the color clothes on Tuesday and put them on the clothesline to dry; don't walk barehead in the hot sun; cook pumpkin fritters in very hot sweet oil; soak your little clothes right after you take them off; when buying cotton to make yourself a nice blouse, be sure that it doesn't have gum on it, because that way it won't hold up well after a wash; soak salt fish overnight before you cook it; is it true that you sing benna in Sunday School?; always eat your food in such a way that it won't turn someone else's stomach; on Sundays try to walk like a lady and not like the slut you are so bent on becoming; don't sing benna in Sunday School; you mustn't speak to wharf-rat boys, not even to give directions; don't eat fruits on the street—flies will follow you; *but I don't sing benna on Sundays at all and never in Sunday School;* this is how to sew on a button; this is how to make a buttonhole for the button you have just sewed on; this is how to hem a dress when you see the hem coming down and so to prevent yourself from looking like the slut I know you are so bent on becoming; this is how you iron your father's khaki shirt so that it doesn't have a crease; this is how you iron your father's khaki pants so that they don't have a crease; this is how you grow okra—far from the house, because okra tree harbors red ants; when you are growing dasheen, make sure it gets plenty of water or else it makes your throat itch when you are eating it; this is how you sweep a corner; this is how you sweep a whole house; this is how you sweep a yard; this is how you smile to someone you don't like too much; this is how you smile to someone you don't like at all; this is how you smile to someone you like completely; this is how you set a table for tea; this is how you set a table for dinner; this is how you set a table for dinner with an important guest; this is how you set a table for lunch; this is how you set a table for breakfast; this is how to behave in the presence of men who don't know you very well, and this way they won't recognize immediately the slut I have warned you against becoming; be sure to wash every day, even if it is with your own spit; don't squat down to play marbles—you are not a boy, you know; don't pick people's flowers—you might catch something; don't throw stones at blackbirds, because it might not be a blackbird at all; this is how to make a bread pudding; this is how to make doukona; this is how to make pepper pot; this is how to make a good medicine for a cold; this is how to make a good medicine to throw away a child before it even becomes a child; this is how to catch a fish; this is how to throw back a fish you don't like, and that way something bad won't fall on you; this is how to bully a man; this is how a man bullies you; this is how to love a man, and if this doesn't work there are other ways, and if they don't work don't feel too bad about giving up; this is how to spit up in the air if you feel like it, and this is how to move quick so that it doesn't fall on you; this is how to make ends meet; always squeeze bread to make sure it's fresh; *but what if the baker won't let me feel the bread?;* you mean to say that after all you are really going to be the kind of woman who the baker won't let near the bread?

- ♦ Control of rate is essential here. What helped you decide when to vary the pace of the story?
- ♦ How did you keep lively the character who speaks the italicized lines?

Lucille Clifton proves the old folktale that the people could fly is still alive. There is a wealth of dignity and experience in these lines, so take the time to let your body recognize *the creek,* feel *the challenge,* do *what it has to do.*

Affirmative Action

LUCILLE CLIFTON

driving through virginia
we pause at a creek called
Difficult Run.

sunday morning.
we have been here before.

we have survived the Mississippi.
the Atlantic and the Nile. there we were
bundled into boats and the captain
hated us.

he still does. he will do
whatever he can to drown us,

but we are not surprised
by the captains, the waters, the long
and difficult run. the people

can fly if they have to.
we lift ourselves across.

- ◆ How did you embody the fulcrum? What did your voice sound like?
- ◆ Just before the final line, the speaker seems to inhale. Why?

As in the previous poems, there is no mistaking the strong kinetic and kines-thetic imagery throughout this selection. Although the style may seem closer to prose than to poetry, don't neglect the contribution of the lines as units of the thought progression. The insistent I is varied sufficiently by the insertions of indirect discourse to help control the pressure and rush of the bulk of the poem. The fulcrum is clear and comes just in time for the persona and for us. The last long sentence is gentle, and this contrast is helped considerably by the line lengths and punctuation.

The Race

SHARON OLDS

When I got to the airport I rushed up to the desk
and they told me the flight was cancelled. The doctors had
said my father would not live through the night
and the flight was cancelled. A young man with a
dark blond mustache told me
another airline had a non-stop
leaving in seven minutes—see that
elevator over there well go
down to the first floor, make a right you'll
see a yellow bus, get off at the
second Pan Am terminal—I
ran, I who have no sense of direction
raced exactly where he'd told me, like a fish
slipping upstream deftly against the
flow of the river. I jumped off that bus with my
heavy bags and ran, the bags
wagged me from side to side as if to
prove I was under the claims of the material, I
ran up to a man with a white flower on his breast,
I who always go to the end of the line, I said
Help me. He looked at my ticket, he said make a
left and then a right go up the moving stairs and then
run. I raced up the moving stairs
two at a time, at the top I saw the
long hollow corridor and

then I took a deep breath, I said
goodbye to my body, goodbye to comfort, I
used my legs and heart as if I would
gladly use them up for this, to
touch him again in this life. I ran and the
big heavy dark bags
banged me, wheeled and swam around me like
planets in wild orbits—I have seen
pictures of women running down roads with their
belongings tied in black scarves
grasped in their fists, running under serious
gray historical skies—I blessed my
long legs he gave me, my strong
heart I abandoned to its own purpose, I
ran to Gate 17 and they were

just lifting the thick white
lozenge of the door to fit it into the
socket of the plane. Like the man who is not
too rich, I turned to the side and
slipped through the needle's eye, and then I
walked down the aisle toward my father. The jet was
full and people's hair was shining, they were
smiling, the interior of the plane was filled with a
mist of gold endorphin light,
I wept as people weep when they enter heaven,
in massive relief. We lifted up
gently from one tip of the continent and
did not stop until we set down lightly on the
other edge, I walked into his room and
watched his chest rise slowly and
sink again, all night
I watched him breathe.

- ◆ How did you show that your muscles remembered the effort of
  the race?

*Langston Hughes was able to condense and make vivid the history of his race
from its beginnings through the first quarter of the twentieth century in this
brief poem. The repetitions are, of course, a strong unifying factor, as are the
motifs. Be careful that they do not obscure the variety and progression. The
pride and strength of the persona as he speaks in the first person but also as a
voice for an entire race will influence empathy and muscle tone. Don't let the
repetition at the beginning of lines become patterned. Allow the verbs to provide the clues for handling them.*

⊚ The Negro Speaks of Rivers

LANGSTON HUGHES

I've known rivers:
I've known rivers ancient as the world and older than the flow of
   human blood in human veins.
My soul has grown deep like the rivers.
I bathed in the Euphrates when dawns were young.
I built my hut near the Congo and it lulled me to sleep.
I looked upon the Nile and raised the pyramids above it.
I heard the singing of the Mississippi when Abe Lincoln went
   down to New Orleans, and I've seen its muddy bosom turn all
   golden in the sunset.

I've known rivers:
Ancient, dusky rivers.

My soul has grown deep like the rivers.

- ◆ What physical differences occurred in your persona before the eighth line and before the tenth line? Why?

The old lady whose words we hear in this poem obviously once loved being alive and physically responsive. Be sure to emphasize her memory of the joy of her body. Note the inner strength and fire suggested in the two-line stanza. Rhythm of content reflects the rhythm of her life as she remembers the past, is frozen in the present, and yearns for what is to come.

Old Lady's Winter Words

THEODORE ROETHKE

To seize, to seize,—
I know that dream.
Now my ardors sleep in a sleeve.
My eyes have forgotten.
Like the half-dead, I hug my last secrets.
O for some minstrel of what's to be,
A bird singing into the beyond,
The marrow of God, talking,
Full merry, a gleam
Gracious and bland,
On a bright stone.
Somewhere, among the ferns and birds,
The great swamps flash.
I would hold high converse
Where the winds gather,
And leap over my eye,
An old woman
Jumping in her shoes.
If only I could remember
The white grass bending away,
The doors swinging open,
The smells, the moment of hay,—
When I went to sea in a sigh,
In a boat of beautiful things.
The good day has gone:
The fair house, the high
Elm swinging around

With its deep shade, and birds.
I have listened close
For the thin sound in the windy chimney,
The fall of the last ash
From the dying ember.
I've become a sentry of small seeds,
Poking alone in my garden.
The stone walks, where are they?
Gone to bolster a road.
The shrunken soil
Has scampered away in a dry wind.
Once I was sweet with the light of myself,
A self-delighting creature,
Leaning over a rock,
My hair between me and the sun,
The waves rippling near me.
My feet remembered the earth,
The loam heaved me
That way and this.
My looks had a voice;
I was careless in growing.

If I were a young man,
I could roll in the dust of a fine rage.

The shadows are empty, the sliding externals.
The wind wanders around the house
On its way to the back pasture.
The cindery snow ticks over stubble.
My dust longs for the invisible.
I'm reminded to stay alive
By the dry rasp of the recurring inane,
The fine soot sifting through my south windows.
It is hard to care about corners,
And the sound of paper tearing.
I fall, more and more,
Into my own silences.
In the cold air,
The spirit
Hardens.

- ◆ Did your old lady have a clearly lived past *before* she began to speak? How did you demonstrate this to your audience?

This persona's body remembers everything. What he says may seem philo-
sophical, but it is clearly the product of muscle memory, sense imagery, and
empathy. Anthony Swofford dedicates his book to his fellow marines (jarheads)
of the Surveillance and Target Acquisition Platoon, Second Battalion, Seventh
Marines, August 1990–April 1991, with whom he served in Operation Desert
Storm. This chapter—almost at the end of the book—summarizes much of
what he has concluded. Give him full rein to think. Crucially, he lets his audi-
ence draw the conclusion. Give them time to think, too.

 FROM *Jarheads*

ANTHONY SWOFFORD

To be a marine, a true marine, you must kill. With all of your training, all of your expertise, if you don't kill, you're not a combatant,
even if you've been fired at, and so you are not yet a marine: receiving fire is easy—you've either made a mistake or the enemy is
better than you, and now you are either lucky or dead but not a
combatant. You will receive a Combat Action Ribbon, and if un-
lucky enough to have been hit but not fatally, a Purple Heart, or if
you're hit fatally, your mother will receive your Purple Heart, but

whether you are dead or not, you haven't, with your own hands, killed a hostile enemy soldier. This means everything.

Sometimes you wish you'd killed an Iraqi soldier. Or many Iraqi soldiers, in a series of fierce firefights while on patrol, with dozens of well-placed shots from your M40A1, through countless calls for fire. During the darkest nights you'd even offer your life to go back in time, back to the Desert for the chance to kill. You consider yourself less of a marine and even less of a man for not having killed while at combat. There is a wreck in your head, part of the aftermath, and you must dismantle the wreck.

But after many years you discover that you cannot dismantle the wreck, so you move it around and bury it.

It took years for you to understand that the most complex and dangerous conflicts, the most harrowing operations, and the most deadly wars, occur in the head.

You are certain you'd be no better or worse a man if you'd killed one or all of the men you sometimes fantasize about killing. Probably, you are incorrect, and you would be insane or dead by your own hand if you'd killed one or all of those men. You would've been a great killer. You would've been a terrible killer.

If you'd killed those men, you would've told your mother, "No, I never killed anyone," and even though you have indeed killed no one and have told your mother this, still she has said, numerous times, while weeping, "I lost my baby boy when you went to war. You were once so sweet and gentle and now you are an angry and unhappy man."

- ◆ Why does the author cast this chapter in the second person ("you")? Is it easier for the narrator to address these thoughts to another person? Why?

- ◆ What happened during the third paragraph that permitted you to conclude what is described in paragraph 4? How did you show that discovery to your audience?

Let your muscles respond to this famous speech on the seven ages of man. Remember the importance of muscle tone. Keep the progression firm and unified, but allow time for the physical and emotional transitions. The person himself does not age, but he visualizes and empathizes.

FROM **As You Like It**

WILLIAM SHAKESPEARE

ACT II, SCENE 7

JAQUES: All the world's a stage,
And all the men and women merely players.
They have their exits and their entrances,
And one man in his time plays many parts,
His acts being seven ages. At first the infant,
Mewling and puking in the nurse's arms.
Then the whining school-boy, with his satchel
And shining morning face, creeping like snail
Unwillingly to school. And then the lover,
Sighing like furnace, with a woeful ballad
Made to his mistress' eyebrow. Then a soldier,
Full of strange oaths, and bearded like the pard,
Jealous in honor, sudden, and quick in quarrel,
Seeking the bubble reputation
Even in the cannon's mouth. And then the justice,
In fair round belly with good capon lin'd,
With eyes severe and beard of formal cut,
Full of wise saws and modern instances;
And so he plays his part. The sixth age shifts
Into the lean and slipper'd pantaloon,
With spectacles on nose and pouch on side,
His youthful hose, well sav'd, a world too wide
For his shrunk shank, and his big manly voice,
Turning again toward childish treble, pipes
And whistles in his sound. Last scene of all,
That ends this strange eventful history,
Is second childishness and mere oblivion,
Sans teeth, sans eyes, sans taste, sans everything.

- ◆ How did your Jaques incorporate the kinesthetic imagery in performance?

Here is a work in which bodies dominate the telling as well as the tale. Don't miss the implications of the author's decision to cast this tale in the present tense, so that the speaker's outward voice and body maintain a composure that may not live inside. Although she says a great deal, she leaves out a great deal more. Can her body and voice suggest some of what is left unsaid?

Admission of Failure

PHYLLIS KOESTENBAUM

The hostess seats a girl and a young man in a short-sleeve sport shirt with one arm missing below the shoulder. I'm at the next table with my husband and son, Andy's Barbecue Restaurant, an early evening in July, chewing a boneless rib eye, gulping a dark beer ordered from the cocktail waitress, a nervous woman almost over the hill, whose high heel sandals click back and forth from the bar to the dining room joined to the bar by an open arch. A tall heavy cook in white hat is brushing sauce on the chicken and spareribs rotating slowly on a squeaking spit. Baked potatoes heat on the oven floor. The young man is eating salad with his one hand. He and his girl are on a date. He has a forties' movie face, early Van Johnson before the motorcycle accident scarred his forehead. He lost the arm recently. Hard as it is, it could be worse. I would even exchange places with him if I could. *I want to exchange places with the young armless man in the barbecue restaurant.* He would sit at my table and I would sit at his. After dinner I would go in his car and he would go in mine. I would live in his house and work at his job and he would live in my house and do what I do. I would be him dressing and undressing and he would be me dressing and undressing. Our bill comes. My husband leaves the tip on the tray; we take toothpicks and mints and walk through the dark workingmen's bar out to the parking lot still lit by the sky though the streetlights have come on as they do automatically at the same time each night. We drive our son, home for the summer, back to his job at the bookstore. As old Italians and Jews say of sons from five to fifty, he's a good boy. I have worked on this paragraph for more than two years.

- ◆ Where did that final sentence come from? How did you prepare your audience for that revelation?

- ◆ Where does this narrator focus her attention? What do her husband and her son see while she does this?

Bibliography

For the Student

These works offer practical and theoretical approaches to training the body for performance:

King, Nancy R. *A Movement Approach to Acting.* Englewood Cliffs, NJ: Prentice-Hall, 1981.
A program for movement training that begins with the performer's self-awareness and advances to difficult stage movement.

Nelson, Cary. *The Incarnate Word: Literature as Verbal Space.* Urbana: University of Illinois Press, 1973.
A broad and liberating explanation of the ways in which literature exists in the embodiment of language.

Vernon, John. *Poetry and the Body.* Urbana: University of Illinois Press, 1979.
This study argues that poetic experience is essentially a kinetic experience activated through the reader's imaginative participation.

For the Instructor

Contemporary literary and critical theory is deeply concerned with questions of "the body" and its relationship to texts and performative speech acts. These two works deftly describe this trend in cultural analysis:

Butler Judith. *Bodies That Matter.* New York: Routledge, 1993.

Grosz, Elizabeth. *Volatile Bodies.* Bloomington: Indiana University Press, 1994.

From another perspective

DeChaine, D. Robert. "Affect and Embodied Understanding in Musical Experience," *Text and Performance Quarterly* 22, no. 2 (2002): 79–98.
Arguing for the body as a site of knowledge, DeChaine accounts for the power of music as a bodily experience.

For the Student and the Instructor

Not all bodies and voices can do the same things, but voices are great within us. A lively and empowering literature from within the disabled community expands horizons. These books will help you discover those voices:

Baird, Joseph L., and Deborah S. Workman, eds. *Towards Solomon's Mountain: The Experience of Disability in Poetry.* Philadelphia: Temple University Press, 1986.

Fries, Kenny, ed. *Staring Back: The Disability Experience from Inside Out.* New York, Plume, 1997.

Shaw, Barrett, ed. *The Ragged Edge: The Disability Experience from the First Fifteen Years of "The Disability Rag."* Louisville, KY: Advocado Press, 1994.

PART TWO

Interpretation of Prose

**No difference between man and beast
is more important than syntax.**
Herbert Read
English Prose Style

CHAPTER FIVE

Style and Types in Fiction and Nonfiction

EXPECT THIS!

This chapter explores the distinctive components of nondramatic prose and considers the characteristics of style and the types of nonfiction you are likely to encounter. We touch only briefly on narrators here, because we focus exclusively on understanding them in the next chapter. By the end of this chapter, then, you should be able to:

- Describe the principle components of prose style.

- Explain the functions and effects of paragraphs.

- Discuss the ways in which syntax establishes meaning and contributes to the function and effects of sentences.

- Recognize, and perform appropriately, the variety of speech phrases.

- Compare the effects of diction (word choice).

- Demonstrate the roles of tone color in prose and in performance.

- Inform your rehearsal by responding to rhythm in prose.

- Show how to balance sentences.

- Consider the components and effects of description.

- Define and illustrate the most common types of prose: factual prose; personal essays; journals, letters, and diaries; oral histories; family stories; and folktales.

Prose writing ranges

in type from a

chemistry textbook

to a stream-of-

consciousness novel

to a trial transcript

to a public oration.

Selections Discussed in This Chapter

In explaining some topics, we mention texts that are reprinted either within the chapter itself or at the end of a chapter. Use the guide below for quick reference to acquaint yourself with selections you may not fully recall.

Author	Title	Location
Jamaica Kincaid	"Girl"	Chapter 4, page 161
Antoine de Saint-Exupéry	from *Wind, Sand and Stars*	Chapter 5, page 180
Henry James	from *The Spoils of Poynton*	Chapter 5, page 180
Virginia Woolf	from *The Common Reader*	Chapter 5, page 181
Jonathan Swift	from *Gulliver's Travels*	Chapter 5, page 181
John Donne	from *Devotions, XVII*	Chapter 5, page 181
William Shakespeare	from *Henry IV, Part I*	Chapter 5, page 182
Bergen Evans	from *The Natural History of Nonsense*	Chapter 5, page 183
Lillian Hellman	from *Pentimento*	Chapter 5, page 184
Gladys Schmitt	from *The Godforgotten*	Chapter 5, page 186
Eudora Welty	from "June Recital"	Chapter 5, page 198
Amy Tan	from *The Joy Luck Club*	Chapter 5, page 200
John C. Dann, ed.	from *The Revolution Remembered*	Chapter 5, page 203
Al Santoli, ed.	from *Everything We Had*	Chapter 5, page 205
Joan Didion	from "The Seacoast of Despair"	Chapter 5, page 207
Jane Gould Tortillot	from *Women's Diaries of the Westward Journey*	Chapter 5, page 213
Dana Tierney	"The Makeup Artist"	Chapter 5, page 217
Studs Terkel	"Terry Pickens," from *Working*	Chapter 5, page 221
Lynda Barry	"KEEP OUT! (A Boy's Bedroom)"	Chapter 5, page 224
Raymond Carver	"Popular Mechanics"	Chapter 6, page 272
Anna Deavere Smith	from *Fires in the Mirror*	Chapter 7, page 313

IN PART I, WE DISCUSSED MANY ASPECTS OF ANALYSIS THAT are common to all types of writing. We showed how interpreters use the knowledge gained through responsive analysis and through observing the performance that surrounds them to communicate literature with both their voices and their bodies. Part II concerns prose. Parts III and IV deal with drama and poetry, respectively.

Classifying material as prose, drama, or poetry, with smaller subdivisions, should be regarded as only a convenience. Our concern is not with literary labels, except insofar as these labels help us to understand the material. Rather, we're interested in communicating literature to listeners. Classification serves only as a starting point for detailed analysis.

An interpreter soon discovers the problems and advantages in each type of literature and then goes beyond this generalization to the specific, individual variations within a particular selection. Regardless of its form or type, each selection should be approached as an individual example. Before we consider various kinds of literature, we review some aspects of literary style found in all prose writing. Because subsequent chapters are devoted to narration, drama, and poetry, we focus here on nondramatic prose.

Nondramatic prose can take many forms: an encyclopedia, a user's manual for your DVD player, a personal essay, a "blog" entry, a letter, an oral history, this textbook. Such diverse components share some important characteristics, and for the interpreter none is more instructive for performance than "style." After reviewing the general topic of style, we focus on increasingly narrow components in more and more detail. Specifically, we first explore the role of paragraphs, move to sentences (those things that paragraphs are made of), zero in on speech phrases (what sentences are made of), and conclude with words themselves: why they are chosen (*diction*), how they sound (*tone color*), how they live with neighboring words (*rhythm*). Not every selection you choose will demonstrate an equal interest in all of these characteristics, but no good prose we know ignores any of them. As usual, your careful analysis will tell you how your selection is constructed, and, with that knowledge, you can construct the performance that will convey that knowledge to your audience.

Style

The word *style* comes from the Latin *stilus*, which means a pointed instrument for writing. Even today, each writer has a different way of using a writing instrument; and, although that instrument may now be a word processor rather than a quill, we think of each author as having a distinctive style. By the end of the sixteenth century, the word *style* came to mean a manner of writing or speaking.

George Bernard Shaw said, "He who has nothing to assert has no style." Style demonstrates character. How you dress and what you wear are always part of who you are. Style therefore consists of:

- Overall organization of ideas: How do we get from the first sentence to the last sentence?

- Steps in developing the central idea: How do the major thought units (which are paragraphs in prose) follow each other?

- Syntactical characteristics of the sentences: Is the sentence long or short, direct or meandering, simple or elaborate?

- Word choice and the relationship between words in a sentence: Why *this* now, why *these* modifiers, why *these* sounds?

Because your performance uses your body and your voice, you are also likely to be concerned with (1) speech phrases; (2) the way words combine, repeat, or rearrange the same sounds; and (3) the location of stresses that clarify meaning.

As British novelist Arnold Bennett said, "When a writer conceives an idea he conceives it in a form of words. That form of words is his style." Style, then, reveals itself in the ways *this* language conveys *this* meaning in *this* context. Just as you are shaped by your history, your general philosophy of life, your age, and your cultural heritage, so style reflects the author's attitudes toward the subject matter and toward the intended audience—the readers. Finally, style is also a mode of performance. The interpreter's goal must be to match the style of performance with the style of the writing.

Paragraphs

The first step in examining the style of a selection is to become aware of its general organization. The next step is to discover how the organization and arrangement of the elements make up the whole. In prose this process involves a consideration of the major thought units: *paragraphs.*

Each paragraph advances thought. The length and complexity of the unit and of the sentences that compose it reflect both the author's approach to the thought and the pace and the depth at which the idea is developed. In general, short, simple sentences and paragraphs indicate a direct approach and suggest immediacy of experience (as in "Terry Pickens" from *Working,* at the end of this chapter). Long, complicated sentences and paragraphs usually suggest a more sophisticated and evaluative approach, perhaps an intellectualization of experience or a reflection on past experiences. Joan Didion uses only five paragraphs in "The Seacoast of Despair" (at the end of this chapter) to explore the reverberating ironies of Newport, Rhode Island, and even the briefest paragraph (the first) elaborates ornately (like the Newport mansions she describes) on the unique mix of her reflections.

Nevertheless, some authors can use quite complicated sentences to create a very different impact. For example, you have already encountered Jamaica Kincaid's "Girl" (at the end of Chapter 4). This tale lives in one massive paragraph that is—except for the interruptions—one extraordinarily long sentence. Clearly, this speaker has a *lot* to say and wants to be sure to get it all in. Much the same motivation prompts the speaker of Lynda Barry's "KEEP OUT! (A Boy's Bedroom)" (at the end of this chapter). Consistently among Didion, Kincaid, and Barry, though, as the paragraph progresses, the thoughts develop—always in the character of the speaker.

Writers suggest relationships and importance by what they put together in paragraphs. An author may combine several relevant examples of a key idea in one paragraph, or each idea may require an explanation that is its own paragraph. Because paragraphs support the main thought, each deals with a particular point and ends only when that point has been developed. Still, in each paragraph's development you are likely to find a slight climax, where a logical point or an emotional level emerges and prepares the way for others to follow. Thus paragraphs serve as the steppingstones to the main climax and the conclusion, and they are as long or as short as the speaker requires to extend the argument or speed up the outcome. Compare, for example, the wide variety of paragraph lengths Amy Tan uses in the segment from *The Joy Luck Club* (at the end of this chapter). When the daughter confronts her mother most virulently, the paragraphs are brief, direct, and sharp; in moments of retrospection or consideration, they are longer, more indirect, and descriptive. Alternating these paragraph types helps create a characteristic rhythm.

Sentences

Sentences present the most immediate—and sometimes the peskiest—practical concerns to interpreters. Problems may arise because of the length, the grammatical construction, or the syntax of the sentences. Syntax describes the way words are grouped to show their relationship to each other and to demonstrate degrees of importance.

How do we solve the problems that sentences present? Suggestions for solutions are in the sentences themselves. Note first the elementary syntactical distinctions. Is this a simple sentence? complex? compound? How long is the sentence? How are its components arranged? What does the order of words tell you about importance and impression? Are more elaborate structural devices used, such as parallelism or balanced construction? Your answers will guide your use of pause, rate, emphasis, and inflection in your performance.

Let's look at an example. Contrast the syntax in these two sentences: "All the marigolds and pinks in the bungalow gardens were bowed to earth with wetness" and "Drenched were the cold fuchsias." In the first sentence, the order is normal and easily leads to the completed thought.

We get an extended view of numerous flower beds. In the second sentence, however, "drenched" is given strong emphasis by its uncommon position at the beginning of the sentence, and our focus is on the degree of wetness, which is intensified by "cold." "Drenched" is much wetter than "wetness."

Let's try another example. The writer of the following excerpt is describing how he felt when landing his plane after a dangerous and fantastic flight. He is unable to reflect on the experience and cannot translate it through his intellect into an ordered pattern. He isn't quite sure what he thinks. The succession of short sentences that combine statements, questions, and an exclamation gives an almost breathless sense of the writer's emotional exhaustion and his inability to put his experience into words:

> Had I been afraid? I couldn't say. I had witnessed a strange sight. What strange sight? I couldn't say. The sky was blue and the sea was white. I felt I ought to tell someone about it since I was back from so far away! But I had no grip on what I had been through.[1]

Try reading these sentences aloud. What happened to your rate? Where did you pause? Why?

Longer sentences probably need to be broken down into speech phrases when they are read aloud. Long modifying phrases and clauses (italicized in the following examples) present the interpreter with a special challenge. Try to determine the core of the sentence.

Modifiers (adjectives, adverbs, and phrases that qualify some assertion being made) at the beginning of a sentence prepare readers for the main idea and orient them toward it, and you must build up to the key words of the thought. A sentence whose elements occur out of the normal order so that the meaning is held up until near the very end of the sentence is said to be of *periodic* construction. Because the periodic sentence delays the completion of meaning, it creates suspense. When it breaks the usual sentence pattern and alters the normal stresses, it can be especially emphatic:

> *Wandering through clear chambers where the general effect made preferences almost as impossible as if they had been shocks, pausing at open doors where vistas were long and bland,* she would, *even if she had not already known,* have discovered for herself that Poynton was the record of a life.[2]

Modifiers in the middle of a sentence interrupt the main flow of the thought, even while commenting on some elements within it. The meaning should be sustained, and the thread of the principal idea should be carried from one key word to another over the intervening

1. Antoine de Saint-Exupéry, *Wind, Sand and Stars.*
2. Henry James, *The Spoils of Poynton.* (Emphasis added.)

material. At the same time, the contribution of those subordinate elements to the whole should not be ignored:

> The book in question, *which is at once a lasting contribution to English literature and a mere farrago of pretentious mediocrity,* was published about two months ago.[3]

Modifiers at the end of a sentence continue the main idea, expanding or qualifying it, although the skeletal frame of the thought is already complete without them:

> I was at incredible pains in cutting down some of the largest trees for oars and masts, *wherein I was, however, much assisted by his Majesty's shipcarpenters, who helped me in smoothing them after I had done the rough work.*[4]

Negotiating such sentences requires careful analysis and clear-sighted rehearsal. Pitch and vocal quality are two especially useful tools to employ in traversing long sentences. Once your analysis reveals the core of the sentence, plan to use your most comfortable, optimum pitch for those words. Then, *slightly* alter your pitch (or tempo or volume) for the modifying segments of the sentence, taking care not to make the differences so striking that it seems two different speakers are living in one sentence. If one vocal quality is established as the core of the sentences (or of the paragraph), your flexibility can suggest to your audience the ways in which the sentences are modified and attired.

Sentences that demonstrate *parallelism,* or balanced construction, challenge interpreters in another way. Keep the parallel elements equal in *value* (although they may be unequal in number of words or the amount of time it takes to say the words) while at the same time pointing out the connection or contrast. The most obvious form of parallelism is two independent clauses connected by a conjunction; the two clauses explore related ideas and thus are related in grammatical construction. They have, roughly speaking, equal value. Usually you find the connective *and* (or sometimes a comma or a semicolon standing in for a conjunction) as the signpost pointing out the coordination of the two parts.

The parallels may be evenly balanced against each other:

> No man is an island, entire of itself;
> every man is a piece of the continent, a part of the main.[5]

You can easily demonstrate the parallelism by lining up the parts:

| No man | is an island, | entire of itself; |
| every man | is a piece of the continent, | a part of the main. |

---

3. Virginia Woolf, *The Common Reader.* (Emphasis added.)
4. Jonathan Swift, *Gulliver's Travels.* (Emphasis added.)
5. John Donne, *Devotions, XVII.*

The parallelism also may be a series of elaborately wrought *analogies* (comparisons) and *antitheses* (opposites) that are reflected in the form in which the sentence is cast. Look at this example from Shakespeare's *Henry IV, Part I:*

> Harry, I do not only marvel where thou spendest thy time, but also how thou art accompanied; for though the camomile, the more it is trodden on the faster it grows, yet youth, the more it is wasted the sooner it wears.[6]

This sentence can be represented as follows:

Harry, I do	not only	marvel	where thou spendest thy time,
	but also		how thou art accompanied;
		for though	the camomile,
			the more it is trodden on
			the faster it grows,
		yet	youth,
			the more it is wasted
			the sooner it wears.

Remember that at the level of syntax, parallelism indicates parts of a sentence that are *equal in value* although they may be *unequal in length or number of syllables.* The ideas balance each other and contribute to each other.

Skillful writers vary both the length and the structure of sentences and hold their readers' sustained attention by the use of subtle shifts of emphasis and pattern. Although variety and rhythm in style are controlled by the writer, the interpreter also employs shifts in pace and tone to hold the audience's attention.

Speech Phrases

Speech phrases may seem more important to the interpreter than to the writer. The relative lengths of units within the sentence as well as the location of stresses become integral parts of the sound pattern. The division of a sentence into speech phrases is dictated by (1) its punctuation; (2) its grammatical structure; and (3) by the need to make mood and idea clear to an audience.

Punctuation is the first guide, even though it is meant for the eye rather than the ear. A comma, for example, prevents the eye from running ahead and mistaking the sense of the sentence, but in oral reading a comma does not always demand a pause. Again, changing your pitch, your tempo, or your volume can often serve the same purpose less obtrusively than a pause.

Important clues are given by semicolons, colons, parentheses, and dashes. A *semicolon* marks a turn of the thought or a definite separation

---

6. William Shakespeare, *Henry IV, Part I.*

between two aspects of the same thought, and it usually requires a slight pause to make the relationship clear to the listeners. *Parentheses* and *dashes,* in pairs, also mark off distinct speech phrases, which are often interpolated ideas across which the main thought of the sentence should be carried. Again, a shift in pitch or tempo or volume can help. (Long interpolations, of course, need to be further subdivided for convenience and clarity when you are reading aloud.) A *single dash* or a *colon* often marks the pause that occurs just before a summing-up and implies a reference to some previous portion of the sentence. Often, a brief pause helps out.

Punctuation does not, unfortunately, serve as an infallible guide when speech phrases are performed. In fact, punctuation alone is often inadequate for aural comprehension, and you may need to insert slight pauses to emphasize similar or contrasting ideas, as in the following example:

> The same cartoon humor that shows goats munching tin cans depicts ostriches swallowing alarm clocks, monkey wrenches, and cylinder heads.[7]

Although the punctuation is correct in this sentence, a slight pause between "cans" and "depicts" helps balance the parallel ideas when the sentence is read aloud. The following single-sentence paragraph gives an even better example of the problem:

> There is an amusing belief among many country boys, for instance, that an owl has to turn his head to watch you and must watch you if you are near him, so that if you will only walk completely around him he will wring his own neck.[8]

If this sentence were read aloud without a pause or any attention to the author's punctuation, it would quickly lose an audience in a maze of clauses. When it is read aloud with each mark of punctuation reflected in a change of pitch, pace, or volume, the sentence becomes somewhat clearer but still needs work: the punctuation does not take care of the parallel values in "that an owl has to turn his head to watch you and must watch you if you are near him," or of the suspension of thought from "so that" to "he will wring his own neck." Therefore, you need to break down these long units into shorter speech phrases. Be careful, of course, not to perform simply the parts and ignore the whole.

Balancing Sentences

Some sentences may seem much too long to sustain your audience's attention. The following two sentences (one paragraph from the chapter in Lillian Hellman's *Pentimento* in which she describes the life of her cousin Bethe after Bethe's arrival in New Orleans) are good examples:

7. Bergen Evans, *The Natural History of Nonsense.*
8. Ibid.

Bethe for a short time lived in the modest house on Prytania Street, sleeping on a cot in the dining room, rising at five o'clock to carry it to the back porch, to be the first to heat the water, to make the coffee, to roll and bake the German breakfast rolls that nobody liked. Then, to save the carfare, she walked the long distance to the end of Canal Street, where she carried shoe box stacks back and forth all day, for the German merchant who ran a mean store for sailors off the wharves.[9]

Every sentence (especially very long sentences like these) has a *fulcrum*, or balancing point. Indeed, paragraphs, stanzas, poems, stories, all have fulcrums: that point where the action and language pivot or balance. Sentences have their own point of balance, where the weight of the words in the first segment roughly equals the weight of the words in the second segment. Remember, there need not be exactly the same number of words or syllables in both components (as you know, one large adult can balance five or six small children on a seesaw); but the weight of sense in the two parts of a sentence should be equal.

In the first of Hellman's sentences, then, where would you place the fulcrum? A case can be made for one or two other places, but the most even balance for this sentence occurs if the fulcrum is placed after "Prytania Street." Thus, the first half of the sentence concerns Bethe's first weeks in New Orleans: "Bethe for a short time lived in the modest house on Prytania Street." The second half of the sentence describes Bethe's life in the house as a succession of activities: "sleeping on a cot in the dining room, rising at five o'clock to carry it to the back porch, to be the first to heat the water, to make the coffee, to roll and bake the German breakfast rolls that nobody liked."

If you consider these parts equal in substance (although they are clearly unequal in numbers of syllables or in the time needed to speak them), your performance must demonstrate their relationship in a vocal and physical way. We have to see and hear that, to Bethe, living in the house means completing all these tasks—and that's even before leaving for work! If you make each of the tasks in the second part more difficult or onerous because it follows and precedes its neighbors, the audience can have a fuller idea of what Bethe's life was like. You and they will understand why Hellman (who could also write effective short sentences) made this one so long.

Now consider the second sentence. This sentence, which describes a typical workday for the immigrant woman, has a much more familiar structure than the first sentence. Where does the sentence logically and substantively divide? Whereas some might place the fulcrum after "Then" (although as a performance decision it seems eccentric), others would more effectively place the fulcrum after "Canal Street," nicely paralleling the fulcrum of the prior sentence. One part of the sentence

9. Lillian Hellman, *Pentimento*.

then describes how Bethe got to work, and the other part tells what she did when she got there. Again, the fulcrum clarifies the arrangement of Bethe's day and helps us see clearly the progress and purpose of the sentence.

Diction: The Choice of Words

Our discussion of words as an aspect of style to some extent overlaps our earlier discussion of words as an aspect of content, for style and content are obviously inseparable. Nevertheless, the writer's choice of words is a vital part of style and deserves special attention.

We have already made a distinction between the denotations and the connotations of words. Now we should remind ourselves of another important aspect of literary style—the writer's use of *allusions, similes,* and *metaphors.* These three types of figures of speech are all means of comparing one thing to another; thus, they are instruments of conveying connotative meaning. *Allusions* refer to something that persons who share our experiences understand ("I hope tonight won't be another Thanksgiving dinner."). *Similes* describe what things are like (*simile* means "like" in Latin), and you recognize them because they usually have " like" or "as" or "as if" introducing them ("I feel like a million dollars now!"). *Metaphors* (the word comes from the Greek for "transfer") use terms from one "world" and apply them to another "world" ("He has a heart of stone" or "She's a real piece of work!"). You will find these three figures of speech in all types of writing, but they are basic to description. They contribute primarily to harmony by intensifying theme or underscoring attitude. This is certainly the function of the simile in Eudora Welty's "June Recital" (the studio "decorated like the inside of a candy box") that sets the tone for the excerpt (at the end of this chapter).

The length of words is a practical concern for the interpreter who is reading aloud, but from the point of view of style, what is important is whether words are formal, informal, or even colloquial and whether they are unusual or common in everyday speech. In any case, you should evaluate the words in terms of the prevailing tone of the selection. This sentence from Woolf's *The Common Reader,* which appeared earlier in the chapter, is a delightful example of how word choice can shift within a single sentence to underscore attitude:

> The book in question, which is at once a lasting contribution to English literature and a mere farrago of pretentious mediocrity, was published about two months ago.[10]

Woolf begins with the straightforward, factual "The book in question." This is also the tone of the closing phrase. In the middle of the sentence,

10. Virginia Woolf, *The Common Reader.*

however, are the almost classic academic reference to "a lasting contribution to English literature" and the cutting, deliberately elaborate "mere farrago of pretentious mediocrity." It is amusing to know that *farrago* means "hodgepodge" and comes from a Latin word meaning "mixed fodder for cattle." The shift in style reveals the persona's true attitude.

Tone Color: The Sounds of Words

The sounds of the words an author has chosen are especially important for the interpreter, whose task is to translate the written symbols into sound symbols for the audience. Writers carefully establish harmony between what they are describing and the sounds of the words with which they choose to describe it. Of course the words, not the separate sounds, carry the meaning; and it is the connotations of the words that influence the interpreter's pace and vocal quality. There are, for instance, more factors affecting the way one would say *sleep, slap, slip,* and *slop* than merely different vowels. Nevertheless, certain combinations of sounds slow the pace or give a sharpness to separate words, whereas other combinations produce a liquid, fluent effect. A repeated or recurrent vowel sound is called *assonance* (smile–time). Repeated or recurrent consonant sounds are called *consonance* (bold–bled). Words comprise both vowels and consonants, of course, and what that combination provides is called *tone color*. Take a moment now to read the following pair of examples aloud several times, fully realizing the imagery and noting carefully how your voice and your body are responding to them:

> The world was more wintry than he had expected. Hoarfrost lay white over the hard refrozen edges of things—the thatch that roofed the hovels, the ridges of mud, and the stones and rubbish in the lane.[11]

> The weather was airy and light; the stars came nightly into their appointed places; there were rills and cresses and kindling sticks, and fish for the catching in some of the streams.[12]

Now listen to how the sounds of the words in combination enhance and reinforce that imagery—and vice versa. The strong contrast in the syntax sets up a harmonious rhythm in each example. When a skilled interpreter handles these brief descriptions of weather, both the interpreter and the audience can enjoy them.

---

11. Gladys Schmitt, *The Godforgotten*.
12. Ibid., 301.

Rhythm in Prose

Another important guide for the interpreter is the rhythm of a prose selection. All well-written prose has *rhythm*—not the formal, patterned rhythm of poetry but a controlled flow of words that makes relationships clear and causes emphasis to fall on important words.

We have already mentioned *rhythm of content*, which is established by the organization and progression of thoughts and emotions. This type of rhythm depends on the placement of key words and phrases and of the major and minor climaxes, both logical and emotional, throughout the entire selection.

There is also a *rhythm in structure* that becomes evident when prose is read aloud. This prose rhythm is established by the length and grammatical construction of the sentences and speech phrases and by the position of the stresses. As you group words into thought units and speech phrases, separating them with pauses of varying duration, you are creating cadences. A *cadence* is a flow of sound. Words grouped together form a flow of sound. When a pause interrupts this flow, whether it is a terminal pause at the end of a sentence or a brief pause to set off a speech phrase, a cadence occurs, which helps to create prose rhythm.

The rate at which the flows of sound are uttered and the number of syllables within the flows affect the rhythm pattern. A numerical measurement of the cadences in prose is usually not necessary, although it may prove interesting and helpful. The interpreter whose ear is trained is aware of the existence and contribution of cadences.

Stress in prose results from a number of factors: the demands of proper pronunciation, the need for clarity, the development of contrast, or the combining of particular sounds. The sentences from *Pentimento* quoted earlier illustrate this. The use of numerous one-syllable words in sequence, for instance, may produce a sharp staccato rhythm, especially if the content is forceful in meaning and if the cadences established by the length of sentences and speech phrases are short. The brief excerpt from *Wind, Sand and Stars* near the beginning of this chapter provides an interesting illustration of this type of cadence.

Description

Most writing can be roughly classified as *dialogue* (characters talking to characters), *narration* (storyteller relating a tale), or *description* (speaker focusing attention on sensory experience). Most often we find these categories combined: a character in a play who tells the Prince about her past life with a wicked stepmother is *describing* and *narrating* in *dialogue.* Most familiar narratives (in poetry or in prose) contain both dialogue and description. Indeed, the stories we tell in everyday life commonly combine both parts: we are eager to describe what people said or what they were wearing or how they acted. We discuss narration more thoroughly in Chapter 6 and dialogue in Chapters 6, 7, and 8. Here we concentrate on description.

Descriptive writing appeals to the senses. It explores the sensory qualities of people, places, things, and events and wants to achieve vividness and clarity. It engages us physically as well as emotionally because it tells us how something looks, sounds, smells, or tastes. It may describe texture or pressure, heat or cold. It may show movement, energy, or light or may even convey a sense of bulkiness or weightlessness. In its rich appeals to the senses, descriptive writing is important in evoking empathic response.

Description can range in length from a few words to several paragraphs. Whatever the length, when you examine a unit of descriptive writing, you make associations from your own experience. You should follow this response with an objective analysis that enables you to communicate the experience that exists *within* the literature. Suppose, for example, that the subject is a dangerous storm at sea. You might never have known such an experience, but you imagine you would be terrified. The author, however, finds the storm exhilarating. Thus, you need to substitute your imagined fearful response with the memory of another experience that had an exhilarating effect on you in order to convey the emotion in the writing correctly. An interpreter embodies the emotional experience within the framework of the writing, not simply his or her personal response.

Remember the sense of the entire thought unit. Consider, for instance, the thermal implications of the word *hot.* When the word is used in a phrase such as "hot shower after a long hike," one has natural tendency to let the accompanying suggestion of relaxation show in one's muscles, in the slower tempo of the words, and in a more relaxed vocal tone. If, on the other hand, the word is used in the context of "Ouch! That water is hot!" your muscles become tense, the tempo of the words quickens, and the force and tension of your voice increase. In short, always combine the image-bearing word or phrase with the whole unit of thought.

Response to imagery affects your muscle tone and consequently the audience's empathic and emotional response. This is particularly true in the case of appeals to motor responses, but the attendant emotional associations the author has achieved through references to sights, sounds, tastes, and smells also make an empathic contribution.

When you have worked out the various images, consider next what aspects of the imagery contribute most to the total context and impact of the selection. How can you perform particular images in such a way that they are a unifying force, and not a catalog of separate items? In other words, which sense appeals contribute to *unity* and *harmony,* and which add *variety* and *contrast* within that unity? When the images are considered in relation to the whole, some contribute more than others and should be stressed. Those that provide variety within this unity may be played down.

Seeing is believing. Audience members rely on you to see what they are unable to see. Your description is their only means of understanding what the author wants them to see. Until you see it clearly, no audience will be able to see it reflected in your voice and body. The elocutionists used to say, "Impression before expression." *See* what you are describing before telling your audience about it. Unless you do, the audience loses.

You may be tempted to overemphasize some especially vivid images, but remember that too much stress on one descriptive detail may destroy the greater unity of the material. In your performance, use the descriptive elements in the same way you use every other aspect of content and form—unobtrusively. Elements are only *parts* of the whole. The final step in preparation is to put the material back together so that all parts are coordinated.

Types of Prose

Prose writing ranges in type from a chemistry textbook to a stream-of-consciousness novel to a trial transcript to a public oration. The numerous subdivisions frequently overlap, and authors shape and combine types of prose to suit their own purposes. A sociology textbook is likely to include case studies of dysfunctional families that might even feature personal testimony from survivors. A commencement address can tell a vivid story of one scholar's success. A transcript of everyday conversation is likely to be loaded with short scenes and little tales. We look briefly here at some of the broader categories and consider them unmixed with other types. You will note that each type of prose moves (in its own way) toward story. Humans have an insatiable craving for stories; we use them to make sense out of how and why we live. They take as many shapes as there are storytellers.

Factual Prose

The interpreter is not likely to be working extensively with strictly factual prose. Obviously, you would seldom perform material from an encyclopedia. Nevertheless, you may encounter a few sentences or paragraphs in an essay that are technically factual and out of which the personal reflections of the author develop.

Factual prose, in the strictest definition of the term, is writing in which the author gives verifiable information. It states that something is so.

The writer's personal comments are kept to a minimum. Unadulterated examples of this type of writing are probably found only in books on science and mathematics, where the reader is told, for instance, that "in an isosceles triangle the angles opposite the equal sides are themselves equal," or in an encyclopedia, which states on good authority that John Milton was born in England in 1608 and died in 1674. Objective journalistic reporting also may be considered factual when it limits itself to the simple formula of "who, where, when, what," and possibly "how" and "why." Factual prose informs, defines, and explains.

The interpreter is more likely to deal with prose in which the author is concerned with the implication or interpretation of the facts. Sometimes the facts provide a touch of humor or satire; in other cases, the implied comment of the author is the desired end. The interpreter discovers how the author arranges and shapes the information and ensures that this same purpose is communicated to the audience.

Personal Essays

Personal essays offer a wide variety of material to interest an audience. Their content includes broad humor, philosophy, politics, and religion. The writer's personality and values are reflected in the facts and concrete objects that have been selected. Such associations and connotations lead readers and listeners beyond the denotations of words and phrases.

For example, Jacques Barzun describes a certain mathematics teacher by saying, "He would put the chalk to his lips, make a noise like a straining gear box, and write out the correct result." We have no idea what the man looks like, and we do not need to. The depiction of his characteristic gesture of putting chalk to his lips calls forth in us a mental picture of bemused, pedantic concentration. The "noise like a straining gear box" suggests that he is more of a machine than a man, and when the gears start to move, out comes the answer!

Often, especially in humorous essays, an author chooses to write in the first person, whether the selection is autobiographical or not. Certainly we are not expected to believe that James Thurber, for instance, actually experienced all the incidents he recorded in the first person! We are really not so concerned about the actual physical identity of the speaker as we are with the author's wit and sense of the ridiculous that has ordered the details of the incidents for our enjoyment. We are often concerned with the age, sex, or social position of the speaker; but we care about these details as they relate to the speaker's situation and to the comments the author makes by implication or direct statement.

Sometimes essayists choose topics that, on first glance, may seem far from the interests of a general audience. In "The Seacoast of Despair" (at the end of this chapter), Joan Didion visits Newport, Rhode Island, to view the "vast, stone, *fin de siècle* cottages in which certain rich Americans once summered." For such a visit to mean something other than a travelogue without slides, her interest—or what she discovers—has to appeal more broadly. Indeed, the best personal essays make clear that what may superficially seem a peculiar concern in fact engages concerns we all share. (Remember our discussion of *universality* in Chapter 1.) Didion makes precisely this point in the final paragraph (a common place to find such revelations in personal essays). Rather than an elegant summer colony, she sees Newport as "a fantastically elaborate stage setting for an American morality play in which money and happiness are presented as antithetical." Didion leaves us with a haunting image of death and loss among the stones of Newport.

Writers use references for their universal appeal. You need never have visited Newport—or even have known that it exists—to understand that money and happiness don't always go together. You need not care about the lifestyles of America's rich and famous in 1900 to be intrigued by the fact that the country's wealthiest families created monuments "to unhappiness, to restrictiveness, to entrapment in the mechanics of living." Didion chose these images and examples in part because of the topic and in part because of who she is. When you understand what all of the words mean *and* suggest, in themselves and in their contexts, you begin to understand the author and why the message is shaped so characteristically. Convey that discovery to your audience.

Journals, Diaries, and Letters

Journals and diaries often make excellent selections for performance, because they provide intimate glimpses into special moments in the lives of interesting people, or we see famous people engaged in being "people" rather than in what makes them "famous." Ostensibly, most diaries are written for the writer's private pleasure. They are likely to be less formal than essays, which are intended for public consumption. The organization of diaries is often dictated by highly subjective associations. A careful examination of the elements of style helps you learn about the writer's personality and reveals attitudes and degrees of emotional involvement. A diary or a journal remains a very personal statement and in the past often was the only tool for an *individual* to record his or her impressions of the world. Find out as much as possible about the writer's life and times. See how the writing of the diary arose from the environment the author inhabited, the way the author lived, and how the world impinged on the author's goals. Why did *this* author need a diary or journal?

For example, Jane Gould Tortillot's diary (from *Women's Diaries of the Westward Journey,* excerpted at the end of this chapter) typifies one reason to write: the need to record impressions and relate events, to find some sense in the jumble of experience, to aid memory when recollecting in tranquillity. In that respect, diaries and journals are kin to photo albums and video recordings—providing ways to see, and see again, where we were and where we are. For the interpreter, however, there is an element of danger in this idea. You must have sufficient projection, both psychological and vocal, to hold your audience's attention and interest. One of the ways to achieve this delicate balance between private thoughts and public expression of them in performance is to allow the writer to appear to be "thinking aloud" as he or she orders his or her thoughts and enters them in the diary. This procedure helps you remain actively engaged in organizing and expressing the entire entry.

Over the past decade, technology has encouraged a hybrid form of diary/journal/personal narrative on the Internet. Many people have developed personal homepages where they record significant moments in their lives and post photos of loved ones. These decidedly public records (anyone who knows the website's address can access them) can become even more elaborate, featuring audio and video images and many hypertext links, in addition to the straight text that records the individual's thoughts and (often) invites viewers to respond. The most elaborate of these recorders—called bloggers (derived from the contraction of *Web* and *logging*)—often add new material several times a day and can develop loyal followers. The topics they record, the language they use, the way they format their entries, the extent and sophistication of their essential hypertext links, the interpolation of video with audio and with text: all these evoke the character of individual bloggers. In part, bloggers have motives in common with other tellers of personal narrative (see below), but they have also combined the very traditional habit of "commonplace books" (in which individuals in the eighteenth and nineteenth centuries recorded important events, thoughts, poetry, news clippings, and the like) with the interests of a tech-savvy audience that finds the Web the most convenient means to satisfy traditional curiosity about other humans. As a performance possibility for a solo interpreter, blogs would prove very challenging, in part because of the complexity of the components and in part because of the editing they would require. But precisely those problems could intrigue a group performance. (We discuss group performances in Chapter 11.) For now, blogging serves as contemporary evidence that the need to record and share our lives has never diminished.

Much of the appeal of letters is undoubtedly the same as that of diaries and journals. Letters, however, present an added problem for the interpreter. First, you need to distinguish whether they are public or private letters. Public letters (an epistle by Paul, for example) may be handled very much as you would approach an oration or a public address. They are usually didactic, having been designed to persuade a large group of listeners or readers to a course of action or to the acceptance of an idea. The writer selects details with strong universal appeal and refers to matters with which the intended audience is easily familiar. The writer of a public letter is speaking to a specific audience. Imagine that this particular audience and your own audience are identical. This approach helps achieve directness. Address your listeners in the persona of the writer or, more probably, in the persona of someone selected to present the letter to the intended audience.

Private letters involve a more complex relationship between writer and recipient, and you need to find out as much as possible about both parties. The letter you are reading may be the reply to a letter received earlier by the writer; consequently, a chain of references may have to be investigated. The method of organization and the style of writing reflect the purpose of the letter as well as the relationship between the writer and the person to whom the letter is addressed. (See the letter Emily Dickinson sent her brother, at the end of this chapter.)

Sometimes you might be more interested in the reaction of the recipient than you are in the writer. In this case, read the letter as if you are the one to whom it is addressed. To succeed in this approach, you must cope with a twofold problem: how to use the writer's style effectively and, at the same time, how to suggest the reaction of another person. Obviously, this is easier when the relationship between the two people is clearly drawn or is so well known that the response is predictable. Letters are often used in this way within a play or narrative where the characters have been well established. The letter becomes virtually a part of the plot and motivation.

Oral Histories

Increasingly, interpreters have found wonderful material for performance in collections of oral histories, testimony, depositions, and transcripts. In preparing such material, an editor's skill is at least as important as the speaker's. Because the words began as speech, they carry with them an immediacy and a conviction that can be startling. In the past four decades, perhaps no one more than Studs Terkel has developed the art of oral history. In such works as *Hard Times*, *Division Street*, *Working*, and *The Good War*, Terkel (with his tape recorder) speaks with people from every level of society and in every possible occupation. He asks them to tell him what they have learned about their own lives, a special period, or an event. Then, with the skill of an artist, he splices together their words to make powerfully funny or poignant testimony to the human condition. We see people whom we may easily know expressing something both unique and timeless. See "Terry Pickens" from *Working* at the end of this chapter.

Oral history projects frequently flourish where archives are housed and often can be the source of impressive and moving material for performance. At the end of this chapter, for example, are selections in which two veterans of the Revolutionary War tell what they discovered about themselves from fighting. If you compare their testimony to the oral history in Al Santoli's *Everything We Had* (at the end of this chapter) or to Anthony Swofford's recollections in *Jarhead* (at the end of Chapter 4), you'll discover how little war's impact has changed. Sometimes court records provide exciting exchanges between litigants in important cases. Even the *Congressional Record* offers, on occasion, impressive speeches and exchanges between debating members of Congress. Also, don't neglect the various collections of memorabilia—letters, notes, journal entries, and reminiscences—that are assembled to mark historic events or to portray a locale or historic period. With careful editing, such prose works can give vivid and powerful glimpses of the personalities who shaped our lives, either in great office or in unrecognized occupations. Such material records the immediate voices of people struggling to make themselves understood. These records are too rich a source for interpreters to overlook.

Family Storytelling: The Tales of Everyday Life

Oral histories and reflections and testimonies are the most public forms of the storytelling that fills our everyday lives. This impulse to spin a tale is grounded in our earliest memories: as children we are taught through commonplace tales much more frequently than we are read to or allowed to watch videos. We naturally share narratives at home before we encounter the world, and our earliest play constitutes telling stories. As we get older, our hunger for stories is never satisfied. We share tales around the water cooler each morning at work, in the afternoon over coffee or sewing, in the evening when we recount the day's events.

It's no secret *why* personal narratives so engage us. They are our unique way of making sense of what happens to us. They reward us for the telling in all the ways in which performing rewards us: attention, communication, communion, connection. Personal narratives are themselves performances. Like other performances, they live in context with all the social pressures that engage us. They merit all the scrutiny demanded by complex issues of representation, identity, and sociopolitical discourse. Indeed, interest in the performance of personal narratives— and the ethical problems such performance invokes—has mushroomed in recent years, and the study is not limited to published stories.

Briefly, context is crucial. Is the narrative your own story, or is it the recorded words of someone else? In performance, of course, this distinction blurs; often it's difficult to tell, and some audiences don't seem to care. Here questions of locus become extremely pertinent. If you perform your own narrative, the audience is implicit. If you perform the narrative of another, what is the relationship between the speaker and the audience to whom the other spoke? Obviously, we tell to a close friend some kinds of things that we wouldn't disclose to a casual acquaintance.

Kristin Langellier focuses our attention to the ways "immediacy" and "proximity" characterize two modes of telling personal narratives; she terms them "narrative mode" and "conversational mode." Narratives in the *narrative mode* are clearly more open to strangers and therefore likely to be more guarded in what is disclosed; they are crafted or at least organized in a linear fashion to build to a logical and emotional climax. They may omit or embellish events for the sake of a "better" story. In contrast, narratives in the *conversational mode* are told usually in small groups of intimates as parts of conversation or the sharing of experiences. They are interruptable, circular, or spiral in construction; they are open-ended (there may not be a logical climax, although emotional climaxes do occur); they feature descriptive detail and circumstances; and they most often seek corroboration from audience members. Narratives—even very informal ones—are often more contrived than conversations, which encourage all the participants to contribute, to interact, to build the story together.[13]

The power of many of these kinds of performances has been radically demonstrated by Anna Deavere Smith, an actress who records a wide range of respondents caught up in fierce social trauma (for example, the simmering racial tensions in Crown Heights, New York, depicted in *Fires in the Mirror*) and then, herself, carefully performs all these subjects. Taken together, the characters telling stories respond (sometimes unconsciously, sometimes quite calculatedly) to each other. Moreover, the gradually revealed context in which they comment itself becomes compelling and dramatic. (See the selection included at the end of Chapter 7.) Personal narratives mark another potent example of our continuing hunger for stories.

Folktales

We have seen some of the ways in which storytelling pervades our families and our contemporary society, but the art pervades all levels of all societies. Traditional oral cultures depended on storytelling as much as does the postmodern world. Today there are fewer oral cultures than existed several hundred years ago, but the craving for stories remains undiminished. The skills that emerged around fires still seduce us

13. Kristin M. Langellier, "Personal Narratives: Perspectives on Theory and Research," *Text and Performance Quarterly* 9 (July, 1989): 243–76. See the bibliography at the end of this chapter for several useful sources on the topic.

today. Centuries-old folktales and their narrators—uniquely gifted men and women who tap the magic and mystery of ancient tales—represent the source of oral interpretation. Before an audience of hundreds, or with just a few lucky people around a fire, storytellers charm and enchant with tales whose meaning is larger (and often more touching) than can be easily explained.

Folktales, like folk songs, appeal to the ear and to human interest in organizing experience and learning from encounters with the world. Storytellers mine the vast resources of folktales, which live in all cultures and have thrived in all times. An authoritative collection of these tales is Antti Aarne and Stith Thompson's *The Types of the Folktale*, which catalogs the vast range of international folktales that have surmounted the barriers of language, geography, and culture. Of course, merely consulting this monument of research doesn't make one a storyteller. Often several versions of a particular story feature markedly different motifs. These differences are the verbal fingerprints of particular storytellers, who, at the moment of telling, shaped the events and dialogue and characters specifically to engage the attentive audience. For example, a storyteller who was adept with dialects may have included several speaking characters to demonstrate that facility; a storyteller who sang well or made realistic birdcalls may have incorporated those skills into a story.

Storytellers aren't verbal in the way writers of stories are verbal. Of course, both use words as the medium to convey the story, but the storyteller—working in the immediacy of performance—can't revise, edit, or erase. Storytellers constantly move the tale forward while engaging an audience eagerly listening at their feet. The story the audience sees and hears occurs not so much as carefully marshaled words (although, of course, tellers plan carefully the kinds of vivid language and compelling dialogue they intend to use). Rather, the audience experiences a series of pictures or images that the storyteller explores, or the audience confronts a succession of incidents that build to the point the teller wants to illustrate or celebrate. Each telling of the same tale by the same teller results in a new story that naturally resembles its predecessors in most ways yet differs significantly in ways chosen by the teller to tailor the story for each unique performance.

If you find this method of composition daunting, consider the favorite stories you tell. If, for example, at your ninth birthday party your Uncle Waldo hired a clown who threw cream pies at all the adults, it is likely that you've told this story many times. You don't think about organization or which words to use. Rather, your familiarity with the events and the characters (your friends, your parents, Uncle Waldo, and Aunt Prudence) makes them appear full-blooded in your consciousness. You proceed through the events so often that sometimes you omit the little incidents that detract from the big event (your cousin Marvin's water pistol, say, or your father's multicolored shorts) to focus on the clown or on the coconut cream pies your mother made for the grownups. You've told this tale often enough to know when to pause, when to move the narrative line, where to direct your audience's gaze, and where to expand the narrative. You know the story is surefire, and you enjoy telling it. Each time you tell it, you feel more confident. You don't need to write it down; you've lived it!

Storytellers have been recorded—both electronically on audio- and videotape and literarily in printed recensions or retellings—and students can consult these resources. Recordings, however, are not, finally, the experiences, any more than saying the words someone else said at another place and in another time will create again the magic for your audience. Nevertheless, you can begin to test your own abilities as a teller of tales by consulting recordings. In addition, your own experiences can be further developed by attending storytelling festivals and listening carefully to how others tell the tales that have been told for centuries. In this manner storytellers have always developed. First, awed by the wonder of the teller, they undertake to study (and, sometimes, convincingly imitate) storytellers who strike their interest. Then they make their own stories. Finally, they develop their own personal storytelling style. The opportunities are endless. In storytelling we can find the earliest, easiest, most accessible entry to understanding another culture's rich wisdom and profiting from its special sources of grace and wonder.

Short Stories and Novels

This chapter has focused on nondramatic prose, but the components of prose are equally influential when used in the forms of prose you probably find most familiar: short stories, novellas (*long* short stories), and novels. Every stylistic component we have discussed—the use and variation of paragraphs, the variety of sentence structures, the revelatory word choice, the vast array of possible uses for speech phrases, the influences of tone color and rhythm, and the rewards of vivid description—operates in short stories and novels in the same ways we have discussed here. But short stories and novels differ from the prose we have discussed in the presence of a narrator. The interpreter embodies and evokes the persona in all prose selections; in short stories and novels, that persona is a narrator. The next chapter explores the narrator's shaping role in short stories and novels.

Selections for Analysis and Oral Interpretation

In addition to the following excerpts, you will find some interesting descriptive passages in the selections in earlier chapters and within the narratives in Chapter 6.

The style here is as packed as the recital room. Pay particular attention to the shift in imagery as you reach the last paragraph.

 FROM **June Recital**

EUDORA WELTY

The night of the recital was always clear and hot; everyone came. The prospective audience turned out in full oppression.

In the studio decorated like the inside of a candy box, with "material" scalloping the mantel shelf and doilies placed under every movable object, now thus made immovable, with streamers of white ribbons and nosegays of pink and white Maman Cochet roses and the last MacLain sweetpeas dividing and re-dividing the room, it was as hot as fire. No matter that this was the first night of June; no electric fans were to whir around while music played. The metronome, ceremoniously closed, stood on the piano like a vase. There was no piece of music anywhere in sight.

When the first unreasoning hush—there was the usual series—fell over the audience, the room seemed to shake with the agitation of palmetto and feather fans alone, plus the occasional involuntary tick of the metronome within its doors. There was the mixture together of agitation and decoration which could make every little forthcoming child turn pale with a kind of ultimate dizziness. Whoever might look up at the ceiling for surcease would be floundered within a paper design stemming out of the chandelier, as complicated and as unavailing as a cut-out paper snowflake.

Now Miss Eckhart came into the room all changed, with her dark hair pulled low on her brow, and gestured for silence. She was wearing her recital dress which made her look larger and closer-to than she looked at any other times. It was an old dress: Miss Eckhart disregarded her own rules. People would forget that dress between times and then she would come out in it again, the untidy folds not quite spotlessly clean, gathered about her bosom and falling heavy as a coat to the sides; it was tawny crepe-back satin. There was a bodice of browning lace. It was as rich and hot and deep-looking as a furskin. The unexpected creamy flesh on her upper arms gave her a look of emerging from it.

Miss Eckhart, achieving silence, stood in the shadowy spot directly under the chandelier. Her feet, white-shod, shod by Mr. Sissum for good, rested in the chalk circle previously marked on the floor and now, she believed, perfectly erased. One hand, with its countable little muscles so hard and ready, its stained, blue nails, went to the other hand and they folded quite still, holding nothing, until they lost their force by lying on her breast and made a funny little house with peaks and gables. Standing near the piano but not near enough to help, she presided but not with her whole heart on guard against disaster; while disaster was what remained on the minds of the little girls. Starting with the youngest, she called them out.

So they played, and except Virgie, all played their worst. They shocked themselves. Parnell Moody burst into tears on schedule. But Miss Eckhart never seemed to notice or to care. How forgetful she seemed at exactly the moments she should have been agonized! You expected the whip, almost, for forgetting to repeat before the second ending, or for failing to count ten before you came around the curtain at all; and instead you received a strange smile. It was as though Miss Eckhart, at the last, was grateful to you for *anything*.

- Did you take the time to allow your narrator to experience each image without being rushed?

- How hot was the room?

Consider this much cooler, very different, piano recital. Amy Tan's The Joy Luck Club *collects the stories of four mothers and four daughters as they learn from each other's experiences. In this segment Jing-Mei Woo discovers that her pleasures in deceiving her deaf piano teacher Old Chong and in thwarting her mother's plans for her to be a prodigy carry serious consequences. She recalls these events many years later, but has she forgotten how she felt?*

 FROM **The Joy Luck Club**

AMY TAN

A few weeks later, Old Chong and my mother conspired to have me play in a talent show which would be held in the church hall. By then, my parents had saved up enough to buy me a secondhand piano, a black Wurlitzer spinet with a scarred bench. It was the showpiece of our living room.

For the talent show, I was to play a piece called "Pleading Child" from Schumann's *Scenes from Childhood*. It was a simple, moody piece that sounded more difficult than it was. I was supposed to memorize the whole thing, playing the repeat parts twice to make the piece sound longer. But I dawdled over it, playing a few bars and then cheating, looking up to see what notes followed. I never really listened to what I was playing. I daydreamed about being somewhere else, about being someone else.

The part I liked to practice best was the fancy curtsy: right foot out, touch the rose on the carpet with a pointed foot, sweep to the side, left leg bends, look up and smile.

My parents invited all the couples from the Joy Luck Club to witness my debut. Auntie Lindo and Uncle Tin were there. Waverly and her two older brothers had also come. The first two rows were filled with children both younger and older than I was. The littlest ones got to go first. They recited simple nursery rhymes, squawked out tunes on miniature violins, twirled Hula Hoops, pranced in pink ballet tutus, and when they bowed or curtsied, the audience would sigh in unison, "Awww," and then clap enthusiastically.

When my turn came, I was very confident. I remember my childish excitement. It was as if I knew, without a doubt, that the prodigy side of me really did exist. I had no fear whatsoever, no nervousness. I remember thinking to myself, This is it! This is it! I looked out over the audience, at my mother's blank face, my father's yawn, Auntie Lindo's stiff-lipped smile, Waverly's sulky expression. I had on a white dress layered with sheets of lace, and a pink bow in my Peter Pan haircut. As I sat down I envisioned people jumping to their feet and Ed Sullivan rushing up to introduce me to everyone on TV.

And I started to play. It was so beautiful. I was so caught up in how lovely I looked that at first I didn't worry how I would sound. So it was a surprise to me when I hit the first wrong note and I realized something didn't sound quite right. And then I hit another and another followed that. A chill started at the top of my head and began to trickle down. Yet I couldn't stop playing, as though my hands were bewitched. I kept thinking my fingers would adjust themselves back, like a train switching to the right track. I played this strange jumble through two repeats, the sour notes staying with me all the way to the end.

When I stood up, I discovered my legs were shaking. Maybe I had just been nervous and the audience, like Old Chong, had seen me go through the right motions and had not heard anything wrong at all. I swept my right foot out, went down on my knee, looked up and smiled. The room was quiet, except for Old Chong, who was beaming and shouting, "Bravo! Bravo! Well done!" But then I saw my mother's face, her stricken face. The audience clapped weakly, and as I walked back to my chair, with my whole face quivering as I tried not to cry, I heard a little boy whisper loudly to his mother, "That was awful," and the mother whispered back, "Well, she certainly tried."

And now I realized how many people were in the audience, the whole world it seemed. I was aware of eyes burning into my back. I felt the shame of my mother and father as they sat stiffly throughout the rest of the show.

We could have escaped during intermission. Pride and some strange sense of honor must have anchored my parents to their chairs. And so we watched it all: the eighteen-year-old boy with a fake mustache who did a magic show and juggled flaming hoops while riding a unicycle. The breasted girl with white makeup who sang from *Madama Butterfly* and got honorable mention. And the eleven-year-old boy who won first prize playing a tricky violin song that sounded like a busy bee.

After the show, the Hsus, the Jongs, and the St. Clairs from the Joy Luck Club came up to my mother and father.

"Lots of talented kids," Auntie Lindo said vaguely, smiling broadly.

"That was somethin' else," said my father, and I wondered if he was referring to me in a humorous way, or whether he even remembered what I had done.

Waverly looked at me and shrugged her shoulders. "You aren't a genius like me," she said matter-of-factly. And if I hadn't felt so bad, I would have pulled her braids and punched her stomach.

But my mother's expression was what devastated me: a quiet, blank look that said she had lost everything. I felt the same way, and it seemed as if everybody were now coming up, like gawkers at the scene of an accident, to see what parts were actually missing. When we got on the bus to go home, my father was humming the busy-bee tune and my mother was silent. I kept thinking she wanted to wait until we got home before shouting at me. But when my father unlocked the door to our apartment, my mother walked in and then went to the back, into the bedroom. No accusations. No blame. And in a way, I felt disappointed. I had been waiting for her to start shouting, so I could shout back and cry and blame her for all my misery.

I assumed my talent-show fiasco meant I never had to play the piano again. But two days later, after school, my mother came out of the kitchen and saw me watching TV.

"Four clock," she reminded me as if it were any other day. I was stunned, as though she were asking me to go through the talent-show torture again. I wedged myself more tightly in front of the TV.

"Turn off TV," she called from the kitchen five minutes later.

I didn't budge. And then I decided. I didn't have to do what my mother said anymore. I wasn't her slave. This wasn't China. I had listened to her before and look what happened. She was the stupid one.

She came out from the kitchen and stood in the arched entryway of the living room. "Four clock," she said once again, louder.

"I'm not going to play anymore," I said nonchalantly. "Why should I? I'm not a genius."

She walked over and stood in front of the TV. I saw her chest was heaving up and down in an angry way.

"No!" I said, and I now felt stronger, as if my true self had finally emerged. So this was what had been inside me all along.

"No! I won't!" I screamed.

She yanked me by the arm, pulled me off the floor, snapped off the TV. She was frighteningly strong, half pulling, half carrying me toward the piano as I kicked the throw rugs under my feet. She lifted me up and onto the hard bench. I was sobbing by now, looking at her bitterly. Her chest was heaving even more and her mouth was open, smiling crazily as if she were pleased I was crying.

"You want me to be someone that I'm not!" I sobbed. "I'll never be the kind of daughter you want me to be!"

"Only two kinds of daughters," she shouted in Chinese. "Those who are obedient and those who follow their own mind! Only one kind of daughter can live in this house. Obedient daughter!"

"Then I wish I wasn't your daughter. I wish you weren't my mother," I shouted. As I said these things I got scared. It felt like worms and toads and slimy things crawling out of my chest, but it also felt good, as if this awful side of me had surfaced, at last.

"Too late change this," said my mother shrilly.

And I could sense her anger rising to its breaking point. I wanted to see it spill over. And that's when I remembered the babies she had lost in China, the ones we never talked about. "Then I wish I'd never been born!" I shouted. "I wish I were dead! Like them!"

It was as if I had said the magic words. Alakazam!—and her face went blank, her mouth closed, her arms went slack, and she backed out of the room, stunned, as if she were blowing away like a small brown leaf, thin, brittle, lifeless.

- ◆ How did your voice and body create the embarrassment the persona recalls?

- ◆ What did you do to create the increasing tensions in the last fifteen paragraphs? Why are increases in volume not enough?

Moses Hall and Garret Watts were foot soldiers in the Revolutionary War. In the following selections they recount their wartime experiences for a federal pension board many years after the events had occurred. Note carefully how vivid these recollections are; be sure to make your audience feel their impact.

FROM The Revolution Remembered

JOHN C. DANN, EDITOR

Moses Hall

Moses Hall served in a troop that had just defeated a detachment of British soldiers and mercenaries (Tories).

The evening after our battle with the Tories, we having a considerable number of prisoners, I recollect a scene which made a lasting impression upon my mind. I was invited by some of my comrades to go and see some of the prisoners. We went to where six were standing together. Some discussion taking place, I heard some of our men cry out, "Remember Buford," and the prisoners were immediately hewed to pieces with broadswords. At first I bore the scene without any emotion, but upon a moment's reflection, I felt such horror as I never did before nor have since, and, returning to my quarters and throwing myself upon my blanket, I contemplated the cruelties of war until overcome and unmanned by a distressing gloom from which I was not relieved until commencing our march next morning before day by moonlight. I came to Tarleton's camp, which he had just abandoned leaving lively rail fires. Being on the left of the road as we marched along, I discovered lying upon the ground something with appearance of a man. Upon approaching him, he proved to be a youth about sixteen who, having come out to view the British through curiosity, for fear he might give information to our troops, they had run him through with a bayonet and left him for dead. Though able to speak, he was mortally wounded. The sight of this unoffending boy, butchered rather than be encumbered in the [illegible] on the march, I assume, relieved me of my distressful feelings for the slaughter of the Tories, and I desired nothing so much as the opportunity of participating in their destruction.

- ◆ What difficulties did your Hall undergo in retelling his story? Why? How did your audience notice this in your performance?

Garret Watts

Garret Watts served in the Continental army under Generals de Kalb and Dickson; he recalls a vivid moment from a battle with British forces under Lord Cornwallis.

The two armies came near each other at Sutton's about twelve or one o'clock in the night (this was in the year 1780). The pickets fired several rounds before day. I well remember everything that occurred the next morning: I remember that I was among the nearest to the enemy; that a man named John Summers was my file leader; that we had orders to wait for the word to commence firing; that the militia were in front and in a feeble condition at that time. They were fatigued. The weather was warm excessively. They had been fed a short time previously on molasses entirely. I can state on oath that I believe my gun was the first gun fired, notwithstanding the orders, for we were close to the enemy, who appeared to maneuver in contempt of us, and I fired without thinking except that I might prevent the man opposite from killing me. The discharge and loud roar soon became general from one end of the lines to the other. Amongst other things, I confess I was amongst the first that fled. The cause of that I cannot tell, except that everyone I saw was about to do the same. It was instantaneous. There was no effort to rally, no encouragement to fight. Officers and men joined in the flight. I threw away my gun, and, reflecting I might be punished for being found without arms, I picked up a drum, which gave forth such sounds when touched by the twigs I cast it away. When we had gone, we heard the roar of guns still, but we knew not why. Had we known, we might have returned. It was that portion of the army commanded by de Kalb fighting still. De Kalb was killed. General Dickson was wounded in the neck and a great many killed and wounded even on the first firing. After this defeat, many of the dispersed troops proceeded to Hillsboro in North Carolina. I obtained a furlough from General Dickson and had permission to return home a short time. This last tour was for the space of three months and truly laborious.

- How did your body behave when Watts admitted he was a deserter?

Clearly the ravages of war and the desolation of combatants haven't changed. Listen to James Bombard's recollection of his friend Hunter Shotwell, a personal narrative rich with performance possibilities. Be careful to let us see the inner turmoil that still rages in his thoughts, nicely contrasting to the calm that concludes the excerpt. You might want to imagine the conversation James Bombard would have with Anthony Swofford, whose Jarhead *appears at the end of Chapter 4.*

 FROM **Everything We Had**

AL SANTOLI, EDITOR

James Bombard

Rifle Platoon Leader, 101st Airborne Division, Phan Rang, December 1967– February 1968

I can remember sitting at McCord Air Base before I went to Vietnam with a friend of mine, Hunter Shotwell, he and his wife. He was a West Pointer and had been to Vietnam before the build-up as an adviser. He was from Massachusetts. He had a beautiful wife and a little child, it was beautiful. I said to him, "Hunter, why are you going back? You're going to get out of the Army." He wanted to be a lawyer. He wanted to set his life in motion. And he said, "I'm going back because I am a soldier." I said, "But you're leaving the military." He said, "But I believe in the nation and I believe that this is my duty. I went to West Point. I am leaving, but I must shoulder the responsibility of leadership." Hunter was a patrician and from a good family. Hunter and I and his wife proceeded to have a few beers and we were pretty mellow when we left together that day. We had served together in the 82nd, we were very close. He had been a hockey player and I was a hockey player, and we had a lot to talk about. He represented everything that was good about the country, the future of the country—it was bright, he was bright, he was handsome. He was everything that our generation stood for.

Right after the Tet offensive I found out that Hunter Shotwell had been killed. And I couldn't help but feel that had been such a loss, such a waste. I had seen other people killed, I had experienced the loss of many friends closer than Hunter was to me, guys I was

in the field with. . . . But somehow his death to me was the most significant, the most moving. Somehow I saw that he had served, he had shouldered his responsibility and yet he had done it again. The nation shouldn't have asked him to do it again. He represented to me what was good and right in the nation. And he was destroyed. I thought of his little child and his wife, what that did to them. And with that death and many like his, with each death a little bit of the fiber of what was good in this country was being destroyed. That's what bothered me.

I didn't see Hunter Shotwell get killed, but I felt like I had. There were many people close to us in the field who were killed. Doc Brown. I remember Doc Brown was a medic who always read philosophy and never took a bath and would always tell everybody to clean up and wash for infection: "Do as I say, not as I do." He would read Saint Thomas and he was a confirmed atheist and he would philosophize. But in the field he was tremendously skilled as a medic and also very daring, and he was killed the day I was wounded. He was moving to a man and he was wounded and killed. Here was a man who was an intellectual, a philosopher, a thinker, and he was there. Probably not agreeing with what was happening. But somehow, again, the good was being destroyed.

I think we lost a lot more in Vietnam than the troops we lost. We really didn't lose too many battles. When we met the enemy we usually won. What did we win? We lost more than we won, especially the aftermath of the war. Having served in Vietnam, having served in the infantry, having been wounded, feeling the bullet rip into your flesh, the shrapnel tear the flesh from your bones and the blood run down your leg, and feeling like you're gonna piss in your pants and it's the blood running down your leg. To put your hand on your chest and to come away with your hand red with your own blood, and to feel it running out of your eyes and out of your mouth, and seeing it spurt out of your guts, realizing you were dying . . .

I had been hit the second time by a direct hit from a mortar. I was ripped open from the top of my head to the tip of my toes. I had forty-five holes in me and I was bleeding everywhere. I can remember saying to myself, "My God, I'm dying." And at that split second, I was calm. Completely, completely at peace with myself.

- ◆ How did you demonstrate Bombard's *thinking* while speaking?
- ◆ Where did you place the fulcrum in this testimony? How did your audience know?

One critic called this "the finest essay written in the second half of the twentieth century." You don't have to share that esteem to recognize Didion's characteristic attention to precise detail or to recognize that something about all the excess of Newport attracts her at least as much as it troubles her.

FROM The Seacoast of Despair

JOAN DIDION

I went to Newport not long ago, to see the great stone *fin-de-siècle* "cottages" in which certain rich Americans once summered. The places loom still along Bellevue Avenue and Cliff Walk, one after another, silk curtains frayed but gargoyles intact, monuments to something beyond themselves; houses built, clearly, to some transcendental point. No one had made clear to me exactly what that point was. I had been promised that the great summer houses were museums and warned that they were monstrosities, had been assured that the way of life they suggested was graceful beyond belief and that it was gross beyond description, that the very rich were different from you and me and yes, they had lower taxes, and if "The Breakers" was perhaps not entirely tasteful, still, *où sont les croquet wickets d'antan.* I had read Edith Wharton and I had read Henry James, who thought that the houses should stand there always, reminders "of the peculiarly awkward vengeances of affronted proportion and discretion."

But all that turns out to be beside the point, all talk of taxes and taste and affronted proportion. If, for example, one pursues the course, as Mrs. Richard Gambrill did in 1900, of engaging the architect who did the New York Public Library, approving plans for an eighteenth-century French château on a Rhode Island beach, ordering the garden copied after one Henry VIII gave to Anne Boleyn, and naming the result "Vernon Court," one moves somehow beyond the charge of breached "discretion." Something else is at work here. No aesthetic judgment could conceivably apply to the Newport of Bellevue Avenue, to those vast follies behind their handwrought gates; they are products of the metastasis of capital, the Industrial Revolution carried to its logical extreme, and what they suggest is how recent are the notions that life should be "comfortable," that those who live it should be "happy."

"Happiness" is, after all, a consumption ethic, and Newport is the monument of a society in which production was seen as the moral point, the reward if not exactly the end, of the economic process. The place is devoid of the pleasure principle. To have had the money to build "The Breakers" or "Marble House" or "Ochre Court" and to choose to build at Newport is in itself a denial of possibilities; the island is physically ugly, mean without the saving grace of extreme severity, a landscape less to be enjoyed than dominated. The prevalence of topiary gardening in Newport suggests the spirit of the place. And it was not as if there were no other options for these people: William Randolph Hearst built not at Newport but out on the edge of the Pacific. San Simeon, whatever its peculiarities, is in fact *la cuesta encantada,* swimming in golden light, sybaritic air, a deeply romantic place. But in Newport the air proclaims only the sources of money. Even as the sun dapples the great lawns and the fountains plash all around, there is something in the air that has nothing to do with pleasure and nothing to do with graceful tradition, a sense not of how prettily money can be spent but of how harshly money is made, an immediate presence of the pits and the rails and the foundries, of turbines and pork-belly futures. So insistent is the presence of money in Newport that the mind springs ineluctably to the raw beginnings of it. A contemplation of "Rosecliff" dissolves into the image of Big Jim Fair, digging the silver out of a mountain in Nevada so that his daughter might live in Newport. "Old Man Berwind, he'd turn in his grave to see that oil truck parked in the driveway," a guard at "The Elms" said

to me as we surveyed the sunken garden there. "He made it in coal, soft coal." It had been on my mind as well as on the guard's, even as we stood in the sunlight outside the marble summer house, coal, soft coal, words like *bituminous* and *anthracite*, not the words of summer fancy.

In that way Newport is curiously Western, closer in spirit to Virginia City than to New York, to Denver than to Boston. It has the stridency usually credited to the frontier. And, like the frontier, it was not much of a game for women. Men paid for Newport, and granted to women the privilege of living in it. Just as gilt vitrines could be purchased for the correct display of biscuit Sèvres, so marble stairways could be bought for the advantageous display of women. In the filigreed gazebos they could be exhibited in a different light; in the French sitting rooms, in still another setting. They could be cajoled, flattered, indulged, given pretty rooms and Worth dresses, allowed to imagine that they ran their own houses and their own lives, but when it came time to negotiate, their freedom proved *trompe l'oeil*. It was the world of Bailey's Beach which made a neurasthenic of Edith Wharton, and, against her will, the Duchess of Marlborough of Consuelo Vanderbilt. The very houses are men's houses, factories, undermined by tunnels and service railways, shot through with plumbing to collect salt water, tanks to store it, devices to collect rain water, vaults for table silver, equipment inventories of china and crystal and "Tray cloths—fine" and "Tray cloths—ordinary." Somewhere in the bowels of "The Elms" is a coal bin twice the size of Julia Berwind's bedroom. The mechanics of such houses take precedence over all desires or inclinations; neither for great passions nor for morning whims can the factory be shut down, can production—of luncheons, of masked balls, of *marrons glacés*—be slowed. To stand in the dining room of "The Breakers" is to imagine fleeing from it, pleading migraine.

What Newport turns out to be, then, is homiletic, a fantastically elaborate stage setting for an American morality play in which money and happiness are presented as antithetical. It is a curious theatrical for these particular men to have conceived, but then we all judge ourselves sometime; it is hard for me to believe that Cornelius Vanderbilt did not sense, at some point in time, in some dim billiard room of his unconscious, that when he built "The Breakers" he damned himself. The world must have seemed greener to all of them, out there when they were young and began laying the rails or digging for high-grade ore in the Comstock or daring to think that they might corner copper. More than anyone else in the society, these men had apparently dreamed the dream and made it work. And what they did then was to build a place which seems to illustrate, as in a child's primer, that the production ethic led step by step to unhappiness, to restrictiveness, to entrapment in the mechanics of living. In that way the lesson of Bellevue Avenue is more seriously radical than the idea of Brook Farm. Who could fail to read the sermon in the stones of Newport? Who could think that the building of a railroad could guarantee salvation, when there on the lawns of the men who built the railroad nothing is left but the shadows of migrainous women, and the pony carts waiting for the long-dead children?

- This essay is filled with allusions. How did you make sure your audience understood them?

- Did you carefully balance the long sentences? How?

This memoir is probably as physical and spirited as Maya Angelou's early life with her older brother, Bailey. Her fascination with everyone and everything in the Christian Methodist Episcopal Church in Stamps, Arkansas, has not diminished with time. Keep those bodies alive!

FROM I Know Why the Caged Bird Sings

MAYA ANGELOU

In the Christian Methodist Episcopal Church the children's section was on the right, cater-cornered from the pew that held those ominous women called the Mothers of the Church. In the young people's section the benches were placed close together, and when a child's legs no longer comfortably fitted in the narrow space, it was an indication to the elders that that person could now move into the intermediate area (center church). Bailey and I were allowed to sit with the other children only when there were informal meetings, church socials or the like. But on the Sundays when Reverend Thomas preached, it was ordained that we occupy the first row, called the mourners' bench. I thought we were placed in front because Momma was proud of us, but Bailey assured me that she just wanted to keep her grandchildren under her thumb and eye.

Reverend Thomas took his text from Deuteronomy. And I was stretched between loathing his voice and wanting to listen to the sermon. Deuteronomy was my favorite book in the Bible. The laws were so absolute, so clearly set down, that I knew if a person truly wanted to avoid hell and brimstone, and being roasted forever in the devil's fire, all she had to do was memorize Deuteronomy and follow its teaching, word for word. I also liked the way the word rolled off the tongue.

Bailey and I sat alone on the front bench, the wooden slats pressing hard on our behinds and the backs of our thighs. I would have wriggled just a bit, but each time I looked over at Momma, she seemed to threaten, "Move and I'll tear you up," so, obedient to the unvoiced command, I sat still. The church ladies were warming up behind me with a few hallelujahs and Praise the Lords and Amens, and the preacher hadn't really moved into the meat of the sermon.

It was going to be a hot service.

On my way into church, I saw Sister Monroe, her open-faced gold crown glinting when she opened her mouth to return a neighborly greeting. She lived in the country and couldn't get to church every Sunday, so she made up for her absences by shouting so hard when she did make it that she shook the whole church. As soon as she took her seat, all the ushers would move to her side of the church because it took three women and sometimes a man or two to hold her.

Once when she hadn't been to church for a few months (she had taken off to have a child), she got the spirit and started shouting, throwing her arms around and jerking her body, so that the ushers went over to hold her down, but she tore herself away from them and ran up to the pulpit. She stood in front of the altar, shaking like a freshly caught trout. She screamed at Reverend Taylor. "Preach it. I say, preach it." Naturally he kept on preaching as if she wasn't standing there telling him what to do. Then she screamed an extremely fierce "I said, preach it" and stepped up on the altar. The Reverend kept on throwing out phrases like home-run balls and Sister Monroe made a quick break and grasped for him. For just a second, everything and everyone in the church except Reverend Taylor and Sister Monroe hung loose like stockings on a washline. Then she caught the minister by the sleeve of his jacket and his coattail, then she rocked him from side to side.

I have to say this for our minister, he never stopped giving us the lesson. The usher board made its way to the pulpit, going up both aisles with a little more haste than is customarily seen in church. Truth to tell, they fairly ran to the minister's aid. Then two of the deacons, in their shiny Sunday suits, joined the ladies in white on the pulpit, and each time they pried Sister Monroe loose from the preacher he took another deep breath and kept on preaching, and Sister Monroe grabbed him in another place, and more firmly. Reverend Taylor was helping his rescuers as much as possible by jumping around when he got a chance. His voice at one point got so low it sounded like a roll of thunder, then Sister Monroe's "Preach it" cut through the roar, and we all wondered (I did, in any case) if it would ever end. Would they go on forever, or get tired out at last like a game of blindman's bluff that lasted too long, with nobody caring who was "it"?

I'll never know what might have happened, because magically the pandemonium spread. The spirit infused Deacon Jackson and Sister Willson, the chairman of the usher board, at the same time. Deacon Jackson, a tall, thin, quiet man, who was also a part-time Sunday school teacher, gave a scream like a falling tree, leaned back on thin air and punched Reverend Taylor on the arm. It must have hurt as much as it caught the Reverend unawares. There was a moment's break in the rolling sounds and Reverend Taylor jerked around surprised, and hauled off and punched Deacon Jackson. In the same second Sister Willson caught his tie, looped it over her fist a few times, and pressed down on him. There wasn't time to laugh or cry before all three of them were down on the floor behind the altar. Their legs spiked out like kindling wood.

Sister Monroe, who had been the cause of all the excitement, walked off the dais, cool and spent, and raised her flinty voice in the hymn, "I came to Jesus, as I was, worried, wound, and sad; I found in Him a resting place and He has made me glad."

The minister took advantage of already being on the floor and asked in a choky little voice if the church would kneel with him to offer a prayer of thanksgiving. He said we had been visited with a mighty spirit, and let the whole church say Amen.

On the next Sunday, he took his text from the eighteenth chapter of the Gospel according to St. Luke, and talked quietly but seriously about the Pharisees, who prayed in the streets so that the public would be impressed with their religious devotion. I doubt that anyone got the message—certainly not those to whom it was directed. The deacon board, however, did appropriate funds for him to buy a new suit. The other was a total loss.

- How did you keep the turmoil from getting out of control?

- Did you fully embody Sister Monroe? How?

- Did you take enough time for your audience to see all of it happen?

Jane Gould Tortillot kept a diary as she crossed the Great Plains from May to November 1862. On some days she was too busy to make any entries. When she did write, she gave a moving picture of the world of the wagon train; of her husband, Albert; of her life under extraordinarily difficult circumstances. To be sure, she suffered, but she didn't whine. Keep her backbone strong.

 FROM **Women's Diaries of the Westward Journey**

LILLIAN SCHLISSEL, EDITOR

Jane Gould Tortillot

Friday, July 4   Today is the Fourth of July and here we are away off in the wilderness and can't even stay over a day to do any extra cooking. The men fired their guns. We wonder what the folks at home are doing and oh, how we wish we were there. Albert is not well today, so I drive. I have been in the habit of sleeping a while every forenoon, so naturally I was very sleepy driving. Went to sleep a multitude of times, to awaken with a start fancying we were running into gullies. After going a short distance we came in sight of a mail station, on the other side of the river there were several buildings. They are of adobe, I suppose. Nearly opposite on this side of the river we passed a little log hut which is used for a store. It was really a welcome sight after going four hundred miles without seeing a house of any kind. . . .

Saturday, July 5–Tuesday, July 8 . . .

Wednesday, July 9 . . . We hear many stories of Indians depredations, but do not feel frightened yet. . . .

July 10 . . .

Friday, July 11 . . . There was a little child run over by a wagon in Walker's train, who are just ahead of us. The child was injured quite seriously. . . . They sent for a German physician that belongs to our train, to see the child that was injured. He said he thought it would get better.

July 12–July 19 . . .

Sunday, July 20 . . . The men had a ball-play towards night. Seemed to enjoy themselves very much, it seemed like old times.

Monday, July 21 . . . Our men went to work this morning to building a raft. Worked hard all day. Half of the men in the water, too. . . .

Tuesday, July 22 . . . Went to work this morning as early as possible to ferrying the wagons over. Had to take them apart and float the box and cover behind. The two boxes were fastened together by the rods, one before to tow in and the other to load. Worked till dark. We were the last but one to cross tonight. Got some of our groceries wet, some coffee, sugar dissolved.

July 24–July 25 . . .

Saturday, July 26 . . . Annie McMillen had lagged behind, walking, when we stopped. The whole train had crossed the creek before they thought of her. The creek was so deep that it ran into the wagon boxes, so she could not wade. A man on horseback went over for her, and another man on a mule went to help her on. The mules refused to go clear across went where the water was very deep, threw the man off and almost trampled him, but he finally got out safe, only well wet and with the loss of a good hat, which is no trifling loss here.

Sunday, July 27 . . .

Monday, July 28 . . . Came past a camp of thirty-six wagons who have been camped for some time here in the mountains. They have had their cattle stampeded four or five times. There was a woman died in this train yesterday. She left six children, one of them only two days old. Poor little thing, it had better have died with its mother. They made a good picket fence around the grave.

July 29–31, August 1–2 . . .

Sunday, August 3 . . . We passed by the train I have just spoken of. They had just buried the babe of the woman who died days ago, and were just digging a grave for another woman that was run over by the cattle and wagons when they stampeded yesterday. She lived twenty-four hours, she gave birth to a child a short time before she died. The child was buried with her. She leaves a little two year old girl and a husband. They say he is nearly crazy with sorrow. . . .

August 4 . . .

Tuesday, August 5 . . . Did not start very early. Waited for a train to pass. It seems today as if I *must* go home to father's to see them all. I can't wait another minute. If I could only *hear* from them it would do some good, but I suppose I shall have to wait whether I am patient or not. . . .

August 6–9 . . .

Sunday, August 10 . . . Traveled five or six miles when we came to Snake River. We stayed till two o'clock then traveled till about four or five, when *we* from the back end of the train saw those on ahead all get out their guns. In a short time the word came back that a train six miles on had been attacked by the Indians, and some killed and that was cause enough for the arming. In a short time were met by two men. They wanted us to go a short distance from the road and bring two dead men to their camp, five miles ahead.

Albert unloaded his little wagon and sent Gus back with them and about forty armed men from both trains, to get them. We learned that a train of eleven wagons had been plundered of all that was in them and the teams taken and the men killed. One was Mr. Bullwinkle who left us the 25th of last month, at the crossing of Green River. He went on with this Adams train. Was intending to wait for us but we had not overtaken him yet. He was shot eight times. His dog was shot four times before he would let them get to the wagon. They took all that he had in his wagon, except his trunks and books and papers. They broke open his trunks and took all that they contained. (He had six.) It is supposed that they took six thousand dollars from him, tore the cover from his wagon, it was oilcloth. He had four choice horses. They ran away when he was shot, the harnesses were found on the trail where it was cut from them when they went. It was a nice silver one. The Captain had a daughter shot and wounded severely. This happened yesterday. This morning a part of their train and a part of the Kennedy train went in pursuit of the stock. They were surrounded by Indians on ponies, two killed, several wounded and two supposed to be killed. They were never found. One of those killed was Capt. Adams' son, the other was a young man in the Kennedy train. Those that we carried to camp were those killed this morning. Mr. Bullwinkle and the two others were buried before we got to the camp. There were one hundred and fifty wagons there and thirty four of ours. Capt. Kennedy was severely wounded. Capt. Hunter of Iowa City train was killed likewise by an Indian. We camped near Snake River. We could not get George to ride after the news, he *would* walk and carry his loaded pistol to help.

Monday, August 11 . . .   The two men we brought up were buried early this morning with the other three, so they laid five men side by side in this vast wilderness, killed by guns and arrows of the red demons. The chief appeared yesterday in a suit of Mr. Bullwinkle's on the battlefield. . . .

Tuesday, August 12 . . .   Capt. Adams' daughter died this morning from the effects of her wound. Was buried in a box made of a wagon box. Poor father and mother lost one son and one daughter, all of his teams, clothing and four thousand dollars. Is left dependent on the bounty of strangers. . . . In the evening we took in Mrs. Ellen Ives, one of the ladies of the plundered train. Her husband goes in the wagon just ahead of us. She was married the morning she started for California. Not a very pleasant wedding tour. . . .

- ◆ How did you make your audience see the tensions building in Jane at the end of July and the beginning of August?

While the sites and tasks of courage change with the times, the essentials remain. There are crucial ways in which Dana Tierney's mother is close kin of Jane Gould Tortillot. Both are determined survivors: realistic, clear-eyed, and ready to confront any problem life presents them. They typify the kinds of women's storytelling that is receiving increasing attention. Be sure this woman is confident and self-reliant, even if you think her occupational choice is unusual.

The Makeup Artist

DANA TIERNEY

My mother, who is beautiful and takes beauty seriously, was appalled at my sister's final make-over. The people at the funeral home had made her face pumpkiny orange, the lipstick too big on her downturned mouth. Breast heaving, my mother gazed into the coffin and announced to the mortuary cosmetologist, "That's not my daughter in there." She held out her hand. "Give me that sponge." The startled funeral director and staff watched as my mother redid my sister's face herself. So two weeks later I'm explaining to friends: "My mother has gotten a job. . . ."

They try hard to be supportive. "Cosmetologist," they say. "To the dead. At the funeral home. Where they just cremated your sister. *O-k-a-a-y.*"

Before she died of brain cancer at 32, my sister, Dawn, was confined to a wheelchair. Confronted with institutionalizing her, my mother drew herself up: "I *will not* put her in a nursing home. She is *my child.*" She swept back to Dawn's room, where she lighted a joint, inhaled hard and blew the smoke into my sister's mouth until the nausea passed.

My mother took care of Dawn for five years—after she became too heavy to lift, could barely speak or feed herself and was incontinent. So now I'm a little worried. Has my mother finally lost it? After Day 1 on the job, I ask, "How'd it go?"

"Well, my very first person was a man who'd gotten run over by a bulldozer, and part of his ear was gone. Nobody knew what to do. But I ran out and got beeswax. And I tell you, it was miraculous!" I envision my mother's fingers working on a mangled ear, the results like a restored mollusk. "I think I'm pretty good at this," she confides.

At her house, my mother greets me with a little ram's-horn furrow of determination between her eyes. I'm startled at the transformation: normally my mother floats in her long skirts, shark-tooth necklaces and castoff penny loafers. Now she's in a business suit and Naturalizer pumps, leading me briskly up the handicapped ramp, past my sister's now-closed door and back to her own bathroom, where she has assembled the tools of her new trade. I watch her intently arranging makeup brushes according to height, nail polish according to color, and realize the job makes a certain amount of sense: my mother has the pretty woman's reverence for the power of blush and lip liner—and she was a good artist before she became my sister's full-time caretaker.

Mama is shaking a bottle of Chanel Teint Naturel—for her clients, she has decided only Chanel will do. "Honey," she says, "the dead do not have to look like clowns."

I laugh as she brandishes a makeup sponge that looks like a piece of tofu. Sternly, she says, "This job is not a trip to the Lancôme counter."

"O.K." I take a deep breath. "What is it like then?"

"Well, today they brought in Mrs. Griscombe, and they hadn't found her for two days, so she was difficult, needed several layers of foundation." I imagine my mother bending over an insensate body for hours, primping the hair, applying the lipstick, making Mrs. Griscombe as beautiful as she can be, very like what she used to do for my sister. But now it's different. There is no soft "Thank you, Mama," no hand squeeze, no flickering eyelid.

Now I see my mother holding a lifeless hand, filing the nails, applying three layers of polish, putting the final touch on strangers, clinging to a phantom ritual. Over the past few years my mother's hair has turned white; now it's up on her head in a bun wrapped in on itself like a sleeping dove. Touching her own face, she murmurs: "The skin of the dead is like tissue. It tears so easily." Suddenly I remember how in my sister's final days, we couldn't keep our hands off her. Even when we read her the Bible, we hung on, curling up in bed with her, stroking her face, the wisps of her hair. We felt her thready pulse, her heart thudding like an elephant's, six beats a minute, the hugeness of its animation. And after she took her last breath, how quickly her life was over; she was utterly gone, and had turned the color of granite. Even then we couldn't stop touching her.

My sister's ashes rest in a cloisonné urn, and it's just my mother and me and lots of makeup in a quiet house in the mountains. Evening has fallen, and Mama is washing flesh tone out of sponges, still talking about her day. "Mrs. Griscombe. I could not get that woman to smile. Took a lot of coaxing just to get a Mona Lisa out of her. But finally"—she gazes proudly at her own hands—"the family said: 'Oh, she looks wonderful! Like she might get up and walk.'"

- ◆ Whose tale is this? How did your performance demonstrate that?

- ◆ The spirits of the narrator and her mother clearly differ in many respects, but there are crucial signs that this is a daughter's tale about her mother, a family story. What performance choices made their relationship clear to your audience?

The American poet Emily Dickinson didn't always feel "a Funeral, in my Brain," but clearly she often felt the world strongly. In this affectionate and imaginative letter to her brother, Austin, she eagerly awaits his return, but her attention to detail sketches for him much of what he misses. That she misses him greatly needs only the evidence of what her imagination can do in the conclusion: she can re-create summer for him! Yes, the sentences are long, but the speech phrases are clear, and the rhythm is characteristically her own. Could any brother who received such a letter not *hasten to return?*

To Austin Dickinson

EMILY DICKINSON

17 October 1851

We are waiting for breakfast, Austin, the meat and potato and a little pan of your favorite brown bread are keeping warm at the fire, while father goes for shavings.

While we were eating supper Mr Stephen Church rang the door bell very violently and offered to present us with *three barrels of shavings.* We are much overcome by this act of magnanimity and father has gone this morning to claim his proffered due. He wore a palm leaf hat, and his pantaloons tucked in his boots and I could'nt help thinking of *you* as he strode along by the window.

I dont think "neglige" quite becoming to so mighty a man. I had rather a jacket of green and your barndoor apparrel, than all the mock simplicity of a lawyer and a man. The breakfast is so warm and pussy is here a singing and the teakettle sings too as if to see which was loudest and I am so afraid lest kitty should be beaten—yet a *shadow* falls upon my morning picture—where is the youth so bold, the bravest of our fold, a seat is empty here—spectres sit in your chair and now and then nudge father with their long, bony elbows. I wish you were here dear Austin—the dust falls on the bureau in your deserted room and gay, frivolous spiders spin away in the corners. I dont go there after dark whenever I can help it, for the twilight seems to pause there and I am half afraid, and if ever I have to go, I hurry with all my might and never look behind me for I know who I should see.

Before next Tuesday—Oh before the coming stage will I not brighten and brush it, and open the long closed blinds, and with a sweeping broom will I not bring each spider down from its home so high and tell it it may come back again when master has gone—and oh I will bid it to be a tardy spider, to tarry on the way, and I will think my eye is fuller than sometimes, tho' *why* I cannot tell, when it shall rap on the window and come to live again. I am so happy when I know how soon you are coming that I put away my sewing and go out in the yard to think. I have tried to delay the frosts, I have coaxed the fading flowers, I thought I *could* detain a few of the crimson leaves until you had smiled upon them, but their companions call them and they cannot stay away—you will find the blue hills, Austin, with the autumnal shadows silently sleeping on them, and there will be a glory lingering round the day, so you'll know autumn has been here, and the *setting sun* will tell you, if you dont get home till evening. How glad I am you are well—you must try hard to be careful and not get sick again. I hope you will be better than ever you were in your life when you come home *this time,* for it never seemed so long since we have seen you. I thank you for such a long letter, and yet if I might choose, *the next* should be a longer. I think a letter just about *three days* long would make me happier than any other kind of one—if you please, dated at Boston, but thanks be to our Father, you may conclude it *here.* Everything has changed since my other letter— the doors are shut this morning, and all the kitchen wall is covered with chilly flies who are trying to warm themselves—poor things, they do not understand that there are no summer mornings remaining to them and me and they have a bewildered air which is really very droll, did'nt one feel *sorry* for them. You would say t'was a gloomy morning if you were sitting here—the frost has been severe and the few lingering leaves seem anxious to be going and wrap their faded cloaks more closely about them as if to shield them from the chilly northeast wind. The earth looks like some poor old lady who by dint of pains has bloomed e'en till *now,* yet in a forgetful moment a few silver hairs from out her cap come stealing, and she tucks them back so hastily and thinks nobody *sees.* The cows are going to pasture and little boys with their hands in their pockets are whistling to try to keep warm. Dont think that the sky will frown so the day when you come home! She will smile and look happy, and be full of sunshine *then*—and even *should* she frown upon her child returning, there is *another* sky ever serene and fair, and there is *another* sunshine, tho' it be darkness there—never mind faded forests, Austin, never mind silent fields—*here* is a little forest whose leaf is ever green, here is a *brighter* garden, where not a frost has been, in its unfading flowers I hear the bright bee hum, prithee, my Brother, into *my* garden come!

Your very aff

Sister.

- ◆ How did you create the seeming immediacy of Emily Dickinson's brother?

- ◆ There are many shifts in locus in this letter. How did you make each shift apparent to your audience? Where did Austin go when the locus shifted?

Terry Pickens, age 14, is a newsboy. Together with his brother Cliff (who is 12), he serves 111 customers, but Terry's route is more difficult. As he says, "Cliff hasn't got any hills. Mine's all hills." Be sure we see Terry think—he has become a very savvy young man. What question do you suppose Terkel asked to get him started?

 FROM **Working**

STUDS TERKEL

Terry Pickens

I've been having trouble collecting. I had one woman hid from me once. I had another woman tell her kids to tell me she wasn't home. He says, "Mom, newsboy." She says (whispers), "Tell him I'm not home." I could hear it from the door. I came back in half an hour and she paid me. She's not a deadbeat. They'll pay you if you get 'em. Sometimes you have to wait. . . .

If I don't catch 'em at home, I get pretty mad. That means I gotta come back and come back and come back and come back until I catch 'em. Go around about nine o'clock at night and seven o'clock in the morning. This one guy owed me four dollars. He got real mad at me for comin' around at ten o'clock. Why'd I come around so late? He probably was mad 'cause I caught him home. But he paid me. I don't care whether he gets mad at me, just so I get paid.

I like to have money. It's nice to have money once in a while instead of being flat broke all the time. Most of my friends are usually flat broke. I spent $150 this summer. On nothing—candy, cokes, games of pool, games of pinball. We went to McDonald's a couple of times. I just bought anything I wanted. I wonder where the money went. I have nothing to show for it. I'm like a gambler, the more I have, the more I want to spend. That's just the way I am.

It's supposed to be such a great deal. The guy, when he came over and asked me if I wanted a route, he made it sound so great.

Seven dollars a week for hardly any work at all. And then you find out the guy told you a bunch of bull. You mistrust the people. You mistrust your customers because they don't pay you sometimes.

Then you get mad at the people at the printing corporation. You're supposed to get fifty-seven papers. They'll send me forty-seven or else they'll send me sixty-seven. Sunday mornings they get mixed up. Cliff'll have ten or eleven extras and I'll be ten or eleven short. That happens all the time. The printers, I don't think they care. They make all these stupid mistakes at least once a week. I think they're half-asleep or something. I do my job, I don't see why they can't do theirs. I don't like my job any more than they do.

Sunday morning at three—that's when I get up. I stay up later so I'm tired. But the dark doesn't bother me. I run into things sometimes, though. Somebody's dog'll come out and about give you a heart attack. There's this one woman, she had two big German shepherds, great big old things, like three or four feet tall. One of 'em won't bite you. He'll just run up, charging, bark at you, and then he'll go away. The other one, I didn't know she had another one—when it bit me. This dog came around the bush. (Imitates barking.) When I turned around, he was at me. He bit me right there (indicates scar on leg). It was bleeding a little. I gave him a real dirty look.

He ran over to the other neighbor's lawn and tried to keep me from gettin' in there. I walked up and delivered the paper. I was about ready to beat the thing's head in or kill it. Or something with it. I was so mad. I called up that woman and she said the dog had all its shots and "I don't believe he bit you." I said, "Lady, he bit me." Her daughter started giving me the third degree. "What color was the dog?" "How big was it?" "Are you sure it was our yard and our dog?" Then they saw the dogs weren't in the pen.

First they told me they didn't think I needed any shots. Then they said they'd pay for the doctor. I never went to the doctor. It wasn't bleeding a whole lot. But I told her if I ever see that dog again, she's gonna have to get her papers from somebody else. Now they keep the dog penned up and it barks at me and everything. And I give it a dirty look.

There's a lot of dogs around here. I got this other dog, a little black one, it tried to bite me too. It lunged at me, ripped my pants and missed me. (With the glee of W. C. Fields) I kicked it *good*. It still chases me. There are two black dogs. The other one I've kicked so many times that it just doesn't bother me any more. I've kicked his face in once when he was biting my leg. Now he just stays under the bushes and growls at me. I don't bother to give him a dirty look.

There were these two other dogs. They'd always run out in the street and chase me. I kicked them. They'd come back and I'd kick 'em again. I don't have any problems with 'em any more, because they got hit chasin' cars. They're both dead.

I don't like many of my customers, 'cause they'll cuss me if they don't get their papers just exactly in the right place. This one guy cussed me up and down for about fifteen minutes. I don't want to repeat what he called me. All the words, just up and down. He told me he drives past all those blank drugstores on his blank way home and he could stop off at one of 'em and get a blank newspaper. And I'm just a blank convenience.

I was so mad at him. I hated his guts. I felt like taking a lead pipe to him or something. But I kept my mouth shut, 'cause I didn't know if the press guy'd get mad at me and I'd lose my route. You see, this guy could help me or he could hurt me. So I kept my mouth shut.

A lot of customers are considerate but a lot of 'em aren't. Lot of 'em act like they're doing you such a favor taking the paper from you. It costs the same dime at a drugstore. Every time they want you to do something they threaten you: (imitates nasty, nasal voice) "Or I'll quit."

What I really can't stand: you'll be collecting and somebody'll come out and start telling you all their problems. "I'm going to visit my daughter today, yes, I am. She's twenty-two, you know." "Look here, I got all my sons home, see the army uniforms?" They'll stand for like half an hour. I got two or three like that, and they always got something to say to me. I'll have like two hours wasted listening to these people blabbin' before they pay me. Mmm, I don't know. Maybe they're lonely. But they've got a daughter and a son, why do they have to blab in my ear?

A lot of the younger customers have had routes and they know how hard it is, how mean people are. They'll be nicer to you. They tend to tip you more. And they don't blab all day long. They'll just pay you and smile at you. The younger people frequently offer me a coke or something.

Older people are afraid of me, a lot of them. The first three, four weeks—(muses) they seemed so afraid of me. They think I'm gonna rob 'em or something. It's funny. You wouldn't think it'd be like this in a small town, would you? They're afraid I'm gonna beat 'em up, take their money. They'd just reach through the door and give me the money. Now they know you so well, they invite you in and blab in your ear for half an hour. It's one or the other. I really don't know why they're afraid. I'm not old, so I wouldn't know how old people feel.

Once in a while I come home angry, most of the time just crabby. Sometimes kids steal the paper out of people's boxes. I lose my profits. It costs me a dime. The company isn't responsible, I am. The company wouldn't believe you probably that somebody stole the paper.

I don't see where being a newsboy and learning that people are pretty mean or that people don't have enough money to buy things with is gonna make you a better person or anything. If anything, it's gonna make a worse person out of you, 'cause you're not gonna like people that don't pay you. And you're not gonna like people who act like they're doing you a big favor paying you. Yeah, it sort of molds your character, but I don't think for the better. If anybody told me being a newsboy builds character, I'd know he was a liar.

I don't see where people get all this bull about the kid who's gonna be President and being a newsboy made a President out of him. It taught him how to handle his money and this bull. You know what it did? It taught him how to hate the people on his route. And the printers. And dogs.

- ♦ What did you do with your body and voice to let your audience see a 14-year-old boy eager to talk? What was his body doing?

This young man might be a friend of Terry's. Look carefully at how Lynda Barry creates his world through repeated speech phrases, distinctive word choice, and artfully arranged details. Why is this just one paragraph?

KEEP OUT! (A Boy's Bedroom)

LYNDA BARRY

Keep Out. Keep OUT. THIS MEANS YOU. Keep! Out! But Mom always comes in with the bogus excuse of "Here are some clean socks and underwear, I'll put them in your drawer." As if I can't get my own socks and underwear from the laundry room. But no, she just needs any excuse to come into my room and yell, "This room looks like a tornado hit it!" As if she has ever seen anything hit by a tornado. And then she's coming back dragging the vacuum cleaner, as if she has the right to vacuum my room! I go, "MOM, NEVER VACUUM IN HERE!" I got too many important things of life on that floor. Stuff that dropped that I'll need later. And my tarantula, which I swear to God hates my mom so much that the hairs fall off its abdomen, which is what happens to tarantulas when they get freaked, and Mom is always freaking my tarantula with the vacuum. She said I could have a gerbil, so I got a tarantula. Tell me what is the basic difference? I use the same fish tank that leaked all over the dresser and wrecked it, which I had to hear about for 5,000 years because that was her dresser when she was a kid. LIKE IT'S MY FAULT THE

FISH TANK LEAKED AND I DIDN'T NOTICE UNTIL ALL THE WATER WAS OUT! WHAT ABOUT MY FISH, MOM, HUH? So that's why the dresser is all warped. It took a while for the water to leak out. I just thought it was evaporating superfast. I thought it was like a freak of the environment of my bedroom. CAN I HELP IT IF IT WAS LEAKING DOWN THE SIDE OF THE DRESSER I NEVER LOOK AT, MOM? And then you'd think that if it was already wrecked she wouldn't care if I put my eyeball stickers on the mirror and the wood, right? A normal person would normally think, It's

Already Wrecked So What's the Dif. But she has a total attack and she has another total attack that I put eyeball stickers on my bed, IT IS MY BED BUT SHE HAS A TOTAL ATTACK, because it was her brother's bed or her cousin's bed or someone of her family's bed WHO IS OBVIOUSLY MORE IMPORTANT THAN HER SON WHO JUST WANTS TO PUT HIS EYEBALL STICKERS WHERE HE WANTS EXCEPT HE CAN'T BECAUSE HE LIVES IN A CONCEN-TRATION CAMP. Same goes for tape and nail holes in the wall. I go, "Mom, how am I supposed to put up my posters, then?" and she goes, "Oh, I'll buy you a bulletin board." THAT BULLETIN BOARD RIGHT THERE THAT I FILLED UP IN THREE SECONDS! I said, Forget it, man, this is boag, I'm using tape and then she has another total attack and makes me sign a Family Contract that when I leave for college I will personally paint my own room and sand down the tape marks or whatever it is you do with tape marks, which I will have to figure out because as you have noticed there is hardly no wall showing. That is my goal. Total posters. Including the ceiling. Oh, that's another thing. You notice the green light bulbs, right? At first when I bought them WITH MY OWN MONEY, MOM, she to-tally freaked because "Green light bulbs, green light bulbs? The neighbors will think you are growing drugs!" I go, Mom, what kind of drugs do you grow with green light bulbs? And she freaked and we had to have a family meeting where my dad was even there, which is totally weird because I think the total times my dad has even been in my room is like around zero AND NOW HE GETS A VOTE ON MY LIFE? Mom was freaking because she said it brought the value of the house down because my bedroom used to be in the front where the world could see it so that is how I scored this room that used to be my sister's. It smelled like a girl for around a month, during which I couldn't have no one over, but it was worth it for the green light bulbs. Don't they make you feel so peaceful? Wait. Listen to this song. Isn't it the perfect combination? I want to just listen to my station and lie in the peaceful green light, and let my tarantula free. Its name is Dana, for this girl Dana Speers at my school who I swear to God looks just like a tarantula but in a cool way. No one I know knows I named it Dana. They think I named it Boris. It would be embarrassing if people knew. My mom would get all happy. "Oh, a girl in my son's life!" So if she comes in call it Boris. Actually, I snuck the actual Dana Speers up here to meet Dana Speers the tarantula. Dana Speers is a more interesting girl than normal. You wouldn't even think she's a girl from the way she is. She doesn't make no one nervous. I have sat right here and the actual Dana Speers has sat right where you are and we let the tarantula Dana Speers walk from my hand onto her hand, you know, that thing of letting a tarantula walk on you? And it was a trip because no hairs fell off the tarantula

Dana Speers's abdomen when we did that. Which shows you what I said about the actual Dana Speers. And she, the actual Dana, has these superlong eyelashes and eyebrows, which some people think is freaky because it does look slightly monstery because there's hair all around her eyes, even right here in the corner part, which I think looks insanely cool and you know that thing where if you get an eyelash from someone you can wish on it? And maybe even an eyebrow hair counts, too, I don't know. I just know for sure that one eyelash fell off of the actual Dana Speers when she was last over, but it would have been too weird of me to go for it while she was sitting there, so I waited until after she left and I am still looking for it because I got a really good wish I want to make and that's why I don't want my mom to vacuum in here. That and also she might suck up my tarantula.

- What is the persona *doing* during all this talk? Why?
- Who is the audience for the segments printed in capital letters?

Bibliography

For the Instructor

Abrahams, Roger D. *Singing the Master: The Emergence of African-American Culture in the Plantation South.* New York: Penguin Books, 1992.
An exploration of how corn-shucking ceremonies in the antebellum South created and maintained a subversive African American identity.

Conquergood, Dwight. "Poetics, Play, Process, and Power: The Performative Turn in Anthropology." *Text and Performance Quarterly* 9, no. 1 (1989): 82–88.
A concise account of current ethical concerns in anthropological and performance scholarship.

Diamond, Elin, ed. *Performance and Cultural Politics.* New York: Routledge, 1996.
A wide-ranging and provocative collection of essays that navigate the relationships between performance, culture, and history.

Fine, Elizabeth. *The Folklore Text: From Performance to Print.* Bloomington: Indiana University Press, 1984.
An interesting discussion of the techniques of preserving nonfictional spoken texts and their relationship to literature.

Fuoss, Kirk W. *Striking Performances/Performing Strikes.* Jackson: University Press of Mississippi, 1997.

A look at how communal identities were created and contested through two "cultural performances"—the Workers Alliance of America's 1936 takeover of the New Jersey state assembly and the General Motors sitdown strike of 1936–1937.

Haedicke, Susan C., and Tobin Nellhaus, eds. *Performing Democracy: International Perspectives on Urban Community-Based Performance.* Ann Arbor: University of Michigan Press, 2001.
Theorizing about the contested notion of community, this collection of essays considers how performance empowers marginalized groups for social change and maintains the cohesion of a community under assault.

Jefferson, Gail. "On the Poetics of Ordinary Talk." *Text and Performance Quarterly* 16, no. 1 (1996): 1–61.
An exhaustive and compelling analysis of the "wild side of conversational analysis" by one of the most widely respected authorities in the field.

Ong, Walter J. "Before Textuality: Orality and Interpretation." *Oral Tradition* 3, no. 3 (1988): 259–69.
An account of the relationship between reading and nonliterary communication by one of the leading scholars of the oral traditions.

Roach, Joseph. *Cities of the Dead: Circum-Atlantic Performance.* New York: Columbia University Press, 1996.
Considering theatrical, musical, cultural, and textual performances from the eighteenth century to the present, Roach explores how performance constitutes history and identity in the Atlantic rim.

Sauceda, James Steven. "The 'Wordloosed Soundscript:' Performing James Joyce's *Finnegans Wake.*" *Text and Performance Quarterly* 10, no. 2 (1990): 123–42.
Sauceda demonstrates how orality makes assessible one of the most difficult texts in Western literature.

Taylor, Diana. *Disappearing Acts: Spectacles of Gender and Nationalism in Argentina's "Dirty War."* Durham: Duke University Press, 1997.
A look at how performance constructs and rearticulates gender and national identity in Argentina's "Dirty War" (1976–1983).

Personal Narrative

The explosion of interest in personal narratives—in print, on film, in video, online, in dance, in music—has elicited much useful commentary. These items also include useful bibliographies:

Baldwin, K. "Woof! A Word on Women's Roles in Family Storytelling." In *Women's Folklore, Women's Culture: Publication of the American Folklore Society,* n.s., 8, edited by Rosan A. Jordan and Susan J. Kalcik. Philadelphia: University of Pennsylvania Press, 1985.
Dailey, Sheron J., ed. "The Personal Narrative: Problems and Possibilities." In *The Future of Performance Studies: Visions and Revisions,*

199–301. Annandale, VA: National Communication Association, 1998.

Langellier, Kristin M. "Personal Narrative, Performance Performativity: Two or Three Things I Know for Sure." *Text and Performance Quarterly* 19 (1999): 123–44.

Well, you know or don't you kennet or haven't I told you every telling has a taling and that's the he and the she of it. Look, look, the dusk is growing!

James Joyce
Finnegans Wake

CHAPTER SIX

Narration

This chapter is devoted to a thorough study of narration—how we tell stories. By the end of the chapter, you should be able to:

- Determine the point of view of the narrator: first person, second person, third person, omniscient.

- Decide who is being addressed.

- Define the characters who live in the story, understand their relationships, and select characteristic details for performance.

- Portray dialogue consistent with the characters and with the narrator's description, discriminating between direct discourse, indirect discourse, and narrator-transformed discourse.

- Describe the setting as both locale and style.

- Tactfully excerpt or cut a text to adapt it to performance constraints.

- Consolidate elements of prose style (from Chapter 5) with characteristics of narration (from this chapter) to rehearse and perform stories, novels, and other prose fiction.

Stories help us make sense of who we are and what happens to us, and good stories can't be separated from good storytelling.

Selections Discussed in This Chapter

In explaining some topics, we mention texts that are reprinted either within the chapter itself or at the end of a chapter. Use the guide below for quick reference to acquaint yourself with selections you may not fully recall.

Author	Title	Location
Kate Chopin	"The Story of an Hour"	Chapter 2, page 44
Michael Lassell	"How to Watch Your Brother Die"	Chapter 2, page 75

(continued)

Author	Title	Location
Elizabeth Bowen	from "The Little Girls"	Chapter 3, page 110
Toni Cade Bambara	"The Lesson"	Chapter 3, page 119
Maya Angelou	from *I Know Why the Caged Bird Sings*	Chapter 5, page 211
Homer	from *The Odyssey*	Chapter 6, page 234
Eudora Welty	from *Losing Battles*	Chapter 6, page 239
Flannery O'Connor	from "Greenleaf"	Chapter 6, page 244
Dylan Thomas	from *Quite Early One Morning*	Chapter 6, page 247
Bernard Malamud	"The Prison"	Chapter 6, page 254
John Updike	"A & P"	Chapter 6, page 259
Ann Beattie	"Snow"	Chapter 6, page 265
Toni Morrison	from *Sula*	Chapter 6, page 267
David Leavitt	from *The Lost Language of Cranes*	Chapter 6, page 269
Raymond Carver	"Popular Mechanics"	Chapter 6, page 272
Miloš Macourek	"Jacob's Chicken"	Chapter 6, page 273

WE ALL TELL STORIES. STORIES ABOUND IN EVERYDAY LIFE. They help us to make sense of who we are and what happens to us. It is impossible to live without them. These narratives emerge naturally—because something extraordinary just happened to you at the mall that you have to talk about, or because you want to hear about your cousin's honeymoon. Good stories are good because the lively description helps us see what the teller sees, because the people who populate the story speak up when they need to be heard, because—in short—always at the center is a teller, *telling* the tale. These natural narratives are the foundation for stories in which incident and language are carefully shaped and refined, structured and polished like a work of art. The skills you practice all the time as a natural storyteller are the best foundation for the skills you'll need in performing narration. As you know from your experience, good stories can't be separated from good storytelling.

Bill Buford claims that a story is "a piece of writing that makes the reader want to find out what happens next." And we have all found ourselves reading on even when other claims—burning cookies, a bus stop, a good night's sleep—would have us put down the book. But stories are more than plot. Whether cast in prose or in verse (or even in cinematic or visual terms), *narration* includes the *telling* (remember that active form) by a *narrator* (without whom there would be no tale) of something that has happened or that might happen, either to the narrator or to someone else.

When you perform narration, you need to answer five important questions. When you can answer them fully, you will be amply prepared. Let's explore each of them:

1. Who is telling the story? To whom?

2. What is going on here, exactly?

3. What sort of people live in this story?

4. What are they saying to each other?

5. Where is all of this taking place?

As you have come to expect from us, answer any of these five questions and up crops a fresh cluster of other questions. If you are fully informed about each one of them, you will be well on your way to successful and engaging performances of narration.

We said that we have often been glued to a story, turning the pages as rapidly as we can to find out what happens next. It may *seem* that each page is filled with action because the narrator has discreetly focused attention on events and we (because we willingly succumb to such skill) go along. Maybe this is the most obvious proof that the manner of telling the story is as important as the events, because whoever tells the tale shapes *how* it is told, moves the events at the proper pace, and leads us to the planned conclusion. We may not notice that we are being led, but along the way we encounter all those telling details that make the story unique. These are the verbal fingerprints of the narrator, the characteristics that vividly reveal what kind of person this storyteller is. That's where to begin your analysis. "What sort of person is telling this story?"

Who Is Telling the Story? Point of View

Every story has a storyteller, a person who selects what we see and hear, chooses the perspective from which we view the action, determines the details on which we linger, and decides how long it takes us to traverse time. Every story is shaped by its narrator, who establishes a *point of view,* a way to experience the world from a particular vantage point. Every narrator sets for us—by the position from which the action is viewed *and* by his or her unique personality—a characteristic way of showing and telling. In turn, this characteristic way of telling a story tells us about the narrator, too.

In a film, everything we see has been selected by the eye of the camera. Although we might want desperately to see something else, we see the scene only for as long as the camera wants us to watch it, only at the distance from which the camera wants us to see it, and lit in the manner the camera allows. Similarly, the narrator in a story selects and organizes what we see and hear, telling us what we must know or allowing us to overhear characters carrying on dialogue from which we draw our own conclusions. Storytellers have different attitudes and manners. Objective, clinical, cut-and-dried, black-and-white news stories look and feel different from stories that jump around in time and locale and are full of vivid happenings with improbable people doing impossible things. At the center of a story, shaping, controlling, refining, and guiding us through the narrative, is what Henry James calls the "central intelligence." Your first task as an interpreter is to understand the narrator.

First-Person Narrators

Two brief passages demonstrate how palpably present that central intelligence can be. The first is from *The Odyssey*:

> Tell me, Muse, of the man of many ways, who was driven far journeys, after he had sacked Troy's sacred citadel. Many were they whose cities he saw, whose minds he learned of, many the pains he suffered in his spirit on the wide sea, struggling for his own life and the homecoming of his companions.[1]

By the second syllable we know that the story is being told by a specific somebody. "*Tell me*, Muse," the narrator says. The invocation of the Muse and the simplicity and confidence of the words further suggest that the narrator is awed by the hero and his journey. Only if he is inspired by the gods can he convey the story of the "god-like Odysseus." Although the narrator seems to be at some distance from the events, they still impress him. These first few lines summarize the ordeal that is revealed in the story ahead, and the majesty in the words gives emotional impact to the beginning of this great tale.

Now look at the first paragraph of John Updike's "A & P" (the entire story can be found at the end of this chapter):

> In walks these three girls in nothing but bathing suits. I'm in the third checkout slot, with my back to the door, so I don't see them until they're over by the bread. The one that caught my eye first was the one in the plaid green two-piece. She was a chunky kid, with a good tan and a sweet broad softlooking can with those two crescents of white just under it, where the sun never seems to hit, at the top of the back of her legs. I stood there with my hand on a box of HiHo crackers trying to remember if I rang it up or not. I ring it up again and the customer starts giving me hell. She's one of these cash-register-watchers, a witch about fifty with rouge on her cheekbones and

1. Homer, *The Odyssey*, trans. Richmond Lattimore (New York: Harper and Row, 1967), 27.

no eyebrows, and I know it made her day to trip me up. She's been watching cash registers for fifty years and probably never seen a mistake before.[2]

Here we meet Sammy, a boy with his eye on three girls. How else is he identified? What—precisely—is he doing? Where is he doing it? It's going to get him into trouble before the paragraph is over! He is clearly interested in the girls and in their bathing suits, and he takes time from his tasks to describe the cut and color of one suit. Is his mind on his work? He addresses us as if we were his friends. The vivid impression these girls make is marked for both Sammy *and us* by the use of the present tense in the first sentence. What happens to tense as the paragraph progresses?

We are located quickly in the familiar world of the A & P: we recognize the grocery store, and we know about lanes, checkers, cash-register-watchers, and HiHo crackers. We know the landscape; Sammy's ready to tell us about these three girls.

Sammy is obviously not the disembodied voice of Homer and he is surely not Updike, the author. The persona, whether Sammy or Homer's narrator, is simply the teller of a tale vivid and important enough to be worth telling to us; his language makes us his peers. Both *The Odyssey* and "A & P" are written in *first-person narration.* They are told by different narrators, yet each narrator is lively and present, telling us something that happened to him.

In *first-person narration,* the person telling the story speaks directly to the reader as "I," and he or she is also the "eye" of the story. Sometimes the "I" is physically identified, as in Updike's story. In other cases, as with the narrator of Homer's epic, the "I" is not physically identified, although he or she definitely demonstrates a characteristic personality. The narrator may observe from either afar or quite near the events, may participate in the actions described or merely report what happens to others, or may report and evaluate as well. But whatever the degree of physical presence in the story, the narrator remains very much at the center of things. The narrator's personality selects, shapes, and colors everything we see and hear.

First-person narrators are peculiarly convinced of their own vision. They *know* it because it happened to them. Like most people who live through experiences they want to talk about later, first-person narrators are incapable of complete objectivity. They shape events to favor themselves and to prove their antagonists unreasonable, unattractive, and irresponsible. Such qualities do not make first-person narrators less interesting people; on the contrary, the foibles, idiosyncracies, and peculiar diction and vision of these unreliable narrators may present a delightful challenge to the interpreter. The narrator, revealed in the way the story is told, becomes a full-blooded character, unquestionably the

2. John Updike, "A & P."

most important character you will present. You must find within your body and your voice sufficient similarities to the body and voice of the storyteller to convince the audience that they are listening to a story told by someone to whom all of this actually happened.

First-person narrators, then, may be either *central participants* in the action of the story (like Sammy) or *observers* (like Homer's narrator). Each posture presents both benefits and liabilities to interpreters and their audiences. If you perform a first-person story with an actively involved narrator, you obviously have immediate access to many of the events; you know precisely what is going on inside one of the major characters. You are also restricted, however, to that person's perception of the events, and you may find yourself the victim of some fancy elaboration of the truth. If your narrator is chiefly observing the events, you get a much less subjective (though not entirely objective) picture of what is happening, but you do not get the inner concerns of any of the major characters.

Consider an automobile accident. Obviously, the driver of the car knew exactly what *he* was doing and thinking when the truck pulled out in front of him, but he could not see (and could not know) about the truck driver's fears about being late or the little puppy that jumped into the trucker's vision and caused the truck to swerve and collide with the car. Someone watching from the street corner may have seen many of these events happen, more or less clearly, but wouldn't know about any of the internal concerns of the participants. In either case, regardless of whose testimony we hear, the narrator remains at the center of the story, and when we hear the words of the characters, we hear them and see them *through* the voice of the narrator.

Second-Person Narrators

Among the most intriguing developments in contemporary fiction has been the explosion of interest in second-person narrators. Although such narratives do not appear as frequently as first- or third-person narratives, many strong second-person stories have been published in the last decade.[3] Recall the opening lines of Michael Lassell's narrative poem "How to Watch Your Brother Die" (Chapter 2):

> When the call comes, be calm.
> Say to your wife, "My brother is dying. I have to fly to California."
> Try not to be shocked that he already looks like a cadaver.
> Say to the young man sitting by your brother's side, "I'm his brother."
> Try not to be shocked when the young man says,
> "I'm his lover. Thanks for coming."

3. John Capecci deftly explored the performance opportunities in second-person narratives; his research informs the next few paragraphs. See the bibliography at the end of this chapter.

Two characteristics distinguish *second-person narration*. First, an explicit "you" partakes of the events within the tale. This "you" may be manifested directly in "your wife" or "your brother" or appear indirectly in the implied "you" in "When the call comes, [you] be calm." Second, two "clocks" appear to be running simultaneously within the story: the clock that times the events of the story and the clock that times the narrator's telling of the tale to the audience. For example, many hours—if not an entire day—occur between the point when "you" receive the call and when "you" walk into the hospital room to see "your brother"; in this narration, then, the clock was speeded up to get us to the hospital as rapidly as possible and, once we arrived, the clock returned to regular speed for "you" to see "your brother" and to meet the lover. The clock is flexible, then, and it colors what happens in the story.

These two characteristics (an explicit "you" involved in the tale and a flexible clock) can be manipulated in many different ways. Any attempt to classify all second-person narrators is bound to be incomplete. In addition, ingenious authors make categories still more troubling. For our purposes, however, we can identify four kinds of second-person narrators. Each gives a different answer to the questions "Who is the speaker *addressing?*" and "Who is the *you* being mentioned?"

1. The narrator may speak to someone *not* acting within the story who is within, or outside of, the situation being described—say, a patient addressing a therapist, describing a crucial event in the patient's life.

2. A narrator may specifically address someone who is clearly acting and involved in the story (as in Ann Beattie's "Snow," at the end of this chapter).

3. A narrator can really address himself or herself disguised as a "you," giving a confessional or highly personal impression ("How to Watch Your Brother Die" is an example).

4. There is the impersonal "you" with little or no specificity, the "you" of travel guides ("If you turn left at the next corner, Santa Cecilia will be the large building immediately in front of you") or cookbooks ("Now, you gradually fold in the beaten egg whites").

When you discover who "you" is and determine the essential characteristics of "you," you begin a rehearsal process that involves all of the challenges of storytelling. Once you know the type of second-person narrator, you can gauge the ambiguity operating in the work. Sometimes narrators leave details unspecified to give readers more room to fill in. You'll probably want to define clearly some things about "you"—the physical and vocal effects "you" has on the narrator, for example. The narrator needs clear definition. Because the story focuses on "you," clues about the speaking character's body and voice may *appear* elusive. Look carefully at the word choice of the narrator, at what details the narrator chooses to include and to exclude, and you will begin to discover the distinctive flesh and blood who is telling the tale.

Experiments with second-person narrators help us to understand our experiences with first- and third-person narrators. Such tales broaden the field of material available for performance and make immediate and tangible other, new ways for tellers to tell stories. Moreover, second-person narrators encourage creative solutions to performance problems.

Although there is much to recommend attempting a narrative featuring a second-person narrator, there are risks. If you are performing for audiences unfamiliar with the form, you will need to do some careful preparation during your introduction. The technical demands for clearly locating and placing the explicit "you" may require more rehearsal time than usual. The spontaneity of the narrator may make memorization necessary. None of these challenges ought to discourage you from the attempt, however; just take them up with open eyes.

Third-Person Narrators

You are probably most familiar with third-person narration: consider Chopin's "The Story of an Hour" (Chapter 2), Bowen's "The Little Girls" (Chapter 3), and Bissinger's "Friday Night Lights" (Chapter 4). Yet, for most beginning interpreters, this may be the most troubling narrative posture of all. The challenge arises chiefly because the narrator *seems* to fade from existence or to resemble some disembodied voice. It is easy to see who is speaking in first-person narratives, and the persona in second-person narratives is always mentioned (either directly or indirectly). Third-person narrators can *seem* like uninflected reporters simply stating facts. Don't be fooled by appearances. Third-person narrators are lively, full-blooded individuals who only *appear* to conceal themselves. Discovering the ways in which they make their presence known requires careful scrutiny, keen deductive powers, and a responsive imagination.

There are many different forms of third-person narrators, and any extended study of narration will require you to become familiar with all of them. For our purposes, we divide third-person narrators into two broadly inclusive groups: objective observers and omniscient observers. Generally, *objective observers* simply recount the events, incidents, dialogue, and activity that could be related by any reasonable individual present at the scene. *Omniscient observers* have all of these powers; in addition, they can access the internal life of a character or characters. Omniscience can be limited to one or a few characters. Although these narrators *can* tell us about the inner fears and hopes, concerns, past, and future of any character who interests them, they do not *have* to tell us, and in every case they choose the time to tell us. In all third-person narration, though, careful examination of diction, grammar, and syntax (as we learned in Chapter 5) helps reveal the narrators' personalities. Which events do they dwell on? Which do they pass over? Inspect the relationship they establish with the characters in their tales. Some careful deductions will begin to flesh out the personality who is telling a particular tale and whom you must communicate to your audience.

Look at the opening of Eudora Welty's *Losing Battles:*

When the rooster crowed, the moon had still not left the world but was going down on flushed cheek, one day short of the full. A long thin cloud crossed it slowly, drawing itself out like a name being called. The air changed, as if a mile or so away a wooden door had swung open, and a smell, more of warmth than wet, from a river at low stage, moved upward into the clay hills that stood in darkness.

Then a house appeared on its ridge, like an old man's silver watch pulled once more out of its pocket. A dog leaped up from where he'd lain like a stone and began barking for today as if he meant never to stop.

Then a baby bolted naked out of the house. She monkey-climbed down the steps and ran open-armed into the yard, knocking at the walls of flowers still colorless as faces, tagging in turn the four big trees that marked off the corners of the yard, tagging the gatepost, the well-piece, the birdhouse, the bell post, a log seat, a rope swing, and then, rounding the house, she used all her strength to push over a crate that let a stream of white Plymouth Rocks loose on the world. The chickens rushed ahead of the baby, running frantic, and behind the baby came a girl in a petticoat. A wide circle of curl-papers, paler than the streak of dawn, bounced around her head, but she ran on confident tiptoe as though she believed no eye could see her. She caught the baby and carried her back inside, the baby with her little legs still running like a windmill.

The distant point of the ridge, like the tongue of a calf, put its red lick on the sky. Mists, void, patches of woods and naked clay, flickered like live ashes, pink and blue. A mirror that hung within the porch on the house wall began to flicker as at the striking of kitchen matches. Suddenly two chinaberry trees at the foot of the yard lit up, like roosters astrut with golden tails. Caterpillar nets shone in the pecan tree. A swollen shadow bulked underneath it, familiar in shape as Noah's Ark—a school bus.

Then as if something came sliding out of the sky, the whole tin roof of the house ran with new blue. The posts along the porch softly bloomed downward, as if chalk marks were being drawn, one more time, down a still misty slate. The house was revealed as if standing there from pure memory against a now moonless sky. For the length of a breath, everything stayed shadowless, as under a lifting hand, and then a passage showed, running through the house, right through the middle of it, and at the head of the passage, in the center of the front gallery, a figure was revealed, a very old lady seated in a rocking chair with head cocked, as though wild to be seen.

Then Sunday light raced over the farm as fast as the chickens were fly-ing. Immediately the first straight shaft of heat, solid as a hickory stick, was laid on the ridge.

Miss Beulah Renfro came out of the passage at a trot and cried in the voice of alarm which was her voice of praise, "Granny! Up, dressed, and waiting for 'em! All by yourself! Why didn't you holler?"[4]

There is no "I" in this account of dawn in the rural South, but there is a very strong "eye." Even though this account is in the past tense, the om-niscient observer gives us a sense of immediacy. A distinct personality emerges as each sentence reveals details of the farm as well as the char-acter of the storyteller.

The passage is rich in imagery and metaphor. Ask yourself what sort of person is seeing this scene and describing it? What do the metaphors tell about the character of the narrator? The moon is going down "on flushed cheek." As the sun creeps nearer to the top of the ridge, the farm-house appears "like an old man's silver watch pulled once more out of its pocket." The dog has been lying "like a stone." The naked baby "monkey-climbed" down the steps. The narrator knows that the chickens let loose in the new light are Plymouth Rocks. The curl-papers in the girl's hair are "paler than the streak of dawn." The baby's legs are "running like a windmill." The point of the ridge is "like the tongue of a calf." The mirror on the porch wall begins to flicker "as at the striking of kitchen matches." The shadows of the porch posts are like "chalk marks . . . being drawn." The heat that comes with Sunday's first light is "solid as a hickory stick."

What kind of person uses such images? Is the speaker a stranger in these parts or a part of the world of the story? Do the images and metaphors arise out of the world of the story, or do they seem literary or sophisticated when compared with the setting and the characters?

Of course, the narrator knows the locale; the figures of comparison are homely, a part of the world of the story. The heat is solid like a hick-ory stick, an object that belongs to the people of the story, just like the bulky school bus and the shadows like chalk on slate. These metaphors all suggest the air of "country school" that hangs about the dawn in the rural South even on a Sunday. The narrator does not stand aloof from the characters and events in the story but seems rather to be a member of their community, one whose vision of this morning light is infused with affection for the land and its people.

Sometimes a film begins with wide shots that set the scene and give a sense of atmosphere before the camera moves in as the main charac-ters are introduced. Similarly, this narrator glides smoothly over the landmarks of the farm, as light glides, and saves till the end the charac-

4. Eudora Welty, *Losing Battles.*

ter who is to be the central figure in the novel: the old lady seated in the rocker. Granny, whose birthday celebration is the occasion of the novel, has been up and dressed long before dawn. She was sitting there from the first word of the description but is not mentioned until the sun is fully up, and its light, as well as the narrator's eye, reveals her.

We see, then, that third-person narration (like first-person narration) has both advantages and disadvantages. Objective observers clearly are for some the most reliable of storytellers, because all they tell is what has verifiably occurred. This "just the facts, nothing but the facts" approach can allow an audience to deduce relationships and attitudes and temperament for themselves. At the same time, this form of narration tends to be less gripping and can be difficult to sustain over a long tale. Omniscient observers—in all of the many forms this narrative type takes— ideally provide us with access to the past, future, and internal life of characters. Like all the other narrators, however, omniscient observers can withhold information at crucial times, and their interest in a given character may inhibit or even preclude equal interest in another character. Nevertheless, *both kinds of third-person narrators are real people.* A narrator does not have to appear as a character in a story to breathe, sympathize, or grieve. Personality cannot help but emerge in all the little details that reveal the soul. Certainly, clear attitudes, reflected in the words the narrator selects, the images the narrator chooses, the angle of vision the narrator employs, and the incidents themselves selected for narration, are all integral clues to the sensibility telling the tale.

What Is Going on Here? Action and Plot

Once you understand who is telling a story, you need to understand precisely what is going on, how the narrative moves, and where it is going. You should ask of every story, "What is its action?" *Action* is the sequence of visible or discernible physical happenings, the movement that courses through events. How is the action of a story different from its plot? *Plot* is the term used to describe the scheme or plan or design of the action. Plot orders action and arranges it in a pattern. The plot may involve psychological or physical action, and it may turn when one of the characters undergoes a change that affects the outcome of the story.

The *crisis* of a narrative is the turning point of the action. Like the fulcrum in a poem, the crisis serves as the "point of no return"; it is that point after which there can be only one possible resolution.

Conflict is essential in narrative; it causes action and plot. As you know, most works of literature involve people facing problems. (There's not much interest in people who are happy, at peace, and have nothing to do.) In both comedy and tragedy, characters face obstacles: comic characters tend to overcome their problems, and tragic characters succumb to them. There are, however, always some obstacles, some types of conflict. They may be internal and psychological, or external and social. Frequently, external and internal conflicts combine, one accenting the other or causing the other. Characters may fight city hall, nature, their in-laws, society, massive machines, repressive traditions, or even an idea whose time has come—but they all fight something.

Conflict need not be completely explained or absolutely real; there need not even be an absolute logic in the design of the events. But each element must obey the rules the story sets up for itself. Sometimes the shifts in time (of the kind that we discussed under "Second-Person Narrators") can confuse us. We are told the details of the events in the order the narrator chooses, which need not be the order in which they occurred. Narrators can refrain from telling us something—like the fact that Granny was up and dressed before the narrator began to speak in *Losing Battles*—or they can skip back and forth between events and make what happened at very different times *seem* to be immediate (listen to the narrator of Harlan Coben's "The Key to My Father" at the end of this chapter).

The shifts in time may seem illogical *outside* the tale, but meaning arises from the way in which the timing makes sense to the narrator. Similarly, characters can engage in behavior that may mystify us, but that behavior never puzzles the narrator in the same way. Characters do whatever odd or normal thing they do because the narrator wants it that way, wouldn't have it any other way, and (in fact!) planned it that way all along. So, the child in David Leavitt's *The Lost Language of Cranes* responds only to the angular movements and jagged sounds of cranes. The man and woman seem unfazed by the violent end their quarreling ensures in Raymond Carver's "Popular Mechanics." (Both selections appear at the end of this chapter.) Obviously, characters do what they must to live in the worlds of their stories. If narratives—indeed, if any works of art—can be said to obey rules at all, they obey the rules they set for themselves.

What Sort of People Live in This Story? Character

At this point in our analysis, you have discovered who is telling the story and the general action (as ordered in the plot) of the tale itself. Now, discover what sort of people the story is about. Without a narrator, of course, there would be no action; without action, the characters would have nothing to do. Indeed, there would be no characters, because we understand characters by examining what they do, what they say, and what others say about them. First and last, it is the people we encounter—the characters—who grasp us most when we read.

Narrative creates character through action. We learn about people from what others—including the narrator—say about them. We learn about character from the manner in which the narrator supplies all this information. (Setting, which we discuss later, also affects people and personality.) Most often personality, habit, and response motivate a character to react to the forces that shape a story.

A third-person narrator may tell you all you need to know about a character's appearance, behavior, speech, or thoughts. To consolidate these clues, add material from your own life and experiences. Be sure to understand exactly why characters refer to each other in the manner they do. If Clara calls George a "bonehead," you'll want to know what George calls her before you take her word as truth. Unreliable first-person narrators often change the truth of an event to suit their preferences.

Some of the characters whom you encounter may be simple. Depth and development of character are not requirements for successful stories. Little Red Riding Hood simply wants to get to her grandmother's house, and the tortoise beats the hare chiefly because he doesn't stop to munch a carrot. Not much more is needed, since the situation itself or the attitude of the storyteller to the events is what interests us. (See Macourek's "Jacob's Chicken" at the end of this chapter.)

Fuller characters—those that E. M. Forster calls "round characters"[5]—require an internal life that both corresponds to and illumines the external makeup of the character. Sometimes the physical lives of the characters predominate; sometimes the psychological components are primary. Most often, both aspects together sketch the outlines of the character—as happens with Tony/Tommy in Bernard Malamud's "The Prison" (at the end of this chapter). Whatever component is emphasized, in performance the characters must be totalities. Only for purposes of analysis can we separate their components. As in life, so in narrative: the character is greater than the sum of his or her attributes.

What Are They Saying to Each Other? Dialogue

Almost every narrator at some point allows the characters to speak for themselves, providing the audience immediate access to the scene of the story, affording variety through distinctive personalities and speech rhythms, and emphasizing vividness in characterization. Although it

5. E. M. Forster, *Aspects of the Novel* (New York: Harcourt, Brace and Company, 1927).

may be useful for the writer and seductive to the reader, dialogue can cause trouble for the interpreter.

Dialogue may be in the form of direct discourse, indirect discourse, or narrator-transformed discourse. *Direct discourse* is the verbatim recording of the words the character is speaking. It is usually marked by quotation marks, although you cannot always depend on authors to use them; in "Popular Mechanics" Raymond Carver doesn't. Dialogue tags like "she said" are not much help either, for they do not always precede or follow a speech. Direct discourse introduces in the place of narration the total presence of a character, as if the narrator has momentarily stepped aside to allow the character to assume fully the telling of the tale. Characters speak because they wish to be heard, if only by themselves. (Isn't that one reason why you talk to yourself?) Audiences should always be aware of who is speaking and who is listening and the listener's effect on the speaker.

Indirect discourse reports the words the characters spoke and depends on an articulated or assumed "that." For example, in "she admitted she loved and adored chocolate cake," only the first two words are unquestionably pure narration. The remainder blends both the narrator's reporting and the character's declaration. Thus, in performance the interpreter must make clear who is speaking by suggesting the personality of the character through the skillful use of body, voice, and the appropriate mental and physical attitude while not neglecting the narrator.

Indirect discourse blends the presence of the narrator with the presence of the character, so that narrator and character seem to be seen and heard simultaneously. The degree to which the narrator adopts the language, diction, and sentiments of the character guides the blend of narrator and character that the audience sees and hears. A remembered remark, for example, would carry less of the character's attitude than a reiterated demand would, although the narrator and character appear in both cases. Narrators commonly use indirect discourse in either simple grammatical sentences like "He said that . . ." or in more complex forms such as "She remembered having heard him say that. . . ."

To clarify, examine this sentence from Flannery O'Connor's "Greenleaf":

(1)   "I thank God for ever thang," said Mr. Greenleaf.

Now compare it with these two sentences:

(2)   Mr. Greenleaf said that he thanked God for ever thang.
(3)   Then Greenleaf acknowledged divine providence.

Sentence 1 clearly demonstrates direct discourse: from the opening quotation marks the character fully assumes the line, and the narrator does not reappear until the dialogue tag at the end of the sentence. Sentence 2 blends the character and the narrator; but because the narrator has clearly adopted the characteristic diction and figures of speech of the character ("ever thang"), this sentence demonstrates more of the character's attitude than the narrator's, an example of indirect discourse. Sentence 3 has a narrator who has retained only the character's idea and has transformed it into his or her own language—language that is much more sophisticated than the character's. In performance this would be seen as a narrator who dominates, but does not obliterate, the character as is typical in narrator-transformed discourse. In each of these cases, though, remember that your decisions on how to perform a line rest on stylistic as well as literal clues, since style reveals background, attitudes, and the degree of mental or emotional tension of the moment.

Understanding the differences among these three kinds of discourse can help you understand the various technical ways in which an interpreter can persuade an audience to believe that they are seeing before them not a student in a class but a character in a story. To achieve such belief, you must solve the technical problems that arise from performing dialogue. We discuss some of the techniques here. Because techniques for creating character are useful in narration as well as drama, look also at the section "Embodying Characters" in Chapter 8, page 343.

Creating Character

Remember that characters are persons with bodies and voices. Read the story carefully to find all of the clues the narrator gives about the characters in the story. Note carefully the kinds of language the characters use, the kinds of things others say to and about the characters. Then begin to observe—very carefully—the world around you.

Have you ever had to use crutches? What did it feel like? Have you ever tried to descend stairs using them? Have you observed a close friend or family member trying to cope with the shifting weight and awkward movement that always seem to accompany the use of crutches? Your own age and gender are immaterial at this point, but when you have some of these clues, you have begun to characterize "Eva" in Toni Morrison's heart-wrenching *Sula* (at the end of this chapter). But you have only *just* begun. Now, start listening closely to women's speech—especially to older, African American women. What vocal patterns can you detect? Begin to play with your voice. See if you can make yourself sound as if you had lived Eva's past. Your first efforts are not likely to be pretty, but have courage and stay with it. Next, try to add your body. You might feel out of place if you are not African American and not female. How can you make *your* body resemble that of someone on crutches? With a voice and body it is often much easier to understand what makes characters tick, and you will have a firm foundation on which to create richer people. If you stay with *Sula* (and we recommend it highly), you will have to repeat the process with Eva's son, Plum, a teenage addict so strung out on drugs that he slips easily between the world he inhabits with his mother and the world he creates in his intoxication. He will have an entirely different body and voice; Morrison gives us many rich clues. And still other characters live in the story, so you must duplicate the process for each of them, too.

You have established some external characteristics for the audience, but these will simply be externals until you provide the personality that sparks the voice and body to life. Are you thinking about these people in the worlds that they inhabit? Have you examined the part they play in the action of the tale?

Of course, no character exists apart from a story. That is why you should know as much as possible about the persons you are performing. Review the whole story. Glean whatever clues you can from the information given, remembering that this overall view places the characters in proper perspective. Determine the character's gender, age, and maturity. Then define the personal characteristics that distinguish the character's attitude, degree of emotional intensity, and any peculiar or important personal traits. Be sure to notice explicit descriptions about how words are spoken or what state of mind has prompted them. Narrative writing is uniquely able to stop action and examine motive. Don't miss the implicit clues contained in the style of the speech, in the narrator's understanding of and sympathy with the character, and in the way in which the character's position is presented to the audience. Finally, remember that however bizarre these characters may seem to you, they are real in their own worlds. Create them to live there on their terms, not within your world. Here concentration will become increasingly important; only if you commit yourself to the character's life can your audience fully perceive the character's goals. Once you have completed this process for one speaking character, repeat it for all the major characters in the passage you are reading.

When you perform dialogue, imagine vividly the person who is being addressed, and *speak directly* to that person. See that person vividly in front of you, established at a position slightly above and beyond the audience. (See "Placing Action Out Front," in Chapter 2, page 35.) This technique permits the audience to sit in the middle of the tension that ties the characters together and that prompts them to speak. It also protects any particular audience member from feeling directly addressed. Your mental and vocal projection should therefore be strong enough to carry slightly beyond the last row. When you resume the words of the narrator and describe or summarize, you will be able to speak directly to your audience and to establish rapport with them. If several characters speak in rapid succession, establish a place (a point of focus) for each of them, once again slightly above and beyond the audience. You may wish to consult Chapter 8, particularly the section "Physical Focus" (page 350), for further discussion of the ways to solve this kind of problem.

Dialogue has different levels of intensity. Seek the degree of forcefulness that suggests the character's emotional and psychological state at the moment of speaking. Casual comments can be delivered with less power than are pleas for freedom but can be awesome in their impact (as are Eva's last words to her son in *Sula*). Mind you, *mental* focus does not relax, but people ask for the butter more often than they scream for help. The key is spontaneity, since it acknowledges the other characters and motivates responses.

Although you may feel at this point that there isn't anything else you can learn about a story, much remains to be understood.

Where Is All This Taking Place? Setting

Setting is a matter not only of locale but also of style. Narrators see the world through various spectacles. Where they allow their characters to interact and speak is as much a part of the tale as it is a choice of the teller. If we learn that "Aunt Tillie Beta pours her tea each afternoon as the sun strikes four against the walnut bureau," we see not only the aunt's habit but also her residence; the narrator acknowledges her ritual by permitting the sun to toll its time as solemnly as a clock. Compare that serenity to the following sentence that Dylan Thomas employs in one of the stories from *Quite Early One Morning*:

> I was born in a large Welsh town at the beginning of the Great War—an ugly, lovely town (or so it was and is to me), crawling by a long and splendid curving shore where truant boys and sandfield boys and old men from nowhere, beach-combed, idled and paddled, watched the dock-bound ships or the ships steaming away into wonder and India, magic and China, countries bright with oranges and loud with lions; threw stones into the sea for the barking outcast dogs; made castles and forts and harbours and race tracks in the sand; and on Saturday summer afternoons listened to the brass band, watched the Punch and Judy, or hung about on the fringes of the crowd to hear the fierce religious speakers who shouted at the sea, as though it were wicked and wrong to roll in and out like that, whitehorsed and full of fishes.[6]

6. Dylan Thomas, *Quite Early One Morning* (New York: New Directions, 1954).

What an abundance of things to see and hear and smell and touch! And the rush of activity—presented in one massive, breathless sentence—surrounds the reader utterly. Notice how Thomas couples the items in the catalog: the town is ugly *and* lovely; boys *and* old men beach-comb, idle, *and* paddle; the sea that licks that splendid shore carries men to wonder *and* magic. Also, brass bands *and* summers; puppet plays *and* town prophets; charging *and* pulling seas finally full of nothing scarier than fishes: what a wonderful, breathless world he envisions!

To perform the story, you need to capture that world. Develop a keen visual and physical sense, so that in performance the whirling scene is all around you and your audience. Don't utter the first syllable until you see it all. Let your audience see the shore and the boys, and then (as in an aerial shot in a film) move to the ships and the stones, and continue on through the town. A gesture by the narrator might locate those most important places as they pass before you; let that palpable, living world motivate your description. Put Thomas's world there, in front of you. Tell your listeners about it!

Although not every scene is as boisterous as this one, every scene affects the characters as it locates the action. Travel and adventure stories, in particular, use place as a crucial element in the telling of the tale because landscape, climate, and time of day inevitably affect the characters. Biographies and autobiographies, histories and historical fiction—all depend on an audience's acceptance of the vividness of the period, a sense that life was lived fully. Even the most fantastic story uses setting as an element to persuade an audience of the internal reality of the world of the tale, affecting the characters in obvious or subtle, superficial or profound ways.

Cutting and Excerpting

Only rarely does a poem, story, or play fit exactly all of the many requirements that performers impose on texts: the right length, balance of characters, distribution of lines and action, and level of challenge. Consequently, interpreters take on works that, in one way or another, do not measure up. They must cut or excerpt the text.

As we have stressed, interpretation seeks to communicate a work of literary art in its intellectual, aesthetic, and emotional entirety. This does not necessarily mean that you must perform every syllable of a work; indeed, the *essence* of an entire piece of literature can successfully be conveyed through performance of only a selection from it. We distinguish between excerpting a segment from a longer work and cutting, or abridging, a work in an attempt to encompass the entire work in a short amount of time. Guard against the problems and dangers in both methods.

In *excerpting* from a longer work, the interpreter chooses a scene or passage that, when taken on its own, displays a totality of action, theme, or character development. Toni Cade Bambara's "The Lesson" (Chapter 3) offers several episodes that can be successfully excerpted, as does Philip Roth's "The Conversion of the Jews" (at the end of this chapter). In each of these selections, various brief segments seem to be relatively complete. In excerpting a segment, supply—in a *brief* introduction or in transitional comments—all the information necessary for the audience to understand fully what has happened to that point in the story. *Leave the segment itself uncut.* Don't make interlinear or internal cuts, since you've selected the segment specifically because it conforms to the various requirements imposed by the particular performance situation.

A long chapter that boasts a particularly attractive opening scene and a vivid conclusion might tempt an interpreter to splice the two sections together. However, the splicing itself can dangerously impair the delicate rhythms established by the author. Why not admit frankly that you are presenting two scenes from the same chapter? Perform the whole compelling opening; then, in your own words, fill in the transition with whatever information is necessary for the audience to understand the conclusion, which you then perform as the author wrote it. This method has at least three special benefits. First, you can more accurately suggest the intellectual, aesthetic, and emotional entirety of the complete work because you have not tampered with the internal tempo or development of its segments. Second, you can deal with the smaller segments more effectively in short periods of rehearsal time. Finally, because the segments themselves are more easily manageable, you have a better chance of capturing your audience's attention and appreciation. Best of all, of course, is the fact that excerpting allows you to select scenes from any work of literature that you want. You'll never perform all of *Moby Dick* (at least for one audience), but numerous crucial scenes within that novel can be presented rewardingly.

Cutting differs from excerpting in that it imposes on diverse or unrelated words, lines, or scenes a false consecutiveness or immediate relationship not intended or prepared by the author. Some interpreters refuse to eliminate anything from what they perform because they do not wish to impose on the work a pattern or scheme that violates its integrity. For other interpreters, cutting presents no particular problem. A performance may be restricted by time, by financial or physical resources, or sometimes by the intent of the performance. Whatever the limitations, approach the task of cutting literature with respect and concern. The life of the work you seek to communicate in performance is at stake.

You should be fully aware of all of the problems that cutting can create. Of course, cutting a character who has one or two lines, such as a maid or an attendant lord whose chief responsibility is to announce an arrival or present a prop, usually does not impair the excitement of the scene. Be sure, however, that the arriving character or the prop is not central to the scene itself.

Tempo and rhythm can be destroyed when you cut carelessly. Recall Mrs. Mallard's discovery of the new life approaching her in Kate Chopin's "The Story of an Hour" (Chapter 2). At one point Mrs. Mallard says, "Free, free, free!" and later "Free! Body and soul free!" The performer needs these repetitions to demonstrate her growing awareness; cutting them entirely (or even in part) would alter the delicate rhythm that Chopin's narrator establishes. Recognize the care with which Miloš Macourek uses repetition to establish his narrator in "Jacob's Chicken." You may think that the repetitions merely restate the same things; rather, they delightfully reveal the speaker's enthusiasms and character. Cutting them would kill the story.

A cut that may seem small and insignificant can strongly affect the sense of the story. You may be tempted to cut the final paragraph of the excerpt from Maya Angelou's *I Know Why the Caged Bird Sings* (Chapter 5). After all, the turmoil is over and the preceding paragraph ends nicely with the final image of the congregation saying "Amen." Still, that final paragraph relates Reverend Taylor's decision on the following Sunday to take as his text St. Luke's account of the Pharisees, a pointed reference to (though missed by) his flock. If you cut the final paragraph, you miss the "what happened next" of the story.

So alter a text with care and tact. We do not say that you should never cut. Sensitive and experienced interpreters undertake cutting with great caution. If they can avoid cutting, they do so. Think carefully and completely about what you are about to do. Don't let cutting be your choice simply because it seems you'll never master the line. Judge honestly what you will gain and what you will lose if you eliminate a line or a few sentences.

Analyzing the Rehearsal and the Performance

Before we concentrate on how successfully you performed narration and prose, review the questions in the "Analyzing the Rehearsal and the Performance" sections in Chapters 2 and 4. Recall the problems that cropped up in your earlier readings. Have you improved your ability to concentrate? Have you paid clear and consistent attention to variety and contrast? Has your voice contributed to the unity and harmony of the selection? Has your body become more responsive to the imagery, particularly the kinesthetic images of your selection?

Such questions will never disappear from your performance analysis because whatever literature you select will challenge you in new and exciting ways. Don't allow yourself to become discouraged if some aspect of your performance seems to resist improvement. Some skills require considerably more effort than may be apparent. No one is instantly proficient at playing tennis or the violin. Constant, careful, and consistent concentration and commitment will produce the kinds of results you anticipate.

One further thought about progress: Be sure to listen carefully to and watch closely every other performer you can. You can always learn something instructive. Don't, however, measure your own progress against that of others in your class. You are better off gauging your developing prowess against the fine difficulty of the works you choose to perform. The most significant development in performance comes from valiant efforts with literature that cause you to reach slightly beyond your grasp. Nothing is gained by repeating the easy.

If you have not yet begun to experiment, why not do so? If you have performed only verse thus far, now is the time to try prose. Have you been concentrating on contemporary literature? Try a passage from one of the classic authors. Have you yet attempted personae whose gender is opposite to yours? What about characters of different ages and backgrounds and dialects? The function of any class in oral interpretation is not to confirm you in your ability to perform melancholy young women disappointed in love or brash and joking dudes who always crack up audiences. Rather, oral interpretation asks that you experience all of the human condition. Keep exploring yourself and your performance possibilities.

Now, together let's explore some common problems in performing prose. Again, try to respond to the questions as honestly as you can. Ask a classmate to help.

- Did your analysis of the style of the writer suggest physical and vocal analogies to the literature? How did your compound and complex sentences look and sound?

- Did your body and voice manifest the personality apparent in the speaker's word choice? Were you consistent?

- Did you balance each sentence, locating the precise point for the most efficient placement of the fulcrum?

- Did you control your physical and vocal resources to shape each sentence (and each paragraph) to the shape of the thought?

- Were you attentive to parallel structure? Did you carefully attend to each speech phrase?

- Did you allow your body and voice to reflect the fullest possible engagement with the tone color?

- Did you carefully construct an internal and external life for your narrator? Was your audience always certain who was in charge? Did you permit the narrator to relinquish dominance during passages of scene and discourse?

- Were your characters as full-blooded as those of the narrator? Did your narrator blend into the characters in the passage? Why?

- Did you center the narrator's interest on the action and plot? Were your body and voice in control of the events?

- Did the dialogue passages seem spontaneous and unforced? Was your audience certain who was speaking?

- Did you excerpt without internal cutting?

These questions can also help you focus on the performance of others. In your classroom discussion, try to describe as precisely as possible at least two or three of the following concerns:

1. The nature of the narrator you *saw* and *heard:* his or her age and attitude toward events, characters, setting, and the audience to whom the tale is told

2. The relationships between the narrator and the characters, as demonstrated by the performer

3. The internal and external lives of the narrator and characters, as demonstrated by the performer

4. Performance behavior that gave life to personalities in the story

5. Facility in the management of dialogue, as demonstrated by the performer

6. The immediacy of the tale being told, as it is shown in the performance

When differences of opinion arise, return to the literature being performed. Your job as critic is to describe what you saw and heard and then to compare that performance with the text you know. Possibly you have performed the same passage yourself and thus know some of the problems more thoroughly than your classmates. Still, keep your attention directed to what happened in the performance you *saw* and *heard*, not to what might have happened or what didn't happen. It isn't very helpful to say to a performer, "I didn't see any anger in Rosa's response to Tommy." Rather, try to describe exactly what you did see and hear—for example, "I saw a Rosa who seemed very calm and relaxed; your rate and volume were very easygoing." Once you combine your responses with those of other audience members and with those of the performer, reexamine the story to find precisely how Rosa ought to sound and behave.

Performing takes courage. If you want to improve, it helps to feel secure enough with your fellow students to experiment. Such freedom is difficult to achieve if you expect to get "torn apart" each time you perform. Discussion of a performance permits everyone to learn *if* everyone listens carefully and everyone thinks for a moment before speaking. Any given performance is a step on the route to the best possible performance. If you genuinely want to be helped by your classmates, be genuinely helpful in what you say to them.

REMEMBER THIS!

The texture and richness of a good storyteller, we have learned, is the product of a number of qualities working simultaneously—in the story and in performance. Don't lose sight of the following crucial elements when you create the narrator in the tale you select:

- A clear sense of point of view: Is my narrator a first-person narrator (observing or participating, a second-person narrator, or a third-person narrator (objective or omniscient)?

- A full sense of audience: Who is my narrator talking to?

- A firm grasp of character: What kind of people live in this story, what do they do with each other, and what are their relationships?

- A confident command of dialogue: Is the character speaking directly, indirectly, or through the narrator's transformation?

- A thorough understanding of setting: How does where the characters interact affect what they do and what they say?

- Deferential scissors when cutting or excerpting: Did I cut as little as possible, and did I endanger the literature?

There are a lot of narrators waiting to be brought to life!

Selections for Analysis and Oral Interpretation

Because the narrator in this story understands Tommy's frustration much better than Tommy himself does, the audience receives a rich and complex picture of the young man's entrapment, his grim existence, and his future. Pay careful attention to the ways in which Bernard Malamud's language indicates shifts in the closeness of narrator and central character.

The Prison

BERNARD MALAMUD

Though he tried not to think of it, at twenty-nine Tommy Castelli's life was a screaming bore. It wasn't just Rosa or the store they tended for profits counted in pennies, or the unendurably slow hours and endless drivel that went with selling candy, cigarettes, and soda water; it was this sick-in-the-stomach feeling of being trapped in old mistakes, even some he had made before Rosa changed Tony into Tommy. He had been as Tony a kid of many dreams and schemes, especially getting out of this tenement-crowded, kid-squawking neighborhood, with its lousy poverty, but everything had fouled up against him before he could. When he was sixteen he quit the vocational school where they were making him into a shoemaker, and began to hang out with the gray-hatted, thick-soled-shoe boys, who had the spare time and the mazuma and showed it in fat wonderful rolls down in the cellar clubs to all who would look, and everybody did, popeyed. They were the ones who had bought the silver caffe espresso urn and later the television, and they arranged the pizza parties and had the girls down; but it was getting in with them and their cars, leading to the holdup of a liquor store, that had started all the present trouble. Lucky for him the coal-and-ice man who was their landlord knew the leader in the district, and they arranged something so nobody bothered him after that. Then before he knew what was going on—he had been frightened sick by the whole mess—there was his father cooking up a deal with Rosa Agnello's old man that Tony would marry her and the father-in-law would, out of his savings, open a candy store for him to make an honest living. He wouldn't spit on a candy store, and Rosa was too plain and lank a chick for his personal taste, so he beat it off to Texas and bummed around in too much space, and when he came back everybody said it was for Rosa and the candy store, and it was all arranged again and he, without saying no, was in it.

That was how he had landed on Prince Street in the Village, working from eight in the morning to almost midnight every day, except for an hour off each afternoon when he went upstairs to sleep; and on Tuesdays, when the store was closed and he slept some more and went at night alone to the movies. He was too tired always for schemes now, but once he tried to make a little cash on the side by secretly taking in punchboards some syndicate was distributing in the neighborhood, on which he collected a nice cut and in this way saved fifty-five bucks that Rosa didn't know about; but then the syndicate was written up by a newspaper, and the punchboards all disappeared. Another time, when Rosa was at her mother's house, he took a chance and let them put in a slot machine that could guarantee a nice piece of change if he kept it long enough. He knew of course he couldn't hide it from her, so when she came and screamed when she saw it, he was ready and patient, for once not yelling back when she yelled, and he explained it was not the same as gambling because anybody who played it got a roll of mints every time he put in a nickel. Also the machine would supply them a few extra dollars cash they could use to buy television so he could see the fights without going to a bar; but Rosa wouldn't let up screaming, and later her father came in shouting that he was a criminal and chopped the machine apart with a plumber's hammer. The next day the cops raided for slot machines and gave out summonses wherever they found them, and though Tommy's place was practically the only candy store in the neighborhood that didn't have one, he felt bad about the machine for a long time.

Mornings had been his best time of day because Rosa stayed upstairs cleaning, and since few people came into the store till noon, he could sit around alone, a toothpick in his teeth, looking over the *News* and *Mirror* on the fountain counter, or maybe gab with one of the old cellar-club guys who had happened to come by for a pack of butts, about a horse that was running that day or how the numbers were paying lately; or just sit there, drinking coffee and thinking how far away he could get on the fifty-five he had stashed away in the cellar. Generally the mornings were this way, but after the slot machine, usually the whole day stank and he along with it. Time rotted in him, and all he could think of the whole morning, was going to sleep in the afternoon, and he would wake up with the sour remembrance of the long night in the store ahead of him, while everybody else was doing as he damn pleased. He cursed the candy store and Rosa, and cursed, from its beginning, his unhappy life.

It was on one of these bad mornings that a ten-year-old girl from around the block came in and asked for two rolls of colored tissue paper, one red and one yellow. He wanted to tell her to go to hell and stop bothering, but instead went with bad grace to the rear, where Rosa, whose bright idea it was to keep the stuff, had put it. He went from force of habit, for the girl had been coming in every Monday since the summer for the same thing, because her rock-faced mother, who looked as if she arranged her own widowhood, took care of some small kids after school and gave them the paper to cut out dolls and such things. The girl, whose name he didn't know, resembled her mother, except her features were not quite so sharp and she had very light skin with dark eyes; but she was a plain kid and would be more so at twenty. He had noticed, when he went to get the paper, that she always hung back as if afraid to go where it was dark, though he kept the comics there and most of the other kids had to be slapped away from them; and that when he brought her the tissue paper her skin seemed to grow whiter and her eyes shone. She always handed him two hot dimes and went out without glancing back.

It happened that Rosa, who trusted nobody, had just hung a mirror on the back wall, and as Tommy opened the drawer to get the girl her paper this Monday morning that he felt so bad, he looked up and saw in the glass something that made it seem as if he were dreaming. The girl had disappeared, but he saw a white hand reach into the candy case for a chocolate bar and for another, then she came forth from behind the counter and stood there, innocently waiting for him. He felt at first like grabbing her by the neck and socking till she threw up, but he had been caught, as he sometimes was, by this thought of how his Uncle Dom, years ago before he went away, used to take with him Tony alone of all the kids, when he went crabbing to Sheepshead Bay. Once they went at night and threw the baited wire traps into the water and after a while pulled them up and they had this green lobster in one, and just then this fat-faced cop came along and said they had to throw it back unless it was nine inches. Dom said it was nine inches, but the cop said not to be a wise guy so Dom measured it and it was ten, and they laughed about that lobster all night. Then he remembered how he had felt after Dom was gone, and tears filled his eyes. He found himself thinking about the way his life had turned out, and then about this girl, moved that she was so young and a thief. He felt he ought to do something for her, warn her to cut it out before she got trapped and fouled up her life before it got started. His urge to do this was strong, but when he went forward she looked up frightened because he had taken so long. The fear in her eyes bothered him and he didn't say anything. She thrust out the dimes, grabbed at the tissue rolls and ran out of the store.

He had to sit down. He kept trying to make the desire to speak to her go away, but it came back stronger than ever. He asked himself what difference does it make if she swipes candy—so she swipes it; and the role of reformer was strange and distasteful to him, yet he could not convince himself that what he felt he must do was unimportant. But he worried he would not know what to say to her. Always he had trouble speaking right, stumbled over words, especially in new situations. He was afraid he would sound like a jerk and she would not take him seriously. He had to tell her in a sure way so that even if it scared her, she would understand he had done it to set her straight. He mentioned her to no one but often thought about her, always looking around whenever he went outside to raise the awning or wash the window, to see if any of the girls playing in the street was her, but they never were. The following Monday, an hour after opening the store he had smoked a full pack of butts. He thought he had found what he wanted to say but was afraid for some reason she wouldn't come in, or if she did, this time she would be afraid to take the candy. He wasn't sure he wanted that to happen until he had said what he had to say. But at about eleven, while he was reading the *News,* she appeared, asking for the tissue paper, her eyes shining so he had to look away. He knew she meant to steal. Going to the rear he slowly opened the drawer, keeping his head lowered as he sneaked a look into the glass and saw her slide behind the counter. His heart beat hard and his feet felt nailed to the floor. He tried to remember what he had intended to do, but his mind was like a dark, empty room so he let her, in the end, slip away and stood tongue-tied, the dimes burning his palm.

Afterwards, he told himself that he hadn't spoken to her because it was while she still had the candy on her, and she would have been scared worse than he wanted. When he went upstairs, instead of sleeping, he sat at the kitchen window, looking out into the back yard. He blamed himself for being too soft, too chicken, but then he thought, no there was a better way to do it. He would do it indirectly, slip her a hint he knew, and he was pretty sure that would stop her. Sometime after, he would explain to her why it was good she had stopped. So next time he cleaned out this candy platter she helped herself from, thinking she might get wise he was on to her, but she seemed not to, only hesitated with her hand before she took two candy bars from the next plate and dropped them into the black patent leather purse she always had with her. The time after that he cleaned out the whole top shelf, and still she was not suspicious, and reached down to the next and took something different. One Monday he put some loose change, nickels and dimes, on the candy plate, but she left them there, only taking the candy, which bothered him a little. Rosa asked him what he was mooning about so much and why was he eating chocolate lately. He didn't answer her, and she began to look suspiciously at the women who came in, not excluding the little girls; and he would have been glad to rap her in the teeth, but it didn't matter as long as she didn't know what he had on his mind. At the same time he figured he would have to do something sure soon, or it would get harder for the girl to stop her stealing. He had to be strong about it. Then he thought of a plan that satisfied him. He would leave two bars on the plate and put in the wrapper of one a note she could read when she was alone. He tried out on paper many messages to her, and the one that seemed best he cleanly printed on a strip of cardboard and slipped it under the wrapper of one chocolate bar. It said, "Don't do this any more or you will suffer your whole life." He puzzled whether to sign it A Friend or Your Friend and finally chose Your Friend.

This was Friday, and he could not hold his impatience for Monday. But on Monday she did not appear. He waited for a long time, until Rosa came down, then he had to go up and the girl still hadn't come. He was greatly disappointed because she had never failed to come before. He lay on the bed, his shoes on, staring at the ceiling. He felt hurt, the sucker she had played him for and was now finished with because she probably had another on her hook. The more he thought about it the worse he felt. He worked up a splitting headache that kept him from sleeping, then he suddenly slept and woke without it. But he had awaked depressed, saddened. He thought about Dom getting out of jail and going away God knows where. He wondered whether he would ever meet up with him somewhere, if he took the fifty-five bucks and left. Then he remembered Dom was a pretty old guy now, and he might not know him if they did meet. He thought about life. You never really got what you wanted. No matter how hard you tried you made mistakes and couldn't get past them. You could never see the sky outside or the ocean because you were in a prison, except nobody called it a prison, and if you did they didn't know what you were talking about, or they said they didn't. A pall settled on him. He lay motionless, without thought or sympathy for himself or anybody.

But when he finally went downstairs, ironically amused that Rosa had allowed him so long a time off without bitching, there were people in the store and he could hear her screeching. Shoving his way through the crowd he saw in one sickening look that she had caught the girl with the candy bars and was shaking her so hard the kid's head bounced back and forth like a balloon on a stick. With a curse he tore her away from the girl, whose sickly face showed the depth of her fright.

"Whatsamatter," he shouted at Rosa, "you want her blood?"

"She's a thief," cried Rosa.

"Shut your face."

To stop her yowling he slapped her across her mouth, but it was a harder crack than he had intended. Rosa fell back with a gasp. She did not cry but looked around dazedly at everybody, and tried to smile, and everybody there could see her teeth were flecked with blood.

"Go home," Tommy ordered the girl, but then there was a movement near the door and her mother came into the store.

"What happened?" she said.

"She stole my candy," Rosa cried.

"I let her take it," said Tommy.

Rosa stared at him as if she had been hit again, then with mouth distorted began to sob.

"One was for you, Mother," said the girl.

Her mother socked her hard across the ear. "You little thief, this time you'll get your hands burned good."

She pawed at the girl, grabbed her arm and yanked it. The girl, like a grotesque dancer, half-ran, half-fell forward, but at the door she managed to turn her white face and thrust out at him her red tongue.

- How did you embody the relationship between the narrator and Tommy?

- How much of Tommy did we see during indirect discourse? How does that change during the story?

The narrator of this story by John Updike treats us as his friends, and the events he tells us about have affected him deeply, but he is not lugubrious. Don't let him become overbearing or dimwitted, either. Why does he quit his job?

 A & P

JOHN UPDIKE

In walks these three girls in nothing but bathing suits. I'm in the third checkout slot, with my back to the door, so I don't see them until they're over by the bread. The one that caught my eye first was the one in the plaid green two-piece. She was a chunky kid, with a good tan and a sweet broad soft-looking can with those two crescents of white just under it, where the sun never seems to hit, at the top of the backs of her legs. I stood there with my hand on a box of HiHo crackers trying to remember if I rang it up or not. I ring it up again and the customer starts giving me hell. She's one of these cash-register-watchers, a witch about fifty with rouge on her cheekbones and no eyebrows, and I know it made her day to trip me up. She'd been watching cash registers for fifty years and probably never seen a mistake before.

By the time I got her feathers smoothed and her goodies into a bag—she gives me a little snort in passing, if she'd been born at the right time they would have burned her over in Salem—by the time I get her on her way the girls had circled around the bread and were coming back, without a pushcart, back my way along the counters, in the aisle between the checkouts and the Special bins. They didn't

even have shoes on. There was this chunky one, with the two-piece—it was bright green and the seams on the bra were still sharp and her belly was still pretty pale so I guessed she just got it (the suit)—there was this one, with one of those chubby berry-faces, the lips all bunched together under her nose, this one, and a tall one, with black hair that hadn't quite frizzed right, and one of these sunburns right across under the eyes, and a chin that was too long—you know, the kind of girl other girls think is very "striking" and "attractive" but never quite makes it, as they very well know, which is why they like her so much—and then the third one, that wasn't quite so tall. She was the queen. She kind of led them, the other two peeking around and making their shoulders round. She didn't look around, not this queen, she just walked straight on slowly, on these long white prima-donna legs. She came down a little hard on her heels, as if she didn't walk in her bare feet that much, putting down her heels and then letting the weight move along to her toes as if she was testing the floor with every step, putting a little deliberate extra action into it. You never know for sure how girls' minds work (do you really think it's a mind in there or just a little buzz like a bee in a glass jar?) but you got the idea she had talked the other two into coming in here with her, and now she was showing them how to do it, walk slow and hold yourself straight.

She had on a kind of dirty-pink—beige maybe, I don't know—bathing suit with a little nubble all over it and, what got me, the straps were down. They were off her shoulders looped loose around the cool tops of her arms, and I guess as a result the suit had slipped a little on her, so all around the top of the cloth there was this shining rim. If it hadn't been there you wouldn't have known there could have been anything whiter than those shoulders. With the straps pushed off, there was nothing between the top of the suit and the top of her head except just *her,* this clean bare plane of the top of her chest down from the shoulder bones like a dented sheet of metal tilted in the light. I mean, it was more than pretty.

She had sort of oaky hair that the sun and salt had bleached, done up in a bun that was unraveling, and a kind of prim face. Walking into the A & P with your straps down, I suppose it's the only kind of face you *can* have. She held her head so high her neck, coming up out of those white shoulders, looked kind of stretched, but I didn't mind. The longer her neck was, the more of her there was.

She must have felt in the corner of her eye me and over my shoulder Stokesie in the second slot watching, but she didn't tip. Not this queen. She kept her eyes moving across the racks, and stopped, and turned so slow it made my stomach rub the inside of my apron, and buzzed to the other two, who kind of huddled against her for relief, and then they all three of them went up the cat-and-dog-food-breakfast-cereal-macaroni-rice-raisins-seasonings-spreads-spaghetti-soft-drinks-crackers-and-cookies aisle. From the third slot I look straight up this aisle to the meat counter, and I watched them all the way. The fat one with the tan sort of fumbled with the cookies, but on second thought she put the package back. The sheep pushing their carts down the aisle—the girls were walking against the usual traffic (not that we have one-way signs or anything)—were pretty hilarious. You could see them, when Queenie's white shoulders dawned on them, kind of jerk, or hop, or hiccup, but their eyes snapped back to their own baskets and on they pushed. I bet you could set off dynamite in an A & P and the people would by and large keep reaching and checking oatmeal off their lists and muttering "Let me see, there was a third thing, began with A, asparagus, no, ah, yes, applesauce!" or whatever it is they do mutter. But there was no doubt, this jiggled them. A few house-slaves in pin curlers even looked around after pushing their carts past to make sure what they had seen was correct.

You know, it's one thing to have a girl in a bathing suit down on the beach, where what with the glare nobody can look at each other much anyway, and another thing in the cool of the A & P, under the fluorescent lights, against all those stacked packages, with her feet paddling along naked over our checkerboard green-and-cream rubber-tile floor.

"Oh Daddy," Stokesie said beside me. "I feel so faint."

"Darling," I said. "Hold me tight." Stokesie's married, with two babies chalked up on his fuselage already, but as far as I can tell that's the only difference. He's twenty-two, and I was nineteen this April.

"Is it done?" he asks, the responsible married man finding his voice. I forgot to say he thinks he's going to be manager some sunny day, maybe in 1990 when it's called the Great Alexandrov and Petrooshki Tea Company or something.

What he meant was, our town is five miles from a beach, with a big summer colony out on the Point, but we're right in the middle of town, and the women generally put on a shirt or shorts or something before they get out of the car into the street. And anyway these are usually women with six children and varicose veins mapping their legs and nobody, including them, could care less. As I say, we're right in the middle of town, and if you stand at our front doors you can see two banks and the Congregational church and the newspaper store and three real-estate offices and about twenty-seven old freeloaders tearing up Central Street because the sewer broke again. It's not as if we're on the Cape; we're north of Boston and there's people in this town haven't seen the ocean for twenty years.

The girls had reached the meat counter and were asking McMahon something. He pointed, they pointed, and they shuffled out of sight behind a pyramid of Diet Delight peaches. All that was left for us to see was old McMahon patting his mouth and looking after them sizing up their joints. Poor kids, I began to feel sorry for them, they couldn't help it.

Now here comes the sad part of the story, at least my family says it's sad, but I don't think it's so sad myself. The store's pretty empty, it being Thursday afternoon, so there was nothing much to do except lean on the register and wait for the girls to show up again. The whole store was like a pinball machine and I didn't know which tunnel they'd come out of. After a while they come around out of the far aisle, around the light bulbs, records at discount of the Caribbean Six or Tony Martin Sings or some such gunk you wonder they waste the wax on, sixpacks of candy bars, and plastic toys done up in cellophane that fall apart when a kid looks at them anyway. Around they come, Queenie still leading the way, and holding a little gray jar in her hand. Slots Three through Seven are unmanned and I could see her wondering between Stokes and me, but Stokesie with his usual luck draws an old party in baggy gray pants who stumbles up with four giant cans of pineapple juice (what do these bums *do* with all that pineapple juice? I've often asked myself) so the girls come to me. Queenie puts down the jar and I take it into my fingers icy cold. Kingfish Fancy Herring Snacks in Pure Sour Cream: 49¢. Now her hands are empty, not a ring or a bracelet, bare as God made them, and I wonder where the money's coming from. Still with that prim look she lifts a folded dollar bill out of the hollow at the center of her nubbled pink top. The jar went heavy in my hand. Really, I thought that was so cute.

Then everybody's luck begins to run out. Lengel comes in from haggling with a truck full of cabbages on the lot and is about to scuttle into that door marked MANAGER behind which he hides all day when the girls touch his eye. Lengel's pretty dreary, teaches Sunday school and the rest, but he doesn't miss that much. He comes over and says, "Girls, this isn't the beach."

Queenie blushes, though maybe it's just a brush of sunburn I was noticing for the first time, now that she was so close. "My mother asked me to pick up a jar of herring snacks." Her voice kind of startled me, the way voices do when you see the people first, coming out so flat and dumb yet kind of tony, too, the way it ticked over "pick up" and "snacks." All of a sudden I slid right down her voice into her living room. Her father and the other men were standing around in ice-cream coats and bow ties and the women were in sandals picking up herring snacks on toothpicks off a big glass plate and they were all holding drinks the color of water with olives and sprigs of mint in them. When my parents have some-body over they get lemonade and if it's a real racy affair Schlitz in tall glasses with "They'll Do It Every Time" cartoons stenciled on.

"That's all right," Lengel said. "But this isn't the beach." His re-peating this struck me as funny, as if it had just occurred to him, and he had been thinking all these years the A & P was a great big dune and he was the head lifeguard. He didn't like my smiling—as I say he doesn't miss much—but he concentrates on giving the girls that sad Sunday-school-superintendent stare.

Queenie's blush is no sunburn now, and the plump one in plaid, that I like better from the back—a really sweet can—pipes up, "We weren't doing any shopping. We just came in for the one thing."

"That makes no difference," Lengel tells her, and I could see from the way his eyes went that he hadn't noticed she was wearing a two-piece before. "We want you decently dressed when you come in here."

"We *are* decent," Queenie says suddenly, her lower lip pushing, getting sore now that she remembers her place, a place from which the crowd that runs the A & P must look pretty crummy. Fancy Herring Snacks flashed in her very blue eyes.

"Girls, I don't want to argue with you. After this come in here with your shoulders covered. It's our policy." He turns his back. That's policy for you. Policy is what the kingpins want. What the others want is juvenile delinquency.

All this while, the customers had been showing up with their carts but, you know, sheep, seeing a scene, they had all bunched up on Stokesie, who shook open a paper bag as gently as peeling a peach, not wanting to miss a word. I could feel in the silence everybody getting nervous, most of all Lengel, who asks me, "Sammy, have you rung up their purchase?"

I thought and said "No" but it wasn't about that I was thinking. I go through the punches, 4, 9, GROC, TOT—it's more complicated than you think, and after you do it often enough, it begins to make a little song, that you hear words to, in my case "Hello *(bing)* there, you *(gung)* hap-py *pee*-pul *(splat)!*—the *splat* being the drawer flying out. I uncrease the bill, tenderly as you may imagine, it just having come from between the two smoothest scoops of vanilla I had ever known were there, and pass a half and a penny into her narrow pink palm, and nestle the herrings in a bag and twist its neck and hand it over, all the time thinking.

The girls, and who'd blame them, are in a hurry to get out, so I say "I quit" to Lengel quick enough for them to hear, hoping they'll stop and watch me, their unsuspected hero. They keep right on going, into the electric eye; the door flies open and they flicker across the lot to their car, Queenie and Plaid and Big Tall Goony-Goony (not that as raw material she was so bad), leaving me with Lengel and a kink in his eyebrow.

"Did you say something, Sammy?"

"I said I quit."

"I thought you did."

"You didn't have to embarrass them."

"It was they who were embarrassing us."

I started to say something that came out "Fiddle-de-doo." It's a saying of my grandmother's, and I know she would have been pleased.

"I don't think you know what you're saying," Lengel said.

"I know you don't," I said. "But I do." I pull the bow at the back of my apron and start shrugging it off my shoulders. A couple customers that had been heading for my slot begin to knock against each other, like scared pigs in a chute.

Lengel sighs and begins to look very patient and old and gray. He's been a friend of my parents for years. "Sammy, you don't want to do this to your Mom and Dad," he tells me. It's true, I don't. But it seems to me that once you begin a gesture it's fatal not to go through with it. I fold the apron, "Sammy" stitched in red on the pocket, and put it on the counter, and drop the bow tie on top of it. The bow tie is theirs, if you've ever wondered. "You'll feel this for the rest of your life," Lengel says, and I know that's true, too, but remembering how he made that pretty girl blush makes me so scrunchy inside I punch the No Sale tab and the machine whirs "pee-pul" and the drawer splats out. One advantage to this scene taking place in summer, I can follow this up with a clean exit, there's no fumbling around getting your coat and galoshes, I just saunter into the electric eye in my white shirt that my mother ironed the night before, and the door heaves itself open, and outside the sunshine is skating around on the asphalt.

I looked around for my girls, but they're gone, of course. There wasn't anybody but some young married screaming with her children about some candy they didn't get by the door of a powder-blue Falcon station wagon. Looking back in the big windows, over the bags of peat moss and aluminum lawn furniture stacked on the pavement, I could see Lengel in my place in the slot, checking the sheep through. His face was dark gray and his back stiff, as if he'd just had an injection of iron, and my stomach kind of fell as I felt how hard the world was going to be to me hereafter.

- ◆ We must see Sammy clearly. How did you show your audience the audience he is telling his story to?

In this second-person narration, Ann Beattie quietly, chillingly, and achingly details a memory that will not leave the speaker. We must see the description completely if we are to understand its powerful impact. Take your time: this memory haunts.

Snow
ANN BEATTIE

I remember the cold night you brought in a pile of logs and a chipmunk jumped off as you lowered your arms. "What do you think *you're* doing in here?" you said, as it ran through the living room. It went through the library and stopped at the front door as though it knew the house well. This would be difficult for anyone to believe, except perhaps as the subject of a poem. Our first week in the house was spent scraping, finding some of the house's secrets, like wallpaper underneath wallpaper. In the kitchen, a pattern of white-gold trellises supported purple grapes as big and round as Ping-Pong balls. When we painted the walls yellow, I thought of the bits of grape that remained underneath and imagined the vine popping through, the way some plants can tenaciously push through anything. The day of the big snow, when you had to shovel the walk and couldn't find your cap and asked me how to wind a towel so that it would stay on your head—you, in the white towel turban, like a crazy king of the snow. People liked the idea of our being together, leaving the city for the country. So many people visited, and the fireplace made all of them want to tell amazing stories: the child who happened to be standing on the right corner when the door of the ice-cream truck came open and hundreds of Popsicles cascaded out; the man standing on the beach, sand sparkling in the sun, one bit glinting more than the rest, stooping to find a diamond ring. Did they talk about amazing things because they thought we'd turn into one of them? Now I think they probably guessed it wouldn't work. It was as hopeless as giving a child a matched cup and saucer. Remember the night, out on the lawn, knee-deep in snow, chins pointed at the sky as the wind whirled down all that whiteness? It seemed that the world had been turned upside down, and we were looking into an enormous field of Queen Anne's lace. Later, headlights off, our car was the first to ride through the newly fallen snow. The world outside the car looked solarized.

You remember it differently. You remember that the cold settled in stages, that a small curve of light was shaved from the moon night after night, until you were no longer surprised the sky was black, that the chipmunk ran to hide in the dark, not simply to a door that led to its escape. Our visitors told the same stories people always tell. One night, giving me a lesson in storytelling, you said, "Any life will seem dramatic if you omit mention of most of it."

This, then, for drama: I drove back to that house not long ago. It was April, and Allen had died. In spite of all the visitors, Allen, next door, had been the good friend in bad times. I sat with his wife in their living room, looking out the glass doors to the backyard, and there was Allen's pool, still covered with black plastic that had been stretched across it for winter. It had rained, and as the rain fell, the cover collected more and more water until it finally spilled onto the concrete. When I left that day, I drove past what had been our house. Three or four crocus were blooming in the front—just a few dots of white, no field of snow. I felt embarrassed for them. They couldn't compete.

This is a story, told the way you say stories should be told: Somebody grew up, fell in love, and spent a winter with her lover in the country. This, of course, is the barest outline, and futile to discuss. It's as pointless as throwing birdseed on the ground while snow still falls fast. Who expects small things to survive when even the largest get lost? People forget years and remember moments. Seconds and symbols are left to sum things up: the black shroud over the pool. Love, in its shortest form, becomes a word. What I remember about all that time is one winter. The snow. Even now, saying "snow," my lips move so that they kiss the air.

No mention has been made of the snowplow that seemed always to be there, scraping snow off our narrow road—an artery cleared, though neither of us could have said where the heart was.

- ◆ In the next-to-last paragraph, how did you demonstrate what the narrator is thinking? doing? feeling?

This excerpt from Toni Morrison's novel moves powerfully. Consider the rich, haunting motifs: Eva as a white bird of prey "swinging and swooping" and her "flight" down the stairs as she preys on/prays for her son, Plum. Plum is a drug addict. Is that enough to explain Eva's terrifying decision? How could her life have led her to this assault? The care with which Morrison constructs her fiction consistently rewards attention.

 FROM Sula

TONI MORRISON

So late one night in 1921, Eva got up from her bed and put on her clothes. Hoisting herself up on her crutches, she was amazed to find that she could still manage them, although the pain in her armpits was severe. She practiced a few steps around the room, and then opened the door. Slowly, she manipulated herself down the long flights of stairs, two crutches under her left arm, the right hand grasping the banister, the sound of her foot booming in comparison to the delicate pat of the crutch tip. On each landing she stopped for breath. Annoyed at her physical condition, she closed her eyes and removed the crutches from under her arms to relieve the unaccustomed pressure. At the foot of the stairs she redistributed her weight between the crutches and swooped on through the front room, to the dining room, to the kitchen, swinging and swooping like a giant heron, so graceful sailing about in its own habitat but awkward and comical when it folded its wings and tried to walk. With a swing and a swoop she arrived at Plum's door and pushed it open with the tip of one crutch. He was lying in bed barely visible in the light coming from a single bulb. Eva swung over to the bed and propped her crutches at its foot. She sat down and gathered Plum into her arms. He woke, but only slightly.

"Hey, man. Hey. You holdin' me, Mamma?" His voice was drowsy and amused. He chuckled as though he had heard some private joke. Eva held him closer and began to rock. Back and forth she rocked him, her eyes wandering around his room. There in the corner was a half-eaten store-bought cherry pie. Balled-up candy wrappers and empty pop bottles peeped from under the dresser. On the floor by her foot was a glass of strawberry crush and a *Liberty* magazine. Rocking, rocking, listening to Plum's occasional chuckles, Eva let her memory spin, loop and fall. Plum in the tub that time as she leaned over him. He reached up and dripped water into her bosom and laughed. She was angry, but not too, and laughed with him.

"Mamma, you so purty. You so purty, Mamma."

Eva lifted her tongue to the edge of her lip to stop the tears from running into her mouth. Rocking, rocking. Later she laid him down and looked at him a long time. Suddenly she was thirsty and reached for the glass of strawberry crush. She put it to her lips and discovered it was blood-tainted water and threw it to the floor. Plum woke up and said, "Hey, Mamma, whyn't you go on back to bed? I'm all right. Didn't I tell you? I'm all right. Go on, now."

"I'm going, Plum," she said. She shifted her weight and pulled her crutches toward her. Swinging and swooping, she left his room. She dragged herself to the kitchen and made grating noises.

Plum on the rim of a warm light sleep was still chuckling. Mamma. She sure was somethin'. He felt twilight. Now there seemed to be some kind of wet light traveling over his legs and stomach with a deeply attractive smell. It wound itself—this wet light—all about him, splashing and running into his skin. He opened his eyes and saw what he imagined was the great wing of an eagle pouring a wet lightness over him. Some kind of baptism, some kind of blessing, he thought. Everything is going to be all right, it said. Knowing that it was so he closed his eyes and sank back into the bright hole of sleep.

Eva stepped back from the bed and let the crutches rest under her arms. She rolled a bit of newspaper into a tight stick about six inches long, lit it and threw it onto the bed where the kerosene-soaked Plum lay in snug delight. Quickly, as the *whoosh* of flames engulfed him, she shut the door and made her slow and painful journey back to the top of the house.

Just as she got to the third landing she could hear Hannah and some child's voice. She swung along, not even listening to the voices of alarm and the cries of the Deweys. By the time she got to her bed someone was bounding up the stairs after her. Hannah opened the door. "Plum! Plum! He's burning, Mamma! We can't even open the door! Mamma!"

Eva looked into Hannah's eyes. "Is? My baby? Burning?" The two women did not speak, for the eyes of each were enough for the other. Then Hannah closed hers and ran toward the voices of neighbors calling for water.

- ◆ What did it cost Eva to make her move? How did you show that to your audience?

This chapter from David Leavitt's novel spotlights Jerene, one of the characters who interacts with the novel's protagonist. Let her increasing fascination with the account she reads be apparent to the audience, and then let them see where she makes the material she read her own.

FROM The Lost Language of Cranes

DAVID LEAVITT

The Crane-Child

Jerene found it by accident. She was working in the library one afternoon—wasting time, really—skimming through indexes of psychoanalytic journals and papers in search of something, anything that would give her a clue, a new grounding, that would illuminate the way out of the mammoth, unruly dissertation in which she was lost. Over a period of seven years its subject had changed a dozen times—from child abandonment to the phenomenology of adoption, and onto lost languages, children babbling in their bedrooms. Still her fellowship had been renewed, and would be renewed indefinitely, it seemed, for many of the professors on the philosophy faculty thought her a genius in the raw, a great philosophical mind, while the rest feared she might go off the deep end if they turned her down for money, feared she might come in with a sawed-off shotgun and blow their brains out, like that deranged mathematics graduate student at Stanford. Scanning the index, a little bored, beginning to think about lunch, she read the abstract of a case history that intrigued her. It was in a collection of psychoanalytic papers, shelved in a distant stack. She followed the trail of the call number; took the book from a shelf; read the article quickly the first time, a little anxious, skipping sentences to find the thesis as she had trained herself long ago to do. She read it again, slowly. By the

time she was finished she was breathing unevenly, loudly, her foot drumming the dark metal floor of the stacks, her heart pounding.

A baby, a boy, called Michel in the article, was born to a disoriented, possibly retarded teenager, the child of a rape. Until he was about two years old, he lived with his mother in a tenement next to a construction site. Every day she stumbled in and around and out of the apartment, lost in her own madness. She was hardly aware of the child, barely knew how to feed or care for him. The neighbors were alarmed at how Michel screamed, but when they went to knock at the door to ask her to quiet him, often she wasn't there. She would go out all hours, leaving the child alone, unguarded. Then one day, quite suddenly, the crying stopped. The child did not scream, and he did not scream the next night either. For days there was hardly a sound. Police and social workers were called. They found the child lying on his cot by the window. He was alive and remarkably well, considering how severely he appeared to have been neglected. Quietly he played on his squalid cot, stopping every few seconds to look out the window. His play was unlike any they had ever seen. Looking out the window, he would raise his arms, then jerk them to a halt; stand up on his scrawny legs, then fall; bend and rise. He made strange noises, a kind of screeching in his throat. What was he doing? the social workers wondered. What kind of play could this be?

Then they looked out the window, where some cranes were in operation, lifting girders and beams, stretching out wrecker balls on their single arms. The child was watching the crane nearest the window. As it lifted, he lifted; as it bent, he bent; as its gears screeched, its motor whirred, the child screeched between his teeth, whirred with his tongue.

They took him away. He screamed hysterically and could not be quieted so desolate was he to be divided from his beloved crane. Years later, Michel was an adolescent, living in a special institution for the mentally handicapped. He moved like a crane, made the noises of a crane, and although the doctors showed him many pictures of toys, he only responded to the pictures of cranes, only played with the toy cranes. Only cranes made him happy. He came to be known as the "crane-child." And the question Jerene kept coming up against, reading the article, was this: What did it sound like? What did it feel like? The language belonged to Michel alone; it was forever lost to her. How wondrous, how grand those cranes must have seemed to Michel, compared to the small and clumsy creatures who surrounded him. For each, in his own way, she believed, finds what it is he must love, and loves it; the window becomes a mirror; whatever it is that we love, that is who we are.

After Jerene xeroxed the article, she left the library. There was a brisk wind outdoors; she turned her collar up. Some construction was going on nearby—cranes working, lifting beams to the hardhatted men who swarmed the precarious frame of a rising condominium. The cranes looked like a species of gigantic, long-limbed insect. Transfixed, Jerene approached the makeshift wooden fence that surrounded the construction site. There was a crudely cut peephole in the fence, and through it she stared at the vast pit from which the building would rise, watched the cranes lunge and strain. She stood in the deafening roar of the cranes. In the grinding, the churring, the screeching, in the universe of the cranes, the womb of the cranes, she stood there, eyes open, and listened.

- How did you demonstrate the narrator's comfortable relationship with Jerene?

- Does Jerene become a crane-child? Why?

Light—and its gradual disappearance—figure prominently in this grim tale. A related kind of ambiguity haunts the events, too, now revealing a gesture, then disguising or obscuring an action. The characters' struggle may make you gasp, but look carefully at the restraint of the narrator's language. How do you reconcile these different postures?

Popular Mechanics

RAYMOND CARVER

Early that day the weather turned and the snow was melting into dirty water. Streaks of it ran down from the little shoulder-high window that faced the backyard. Cars slushed by on the street outside, where it was getting dark. But it was getting dark on the inside too.

He was in the bedroom pushing clothes into a suitcase when she came to the door.

I'm glad you're leaving! I'm glad you're leaving! she said. Do you hear?

He kept on putting his things into the suitcase.

Son of a bitch! I'm so glad you're leaving! She began to cry. You can't even look me in the face, can you?

Then she noticed the baby's picture on the bed and picked it up.

He looked at her and she wiped her eyes and stared at him before turning and going back to the living room.

Bring that back, he said.

Just get your things and get out, she said.

He did not answer. He fastened the suitcase, put on his coat, looked around the bedroom before turning off the light. Then he went out to the living room.

She stood in the doorway of the little kitchen, holding the baby.

I want the baby, he said.

Are you crazy?

No, but I want the baby. I'll get someone to come by for his things.

You're not touching this baby, she said.

The baby had begun to cry and she uncovered the blanket from around his head.

Oh, oh, she said, looking at the baby.

He moved toward her.

For God's sake! she said. She took a step back into the kitchen.

I want the baby.

Get out of here!

She turned and tried to hold the baby over in a corner behind the stove.

But he came up. He reached across the stove and tightened his hands on the baby.

Let go of him, he said.

Get away, get away! she cried.

The baby was red-faced and screaming. In the scuffle they knocked down a flowerpot that hung behind the stove.

He crowded her into the wall then, trying to break her grip. He held on to the baby and pushed with all his weight.

Let go of him, he said.

Don't, she said. You're hurting the baby, she said.

I'm not hurting the baby, he said.

The kitchen window gave no light. In the near-dark he worked on her fisted fingers with one hand and with the other hand he gripped the screaming baby up under an arm near the shoulder.

She felt her fingers being forced open. She felt the baby going from her.

No! she screamed just as her hands came loose.

She would have it, this baby. She grabbed for the baby's other arm. She caught the baby around the wrist and leaned back.

But he would not let go. He felt the baby slipping out of his hands and he pulled back very hard.

In this manner, the issue was decided.

- There are crucial shifts in tempo throughout this brief story. How did you show your audience the changes in thought that accompany these shifts?

- How did you show your audience the physical struggle?

Here is a tale about telling tales and about how, remarkably, tales can come true. The pattern of speech, the repetitions, the slightly varied details, and the marvelously believing children all present tempting challenges to a performer. Be sure that your telling is both as fantastic and as true as the story.

⌾ Jacob's Chicken

MILOŠ MACOUREK (TRANSLATED FROM THE CZECH
BY DAGMAR HERRMANN)

A chicken is a chicken, you all know how a chicken looks, sure you do, so go ahead and draw a chicken the teacher tells the children, and all the kids suck on crayons and then draw chickens, coloring them black or brown, with black or brown crayons, but wouldn't you know it, look at Jacob, he draws a chicken with every crayon in the box, then borrows some from Laura, and Jacob's chicken ends up with an orange head, blue wings and red thighs and the teacher says that's some bizarre chicken, what do you say children, and the kids roll with laughter while the teacher goes on, saying, that's all because Jacob wasn't paying attention, and, to tell the truth, Jacob's chicken really looks more like a turkey, but then not quite, for it also resembles a sparrow and also a peacock, it's as big as a quail and as lean as a swallow, a peculiar pullet, to say the least, Jacob earns an F for it and the chicken, instead of being hung on the wall, migrates to a pile of misfits on top of the teacher's cabinet, the poor chicken's feelings are hurt, nothing makes it happy about being on top of a teacher's cabinet, so, deciding not to be chicken, it flies off through the open window.

But a chicken is a chicken, a chicken won't fly too far, hence it ends up next door in a garden full of white cherries and powder-blue currants, a splendid garden that proudly shows its cultivator's love, you see, the gardener, Professor Kapon, a recognized authority, is an ornithologist who has written seven books on birds and right now is finishing his eighth, and as he puts the last touches to it, he suddenly feels weary, so he goes out to do some light gardening and toss a few horseshoes, which is easy and lets him muse over birds, there are tons of them, so many birds, Professor Kapon says to himself, but there isn't a single bird that I discovered, he feels down, flips a horseshoe and dreams a love-filled dream about an as-yet-unknown bird when his eye falls on the chicken picking the baby-blue currants, the rare blue currants that dammit he didn't grow for chicken feed, now that would make anyone's blood boil, the professor is incensed, he is furious, he seems unable to zap the chicken, so in the end he just catches it, flings it over the fence, the chicken flies off, and voilà, Professor Kapon follows, he flies over the fence in pursuit of the chicken, grabs it and carries it home, quite an unusual chicken, that one, bet nobody has seen one quite like it, an orange head, blue wings and red thighs, the professor jots it all down, looks like a turkey, but then not quite, reminds one of a sparrow but also of a peacock, it's as big as a quail and as lean as a swallow, and after he has written it all down for his eighth book, the professor, all quivers, bestows upon the chicken his own name and carries it to the zoo.

A chicken is a chicken, who would fuss over a chicken, you think, but this one must be well worth the bother for the whole zoo is in an uproar, such rarity turns up perhaps once in twenty years, if that often, the zoo director is rubbing his hands, the employees are building a cage, the painter has his hands full and the director says the cage must sparkle and make the bed soft, he adds, and already there appears a nameplate, Kapon's chicken, *Gallina kaponi,* it sounds lovely, doesn't it, what do you say, it sounds, actually, how about it, the chicken is having the time of its life, it's moved to tears by all this care, it really can't complain, it has become the zoo's main attraction, the center of attention, the zoo has never had so many visitors, says the cashier, and the crowds are growing larger by the minute, wait, look, there is our teacher with the whole class in front of the cage, explaining, a while ago you saw the Przewalski horse and here you have another unique specimen, the so-called Kapon's chicken or *Gallina kaponi* that looks somewhat like a turkey but not quite, resembles a sparrow and also a peacock, it's as big as a quail and as lean as a swallow, why, look at that gorgeous orange head, the blue wings, the scarlet thighs, the children are agog, they sigh, what a beautiful chicken, ain't that right, teacher, but Laura, as if struck by lightning, pulls on teacher's sleeve and says, that's Jacob's chicken, I bet you it is, the teacher becomes irked, this silly child's ridiculous notions, what Jacob's chicken is she prattling about and, come to think of it, where is Jacob anyhow, again he is not paying attention, now, wouldn't you know, there, just look at him, there he is, in front of an anteater's cage, watching an anteater when he is supposed to be looking at Kapon's chicken, Jacob, the teacher yells at the top of her lungs in a high-pitched voice, next time you'll stay home, Jacob, I've had enough aggravation, which shouldn't surprise anyone, for something like that would make anybody's blood boil.

- ◆ Have you decided for yourself precisely what Jacob's chicken looked like? Will you show your audience your drawing?

- ◆ Although there are no quotation marks, there are lots of characters. How did you distinguish among them?

One virtue of this work of fiction is its remarkable immediacy, an uncanny ability to sound like a personal narrative. The vivid details seem spontaneously recalled, in part because of the narrator's skillful manipulation of tense. Be sure your Marc takes the time to remember everything.

◎ The Key to My Father
HARLAN COBEN

Let's get something straight right away: my father was hopelessly unhip. He was the corporeal embodiment of an Air Supply eight-track. He'd come home from work, shed the powder-blue suit with reversible vest, the tie so polyester it would melt during the heat waves, the V-neck Hanes undershirt of startling white, the gray socks bought by the dozen at Burlington Coat Factory. He'd don a logo T-shirt that was compulsorily a size too snug, if you know what I mean, and shorts that were, uh, short, like something John McEnroe wore at Wimbledon in 1979.

His sunglasses were big, too big. They might have worked on Sophia Loren but on Dad they looked like manhole covers. He had thin legs. My mom teased him about this, this 6-foot-2 man with the barrel chest and olive skin, teetering on spindly legs. His hair, as described by my mother, was "tired," wispy and flyaway. He had big arms. To his children, they looked like oak branches. The biceps would grow spongy with the years. But they never had time to fully atrophy.

He would play ball with us, but he was a terrible athlete. I remember going to that Little League coaches' softball game, the one they have at the end of every season, and watching my father—this man who had taught me to keep my elbow up and back foot planted—take to the plate and ground out weakly to third. Three times in a row. To his credit, he never made excuses. "You," he'd tell me. "You're an athlete. Me, I'm a spaz."

His after-shave was Old Spice. There had been a radical period when he tried an eau called Royal Copenhagen—someone had given him a gift set and damned if he was going to let it go to waste—but he veered back onto his Old Spice route. That is still my strongest bar mitzvah recollection—that smell. No, I can't tell you what part of the haphtara I recited from the pulpit of B'nai Jeshurun. Something from Ezekiel, I think. But there's that part in the ceremony where the father blesses the son. My father bent down and whispered in my ear. He said something about loving me and being proud—much as I want to, I can't remember the exact words—and then he kissed me on the cheek. I remember the feel of his cheek on mine, the catcher's-glove hand cupping my head, and the smell of Old Spice.

On Saturday mornings, we went to Seymour's luncheonette on Livingston Avenue for a milkshake and maybe a pack of baseball cards. I'd sit on a stool at the counter and twirl. He'd stand next to me, always, as if that was what a man did. He'd lean against the counter and eat—too quickly, I think. He was never fat but he was always on the wrong side of the weight curve. He was uneven about physical activity. He'd discover a workout program, do it for three months, go idle for about six, find something new. Rinse, repeat. Like with shampoo.

He hated his job. He never told me this. He dutifully went to work every day. But I knew. He didn't have a lot of friends either, but that was by choice. He could have been a popular man. People liked him. He could feign charm and warmth, but there was a coldness there. He cared only about his family and he cared with a ferocity that both frightened and exhilarated. You know those stories about someone lifting a car to save a trapped loved one? It took little to imagine him performing such a feat. The world was his family—the rest of the planet's inhabitants no more than the periphery, deep background, scenery.

The night was his domain. He slept lightly, too lightly. I wonder if that is to blame, the way he'd startle awake. I would try my hardest to tiptoe past his door, but no matter how great my stealth, he would jerk upright in his bed as if I'd dropped a Popsicle on his stomach. Every night the same thing:

"Marc?" he'd shout.

"Yes, Dad."

"Something wrong?"

"Just going to the bathroom," I'd say. "I've been going by myself since I was 14."

During my freshman year at college, after a particularly debauched frat party, I was struck by a strange realization: this was the first time I'd woken up sick without my father present. His hand was not on my forehead. He was not speaking softly or rubbing my back. I was alone.

I blame myself for what happened.

Three days before my college graduation, I dropped my father off at the airport. We were late. He ran to catch his flight. That is the image I can't shake all these years later. My father, hopelessly unhip and out of shape, running for that stupid flight so he could be at a meeting that meant nothing to anybody.

Six hours later, he called from the Comfort Suite in Tampa. "Let me speak to your mother."

I handed her the phone. I watched her listen. I saw her face turn white.

"What?" I asked.

"He's having chest pains, but he says he's fine."

And I knew. And she knew. I called the front desk. I told them to send an ambulance. I called my father back. "I told the front desk to send somone up," and then my father said the most frightening thing of all: "O.K."

No argument, no brave front, no I'm fine.

"But I have to find the room key first," he added.

"What?"

"They'll be here soon. I have to go. I have to find the key."

"Forget the key."

"You might need it."

"For what?"

But he hung up. And again I knew. He had never been ill, but I knew. With my father's strength, you somehow still sensed the fragile.

My mother and I rushed to the airport. I called the hotel from a pay phone. They just wheeled him out of the lobby, I was told. Wheeled him out. I pictured the oxygen mask on his face. I imagined him as I had never seen him: afraid.

He liked building things, my father, but he was bad with his hands. He gardened on weekends, but our shrubs never looked right, not like the shrubs that belonged to the Bauers, who lived next door. Their lawn looked as if it had been trimmed for a P. G. A. event. Ours had dandelions tall enough to go on the adult rides at Six Flags.

My father fought in the Korean War but never talked about it. I didn't even know he'd been in the military until I explored his junk drawer when I was 8 and found a bunch of medals in the bottom. They were loose in the drawer, mingling with spare change.

Our plane had a stopover at the Atlanta airport, the epicenter of the stopover. I called the hospital. The nurse assured me that my father was fine. But I didn't believe her. She transferred me to the doctor. I told the doctor I was calling about my father, that I was his son. The doctor did that calm voice thing and asked me my name. He told me, Marc—using my name so often it became like an annoying tick—that my father was in serious condition. Marc, that they are going to operate in a few minutes. I felt my legs go. He's awake and comfortable, the doctor told me. He understands what is happening. I asked to speak to him. "The phone cord won't reach, Marc," the doctor said.

"Tell him we're on our way," I insisted. "I will." But I didn't believe him.

My father always longed for a Cadillac. He got one when he turned 52. He listened only to AM radio. Every once in a while a certain song would come on and he'd turn it up. His face would change. The lines would soften. He'd lean back and steer with his wrists and whistle.

By the time we arrived at the hospital, night had fallen. I sat in the waiting room. He was still in surgery. My mother did not speak, something that is usually accompanied by a parting sea or burning bush. I began to make deals with whatever higher power would listen, you know the kind, about what I'd do, what I'd risk, what I'd trade, if only it could be morning again and we could leave for that damn plane a few minutes earlier and if he hadn't run to catch that flight, if he'd just walked instead, if he didn't devour his food, if he kept up with an exercise program, if I'd been an easier son.

At 4 a.m., that awful hospital beeping sound echoed down the still corridor, then a rush that stole our breath. The air was suddenly gone. And so, too, was my father.

We bury him on Father's Day. The weather is, of course, spectacular, mocking my gloom. The men his age come up to me and tell me all about their own heart problems, about their close calls, about how lucky they've been. I look through them, wondering why they are the ones who get to stand before me, happily breathing. I wish them ill. I call his former boss, the one who sold the company and made my father stuff envelopes with his résumé at the age of 56. I tell him that if he shows up at the funeral, I'll punch him in the face. He, too, is to blame.

I wonder if my father was scared near the end or if he went into surgery thinking it would all be O.K. Don't know, of course. There is a lot I don't know. I don't know what my father wanted out of life. I don't know what he wanted to be when he was a young man, before I came around and changed everything. He never expressed any of that to me. And I never asked.

A week after the funeral, I call his doctor down in Tampa.

"He died alone," I say.

"He knew you were there."

"You didn't tell him."

"I did."

"What did he say?"

The doctor takes a second. "He said for you to check his pocket."

"What?"

"You'd need a place to stay overnight. He said to check his pocket."

Cradling the phone, I go to the closet where his belongings, still in the plastic hospital bag the nurse handed me, are hanging. I break the seal. The Old Spice scent is faint but there. I dig past the Hanes V-Neck and find his pants.

"What else?" I ask.

"Pardon?"

"What else did he say?"

"That's it."

"Those were his final words? Check his pocket?"

His voice is suddenly soft. "Yes."

My fingers slip into the pocket of his pants and hit something metallic. I pull it out. The hotel key. He'd found it after all. He put it in his pocket. His last words, his last act, for us.

I still have the key; I keep it in a drawer with his medals.

- ◆ How did you negotiate the frequent shifts in locus to be sure your audience always knew where you were and who was talking?

◆ How much of the father can you recognize in the son? What performance choices you made enabled your audience to see and hear their resemblance?

Because so much of Philip Roth's story begins during a scene, the narrator emerges only gradually as the tale unfolds. Don't be tempted to skimp on preparation, for the narrator's complex understanding of Ozzie's dilemma is central to the total effect of the story. Ozzie and Itzie are two full-blooded 12-year-old boys who are radically different yet remarkably similar.

 FROM **The Conversion of the Jews**

PHILIP ROTH

"You're a real one for opening your mouth in the first place," Itzie said. "What do you open your mouth all the time for?"

"I didn't bring it up, Itz, I didn't," Ozzie said.

"What do you care about Jesus Christ for anyway?"

"I didn't bring up Jesus Christ. He did. I didn't even know what he was talking about. Jesus is historical, he kept saying. Jesus is historical." Ozzie mimicked the monumental voice of Rabbi Binder.

"Jesus was a person that lived like you and me," Ozzie continued. "That's what Binder said—"

"Yeah? . . . So what! What do I give two cents whether he lived or not. And what do you gotta open your mouth!" Itzie Lieberman favored closed-mouthedness, especially when it came to Ozzie Freedman's questions. Mrs. Freedman had to see Rabbi Binder twice before about Ozzie's questions and this Wednesday at four-thirty would be the third time. Itzie preferred to keep *his* mother in the kitchen; he settled for behind-the-back subtleties such as gestures, faces, snarls and other less delicate barnyard noises.

"He was a real person, Jesus, but he wasn't like God, and we don't believe he is God." Slowly, Ozzie was explaining Rabbi Binder's position to Itzie, who had been absent from Hebrew School the previous afternoon.

"The Catholics," Itzie said helpfully, "they believe in Jesus Christ, that he's God." Itzie Lieberman used "the Catholics" in its broadest sense—to include the Protestants.

Ozzie received Itzie's remark with a tiny head bob, as though it were a footnote, and went on. "His mother was Mary, and his father probably was Joseph," Ozzie said. "But the New Testament says his real father was God."

"His *real* father?"

"Yeah," Ozzie said, "that's the big thing, his father's supposed to be God."

"Bull. "

"That's what Rabbi Binder says, that it's impossible—"

"Sure it's impossible. That stuff's all bull. To have a baby you gotta get laid," Itzie theologized. "Mary hadda get laid."

"That's what Binder says: 'The only way a woman can have a baby is to have intercourse with a man.'"

"He said *that*, Ozz?" For a moment it appeared that Itzie had put the theological question aside. "He said that, intercourse?" A little curled smile shaped itself in the lower half of Itzie's face like a pink mustache. "What you guys do, Ozz, you laugh or something?"

"I raised my hand."

"Yeah? Whatja say?"

"That's when I asked the question."

Itzie's face lit up. "Whatja ask about—intercourse?"

"No, I asked the question about God, how if He could create the heaven and earth in six days, and make all the animals and the fish and the light in six days—the light especially, that's what always gets me, that He could make the light. Making fish and animals, that's pretty good—"

"That's damn good." Itzie's appreciation was honest but unimaginative: it was as though God had just pitched a one-hitter.

"But making light . . . I mean when you think about it, something," Ozzie said. Anyway, I asked Binder if He could make all that in six days, and He could *pick* the six days he wanted right out of nowhere, why couldn't He let a woman have a baby without having intercourse."

"You said intercourse, Ozz, to Binder?"

"Yeah."

"Right in class?"

"Yeah."

Itzie smacked the side of his head.

"I mean, no kidding around," Ozzie said, "that'd really be nothing. After all that other stuff, that'd practically be nothing."

Itzie considered a moment. "What'd Binder say?"

"He started all over again explaining how Jesus was historical and how he lived like you and me but he wasn't God. So I said I un-der*stood* that. What I wanted to know was different."

What Ozzie wanted to know was always different. The first time he had wanted to know how Rabbi Binder could call the Jews "The Chosen People" if the Declaration of Independence claimed all men to be created equal. Rabbi Binder tried to distinguish for him between political equality and spiritual legitimacy, but what Ozzie wanted to know, he insisted vehemently, was different. That was the first time his mother had to come.

Then there was the plane crash. Fifty-eight people had been killed in a plane crash at La Guardia. In studying a casualty list in the newspaper his mother had discovered among the list of those dead eight Jewish names (his grandmother had nine but she counted Miller as a Jewish name); because of the eight she said the plane crash was "a tragedy." During free-discussion time on Wednesday Ozzie had brought to Rabbi Binder's attention this matter of "some of his relations" always picking out the Jewish names. Rabbi Binder had begun to explain cultural unity and some other things when Ozzie stood up at his seat and said that what he wanted to know was different. Rabbi Binder insisted that he sit down and it was then that Ozzie shouted that he wished all fifty-eight were Jews. That was the second time his mother came.

"And he kept explaining about Jesus being historical, and so I kept asking him. No kidding, Itz, he was trying to make me look stupid."

"So what he finally do?"

"Finally he starts screaming that I was deliberately simple-minded and a wise guy, and that my mother had to come, and this was the last time. And that I'd never get bar-mitzvahed if he could help it. Then, Itz, then he starts talking in that voice like a statue, real slow and deep, and he says that I better think over what I said about the Lord. He told me to go to his office and think it over." Ozzie leaned his body towards Itzie. "Itz, I thought it over for a solid hour, and now I'm convinced God could do it."

Ozzie had planned to confess his latest transgression to his mother as soon as she came home from work. But it was a Friday night in November and already dark, and when Mrs. Freedman came through the door she tossed off her coat, kissed Ozzie quickly on the face, and went to the kitchen table to light the three yellow candles, two for the Sabbath and one for Ozzie's father.

When his mother lit the candles she would move her two arms slowly towards her, dragging them through the air, as though persuading people whose minds were half made up. And her eyes would get glassy with tears. Even when his father was alive Ozzie remembered that her eyes had gotten glassy, so it didn't have anything to do with his dying. It had something to do with lighting the candles.

As she touched the flaming match to the unlit wick of a Sabbath candle, the phone rang, and Ozzie, standing only a foot from it, plucked it off the receiver and held it muffled to his chest. When his mother lit candles Ozzie felt there should be no noise; even breathing, if you could manage it, should be softened. Ozzie pressed the phone to his breast and watched his mother dragging whatever she was dragging, and he felt his own eyes get glassy. His mother was a round, tired, gray-haired penguin of a woman whose gray skin had begun to feel the tug of gravity and the weight of her own history. Even when she was dressed up she didn't look like a chosen person. But when she lit candles she looked like something better; like a woman who knew momentarily that God could do anything.

After a few mysterious minutes she was finished. Ozzie hung up the phone and walked to the kitchen table where she was beginning to lay the two places for the four-course Sabbath meal. He told her that she would have to see Rabbi Binder next Wednesday at four-thirty, and then he told her why. For the first time in their life together she hit Ozzie across the face with her hand.

All through the chopped liver and chicken soup part of the dinner Ozzie cried; he didn't have any appetite for the rest.

On Wednesday, in the largest of the three basement classrooms of the synagogue, Rabbi Marvin Binder, a tall, handsome, broad-shouldered man of thirty with thick strong-fibered black hair, removed his watch from his pocket and saw that it was four o'clock. At the rear of the room Yakov Blotnik, the seventy-one-year-old custodian, slowly polished the large window, mumbling to himself, unaware that it was four o'clock or six o'clock, Monday or Wednesday. To most of the students Yakov Blotnik's mumbling, along with his brown curly beard, scythe nose, and two heel-trailing black cats, made of him an object of wonder, a foreigner, a relic, towards whom they were alternately fearful and disrespectful. To Ozzie the mumbling had always seemed a monotonous, curious prayer; what made it curious was that old Blotnik had been mumbling so steadily for so many years. Ozzie suspected he had memorized the prayers and forgotten all about God.

"It is now free-discussion time," Rabbi Binder said. "Feel free to talk about any Jewish matter at all—religion, family, politics, sports—"

There was silence. It was a gusty, clouded November afternoon and it did not seem as though there ever was or could be a thing called baseball. So nobody this week said a word about that hero from the past, Hank Greenberg—which limited free discussion considerably.

And the soul-battering Ozzie Freedman had just received from Rabbi Binder had imposed its limitation. When it was Ozzie's turn to read aloud from the Hebrew book the rabbi had asked him petulantly why he didn't read more rapidly. He was showing no progress. Ozzie said he could read faster but that if he did he was sure not to understand what he was reading. Nevertheless, at the rabbi's repeated suggestion Ozzie tried, and showed a great talent, but in the midst of a long passage he stopped short and said he didn't understand a word he was reading, and started in again at a drag-footed pace. Then came the soul-battering.

Consequently when free-discussion time rolled around none of the students felt too free The rabbi's invitation was answered only by the mumbling of feeble old Blotnik.

"Isn't there anything at all you would like to discuss?" Rabbi Binder asked again, looking at his watch. "No questions or comments?"

There was a small grumble from the third row. The rabbi requested that Ozzie rise and give the rest of the class the advantage of his thought.

Ozzie rose. "I forget it now," he said, and sat down in his place.

Rabbi Binder advanced a seat towards Ozzie and poised himself on the edge of the desk. It was Itzie's desk and the rabbi's frame only a dagger's-length away from his face snapped him to sitting attention.

"Stand up again, Oscar," Rabbi Binder said calmly, "and try to assemble your thoughts."

Ozzie stood up. All his classmates turned in their seats and watched as he gave an unconvincing scratch to his forehead.

"I can't assemble any," he announced, and plunked himself down.

"Stand up!" Rabbi Binder advanced from Itzie's desk to the one directly in front of Ozzie; when the rabbinical back was turned Itzie gave it five-fingers off the tip of his nose, causing a small titter in the room. Rabbi Binder was too absorbed in squelching Ozzie's nonsense once and for all to bother with titters. "Stand up, Oscar. What's your question about?"

Ozzie pulled a word out of the air. It was the handiest word. "Religion."

"Oh, now you remember?"

"Yes."

"What is it?"

Trapped, Ozzie blurted the first thing that came to him. "Why can't He make anything He wants to make!"

As Rabbi Binder prepared an answer, a final answer, Itzie, ten feet behind him, raised one finger on his left hand, gestured it meaningfully towards the rabbi's back, and brought the house down.

Binder twisted quickly to see what had happened and in the midst of the commotion Ozzie shouted into the rabbi's back what he couldn't have shouted to his face. It was a loud, toneless sound that had the timbre of something stored inside for about six days.

"You don't know! You don't know anything about God!"

The rabbi spun back towards Ozzie. "What?"

"You don't know—you don't—"

"Apologize, Oscar, apologize!" It was a threat.

"You don't—"

Rabbi Binder's hand flicked out at Ozzie's cheek. Perhaps it had only been meant to clamp the boy's mouth shut, but Ozzie ducked and the palm caught him squarely on the nose.

The blood came in a short, red spurt on to Ozzie's shirt front.

The next moment was all confusion. Ozzie screamed, "You bastard, you bastard!" and broke for the classroom door. Rabbi Binder lurched a step backwards, as though his own blood had started flowing violently in the opposite direction, then gave a clumsy lurch forward and bolted out the door after Ozzie. The class followed after the rabbi's huge blue-suited back, and before old Blotnik could turn from his window, the room was empty and everyone was headed full speed up the three flights leading to the roof.

- ◆ Ozzie is serious and intelligent, but he isn't solemn. How did you demonstrate to your audience his continued efforts to understand?

Bibliography

For the Student

Kundera, Milan. *The Art of the Novel.* Translated by Linda Asher. New York: Grove Press, 1988.

A fascinating study of the novel from one of the twentieth century's finest writers.

Moffett, James, and Kenneth R. McElheny. *Points of View: An Anthology of Short Stories.* New York: Mentor, 1995.

A diverse anthology of classic stories divided into sections based on narrative technique.

Pollock, Della. *Telling Bodies: Performing Birth.* New York: Columbia University Press, 1999.

A beautiful, touching, and sometimes humorous account of how narrative produces the ritual and memory of giving birth.

Welty, Eudora. *The Eye of the Story.* New York: Random House, 1978.

Welty's essays explore the function of narrator-characters in contemporary fiction.

For the Instructor

Booth, Wayne C. *The Rhetoric of Fiction.* 2nd ed. Chicago: University of Chicago Press, 1983.

The expanded second edition of this classic explores the social influences of prose fiction.

Capecci, John. "Performing the Second Person." *Text and Performance Quarterly* 9, no. 1 (1989): 42–52.
A concise discussion of performance problems and opportunities in second-person narration; useful bibliography.

Cohn, Dorrit. *Transparent Minds: Narrative Modes for Representing Consciousness in Fiction.* Princeton: Princeton University Press, 1978.
A detailed presentation of the nuances of first- and third-person narrators in fiction.

Genette, Gerard. *Narrative Discourse.* Translated by Jane E. Lewin. Ithaca, NY: Cornell University Press, 1980.
The magisterial index of the functions and effects of narrative techniques.

Ricoeur, Paul. *Time and Narrative.* Vol. 1. Translated by Kathleen McLaughlin and David Pellauer. Chicago: University of Chicago Press, 1984.
A theoretical and useful discussion of the relationship between time and narrative.

PART THREE

Interpretation of Drama

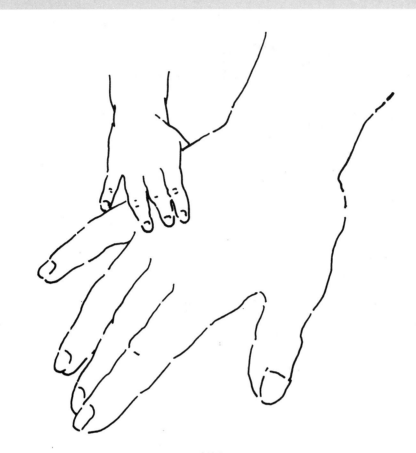

**To make a play
is to make
people; to make
people make**

**themselves; to
make people
make themselves
new. So real.**
May Swenson
   "To Make a Play"

CHAPTER SEVEN

Solo Performance of Drama

EXPECT THIS!

Plays aren't novels, so the characteristics of the solo performance of drama and novels differ in some ways yet are similar in other ways. This chapter explores the *theory* of performing drama by looking at several examples. By the end of this chapter, you should be able to:

- Define the nature of drama.

- Provide four reasons why a solo performer should attempt drama.

- Discuss the similarities and differences between acting and interpretation.

- Sketch the standard ways in which conflict is presented, developed, and resolved.

- Show how character is created by explicit and hidden clues.

- Describe the functions and effects of character interaction.

- Explain how rhythm affects meaning in drama.

- Illustrate style through language, arrangement of idea, and length of thought unit.

- Evaluate the role of scenography in a drama.

- Recognize that synthesis can be achieved with careful rehearsal and playful pleasure in performance.

People in conflict making choices about their lives is the essence of drama.

Selections Discussed in This Chapter

In explaining some topics, we mention texts that are reprinted either within the chapter itself or at the end of a chapter. Use the guide below for quick reference to acquaint yourself with selections you may not fully recall.

Author	Title	Location
Anton Chekhov	from *The Three Sisters*	Chapter 7, page 295
Edward Albee	from *Who's Afraid of Virginia Woolf?*	Chapter 7, page 300
Anna Deavere Smith	from *Fires in the Mirror*	Chapter 7, page 313
Pearl Cleage	from *Flyin' West*	Chapter 7, page 327
Harold Pinter	from *Betrayal, Scene Five*	Chapter 8, page 367

DRAMA IS MORE INTERESTING THAN LIFE—OR IT SHOULD BE. Like real life, dramatic life has a beginning, a middle, and an end; but unlike real life, dramatic life consists of only selected events that take place for a discernible reason. Everything that happens on stage contributes to the conflict. The excitement of the conflict arises from the equality of the matched contestants. Thus, people in conflict making choices about their lives is the essence of drama.

But drama is also make-believe, game, and ritual. The actress playing Juliet only pretends to die, speaking iambic pentameter, while the audience willingly suspends disbelief. The actors must speak and move as they do, not because of their rehearsals or the needs of their audience, but because this is the way real people lead their lives. When you interpret drama, you too must create a completely convincing illusion.

The Nature of Drama

Dramas reveal their unique power only in performance, and that performance can take place in a classroom, on a podium, in an auditorium, with or without a manuscript. The French playwright Molière said that all he needed for a theater was "a platform and a passion or two." The passion, though, must be prompted by a text and live inside the performer, and it must be communicated to an audience. Does that sequence sound familiar to you? It mirrors the process we have used in your first performances and the process we used in understanding the interpretation of prose. This chapter and Chapter 8 are designed to explore and solve the unique challenges that accompany the performance of drama. We presume, however, that you will employ all the advice that we provided in Chapters 3 and 4 about using the voice and body. Similarly, most dramas are written in prose, so the techniques of analysis that we used in Chapters 5 and 6 will come in handy, too. Finally, one distinctive characteristic of drama is character, so also build on the techniques for creating and presenting characters we discussed earlier.

Certain similarities not withstanding, drama differs from prose and from poetry because, as a solo performer, you create not only characters but also the world of the play. Two or three characters may have spoken in the stories you have performed, but (as we learned in Chapter 6), a narrator is there, shepherding the reader/audience to look where and see what the narrator wanted. In drama, characters speak for themselves, revealing (or attempting to conceal) who they are. To achieve the fullest impact, the interpreter needs to concentrate on and convey the character's needs and be committed to transmitting the character's hopes. Concentration and commitment alone are not enough, however. The solo interpreter communicates the drama in a playing space that is reduced to the boundaries sketched by one body and one voice.

In this chapter, then, we examine the fundamental *structural* components of a drama. By carefully scrutinizing one short scene, pointing to the *explicit* clues it provides about its characters, and, more rewardingly, discovering the *hidden* clues it reveals, we explore the ways a drama makes meaning for its audience. That section will be filled with questions for you to answer and will establish the pattern of going back and forth between text and competing performance possibilities, which are the hallmarks of any rehearsal process. Then, together, we will "work a scene"—analyzing carefully how the interaction of characters creates drama. When characters do not clash, there is no drama. Then, with an idea of how character is created and a better sense of how character interaction creates drama, we can explore three other crucial elements of drama: rhythm, style, and scenography. We conclude this chapter with some advice on how to reassemble the parts. In the next chapter, we look at *technical* problems presented by the solo performance of drama. But first, we suspect two questions are itching to be asked—and answered!

Why Perform Drama?

Because the process of performing drama may seem complicated, beginning interpreters frequently ask, "What is to be gained by one person's doing something that was clearly written to be done by a group?" If you have such a doubt, the next few paragraphs are for you.

First, performing drama requires that you coordinate all the skills you use in performing other genres. Mastering the basic skills requires considerable practice. The skills of the solo performer of drama are the skills you use to perform poetry and prose.

Second, the solo performance gives you a unique way of knowing the play. Actors "know" their lines, dancers "know" the steps, typists "know" the keyboard; all acquire a special understanding of what they do. Like an actor, the interpreter communicates the play with body and mind and emotional makeup. Unlike an actor, however, the interpreter takes on *all* the characters. An interpreter's experience will thus be *broader* (though not necessarily deeper) than an actor's because the interpreter's task is to communicate the *entirety* of the play.

Third, an audience benefits from a solo performance because it sees the play from a unique perspective: the shifting focus of the speaking character. A person watching a staged production may be distracted; but in your solo performance no one can upstage you, no one moves on your lines, and no one covers you. The audience sees how individual forces acting on the speaker make the play what it is. Your audience takes part in the play's creation because it imagines the spectacle that you suggest.

Finally, even the play benefits from a solo performance because it has a unique embodiment—you. Your vision informs the audience without all the difficulties that accompany any staged performance (missed light cues, dropped lines, botched blocking). Only the play, the interpreter, and the audience exist. That is why, taken seriously by serious students, solo performance is an exciting way to experience the world of drama.

Not for a minute do we suggest that the solo performance of drama is superior to a staged play, that what actors do interpreters do better, or that drama should always be performed by solo interpreters. Different forms of performance offer different kinds of rewards, and a world without the collaborative excitement of staged theater would dismay us just as much as would a world in which serious students are told not to perform certain types of splendid literature.

What Is the Difference Between Acting and Interpretation?

The other question beginning interpreters ask (though, thankfully, not as often as they used to) is "What is the difference between acting and interpretation?" Your instructor may sigh before answering, for within that question hide decades of debate that today *seems* to have quieted down. For most current-day interpreters, it doesn't so much matter what the performance of literature is called as long as the literature is performed. Contemporary theater itself is not confined to the performance of plays. Novels are staged; performance art thrives; solo performers freely mix verse, dance, musical and visual arts. Today's performance practice celebrates multivocal texts that defy categorization and leave audiences to resolve what they are or what they mean. Students of performance study performing any way they can, any place they find it, any way it's done. Time and change—if not progress—have made the question sometimes seem quaint.

Actors and interpreters work much of the same turf. That they don't always work it in the same way suggests the richness of performance possibilities and the ingenuity of all performers. Any of the most traditional distinctions meet quick rejoinders. If we say that actors usually confine themselves to one character at a time in staged dramas, interpreters point to the multiple casting so common today and remind us that performance is not limited to plays. Because both actors and interpreters maximize the eloquence their bodies and voices provide in embodying texts, you can see how the distinctions between the two can become finer and finer, or less and less useful.

It would be easy (and so tempting) simply to say that acting and interpretation are the same, but that is not really accurate either. In solo performance your body creates the frame from within which half of the scene is played. The other half of the scene exists just beyond the far edge of the audience, where the silent character is responding to the speaking character. A character speaks. The audience sees and hears the fierce demand. Instantly, the performer switches characters and the audience sees and hears the spirited refusal coming from another character. The tension arising from their conflict crackles along a line *parallel* to the sightlines of the audience, who find themselves in the middle of the excitement.

You could retort that actors can do the same thing—and they can. That is one reason why flexible actors often make such good interpreters. Both actors and interpreters share a commitment to the faithful embodiment of the play. Actors are *likelier* to demonstrate their commitment in groups, often with the powerful assistance of scenography (sets and props, costumes, makeup, lights—all the technical wizardry). Solo interpreters create all of the characters in the scene, one at a time. Your body and your voice are a smaller frame than is a big stage, but if you lead your audience carefully, together you can create a different, but equally engaging, world for the drama. Finally, for most students, the differences are less useful than the similarities.

Structural Elements of a Play

Plays are organized on the principles of *unity* and *probability.* We said their basic ingredient is *conflict.* The ways in which conflict is presented, developed, and resolved vary widely. In general, however, the opening scenes of a play are devoted to *exposition* through action and dialogue. Then comes the challenge that introduces the inciting or exciting force. Several such units may develop. The subsequent moves and counter-moves among the characters produce a tightening of conflict (the *rising action*). The rising action comes to a point of decision in the crisis. The *crisis* is that moment of limitation that directs the action to its final outcome. The crisis makes inevitable and brings about the *climax,* the culmination of all the elements of the conflict. The climax is fol-lowed by the *denouement,* or *resolution,* or, in tragedy, the inevitable catastrophe.

Most dramas follow some variation of this general form; in the changes and alterations, each drama achieves its unique pattern. These events or occurrences should not be confused with plot. As we dis-cussed in Chapter 6, plot cannot be separated from the characters. We call *plot* all that the characters say and do, and we know about charac-ters from what they say and do and from what others say about and do to them. A plot is not a play, and a play is not simply its plot. Anton Chekhov's *The Three Sisters,* some people say, is about three women who don't go to Moscow. It is true that the sisters never reach that des-tination. Still, this description shows very little understanding of what the sisters *do* reach, or how they get it, or what it costs, or what happens along the way.

It is very unlikely that you will perform a complete play; you are much more likely to find an exciting scene to excerpt, analyze, and per-form. We do precisely that in the following pages. Remember that iso-lating one scene from its neighboring scenes, and removing from the performance all that led up to the scene as well as what followed the scene, will complicate your performance responsibilities. You will need to respect the scene as it operates within the play from which it was re-moved, and, from the perspective of analysis, you will find much use-ful information about the characters in parts of the play you won't be performing. That is why, when you study a play during rehearsal, you need to proceed carefully, *speech by speech.* You have to be certain that everything that is happening onstage is clear to you. Someone who may not be speaking could be communicating a great deal simply by her presence. In a staged version, the audience would be able to see how that contribution shapes the drama. As a solo performer, you must make that silent presence apparent in the ways in which the speaking character delivers his lines.

Similarly, the ways characters move around the stage help the play to make meaning. Sometimes it will be useful for you to sketch a small stage map that helps you to clarify where everyone is. Obviously, if only two people are in the scene, your job is easier than if there are seven people, six of whom enter or exit during your segment. In any case, don't proceed to the next speech until you are certain—in your body and in your voice—that you understand what the speaker is saying and doing and what everyone else who is onstage (or about to come on-stage) is doing. Are all the others listening to the speaking character? What is on their minds? What are they *not* saying? What is the speaker thinking? What is the speaker doing? What is the speaker trying to hide? Where is everyone looking? What should your audience know about the movement onstage?

Explicit clues about what the characters are thinking are not always provided in the play. Be on the lookout for implicit or even concealed clues in a given scene, speech, line, or word. You need to discover how the scheme of events figures in each play.

Analyzing a Scene

Let us examine a scene to find explicit and hidden clues about character. *The Three Sisters* is a play about time filled with the minutiae of life. Much of the action seems not to get anybody anywhere. But Chekhov recognized what we all know: Only rarely do lives change because of drastic or melodramatic events. Usually, changes "just happen" without our direction—as we drink coffee, turn the pages of a newspaper, or stroll along a walkway overlooking the water.

The following scene is almost at the end of the play. Irina, the youngest sister, converses with her new fiancé, the Baron Nikolai Tuzenbach. For three and one-half acts the Baron has carefully courted Irina; she has quietly rejected each of his tenuous but persistent offers. She dreamed of marrying a Prince Charming who would carry her away on a white horse. Time has pulled that dream apart. Irina has grown up and settled for the Baron. Perhaps he represents her last chance to get out of the small town where her culture and achievements are "like a sixth finger." Settling for the Baron comes at a high price, for he is painfully ugly; but his devotion to Irina never flags, and he even challenges a rival for her affections to a duel. As the scene begins, the Baron is about to leave for that duel. He may die because of it (if he does, his death will destroy even this fragment of Irina's dream), but he will not mention that possibility to Irina.

[*Enter* IRINA *and* TUZENBACH, TUZENBACH *wearing a straw hat;*
   KULYGIN *crosses the stage, calling "Aa-oo, Masha! Aa-oo!"*]

TUZENBACH: That seems to be the only man in town who's glad the officers are leaving.

IRINA: It's understandable. [*Pause*] Our town is going to be empty now.

TUZENBACH: Dear, I'll be back shortly.

IRINA: Where are you going?

TUZENBACH: I must go into town . . . to see my comrades off.

IRINA: That's not true . . . Nikolai, why are you so distracted today?
   [*Pause*] What happened yesterday near the theater?

TUZENBACH [*with a gesture of impatience*]:   I'll come back in an hour and
be with you again. [*Kisses her hands.*] My beloved. . . . [*Looks into her
face.*] It's five years now that I have loved you, and I still can't get used
to it, and you seem always more beautiful to me. What lovely, wonderful hair! What eyes! Tomorrow I shall carry you off, we'll work, and be
rich, and my dreams will come true. You shall be happy. There is only
one thing, only one: you do not love me!

IRINA: That is not within my power! I'll be your wife, faithful and obedient, but it's not love, I can't help it! [*Weeps.*] I have never in my life
been in love. Oh, how I have dreamed of love, dreamed of it for a long
time now, day and night, but my soul is like a fine piano that is locked,
and the key lost. [*Pause*] You look troubled.

TUZENBACH: I haven't slept all night. There is nothing in my life so
terrible as to frighten me, only that lost key racks my soul and will not
let me sleep. . . . Tell me something. . . . [*Pause*] Tell me something. . . .

IRINA: What? What shall I say? What?

TUZENBACH: Something.

IRINA: Don't! Don't! [*Pause*]

TUZENBACH: What trifles, what silly little things in life will suddenly,
for no reason at all, take on meaning. You laugh at them just as you've
always done, consider them trivial, and yet you go on, and you feel
that you haven't the power to stop. Oh, let's not talk about that! I feel
elated, I see these fir trees, these maples and birches, as if for the first
time, and they all gaze at me with curiosity and expectation. What
beautiful trees, and, in fact, how beautiful life ought to be with them!
[*A shout of: "Aa-oo! Yoo-hoo!"*] I must go, it's time. . . . There's a tree
that's dead, but it goes on swaying in the wind with the others. So it
seems to me that if I die, I'll still have a part in life, one way or another.
Good-bye, my darling. . . . [*Kisses her hands.*] The papers you gave me
are on my table, under the calendar.

IRINA: I am coming with you.

TUZENBACH: [*alarmed*]:   No, no! [*Quickly goes, then stops in the avenue.*]
Irina!

IRINA: What?

TUZENBACH: [*not knowing what to say*]:   I didn't have any coffee this
morning. Ask them to make me some. [*Quickly goes out.*]

[IRINA *stands lost in thought, then goes to the back of the stage and sits down
   in the swing.*]

On a first reading, not much seems to be happening here: man and woman enter, talk about love, happiness, a piano, some trees, and the man runs off. All true. Let's reread the scene carefully, speech by speech, to see what else is happening.

The Baron enters with Irina. He had renounced his aristocracy to join the army, and now he has even renounced the army—he wants to join Irina and work for their future together. Although Irina has accepted this comically ugly man whom her oldest sister recommended to her, can you imagine her mixed feelings when she gave up her dream of a dashing hero gloriously whisking her off? Irina and the Baron stand onstage together, silent. Each contemplates marriage. Do they touch? The text does not tell us. What do *you* think?

Irina breaks the pause with "Our town is going to be empty now." Tuzenbach looks at his watch (he must not be late for the duel in which he could be—and is—killed) and reassures Irina that he will return shortly. Anxious and distracted, he stumbles through his half-lie about saying good-bye to friends. Irina senses his fear, knows that he's hiding the truth, and gently encourages him to confide in her.

Time presses. This silent Tuzenbach—distressed because he upsets the woman he never dreamed would say yes—resembles the earlier, silent Tuzenbach, who is awed by Irina's beauty. Impatiently he ignores the repeated question with a repeated assurance. He kisses her hand and looks directly into her eyes to repeat the love he has declared so often in the past. (Remember what he looks like, how his looks are a silent reminder to her of how her dreams have shriveled.) Exclaiming over her beautiful eyes and hair, he begins to sketch their future. But notice carefully what he says and how he says it: "Tomorrow I shall carry you off, we'll work, and be rich, and my dreams will come true. You shall be happy."

Consider those personal pronouns carefully. Baron Tuzenbach wants to be sure that *he* fulfills Irina's dreams by taking her away, as a knight rescues a damsel in distress. The kingdom he offers her is the simple life of working together and being rich together. Does one inevitably follow the other? Is work as simple as saying it? When all of this occurs, Tuzenbach assumes, then "my" dreams of five years will all be true. But will they? Will Irina love this ugly man as he loves her? And what of *her* dreams? Tuzenbach knows she doesn't love him. He fears that more than his imminent death. He acknowledges the fear that she doesn't love him, but he assures her that *she'll* be happy. Can he be so certain?

Irina's honest answer isn't meant to be cruel, although it must ravage the Baron, particularly because he is about to duel with a rival for her love. She agrees to be his wife, but with open eyes and without pretenses. Her dreams have evaporated. In their place stands the ugly Baron. She begins to cry over her lost dreams. At least she is passionate about something she *isn't:* her "soul is like a fine piano that is locked, and the key lost."

More time passes. Tuzenbach admits that he does not shrink from the future, even from death; only death without her love tortures him, terrifies him. He is willing not to be the pianist on the piano of her soul; he will settle for being the key, if only she will let him. In bravely disguised misery, they stand silent. Time passes. Then he begs her to speak to him.

Tuzenbach is at his most vulnerable. The only cover is Irina's insipid "What? What shall I say? What?" She isn't being coy or heartless. She doesn't know his future. She doesn't love him, can't love him. Ought she pretend to love him? On the verge of tears and almost numb, he offers one word in isolation; but he gets the response a mother might give a fussing child. He asks for what Irina does not have and cannot give. They stand together, silent again. Time presses.

Tuzenbach's only complaining lines appear here when he speaks of how "trifles" (like duels?) and "silly little things" (like phrases uttered without thinking—even by a woman who has told him that it does not lie in her power to love him?) come to matter. It takes a moment for Tuzenbach's customary optimism to assert itself. He claims that he is curiously happy. He has waited for Irina, and she has agreed. Life *must* be good. Looking around, he sees the trees that enchanted him in the first and second acts (and that will be cut down as soon as the curtain falls): "What beautiful trees, and, in fact, how beautiful life ought to be with them!" With the special clarity of the condemned, he values any world that can make them both so miserable even as it rewards them. The subjunctive mood used in the second half of the line qualifies his future, just as he suddenly stiffens when he hears the call to the duel, a hello that means good-bye. Death waits for them all—it is only a matter of time. But he still will not succumb. Even the dead, dried-up tree partakes somehow of life with the others, is moved as they move, and so Tuzenbach knows that he will live some kind of life after the duel. At last he takes her hand and kisses it.

Irina knows that this emotional farewell is suspicious and moves to protect the man. She will go with him. Tuzenbach, alarmed, refuses to consider it and moves, now, to join those trees both living and dead with whom he has linked himself. He cannot let her know what will happen; she mustn't be hurt. Abruptly he stops, turning once more to glimpse her eyes and her hair and calls out for her. What does he want to say? "Good-bye," and "I love you," and "I'm doing this for you," and "Please just tell me that you love me." Irina, alone, unsure, afraid, confused, echoes what she said before: "What?" What more can she say? He requests some coffee, and in the last moment onstage finds himself caught between saying everything and nothing. Refusing to buckle, he gets one more glimpse. Just as he is about to break, he dashes off. She stands alone. Time passes.

In patterning this scene, Chekhov creates a telling rhythm with long speeches that allow for prolonged self-disclosure (Tuzenbach on Irina's beauty, Irina on her inability to love Tuzenbach, Tuzenbach on the trees) set against brief questions and answers. Midscene the impasse between the two characters is clearest, and the language breaks down almost completely. Yet, under scrutiny, these apparently patternless events reveal careful plotting of *speech, incident,* and potent *silence.* Each of these components furthers the action of the play. Tuzenbach must repeat his love to Irina and then somehow prepare her for the future that might not include him. Irina must make clear to Tuzenbach just what her agreement to marry him does (and does not) include. Neither can leave the stage until these objectives are fulfilled. Their conflict arises from the unresolvable tasks both characters undertake. Through their language, the characters convey their limitations and the degree to which they are willing to expose themselves: Tuzenbach speaks almost constantly. In dismay Irina responds briefly until her one long speech, during which Tuzenbach learns the futility of his hopes. He moves toward her, away from her, and then finally runs off; she tolerates, accepts, endures. Then they are silent.

Admittedly, characters must speak if an audience is to achieve the fullest possible understanding of their lives. But in drama some of the most moving moments are silent ones. That is probably also true of your life, isn't it? Do not presume that nothing happens during a pause. A great deal happens that even words cannot convey. Chekhov places five pauses in this brief scene, all at moments when nothing that the characters can *say* demonstrates their agony as effectively as momentary speechlessness. "What shall I say?" Irina asks. Even together, she and Tuzenbach are more than ever apart and alone.

This brief excerpt is not Chekhov's entire play. As rich as the scene becomes under careful observation, it resonates even more deeply when understood in its proper context. You can never assume that a fragment of a character's life equals its entirety. Does someone who spent a week with you on vacation fully understand you? To know the characters in a play fully, it is necessary to read the entire play. That is also the best first step for performing drama.

Working a Scene

Plays are interactions of characters. Your preparation begins by knowing how and where to look for the clues to understanding these characters. Characters *interact* when confronting one another, so a scene becomes more than simply an aggregate of speeches by different characters. You need to understand the shape of the scene that results when the characters try to live with one another.

We look now at a scene from a different kind of play to see how charting the relationship between characters reveals the trajectory of a scene. To reiterate a crucial point: scenes are *not* entire plays. We include excerpts because you are most likely to perform them and because time and space limitations preclude reprinting and discussing entire plays. That we do not explore complete plays—as we have done with complete stories and complete poems—in no way suggests that you need read only a scene to grasp the richness of a play.

This scene occurs very early in Edward Albee's *Who's Afraid of Virginia Woolf?* George is a 46-year-old associate professor of history; his 52-year-old wife, Martha, is the daughter of the president of the college. It is after two in the morning, and husband and wife have just returned from a party given by Martha's father to welcome new faculty. At the party Martha has met a new biology professor and his wife and has invited them home for a nightcap. George, exhausted and more harassed than usual by his boisterous wife, has complained about their guests' tardiness. Martha retorts:

MARTHA [*after a moment's consideration*]:   You make me puke!

GEORGE: What?

MARTHA: Uh . . . you make me puke!

GEORGE [*thinks about it . . . then . . .*]:   That wasn't a very nice thing to say, Martha.

MARTHA: That wasn't *what?*

GEORGE: . . . a very nice thing to say.

MARTHA: I like your anger. I think that's what I like about you most . . . your anger. You're such a . . . such a simp! You don't even have the . . . the what? . . .

GEORGE: . . . guts? . . .

MARTHA: PHRASEMAKER! [*Pause . . . then they both laugh.*] Hey, put some more ice in my drink, will you? You never put any ice in my drink. Why is that, hunh?

GEORGE [*takes her drink*]:   I always put ice in your drink. You eat it, that's all. It's that habit you have . . . chewing your ice cubes . . . like a cocker spaniel. You'll crack your big teeth.

MARTHA: THEY'RE MY BIG TEETH!

GEORGE: Some of them . . . some of them.

MARTHA: I've got more teeth than you've got.

GEORGE: Two more.

MARTHA: Well, two more's a lot more.

GEORGE: I suppose it is. I suppose it's pretty remarkable . . . considering how old you are.

MARTHA: YOU CUT THAT OUT! [*Pause*] You're not so young yourself.

GEORGE [*with boyish pleasure . . . a chant*]:   I'm six years younger than you are . . . I always have been and I always will be.

MARTHA [*glumly*]:   Well . . . you're going bald.

GEORGE: So are you. [*Pause . . . they both laugh.*] Hello, honey.

MARTHA: Hello. C'mon over here and give your Mommy a big sloppy kiss.

GEORGE: . . . oh, now. . . .

MARTHA: I WANT A BIG SLOPPY KISS!

GEORGE [*preoccupied*]:   I don't *want* to kiss you, Martha. Where *are* these people? Where are these *people* you invited over?

MARTHA: They stayed on to talk to Daddy. . . . They'll be here. . . . *Why* don't you want to kiss me?

GEORGE [*too matter-of-fact*]:   Well, dear, if I kissed you I'd get all excited . . . I'd get beside myself, and I'd take you, by force, right here on the living room rug, and then our little guests would walk in, and . . . well, just think what your father would say about *that.*

MARTHA: You pig!

GEORGE [*haughtily*]:   Oink! Oink!

MARTHA: Ha, ha, ha, HA! Make me another drink . . . lover.

GEORGE [*taking her glass*]:   My God, you can swill it down, can't you?

MARTHA [*imitating a tiny child*]:   I'm firsty.

GEORGE: Jesus!

MARTHA [*swinging around*]:   Look, sweetheart, I can drink you under any goddamn table you want . . . so don't worry about me!

GEORGE: Martha, I gave you the prize years ago. . . . There isn't an abomination award going that you. . . .

MARTHA: I swear . . . if you existed I'd divorce you. . . .

GEORGE: Well, just stay on your feet, that's all. . . . These people are your guests, you know, and. . . .

MARTHA: I can't even see you . . . I haven't been able to see you for years. . . .

GEORGE: . . . if you pass out, or throw up, or something . . .

MARTHA: I mean, you're a blank, a cipher . . .

GEORGE: . . . and try to keep your clothes on, too. There aren't many more sickening sights than you with a couple of drinks in you and your skirt up over your head, you know. . . .

MARTHA: . . . a zero . . .

GEORGE: . . . your *heads,* I should say. . . .

[*The front doorbell chimes.*]

MARTHA: Party! Party!

GEORGE [*murderously*]:   I'm really looking forward to this, Martha. . . .

MARTHA [*same*]:   Go answer the door.

GEORGE [*not moving*]:   You answer it.

MARTHA: Get to that door, you. [*He does not move.*] I'll fix you, you. . . .

GEORGE [*fake-spits*]:   . . . to you. . . .

[*Door chime again.*]

MARTHA [*shouting . . . to the door*]: C'MON IN! [*To* GEORGE, *between her teeth.*] I said, get over there!

GEORGE [*moves a little toward the door, smiling slightly*]: All right, love . . . whatever love wants. [*Stops.*] Just don't start on the bit, that's all.

MARTHA: The bit? The bit? What kind of language is that? What are you talking about?

GEORGE: The bit. Just don't start in on the bit.

MARTHA: You imitating one of your students, for God's sake? What are you trying to do? WHAT BIT?

GEORGE: Just don't start in on the bit about the kid, that's all.

MARTHA: What do you take me for?

GEORGE: Much too much.

MARTHA [*really angered*]: Yeah? Well, I'll start in on the kid if I want to.

GEORGE: Just leave the kid out of this.

MARTHA [*threatening*]: He's mine as much as he is yours. I'll talk about him if I want to.

GEORGE: I'd advise against it, Martha.

MARTHA: Well, good for you. [*Knock.*] C'mon in. Get over there and open the door!

GEORGE: You've been advised.

MARTHA: Yeah . . . sure. Get over there!

GEORGE [*moving toward the door*]: All right, love . . . whatever love wants. Isn't it nice the way some people have manners, though, even in this day and age? Isn't it nice that some people won't just come breaking into other people's houses even if they *do* hear some subhuman monster yowling at 'em from inside . . . ?

MARTHA: SCREW YOU!

[*Simultaneously with* MARTHA'*s last remark,* GEORGE *flings open the front door.* HONEY *and* NICK *are framed in the entrance*]

First, let's be clear: this scene does *not* depict a typical academic couple at home. We must determine exactly what happens in the scene, and then determine how this action arises from the characters' needs and goals as revealed or hidden in what they say and do. Albee's stage directions greatly aid analysis, as does his distinctive use of ellipses to indicate both pause and thought at the same time.

We begin by analyzing this scene together. (You will develop your own method by a process of trial and error as you gain experience with different kinds of plays.) Although we focus here on one scene, the first step is to understand how *all* the scenes make the play. When you have a rough idea of the functions of each scene, begin to look at each scene individually, keeping in mind that what you decide must be consistent with the rest of the play. Carefully follow the patterns of *action and inaction* and *silence and speech*. What do George and Martha say? In what circumstances do they say it? How does what they say further the development of their goals?

Understanding the physical activity that occurs during the scene enables us to understand the changes that constantly occur in George and Martha. Where does Martha drop one role and assume another? There are several such points before the front doorbell chimes. Where does George shift his role? How frequently do his shifts occur? Who changes personality more often? How are George and Martha different by the last line of this scene? Keeping in mind this rough sketch of the ground to be covered, go back to the beginning.

Once you know the content of the scene, you should consider the relationship of the characters to the setting in which they live. Albee has set this scene "in the living room of a house on the campus of a small New England college." George and Martha are sloppy housekeepers; moreover, they have lived here for more than twenty years, and the accumulations of their lives fill this home. Books probably abound. Are they all neatly shelved? Now ask the questions that your answers imply. Might the ashtrays be full? Are the glasses empty and sweating on the table? Is it likely that George has suddenly taken out the vacuum and begun to tidy up? What are they wearing? Does what you know about Martha even from this scene suggest a svelte, haughtily fashionable woman? Might her clothes be tighter, smaller, younger looking than she is? What makes you think so? Does George look like an illustration from *GQ*? How do you know what he looks like?

Consider the differences between George and Martha. How do they compare, contrast, and balance in temperament, maturity, and cultural background? The *variety and contrast* of a play are achieved by pitting telltale differences against each other and by comparing the tiny differences that loom large when so many other things are similar. George appears willing to submit to Martha's abuse. But doesn't he taunt her, too? Both delight in word play; each is able to learn new rules as quickly as the other changes the game. Such interdependence arises out of years of practice, no doubt, as well as out of something fundamental that they share. Look at George and Martha again from this perspective. It has been said that married couples tend to resemble each other after many years. Is this true of George and Martha? Do their similarities outweigh their differences? Why have they stayed together for so long? They fight viciously, so conflict obviously exists. In this scene, apart from the couple's obvious physical differences, what are the chief points of opposition between them? How do these different temperaments appear in the lines? Does either partner obliterate the other? Why or why not?

Such preliminary questions prove that the lives of the characters are both internal and external, as your life is. Your room may look immaculate or messy; you may have a favorite item of apparel, a manner of talking or habit of drinking coffee; but you are surely not just the woman with the southern accent who wears scarves or the man in the bomber jacket who reads *Sports Illustrated.* Characters are much more than their appearance.

Focusing attention on one character at a time (starting with the person who has the most lines), apply the now-familiar process of understanding logical content and giving careful attention to climaxes and focal points, style and rhythm, and the denotative and connotative richness of all the words. Once you are sure of the content, you are ready to fuse external and internal activity to make a character appear to be alive.

We'll start with Martha. Albee describes her as "a large, boisterous woman, 52, looking somewhat younger. Ample but not fleshy." Martha must also be capable of rapid changes in personality: she is a braying woman, a mommy, a tiny child, a vituperative wife, a shouting harridan—all within five minutes. How do these changes occur in Martha? Where do these shifts take place? What do they arise from? Why does shared laughter accelerate the change? Does Martha need to move out of her chair? Why? Is there any difference among the kinds of anger Martha shows? All of these are *outward* characteristics—things your audience *sees* and *hears*. When you know what the audience must see, you can clarify better both what internal life gives rise to these elements and how these responses affect other characters.

Now apply the same kinds of questions to George, whom Albee tellingly describes as "her husband, 46. Thin; hair going gray." Not much to build on there, one might think. But think a minute. George is six years younger than Martha, and he taunts her with this fact. He is described as "her husband," an adjunct to her, rather than a man or a history professor or a "failure," though he is all of these things, too. His physical spareness—borne out in his lines and perhaps even in his volume—contrasts with her abundance. His mildness is not passivity, because he is capable of annoying her. Is there any way in which "giving in" can be a victory? Does "submission" mean a loss of dignity? Is it ever easier to do something than to fight about it? Martha calls George "a blank, a cipher" and moments later "a zero." Is he? Are they unequally matched? George opens the door at the end of the scene, as Martha has ordered. Why? He is clearly the more physically active of the two in this scene. Does this movement parallel another kind of flexibility, his submissiveness, or both?

The interpreter of drama needs to know how a character looks, lives, thinks, and behaves long before the play or the scene takes place. The playwright does not always give this information. Depend on your knowledge of human nature and your skills at observing others to supply the omitted details. Behind the exterior are the motivations. You are dealing with human actions and reactions, and the more you know of your fellow creatures, the more easily you can understand and communicate to the audience the complexities of the characters in the play.

With the *physical, psychological,* and *emotional* background filled in, the interpreter can begin to study the sources of the incidents in the play. From examining this segment can you project what George and Martha were doing immediately *before* their entrance? Did George enjoy his father-in-law's party? Did he remember the young biology professor? Why did George and Martha go to the party? Why did Martha remember the biology professor? Why did they leave the party? Why do you suppose Martha put off telling her husband about the late guests? Did George expect any of this? Are they both prepared for what happens in the scene?

Characters in drama, like people in life, represent at least the sum of their past experiences. All people respond to the pressures and needs of a given situation on the basis of the events of their past. Psychologists have taught us how much of adult human behavior and personality is really a response, a *reaction,* both to the world as it was learned in childhood and also to the primal relationship of parent and child. Such substance renders much of the excitement of this scene, and many of its difficulties as well. How do George and Martha live with each other? Why have they put up with each other's abuse for so long? They are not a couple who would refuse to consider divorce from any religious scruple. Martha mentions divorce, surely not for the first time. Can you fight over something you don't care about? The first act is called "Fun and Games," and both characters change considerably, even during this scene. How do they know when a new game is being played? George appears to submit to Martha. Does Martha ever give in to George? How do they "weigh out" in the match between them? They certainly laugh a great deal—together and separately. Does one person's laughter ridicule or scorn the other? What is so funny about "PHRASEMAKER," which elicits their first laugh together? When George cautions Martha not to "start in on the bit about the kid," is it a threat, a taunt, or a caution? Does he expect Martha to obey him? Does either partner surprise the other? Why?

Incorporate the answers to all of these questions—and many others that will occur to you—into your performance. Sometimes, beginning interpreters become so enamored of a favorite character in a play or a scene that the rest of the characters never appear or they appear only to feed lines to the real star. Continue careful analysis of *each* character, studying each as an individual and evaluating his or her relationship to every other individual. Remember that your responsibility is to the *scene* as a whole, to the play Albee wrote. Balance your own observations with the play's truth, keeping in mind that although the audience wants to see and hear you (which will happen in any case), they also want to see and hear Albee's play. Make sure they get both.

We have seen how characters emerge from what they say and what they do, and how understanding character requires careful reading, thoughtful questioning, a good grounding in human psychology. We just saw how characters, by *interacting with each other,* create the drama of a scene, provide the tension that compels an audience to listen and watch. The play thrives, however, because the interactions are shaped and arranged to rivet our attention, and the pattern of the arrangement creates a scene's distinctive rhythm. We discussed rhythm in Chapter 5 (and will discuss its role in poetry in Chapter 10); all of these discussions overlap in some areas.

Rhythm

When your characters begin to take on life, rehearsals can be exhilarating. As the interactions ignite, you will be energized by the vitality you create and tap. Interaction becomes fluent as the rhythm of the individuals' speeches becomes more obvious to you. At the same time, how the speeches work off each other will become more apparent and important, because the tempo of the interaction provides the foundation for rhythm. Rhythm in a play is extremely interesting and complex. First, at the stylistic level, the individual speech rhythm of each character is revealed: Irina is a woman of few words, most of the time; Martha has no trouble speaking up without restraint and without a censor. Second, fluctuations of emotional tension—as anger rises and subsides, or laughter is shared or separated—reveal rhythm in both content and form. Third, there is the inevitable alternation between activity and stillness: Irina stands in one place for the entire scene; Martha probably stays seated; Tuzenbach and George move frequently. The alternation between their various modes of living on stage contributes to the play's rhythm. (Of course, because a play depends on action for development, no part of a good play is really passive: drama imitates *action*.)

This alternation between active and passive elements affects the tempo at which the various scenes and speeches move. It also determines the speed with which they build toward minor climaxes and finally toward the main climax, whether in action or character development or both. In a well-written play, static scenes are used sparingly and are governed by the same principles that influence the writer of narrative prose: the need for relaxation from tension and intense activity and the need to channel the audience's concentration into an area that is different in kind if not in degree.

In *Who's Afraid of Virginia Woolf?* and *The Three Sisters,* changes in rhythm are caused by changes of content as well as by stylistic, linguistic, grammatical, or syntactical changes. The words Chekhov uses range from spare to elaborate, but each word exists because at that particular moment with those people, at that point in their lives, only that combination of words expresses the complexity of their characters. Albee allows George and Martha to complete each other's lines. We learn their characteristic attitudes through techniques that include careful management of punctuation and pause. The patterning of silences to achieve a specific tempo appears often in contemporary drama. Harold Pinter, in particular, has elevated the pause to a dramatic force that can be both menacing and pitiful, ominous and poetic. (See his *Betrayal* at the end of Chapter 8.) Pauses occur because words fail the characters. Maybe you've had the same experience in your own life.

Style

Style includes what a character omits as well as what he or she says. Playwrights don't leave characters speechless because they ran out of ink or couldn't think of anything for them to say. In discovering the elements of dialogue style, interpreters learn about another part of a character's life. The *language* a character uses reveals background and attitude. The *arrangement of ideas* gives a clue to the person's clarity of thinking and is likely to reflect intensity of emotion. The *length of the thought units* also may reveal much about a character's personality, forcefulness, and authority as well as the degree of psychological tension. In *Fires in the Mirror,* Anna Deavere Smith uses line length much as a poet does to suggest the rhythm of the characters' speech and takes special care to describe how such pauses are filled (see the excerpt at the end of this chapter).

Some contemporary dramas expand traditional concepts of style. Sometimes the motivation for speech or action is confined to the character's mind and formed by a sense of isolation from the world or by the belief that the people, the world, life, love, and death are equally absurd and that speech and action are pointless. In a play, of course, such characters still speak, but sometimes their dialogue takes the form of extremely long near-monologues, or soliloquies. Often these monologues are subjectively motivated and highly repetitive, and sometimes the character's action is violent or static, impotent. Such monologues are nonetheless richly rewarding vehicles for the solo performer because they stretch your physical and vocal capacity, expand your ability to capitalize on your own responsiveness to emotional and sense imagery, and are exhausting in the best senses. (See Wesley's monologue from the beginning of *Curse of the Starving Class* at the end of Chapter 8.) Mind you, we do not suggest that traditional drama is a day at the beach, and if you have more experience in today's performance art, Shakespeare and Goldsmith will challenge you at least as much as Soyinka or Shepard and will do so in very different ways.

Scenography

When you go to the theater, you are likely to see costumed performers on a carefully lighted stage that probably has properties and set pieces to suggest the period and social status of the world of the play. These technical achievements can astonish an audience. Watch a three-masted ship in full sail explode into flames under a starry sky while seventy-eight choristers and six principals in seventeenth-century Venetian costume sing lustily—the spectacle will amaze you. Dramatists usually have little difficulty establishing setting because they can put whatever information is necessary into stage directions and descriptions that precede or come between the scenes. Renaissance dramatists evoke setting within the speeches of the characters; contemporary dramatists specify lighting, setting, and costume. Some playwrights provide voluminous and minute descriptions for almost every second. In whatever period, drama always has been partly spectacle.

A solo performer, on the other hand, most often appears in street clothes, sometimes behind a lectern, even carrying a script. How can this interpreter hope to compete with the visually pleasing sets and costumes that surround actors? Carefully consider what you are doing. The technical resources that create visual statements in realistic dramas do not exist for the solo interpreter. Such resources, however, aren't any more necessary to the interpreter than they were to Shakespeare or Sophocles. Although spectacle is part of drama, the spectacle need not be the *fact* of a staged production. Some realistic dramas of the late nineteenth and early twentieth centuries attempted to convince the audience of the reality of stage activity by featuring objects and details of real life (real bacon frying in a real cast-iron skillet over a real fire built on real sod). Proponents of these outlandish experiments (the real sod, after all, rested on a stage and was lit by stage lights) forget that belief is not as much a matter of what goes on in front of the audience's eyes as it is a matter of what goes on inside the audience's minds. There, illusion is made real. Absolutely crucial stage directions and descriptions can always be given by the performer (*not* the characters) before the performance begins. Audiences do not expect one performer to be eighty-four performers, nor do they expect the lavish spectacle of the stage. Your listeners will assist in creating the scenographic elements in the performance with their imaginations. They can do this quite well when their imaginations are carefully guided and you give them enough space to create. Indeed, that is *their* part in your performance.

Sometimes, of course, the interpreter is called on to describe some intensely interpersonal activity that one person simply cannot duplicate—a pie fight, swordplay resulting in death, a wrestling match, a kiss. Or the interpreter is presented with some vast or intricate set piece or design requirement. Under such circumstances it is far wiser for the performer (*not* one of the characters) to describe the action as the playwright describes it in the stage directions.

Scenography also conveys period manners, social customs, and economic conditions to an audience. All affect the characters. Writers of narratives can (and often do) remind their readers of the physical and psychological impact of surroundings on character. Interpreters of drama should constantly scrutinize the world they are attempting to suggest to be sure that the telltale parts clearly appear in their performance. Tuzenbach keenly feels the impact of the birches as he and Irina stand in front of the house. George surely feels once again the messiness of his house as it is to be seen for the first time by the guests. Both stand and move at least in part in response to their respective environments.

Place can establish a motive, motivate an action, describe a world, limit alternatives, or impede the achievement of a goal. Properties and various details of the sets may also play an important part in the action. In *Flyin' West* (at the end of this chapter) Sophie spends much of the first half of the scene chewing black licorice. She offers Miss Leah a piece, and both characters discuss it. Should you search the local drugstore for the right prop? Well, if you find the genuine article and insist on using it as Sophie, won't you have to remove it from your mouth when Miss Leah speaks? Better to imagine you are chewing and show your audience that you are; they will believe you (and probably thank you for not making them witness your spitting it out!).

Putting It Together

If all these responsibilities and problems you are likely to encounter in performing drama seem daunting, some words of encouragement may help. First, the solo performance *can* be done. We have been awed by the richly rewarding performances that occur when serious students work conscientiously. In drama, perhaps more than in any other genre, the key is not to take anything for granted: take the time for a *thorough* rehearsal of a three-minute segment rather than expect the same amount of rehearsal to prepare you for a five-minute scene. Next, don't expect it all to happen instantly. You know how long you took on your earlier performances. Allot yourself at least half again as much time to work up this performance. Last, remember our opening comments about drama as "play." If you have rehearsed carefully, you have every reason to enjoy what you are doing. If you have studied the scene carefully, you won't be surprised.

Perhaps the most difficult thing about interpreting drama, aside from the purely mechanical or technical problems of suggesting character and action (which we explore in the next chapter), is keeping the numerous threads of character development and reaction separated yet related. This demands careful preparation and a high degree of concentration during performance. The interpreter must check carefully, especially during preparation, to avoid presenting a mere series of character sketches, each complete in itself but unrelated to the others.

Besides having a thorough knowledge of each character, you should have a constant awareness of relationships and of progressions in these relationships. As the actor must learn to *hear* the speeches of other characters, the interpreter must learn to *have heard,* to be sure each character is responding to what has gone before. All the characters must stay "in scene" and be ready to pick up the progression as they speak.

Thus, the interpreter needs to select for each character enough significant physical and vocal details so that the listeners can themselves fill in the outline to make a three-dimensional, believable person. Each personality in each play presents its own slightly different problems. Some suggestions for handling mechanical details—and they are suggestions only—are given in the next chapter.

REMEMBER THIS!

This chapter has focused on the theoretical foundations of the solo performance of drama to inform the technical responsibilities we discuss in the next chapter. Some of what we suggest may seem complicated or inaccessible, but if you keep these points in mind, you will succeed:

- Drama requires character in action.

- Solo performance of drama offers unique rewards.

- Actors and interpreters are similar and different.

- Conflict is essential to drama but can be presented, developed, and resolved in many different ways.

- Characters are composed of what they say, what they do, what they don't say, what they avoid, and how they interact with each other.

- Rhythm, style, and scenography all affect the ways in which plays make meaning.

- Synthesis requires careful rehearsal and playful pleasure.

This scene opens the second act of Fifth of July. *Shirley, age 14, is the somewhat precocious and self-dramatizing niece of Jed's lover, Ken. All have assembled at the Talley farm near Lebanon, Missouri, for a celebration presided over by Sally, Ken's aunt and Shirley's great-aunt. Jed—an almost silent listener—is essential for Shirley to achieve her effect. Don't let either character become outlandish.*

 FROM **Fifth of July**

LANFORD WILSON

The porch. JED *is sitting in the sunshine, referring back and forth between two books, trying to compose a letter on a legal-size yellow pad. A bell tolls in the distance, fifteen seconds between each deep, heavy stroke.*

SHIRLEY *enters. She enjoys being alone with* JED *for a moment. She looks out over the garden, quite forgetting that* JED *does not see her there. She notices the bell.*

SHIRLEY: Oh! Listen!

JED: (*Jumps a foot*) Oh, God.

SHIRLEY: "Ask not for whom the bell tolls . . ."

JED: It tolls for Harley Campbell.

SHIRLEY: Who?

JED: Your Aunt Sally went to the funeral. They ring the bell before the service and after the service.

SHIRLEY: Oh. Oh, God, now it sounds horrible. Oh, God, that's mournful.

JED: If the man made more than a hundred thousand a year and left a widow, they ring it all during the service as well.

SHIRLEY: We, of course, are the first. (*He looks at her, not understanding*) To arise this morning.

JED: You're the last.

SHIRLEY: Last?

JED: You're up in time for brunch. . . .

SHIRLEY: Gwen is up?

JED: Yeah. And on the phone.

SHIRLEY: Uncle Kenny's up?

JED: Yeah, Sally and I had breakfast at seven, I drove her to church, woke up Ken, and we made an herbal anti-fungus concoction guaranteed to fail, and sprayed thirty-five phlox plants. With Wes's, uh . . . supervision.

SHIRLEY: (*Adjusts*) Oh. Yes . . . I slept . . . fitfully. I tossed, I . . .

JED: Turned?

SHIRLEY: I had this really weird dream. I was being chased by a deer. All through the woods, over bridges, this huge deer. What does a dream like that mean?

JED: Did he have antlers?

SHIRLEY: I don't remember. Why? (JED *goes back to his books*)

JED: If you happen to dream about seven fat cows and seven lean cows, I know what that one means.

SHIRLEY: I would never dream of a cow.

JED: Not a feisty young heifer? Jumping fences, trying to get into the corn?

SHIRLEY: Oh, please. I certainly hope you don't think of me like that! I am not a common cow! I am a . . . flower, Jed. Slowly and frighteningly opening her petals onto the spring morning. A trimu-a-timulus, a timu—

JED: What? A mimulus? You're probably a mimulus.

SHIRLEY: What's a mimulus?

JED: Mimulus is a wild flower. Pinkish-yellow, the monkey flower, they call—

SHIRLEY: No, not that one. Not a monkey flower! I am a . . .

JED: What?

SHIRLEY: Well, not—I don't know. And it's important, too. But . . . I can *see* it. A nearly white, small, single . . .

JED: What about an apple blossom? The first tree of spring to—

SHIRLEY: No, oh, God, no. And grow into an apple? A fat, hard, red, bloated, tasteless apple? For some crone to bake in a pie for her ditchdigger husband to eat without even knowing it? Oh, God. Never. I'm more than likely the daughter of an Indian chief. My mother was very broad-minded and very promiscuous.

JED: So I've heard.

SHIRLEY: (*Thinks*) I am a blossom that opens for one day only . . . and I fall. I am not pollinated. It's too early for the bees. They don't find me. And I fade. Dropping my petals one by—what kind of flower is that? (*She thinks a moment*) A wild rose?

JED: No, you wouldn't flower till May at the earliest. There'd be bees lined up around the block.

SHIRLEY: Well, *what?* God. Daisies are when? (*He shakes his head*) Peony?

JED: There are some anemones . . . that bloom very early.

SHIRLEY: An anemone . . .

JED: The original ones are from Greece, so they're all claimed by heroes who fell in battle and their blood seeped into the ground and anemones sprang up, but I think they've found one or two somewhere else that haven't been claimed yet. I have a picture of them somewhere.

SHIRLEY: Could you find it?

JED: It's around; I'll look it up.

SHIRLEY: (*Hand on sleeve*) Jed. Thank you. This is, you know, very
   important to me.

JED: (*Mock seriousness*) Shirley. It's important to us all.

SHIRLEY: I know.

JED: We don't dwell on it because we try to spare you the pressure of
   all our expectations. We multitudes.

SHIRLEY: I know. But don't. Don't spare me. It makes me strong.

- How did you show the audience the seriousness underlying
  Shirley's humor and the humor underlying Jed's seriousness?

In the early 1980s, Anna Deavere Smith began to create a series of
performance pieces by "interviewing people and later performing
them using their own words" in an attempt to "find American character in the ways that people speak." Her research took her to the racially
polarized world of Crown Heights, Brooklyn, in the summer of 1991.
A 7-year-old black boy was killed by a car in a rabbi's motorcade, and a
Jewish student was slain by blacks in retaliation. From the interviews
Deavere conducted with numerous adversaries, victims, and eyewitnesses, she collected more than two dozen speakers in a dazzling portrait of contemporary ethnic turmoil. About her search Smith writes:

> My sense is that American character lives not in one place or the other, but
> in the gaps between places, and in our struggle to be together in our dif-
> ferences. It lives not in what has been fully articulated, but in what is in the
> process of being articulated, not in the smooth-sounding words, but in the
> very moment that the smooth-sounding words fail us.

*Pay careful attention to how Smith re-creates these two speakers. Note partic-
ularly how the length of the line encourages certain rhythmic experimentation,
always keeping in mind that silence does not mean absence of thought or concentration. Respect the integrity with which these people speak: you are taking
their words right out of their mouths.*

 FROM **Fires in the Mirror**

ANNA DEAVERE SMITH

Bad Boy
Anonymous Young Man

(*Evening. Spring. A recreation room. Young Man is wearing a black jacket
over his clothes. He has a gold tooth. He has some dreadlocks, and a very odd-
shaped multicolored hat. He is soft-spoken, and has a direct gaze. He seems to
be very patient with his explanation.*)

That youth,
that sixteen-year-old
didn't murder that Jew.
(*Pause*)
For one thing,
he played baseball, right?

314

He was a atha-lete,
right?
A bad boy
does
bad things.
Only a bad boy coulda stabbed the man.
Somebody who
does those type a things,
or who sees
those types a things.
A atha-lete
sees people,
is interested in athletics,
stretchin',
exercisin',
goin' to his football games,
or his baseball games.
He's not interested
in stabbin'
people.
So
it's not in his mind
to stab,
to just jump into somethin',
that he has no idea about
and
sta—
and kill a man.
A bad boy,
somebody who's groomed in badness,
or did badness
before,
stabbed the man.
Because I used to be a atha-lete
and I used to be a bad boy,
and when I was a atha-lete,
I was a atha-lete.
All I thought about was atha-lete.
I'm not gonna jeopardize my athleticism
or my career to do anything
that bad people do.
And when I became a bad boy
I'm not a athalete no more.
I'm a bad boy,
and I'm groomin' myself in things that is bad.

You understand, so
he's a athalete,
he's not a bad boy.
It's a big difference.
Like,
mostly the Black youth in Crown Heights have two things to do—
either DJ or be a bad boy, right?
You either
DJ, be a MC, a rapper
or Jamaican rapper,
ragamuffin,
or you be a bad boy,
you sell drugs or you rob people.
What do you do?
I sell drugs.
What do you do?
I rap.
That's how it is in Crown Heights.
I been livin' in Crown Heights mosta my life.
I know for a fact that that youth, that sixteen-year-old,
didn't kill that Jew.
That's between me and my Creator.

- ◆ How did you demonstrate the speaker's physical confidence?

- ◆ How did the language suggest postures and gestures for you?

The Coup
Roslyn Malamud

(Spring. Midafternoon. The sunny kitchen of a huge, beautiful house on Eastern Parkway in Crown Heights. It's a large, very well equipped kitchen. We are sitting at a table in a breakfast nook area, which is separated by shelves from the cooking area. There is a window to the side. There are newspapers on the chair at the far side of the table. Mrs. Malamud offers me food at the beginning of the interview. We are drinking coffee. She is wearing a sweatshirt with a large sequined cat. Her tennis shoes have matching sequined cats. She has on a black skirt and is wearing a wig. Her nails are manicured. She has beautiful eyes that sparkle and are very warm, and a very resonant voice. There is a lot of humor in her face.)

Do you know what happened in August here?
You see when you read the newspapers.
I mean my son filmed what was going on,
but when you read the newspapers . . .
Of course I was here

I couldn't leave my house.
I only would go out early during the day.
The police were barricading here.
You see,
I wish
I could just like
go on television.
I wanna scream to the whole world.
They said
that the Blacks were rioting against the Jews in Crown Heights
and that the Jews were fighting back.
Do you know that the Blacks who came here to riot were not my
neighbors?
I don't love my neighbors.
I don't know my Black neighbors.
There's one lady on President Street—
Claire—
I adore her.
She's my girl friend's next-door neighbor.
I've had a manicure
done in her house and we sit and kibbitz
and stuff
but I don't know them.
I told you we don't mingle socially
because of the difference
of food
and religion
and what have you here.
But
the people in this community
want exactly
what I want out of life.
They want to live
in nice homes.
They all go to work.
They couldn't possibly
have houses here
if they didn't
generally—They have
two,
um,
incomes
that come in.
They want to send their kids to college.
They wanna live a nice quiet life.

They wanna shop for their groceries and cook their meals and go to
their Sunday picnics!
They just want to have decent homes and decent lives!
The people who came to riot here
were brought here
by this famous
Reverend Al Sharpton,
which I'd like to know who ordained him?
He brought in a bunch of kids
who didn't have jobs in
the summertime.
I wish you could see the *New York Times,*
unfortunately it was on page twenty,
I mean, they interviewed
one of the Black girls on Utica Avenue.
She said,
"The guys will make you pregnant
at night
and in the morning not know who you are."
(*Almost whispering*)
And if you're sitting on a front stoop and it's very, very hot
and you have no money
and you have nothing to do with your time
and someone says, "Come on, you wanna riot?"
You know how kids are.
The fault lies with the police department.
The police department did nothing to stop them.
I was sitting here in the front of the house
when bottles were being thrown
and the sergeant tells five hundred policemen
with clubs and helmets and guns
to duck.
And I said to him,
"You're telling them to duck?
What should I do?
I don't have a club and a gun."
Had they put it—
stopped it on the first night
this kid who came from Australia . . .
(*She sucks her teeth*)
You know,
his parents were Holocaust survivors, he didn't have to die.
He worked,
did a lot of research in Holocaust studies.
He didn't have to die.

What happened on Utica Avenue
was an accident.
JEWISH PEOPLE
DO NOT DRIVE VANS INTO SEVEN-YEAR-OLD BOYS.
YOU WANT TO KNOW SOMETHING? BLACK PEOPLE DO
    NOT DRIVE
VANS INTO SEVEN-YEAR-OLD BOYS.
HISPANIC PEOPLE DON'T DRIVE VANS INTO SEVEN-YEAR-
    OLD BOYS.
IT'S JUST NOT DONE.
PEOPLE LIKE JEFFREY DAHMER MAYBE THEY DO IT.
BUT AVERAGE CITIZENS DO NOT GO OUT AND TRY TO KILL
(*Sounds like a laugh but it's just a sound*)
SEVEN-YEAR-OLD BOYS.
It was an accident!
But it was allowed to fester and to steam and all that.
When you come here do you see anything that's going on, riots?
No.
But Al Sharpton and the likes of him like *Dowerty*,
who by the way has been in prison
and all of a sudden he became Reverend *Dowerty*—
they once did an exposé on him—
but
these guys live off of this,
you understand?
People are not gonna give them money,
contribute to their causes
unless they're out there rabble-rousing.
My Black neighbors?
I mean I spoke to them.
They were hiding in their houses just like I was.
We were scared.
I was scared!
I was really frightened.
I had five hundred policemen standing in front of my house
every day
I had mounted police,
but I couldn't leave my block,
because when it got dark I couldn't come back in.
I couldn't meet anyone for dinner.
Thank God, I told you my children were all out of town.
My son was in Russia.
The coup
was exactly the same day as the riot
and I was very upset about it.

He was in Russia running a summer camp
and I was very concerned when I had heard about that.
I hadn't heard from him
that night the riot started.
When I did hear from him I told him to stay in Russia, he'd be safer
there than here.
And he was.

♦ Once again, physical presence is crucial in creating character. How
did you demonstrate the speaker's conviction? her agitation? her
humor?

By this point in Othello, *Iago has convinced the black general Othello that his
young, white wife Desdemona has been unfaithful. We know the claim is utterly
false, but Iago's sinuous skill has all but obliterated Othello's reason. Professional
performers spend lifetimes returning to these characters, fascinated by the challenge of language, emotional range, and power. Be courageous and make a start.*

 FROM **Othello**

WILLIAM SHAKESPEARE

ACT III, SCENE 3

IAGO: I see, [sir], you are eaten up with passion;
    I do repent me that I put it to you.
    You would be satisfied?
OTHELLO: What? nay, and I will.
IAGO: And may; but how? How satisfied, my lord?
    Would you, the [supervisor], grossly gape on?   395
    Behold her topp'd?
OTHELLO: Death and damnation! O!
IAGO: It were a tedious difficulty, I think,
    To bring them to that prospect; damn them then,
    If ever mortal eyes do see them bolster
    More than their own. What then? How then?   400
    What shall I say? Where's satisfaction?
    It is impossible you should see this,
    Were they as prime as goats, as hot as monkeys,
    As salt as wolves in pride, and fools as gross
    As ignorance made drunk. But yet I say,   405
    If imputation and strong circumstances

395 supervisor: *onlooker, spectator.*   **398–99 damn . . . ever:** *i.e. to condemn them only
if.*   **399 bolster:** *go to bed together.*   **400 More:** *other (eyes).*   **402 see:** *i.e. contrive to
be an actual witness of.*   **403 prime:** *lustful.*   **404 salt:** *lecherous.*   **pride:** *heat.*

Which lead directly to the door of truth
Will give you satisfaction, you might have't.
OTHELLO: Give me a living reason she's disloyal.
IAGO: I do not like the office;   410
   But sith I am ent'red in this cause so far
   (Prick'd to't by foolish honesty and love),
   I will go on. I lay with Cassio lately,
   And being troubled with a raging tooth,
   I could not sleep.   415
   There are a kind of men, so loose of soul,
   That in their sleeps will mutter their affairs;
   One of this kind is Cassio.
   In sleep I heard him say, "Sweet Desdemona,
   Let us be wary, let us hide our loves";   420
   And then, sir, would he gripe and wring my hand;
   Cry, "O sweet creature!" then kiss me hard,
   As if he pluck'd up kisses by the roots
That grew upon my lips; [then] laid his leg   425
   [Over] my thigh, and [sigh'd], and [kiss'd], and then
   [Cried], "Cursed fate that gave thee to the Moor!"
OTHELLO: O monstrous! monstrous:
IAGO: Nay, this was but his dream
OTHELLO: But this denoted a foregone conclusion.
IAGO: 'Tis a shrewd doubt, though it be but a dream,
   and this may help to thicken other proofs   430
   That do demonstrate thinly.
OTHELLO: I'll tear her all to pieces
IAGO: Nay, yet be wise; yet we see nothing done
   She may be honest yet. Tell me but this,
   Have you not sometimes seen a handkerchief
   Spotted with strawberries in your wive's hand?   435
OTHELLO: I gave her such a one; 'twas my first gift.
IAGO: I know not that; but such a handkerchief
   (I am sure it was your wive's) did I to-day
   See Cassio wipe his beard with.
OTHELLO: If it be that—
IAGO: If it be that, or any [that] was hers,   440
   It speaks against her with the other proofs.
OTHELLO: O that the slave had forty thousand lives!
   One is too poor, too weak for my revenge.
   Now do I see 'tis true. Look here, Iago,

---

421 gripe: *grip, clasp.*   **428 foregone conclusion:** *act already performed.*   **429 shrewd doubt:** *strong reason for suspicion.*   **430 thicken:** *substantiate.*   **435 wive's:** *wife's.*   **442 the slave:** *i.e. Cassio.*

All my fond love thus do I blow to heaven.   445
'Tis gone.
Arise, black vengeance, from the hollow hell!
Yield up, O love, thy crown and hearted throne
To tyrannous hate! Swell, bosom, with thy fraught,
For 'tis of aspics' tongues!

IAGO: Yet be content.   450

OTHELLO: O blood, blood, blood!

IAGO: Patience, I say; your mind [perhaps] may change.

OTHELLO: Never, Iago. Like to the Pontic Sea,
Whose icy current and compulsive course
Nev'r [feels] retiring ebb, but keeps due on   455
To the Propontic and the Hellespont,
Even so my bloody thoughts, with violent pace,
Shall nev'r look back, nev'r ebb to humble love,
Till that a capable and wide revenge   459
Swallow them up. [*He kneels.*] Now by yond marble heaven,
In the due reverence of a sacred vow
I engage my words.

IAGO: Do not rise yet. [*Iago kneels.*]
Witness, you ever-burning lights above,
You elements that clip us round about,
Witness that here Iago doth give up   465
The execution of his wit, hands, heart,
To wrong'd Othello's service! Let him command,
And to obey shall be in me remorse,
What bloody business ever.   [*They rise.*]

OTHELLO: I greet thy love,
Not with vain thanks, but with acceptance bounteous,
And will upon the instant put thee to't: 471
Within these three days let me hear thee say
That Cassio's not alive.

IAGO: My friend is dead; 'tis done at your request.
But let her live.

OTHELLO: Damn her, lewd minx! O, damn her, damn her!   476
Come go with me apart, I will withdraw
To furnish me with some swift means of death
For the fair devil. Now art thou my lieutenant.

IAGO: I am your own for ever.   *Exeunt.*

---

448 hearted: *established in my heart.*   **449 fraught:** *burden.*   **450 aspics':**
asps'.   **453 Pontic Sea:** *Black Sea.*   **459 capable:** *capacious, comprehensive.*
460 marble: *shining (?) or enduring, changeless (cf. marble-constant, in Antony and
Cleopatra, V.ii.240) (?).*   **464 clip:** *embrace.*   **466 execution:** *action.*   **468–69 to . . .
ever:** *in Othello's service even the cruellest acts will be as allowable as if they were gentle
and prompted by pity (remorse).*   **476 minx:** *wanton.*

♦ On what line does Othello relinquish his last shred of doubt? How did you show this to your audience? What did your Iago do to mark the victory?

This scene comes from the second act of Oliver Goldsmith's eighteenth-century comedy of manners. Marlow, a wealthy Londoner, has come to visit his father's old friend, Mr. Hardcastle, and, at his father's insistence, to pay court to Miss Kate Hardcastle. However, he and his friend Hastings got lost on their journey and have been duped onto believing that they have stumbled on a roadside inn. Neither of the young Londoners has ever met the Hardcastles, and thus neither suspects the trick. Kate and her cousin, Miss Neville, pretend to be at the "inn" quite by chance, so the following interview can occur. Marlow has confessed to his friend that, although he is very much at home with barmaids and "easy" women, he finds conversation with a lady excruciating. Kate has been warned of Marlow's shyness, and she enjoys herself immensely at his expense. People enter and leave frequently in this scene; thus, it provides a solo performer good practice in managing stage business.

 FROM **She Stoops to Conquer**

OLIVER GOLDSMITH

(*Enter* MARLOW *alone.*)

MARLOW: The assiduities of these good people tease me beyond bearing. My host seems to think it ill manners to leave me alone, and so he claps not only himself, but his old-fashioned wife on my back. They talk of coming to sup with us, too; and then, I suppose, we are to run the gauntlet through all the rest of the family.—What have we got here?—

(*Enter* HASTINGS *and* MISS NEVILLE.)

HASTINGS: My dear Charles! Let me congratulate you!—The most fortunate accident!—Who do you think is just alighted?
MARLOW: Cannot guess.
HASTINGS: Our mistresses, boy, Miss Hardcastle and Miss Neville. Give me leave to introduce Miss Constance Neville to your acquaintance. Happening to dine in the neighbourhood, they called, on their return, to take fresh horses here. Miss Hardcastle has just stepped into the next room, and will be back in an instant. Wasn't it lucky? eh!
MARLOW (*aside*):   I have just been mortified enough of all conscience, and here comes something to complete my embarrassment.
HASTINGS: Well! but wasn't it the most fortunate thing in the world?

MARLOW: Oh! yes. Very fortunate—a most joyful encounter.—But our dresses, George, you know, are in disorder.—What if we should postpone the happiness till tomorrow?—Tomorrow at her own house.—It will be every bit as convenient—and rather more respectful.—Tomorrow let it be. (*Offering to go.*)

MISS NEVILLE: By no means, sir. Your ceremony will displease her. The disorder of your dress will shew the ardour of your impatience. Besides, she knows you are in the house, and will permit you to see her.

MARLOW: Oh! the devil! how shall I support them? Hem! hem! Hastings, you must not go. You are to assist me, you know. I shall be confoundedly ridiculous. Yet, hang it! I'll take courage. Hem!

HASTINGS: Pshaw, man! it's but the first plunge, and all's over. She's but a woman, you know.

MARLOW: And of all women, she that I dread most to encounter!

(*Enter* MISS HARDCASTLE, *as returned from walking.*)

HASTINGS (*introducing them*):   Miss Hardcastle. Mr Marlow. I'm proud of bringing two persons of such merit together, that only want to know, to esteem each other.

MISS HARDCASTLE (*aside*):   Now, for meeting my modest gentleman with a demure face, and quite in his own manner. (*After a pause, in which he appears very uneasy and disconcerted.*) I'm glad of your safe arrival, sir—I'm told you had some accidents by the way.

MARLOW: Only a few, madam. Yes, we had some. Yes, madam, a good many accidents, but should be sorry—madam—or rather glad of any accidents—that are so agreeably concluded. Hem!

HASTINGS (*to him*):   You never spoke better in your whole life. Keep it up, and I'll insure you the victory.

MISS HARDCASTLE: I'm afraid you flatter, sir. You that have seen so much of the finest company can find little entertainment in an obscure corner of the country.

MARLOW (*gathering courage*):   I have lived, indeed, in the world, madam; but I have kept very little company. I have been but an observer upon life, madam, while others were enjoying it.

MISS NEVILLE: But that, I am told, is the way to enjoy it at last.

HASTINGS (*to him*):   Cicero never spoke better. Once more, and you are confirmed in assurance for ever.

MARLOW (*to him*):   Hem! Stand by me, then, and when I'm down, throw in a word or two to set me up again.

MISS HARDCASTLE: An observer, like you, upon life, were, I fear, disagreeably employed, since you must have had much more to censure than to approve.

MARLOW: Pardon me, madam. I was always willing to be amused. The folly of most people is rather an object of mirth than uneasiness.

HASTINGS (*to him*):   Bravo, bravo. Never spoke so well in your whole life. Well, Miss Hardcastle, I see that you and Mr Marlow are going to be very good company. I believe our being here will but embarrass the interview.

MARLOW: Not in the least, Mr Hastings. We like your company of all things. (*To him.*) Zounds! George, sure you won't go? How can you leave us?

HASTINGS: Our presence will but spoil conversation, so we'll retire to the next room. (*To him.*) You don't consider, man, that we are to manage a little *tête-à-tête* of our own.

(*Exeunt.*)

MISS HARDCASTLE (*after a pause*):   But you have not been wholly an observer, I presume, sir: the ladies, I should hope, have employed some part of your addresses.

MARLOW (*relapsing into timidity*):   Pardon me, madam, I—I—I—as yet have studied—only—to—deserve them.

MISS HARDCASTLE: And that some say is the very worst way to obtain them.

MARLOW: Perhaps so, madam. But I love to converse only with the more grave and sensible part of the sex.—But I'm afraid I grow tiresome.

MISS HARDCASTLE: Not at all, sir; there is nothing I like so much as grave conversation myself: I could hear it for ever. Indeed, I have often been surprised how a man of sentiment could ever admire those light airy pleasures, where nothing reaches the heart.

MARLOW: It's—a disease—of the mind, madam. In a variety of tastes there must be some who, wanting a relish for—um-a-um.

MISS HARDCASTLE: I understand you, sir. There must be some, who, wanting a relish for refined pleasures, pretend to despise what they are incapable of tasting.

MARLOW: My meaning, madam, but infinitely better expressed. And I can't help observing—a—

MISS HARDCASTLE (*aside*):   Who could ever suppose this fellow impudent upon some occasions. (*To him.*) You were going to observe, sir—

MARLOW: I was observing, madam—I protest, madam, I forget what I was going to observe.

MISS HARDCASTLE (*aside*):   I vow and so do I. (*To him.*) You were observing, sir, that in this age of hypocrisy—something about hypocrisy, sir.

MARLOW: Yes, madam. In this age of hypocrisy, there are few who upon strict inquiry do not—a—a—a—

MISS HARDCASTLE: I understand you perfectly, sir.

MARLOW (*aside*):   Egad! and that's more than I do myself!

MISS HARDCASTLE: You mean that in this hypocritical age there are few that do not condemn in public what they practise in private, and think they pay every debt to virtue when they praise it.

MARLOW: True, madam; those who have most virtue in their mouths, have least of it in their bosoms. But I'm sure I tire you, madam.

MISS HARDCASTLE: Not in the least, sir; there's something so agreeable and spirited in your manner, such life and force—pray, sir, go on.

MARLOW: Yes, madam. I was saying—that there are some occasions—when a total want of courage, madam, destroys all the—and puts us—upon a—a—a—

MISS HARDCASTLE: I agree with you entirely, a want of courage upon some occasions assumes the appearance of ignorance, and betrays us when we most want to excel. I beg you'll proceed.

MARLOW: Yes, madam. Morally speaking, madam—but I see Miss Neville expecting us in the next room. I would not intrude for the world.

MISS HARDCASTLE: I protest, sir, I never was more agreeably entertained in all my life. Pray go on.

MARLOW: Yes, madam. I was—but she beckons us to join her. Madam, shall I do myself the honour to attend you?

MISS HARDCASTLE: Well then, I'll follow.

MARLOW (*aside*):   This pretty smooth dialogue has done for me. (*Exit.*)

MISS HARDCASTLE (*alone*):   Ha! ha! ha! Was there ever such a sober sentimental interview? I'm certain he scarce looked in my face the whole time. Yet the fellow, but for his unaccountable bashfulness, is pretty well, too. He has good sense, but then so buried in his fears, that it fatigues one more than ignorance. If I could teach him a little confidence, it would be doing somebody that I know of a piece of service. But who is that somebody?—that, faith, is a question I can scarce answer. (*Exit.*)

- Is Kate malicious or playful? What prompts her toying with Marlow?

- You need to keep four different bodies and voices distinct in this scene. What one specific physical or vocal element was unique for each character?

This scene opens Pearl Cleage's Flyin' West. It takes place on a fall evening in 1898, outside the all-black town of Nicodemus, Kansas. Large groups of African American homesteaders left the South after the Civil War to settle all-black communities in the West. Their dreams were shattered when many western states enacted Jim Crow laws as cruel as any in the South. As the play opens, Sophie, a 36-year-old black woman born into slavery, returns to the home she shares with Fan and, more recently, Miss Leah, a 73-year-old former slave. She stuffs a letter into an overflowing desk, withdraws a long strip of black licorice, and starts to chew. Miss Leah enters, unsteadily. She has no cane and thus uses the furniture to steady her walk. She is looking for something and is exasperated. Sophie does not notice her, but Miss Leah immediately notices the window Sophie has opened. Keep these women alive in themselves and with each other.

 FROM Flyin' West

PEARL CLEAGE

MISS LEAH: Well, ain't you somethin'!

SOPHIE: I didn't know you were up, Miss Leah. Want a piece?

(SOPHIE *gets up and closes the window, stokes the fire, etc.*)

MISS LEAH: I hate licorice. (MISS LEAH *stumbles a little.* SOPHIE *moves to steady her and is stopped by a "don't you dare" look from* MISS LEAH.)

SOPHIE: You miss your cane?

MISS LEAH: I don't need no cane! I told you that before. You can lay it next to my bed or prop it against my chair like it walked out there on its own. It still ain't gonna make me no never mind. I don't want no cane and I don't need no cane.

SOPHIE: Suit yourself! (*Takes another bite of licorice as she hangs her coat.* MISS LEAH's *shawl is hanging there in plain view.* SOPHIE *starts to reach for it, stops, ignores it and begins putting things away.* MISS LEAH *finally speaks with cold dignity.*)

MISS LEAH: I am looking for my shawl, if you must know.

SOPHIE: It's right . . .

MISS LEAH: Don't tell me! If you start tellin' me, you'll just keep at it 'til I won't be able to remember a darn thing on my own.

SOPHIE: I'll make some coffee.

MISS LEAH: I don't know why. Can't nobody drink that stuff but you.

SOPHIE: It'll warm you up.

MISS LEAH: It'll kill me.

SOPHIE: Well, then, you haven't got much time to put your affairs in order.

MISS LEAH: My affairs are already in order, thank you. (*Pulls her chair as far from the window as possible and sits with effort.*) It's too cold for first October. (*Shivering*) Where's my shawl? Don't tell me!

SOPHIE: I brought you some tobacco.

MISS LEAH: What kind?

SOPHIE: The kind you like.

MISS LEAH: (*Pleased in spite of herself*) Well, thank you, Sister Sophie. Maybe a good pipe can cut the taste of that mess you cookin' up in Fan's good coffee pot. (*She proceeds to make a pipe while* SOPHIE *makes coffee.*) What are we celebrating?

SOPHIE: We are celebrating my ability not to let these Nicodemus Negroes worry me, no matter how hard they try.

MISS LEAH: Then we ought to be drinking corn whiskey. (*She lights the pipe and draws on it contentedly.*) Are you still worrying about the vote?

SOPHIE: I just told you. I'm celebrating an end to worrying. (*A beat*) I rode in by way of the south ridge this morning. Smells like snow up there already.

MISS LEAH: What were you doing way over there?

SOPHIE: Just looking . . .

MISS LEAH: Ain't you got enough land to worry about?

SOPHIE: I'll have enough when I can step outside my door and spin around with my eyes closed and wherever I stop, as far as I can see, there'll be nothing but land that belongs to me and my sisters.

MISS LEAH: Well, I'll try not to let the smoke from my chimney drift out over your sky.

SOPHIE: That's very neighborly of you. Now drink some of this.

MISS LEAH: (*Drinks and grimaces*) Every other wagon pull in here nowadays got a bunch of colored women on it call themselves homesteadin' and can't even make a decent cup of coffee, much less bring a crop in! When I got here, it wasn't nobody to do nothin' for me but me . . .

SOPHIE and MISS LEAH: (*Together*) . . . and I did everything there was to be done and then some . . .

MISS LEAH: That's right! Because I was not prepared to put up with a whole lotta mouth. Colored men always tryin' to tell you how to do somethin' even if you been doin' it longer than they been peein' standin' up. (*A beat*) They got that in common with you.

SOPHIE: I don't pee standing up.

MISS LEAH: You would if you could! (*Sips coffee and grimaces again*)

SOPHIE: Put some milk in it, Miss Leah.

MISS LEAH: When I want milk, I drink milk. When I want coffee, I want Fan's coffee.

SOPHIE: Suit yourself. (*A beat*) People were asking about Baker at the land office.

MISS LEAH: What people?

SOPHIE: White people. Asked me if I had heard anything from him.

MISS LEAH: Ain't no white folks looking to settle in no Nicodemus, Kansas.

SOPHIE: It's some of the best land around here. You said it yourself.

MISS LEAH: Ain't nothin' good to no white folks once a bunch of colored folks get set up on it!

SOPHIE: There's already a new family over by the Gaddy's and a widower with four sons between here and the Jordan place. They've probably been looking at your place, too.

MISS LEAH: Who said so?

SOPHIE: Nobody said anything. I just mean since you've been staying with us for awhile.

MISS LEAH: Well, I ain't no wet behind the ears homesteader. I own my land. Free and clear. My name the only name on the deed to it. Anybody lookin' at my land is countin' they chickens. I made twenty winters on that land and I intend to make twenty more.

(*While* MISS LEAH *fusses,* SOPHIE *quietly goes and gets her shawl and gently drops it around her shoulders.*)

SOPHIE: And then what?

MISS LEAH: Then maybe I'll let you have it.

SOPHIE: You gonna make me wait until I'm old as you are to get my hands on your orchard?

MISS LEAH: That'll be time enough. If I tell you you can have it any sooner, my life won't be worth two cents!

SOPHIE: You don't really think I'd murder you for your land, do you?

(MISS LEAH *looks at* SOPHIE *for a beat before drawing deeply on her pipe.*)

MISS LEAH: I like Baker. And Miz Baker sweet as she can be. They just tryin' to stay in the city enough for her to get her strength back and build that baby up a little.

SOPHIE: She'll never make it out here and you know it.

MISS LEAH: Losing three babies in three years takes it out of you, girl!

SOPHIE: They wouldn't have made it through the first winter if Wil Parrish hadn't been here to help them.

MISS LEAH: You had a lot of help your first coupla winters, if I remember it right.

SOPHIE: And I'm grateful for it.

MISS LEAH: Some of us were here when you got here. Don't forget it!

SOPHIE: All I'm trying to say is the Bakers have been gone almost two years and he hasn't even filed an extension. It's against the rules.

MISS LEAH: Against whose rules? Don't nobody but colored folks know they been gone that long no way. Them white folks never come out here to even check and see if we're dead or alive. You know that good as the next person. (*A beat*) Sometimes I suspect you think you the only one love this land, Sister, but you not.

SOPHIE: What are you getting at?

MISS LEAH: Just the way you were speechifyin' and carryin' on in town meetin' last week like you the only one got a opinion that matter.

SOPHIE: Why didn't the others speak up if they had so much to say?

MISS LEAH: Can't get a word in edgewise with you goin' on and on about who ain't doin' this and that like they 'spose to.

SOPHIE: But you know I'm right!

MISS LEAH: Bein' right ain't always the only thing you got to think about. The thing you gotta remember about colored folks is that the stuff they don't say when they want to, they just gonna say it double time later. That's why you gonna lose that vote if you ain't careful.

SOPHIE: It doesn't make sense. A lot of the colored settlements have already passed rules saying nobody can sell to outsiders unless everybody agrees.

MISS LEAH: Ain't nobody gonna give you the right to tell them when and how to sell their land. No point in ownin' it if you can't do what you want to with it.

SOPHIE: But half of them will sell to the speculators! You know they will!

MISS LEAH: Then that's what they gonna have to do.

SOPHIE: We could have so much here if these colored folks would just step lively. We could own this whole prairie. Nothing but colored folks farms and colored folks wheat fields and colored folks cattle. Everywhere you look nothing but colored folks! But they can't see it. They look at Nicodemus and all they can see is a bunch of scuffling people trying to get ready for the winter instead of something free and fine and all our own. Most of them don't even know what we're doing here!

MISS LEAH: That's cause some of them ain't never had nothin' that belonged to 'em. Some of them come cause they can't stand the smell of the city. Some of them just tired of evil white folks. Some of 'em killed somebody or wanted to. All everybody got in common is they plunked down twelve dollars for a piece of good land and now they tryin' to live on it long enough to claim it.

SOPHIE: Everybody isn't even doing that.

MISS LEAH: Everybody doin' the best they can, Sister Sophie.

SOPHIE: And what happens when that isn't good enough?

MISS LEAH: Then they have to drink your coffee!

- ◆ These women have known each other for a long time and shared much history. How did you demonstrate this shared past to your audience?

- ◆ This dialogue requires quick response and then silence to achieve its full rhythm. What else makes the women's speech characteristic?

Bibliography

These works consider the development of dramatic theory primarily in the West. For practical texts on theatrical technique, consult the bibliography at the end of Chapter 8.

Boon, Richard, and Jane Plastow. *Theatre Matters: Performance and Culture on the World Stage.* Cambridge: Cambridge University Press, 1998.
   An engaging collection of essays that explores the capacity of theatrical performance to make social and political interventions in several developing nations.

Dukore, B. F., ed. *Dramatic Theory and Criticism: Greeks to Grotowski.* New York: Holt, Rinehart and Winston, 1974.
   A collection of important perspectives in dramatic theory.

Fuchs, Elinor. *The Death of Character: Perspective on Theatre After Modernism.* Bloomington: Indiana University Press, 1996.
A thoughtful discussion on the nature of postmodern theater.

Grene, Nicholas. *The Politics of Irish Drama: Plays in Context from Boucicault to Friel.* Cambridge: Cambridge University Press, 1999.
An account of the "three-way relationship" between subject, playwright, and audience in twentieth-century Irish theater that sheds considerable light on the links between performance and its social-cultural context.

Keir, Elam. *The Semiotics of Theatre and Drama.* New York: Routledge, 1988.
A view of stage performance as structural semiotics.

Sidnell, Michael J., with D. J. Conacher et at. *Sources of Dramatic Theory.* New York: Cambridge University Press, 1991.
A collection of various perspectives on the development of contemporary dramatic theory.

Worthen, William B. *Modern Drama and the Rhetoric of Theater.* Berkeley: University of California Press, 1992.
A thoughtful consideration of theater's persuasive power of representation.

Technique is a test of a man's sincerity.

Ezra Pound

CHAPTER EIGHT

Technique in Drama

EXPECT THIS!

With our foundation in the analysis of drama, we focus here on how to communicate it: the techniques required for the solo performer. By the end of this chapter, you should be able to:

- Isolate what your audience must see and what they can't see.

- Explain why technique is the economical management of a performer's resources.

- Demonstrate control in emotional response and in creating character.

- Select appropriate instances for memorizing.

- Decide how much scene setting is necessary and how to supply it.

- Understand when properties are essential and when obtrusive.

- Find and imagine appropriate bodies for characters, and devise appropriate voices for characters.

- Coordinate bodies and voices of characters, and distinguish gender roles in performance.

- Determine what physical contact the audience must see and how they can see it through the speaking character.

- Achieve the essential illusion of interplay of characters.

- Pick up cues automatically.

- Resolve problems of physical focus, and polish an appropriate method of focus and angle of placement.

- Use efficiently or set aside the reading stand.

- Practice cutting and excerpting with integrity and tact.

Technique is the economical management of the performer's resources.

Selections Discussed in This Chapter

In explaining some topics, we mention texts that are reprinted either within the chapter itself or at the end of a chapter. Use the guide below for quick reference to acquaint yourself with selections you may not fully recall.

Author	Title	Location
Anton Chekhov	from *The Three Sisters*	Chapter 7, page 295
Edward Albee	from *Who's Afraid of Virginia Woolf?*	Chapter 7, page 300
Lanford Wilson	from *Fifth of July*	Chapter 7, page 311
Anna Deavere Smith	from *Fires in the Mirror*	Chapter 7, page 313
William Shakespeare	from *Othello*	Chapter 7, page 320
Oliver Goldsmith	from *She Stoops to Conquer*	Chapter 7, page 323
Sam Shepard	from *Curse of the Starving Class*	Chapter 8, page 362
William Shakespeare	from *Romeo and Juliet*	Chapter 8, page 365
Harold Pinter	from *Betrayal, Scene Five*	Chapter 8, page 367

PERFORMING DRAMA IS THE MOST TECHNICALLY CHALLENGing task an interpreter can undertake. It can also be the most rewarding. The challenges and the rewards follow from the same source: drama's unique reliance on speaking characters to introduce, develop, and resolve conflict. Like the interpreter of prose and of poetry, the interpreter of drama responds emotionally, mentally, and physically to the aesthetic entirety of the literature. Like the interpreter of other forms, the interpreter of drama skillfully uses body and voice to persuade the audience to collaborate in creating scene and character. But unlike interpreters of poetry and of prose, the solo performer presents *only* character—only the *speaking* character. An audience always needs to see and hear a full-blooded character; no poet or narrative persona intervenes. The interpreter of drama is all character, all the time.

To achieve the goal of total immersion in characters, interpreters must solve a number of technical problems. Most of them arise because the interpreter is trying to persuade audience members to believe that the one performer they see in front of them can become several, often very different, people. As a performer of drama, then, you need to focus your audience's attention as tightly as possible on what *is* present and make that so compelling that the audience will momentarily forget what is *not* present. Because we have laid our foundation for understanding drama in the prior chapter, this chapter suggests several ways you can solve some of the peskiest problems. Also, we highlight Rehearsal Tips in the form of questions intended to help you solve problems during rehearsal. Our suggestions are *not* rules, however. As with prose and with poetry, when you perform drama often enough, you will begin to develop your individual method of handling the problems posed by each scene. Remember: technical facility is at its most accomplished when the audience doesn't notice it.

Technique in Interpretation

An interpreter spends a great deal of time and effort training voice and body. As we discussed in Chapter 7, you may often have to go over and over a difficult speech or exchange or scene, working it out the way a dancer perfects a complicated step. Such in-depth rehearsal brings your unique resources to a level that allows you to communicate the scene. Of course, no audience comes to see a rehearsal. You work thoroughly *before* a performance in order to focus your audience's attention on the material you are performing.

Technique is the economical management of a performer's resources. Every work of art demands some technique uniquely refined by each artist. Although one artist's technique differs from another's, there are some fundamental similarities. What is achieved must be more than just a lecture or demonstration of technique. Technical mastery of body and voice allows the interpreter to communicate to the audience all the discoveries made during rehearsal.

Sometimes beginning actors misunderstand technique. They believe that a technically proficient actor is a hollow performer who substitutes a supple body and resonant voice for the character's life. At the opposite pole, technically proficient performers retort that the internal-reality performer merely displays personal anguish that has nothing to do with the character's life. Both extremes typify selfish performers, whether actors or interpreters. Without the ability to project and refine gesture, internal commitment to the reality of the play is worthless. Without internal commitment, technical mastery simply shows—with striking clarity—how empty the interpreter really is. As you become more familiar with the performance of drama, it will become increasingly apparent to you that certain kinds of gestures or vocal habits can impress your audience. You will be developing a bag of tricks. Tricks are not technique. Tricks deceive in order to puzzle or amuse. *Technique refines and clarifies.* Skill in execution and economy in performance present the selection instead of the performer. Lose the tricks.

Control

Beginning performers sometimes believe that an interpreter should not respond emotionally to a scene during performance or rehearsal. Make no mistake, controlling the outward manifestations of an emotion is not suppressing it. You well know that when you must "hold your tongue," you do not eliminate emotional involvement. Both audience and interpreter have as their goal the fullest possible life for the scene or the play. Interpreters should always remember that the characters, the action, the author's intentions, and their own personal preferences should all be directed to the life of the play. None is an end in itself. You manage your emotional commitment as you do the other components of your performing instrument, remembering, of course, that *you* manage *them*, they do not manage you. The principle of *aesthetic distance* (that self-referencing power that enables us to see ourselves as others see us) does not require lessened intensity in commitment or in execution; it requires greater control.

Suppose that you have chosen to perform the segment from *The Three Sisters* that we examine in Chapter 7. Suppose, further, that you once had an admirer whose attentions made you uncomfortable. You think, understandably, that this scene was made for you. But you are neither Irina nor Tuzenbach. You have none of their history, their environment, their future. And, what is more, *they* are not living in the twenty-first century. They never encountered e-mail, Starbucks, or reality television. True, you share with both characters some sense of who they are and what makes them tick. But, in an excess of sympathy, you can't make Irina succumb to Tuzenbach's pitiful pleas, nor can you make Tuzenbach attractive. Your life is not the play's life because *you* are not an author's creation bound in a book. You contribute what you know and then stretch to fill the play.

This concept may be the single most difficult principle for performers to understand. Yet it is the one principle that, if ignored, leads to the most trouble in performance. *Control in a scene is like paying taxes: If you give less than required, you get into trouble. If you give more, you are either foolish or careless.* Interpreters in control of a scene spend just *enough* resources to be sure that the audience fully experiences the life of the drama. They don't take so much space that there's no room for the audience. As performers, they may not be experiencing precisely the same emotions as is the audience, but as characters, they are suggesting the emotional fullness of the role. Interpreters should not confuse their personal response to a character's plight (from the examples we used in Chapter 7, sorrow at Irina's loss or anger at Martha) with the intention of the character, and they should channel the *character's* intention into the *scene's* intention. What is more, by controlling their personal response to the scene, interpreters give the audience room to fulfill its part in the experience. An audience wants to focus on the life in the scene, not on the personal travails and traumas of the interpreter as a performer. Excessive displays only display excess.

Memorizing Lines

Happily, we are now past the days when interpreters were told that memorizing means acting. Frequent rehearsal of a scene or a passage often allows the performer to become so familiar with the speech that the words become inevitable parts of the character. They should be. It is not absolutely necessary to memorize a scene—and surely it would be extraordinarily difficult to memorize an entire play. Still, memorizing may sometimes be useful, if not essential.

When two or three characters share rapid, short dialogue (see Jed and Shirley in *Fifth of July* or Iago and Othello in *Othello,* both at the end of Chapter 7), memorizing allows the pace of the scene to continue unabated. Sometimes transitions between characters are intricate, and one character may interrupt the speaker with one or two words. In such cases it is far easier to memorize all the lines surrounding the interruptions to ensure that the audience has the benefit of your full-front placement and projection in clarifying the change in character. A particularly involved gesture demanded by the scene may prohibit consulting a text. In this case, if you move tentatively away from the text, you can make your audience nervous. Generally, it is more graceful to pick up the lines that you don't know by glancing at the text while you are speaking lines that you *do* know. Your rehearsal will have been extensive enough so that a key word or phrase triggers the rest of the line in your mind. Memorizing here can help you enormously because it allows you to spend your resources directly on the audience. If you are tied to the text, with your face forever buried, no audience will ever see the life of the characters. Even exemplary vocal projection suffers when directed to the floor.

However, memorizing carries with it some problems. The most dangerous pitfall is a *set-speech* attitude: the type of delivery made by children who have had their "piece" drummed into them for the grade-school pageant and say all the words as rapidly as they can—and with very little sense of what they are saying. This lifelessness shows that the performer has memorized the text—but little more. Words mean ideas, hopes, and actions; words communicate and disclose the world that lives within the play. When a performer simply rattles off words, all the audience perceives is the rattling off of words.

Perhaps the best method to understand the needs of a scene is to ask whether the scene can be presented most fully if it is completely memorized, memorized in small or large part, or presented entirely from the text. Think carefully and keep this question as your guide: *During this scene, what does the audience need to see?*   **Rehearsal Tip 1**

Setting the Scene

When people attend a play, they usually receive programs with the characters' names, actors' names, setting and time, act divisions, and program notes. The interpreter, on the other hand, individually presents all of these elements, but the burden isn't as vast as it may sound.

The audience probably knows your name already. Your concern should be with the characters who appear in your scene. Be sure that whatever information you give is restricted to what is needed in the scene you are performing. The *Dramatis Personae* usually lists whatever additional information an audience should know, although if you begin the play after the opening curtain, it is helpful to tell your audience what has happened prior to the first line of your scene. You might also take the time at the beginning to indicate the arrival of any characters who will appear later during the scene.

As you begin, remember that the image you present to the audience is the general *frame* of your performance. The audience focuses its attention within this frame. If you plan to move about the performance area during your scene, you might prepare your audience in the introduction. As the scene begins, you will not repeat each character's name because the characterizations you present, coupled with your placement of characters out front, should clarify that matter sufficiently for the audience.

When stage directions appear important, they can be incorporated into the performance by the performer (*not* by the characters), speaking directly to the audience—as a narrator does with summary in a story. You may want to give some indication of time and locale, if they are not made clear by the lines of the play *and* if they are crucial to understanding the scene. If there is a rapid passage of time between two or three scenes you have selected to perform, relay this fact to the audience at the least obtrusive moment during your performance, usually at the end of one scene or just prior to an important segment. Once again **Rehearsal Tip 2** answer this question: *Is the performance fuller with this information supplied explicitly rather than understood implicitly?*

Sometimes it is necessary to provide scenographic information that is crucial to an understanding of the scene. In Roslyn Malamud's monologue, "The Coup," from *Fires in the Mirror* (Chapter 7), the comfortable setting and costume are essential to the persona's attitude. Sometimes the lines of the play themselves set the scene much more effectively than does any explanation by the performer. It is not necessary for an audience to know minor details when the broadest outline can allow them both to follow the playwright's requirements and complete the details in their imaginations.

Entrances and exits during a scene may cause some difficulty. If a character's exit occurs at the close of a speech and completes a key scene, the interpreter may simply turn away. If there are elaborate activities accompanying the departure, the performer (*not* the character) may describe the action: "She pauses a moment, slipping on the long white gloves, gently grasping the parasol in her left hand, and turning ever so delicately toward the French doors, where she finds herself moments later as the curtain falls." If the audience's attention should remain with the character or characters onstage (as it does with Irina, after Tuzenbach runs off to the duel in *The Three Sisters* in Chapter 7), adjust the description to reflect the departing character's activity while allowing the remaining characters to resume the scene. If a character enters midscene or later, you may have to give that identification with a two- or three-word description. Place such an entrance according to the world you and your audience have created ("She enters from the porch"), rather than from some stage-setting location ("She enters up left"). The world of the play includes your audience.

When a character enters or departs during another character's speech, careful handling of placement of character and offstage focus can indicate to the audience that someone has either entered or left the room. You can welcome an arriving character or bid farewell to a departing character with the slight rise in mental and vocal projection, reaching over the greater distance. (Try these techniques with Lady Capulet's departure in *Romeo and Juliet* or with Wesley's responses to Ella in *Curse of the Starving Class*, both at the end of this chapter.) As a guide, keep in mind this question: *How can I lead my audience to understand the*   **Rehearsal Tip 3** *activity of this scene without diverting their attention from the scene itself?*

Audiences want to believe. They like to participate in the creation of the world of the scene, provided you give them room and do not give them false clues. Present your suggestions with economy.

Properties

Properties can cause many types of (often unnecessary) problems for performers. In our experience, real properties are often more trouble than reward. If you use real properties, be sure that *all* the characters who appear in the scene use the *same* prop, or you will be asking your audience both to permit and to dismiss reality without regard for the play's requirements.

Sometimes, however, you may choose to present a mimed prop. If anything, mimed props should be treated more carefully than real properties because the performer carefully establishes, nurtures, and concludes their existence. The danger is that the scene might become a scene about a prop rather than a scene in which the prop helps the characters in their attempts to reach their goals. Use the imaginary prop only insofar as it touches the characters' lives and the scene's purpose.

In the potion scene in *Romeo and Juliet,* Juliet has a vial. Stage tradition suggests that she lift it high for the audience to see, just as she shows a dagger later in the same speech. An interpreter with a text faces some problems in trying to juggle book, bottle, and knife. We think the energy used in finding and mastering the props would be better spent in rehearsing the scene and attempting to convey Juliet's dilemma, which, after all, is what you want your audience to remember. By barely sketching the gesture of holding a vial in hand, you can convey the mixture of fear and anticipation with which Juliet regards the liquid. If you project the muscle response that accompanies that tension, you will further create the power that piece of glass has over Juliet. This, after all, is the point of the scene. When, a few lines later, Juliet picks up the dagger, you can establish the presence of the knife by a similar gesture, slightly to the right or left of wherever you have placed the vial. As your body remembers what your muscles did in picking up the dagger, you can persuade the audience that Juliet is considering hefting the dagger. If you have suggested the action economically, the only performance action an observer strolling by may in fact see is the opening of a hand. The audience, though, will imagine that Juliet has considered and rejected the dagger and has returned to the vial to complete the scene. Perhaps at the end your Juliet will raise her hand and touch her lips with her fingers, almost in a farewell kiss.

Some students who understand completely the problems of handling real properties fall into the opposite trap: too much explicit gesture, or *mimetic,* gesture. They end up shuttling imaginary properties from hand to lectern to floor, plucking others out of the air and resting them on nothingness, then blithely walking through a wall and over a sleeping baby they had asked their audiences to imagine. Extremely physical, overt representations very rarely succeed. Often, elaborate gestures soak up the tension created by the fullest response a scene demands. Worst of all, some students rack their imaginations to find a gesture to elaborate every statement, as though waving hands and arms were part of the drama. Your goal is to create characters who are distinctly different and whose behavior and speech enable audience members to see the scene in *their* minds and feel the tension in *their* muscles. The point of the scene in *Romeo and Juliet* is not how many "things" surround the performer but how agonized is Juliet's decision. *Suggestion* keeps you from plucking at the air; *empathy* allows the audience to feel with the characters; and your skillfully *controlled intensity* pinpoints the conflict.

Embodying Characters

Characters have bodies. You have a body. You will often select scenes in which these two bodies are anything but identical. Indeed, one of the rewards of drama for the solo performer is precisely this freedom to undertake characters and roles in which you would never be cast. Do not be daunted by the fact that a character may have a physical life greatly unlike your own. One of the most enriching—and challenging—parts of the rehearsal period is your discovery of the ways your body and the characters' bodies are similar, and the (often) many more ways you must expand or adapt your physical resources to match those of the characters. We said in Chapter 4 that your responsiveness and genuine imaginative engagement will lead you to find unique ways to create this match. So don't be put off by physical (or vocal) demands that you encounter in the text. Rather, consider them the challenges that will stretch your unique performing instrument. If you are still unsure, relax; our discussion of "Coordinating Bodies and Voices of Characters" and "Physical Focus," a bit later, offer much practical advice.

As an interpreter, you feel in your muscles the physical lives of the characters in the scene. It is sometimes helpful to go through the entire selection and develop a physical technique for each character, one at a time, concentrating wholly on those speeches and actions as if you were going to act that part—and only that part—on the stage. In making this type of study, you will use the other characters merely as line feeders until you feel that the main character is clearly and lastingly instilled in your mind, muscles, and voice. Then, one by one, allow the other characters to emerge with their individualities, progressions, and interrelationships. You may find it helpful to "walk" the characters—that is, to rehearse relevant business exactly as if you were going to do it in a staged version with properties and scenery. All this is an invaluable aid to timing, pace, and muscle tension, as well as to the motivation of changes in thought, the means for suggesting the character to your audience. After the habits of preparation are established, the process becomes less puzzling, because you know what you are looking for and where to find it.

After the characters are clearer, the next step is vocal and physical selectivity. You have created an explicit character with individual mental, emotional, physical, and vocal traits. Now, decide which vocal elements—such as tempo, rhythm, inflection, range, and quality—will most accurately and swiftly suggest each character to the audience. The interpreter here depends primarily on posture, muscle tone, and kinesthetic response to suggest physical characteristics.

The time spent in rehearsing the actual business is by no means lost, however, because the *memory* of it will add to the vitality, pace, and general effectiveness of the performance. This principle of muscle memory is sometimes referred to as the *theory of remembered action.* Muscle memory affects the reader's empathy and aids in suggesting hurry or leisure, activity or passivity, tension or relaxation as the scenes progress. Answer this question: *Which significant physical and vocal details will permit the listeners to fill in a three-dimensional, believable person?*

Rehearsal Tip 4

Coordinating Bodies and Voices of Characters

As an interpreter, you work with the audience to create the life of the character. You *suggest* characters to the audience, but that does not diminish your responsibility to give a full performance. Nor does it alter the need for real people—not shadows—to speak the lines.

All characters have bodies. Sometimes they are buried up to their necks, sometimes they are chained to garbage cans, sometimes they appear odd or marvelously strange or fiendishly elusive, but in performance, they all have bodies. The performer's body should be sufficiently flexible to suggest a character without worrying about wigs, noses, humps, pirouettes, or gymnastics.

Gender Roles

The most common concern is the matter of gender. Can a male performer ever persuade an audience that he is really Irina or Martha? How can a female ever convince an audience that she is Othello? Remember, audiences want to believe. You are not asking them to believe you are physically a particular character. Rather, you are asking them to join you in creating a character who behaves and thinks in the fashion you are suggesting and who happens to be a male or a female. Like age and infirmity, gender is finally a matter of characterization; yet neither age, infirmity, nor gender alone is sufficient to create a character.

Faced with the problem of performing a character of the opposite sex, the interpreter should first determine precisely the size and shape of the character. Not all women look like Martha; not all men look like George. Try to find real people in real life who seem to you to look like the character. See how they carry themselves; watch them walk. Be on the lookout for people who may provide you with the perfect telltale gesture to clarify a goal or finish a scene. Note in particular what happens to a person's hips, thighs, shoulders, and hands as the person moves, walks, and sits. As movement takes place, what happens to the center of gravity? Actors sometimes find animals that resemble their characters and watch them carefully. Use any technique you need, but be sure that you are fully aware of how the body moves. Know what your character *would* embody.

Now look at what you have to work with—yourself. Where do you carry your weight? Are there similarities between the ways you and your characters move that you can use? Some men may find that the way they sit is similar to the way that Martha sits; some women may find that they make certain motions that resemble the way in which Tuzenbach looks back at Irina. You probably will develop many of the character's gestures and motions from observation. Try different things with your own body. Use a full-length mirror, and practice alone because then you can concentrate better on the way you know you want to look.

Some interpreters have limited mobility or are disabled. If you use a wheelchair, you may at first reject flamboyantly physical characters. Although your decision is understandable, our experience suggests that by doing so you place needless restrictions on yourself. Remember, you are asked to join with your audience in creating the character. Your audience can imagine wildly physical events if they are guided by a performer whose spirit embodies such physicality. If you have musculoskeletal disabilities that inhibit your fluency of gesture, let your audience complete *that* part of your performance; be sure that you fully suggest the personality and attitude of the character. Every interpreter creates with the unique instrument of an individual body and voice. Work to achieve the fullest responsiveness with the resources you have, and focus on the interplay of spirit and attitude that are essential for character.

Women who want to perform male characters have found that, generally, (1) straightening their shoulders, (2) increasing the feel of weight in their forearms and hands, and (3) broadening their stance will get them moving in the right direction. Not all male characters will require all of these elements; some will require none. These are simply ways to start the trial-and-error process. Men who want to perform female characters have found that, generally, (1) narrowing their base of support, (2) lightening the weight in their hands, forearms, and upper legs, and (3) drawing in their shoulders will help them begin to suggest some female characters. Once again, this is simply one way to begin the process. It is not the end.

Clothes and Voice

Once you have developed a character's body, put some clothes on it. Your clothes may restrict movement in ways that period costume does not, and vice versa. If you intend, for example, to perform a scene from *She Stoops to Conquer* (Chapter 7) in jeans, you need to know how Kate Hardcastle's body and movement can be suggested by yours. Costumes enforce specific kinds of postures: because of his rage and desolation, Othello would not be able to stand at attention successfully. Corsets, skirts, and swords all hamper agility and restrict freedom of gesture. Although you won't be costumed in period attire in performance, your body can respond as if you are.

When you are wearing what you will wear in the performance—and you imagine what you see the character wearing—proceed through the range of movement in the body of the *character*. Note how your body moves through the passages in the scene; try any particularly active movement several times. If you are using the lectern, does it inhibit any activity? How does your costumed body feel in that frame?

Finally, what voice emerges from the body you have made and dressed? Try not to force wide variations in pitch, range, or volume. Does this newly costumed body create a voice by itself? Without imposing any preconceptions on the voices, try the central lines for each body you have created. Run the scene entirely as the character you have created, moving as the character might in a staged version. How does it feel and sound? Don't expect instant success. You will need to practice. Work through the scene again, this time without saying a word. Do you remember what differences the voice made? What the body felt like? How the voice and the body together arose from the situation? Listen to people whose voices sound like your characters (they are not likely to be the same people whose *bodies* resembled your characters), and try those voices out on the new bodies. You have begun to build characters, and that is the beginning of building a scene.

Special Situations

Sometimes characters with physical disabilities pose special problems. The best way to deal with these characters is to examine how the disability affects their *living in the scene*. How do their bodies differ *specifically*? Is it simply that they gesture more slowly and deliberately, or is the character showing pain with each movement? Remember that habit creates character.

Avoid stock physical attributes for characters. It is true that some old people have voices that crack piteously, but not all old voices crack. It is true that age bends some men and women, but you probably know old people who are erect and vigorous and who would slap you if you called them "feeble."

Specific detail is the key to effective depiction of characters. Each moment and each movement should offer a new bit of information for the audience. Each must contribute *something useful* and *something different* to the picture the audience is assembling and to which they are adding their own discoveries as well. Each movement arises out of the prior movement, prepares the following movement, and suggests the complexity that makes a character a vital human being. Bodies and characters are never divorced; they never cease their intricate dance of information.

Physical Contact

Physical contact is difficult for the solo performer, but audiences want to believe. At the movies, we believe that flickering shadows are real people. True, anything that requires repeated, flesh-on-flesh contact cannot be duplicated successfully by one person. If a swordfight, or a boxing match, or a pistol whipping, or even a kiss is what motivates the plot or initiates crucial character development, it may be wiser to narrate the conflict and allow the audience to stage the scene more fully in their imagination.

Sometimes, though, scenes that *appear* on first or second reading to be intensely physical are in fact marvelous opportunities for the solo performer to stretch the possibilities of the craft and challenge technical facility. The key here is to remember that what the audience always sees is the speaking character. As the line shifts, so does the speaking character. Ask yourself how the activity immediately *touches* the speaking character. Using the speaking character as the recipient or initiator of the action, reconsider the scene. What can the *speaking* character do that will suggest activity on the part of the *silent* characters? Such behavior is called *reflexive physical activity* because it reflects activity by someone other than the speaker.

For example, suppose a silent character picks up a vase to throw at the speaking character. If the speaking character keeps focus on the silent character and on the raised vase, increasing the tension, excitement, and volume, the audience will believe that something they can't see is causing the character's increased concern. When the silent character finally lets the object fly, the speaker can cringe or dodge the vase as it narrowly misses him or, if it finds its mark, can quickly grasp his forehead to cover the blood and then complete the speech, still suffering from the blow. Take the famous moment in *Othello* when Iago is seized by the throat. Othello says:

> Villain, be sure thou prove my love a whore,
> Be sure of it, give me the ocular proof,
> Or by the worth of man's eternal soul,
> Thou hadst been better have been born a dog,
> Than answer my wak'd wrath.

Traditional stage practice has Othello throttling Iago, who manages to croak out only, "Is 't come to this?" An interpreter (who of course knows the lines so well he or she need not consult the text) can focus on the imagined Iago and let the outstretched arms and tensed, spread fingers suggest the writhing man as Othello speaks. Then, simply by clasping those outstretched hands together at the moment Iago begins to speak, the interpreter changes persona, hoarsely rasping Iago's line. Othello immediately resumes talking, "his" hands still around the throat of Iago, whom Othello can thrust away in disgust when he chooses.

It is impossible to formulate general rules that can be applied to all types of physical contact scenes; each presents its own problems, and each interpreter is at a different level of technical proficiency. Remember that technique manages your *resources*, and audience belief is one of them. To help you determine some workable solutions to try in re-

Rehearsal Tip 5   hearsal, ask yourself: *How explicit must I be for the audience to believe the action? Will the technique I have chosen draw the audience's attention away from the scene?*

Interplay of Characters

After you have discovered a body and a voice for each character in your scene and decided how to cope with the characters' physical contact, more remains. The characters need to listen to one another. Obviously, you cannot perform listening as one character while you are speaking as another. Interpreters of drama develop the ability to pick up a speech midway into a train of thought, to "have heard." This requires split-second response and complete control of the characters. You are going to become not split personalities but rather *compound* ones, each with a sharp focus on what is happening, where it is happening, and how what is happening affects everyone else. Drama arises from the interplay of the characters whose goals engage one another because they either share these goals or oppose them. You do not want your audience to feel that they are watching a number of people speaking from a series of disconnected islands.

It is now time to repeat some of the questions that you asked at the beginning of your preparation. When the bodies of the characters have been assembled, ask yourself again: "Why are these two people continuing to talk to each other?" "What keeps them onstage dealing with one another?" "What does this character hope to gain by continuing his attention to that character?" Relationships are built through the sequences of speeches; as each character speaks, the other listens carefully and joins the dialogue without a pause when the first stops speaking, having heard what the speaker just said.

Characters interacting in this way seem to be together on the same stage, carrying on their conversations, creating the tension that is the heartbeat of the *scene,* the interpreter's real goal. When characters at last begin to live in the scene, they *lean into* the action. This does not mean that they incline their bodies forward over the reading stand, although they may do that. Characters need to get at the object of their discussion, there, in front of them. Their intention is to connect with another character, to whom they speak with earnest conviction. If the character who is being addressed moves, the speaking character follows, always keeping the person clearly in focus as the object of the speech. Then, one character is dropped and, instantly, before the audience can see a gap, the next character is speaking. Such seamless skill requires considerable rehearsal but contributes mightily to the impact of a scene.

Look at an interchange near the end of *Scene Five* of Pinter's *Betrayal* (the entire scene is at the end of this chapter). Robert has discovered his wife's infidelity with an old friend, Jerry. These speeches are brief but full of import:

> EMMA: We're lovers.
> ROBERT: Ah. Yes. I thought it might be something like that, something along those lines.
> EMMA: When?
> ROBERT: What?
> EMMA: When did you think?
> ROBERT: Yesterday. Only yesterday. When I saw his handwriting on the letter. Before yesterday I was quite ignorant.
> EMMA: Ah.

These characters know each other very well, and because they have a long prior life together and have come to know well each other's vulnerabilities, Emma anticipates *some* of Robert's reaction to her confession. He lets her stew silently in the pauses between his "Ah" and his "Yes." The interpreter, in character as Robert, can consider the imagined Emma before him, watching her carefully as she awaits his fuller response. Withholding his elaboration becomes a kind of silent torture, as he very well knows. Then they have the quick exchange of questions, each uttered almost simultaneously. Robert again considers Emma and again watches her draw conclusions from each of his statements. Only then is she permitted her "Ah," as fraught with the unspoken as was his.

Picking Up Cues

In picking up cues, the solo performance of drama is at its most artificial, and thus, for the performer, the potential liabilities are the most dangerous. Poor planning, lack of foresight, or insufficient rehearsal can destroy all the effort that has been made. During transitions, remember to focus on the audience's attention on *what is there* (the speaking character) and not to distract them with *what isn't there.* There are no empty spaces in life, and there should be no empty spaces in the scene either. You are laboring to achieve the totality of the scene, and lapses break or kill the continuity.

When audience members constantly see the character, they do not have time to see the machinery of the interpreter's efforts. They do not have time to see the performer groping for lines or pausing to think about what comes next. Try to ensure that whatever posture one character may be in at the conclusion of her or his line is not so extreme as to require the next character to make any extravagant movement. This does not mean that characters cannot move. It means that wild postures or gestures should be adjusted and resolved by the time the speech is concluded, so that the performer is in a posture that is neutral enough to conclude one character and begin the next fluently. Without the need for any excessive or radical alteration in posture, the interpreter can shift the focus to the new character and begin the new line "effortlessly," and the audience will not be jolted.

Thorough rehearsal helps these transitions to come more readily to the performer. Vocal and physical changes will occur so rapidly that an audience will not have time for a lapse in belief. Begin your rehearsal so that there is enough time to evolve the habits of each character and to develop ease in assuming characters. Many brief practice sessions are far superior to one long session, for the interpreter must live with the characters to get to know them. One general question subsumes many **Rehearsal Tip 6** other allied concerns: *How can a performer focus the audience's attention on what is there and divert attention from what isn't there?*

Physical Focus

As we discussed in Chapters 2 and 6, the action of the scene should move along a line that stretches from the performer through the audience to the opposing character or characters, who exist just above and beyond the listeners' heads. This arrangement places the audience at the center of the interaction, with the interpreter providing the constant source of information and activity within the scene. Characters who are being addressed live at some distance from the speaker who addresses them, and this distance should be bridged by the performer's intensity and commitment. The audience will support and enhance the tension among the characters, but only if you have given them some life to sustain the excitement and direction of the scene. *The physical focus of the scene should exist out front.* Resist those powerful temptations to place other characters on stage, to your right or left, leaving you in profile. Not only would the audience be denied the cues that your face and body can give them, but their attention also would be drawn away from what is in front of them. Keep the characters talking to other characters, and be sure that all the characters exist out front.

Methods of Focus

When the interpreter needs to distinguish between different heights or eye levels for the characters, the difference should not be even slightly exaggerated because, from their perspective, the audience can grossly distort the intended angle of placement. You usually can make sufficient distinction with your eyes, and you need never substantially alter the horizontal angle of your head. This technique may still puzzle you.

Consider this analogy. In a movie, say, *Gone with the Wind*, you see Rhett Butler and Scarlett O'Hara in their final scene together confront each other in front of the staircase. You know that they are talking to each other. But there in front of you at one moment is a tight closeup of Clark Gable speaking directly to *you*; then, in turn, there is a similar closeup of Vivien Leigh's face as she talks directly to *you*. Of course both performers are speaking directly to the camera, and if you had seen the segment staged, you would have seen only the two actors speaking to each other directly. In the film, the camera is interposed between the characters; because the camera is there, so are you. You can see in their eyes and their mouths all of the tension of that moment.

Much the same phenomenon occurs in the solo performance of drama, except that instead of interposing the camera between the characters, the performer puts the audience there. We accept this convention because our experience with watching video renders it perfectly natural for two people who in fact are talking to each other to appear to be addressing the audience. If you keep in mind the analogy between the placement of the camera and that point where the audience enters the excitement of the scene, your initial fears about audience belief may be calmed. But remember that the performers in the film were skillful. They made you believe that their characters were talking to each other. What the camera does is help us see more—and see differently—than we could ever see on a stage.

Action, after all, is the outward manifestation of the interior response, and this gives the interpreter an important clue to the way action should be handled. It is not so much *what* the characters do as *how* they do it that reveals what they are thinking and feeling. If, for example, a character sinks dejectedly into a chair, it is not the process of sitting down that is important; it is the dejection emphasized by the action. Dejection shows itself in the muscle tone of the interpreter's entire body, in the pace of speech, in vocal quality, and in countless other ways. In rehearsal, the staged scene should certainly be practiced in detail, and the act of sitting should be synchronized with the speech so that voice and body are saying the same thing. In an interpreter's performance, however, your sinking into a set-piece chair would pull the scene up on stage instead of keeping it out front. Worse, you would need a chair to sink into, and then you would need to get up in time to deliver the other characters' lines. Such activity draws attention to what isn't there at the expense of what is. Continue standing throughout the scene, and suggest a particular attitude not by an overt bodily activity but by empathy, muscle tone, and whatever aspects of focal technique are appropriate.

Angle of Placement

Onstage, actors move from place to place, and we follow them as they move. Part of the spectacle of a play is formed by the choreography of moving bodies. Understandably, solo interpreters cannot show such compositions in their performances. Through careful character placement, however, they can imply the movement of characters and suggest to the audience something of the essential movement of the play. After all, spatial relationships among characters contribute to their motivations and their lives—and vice versa.

Interpreters clarify the speaker's position by directing comments to specific locales. Too often, however, the angle of character placement is substituted for characterization. It should be merely a tool to assist characterization. Placement of characters comes among the last of the responsibilities the interpreter needs to face.

The most effective method of placing characters in a drama derives its power from the visual activity a staged version of the same play would provide, and it uses the stage picture as its foundation for subtly powerful impact. Picture a scene from Pinter's *Betrayal* (at the end of this chapter). The interpreter plays Emma and Robert. When Emma speaks, her comments are chiefly addressed to Robert; when Robert speaks, he most often addresses Emma. *When playing Robert,* the performer focuses on the imagined Emma, slightly above and beyond the audience's heads, as in this diagram:

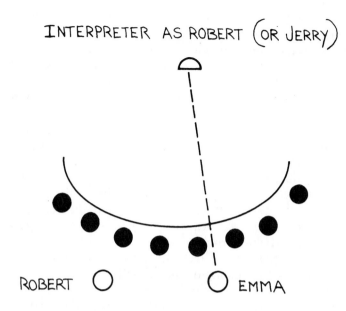

INTERPRETER AS ROBERT (OR JERRY)

ROBERT ○   ○ EMMA

When playing Emma, the performer focuses on the imagined Robert, again slightly above and beyond the audience's head, as in this diagram:

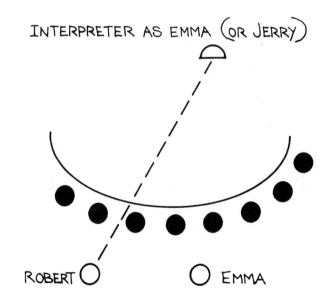

INTERPRETER AS EMMA (OR JERRY)

ROBERT ○   ○ EMMA

That much is easy, because the scene contains only two people. Now, suppose that Jerry (who is Emma's lover and whose letter Robert picks up) appears in the scene. The interpreter—*playing Jerry and addressing Emma*—would direct his focus to the same point he looked at when he was playing Robert. Similarly, were Jerry's lines to Robert, the interpreter would direct his attention to the point he used when Emma addressed Robert.

Won't the audience be confused? you ask. Identical twins aren't identical *people.* The audience won't be confused if the speaking characters are *distinctly drawn in body and voice,* because Emma, Robert, and Jerry are very different people with very different physical and vocal characteristics. Moreover, using this method permits the members of the audience to imagine Emma and Robert and Jerry behind them, in a kind of proximity to each other that permits each of them to move while speaking and allows each speaking character to distinguish the specific target of the speech. This method of character placement emphasizes the movement of the scene and capitalizes on the interpreter's essential ability to create distinct characters.

There are probably as many ways to place action out front as there are skilled interpreters. Another method asks the performer to locate a point for each character. Again, the point is slightly above and slightly beyond the heads of the audience. If you place the points reasonably close to each other, you can locate five or six characters quite easily without turning your head more than 30 degrees. This method ensures that a specific character—Emma, say—always looks at the same point, whether she addresses Robert or the Jerry we imaginatively brought into the scene. Although this method lacks the elegance of conveying stage action, it enables a beginning performer to keep the characters distinct and in order.

Remember, finally, that the method of placement is immeasurably less important than the fullness of character. Audiences will recognize true characters not because you place them in one spot or another but because you communicate their lives with your body and voice, and because you have created *people* in whom the audience can believe. Beginning students sometimes devote great chunks of rehearsal to "getting the angles" and ignore "finding the characters." Whatever method you choose, or if you devise your own method, be sure that the important characters are in the center of the audience and that less important characters are grouped accordingly, only slightly to either side of that center line. If you place characters too far apart, you will constantly be moving your head back and forth, encouraging the audience to pick up on the artificialities of the performing method. The audience will focus attention on what is *not* there, rather than on what *is.*

The method you adopt must give the audience the clearest, least ambiguous information. The audience should always know who is speaking. Whatever the method, any reasonable activity can occur during a given speech, provided that the activity is begun and concluded by the interpreter's focusing at the agreed-upon character point and that the speech remains addressed to characters within the play.

The interpreter generally does not have any direct audience contact during the passages in which *characters talk to characters*. But when you present any narrative material or explanation, you can establish audience contact because you are delivering that material as yourself. Sometimes characters speak directly to the audience, for example, in a soliloquy or an aside (indeed, the characters from Chapter 7's *Fires in the Mirror* speak directly to their audiences as does George in Sondheim's *Sunday in the Park with George* at the end of this chapter). In any case, avoid addressing your words to a single member of the audience, because that person might become uneasy under your constant gaze. Also, you do not want to distract yourself by catching the eye of any individual audience member. If you still find the matter of offstage focus and frontal placement of action puzzling, look at the discussion of "Readers' Theater" in Chapter 11. Some students have found the diagrams we provide there very helpful in clarifying the principles interpreters have to enforce.

Rest easy. The audience is actively involved in creating characters and places and ideas with your guidance. If you are constantly in character, giving your listeners new information, alive and fully aware of the excitement of your scene, the audience will be with you, enthralled, absorbed, and perhaps (even) as exhausted as you are by the conclusion.

The Reading Stand

For some people, the reading stand, or lectern,[1] is one of the traditional hallmarks of the interpreter. The decision to use or forgo a lectern is based on the needs of the material being performed, the amount of time available for rehearsal, and (sometimes) on the exigencies of what happens to be available (interpreters are nothing if not flexible). So, whatever choice you make, recognize that there are a number of reasons for choosing to use a lectern. If you perform with a physical text (a script), the lectern holds it nicely. (If you have memorized your entire selection, a lectern is probably superfluous.)

A lectern allows for greater freedom and flexibility in suggestion. It can serve as a table, a bar, a counter, a ledge, a tray, or any imaginary

---

1. A *lectern* should not be confused with a *podium,* which is an elevated platform on which one stands.

stage piece; it can also support some of the performer's weight. In addition, there is an aesthetic element to the lectern: it frames your performance. Every performer appearing before an audience is a presentational object. Around your person the audience unconsciously sketches in a frame. You—as performer—are responsible for filling that frame with the life of the play. If your frame includes a lectern, the audience is likely to restrict the amount of physical movement they expect from you. (Of course, you can always move toward and away from the lectern.) This restriction, however, carries with it a certain freedom. It encourages the audience to attend carefully to the suggestions you will give them within that frame to create the world of the play. In some staged productions the actor must compete with sets, costumes, and other actors for the audience's attention, and gestures must be sufficiently grand to fill a large space. Because they are restricted, interpreters can—and often do—use substantially more economical activity than do actors. Thus, interpreters become capable of a variety, subtlety, and nuance in their physical world because the audience itself undertakes a unique creative role.

One other practical matter about lecterns should be mentioned: unfortunately, they can obliterate carefully planned gestures and obscure delicate muscle memory. Rehearse with one, if at all possible.

Cutting and Excerpting

In Chapter 6 we discuss some responsible techniques of excerpting. Every interpreter is sooner or later confronted by this delicate task. The safest, most conservative rule regarding cutting and excerpting remains this: the less, the better. Each text is unique, and every performer and performance situation varies from every other. Therefore, we cannot establish any set rules for excerpting. But we are quick to recognize that drama frequently requires some kind of condensation, particularly for a solo interpreter.

Because time limitations can cause problems, it is wisest to excerpt a segment from a longer work that adequately fills the time limit without any internal cutting. You thus benefit from the carefully constructed rhythmic patterns of the play; the intricate, involved structure that sometimes hides itself at first glance emerges during your rehearsal process. Moreover, as you build the scene, you will have all the benefits of the author's craft on your side. If your segment should occur midway in the play, you can describe to the audience what has happened just prior to the scene; if subsequent events are important for an understanding of your passage, you can relate them after you have finished. In the introductory paragraph, each excerpt provides the information an audience needs. If you start at the beginning of a play, your audience can join the performance as if they are watching a staged production, because your performance will present all the required information.

Sometimes, though, it is necessary to cut the material, and you must be extremely careful how you do this. Often a performer's reflexive physical activity can suggest an action that has been performed: a speaking character is allowed to continue speaking while the performer nods to an imaginary butler and mimes the action of picking up a letter from a proffered tray. If this is the butler's only appearance and his only line, the audience will scarcely miss him. If, however, your play is one in which "the butler did it," cutting his appearance here would deprive your audience of crucial information. Before cutting anything, try conscientiously to include everything. If your effort is genuine, you will be surprised at how unnecessary any cutting is. Only extraordinary circumstances should require you to cut more than a few words. If these circumstances arise, at all costs avoid interlinear cutting because it defeats your purpose, misrepresents the play, and confuses the audience. Keep the speech whole.

Analyzing the Rehearsal and the Performance

Begin your analysis with an update and a review. By now you should be familiar with the performance problems that habitually plague you. Have you spent sufficient time on rehearsal? Have you been maintaining concentration? Have you made substantial and serious efforts to transform the literary analysis into performance behavior? Is your body responding more flexibly? Has your voice continued to demonstrate the tone color and vocal variety that mark successful interpretation? As we have said, these questions will never disappear. They will shift focus and degree, of course, with each selection you prepare and each performance you deliver, but the fundamental concerns of interpretation remain the same for beginning students and for veterans.

Performing drama affords another opportunity to broaden your experiences. Drama presents special problems in creating character, managing dialogue, and demonstrating action. These problems, of course, also appear when you are performing narration, and some types of poetry—particularly confessional poems—require similar effort for construction of character. Thus, the skills you develop in these performances rest on the skills you have already established, and they will also be useful when you confront the special problems of performing poetry.

Try to respond, then, to the following questions about your performance of drama not simply in terms of this genre's unique concerns but also in terms of the *process* you undertake in performing any literary selection. Although these questions may seem specifically related to drama, they really are about your development as an interpreter of all kinds of literature.

- Was your commitment to the scene total? Did your audience see only characters during the performance? When did the interpreter emerge? Why? Was it planned?

- Did you carefully analyze the structure of your scene, taking time to establish clearly all the principal components of the action?

- Did your close analytical reading disclose hidden clues about characters? How did the discovery change your rehearsal?

- How did you find appropriate bodies and voices and gestures for the people in your scene?

- How was silence used in your scene? Did your characters fill the silences with their personalities? Did the speaker watch carefully for responses from the silent characters?

- Did you stage the scene for yourself during rehearsal? Did you carefully imagine and define the settings and properties filling the world of the scene? Did you dress the characters appropriately?

- Did your movement through the scene clarify the reason each character speaks and why the character chooses the language used? Did you need a paraphrase to understand the intellectual component of the scene?

- Were properties necessary? Were they kept alive? Did you *economically* suggest stage movement? Did your audience always know where the characters were, in addition to who was speaking? How did you solve the scenographic requirements of the play?

- Were you sensitive to the rhythm of the speeches? Did you allow each character a distinctive vocal timbre?

- Were you in control? Were you too much in control? Have you begun to develop a method for rehearsal? Did memorization intrude? Ought memorization to have been used?

- Were your muscles remembering the bodies you created in rehearsal? Did you make clear why each character remains onstage?

- Did you pick up your cues?

- Did you place the action of the scene directly out front? Did you keep the characters distinct?

- If you used a lectern, was it part of the performance or part of the woodwork? Did you make your physical text part of the performance?

- Did you cut your scene internally? Was it living when you finished?

Also use those questions to focus your responses to the performances of others in your class. Keeping in mind that your chief responsibility is to be descriptive, try to make sure that you say *precisely* what you saw and heard and, most important, try to make sure that what you say is precisely what you mean. If there is some possibility of misunderstanding, take the time to clarify before proceeding. For example, if you say, "I thought the performer seemed out of breath, gasping and choking," when in fact you mean you thought a *character* in the scene demonstrated this behavior, do not be surprised if the interpreter is puzzled. Clear, shared language reveals shared goals. In laboratory sessions a performer might work on a special problem (dialect, for example, or physical debility in a character) and, in his or her attention to this concern, might slight other responsibilities (character placement or volume). Know what the other performer is working on. If you don't know or it isn't apparent, ask. As you know, performers like very much to talk about what they do.

Acknowledging that there are many responsibilities for a performer, as well as fulfilling each of these responsibilities with equal distinction, is a rare—a very rare—achievement. Because something remains to be done, however, does not mean that nothing has been done. Something may have been omitted from a performance in which much more has been included.

Finally, discussing performance can become an enormously humanizing concern, if performer and audience are both primarily concerned with *understanding*. For criticism to be useful, it must be humane. This doesn't mean it cannot be specific or blunt, as the case warrants. It means that the goal for the critic ought to be the same as for the performer: the fullest possible communication of a work of literature. Whatever diverts attention from that goal isn't really worth our time.

REMEMBER THIS!

Although you will not always select drama for performance, many of the skills you acquired in this chapter will serve you well when you perform other genres. Performing prose or performing poetry will be easier if you recall:

- An audience's need to see and to create.

- How to keep control of emotional response.

- When memorizing is essential.

continued

- How scene affects audience creativity.

- Ways to develop and enrich engaging characters.

- Methods to convey physical contact; to maximize the interplay of character; and to clarify physical focus.

- Uses and abuses of reading stands.

- Techniques for sympathetic cutting and excerpting.

Selections for Analysis and Oral Interpretation

Stephen Sondheim won a Pulitzer Prize for Sunday in the Park with George, *a musical that explores the responsibilities of artists by examining the life of the French pointillist painter Georges Seurat. George's girlfriend has left him because he has been obsessed with his work and has neglected their relationship. Now she is looking for him. In this song George makes clear that what caused the problem will always remain. Sondheim composed particularly ravishing music for these lyrics, but everything you need for performing is in the words he wrote. Show us how George thinks. Trust Sondheim's line lengths.*

 FROM **Sunday in the Park with George**

STEPHEN SONDHEIM

Finishing the Hat

> Yes, she looks for me—good.
> Let her look for me to tell me why she left me—
> As I always knew she would.
> I had thought she understood.
> They have never understood,
> And no reason that they should.
> But if anybody could . . .
>
> Finishing the hat,
> How you have to finish the hat.
> How you watch the rest of the world
> From a window
> While you finish the hat.
>
> Mapping out a sky,
> What you feel like, planning a sky.

What you feel when voices that come
Through the window
Go
Until they distance and die,
Until there's nothing but sky.

And how you're always turning back too late
From the grass or the stick
Or the dog or the light,
How the kind of woman willing to wait's
Not the kind that you want to find waiting
To return you to the night,
Dizzy from the height,
Coming from the hat,
Studying the hat,
Entering the world of the hat,
Reaching through the world of the hat
Like a window,
Back to this one from that.

Studying a face,
Stepping back to look at a face
Leaves a little space in the way like a window,
But to see—
It's the only way to see.

And when the woman that you wanted goes,
You can say to yourself, "Well, I give what I give."
But the woman who won't wait for you knows
That, however you live,
There's a part of you always standing by,
Mapping out the sky,
Finishing a hat . . .
Starting on a hat . . .
Finishing a hat . . .
Look, I made a hat . . .
Where there never was a hat . . .

- ◆ Did you find the fulcrum of George's speech? Did your audience see it?

- ◆ What do the last five lines mean?

This excerpt—the opening minutes of Sam Shepard's Curse of the Starving
Class—*combines active dialogue and a long, reflective monologue. Wesley is
methodically throwing pieces of wooden debris into an old wheelbarrow when*

his mother, Ella, just waking up, enters, winding an alarm clock. The tension between the two characters is aggravated by the relationship each has with someone not there. The scene challenges you to keep vivid the ways in which someone absent makes his presence felt—indelibly.

☉ FROM Curse of the Starving Class

SAM SHEPARD

ELLA: (*after a while*) You shouldn't be doing that.

WESLEY: I'm doing it.

ELLA: Yes, but you shouldn't be. He should be doing it. He's the one who broke it down.

WESLEY: He's not here.

ELLA: He's not back yet?

WESLEY: Nope.

ELLA: Well, just leave it until he gets back.

WESLEY: In the meantime we gotta' live in it.

ELLA: He'll be back. He can clean it up then.

(WESLEY *goes on clearing the debris into the wheelbarrow.* ELLA *finishes winding the clock and then sets it on the stove.*)

ELLA: (*looking at clock*) I must've got to sleep at five in the morning.

WESLEY: Did you call the cops?

ELLA: Last night?

WESLEY: Yeah.

ELLA: Sure I called the cops. Are you kidding? I was in danger of my life. I was being threatened.

WESLEY: He wasn't threatening you.

ELLA: Are you kidding me? He broke the door down, didn't he?

WESLEY: He was just trying to get in.

ELLA: That's no way to get into a house. There's plenty of other ways to get into a house. He could've climbed through a window.

WESLEY: He was drunk.

ELLA: That's not my problem.

WESLEY: You locked the door.

ELLA: Sure I locked the door. I told him I was going to lock the door. I told him the next time that happened I was locking the door and he could sleep in a hotel.

WESLEY: Is that where he is now?

ELLA: How should I know?

WESLEY: He took the Packard I guess.

ELLA: If that's the one that's missing I guess that's the one he took.

WESLEY: How come you called the cops?

ELLA: I was scared.

WESLEY: You thought he was going to kill you?

ELLA: I thought—I thought, "I don't know who this is. I don't know who this is trying to break in here. Who is this? It could be anyone."

WESLEY: I heard you screaming at each other.

ELLA: Yes.

WESLEY: So you must've known who it was.

ELLA: I wasn't sure. That was the frightening part. I could smell him right through the door.

WESLEY: He was drinking that much?

ELLA: Not that. His skin.

WESLEY: Oh.

ELLA: (*suddenly cheerful*) You want some breakfast?

WESLEY: No thanks.

ELLA: (*going to refrigerator*) Well I'm going to have some.

WESLEY: (*still cleaning*) It's humiliating to have the cops come to your own house. Makes me feel like we're someone else.

ELLA: (*looking in refrigerator*) There's no eggs but there's bacon and bread.

WESLEY: Makes me feel lonely. Like we're in trouble or something.

ELLA: (*still looking in refrigerator*) We're not in trouble. He's in trouble, but we're not.

WESLEY: You didn't have to call the cops.

ELLA: (*slamming refrigerator door and holding bacon and bread*) I told you, he was trying to kill me!

(*They look at each other for a moment.* ELLA *breaks it by putting the bacon and bread down on the top of the stove.* WESLEY *goes back to cleaning up the debris. He keeps talking as* ELLA *looks through the lower drawers of the stove and pulls out a frying pan. She lights one of the burners on the stove and starts cooking the bacon.*)

WESLEY: (*as he throws wood into wheelbarrow*) I was lying there on my back. I could smell the avocado blossoms. I could hear the coyotes. I could hear stock cars squealing down the street. I could feel myself in my bed in my room in this house in this town in this state in this country. I could feel this country close like it was part of my bones. I could feel the presence of all the people outside, at night, in the dark. Even sleeping people I could feel. Even all the sleeping animals. Dogs. Peacocks. Bulls. Even tractors sitting in the wetness, waiting for the sun to come up. I was looking straight up at the ceiling at all my model airplanes hanging by all their thin metal wires. Floating. Swaying very quietly like they were being blown by someone's breath. Cobwebs moving with them. Dust laying on their wings. Decals peeling off their wings. My P-39. My Messerschmitt. My Jap Zero. I could feel myself lying far below them on my bed like I was on the ocean and overhead they were on reconnaissance. Scouting me. Floating. Taking pictures of the enemy. Me, the enemy.

I could feel the space around me like a big, black world. I listened like an animal. My listening was afraid. Afraid of sound. Tense. Like any second something could invade me. Some foreigner. Something undescribable. Then I heard the Packard coming up the hill. From a mile off I could tell it was the Packard by the sound of the valves. The lifters have a sound like nothing else. Then I could picture my Dad driving it. Shifting unconsciously. Downshifting into second for the last pull up the hill. I could feel the headlights closing in. Cutting through the orchard. I could see the trees being lit one after the other by the lights, then going back to black. My heart was pounding. Just from my Dad coming back. Then I heard him pull the brake. Lights go off. Key's turned off. Then a long silence. Him just sitting in the car. Just sitting. I picture him just sitting. What's he doing? Just sitting. Waiting to get out. Why's he waiting to get out? He's plastered and can't move. He's plastered and doesn't want to move. He's going to sleep there all night. He's slept there before. He's woken up with dew on the hood before. Freezing headache. Teeth covered with peanuts. Then I hear the door of the Packard open. A pop of metal. Dogs barking down the road. Door slams. Feet. Paper bag being tucked under one arm. Paper bag covering "Tiger Rose." Feet coming. Feet walking toward the door. Feet stopping. Heart pounding. Sound of door not opening. Foot kicking door. Man's voice. Dad's voice. Dad calling Mom. No answer. Foot kicking. Foot kicking harder. Wood splitting. Man's voice. In the night. Foot kicking hard through door. One foot right through door. Bottle crashing. Glass breaking. Fist through door. Man cursing. Man going insane. Feet and hands tearing. Head smashing. Man yelling. Shoulder smashing. Whole body crashing. Woman screaming. Mom screaming. Mom screaming for police. Man throwing wood. Man throwing up. Mom calling cops. Dad crashing away. Back down driveway. Car door slamming. Ignition grinding. Wheels screaming. First gear grinding. Wheels screaming off down hill. Packard disappearing. Sound disappearing. No sound. No sight. Planes still hanging. Heart still pounding. No sound. Mom crying soft. Soft crying. Then no sound. Then softly crying. Then moving around through house. Then no moving. Then crying softly. Then stopping. Then, far off the freeway could be heard.

(WESLEY *picks up one end of the wheelbarrow. He makes the sound of a car and pushes it off right, leaving* ELLA *alone at the stove watching the bacon.*)

- ◆ These characters have very different actions. How did you clarify that difference to your audience?

- ◆ Sense memory fills Wesley's monologue. What did you do to ensure that your audience saw and heard you remembering?

The beginning of this famous scene, with its entrances and exits, requires some care to keep the abrupt stage directions from interrupting the dialogue. Juliet's speech, with its problem of properties and her loss of consciousness at the end, has been discussed in this chapter. Watch the buildup of hysteria toward the end of the speech and the resultant problem of balancing the climactic "This do I drink to thee." Juliet is always thinking.

 FROM **Romeo and Juliet**

WILLIAM SHAKESPEARE

ACT IV, SCENE 3

(*Enter* JULIET *and* NURSE.)

JULIET: Ay, those attires are best; but, gentle nurse,
I pray thee, leave me to myself to-night;
For I have need of many orisons
To move the heavens to smile upon my state,
Which, well thou know'st, is cross and full of sin.

(*Enter* LADY CAPULET.)

LADY CAPULET: What, are you busy, ho? Need you my help?
JULIET: No, Madame; we have cull'd such necessaries
As are behoveful for our state to-morrow.
So please you, let me now be left alone,
And let the nurse this night sit up with you;

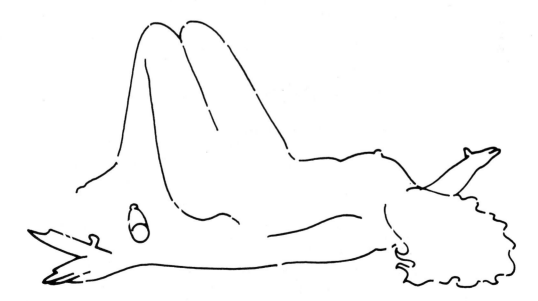

For, I am sure, you have your hands full all,
In this so sudden business.
LADY CAPULET: Good-night.
Get thee to bed, and rest; for thou hast need.

(*Exeunt* LADY CAPULET *and* NURSE.)

JULIET: Farewell! God knows when we shall meet again.
I have a faint cold fear thrills through my veins,
That almost freezes up the heat of life.
I'll call them back again to comfort me.
Nurse! What should she do there?
My dismal scene I needs must act alone.
Come, vial.
What if this mixture do not work at all?
Shall I be married then to-morrow morning?
No, no; this shall forbid it. Lie thou there. (*Laying down her dagger*)
What if it be poison, which the friar
Subtly hath minist'red to have me dead,
Lest in this marriage he should be dishonour'd
Because he married me before to Romeo?
I fear it is; and yet, methinks, it should not,
For he hath still been tried a holy man.
How if, when I am laid into the tomb,
I wake before the time that Romeo
Come to redeem me? There's a fearful point!
Shall I not then be stifled in the vault,
To whose foul mouth no healthsome air breathes in,
And there die strangled ere my Romeo comes?
Or, if I live, is it not very like
The horrible conceit of death and night,
Together with the terror of the place,—
As in a vault, an ancient receptacle,
Where, for this many hundred years, the bones
Of all my buried ancestors are pack'd;
Where bloody Tybalt, yet but green in earth,
Lies fest'ring in his shroud; where, as they say,
At some hours in the night spirits resort;—
Alack, alack, is it not like that I,
So early waking,—what with loathsome smells,
And shrieks like mandrakes' torn out of the earth,
That living mortals, hearing them, run mad;—
O, if I wake, shall I not be distraught,
Environed with all these hideous fears,
And madly play with my forefathers' joints,
And pluck the mangled Tybalt from his shroud,

And, in this rage, with some great kinsman's bone
As with a club, dash out my desperate brains?
O, look! methinks I see my cousin's ghost
Seeking out Romeo, that did spit his body
Upon a rapier's point. Stay, Tybalt, stay!
Romeo, I come! This do I drink to thee.

(*She falls upon her bed, within the curtains.*)

- ◆ What kind of a mother was your Lady Capulet?

- ◆ What caused Juliet finally to drink the potion? Did your audience see that, too?

This play explores the slow denouement of at least three relationships in a complex series of nine scenes that begin in 1977 and recede in time to 1968. Midway through the play Robert and Emma—husband and wife—vacation in Venice, but their sojourn cannot be relaxing for either. Pinter uses "Pause" and "Silence" more eloquently than other modern dramatists, and you must scrupulously follow his directions. Be sure, however, that these pauses are filled with concentration.

 FROM **Betrayal, Scene Five**

HAROLD PINTER

HOTEL ROOM. VENICE, 1973. SUMMER.

EMMA *on bed reading.* ROBERT *at window looking out. She looks up at him, then back at the book.*

EMMA: It's Torcello tomorrow, isn't it?
ROBERT: What?
EMMA: We're going to Torcello tomorrow, aren't we?
ROBERT: Yes. That's right.
EMMA: That'll be lovely.
ROBERT: Mmn.
EMMA: I can't wait.

Pause

ROBERT: Book good?
EMMA: Mmn. Yes.
ROBERT: What is it?
EMMA: This new book. This man Spinks.
ROBERT: Oh that. Jerry was telling me about it.
EMMA: Jerry? Was he?
ROBERT: He was telling me about it at lunch last week.

EMMA: Really? Does he like it?

ROBERT: Spinks is his boy. He discovered him.

EMMA: Oh. I didn't know that.

ROBERT: Unsolicited manuscript.

Pause

You think it's good, do'you?

EMMA: Yes, I do. I'm enjoying it.

ROBERT: Jerry thinks it's good too. You should have lunch with us one day and chat about it.

EMMA: Is that absolutely necessary?

Pause

It's not as good as all that.

ROBERT: You mean it's not good enough for you to have lunch with Jerry and me to chat about it?

EMMA: What the hell are you talking about?

ROBERT: I must read it again myself, now it's in hard covers.

EMMA: Again?

ROBERT: Jerry wanted us to publish it.

EMMA: Oh, really?

ROBERT: Well, naturally. Anyway, I turned it down.

EMMA: Why?

ROBERT: Oh . . . not much more to say on that subject, really, is there?

EMMA: What do you consider the subject to be?

ROBERT: Betrayal.

EMMA: No, it isn't.

ROBERT: Isn't it? What is it then?

EMMA: I haven't finished it yet. I'll let you know.

ROBERT: Well, do let me know.

Pause

Of course, I could be thinking of the wrong book.

Silence

By the way, I went into American Express yesterday.

She looks up.

EMMA: Oh?

ROBERT: Yes. I went to cash some travellers cheques. You get a much better rate there, you see, than you do in an hotel.

EMMA: Oh, do you?

ROBERT: Oh yes. Anyway, there was a letter there for you. They asked me if you were any relation and I said yes. So they asked me if I wanted to take it. I mean, they gave it to me. But I said no, I would leave it. Did you get it?

EMMA: Yes.

ROBERT: I suppose you popped in when you were out shopping yesterday evening?

EMMA: That's right.

ROBERT: Oh well, I'm glad you got it.

Pause

To be honest, I was amazed that they suggested I take it. It could never happen in England. But these Italians . . . so free and easy. I mean, just because my name is Downs and your name is Downs doesn't mean that we're the Mr and Mrs Downs that they, in their laughing Mediterranean way, assume we are. We could be, and in fact are vastly more likely to be, total strangers. So let's say I, whom they laughingly assume to be your husband, had taken the letter, having declared myself to be your husband but in truth being a total stranger, and opened it, and read it, out of nothing more than idle curiosity, and then thrown it in a canal, you would never have received it and would have been deprived of your legal right to open your own mail, and all this because of Venetian *je m'en foutisme*.[2] I've a good mind to write to the Doge of Venice about it.

Pause

That's what stopped me taking it, by the way, and bringing it to you, the thought that I could very easily be a total stranger.

Pause

What they of course did not know, and had no way of knowing, was that I am your husband.

EMMA: Pretty inefficient bunch.

ROBERT: Only in a laughing Mediterranean way.

Pause

EMMA: It was from Jerry.

ROBERT: Yes, I recognised the handwriting.

Pause

How is he?

EMMA: Okay.

ROBERT: Good. And Judith?

EMMA: Fine.

Pause

ROBERT: What about the kids?

EMMA: I don't think he mentioned them.

ROBERT: They're probably all right, then. If they were ill or something he'd have probably mentioned it.

Pause

Any other news?

EMMA: No.

Silence

ROBERT: Are you looking forward to Torcello?

Pause

How many times have we been to Torcello? Twice. I remember how you loved it, the first time I took you there. You fell in love with it. That was about ten years ago, wasn't it? About . . . six months after

---

2. A coarse French version of "I don't give a damn."

we were married. Yes. Do you remember? I wonder if you'll like it as much tomorrow.

Pause

What do you think of Jerry as a letter writer?

She laughs shortly.

You're trembling. Are you cold?

EMMA: No.

ROBERT: He used to write to me at one time. Long letters about Ford Madox Ford. I used to write to him too, come to think of it. Long letters about . . . oh, W. B. Yeats, I suppose. That was the time when we were both editors of poetry magazines. Him at Cambridge, me at Oxford. Did you know that? We were bright young men. And close friends. Well, we still are close friends. All that was long before I met you. Long before he met you. I've been trying to remember when I introduced him to you. I simply can't remember. I take it I *did* introduce him to you? Yes. But when? Can you remember?

EMMA: No.

ROBERT: You can't?

EMMA: No.

ROBERT: How odd.

Pause

He wasn't best man at our wedding, was he?

EMMA: You know he was.

ROBERT: Ah, yes. Well, that's probably when I introduced him to you.

Pause

Was there any message for me, in his letter?

Pause

I mean in the line of business, to do with the world of publishing. Has he discovered any new and original talent? He's quite talented at uncovering talent, old Jerry.

EMMA: No message.

ROBERT: No message. Not even his love?

Silence

EMMA: We're lovers.

ROBERT: Ah. Yes. I thought it might be something like that, something along those lines.

EMMA: When?

ROBERT: What?

EMMA: When did you think?

ROBERT: Yesterday. Only yesterday. When I saw his handwriting on the letter. Before yesterday I was quite ignorant.

EMMA: Ah.

Pause

I'm sorry.

ROBERT: *Sorry?*

Silence

Where does it . . . take place? Must be a bit awkward. I mean we've got two kids, he's got two kids, not to mention a wife . . .

EMMA: We have a flat.

ROBERT: Ah. I see.

Pause

Nice?

Pause

A flat. It's quite well established then, your . . . uh . . . affair?

EMMA: Yes.

ROBERT: How long?

EMMA: Some time.

ROBERT: Yes, but how long exactly?

EMMA: Five years.

ROBERT: *Five years?*

Pause

Ned is one year old.

Pause

Did you hear what I said?

EMMA: Yes. He's your son. Jerry was in America. For two months.

Silence

ROBERT: Did he write to you from America?

EMMA: Of course. And I wrote to him.

ROBERT: Did you tell him that Ned had been conceived?

EMMA: Not by letter.

ROBERT: But when did you tell him, was he happy to know I was to be a father?

Pause

I've always liked Jerry. To be honest, I've always liked him rather more than I've liked you. Maybe I should have had an affair with him myself.

Silence

Tell me, are you looking forward to our trip to Torcello?

- How did you demonstrate that Robert knows of the affair as the scene begins?
- How did you prepare your audience for Emma's confession?

The Nobel laureate Wole Soyinka built this play on an incident that occurred in Nigeria in 1946, but the drama rests in the conflict of the hero, Elesin, and Yoruba tradition. In this scene, Sergeant Amusa—the African policeman employed to carry out the orders of the white colonial administrator—attempts to arrest Elesin on the latter's wedding night. He has not reckoned sufficiently with the women of the community, or with the "mother" of the marketplace, Iyaloja. One of the challenges of this scene is that the women and the girls are not assigned to specific speeches. Why? How does that communal ownership of the part empower the solo performer?

FROM Death and the King's Horseman

WOLE SOYINKA

A swelling, agitated hum of women's voices rises immediately in the background. The lights come on and we see the frontage of a converted cloth stall in the market. The floor leading up to the entrance is covered in rich velvets and woven cloth. The women come on stage, borne backwards by the determined progress of Sergeant Amusa and his two constables who already have their batons out and use them as a pressure against the women. At the edge of the cloth-covered floor however the women take a determined stand and block all further progress of the men. They begin to tease them mercilessly.

AMUSA: I am tell you women for last time to commot my road. I am here on official business.

WOMAN: Official business you white man's eunuch? Official business is taking place where you want to go and it's a business you wouldn't understand.

WOMAN: (*makes a quick tug at the constable's baton*): That doesn't fool anyone you know. It's the one you carry under your government knickers that counts. (*She bends low as if to peep under the baggy shorts. The embarrassed constable quickly puts his knees together. The women roar.*)

WOMAN: You mean there is nothing there at all?

WOMAN: Oh there was something. You know that handbell which the whiteman uses to summon his servants . . . ?

AMUSA: (*he manages to preserve some dignity throughout*): I hope you women know that interfering with officer in execution of his duty is criminal offence.

WOMAN: Interfere? He says we're interfering with him. You foolish man we're telling you there's nothing there to interfere with.

AMUSA: I am order you now to clear the road.

WOMAN: What road? The one your father built?

WOMAN: You are a Policeman not so? Then you know what they call trespassing in court. Or—(*Pointing to the cloth-lined steps*)—do you think that kind of road is built for every kind of feet.

WOMAN: Go back and tell the white man who sent you to come himself.

AMUSA: If I go I will come back with reinforcement. And we will all return carrying weapons.

WOMAN: Oh, now I understand. Before they can put on those knickers the white man first cuts off their weapons.

WOMAN: What a cheek! You mean you come here to show power to women and you don't even have a weapon.

AMUSA: (*shouting above the laughter*): For the last time I warn you women to clear the road.

WOMAN: To where?

AMUSA: To that hut. I know he dey dere.

WOMAN: Who?

AMUSA: The chief who call himself Elesin Oba.

WOMAN: You ignorant man. It is not he who calls himself Elesin Oba, it is his blood that says it. As it called out to his father before him and will to his son after him. And that is in spite of everything your white man can do.

WOMAN: Is it not the same ocean that washes this land and the white man's land? Tell your white man he can hide our son away as long as he likes. When the time comes for him, the same ocean will bring him back.

AMUSA: The government say dat kin' ting must stop.

WOMAN: Who will stop it? You? Tonight our husband and father will prove himself greater than the laws of strangers.

AMUSA: I tell you nobody go prove anyting tonight or anytime. Is ignorant and criminal to prove dat kin' prove.

IYALOJA: (*entering, from the hut. She is accompanied by a group of young girls who have been attending the* BRIDE): What is it Amusa? Why do you come here to disturb the happiness of others.

AMUSA: Madame Iyaloja, I glad you come. You know me. I no like trouble but duty is duty. I am here to arrest Elesin for criminal intent. Tell these women to stop obstructing me in the performance of my duty.

IYALOJA: And you? What gives you the right to obstruct our leader of men in the performance of his duty.

AMUSA: What kin' duty be dat one Iyaloja.

IYALOJA: What kin' duty? What kin' duty does a man have to his new bride?

AMUSA: (*bewildered, looks at the women and at the entrance to the hut*): Iyaloja, is it wedding you call dis kin' ting?

IYALOJA: You have wives haven't you? Whatever the white man has done to you he hasn't stopped you having wives. And if he has, at least he is married. If you don't know what a marriage is, go and ask him to tell you.

AMUSA: This no to wedding.

IYALOJA: And ask him at the same time what he would have done if anyone had come to disturb him on his wedding night?

AMUSA: Iyaloja, I say dis no to wedding.

IYALOJA: You want to look inside the bridal chamber? You want to see for yourself how a man cuts the virgin knot?

AMUSA: Madam . . .

WOMAN: Perhaps his wives are still waiting for him to learn.

AMUSA: Iyaloja, make you tell dese women make den no insult me again. If I hear dat kin' indult once more . . .

GIRL: (*pushing her way through*): You will do what?

GIRL: He's out of his mind. It's our mothers you're talking to, do you know that? Not to any illiterate villager you can bully and terrorise. How dare you intrude here anyway?

GIRL: What a cheek, what impertinence!

GIRL: You've treated them too gently. Now let them see what it is to tamper with the mothers of this market.

GIRL: Your betters dare not enter the market when the women say no!

GIRL: Haven't you learnt that yet, you jester in khaki and starch?

IYALOJA: Daughters . . .

GIRL: No no Iyaloja, leave us to deal with him. He no longer knows his mother, we'll teach him.

(*With a sudden movement they snatch the batons of the two constables. They begin to hem them in.*)

GIRL: What next? We have your batons? What next? What are you going to do?

(*With equally swift movements they knock off their hats.*)

GIRL: Move if you dare. We have your hats, what will you do about it? Didn't the white man teach you to take off your hats before women?

IYALOJA: It's a wedding night. It's a night of joy for us. Peace . . .

GIRL: Not for him. Who asked him here?

GIRL: Does he dare go to the Residency without an invitation?

GIRL: Not even where the servants eat left-overs.

GIRL: (*in turn. In an "English" accent*): Well well it's Mister Amusa. Were you invited? (*Play-acting to one another. The older women encourage them with their titters.*)

—Your invitation card please?

—Who are you? Have we been introduced?

—And who did you say you were?

—Sorry, I didn't quite catch your name.

—May I take your hat?

—If you insist. May I take yours? (*Exchanging the policeman's hats.*)

—How very kind of you.

—Not at all. Won't you sit down?

—After you.

—Oh no.

—I insist.

—You're most gracious.

—And how do you find the place?

—The natives are alright.

—Friendly?

—Tractable.

—Not a teeny-weeny bit restless?

—Well, a teeny-weeny bit restless.

—One might even say, difficult?

—Indeed one might be tempted to say, difficult.

—But you do manage to cope?

—Yes indeed I do. I have a rather faithful ox called Amusa.

—He's loyal?

—Absolutely.

—Lay down his life for you what?

—Without a moment's thought.

—Had one like that once. Trust him with my life.

—Mostly of course they are liars.

—Never known a native tell the truth.

—Does it get rather close around here?

—It's mild for this time of the year.

—But the rains may still come.

—They are late this year aren't they?

—They are keeping African time.

—Ha ha ha ha

—Ha ha ha ha

—The humidity is what gets me.

—It used to be whisky.

—Ha ha ha ha

—Ha ha ha ha

—What's your handicap old chap?

—Is there racing by golly?

—Splendid golf course, you'll like it.

—I'm beginning to like it already.

—And a European club, exclusive.

—You've kept the flag flying.

—We do our best for the old country.

—It's a pleasure to serve.

—Another whisky old chap?

—You are indeed too too kind.

—Not at all sir. Where is that boy? (*With a sudden bellow.*) Sergeant!

AMUSA: (*snaps to attention*): Yessir!

(*The women collapse with laughter.*)

GIRL: Take your men out of here.

AMUSA: (*realising the trick, he rages from loss of face*): I'm give you warning . . .

GIRL: Alright then. Off with his knickers! (*They surge slowly forward.*)

IYALOJA: Daughters, please.

AMUSA: (*squaring himself for defence*): The first woman wey touch me . . .

IYALOJA: My children, I beg of you . . .

GIRL: Then tell him to leave this market. This is the home of our mothers. We don't want the eater of white left-overs at the feast their hands have prepared.

IYALOJA: You heard them Amusa. You had better go.

GIRL: Now!

AMUSA: (*commencing his retreat*): We dey go now, but make you say no say we no warn you.

GIRL: Now!

GIRL: Before we read the riot act—you should know all about that.

AMUSA: Make we go. (*They depart, more precipitately.*)

- ◆ What happens to Amusa's speech during the scene? How did you show this?

Bibliography

These texts offer perspectives on the development of acting and directing technique, primarily for the student.

Cohen, Robert. *Acting Power.* Palo Alto, CA: Mayfield, 1978.
> *Considers intellectual rather than physical approaches to acting preparation.*

Cole, Susan Letzler. *Directors in Rehearsal: A Hidden World.* New York: Routledge, 1992.
> *Considers the practice of theater craft in discussions of major twentieth-century directors.*

Converse, Terry John. *Directing for the Stage.* Colorado Springs, CO: Meriwether, 1995.
> *A useful handbook with many rehearsal exercises for directors.*

Dolan, Jill. *Geographies of Learning: Theory and Practice, Activism and Performance.* Middletown, CT: Wesleyan University Press, 2001.
> *A personal account about the challenges and potential solutions for wedding theory, practice, and progressive advocacy in the production and teaching of theater within the academy.*

Hagan, Uta. *Respect for Acting.* New York: Macmillan, 1973.
> *One of the most important teachers of acting outlines her approach; this text is essential reading for any student of theater.*

Stanislavski, Konstantin. *An Actor Prepares.* Translated by Elizabeth Reynolds Hapgood. New York: Theatre Arts Books, 1970.
> *Perhaps the most influential statement about acting technique in the twentieth century.*

Whitmore, Jon. *Directing Postmodern Theatre.* Ann Arbor: University of Michigan Press, 1994.
> *A thought-provoking book that considers diverse apects of directing for the stage.*

PART FOUR

Interpretation of Poetry

If I read a book and it makes my whole body so cold no fire can ever warm me, I know that it is poetry. If I feel physically as if the top of my head were taken off, I know that it is poetry. Is there any other way?

Emily Dickinson

CHAPTER NINE

Language of Poetry

Poems

are

different.

EXPECT THIS!

This chapter begins our intensive exploration of poetry by examining what poems are made of; Chapter 10 will examine how they are made. By the end of this chapter, you should be able to:

- Define poetic content.

- Recognize the characteristic elements of narrative, lyric, and dramatic poems, and the common variations of each class.

- Determine the unique perspective of the persona in each of the kinds of poems discussed.

- Discuss the interrelationship of experience and language in poetry.

- Unpack the condensed language of poetry by recognizing allusions, figures of speech, sensory appeals, and poetic syntax.

- Exploit tone color in poetry in your performance.

- Integrate titles insofar as the poem demands.

- Keep the poem alive after analysis.

Selections Discussed in This Chapter

In explaining some topics, we mention texts that are reprinted either within the chapter itself or at the end of a chapter. Use the guide below for quick reference to acquaint yourself with selections you may not fully recall.

Author	Title	Location
Maury Yeston	"New Words"	Chapter 2, page 38
Amanda McBroom	"Dreaming"	Chapter 2, page 66
		(continued)

Author	Title	Location
Joanne Gilbert	"Upon Learning That a Junior High School Acquaintance Has Been Nominated for an Academy Award"	Chapter 2, page 74
Alfred, Lord Tennyson	"Ulysses"	Chapter 4, page 154
Sharon Olds	"The Race"	Chapter 4, page 163
Theodore Roethke	"Old Lady's Winter Words"	Chapter 4, page 166
Stephen Sondheim	"Finishing the Hat," from *Sunday in the Park with George*	Chapter 8, page 360
John Keats	"To Autumn"	Chapter 9, page 396
Gerard Manley Hopkins	"The Windhover"	Chapter 9, page 406
Robert Frost	"Wild Grapes"	Chapter 9, page 407
e. e. cummings	"Spring is like a perhaps hand"	Chapter 9, page 410
Mary Stewart Hammond	"Saving Memory"	Chapter 9, page 413
Seamus Heaney	"Mid-Term Break"	Chapter 9, page 414
John Ciardi	"Most Like an Arch This Marriage"	Chapter 9, page 418
Robert Browning	"My Last Duchess"	Chapter 10, page 453
Ovid	"The Story of Baucis and Philemon," from *The Metamorphoses*	Chapter 11, page 495

POEMS ARE DIFFERENT. WE HEAR AND TELL STORIES ALL THE time; we see movies and plays and television dramas. For many people, however, poems seem unfamiliar, peculiar, dense. They are. Precisely the unusualness of some experiences makes poems possible. The many layers of important experiences make poems necessary. The rich complexity of joy or despair makes poems exciting. Poetry's "dense" quality provides interpreters with the perfect opportunity to develop their performance skills.

Broadly speaking, poetry differs from prose in its compactness, in the emotional weight of its content, and in the importance of its patterns. In poetry the content and the form deepen each other. The poet tests words for sound as well as for denotation and connotation. Because poetry is so condensed, an audience profits considerably from the trained interpreter's knowledge and control of vocal quality, inflection, force, rate, and timing that help clarify the meaning and add richness to the associational values of the words.

Poetry exploits rhythm, which is based on an effective combination of sounds and silences and of lighter and heavier stresses. This pattern of sound and stress can be fully realized and appreciated only in performance. Poetry maximizes vocal flexibility and control, and you must keep the content and the sound pattern in harmonious balance so that neither obscures the other. Indeed, the total impact of the poem is achieved only when content and structure are perfectly coordinated.

Thus, to construct a responsive performance, you will need to understand the *nature of poetry*—its content, its forms, and the arsenal of language uses it employs—and the *structure of poetry*—how the parts are assembled and what the variations entail. To that end, this chapter examines "content" in its broadest sense, and Chapter 10 looks at "structure," broadly defined. Need we repeat what by now must seem like a mantra to you: Separating components for analysis is merely a convenience. No poem (and no story and no play) is simply the sum of its parts: the life of a literary work is what eludes dissection.

Poetic Content

In previous chapters logical content (what a piece of writing *says*) and emotional content (how it makes you *feel*) have often been considered separately, although neither lives nor works alone in great literature. In poetry the *logical content* and the *emotive content* merge so completely that it is nearly impossible to determine where one ends and the other begins. We said poetry is dense; another way of putting it is to say that poetry leaves much unsaid. Because poets use fewer words than other writers, the words they do use must give readers enough clues to guide their responses. Thus, poets select every word with utmost care, because each word is going to perform triple or quadruple duty in the poem. Although novelists and playwrights also choose their language with care, they are likely simply to have more space to make their points.

In poetry, each word must complete at least three tasks:

1. Each word carries distinct denotative (dictionary) meaning.

2. Each word connotes (suggests or implies related things) meanings.

3. Each word harmonizes with the sound pattern.

In some poems, each word fulfills even more tasks. If you are a poet, you know well the time spent searching for precisely the right word that can carry all these burdens *and* appear effortlessly "right" in the line.

Finding the right word means the poet can tighten the poem just that much more, which sharpens and refines the emotional impact of the poem and allows it to work on many levels simultaneously. When John Ciardi, in "Most Like an Arch This Marriage" (at the end of this chapter) says, "Till we kiss/I am no more than upright and unset," he means that the union of wife and husband is not settled simply when one kisses the other but that each is unfinished, unstable, and incomplete until their love is shared—both emotionally and physically. Our shabby paraphrase of his exquisite line suggests why the poem succeeds so richly: each word the poet chooses conveys much more than any words we choose.

You might want to reconsider the established concept of content, or what the author has said. Obviously, a poet must say something that the audience understands. But a poet intends to communicate something beyond fact or opinion. Indeed, much poetry does not require an opinion at all; it asks the reader merely to explore an attitude. One does not have to accept this attitude as a philosophy of life, but merely to grant the poet the right to hold it.

Poetry is a record of *experience to be shared*. This does not mean that the experience needs to be explained, nor does it always mean totality of experience. A poem may give us only a segment of an experience. Poets certainly write of facts, but they interpret these facts in the wider areas of human life. A poem may be motivated by an idea, but if the idea were the whole concern, the poet would not need the suggestive richness of sound characteristic of poetry. Poetry, most often, is concerned with an emotional or aesthetic response to an idea. In any case, poetry goes beyond the confines of strictly logical content.

Archibald MacLeish says in his "Ars Poetica":

A poem should not mean
But be.

This statement implies that a poem must be a complete, harmonious entity. Of course, it "means" something, but it also exists beyond purely logical meaning. When you accept the fact that poetry is not only *what it means* but *how it means* (to borrow a phrase from John Ciardi), you are ready to let the poet and the poem begin their communication with you.

The first step in understanding and evaluating a poem is to read the entire work to get a general idea of what it says. This first step may be less objective, less purely "intellectual" with poetry than it is with much prose or drama. At first reading, you may be attracted by the sounds or the rhythm rather than by the denotative meanings of the words. Your initial response to a poem may not be in terms of idea or logical content at all, but rather in terms of emotion. Read the poem aloud several times. Permit yourself the luxury of a completely subjective response before beginning an objective analysis. Give full play to the sound. Instead of working on the poem, let the poem work on you. Enjoyment is a good starting point for appreciation, even if the reason for liking the poem cannot be put into words immediately. And there's no point in performing a poem you don't enjoy.

Do not be discouraged if you find only a very simple, obvious meaning in a poem where someone else finds a great deal of implication. You aren't performing someone else's implications. As your experience with life and poetry increases, you will be better able to draw richer, more extensive associations. Above all, be careful not to get so preoccupied with reading between the lines that you lose sight of the lines themselves.

Classification of Poetry

Poetry has been classified by types according to innumerable systems. Some are based on content, some on structure, and some on combinations of both elements. Many of the classifications overlap, and you will find differences of opinion about the proper category in which certain poems should be placed. Technical names and categories provide handles for grasping the material; they are not poems.

We broadly classify poetry under three major headings: *narrative*, *lyric*, and *dramatic*. These distinctions are based largely on a consideration of the persona—the speaker in the poem. As we learned in Chapter 2, this consideration guides your relation to the audience. As with stories and plays, you should know (1) who is speaking in the poem, (2) to whom the person is speaking, and whether the experience (3) is being revealed directly (as in a narrative poem), (4) is overheard (as in a dramatic poem), or (5) is the personal utterance of a single speaker (as in a lyric poem).

Narrative Poetry

Narrative poetry tells a story or relates a series of events that lead up to a climax. In this respect, narrative poetry mirrors narrative prose. Many of the steps of analysis we discussed in Chapter 6 are helpful here. You should give attention (a) to the establishment of time and place, (b) the development of characters, and (c) the relationships between characters. Consider also (d) setting, (e) situation, and (f) physical and psychological traits of character—and (g) the interdependence of these factors. The persona is the narrator. Narrative poetry often includes dialogue; from your experience with dialogue in narrative prose, you should already know how to handle this element. Also, as in narrative prose, descriptive passages in narrative poetry reinforce setting or effect transitions between key situations. So, you know a great deal about this form already.

When you elect to present a narrative poem, you take the role of a storyteller. This role is no different from that of the tale teller, which we all undertake each day. The progression of events should be your primary concern. Analyze the content carefully to become thoroughly aware of all the aspects of organization. Remember that you are telling a story in poetry. Use the aspects of poetry to enhance the poem's movement and emotional impact.

One of the oldest types of narrative poetry is the *popular ballad,* a form that began before the advent of printing. It is a folk product; its author, anonymous. Over the centuries, many poems have adopted some of the characteristics of the popular ballad, which is a short, swift, stark narrative, simple in plot and with a catchy, infectious metrical pattern. The language is unadorned, and the characters are basically types rather than individuals. The ballad should have an easy flow of sound, but it should also tell a fast-moving and exciting story, often with a surprising ending.

Today, country music is filled with popular ballads about faithless husbands, devoted wives, and the troubles of living in the world. When Tammy Wynette tells you to "Stand by Your Man," or Dolly Parton swears "I Will Always Love You," or Patsy Cline sings about "Walking After Midnight," all of the women partake in the culture of popular ballads. They tell you stories of their own lives (Loretta Lynn's "Coal Miner's Daughter" is a classic example) or of characters' lives (listen to Dolly Parton's "9 to 5"), but in all cases the language sits on music that joins the emotional and logical content and is evoked by the distinctive style of the performer.

Another characteristic of ballads is the refrain, which may help implement the plot but is often primarily rhythmic. Consider Amanda McBroom's "Dreaming" (see Chapter 2). It repeats certain phrases or groups of lines, but the repetitions of words do not necessarily repeat ideas or implications. Rather, they reveal important aspects of the speaker's life and reflect the unique world of the tale. When you undertake refrains, be sure that they do not impede the progress or simply repeat the words but rather continue to show us something distinctive and *new* about the speaker. Because so much of their impact rests on the conviction of the teller and the reality of the tale being told, ballads challenge performers to come up with the gusto that makes them convincing.

The second important type of narrative poetry is the *metrical tale,* which is like a full-length novel or short story in verse. It may be a medieval tale, such as Geoffrey Chaucer's *Canterbury Tales,* or a more modern product, like John Keats's "The Eve of St. Agnes," Robert Frost's "The Death of the Hired Man," or Vikram Seth's *The Golden Gate.* In any case, the process of analyzing its content and organization is comparable to that used for the short story. Descriptions of setting are likely to be fairly explicit, and the relationship between the characters and the setting is important. Moreover, the narrative persona expresses personal attitudes and sympathies from time to time, while still retaining the position of observer.

The third type of narrative poetry is the *epic*. An epic is characterized by its extreme length, by its elevated tone, and especially by the type of events it relates. An epic centers on a hero of superhuman proportions, both morally and physically, whose exploits are of great significance to a tribe, race, or nation. *The Aeneid,* an art epic, and *Beowulf,* a folk epic, are examples of this type of narrative poetry. Most cultures boast long verse works, often sung or chanted originally, that describe their origins and history. Another kind of epic concerns humanity's battle with the forces of evil and the struggle for a divine victory: John Milton's *Paradise Lost* is a prime example. Such epics were not all written in the eighteenth century. Derek Wolcott's *Omeros* is a splendid contemporary version set in the Caribbean. A *mock epic,* exemplified by Alexander Pope's "The Rape of the Lock," applies the grand epic scope and manner to trivial circumstances, such as a haircut, with amusing, satirical effect.

The style of an epic is lofty, the language is highly poetic and exalted, and the sentences are usually complex and elaborate, with numerous clauses and inversions. These aspects of style help suggest the scope of the episodes and the heroic proportions of the participants. Epics are not written about common people who drive to the market for eggs and juice. They involve whole nations and heroes who are larger than life, and they should be given their proper dimension in performance.

Lyric Poetry

Typically, the *lyric* is a short poem, although it may be a long, sustained emotional utterance. It is a strongly unified form of poetry, for all aspects of content are shaped toward the emotional focal point. A lyric poem has been compared to a flash of lightning that illuminates some object in a brief moment of emotional vividness. Lyric poets usually give little, if any, account of what leads up to or follows the emotional experience, since their concern is with *sharing* the experience, not *explaining* it. You, however, may find that sketching in some relevant background in your own mind enhances appreciation and helps set the appropriate mood. The interpreter needs to be in complete control of techniques *before* beginning to perform a lyric poem for an audience. The extreme condensation of the poem allows no time to warm up or to find an equilibrium. Thus, the introduction that the performer provides is exceptionally important; it gets you and the audience ready for something that will be over very soon.

The persona in a lyric poem is usually a single speaker whose primary purpose is to share an emotional experience. Whether the speaker and the poet are the same is a matter of debate among critics. The differences of opinion grow in part out of a semantic problem. For our purposes we assume that the poet is speaking in a "pure" lyric, remembering that poets, like the rest of us, have varying moods and attitudes and complex and many-sided personalities. When we discuss the dramatic lyric, we address the problem of someone who thinks and feels like the poet but who is a clearly distinguishable character. However, we are not concerned in a lyric with the physical being of the poet, his eyes or hair, her voice or gait. Rather, we are dealing with the *emotional and psychological personality of the persona* as it is revealed in the particular poem.

Most lyric poetry must be read more slowly than other forms of writing. Why? *Imagery* is less easy to assimilate than is a story line. Swiftly paced reading does not permit the *sound pattern* to make its full contribution to both *music* and *emotion*. The audience should have time to hear the words, re-create the images, and set up the response. Lyric poetry requires less directness in presentation than narrative writing. Be careful, however, not to read as though you are lost in the clouds. The happy mean is to adopt an attitude of *sharing the experience.* You know that your listeners' emotions cannot be compelled. Your goal is to bring the audience into the poem, not to thrust the poem at them. Share—don't explain.

The emotion that characterizes lyric poetry is often expressed in terms of reflection or description. Thus, the *reflective lyric,* as its name suggests, is the persona's emotional response through recall and reflection or contemplation. The persona recalls an important emotional experience, and the recall is important to the interpreter. Mary Stewart Hammond's "Saving Memory" and Susan Minot's "The Toast" (both at the end of this chapter) exemplify reflective or descriptive lyrics.

The *elegy* is a lyric that expresses grief, usually at someone's death. In Greek verse the elegy had a definite structural form, but English poets use it as a type of emotional expression. Thus, an elegy may assume any conventional metrical pattern or may even be written in free verse. Usually, formality of language and structure lends dignity to the expression of grief and harmonizes with the solemn mystery of death and the sense of personal loss. The persona of Seamus Heaney's "Mid-Term Break" (at the end of this chapter) uses common language and tight, formal restrictions to try to understand his brother's death.

An *ode* is a dignified, relatively long lyric poem that is formal in language and formal, though not necessarily strictly regular, in structure. Like the elegy, the ode was a recognized lyrical form in Greek verse. Designed to be accompanied by music and a highly stylized dance, it consisted of three movements, two of which had identical music and dance patterns. Although these Greek structures have been imitated by English poets, the term *ode* has come to be applied to any sustained lyric utterance of exalted theme, often in commemoration of some important event or experience. In general tone, the ode is more contemplative than active.

Doubtless, the most familiar type of lyric poem is the *sonnet*. The interpreter is likely to spend a great deal of time performing sonnets, in part because the form is so common (Shakespeare alone wrote 154 of them!) and in part because its fixed form presents many challenges. Sonnets are also easy to recognize: they are fourteen lines, and commonly each line has ten syllables. For our purposes, the most interesting question is how such a very restricted (and not very long) form could spawn so many different incarnations and variations. See Edna St. Vincent Millay's "Sonnet XXX" at the end of Chapter 10 for a good example; then look at Gerard Manley Hopkins's "The Windhover" for an equally rigorous but much less orthodox example and, finally, at Susan Minot's "The Toast" for a contemporary variation on the form (the last two are at the end of this chapter).

Poets choose to write sonnets (or any other form) because something in that form seems to embody uniquely the experience they want to share. And, too, there's the personal gratification one experiences when mastering any serious challenge: the 100m butterfly, the 50-yard dash, a flawless béarnaise sauce. It is the impulse that prompts composers to write songs, painters to paint portraits, gardeners to tend roses. There will always be an *easier* way to do almost anything, but easier isn't always richly rewarding. Confronting a sonnet, then, asks that you consider both what the form brings to the experience being related and what the poet brings to the form.

A lyric poem demands your full engagement. This does not mean that you get carried away with your emotions. Remember to leave room in your performance for the audience. But in your earliest preparation, go ahead and indulge in complete subjectivity. Get to know how everything *feels*. Your task in performance will be to *share* the experience in the poem—not to display your personal sensitivity. This sharing requires intelligent control of technique. The more your listeners focus on the material and are unaware of your presence, the more successful your performance will be.

Dramatic Poetry

Many contemporary critics take the position that all poetry is dramatic because speaking is itself an action, because it concerns a person or persons, and because it contains a distinct development or revelation. This approach to analysis can prove helpful. Our discussion of dramatic poetry concerns works that center on a character who is in conflict with internal or external forces and whose development is revealed without a third-person narrator. There are four types of dramatic poetry: *dramatic narrative, dramatic lyric, dramatic monologue,* and *soliloquy.* Although these terms are often used interchangeably, the four types vary slightly in emphasis on character and situation. Knowing the differences among them helps in deciding on the degree of characterization that is necessary for performance. In each case the persona is an identifiable character who speaks directly to an audience, or thinks aloud, or talks to other characters involved in a dramatic situation. Physical setting and historical period are often important considerations.

A *dramatic narrative* is a poem in which the incidents or series of incidents are related by a participant who is affected by the events described. You often find dramatic narratives collected into longer works that explain complex natural or supernatural events. Ovid, in *The Metamorphoses,* describes how the world came into being and how extraordinary events changed (metamorphosed) former persons or things into characteristic landmarks of the world we know. The teller of these tales is often less important than the events themselves, so you can safely assume that a given speaker is a device for revealing the plot or guiding our responses to the changes, rather than a motivating force for the plot's progression. (Look, for example, at Ovid's "The Story of Baucis and Philemon" at the end of Chapter 11. The narrator appears only in the first four lines and returns only in the last six lines.)

The *dramatic lyric,* like any other type of lyric poetry, reflects the poet's subjective responses, thoughts, and aspirations. It is dramatic because the poet reveals these thoughts and emotions through the words of an appropriate character, so that there is added force and vividness to the expression. Tennyson's "Ulysses" (Chapter 4) falls into the general classification of dramatic lyric (although it also shares some of the same characteristics of a dramatic monologue). Emphasize in your character those qualities that make the speaker an appropriate exponent of the philosophy being expressed. Ulysses' essential qualities, for instance, are his mental vigor, maturity, wisdom, authority, and leadership. It is unwise to take too literally his phrase "you and I are old," because he turns immediately to the belief that

Old age hath yet his honor and his toil,

which he reinforces with

   . . . but something ere the end,
Some work of noble note, may yet be done,
Not unbecoming men that strove with Gods.

The poem closes on the positive note that Ulysses is still

   . . . strong in will
To strive, to seek, to find, and not to yield.

The *dramatic monologue* is spoken by a single character who is clearly and distinctly not the poet. The persona directly addresses other characters, who are also affected by the incidents taking place and who help motivate the persona's reactions and train of thought. The other characters do not speak, but they are developed as personalities or at least as forces that act on the speaker. Maury Yeston's "New Words" (Chapter 2) exemplifies this type of dramatic poetry. The speaker is clearly interacting with another (for us, silent) character—"my son"—but the events that occur and the emotions they conjure up arise directly out of the little lesson in which the persona engages. One of the most famous dramatic monologues, Robert Browning's "My Last Duchess," appears at the end of Chapter 10.

Soliloquy differs from dramatic monologue chiefly in conventional ways, namely that the audience accepts the speaker as accurately and honestly revealing his or her inmost thoughts. We believe that speakers do not lie in soliloquy and that they capitalize on this immediate, direct relationship with the audience to express themselves. Recall George's soliloquy "Finishing the Hat" from Stephen Sondheim's *Sunday in the Park with George* (Chapter 8). We learn what George wants from the relationships he undertakes, and we learn as well of his recognition that what matters most to him is his art.

Music and Dramatic Poetry

You will have noted that we frequently refer to music, having cited country singers, musical movies, and songwriters, and having reprinted the lyrics of several songs (Yeston's "New Words," McBroom's "Dreaming," and Sondheim's "Finishing the Hat"). All of these works have been set to music by their authors. Poetry and music have a long, distinguished, and complicated relationship. They have never been entirely separate, partly because songs pattern sound and silence as much as poems do. Today, drama in verse exists almost exclusively in the musical theater, but the opportunities for dramatic verse are livelier today than ever.

Some people object that we don't speak in poetry during everyday life, and that characters' choosing to sing in important emotional moments is unrealistic. Yet most of us hum or whistle or listen to music for a good part of every day. The musical theater simply exploits the desire to exclaim in song. And one reason we like to listen to certain songs is that they speak *for* us, with a richness and depth we may only inadequately grasp. We ask songs to carry our emotional life. And when the words sit on such heart-tugging melodies, the attraction is almost irresistible.

The interpreter who chooses to perform the lyrics of songs must resolve two specific—and related—problems. First, will you perform both the music *and* the lyrics? Recognize that some lyrics need the music to survive; without the superior musical support, the words seem lifeless and obvious. Second, if you choose to perform only the lyrics, take care that the musical setting you may be hearing in *your* ears does not intrude onto what members of your audience hear in *their* ears. To perform only the lyrics, you must concentrate completely on the situation, on the natural music inherent in the words chosen by the lyricist, and on the careful patterning apparent in the poem's structure. Sometimes we have heard gifted performers pass lyrics by with the explanation, "I can't sing." Indeed, some people can't, but we have been impressed (and several performers have surprised themselves) by the genuine attempt. As with any selection, trust your response to the language and situation and your tenacity of purpose.

In summary, all the types of poetry we have discussed—and the countless variations we could not begin to catalog—have *experience* as their foundation. To convey the experience, the poet uses *language* as bricks and mortar. Some kinds of language perform some tasks better than others. The poet searches for language that can fulfill many responsibilities simultaneously; poetry is language multitasking. Thus, after the poet has selected the kind of poem to write based on the experience he or she wants to communicate, the poet selects the language that can turn the experience into poetry.

Figurative Language

We stressed that poetry is a highly condensed form of expression. Although poetry may seem to communicate less directly than prose, it actually makes a more direct appeal. It does not talk about something but attempts, rather, to present the essence of that something by striking at readers through senses, emotions, intellect, and imagination, and calling forth a blended response that gives new insight into experience. Hence, the poet uses words that carry with them not only precise denotations but, perhaps more important, the right connotations as well.

The words the poet uses do not define a concept so much as *expand* it in the reader's consciousness, just as a pebble tossed into a pool sends ever-widening circles rippling out from the point of surface contact. The *implications* of the words take the reader beyond the narrow confines of exact definition into the area of suggested meaning. In examining a poet's choice of words, then, remember that just as a poem not only means something but *is* something beyond meaning, so the words that compose it go beyond fact and information. Indeed, words in poetry mean many things simultaneously. Robert Frost's "Wild Grapes" (at the end of this chapter) exemplifies the rich connotations figurative language conveys.

The fact that poetry simultaneously means different things prompts some people to complain that they can't make sense out of poetry because it isn't clear, specific, or unambiguous. It's true that the ability to untangle complexities comes in handy when reading poetry. You must also be willing to appreciate the possible richness ambiguity can present—poetry being in this respect not so different from situations you may encounter in life. Some people rejoice in the complexity of human nature and in the sometimes odd, sometimes infuriating combination of traits that friends possess. Indeed, one way friendship develops is the mutual recognition of complexities (or, even, contradictions) that we never realized were present. The ability to appreciate a lot of mixed traits and impressions in another will fairly surely predict the ability to enjoy poetry and the figurative language with which it is composed.

Allusions

A poet often achieves condensation and emotional impact by using references to things or ideas or events that we all recognize. These *allusions* embody a wealth of implication. They may contribute materially to the logical meaning of the poem, but they are likely to be most valuable for the associations they set up by implied comparison. When they refer to mythical or historical persons or places, their associational value may be lessened for the reader today. Still, a reader can recognize them easily as allusions and knows that they are explained in encyclopedias or other appropriate reference books.

In some poetry, however, connotative literary allusions may prove more difficult because they may involve the deliberate echo of a phrase or line from another person or literary work to reinforce mood or emotion by inviting comparison or ironic contrast. A poem that skillfully implies reference to other works is Joanne Gilbert's "Upon Learning That a Junior High School Acquaintance Has Been Nominated for an Academy Award" (Chapter 2). The first two lines recall a popular children's story and video (*The Grinch Who Stole Christmas*). Later, the speaker turns a common term for unjustified resentment into a witty expansion ("my sour grapes to/sour wine"). A mention of *The National Enquirer* brings us directly to the supermarket tabloid famous for "revelations" about "celebrities." Later, the object of the poem is called an "Amazon," alluding to the classical women of great strength who overpowered all competitors. Then, in an echo from Shakespeare's *Macbeth*, where the soon-to-be victorious Macduff unnerves Macbeth by stating he "was from his mother's womb/Untimely ripped" (*Macbeth*, V.viii.15–16), the speaker describes the star's battle scar as "a cyst on her egg sac—the whole untimely ripped at her ripening." The next lines refer us outside literature, as the skillful use of line length in "The envelope please . . ./es me" echoes the standard request from the presenter for the envelope which contains the name of the winner. Hearing such echoes brings an added level of understanding and a more complex response to the entire poem. Allusions strengthen a poem's impact.

How does an interpreter deal with allusions? Obviously, you are not going to explain the references to the audience, to stand between poem and audience as a sort of collection of footnotes. However, you cannot share the poem with your audience if you have not assimilated it first yourself. The more thoroughly you understand the allusions, the more fully you will appreciate the poet's purpose in using them—and the more intelligently you can use them in communicating the whole intent of the poem to others. You must, therefore, be familiar enough with the allusions to understand the type of response they are intended to arouse or reinforce. By integrating them into the poem as a self-contained whole, you can use them as a means of drawing the proper empathic response from the audience.

Figures of Speech

Three of the most common figures of speech—*simile, metaphor,* and *analogy*—are all based on comparing one thing to another. These comparisons appeal to our senses and our motor responses. Therefore, they depend on sensory imagery, which we discussed at some length in Chapters 4 and 5.

A *simile* is easily recognized, because it makes an explicit comparison, generally using the word *like* or *as*. It compares two objects of common nature or the particular qualities of one thing to the general qualities of another. Ciardi uses simile in the title of his poem "Most Like an Arch This Marriage," and the rest of the poem articulates the many points of similarity between arches and the wife's and husband's love.

A *metaphor* states that something *is* something else; the comparison is based on some related but not identical factor. It establishes a relationship between two elements that may be dissimilar in their basic components yet have attributes in common, such as "Your eyes are stars." Nikki Giovanni says "Black love is Black wealth" in "Nikki-Rosa" (at the end of this chapter). Sometimes a metaphor expresses a synthesis of thought and feeling so subtle and complex that it becomes an organic or structural part of an entire poem. Indeed, critics often use the term *metaphor* or *metaphorical* to describe writing that goes beyond fact and obvious relationships.

An *analogy* is an extended metaphor and may serve to implement an entire poem. Sharon Olds's "The Race" (Chapter 4) implicitly compares the speaker's desperate striving to make a plane departure with her father's struggle to live and is especially rich in similes and metaphors within the analogy.

These three ways of making comparisons are important for several reasons. First, of course, you should understand what they are and how they function in order to find the total meaning of the poem. More particularly, you need to be aware not only of the objects being compared but of the attributes of those objects that make their comparison acceptable. Finally, you should use your knowledge of sense imagery and empathy to make the comparisons work effectively for the audience.

Two other figures of speech—*metonymy* and *synecdoche*—carry associational values that are somewhat different from those of similes, metaphors, and analogies. *Metonymy* is the use of one word for another that it suggests, such as "a good table" for "good food." *Synecdoche* is the use of a part for a whole, such as "sail" for "boat." The technical difference between these two figures is of minor importance for our discussion. Metonymy and synecdoche are useful whenever they suggest certain characteristics emphasized by the part that is chosen for the whole. For example, *sail* is a more picturesque word than *boat* and could be used to imply majesty; you then might wish to make use of the visual and kinesthetic imagery that would be called up by tall sails against the sky rather than by a tugboat or a coal barge.

Classifying a figure of speech is *not* your major concern. Instead, understand why that figure of speech was used, what it is intended to convey, and what it demands when the material is presented to an audience. If you understand the figures of speech for what they are and for the purpose they serve, you are better equipped for the job of doing justice to the poetry.

In addition to these five figures of speech, two others directly affect the interpreter's communication: *personification* and *apostrophe*. *Personification* is the attribution of human qualities to an abstract or inanimate object. This figure of speech is closely related to simile, metaphor, and analogy—the "comparison" figures—because the poet treats an inanimate object or abstraction as if it were a person, thus giving it definite human characteristics. Keats, for example, uses personification throughout "To Autumn" (see page 396). In the second line, he calls Autumn the "Close bosom-friend of the maturing sun." The personification is most vivid in the second stanza, where Autumn is depicted as "sitting careless on a granary floor," and "on a half-reaped furrow sound asleep," and "by a cider-press" watching "the last oozings hours by hours."

You will find personification a great aid in visualizing poetry because it is easier to re-create a person than an abstraction. Moreover, this device allows for more kinetic and kinesthetic imagery. Don't overlook the animating quality this figure of speech provides.

Frequently, personification is combined with the figure of speech known as *apostrophe*—direct address to an abstraction or to an absent or inanimate object. "To Autumn" consistently uses a combination of personification and apostrophe. The opening line, "Season of mists and mellow fruitfulness," might be taken merely as a reflective thought about the season, if considered by itself. On close examination, however, it is evident that the poet becomes more direct in his approach to the season as the poem progresses, and there can be no doubt about the directness of address in the opening lines of the final stanza:

> Where are the songs of Spring? Ay, where are they?
> Think not of them, *thou* hast *thy* music too . . .

Figurative language enables a writer to express an abstract idea in concrete terms, to make it more vivid by comparing it or relating it to a concrete object or a specific quality. Through figures of speech, poets bring together things that are not ordinarily seen in relation to one another, and thus they open the way to new insights. Clearly, then, sense imagery and figurative language, or literary imagery, are interdependent, and the motor responses to literary and sensory imagery are inseparably tied to emotional response and empathy.

Sensory Appeals

When poems depend strongly on sensory appeals, you should accept and use all of the clues the writer has provided. One of the characteristics of Keats's "To Autumn" is its strong sensory quality; his skill in blending and even combining words to intensify the appeal to the senses makes this poem so rewarding.

The chief purpose of "To Autumn" is to record the sights, sounds, smells, and rich textures of the season. This poem makes no other important comment about life, except perhaps to imply that satisfaction can be found in inevitable change:

> Where are the songs of Spring? Ay, where are they?
> Think not of them, thou hast thy music too . . .

The poet describes autumn, and the poem (which follows in its entirety) lays claim to emotional response through the pleasure this season gives to the senses.

To Autumn
JOHN KEATS

Season of mists and mellow fruitfulness,
   Close bosom-friend of the maturing sun;
Conspiring with him how to load and bless
   With fruit the vines that round the thatch-eaves run;
To bend with apples the mossed cottage-trees,
   And fill all fruit with ripeness to the core;
    To swell the gourd, and plump the hazel shells
   With a sweet kernel; to set budding more,
And still more, later flowers for the bees,
Until they think warm days will never cease,
   For Summer has o'er-brimmed their clammy cells.

Who hath not seen thee oft amid thy store?
   Sometimes whoever seeks abroad may find
Thee sitting careless on a granary floor,
   Thy hair soft-lifted by the winnowing wind;
Or on a half-reaped furrow sound asleep,
   Drowsed with the fume of poppies, while thy hook
      Spares the next swath and all its twinèd flowers:
And sometimes like a gleaner thou dost keep
   Steady thy laden head across a brook;
   Or by a cider-press, with patient look,
   Thou watchest the last oozings hours by hours.

Where are the songs of Spring? Ay, where are they?
   Think not of them, thou hast thy music too,—
While barrèd clouds bloom the soft-dying day,
   And touch the stubble-plains with rosy hue;
Then in a wailful choir the small gnats mourn
   Among the river sallows, borne aloft
      Or sinking as the light wind lives or dies;
And full-grown lambs loud bleat from hilly bourn;
   Hedge-crickets sing; and now with treble soft
   The red-breast whistles from a garden-croft
      And gathering swallows twitter in the skies.

The opening lines have a characteristic complexity of appeals.
"Season of mists" has a strong thermal appeal that combines at once the
warmth of the sun and the coolness of the mists. "Mellow fruitfulness"
carries with it olfactory, gustatory, visual, and kinesthetic appeal, as
well as a continuation of thermal and a possibility of tactile appeal. The
second line brings in a still stronger thermal appeal. The effect is one of
warmth, and it enhances the feeling of drowsiness and almost static
heaviness that recurs in each stanza. The next three lines contain all of
these previous appeals to sensory perception, but with kinetic appeals
added—in fact, with special appeal to kinetic and kinesthetic response:
"load and bless with fruit," "vines that run," "to bend with apples."

Because the appeals are so complex and so closely interwoven, it is almost impossible, and probably unnecessary, to decide which is the primary appeal within a unit of thought. The strength of the appeals shifts
from one type to another almost within a single word. Indeed, the first
five lines include every type of imagery except auditory, and even that
is suggested later in the stanza by "the bees." Clearly, the senses are
working!

As the poem progresses, the visual and auditory appeals become
increasingly important. The second stanza indicates the poet's concern
with the visual by its opening question, "Who hath not seen thee . . . ?"

The third stanza is strongly auditory, with references to "songs" and "music." Within this framework the sensory appeals remain complex. Imagery makes the descriptions vivid and contributes significantly to the unity, harmony, and variety of the poem. The kinesthetic imagery and the kinetic imagery, both of which are made more vivid through personification, will help keep this poem from becoming merely a lush combination of beautiful sounds. The shift to visual and then to auditory imagery in the second and third stanzas will help unravel the complicated sentences and keep the poem moving to its choral finish.

Poetic Syntax

Stanzas (separated groups of a consistent number of lines) provide the main division of organization and content. Within stanzas, sentences are the minor units of thought. In poetry, however, you are likely to find that the syntax of a sentence is more complicated than it is in prose. Recall that poetry revels in condensing emotion, image, and language: the tighter syntax means that you may have to unpack what the poet has so carefully combined.

Poets often achieve this condensation by using long, involved sentences that contain numerous dependent clauses and descriptive phrases. These clauses and phrases are not always adjacent to the words they modify, as we expect them to be in prose. Consequently some care in analysis can help your performance to keep the thread of thought from becoming hopelessly entangled and the poem from seeming to consist merely of unrelated sets of words.

If you encounter an involved sentence, simply recast it in normal word order, identifying the subject, verb, and object, if any, and arranging the clauses and phrases to modify the appropriate parts of the sentence. You should not, however, insist that poetry display the same clarity and syntactical precision as factual prose. Often parts of speech are omitted, and references are implied rather than stated. Normal word order is frequently changed for emotional effect, for heightening of sound qualities, or both.

Hopkins's "The Windhover" demonstrates this *ellipsis* (or omission of words):

> I CAUGHT this morning morning's minion, king-
> dom of daylight's dauphin, dapple-dawn-drawn Falcon, in his riding
> Of the rolling level underneath him steady air, and striding
> High there, how he rung upon the rein of a wimpling wing
> In his ecstasy! then off, off forth on swing,
> As a skate's heel sweeps smooth on a bow-bend; the hurl and gliding
> Rebuffed the big wind.

The sentence, which whirls on for five and one-half lines, begins reasonably enough with the simple "I caught" (meaning "caught sight of" rather than "captured"). The capitalization of "caught" is the poet's and adds a sense of surprise and wonder to the sight. The adverbial phrase "this morning" tells us when the event took place. After this comes the object of the sentence, the windhover, which the poet successively calls "minion," "dauphin," and "Falcon," and we are told what the bird was doing. He was riding and striding, and "he rung upon the rein of a wimpling wing"—that is, he flew upward in spirals by folding or "pleating" or tipping one wing. Then he was off as smoothly as an ice skate cuts a curve, and "the hurl and gliding rebuffed" (snubbed, refused to consider) "the big wind." This, then, is the syntactical skeleton of the sentence.

The next step is to attempt to find the proper relationship of the rest of the words that flesh out this syntactical skeleton. If we want to make a prose paraphrase, we need to add some connectives and phrases to fill in Hopkins's elliptical quality. In the process we obviously destroy much of the beauty of the sound; but that, too, may help prove our point. The sentence might now read:

> This morning I caught (sight of) morning's minion (in his) kingdom, of (which he is) daylight's dauphin (and) dapple-dawn-drawn Falcon, in his riding of the rolling level (which was) underneath him (and which was) steady air and (when he was) striding high there (you should have seen) how he rung upon the rein of a wimpling wing in his ecstasy (and) then (he was) off, off forth on a swing as (smoothly as) a skate's heel sweeps smoothly on a bow-bend (and) the hurl and gliding rebuffed the big wind.

Admittedly, this extremely awkward sentence plods heavily from one detail to the next. We have lost all the "hurl and gliding," the velocity of lift and freedom, and much of the beauty of the sound combinations. Harmony has almost completely disappeared. The insertion of "and" after the exclamation point defeats the poet's own breathless ecstasy at the sight. The substitution of "and" for the colon before the last clause robs it of its conclusive value by making it just one more item rather than a culmination of several.

Now that you understand where the thought is going and how it gets there, go back to the sentence the poet wrote. Control the pace and pauses, and the poet's remarkable imagery and tone color will catch your audience. There's a lot more to unpack in those lines, and there are eight and one-half more ahead!

Tone Color

In addition to connotative values and sensory appeals, other important factors in poetry are the choice and arrangement of words and the sounds of which words are composed. A poet strives for the perfect union of sense and sound and is acutely aware of the contribution that each makes to the other. This attention to the sounds of words separately and in combination is called *tone color.* We discussed it briefly in Chapter 5 in the section on prose style. It is so basic to the sound pattern of poetry, however, that it merits added consideration here.

Tone color is the combination of vowels and consonants to help achieve a particular effect. Clearly, poets do not simply scramble together assorted vowels and consonants: they use words. The choice of words is partially dictated by the way the sounds go together. e. e. cummings's poem "Spring is like a perhaps hand" (at the end of this chapter) owes part of its effectiveness to tone color. The two words "perhaps hand" are characteristic of his remarkable freedom with syntax, using *perhaps* as an adjective to modify *hand.* The connotation is helped, however, by juxtaposing "haps" and "hand," both of which must be said carefully to pronounce the aspirate /h/ and the vowel /æ/. The /p/ and /s/ of "haps" slow the rate, and a slight pause is necessary before the /h/ of "hand." The effect is subtle, but only consider what a difference it would make if the line read, "Spring is perhaps like a hand" or "Perhaps spring is like a hand." This arrangement drastically changes (and even destroys) the meaning, rhythm, and sound values.

The general term *tone color* embraces onomatopoeia and alliteration, assonance, and consonance. *Onomatopoeia* is the use of words whose sounds suggest or reinforce their meaning: for example, *hiss, thud, crack,* and *bubble. Alliteration* is the repetition of identical or nearly identical sounds at the beginnings of two or more adjacent words in a line or phrase. The phrase *"morning morning's minion"* in "The Windhover" is a classic example, and there are many other alliterative combinations in the poem. Many poets use alliteration that operates throughout a large unit or even through an entire brief poem.

The use of identical or closely approximated vowel sounds within words is called *assonance;* the close repetition of identical or approximate consonant sounds within or at the ends of words is called *consonance.* These two techniques are also found throughout "The Windhover": assonance is in the repeated /ɔ/'s; consonance is very strong in the /n/—both sounds permeate "morning morning's minion," and both assonance and consonance occur in "minion," "dauphin," and "Falcon" in the long first line.

Tone color performs several functions in poetry. The amount and richness of it vary with the poem's purpose. The more marked the aesthetic and emotional effect desired, the richer and more complex the tone color is likely to be. One of the most important uses of tone color is to enrich the emotional content. Most authorities agree that it is nearly impossible to divorce the connotation of a word from its sound. Even in everyday conversation, words are colored and their meanings intensified or depreciated by the elongation or shortening of the vowel sounds and by the softening or sharpening of the consonants. Consider the many ways the phrase "Excuse me" is uttered. You can even say it to contradict its denotative meaning! This coloring or intensification through sound is even more marked in poetry when a word is used with others to strengthen the associational values. Thus, tone color makes an important contribution to suggestion.

Tone color implements sense imagery and intensifies empathy. "To Autumn" offers a particularly good example. The opening lines provide unmistakable proof of Keats's concern with sounds:

> Season of *mists* and *mellow fruitfulness,*
>   Close bo*som-friend* of the *maturing sun*

Within these lines, the consonants /s/, /m/, /n/, and /l/ predominate, skillfully combined with rich /u/ and /ə/ sounds, while the lighter vowels in "mists," "mell," "ness," and "friend" keep the effect from becoming monotonous. With such a strong hint in the opening lines, the interpreter should pay particular attention to how Keats combines sounds in the rest of the poem. They vary as the content varies, but in every case, sound, connotation, and sense imagery reinforce each other.

Tone color also changes tempo and give clues to variation in vocal quality. Certain combinations of vowels and consonants allow (even encourage) the reader to speak more rapidly or slowly than other combinations do. A skilled poet is aware of variety of tempo and may have used it. You should look for it and use it, too. Of course, variations in tempo also depend on the content, both emotional and logical, and on the type of imagery they augment.

The last stanza of "To Autumn" contains an excellent example of the use of tone color to provide variety of tempo and vocal quality. The short speech phrases in the form of the questions

> Where are the songs of Spring? Ay, where are they?

help achieve needed variety after the rich, slow sounds of

> Thou watchest the last oozings hours by hours.

which close the preceding stanza. "Think not of them" is likewise light and almost crisp in its sound and its implication of dismissal. Immediately, however, the tempo slows again with "thou hast thy music too," and even more in the next line with "barrèd clouds bloom." The pace picks up slightly on "touch the stubble-plains" but immediately slows again on "rosy hue." This alternation continues throughout the entire stanza. The contrast between "lambs loud bleat from hilly bourn" and the following "Hedge-crickets sing" is particularly effective. Subtle changes indicated by the sounds will demonstrate the needed variety.

Tone color usually does not make a major contribution to unity except within small units or stanzas. An entire poem that is richly laden with the same sound combinations would be extremely difficult to sustain. Tone color, however, is certainly basic to harmony and is valuable in achieving variety and contrast. Its primary function is supportive, and it should be used in its proper relationship with all the other elements you discover in your analysis.

Tone color is another of the elements that make poetry so satisfying to, and in turn so dependent on, the artist/interpreter. To use tone color fully, you should be sure to enunciate clearly but not self-consciously. The poet combined the sounds, and you should accept the responsibility of reproducing them accurately, as they were written.

Titles

An important but sometimes overlooked clue to the meaning of a poem is found in its title. Hopkins identifies his "morning's minion" in the title "The Windhover" and thus helps us untangle the analogy. Roethke clearly identifies the persona in "Old Lady's Winter Words" (Chapter 4). Titles help us to decide what a poem is about as well as guide us on our way.

Sometimes poets give us even more help by introducing the poem with an epigraph, as Hopkins does with the words "To Christ our Lord" just beneath the title of "The Windhover." These brief quotations, frequently from literature or folk sayings, may establish the theme of the poem. Do not ignore them, even if you must translate them from a foreign language.

Admittedly, some poets (like Shakespeare with his sonnets or Emily Dickinson) do not use titles. Then the elements of style within the poem itself reveal the meaning. The poet's choice of words and figures of speech and the way these elements are combined into phrases, line units, sentences, and stanzas should be carefully considered. Method of organization, balance, and proportion give valuable clues to the weight attached to the various phases of thought development. The sound pattern supporting the content often indicates the degree of seriousness and dignity inherent in the attitude. We give this aspect more attention in Chapter 10.

About titles one final point may be made: if the poet gave the poem a title, your audience should know it. The title can become a part of your introduction when it sets the scene or prepares your audience for what follows (as in James Dickey's "The Hospital Window" or William Stafford's "First Grade," both at the end of this chapter). Alternatively, the title can be a part of the poem itself, either because it repeats the poem's first line (as in Wallace Stevens's "The House Was Quiet and the World Was Calm" at the end of this chapter) or because the poem seems to begin *with* the title (as in Corinne Hales's "Power" or Imamu Amiri Baraka's "Preface to a Twenty Volume Suicide Note," both at the end of this chapter). In the first case—where the title lives in the introduction—it is likely to be given by the performer. In the latter case—where the poem begins with the title—it is likely to be delivered by the persona of the poem.

Analysis and Poems

What, then, is the secret of a poem's effectiveness? There are as many answers as there are successful poems. We know that not all poems appeal to all readers, that not all poems stay appealing, and that (happily) some poems that we *used* not to like much have grown on us over the years. In this respect (as in a number of others), our relationship with poems is not unlike our relationships with people: some stay good friends throughout our lives while others drift away, and some people we never understand—or admire or like. With poems, we can be certain only that some transient, universal moment so impressed the poet that it compelled (in this creative mind) sustained life as a poem. The blending of logical and emotional qualities that gave rise to the initial experience, and that got shaped throughout the process of composition, explains some of a poem's effectiveness. The *whole* answer eludes us even after the most careful analysis. For that resistance we are sometimes nettled but ultimately thankful: the poem will persist in being a poem regardless of the measures to which we subject it. An objective study of the component parts enables you to let the poet's technique shape your rehearsal and inform your performance. A poem's essence, though, is not a quantity but an experience. After each step in analysis, the poem needs to be put back together so that it will finally emerge as a complete entity—from its title to its final syllable. Let the poet lead you.

In this chapter we explored the language of poetry, described some useful classifications, and equipped you to discover—in the next chapter—the intricacies of a poem's structure. In pursuit of that discovery, these concepts will come in handy:

- Poems are experiences constructed in language.

- Poetic content denotes, connotes, and harmonizes.

- Poetic experience demands to be shared.

- Poems are, broadly speaking, narrative, lyric, or dramatic—and each type demonstrates a different kind of persona.

- Poetic language is condensed and figurative.

- Poems uniquely exploit tone color.

- Poems value or dismiss titles, as the poem sees fit.

Now, put on your construction boots, gloves, and helmet: in Chapter 10 we're going to see how poems are built!

Selections for Analysis and Oral Interpretation

Don't be deceived by the simplicity of vocabulary and structure in this poem. Use the line lengths exactly as the poet has. The short sentences in the first and last stanzas set off the climaxes. Use them to stop the rush of the action, but remember that they relate strongly to the speaker, her brother, or "the man." Decide who is the major character, but don't neglect the others.

 Power

CORRINE HALES

No one we knew had ever stopped a train.
Hardly daring to breathe, I waited
Belly-down with my brother
In a dry ditch.
Watching through the green thickness
Of grass and willows.
Stuffed with crumpled newspapers,
The shirt and pants looked real enough
Stretched out across the rails. I felt my heart

Beating against the cool ground,
And the terrible long screech of the train's
Braking began. We had done it.

Then it was in front of us—
A hundred iron wheels, tearing like time
Into a red flannel and denim, shredding the child
We had made—until it finally stopped.
My brother jabbed at me,
Pointed down the tracks. A man
Had climbed out of the engine, was running
In our direction, waving his arms,
Screaming that he would kill us—
Whoever we were.
Then, very close to the spot
Where we hid, he stomped and cursed
As the rags and papers scattered
Over the gravel from our joke.

I tried to remember which of us
That red shirt had belonged to,
But morning seemed too long ago, and the man
Was falling, sobbing, to his knees.
I couldn't stop watching.
My brother lay next to me,
His hands covering his ears,
His face pressed tight to the ground.

- ◆ Did your audience see and hear why the persona "couldn't stop
  watching" while her brother's face was "pressed tight to the
  ground"?

*Let the full richness of the sounds come through to increase the lift and sweep
of this poem. The dedication will help you understand the poet's attitude. The
two stresses in the eleventh line were put there by the poet, as were the two
words in capital letters. The poem shifts to direct address to Christ ("my chevalier") in the second stanza. We have been prepared for this by the epigraph.*

The Windhover

GERARD MANLEY HOPKINS

To Christ our Lord

I CAUGHT this morning morning's minion, kingdom of daylight's
    dauphin, dapple-dawn-drawn Falcon, in his riding
  Of the rolling level underneath him steady air, and striding
High there, how he rung upon the rein of a wimpling wing
In his ecstasy! then off, off forth on swing,
  As a skate's heel sweeps smooth on a bow-bend; the hurl and
    gliding
  Rebuffed the big wind. My heart in hiding
Stirred for a bird,—the achieve of, the mastery of the thing!

Brute beauty and valour and act, oh, air, pride, plume, here
  Buckle! AND the fire that breaks from thee then, a billion
Times told lovelier, more dangerous, O my chevalier!

  No wonder of it: sheér plód makes plough down sillion
Shine, and blue-bleak embers, ah my dear,
  Fall, gall themselves, and gash gold-vermilion.

- ◆ What does "Buckle!" in the tenth line mean? How did you demonstrate all those levels to your audience?

Here's another, quite contemporary, example of a sonnet. Like the persona of Hopkins's poem, Minot's speaker recalls a transforming event, but here the exchange is distinctly human and, finally, unresolved. Note how the tightness of the form suggests the speaker's effort at balancing present and past. Why isn't this a full-fledged sonnet?

The Toast

SUSAN MINOT

After I've made it stumbling through the day
And liquid light surrounds the window sill,
After paper buds have furled their wrinkled way
And, tired, I've relaxed my will,
I think of you and of your warm embrace
And recall the disturbed calmness of your face
In repose. And all the sorrow I've contained
This brilliant Tuesday in this lonely place
Vanishes. It topples down the hours strained
Till memory leaves another trace:
The time you smiled and covered me with kisses
And clicked your teeth to mine in a brisk toast,
And I think, At least I have that clinking ghost.

- ◆ How did you negotiate the turns the poem takes, first in line 7, then in line 9?

- ◆ How is line 11 isolated? Why?

"Wild Grapes" calls for considerable attention to locus. The narrative lines, of course, should be directed to the audience. The brother's first instructions are delivered as he stands beside the little girl; his "loud cries" are directed to her as she hangs suspended in the air.

Wild Grapes

ROBERT FROST

What tree may not the fig be gathered from?
The grape may not be gathered from the birch?
It's all you know the grape, or know the birch.
As a girl gathered from the birch myself
Equally with my weight in grapes, one autumn,
I ought to know what tree the grape is fruit of.
I was born, I suppose, like anyone,
And grew to be a little boyish girl

My brother could not always leave at home.
But that beginning was wiped out in fear
The day I swung suspended with the grapes,
And was come after like Eurydice
And brought down safely from the upper regions;
And the life I live now's an extra life
I can waste as I please on whom I please.
So if you see me celebrate two birthdays,
And give myself out as two different ages,
One of them five years younger than I look—
One day my brother led me to a glade
Where a white birch he knew of stood alone,
Wearing a thin head-dress of pointed leaves,
And heavy on her heavy hair behind,
Against her neck, an ornament of grapes.
Grapes, I knew grapes from having seen them last year.
One bunch of them, and there began to be
Bunches all round me growing in white birches,
The way they grew round Leif the Lucky's German;
Mostly as much beyond my lifted hands, though,
As the moon used to seem when I was younger,
And only freely to be had for climbing.

My brother did the climbing; and at first
Threw me down grapes to miss and scatter
And have to hunt for in sweet fern and hardhack;
Which gave him some time to himself to eat,
But not so much, perhaps, as a boy needed.
So then, to make me wholly self-supporting,
He climbed still higher and bent the tree to earth
And put it in my hands to pick my own grapes.
"Here, take a tree-top, I'll get down another.
Hold on with all your might when I let go."
I said I had the tree. It wasn't true.
The opposite was true. The tree had me.
The minute it was left with me alone
It caught me up as if I were the fish
And it the fishpole. So I was translated
To loud cries from my brother of "Let go!
Don't you know anything, you girl? Let go!"
But I, with something of a baby grip
Acquired ancestrally in just such trees
When wilder mothers than our wildest now
Hung babies out on branches by the hands
To dry or wash or tan, I don't know which,

(You'll have to ask an evolutionist)—
I held on uncomplainingly for life.
My brother tried to make me laugh to help me.
"What are you doing up there in those grapes?
Don't be afraid. A few of them won't hurt you.
I mean, they won't pick you if you don't them."
Much danger of my picking anything!
By that time I was pretty well reduced
To a philosophy of hang-and-let-hang.
"Now you know how it feels," my brother said,
"To be a bunch of fox-grapes, as they call them,
That when it thinks it has escaped the fox
By growing where it shouldn't—on a birch,
Where a fox wouldn't think to look for it—
And if he looked and found it, couldn't reach it—
Just then come you and I to gather it.
Only you have the advantage of the grapes
In one way: you have one more stem to cling by,
And promise more resistance to the picker."

One by one I lost off my hat and shoes,
And I still clung. I let my head fall back
And shut my eyes against the sun, my ears
Against my brother's nonsense; "Drop," he said,
"I'll catch you in my arms. It isn't far."
(Stated in lengths of him it might not be.)
"Drop or I'll shake the tree and shake you down."
Grim silence on my part as I sank lower,
My small wrists stretching till they showed the banjo strings.
"Why, if she isn't serious about it!
Hold tight awhile till I think what to do.
I'll bend the tree down and let you down by it."
I don't know much about the letting down;
But once I felt ground with my stocking feet
And the world came revolving back to me,
I know I looked long at my curled-up fingers,
Before I straightened them and brushed the bark off.
My brother said: "Don't you weigh anything?
Try to weigh something next time, so you won't
Be run off with by birch trees into space."
It wasn't my not weighing anything
So much as my not knowing anything—
My brother had been nearer right before.
I had not taken the first step in knowledge;
I had not learned to let go with the hands,

As still I have not learned to with the heart,
And have no wish to with the heart—nor need,
That I can see. The mind—is not the heart.
I may yet live, as I know others live,
To wish in vain to let go with the mind—
Of cares, at night, to sleep; but nothing tells me
That I need to learn to let go with the heart.

◆ Did you make the remembered scene vivid and present to your audience? How?

Trust this poet completely, and use his line lengths exactly as he has put them down. He uses capital letters for a shade of emphasis. Keep the thought suspended across the parentheses, which make a sort of "subpoem" in themselves. The kinesthetic imagery is important.

⊚ Spring is like a perhaps hand

E. E. CUMMINGS

Spring is like a perhaps hand
(which comes carefully
out of Nowhere)arranging
a window,into which people look(while
people stare
arranging and changing placing
carefully there a strange
thing and a known thing here)and

changing everything carefully
spring is like a perhaps
Hand in a window
(carefully to
and fro moving New and
Old things,while
people stare carefully
moving a perhaps
fraction of flower here placing
an inch of air there)and

without breaking anything.

◆ How did your body and voice capture the *perhaps*es? Were they all the same?

This serene poem achieves its distinction as calmly and quietly as the scene it describes. Pay careful attention to the cadences, and give the repetition in the last two couplets your full concentration.

The House Was Quiet and the World Was Calm

WALLACE STEVENS

The house was quiet and the world was calm.
The reader became the book; and summer night

Was like the conscious being of the book.
The house was quiet and the world was calm.

The words were spoken as if there was no book,
Except that the reader leaned above the page,

Wanted to lean, wanted much most to be
The scholar to whom his book is true, to whom

The summer night is like a perfection of thought.
The house was quiet because it had to be.

The quiet was part of the meaning, part of the mind:
The access of perfection to the page.

And the world was calm. The truth in a calm world,
In which there is no other meaning, itself

Is calm, itself is summer and night, itself
Is the reader leaning late and reading there.

◆ Where in your performance did the book, the reader, and the house merge?

◆ How did your voice evoke the poem's progress?

This long, loosely constructed sentence requires careful attention to progression as you move through the numerous ands *into new but closely related minor thought units. The fulcrum begins seven lines from the end, so an awareness of balance and proportion is important.*

Nikki-Rosa

NIKKI GIOVANNI

childhood remembrances are always a drag
if you're Black
you always remember things like living in Woodlawn

with no inside toilet
and if you become famous or something
they never talk about how happy you were to have
your mother
all to yourself and
how good the water felt when you got your bath
from one of those
big tubs that folk in chicago barbecue in
and somehow when you talk about home
it never gets across how much you
understood their feelings
as the whole family attended meetings about Hollydale
and even though you remember
your biographers never understand
your father's pain as he sells his stock
and another dream goes
And though you're poor it isn't poverty that
concerns you
and though they fought a lot
it isn't your father's drinking that makes any difference
but only that everybody is together and you
and your sister have happy birthdays and very good
Christmasses
and I really hope no white person ever has cause
to write about me
because they never understand
Black love is Black wealth and they'll
probably talk about my hard childhood
and never understand that
all the while I was quite happy.

- ◆ What prompted your persona to speak? Did your audience see those memories?

Here is another poem of children and trains, but these mischief makers have quite different intentions. Nevertheless, by the poem's conclusion we see the urge "to hold such power" in the palm is not unlike the attractions Corinne Hales described in "Power." Keep the memory of the experiment—and its results—vivid and tangible.

Saving Memory

MARY STEWART HAMMOND

Summer nights we put pennies on the track.
Even the station was quiet enough for crickets.
Mountains surrounded us, middling high and purple.
No matter where we stood they protected us
with perspective. People call them gentle mountains
but you can die in there; they're thick
with creeper and laurel. Like voodoo,
I drew pictures with a sparkler. A curved line
arced across the night. Rooted in its slope,
one laurel tree big as the mountain holding it.

You can hear the train in the rails,
They're round, not flat, as you'd expect,
and slick. We'd walk the sound, one step, two,
slip, on purpose, in the ballast, hopscotch
and waltz on the ties, watching the big round eye
enter the curve and grow like God out of the purple,
the tracks turning mean, molten silver blazing

dead at us. We'd hula. Tango. And the first
white plume would shoot up screaming long, lonely,
vain as Mamma shooing starlings from her latticed pies.

Sing Mickey Mouse, the second scream rising long, again,
up and up. Stick our right hip out, the third
wailing. Give it a hot-cha wiggle, the fourth
surrounding us. And bidding each other fond adieux,
we'd count to three, turn our backs, flash it a moon,
and materialize, fantastic, run over with light,
the train shrieking to pieces, scared, meaning it,
short, short, short, short, pushing a noise
bigger than the valley. It sent us flying,
flattened, light as ideas, back on the platform,
the Y6B Mallet compound rolling through
southbound, steamborne, out of Roanoke.

It wasn't to make the train jump the track
but to hold the breath-edged piece of copper
grown hot with dying, thin with birth,
wiped smooth of origin and homilies
To hold such power. As big as the eye
of the train, as big as the moon burning
like the sun. All the perspective
curved and gone.

◆ Is there a pun in the title? How did you embody it?

◆ What does your body remember during the third stanza?

The speaker in this tender poem changes his position in the world by the last line. Although he knows what has happened to his brother from the first line, the speaker comes to a special understanding by the last line. Let the rhyme work.

✿ Mid-Term Break

SEAMUS HEANEY

I sat all morning in the college sick bay
Counting bells knelling classes to a close.
At two o'clock our neighbors drove me home.

In the porch I met my father crying—
He had always taken funerals in his stride—
And Big Jim Evans saying it was a hard blow.

The baby cooed and laughed and rocked the pram
When I came in, and I was embarrassed
By old men standing up to shake my hand

And tell me they were "sorry for my trouble."
Whispers informed strangers I was the eldest,
Away at school, as my mother held my hand

In hers and coughed out angry tearless sighs.
At ten o'clock the ambulance arrived
With the corpse, stanched and bandaged by the nurses.

Next morning I went up into the room. Snowdrops
And candles soothed the bedside; I saw him
For the first time in six weeks. Paler now,

Wearing a poppy bruise on his left temple,
He lay in the four foot box as in his cot.
No gaudy scars, the bumper knocked him clear.

A four foot box, a foot for every year.

♦ How did you demonstrate the speaker's dawning understanding
   of the meaning of what happened?

The following two poems "converse" with each other on several levels, but each is a substantial, distinctive statement on its own. Barbara Howes directs our gaze to those moments that conclude the couple's night and (curiously) seems to celebrate separation. In Philip Larkin's poem, the persona remains in bed, although the speaker seems uniquely alone. Obviously, locus—on all its levels— figures prominently in both poems. Be sure that we know where we are.

On Sleeping Together

BARBARA HOWES

Day becomes explicit. From this shared	1
Warmth we grew into together here in bed,	2
Concave as a hammock, we are all one piece	3
At the moment of waking: is that my arm, or his?	4
Still linked and folded, slowly we withdraw	5
Selves and bodies from our world of sleep.	6
Caught in silhouette, heroic figures	7
Dim in the toils of darkness, but now responding	8
To the bravura of conch shell and drum,	9
Alive, we wake; waking, we separate,	10
With ceremony rise to greet the morning.	11

- How did you demonstrate the presence of the other, the partner who, with the speaker, makes up "we"?

- What functions are served by the split in line 10?

Talking in Bed

PHILIP LARKIN

Talking in bed ought to be easiest,
Lying together there goes back so far,
An emblem of two people being honest.

Yet more and more time passes silently.
Outside, the wind's incomplete unrest
Builds and disperses clouds about the sky,

And dark towns heap up on the horizon.
None of this cares for us. Nothing shows why
At this unique distance from isolation

It becomes still more difficult to find
Words at once true and kind
Or not untrue and not unkind.

- What happens between the first and second stanzas? How did you show that thinking to your audience?

- What functions are served by the rhymes? How did they inform your rehearsal?

James Dickey captures the sterility and chill of the hospital remarkably well as he underscores the isolation that it imposes on those who leave a loved one there and return to the outdoor world. (You might want to compare this poem with Sharon Olds's "The Race" in Chapter 4.) The word choice is superior, even when it seems, deliberately, not poetic. Don't neglect the subtle tone color. The kinetic, kinesthetic, and auditory imagery make an excellent contrast to the hospital room. Watch the stanza divisions.

The Hospital Window

JAMES DICKEY

I have just come down from my father.
Higher and higher he lies
Above me in a blue light
Shed by a tinted window.

I drop through six white floors
And then step out onto pavement.

Still feeling my father ascend,
I start to cross the firm street,
My shoulder blades shining with all
The glass the huge building can raise.
Now I must turn round and face it,
And know his one pane from the others.

Each window possesses the sun
As though it burned there on a wick.
I wave, like a man catching fire.
All the deep-dyed windowpanes flash,
And, behind them, all the white rooms
They turn to the color of Heaven.

Ceremoniously, gravely, and weakly,
Dozens of pale hands are waving
Back, from inside their flames.
Yet one pure pane among these
Is the bright, erased blankness of nothing.
I know that my father is there,

In the shape of his death still living.
The traffic increases around me
Like a madness called down on my head.
The horns blast at me like shotguns,
And drivers lean out, driven crazy—
But now my propped-up father

Lifts his arm out of stillness at last.
The light from the window strikes me
And I turn as blue as a soul,
As the moment when I was born.
I am not afraid for my father—
Look! He is grinning; he is not

Afraid for my life, either,
As the wild engines stand at my knees
Shredding their gears and roaring,
And I hold each car in its place
For miles, inciting its horn
To blow down the walls of the world

That the dying may float without fear
In the bold blue gaze of my father.
Slowly I move to the sidewalk

With my pin-tingling hand half-dead
At the end of my bloodless arm.
I carry it off in amazement,

High, still higher, still waving,
My recognized face fully mortal,
Yet not; not at all, in the pale,
Drained, otherworldly, stricken,
Created hue of stained glass.
I have just come down from my father.

♦ How did you make your audience see and hear what caused your persona to stop the traffic?

The simile in the title reverberates throughout the poem, and while the language is dense, it rewards careful scrutiny. What lightens this love song is its brightly colloquial sense of dialogue. Let us see speaker *and* audience.

Most Like an Arch This Marriage

JOHN CIARDI

Most like an arch—an entrance which upholds
and shores the stone-crush up the air like lace.
Mass made idea, and idea held in place.
A lock in time. Inside half-heaven unfolds.

Most like an arch—two weaknesses that lean
into a strength. Two fallings become firm.
Two joined abeyances become a term
naming the fact that teaches fact to mean.

Not quite that? Not much less. World as it is,
what's strong and separate falters. All I do
at piling stone on stone apart from you
is roofless around nothing. Till we kiss

I am no more than upright and unset.
It is in falling in and in we make
the all-bearing point, for one another's sake,
in faultless falling, raised by our own weight.

♦ This poem—like architecture—is both intimate and public. What did you do with your body and voice to demonstrate its openness and its tenderness?

- This poem is also filled with playful language and puns. How do they suggest the speaker's attitude to the beloved?

The language and unique logic of children reveal substantial lessons for adults. To make "first grade" sense of what happens requires a willingness to replace maturity with passion. Like the poem, these children take nothing for granted; neither should you.

 ## First Grade

WILLIAM STAFFORD

In the play, Amy didn't want to be
anybody, so she managed the curtain.
Sharon wanted to be Amy but Sam
wouldn't let anybody be anybody else—
he said it was wrong. "All right," Steve said,
"I'll be me, but I don't like it."
So Amy was Amy and we didn't have the play.
And Sharon cried.

- Each of the events follows a perfectly logical sequence for the children in the class. How did you make *their* logic *your* logic?

This soft-spoken poem is completely devoid of sentimentality. The negation is underscored by the simple word choice and by the conversational relationship of thought units and line lengths in the first four stanzas. Pay particular attention to the single-line stanzas.

Preface to a Twenty Volume Suicide Note

IMAMU AMIRI BARAKA

Lately, I've become accustomed to the way
The ground opens up and envelops me
Each time I go out to walk the dog.
Or the broad edged silly music the wind
Makes when I run for a bus—

Things have come to that.

And now, each night I count the stars,
And each night I get the same number,
And when they will not come to be counted
I count the holes they leave.

Nobody sings anymore.

And then last night, I tiptoed up
To my daughter's room and heard her
Talking to someone, and when I opened
The door, there was no one there . . .
Only she on her knees,
Peeking into her own cupped hands.

- ◆ How did your persona feel when he glimpsed his daughter?

- ◆ How did you demonstrate this attitude to your audience?

Bibliography

Consult the bibliography at the end of Chapter 10 for several sources including handbooks, essays by poets reflecting on poetry, and classic critical statements on poetry.

What I would like to do is to treat words as a craftsman does his wood or stone or what-have-you, to hew, carve, mould, coil, polish and plane them into patterns, sequences, sculptures, fugues of sound . . .

Dylan Thomas

CHAPTER TEN

Structure of Poetry

EXPECT THIS!

This chapter takes you to a construction site—for poems. As you would be at any construction site, you need to be alert, attend to everything, mind your feet(!), and keep your notebook handy. By the end of this chapter, you should be able to:

- Recognize the functions of prosody.

- Describe the most common kinds of verse.

- Explain the role of the stanza in poetry.

- Discuss the variety, function, and effect of the line in poetry.

- Complete a reliable and accurate scansion.

- Illustrate foot prosody, stress prosody, and syllabic prosody.

- Show how line length contributes to the life of the poem.

- Identify primary and secondary cadences, and ascertain their contributions.

- Show how the various kinds of rhyme function.

- Rehearse toward synthesis.

Poets fit their

thoughts into

the structure

they choose.

423

Selections Discussed in This Chapter

In explaining some topics, we mention texts that are reprinted either within the chapter itself or at the end of a chapter. Use the guide below for quick reference to acquaint yourself with selections you may not fully recall.

Author	Title	Location
Alfred, Lord Tennyson	"Ulysses"	Chapter 4, page 154
Stephen Sondheim	"Finishing the Hat," from *Sunday in the Park with George*	Chapter 8, page 360
Robert Frost	"Wild Grapes"	Chapter 9, page 407
Philip Larkin	"Talking in Bed"	Chapter 9, page 416
Stanley Kunitz	"Open the Gates"	Chapter 10, page 433
Elizabeth Bishop	"One Art"	Chapter 10, page 445
Theodore Roethke	"The Waking"	Chapter 10, page 445
Dylan Thomas	"Do Not Go Gentle into That Good Night"	Chapter 10, page 446
T. S. Eliot	"Journey of the Magi"	Chapter 10, page 447
Melvin Dixon	"Heartbeats"	Chapter 10, page 450
Garrett Kaoru Hongo	"Who Among You Knows the Essence of Garlic?"	Chapter 10, page 451
Robert Browning	"My Last Duchess"	Chapter 10, page 453
Edna St. Vincent Millay	"Sonnet XXX," from *Fatal Interview*	Chapter 10, page 457
Victor Hernandez Cruz	"Today Is a Day of Great Joy"	Chapter 10, page 463
Alice Walker	from *Horses Make a Landscape Look More Beautiful*	Chapter 10, page 464

POETRY CONDENSES. IT CONDENSES EMOTIONS, SENSATIONS, incidents, language. Its richness derives from its tightly packed economy: nothing is wasted, and every word has to do double or triple duty. Emotion, language, sensation—all are shaped and ordered to conform with the poet's vision. And something in all that close interaction among poetry's components grabs us, delights or throttles or astonishes. That "something" makes us want to perform one poem rather than another, intrigues us enough to reread it. Precisely that which makes poetry please us makes poetry challenging to perform.

Because poetry condenses, analysis *expands*. Because one word or phrase in a poem is asked to perform several functions simultaneously, we will need much more time to explain what is happening than the poet does to say it (this is one reason why not everyone is a poet). And because poetry requires such discipline to achieve its condensation and organization, the interpreter's analysis is likely to be complex. Poetry depends for its full enjoyment on the perfect blend of sound and sense; and in order to convey that blend, the interpreter needs to know how the poem "works." That is why we study the structure of poetry.

The study of the structure of poetry is called *prosody*. For us, structure includes all of the elements of the language of poetry that we have been discussing: sense imagery, paradoxes, allusions, and other literary imagery—in short, anything that can be patterned in a poem. In this chapter, however, we focus on the devices that produce the sound pattern in a poem. (Obviously, one of them is tone color, which we discussed in Chapter 9, because this element is part style, or language, and part sound patterning.)

Why Study Prosody?

One of the most common questions beginning interpreters pose is "Why do we have to know all this *stuff* about the poem? I like the poem already, and learning about feet and prosody just complicates everything." If you harbor such questions, the following paragraphs are meant for you.

First, your question embodies the single most important requirement for a rich performance: liking the poem you've chosen. If you can't derive pleasure from reading the poem, there's little chance the audience will find much rewarding to see and hear. So let's assume you are ready to build on that pleasure by sharing it with others, presumably because you think they, too, will derive similar pleasure from it. However, you can't share what you don't "own"—that is, you must understand the words and respond to the poem's rhythm and sound. If you don't know the tune, are you likely to sing a song very successfully. W. H. Auden once remarked that the first question he asked when confronting a new poem was always technical: "Here is a verbal contraption. How does it work?" The study of a poem's prosody is one way for us to understand how the verbal contraptions work: how those words cast their spell over us and achieve their extraordinary power and beauty.

We won't pretend that this kind of analysis is simple or quick. In fact, very few useful skills come easy and cheap. And we respect—indeed, we *demand*—mastery from every other practitioner we encounter.

We don't think much of dancers who can't find the beat, and you'd rather have an operation done by a surgeon who has studied extensively and practiced widely before working on you.

The second part of our students' objections usually involves learning all the terms and components of sound patterns. It is perfectly true that this chapter will introduce new vocabulary, and that you can certainly *feel* the rhythm of a poem without being able to name it rightly as "trochaic tetrameter." In any pursuit, however, terminology has to be mastered. You wouldn't ask to play "king" on a pickup basketball team, and you would have no confidence in a mechanic who told you that your car was suffering from "a thingamajig that got stuck near the watchamacallit." We learn technical terms because they provide names for complex information. "Iambic pentameter" calls up a rhythm, pattern, and history in students of poetry much more rapidly (and accurately) than saying, "I like it when it goes da-DUM-da-DUM-da-DUM-da-DUM-da-DUM."

Finally, of course, studying prosody requires us constantly to notice and take account of a lot of "little" things that contribute to the awesome success of the one big thing. We encounter similar situations throughout our lives: anything awesome requires careful, extensive, sometimes grinding repetition. Barry Bonds took batting practice every day he played during the season in which he set a new Major League Baseball record for home runs. Every serious sports team can present copious drill plans, playbooks, and workout schedules. As it is in so much else of life, so it is in poetry: nothing great is achieved without labor. Mastering the structure of poetry will allow you to "own" a poem more richly than you may have suspected possible.

Kinds of Verse

In this chapter we focus on *stanzaic form*, the elements that combine to make stanzas, the "verse paragraphs" of poems. Stanzas are composed of lines, of course, so we examine the length of lines and how lines are composed. Different lines move in different ways, so we explore both the stress and the flow of sounds, and because we are always impressed by sounds, we detect how they are repeated, most obviously in rhyme. All these components of *sound patterns* cry out for the many skills of the interpreter because they fulfill their functions only when the poem lives in performance.

Since the nineteenth century, critics have found it convenient to distinguish between (1) *conventional* (or *traditional*) *types* (or *forms*) of poetry (such as the sonnet, the villanelle, and the sestina) and (2) *free verse.* We use *conventional* to describe some poetry not because the poetry is stodgy or uninspiring but because it follows the requirements for a specific convention: a sonnet, for example, is fourteen lines long with a prescribed pattern of rhyming sounds at the end of each line.

The structure of conventional poetry is based on (1) a clearly discernible pattern of stresses; (2) the grouping of the stresses into traditional patterns called *metrical feet;* (3) the presence of a fixed number of lines in each stanza, each line having a fixed length. The same structure, with only slight variations, usually recurs from stanza to stanza, in both the line lengths and the arrangement of stresses within lines. In some of the strictest forms, specific sounds or words have conventional positions. You might think all these "rules" would function as a straitjacket, but this fixed structural framework actually permits numerous variations in stress patterns and in the location of pauses within lines. In the hands of a master, fulfilling such requirements can exhilarate rather than exhaust. With the notable exception of *blank verse* (which we discuss below), conventional poetry capitalizes on *rhyme:* the repetition of identical or similar sounds (such as *night–light*) at the ends of lines is a pattern called a *rhyme scheme.* Edna St. Vincent Millay's "Sonnet XXX" has all the characteristics of conventional poetry. Susan Minot's "The Toast" is a more recent example of a poem that follows most of them, significantly omitting a crucial line and rhyme (Millay's poem is at the end of this chapter, Minot's at the end of Chapter 9).

Blank verse is a special type of conventional poetry. It doesn't rhyme and has no recurring stanza pattern because the stanzas are divided according to the development of the thought and thus vary in length. Blank verse usually has a definitely prescribed line length of five metrical feet, and a prescribed *prevailing* foot—the *iamb*. Because of the absence of rhyme and the lack of restriction on stanzaic structure in blank verse, skillful poets use this form effectively with narrative and dramatic materials. Shakespeare, an acknowledged master of blank verse in poetic drama, used it to wed nobility of utterance to acceptable rhythms of speech. More recently, Robert Frost used it to sustain the dramatic quality of his long poems and to achieve the difficult feats of making poetry sound like conversation and conversation like poetry; see his "Wild Grapes" at the end of Chapter 9.

Free verse is often considered to be a recent addition to the realm of poetry. The term is modern, and the genre has developed during the last 125 years or so (though it is possible to find earlier examples of free verse). Varying line lengths, and the arrangement of stresses within lines, give the surest indication that a poem is in free verse.

Free verse differs in many other ways from conventional poetry. If a free-verse poem is divided into units at all, they are often irregular in length, although a free-verse poem *may* have quite regular stanzaic division. The free-verse line may vary in length from a single syllable to fifty syllables or more (Walt Whitman succeeds with such long lines quite often). Free verse is frequently not rhymed, though the poet may choose to introduce rhyme to achieve some special effect, as T. S. Eliot does in "Journey of the Magi" (at the end of this chapter). Free verse exhibits no significant pattern of metrical feet, and its rhythm is based on cadence rather than meter.

Successful free verse is not, as the term might suggest, completely lacking in form and discipline. A discoverable rhythmic basis sometimes exists in the number of syllables in the speech phrases within the lines or in the number of heavier stresses within those speech phrases. You can also sometimes discover it by analyzing the number of heavier stresses per line regardless of their relative positioning with lighter stresses. The important point is to find out how the poet works with the content to produce a successful whole.

The strict dichotomy between conventional verse and free verse is becoming much less important in contemporary poetry. Most poets today work *from* rather than *within* strict metrical patterns, so that you often find an interesting combination of the two modes within a single poem. The traditional lines establish a certain expectation; when, a few lines later, you find the insertion of free verse, that expectation is denied, and variety and contrast are underscored. Or a strictly regular line may surprise you with its steady beat and help point to a climax. Stanley Kunitz's poem "Open the Gates" (which we discuss at length later in this chapter) contains an interesting example of this effect.

Most poets writing in free verse still seem to be hearing some standard meters, although they ignore these persistent echoes when they wish. In Garrett Kaoru Hongo's "Who Among You Knows the Essence of Garlic?" (at the end of this chapter), the persona's language and the consistency of line demonstrate remarkable unity, without seeming restrictive. Free verse, then, is not simply the gush of emotional language spilling any old way down the page.

Robert Frost once remarked that writing what some people called free verse was like playing tennis with the net down. Even such a free spirit as Picasso seemed to agree. He admitted that the cubist movement in modern painting could be called a liberation; then he cautioned, "But what the artist gains in the way of liberty, he loses in the way of order." It might make more sense to refer to contemporary free verse as "freed" verse. Study a poem carefully to see how freed it is from traditional patterns, which patterns it continues to employ, and how this freedom and adherence coordinate with the content to produce the poem you admire.

The Stanza

In Chapter 9 we learned that a *stanza* of poetry is roughly comparable to a paragraph, a major *unit of thought.* As such, it is an important factor in the organization. A stanza may also be a *unit of sound,* just as a line of poetry is not only a line of print but also a unit of sound, and a word is not only a symbol for meaning but also a sound or combination of sounds as well. The stanzaic structure often contributes significantly to the poem's pattern of sound. The stanza pattern may divide the poem into nearly identical units of sound when the poem is read aloud. In performance, we tend to separate major divisions in thought by appropriate use of pause and to establish terminations by both pause and vocal inflection. Stanzas help you to determine how to achieve sense.

How stanzaic length contributes to the sound pattern varies considerably from one selection to another. In general, short stanzas and a tight rhyme scheme produce a more apparent sound effect. For example, a poem written entirely in two-line stanzas sets up an extremely close pattern of sounds and silences, especially if each pair of lines completes a thought division. (Consider Melvin Dixon's "Heartbeats" at the end of this chapter.) This important aspect of structural unity might seriously threaten the variety were the poet not very skillful.

In contemporary poetry with a regular stanzaic pattern, the thought units are frequently not identical with the stanzas but run on from one to another. There may be a comma or another punctuation mark that does not indicate a full stop—or, indeed, there may be no punctuation at all—at the end of the last line of a stanza. This pattern appears throughout Victor Hernandez Cruz's poem "Today Is a Day of Great Joy" (at the end of this chapter). Here, punctuation serves as a warning that the thought is unfinished and that the break imposed by the stanza pattern is a suspended break. The poet has chosen the stanzaic pattern but has reserved the right to twist it slightly whenever doing so seems justified by the overall purpose.

Stanza length and composition can be strong factors in the unity, harmony, and rhythm of both content and structure. Variety and contrast are also served by this aspect of structure. A change in stanzaic pattern is sometimes used to emphasize the fulcrum or the climax, as it does in Alice Walker's untitled poem (at the end of this chapter).

Finally, some poems are constructed with a strict stanzaic format (which may also have a strict metrical and rhyming pattern). At the end of this chapter we reprint three contemporary *villanelles:* Elizabeth Bishop's "One Art," Theodore Roethke's "The Waking," and Dylan Thomas's "Do Not Go Gentle Into That Good Night." These are probably the finest examples of the form from the latter half of the twentieth century, but their variety of subject matter and (apparently) effortless colloquial speech encourage careful scrutiny and analysis. Students amazed at all the requirements these poems so gracefully fulfill sometimes ask, "Why would a poet undertake such a burden?" The same question can be asked of anyone who reaches, and is likely to receive the same answer: because it's there.

Whatever contribution stanza length makes to your poem should be part of your growing understanding of the poem. Its importance to you ought to depend largely on its importance to the poem. A poet selects a strictly disciplined form not because it is easier to write but because the form somehow enriches his or her language. Your job is to find what makes that "somehow" effective. If the poet selects long or irregular stanzas, you may assume that the stanzas function primarily as a means of organizing the logical and emotional content.

The Line

Stanzas consist of lines; how lines are shaped is a question of prosody. The three main types of prosody are based on how the individual lines within stanzas are composed. They are usually designated as *metrical* (or *foot*) *prosody, stress prosody,* and *syllabic prosody.* We discuss metrical, or foot, prosody first because it is the most familiar, it combines elements of both stress and syllabic prosody, and, at least until the last few decades, has been the most commonly used in poetry written in English. Get ready to encounter many new terms.

Foot Prosody

The structural rhythm of conventional poetry is based on meter. *Meter* is the pattern set up by a reasonably regular recurrence of an identifiable combination of lighter and heavier stresses within a line. This pattern is discovered through *scansion,* the division of the poetic line into metrical feet. A *metrical foot* is a grouping of such stresses into a unit. The groupings, which were named centuries ago, are useful primarily for making the metrical pattern visually obvious, as the stresses are marked and grouped within the poetic lines. The most common feet in English poetry are the following:

1. *Iamb*—an unstressed syllable followed by a stressed syllable (˘ ´)[1]:

    When I / have fears / that I / may cease/to be

---

1. ´ indicates a stressed syllable; ˘ indicates an unstressed syllable. A slash (/) is used to mark off each combination of lighter and heavier stresses, known as a *foot.*

2. *Anapest*—two unstressed syllables followed by a stressed syllable
   (ˇ ˇ ′):

   ˇ ˇ ′   ˇ   ˇ ′   ˇ   ˇ ′   ˇ   ˇ   ′

   Of my dar / ling—my dar / ling—my life / and my bride

3. *Trochee*—a stressed syllable followed by an unstressed syllable (′ ˇ):

   ′ ˇ   ′ ˇ   ′   ˇ   ′   ˇ

   Tell me / not in / mournful / numbers

4. *Dactyl*—a stressed syllable followed by two unstressed syllables
   (′ ˇ ˇ):

   ′ ˇ ˇ   ′ ˇ ˇ

   Cannon to / right of them

5. *Spondee*—two heavy stresses (′ ′), usually used in combination with
   other types of feet:

   ′ ′   ˇ ′   ˇ ′   ˇ ′

   Beat once / therewith / and beat / no more.

6. *Pyrrhic*—two light stresses (ˇ ˇ), also usually found within another
   basic pattern:

   ˇ ′   ˇ ˇ   ˇ ′   ˇ ˇ   ˇ ′   ˇ ′

   The end / and the / begin / ning in / each oth / er's arms.

Other combinations are possible but are rarely used.

A line is classified according to two characteristics: first, which foot is most frequent: *iambic, anapestic, trochaic,* or *dactylic;* second, the number of those feet it contains: *monometer* (one foot), *dimeter* (two), *trimeter* (three), *tetrameter* (four), *pentameter* (five), *hexameter* (six), and so on. Thus, a line of five iambic feet is spoken of as an *iambic pentameter.*

In almost all conventional poetry, one type of metrical foot prevails. In English poetry, the iamb (ˇ ′) is the most common foot, due in part to stress patterns in spoken English. It is often varied by the trochee (′ ˇ), its reversed counterpart. The next most common is probably the anapest (ˇ ˇ ′), followed by the dactyl (′ ˇ ˇ). Most poets make effective use of variations in the prevalent measure, since variety in unity is the keystone of all art.

Scanning the Poem

Not all stressed syllables receive the same degree or value of stress when the poem is read aloud. The following line might be scanned as a regular iambic pentameter:

ˇ ′   ˇ ′   ˇ ′   ˇ ′   ˇ ′

Not mar / ble, nor / the gild / ed mon / uments

However, in performance, the *relative* values of the stresses would be something like this, where (´) indicates the heaviest stress, (`) indicates a lighter stress, and (˘) indicates the little discernible stress (obviously, there has to be some stress to be audible!):

ˋ ´ ˘ ´ ˘ ´ ˘ ´ ˘ ˋ

Not mar / ble, nor / the gild / ed mon / u ments

In our future diagrams we use only two degrees of stress, lighter (˘) and heavier (´) (although some highly trained phoneticians can detect six or even seven degrees of stress in English). *Relative stress* is one of the peskiest concepts for students to master. Sometimes a fellow student can help you determine stress more accurately than you can, because (after several different soundings) you can't "really hear" what you say. Keep this principle in mind: A syllable receives stress that is (a) heavier, (b) lighter, or (c) the same as the syllables on either side of it. More often than not, the stress differs from one of its neighbors, if not both. Check your "aural scales" carefully when weighing the stresses!

How do you begin to scan a poem? Stress in poetry, as in prose, results from the demands of proper pronunciation. It is simplest to start with the words of more than one syllable, putting the stress where it must fall for pronunciation. *Marble* is of course pronounced *márbĭe*, not *mărbĭe*. If unsure of syllabication, the interpreter should check a pronouncing dictionary. When scanning a poem, you must account for every syllable.

The next step requires you to be familiar not only with what the poem says but with how it means what it says. Note key words that must be emphasized for clarity and general comprehension. What is the attitude of the speaker? Look carefully at words that create mood or contribute sharply to needed variety and contrast. For instance, is a new type of sense imagery introduced? Emphasize it slightly so it will serve its purpose for later lines. The purpose of scanning is to find what the poet has actually done, not to make the lines fit a preconceived pattern.

After these steps, you may discover that a *fairly* regular pattern of lighter and heavier stresses in traditional feet is beginning to emerge. Complete the pattern by filling in whatever syllables have not yet been assigned a degree of stress. Try to conform as nearly as is practical to the predominant type of foot. If no such pattern emerges, perhaps the poet is not interested in stress prosody. Perhaps he or she has used syllabic prosody. This will be easy to determine because you have already marked the stresses. Count up the number of syllables in each line; then look to line lengths, speech phrases, and the number of stresses within them for structural unity.

The relative degree of stress is a matter you must work out for yourself from an understanding of the poem, for there is no one "right" way of reading a poem. Don't lose the *sense* in the insistence of rhythm, and don't lose the *pattern* in working to communicate the sense—these are the twin channel markers you should watch in steering your course. Let the poem lead the way. If meter is the basis of rhythm in the poem, be sure to permit variations.

Stress Prosody

Stress prosody finds its rhythmic base in the number of stresses per line, regardless of their position in relation to each other. Thus, it is often impossible, or at least impractical, to try to group the lighter and heavier stresses into traditional metrical feet. The number of syllables in a line may vary widely, but the number of stresses per line remains consistent or varies only occasionally for a specific effect. This concept of rhythm is important in understanding cadences of poetry and in determining the effectiveness of stresses within flows of sound. Stress prosody can also combine with syllabic prosody (as occurs in Melvin Dixon's "Heartbeats" at the end of this chapter).

Syllabic Prosody

Syllabic prosody is somewhat less common in English; it is the basis of French prosody. During the last century, many poets used syllabic prosody most effectively in combination with foot or stress prosody. *Syllabic prosody* measures flow of sound rather than stresses and depends quite simply on the number of syllables per line. Count them up and see if a rough pattern emerges.

Stanley Kunitz's lyric "Open the Gates" is an excellent example of how at least two of the three systems of prosody work within a single contemporary poem.

Open the Gates

STANLEY KUNITZ

Within / the ci / ty of / the burn / ing cloud,   1

Dragging / my life / behind / me in / a sack,   2

Naked / I prowl, / scourged by / the black   3

Tempta / tion of / the blood / grown proud.   4

> ´ ˘ ˘ ´ ˘ ´ ˘ ´
> Here at / the mon / ument / al door,   5

> ´ ˘ ˘ ´ ˘ ˘ ´ ˘ ˘ ˘ ´
> Carved with the / curious / legend of / my youth,   6

> ˘ ´ ˘ ˘ ´ ´ ˘ ˘ ´
> I brand / ish the great / bone of / my death,   7

> ´ ´ ˘ ´ ˘ ´ ˘ ´
> Beat once / therewith / and beat / no more.   8

> ˘ ´ ˘ ´ ˘ ´ ˘ ´
> The hing / es groan: / a rush / of forms   9

> ´ ˘ ˘ ´ ´ ´ ˘ ´
> Shivers / my name, / wrenched out / of me.   10

> ˘ ´ ˘ ˘ ´ ˘ ˘ ´ ˘ ˘ ˘ ´
> I stand / on the ter / rible thresh / old, and / I see   11

> ˘ ´ ˘ ˘ ˘ ´ ˘ ˘ ˘ ´ ˘ ´
> The end / and the / beginning / in each oth / er's arms.   12

Admittedly, there is more than one way to group the light and heavy stresses into traditional feet, particularly in lines 6, 11, and 12. Let this problem plague a prosodist! Our concern is basically with the relative positioning of the stresses within the line. Let's settle on this scansion for now.

For us, the grouping of stresses into traditional feet is largely a convenient way of seeing the pattern. Can you tell from one play if a football team is going for an aerial game or a ground game? You need to watch the team's successes, fumbles, and reverses. Here the scansion reveals that the meter is *basically* iambic with a great many variations. As a matter of fact, Kunitz uses each of the other five common types of feet at least twice. The only purely iambic line is line 9, which immediately follows the fulcrum.

From our preliminary scansion, then, we discover that the first two lines and the last two lines of "Open the Gates" have five feet and the others have four feet. Each of the four *pentameter* (five-foot) lines has a pyrrhic foot, however, so the stresses per line are consistently four, except for line 8, which is the fulcrum, and line 10, which contains the emotional climax; in those lines, spondees add a fifth stress. Thus, despite the greater length of the opening and closing lines, unity of stress is carefully preserved.

Other interesting details emerge. For instance, line 6 contains eleven syllables yet contains only four heavier stresses. So does the nine-syllable line that follows it. These two lines, which immediately precede the fulcrum, are the only ones with an uneven number of syllables.

An examination of the scansion of this brief poem assures us that there is more to poetic rhythm than a "da-DA da-DA" alternation of light and heavy stresses. Stanley Kunitz has achieved remarkable variety within unity. The chart of this poem on page 438 maps several other ways that collaborate with stress patterns to tighten this poem.

Interpreter's Use of Line Lengths

Because the line functions as a unit of both sound and sense, we need to consider in some detail the twofold discipline that poets have imposed on themselves—and on us—with specific line lengths.

Poets who write conventional poetry divide the stanzas into lines with appropriate lengths. They combine this measure with a more or less regular arrangement of stresses, and perhaps with rhyme at the line ends, to achieve the pattern of sound. After all, poets had some reason for selecting a particular line length, or at least, having selected it, they made some effort to fit their thought units—which also become sound units when the poem is read aloud—into that pattern.

Blank verse presents us with the greatest temptation to ignore line length, partly because the line ends do not have the added reinforcement of rhyme. Yet the best blank verse establishes the line length as one of the components of the rhythmic pattern. The extent to which the poet succeeds at conforming to this discipline is one standard for measuring excellence of achievement. Remember, however, that verse is written in sentences as well as in lines. The line should not obscure the sense. A drop in pitch or a distinct pause at the end of every line produces monotony. Worse, it would distort the sense (because we hear a marked pause as the completion of a thought) and would cancel out one of the chief advantages of the blank verse line—its approximation of the rhythms of conversational speech.

A writer of free verse often uses long sentences so that the flow of sense may be technically uninterrupted for an entire unit (T. S. Eliot does this in most of his poems). If the poet arranges these sentences in lines as long or as short as he or she wants, there must be a reason for the line length chosen. For the interpreter's practical purposes, it can be convenient to take a breath where the free-verse line ends if you need it. It is logical, too, because the breath comes at a division of the thought, or at a point where the poet wishes to reinforce feeling or establish a relationship or progression.

There is an excellent example of such subtle progression in Eliot's "Journey of the Magi" (at the end of this chapter). In the last stanza we find these lines:

All this was a long time ago, I remember,
And I would do it again, but set down
This set down
This: . . .

When the lines are read aloud, their arrangement gives a far different effect from what it would be if the words were arranged as follows:

All this was a long time ago,
I remember, and I would do it again,
But set down this, set down this:

Reread both versions aloud again. Can you hear how the sense changes? What is the speaker considering after the first "down"? after the second? To realize the full contribution of line length to rhythm and to content, then, you must make a pause of *some* kind at the end of each line of poetry.

Of course, pauses vary. The line end that is not called for by punctuation, sentence construction, or overall meaning does not require the kind of pause that is used to end a sentence. Indeed, if the sentence or speech phrase runs over into the next line—a device technically known as *enjambment*[2]—there is no *obvious* hesitation.

Nevertheless, the line length imposes a sense of the boundaries or "shape" of the poem, as marked by the eye in silent reading. In oral interpretation, the voice and the body take over, though not to the point where the physical pattern of the poem obscures meaning, sound, and feeling. Rather, voice and body respond to the length of the line.

Thus, the length, force, and terminal effect of the line-end pauses vary—from a barely perceptible pause, or a slight drawing out or suspension of the terminal vowel sound, to a semistop or "breath pause," to a full pause at the end of the sentence or thought unit. Accordingly, exploit these opportunities for variety. In a caution to poets, Ezra Pound once wrote: "Don't make each line stop dead at the end, and then begin every next line with a heave. Let the beginning of the next line catch the rise of the rhythm wave, unless you want a definite longish pause." Interpreters, too, can apply this advice to their own art.

Believe it, there's still more to say about line length, especially in free verse. Consider the discussion of cadences that follows. And a thorough understanding of the contributions of line length can refine your performance of verse drama and narrative verse, as well as that of many contemporary musical works (see Stephen Sondheim's "Finishing the Hat," at the end of Chapter 8). The important point to remem-

2. From the French *enjambement,* meaning "straddling": that is to say, one leg of the thought on either side of the line end.

ber is that poets fit their thoughts into the structure they choose. Particularly in free verse, the line ends where it ends because that is precisely where the poet wanted the line to end; the line does not end because the poet ran out of ink! This does not mean that in performance each line comes to a thudding conclusion, so that the audience is fully aware of line length. Like tone color, stanzaic patterning, stress patterns, and rhyme, the length of the line contributes to the whole and should be blended with and properly related to all of the elements to permit the *poem* to live in performance.

Cadences

Analyzing cadences is a visual way to map the separate flows of sound within a poem. This process brings together considerations of syllabic prosody (the number of syllables in each line) and stress prosody (the number rather than location of stresses in each line).

A *cadence*, as the term is used here, is simply an uninterrupted flow of sound. Each pause—either briefly or for a longer time—establishes a new cadence. Cadences are measured by the number of syllables they contain.

Earlier we were concerned with the line as a unit of measure. Here, in analyzing cadences, we keep the line in mind, but we also give more attention to the way individual lines may be divided into speech phrases when the poem is performed, and to the length of entire sentences, even if they continue past the line end.

We discussed sentence length and speech phrases within sentences in our examination of prose style in Chapter 5. Analyzing the length and composition of speech phrases and sentences is important in studying prose rhythm. It is absolutely essential in examining poetic rhythm—partly because of the importance of line lengths in poetic structure, and also because cadences, as part of the essential sound pattern on which all poetry depends, should be coordinated with all the other sound factors.

A *primary cadence* is the number of syllables in an entire sentence. *Secondary cadences* refer both to line lengths and to the speech phrases within the lines. Of course, merely counting up syllables does not give us the total picture. Cadences should always be considered in relation to two other elements that exist within them: the number and arrangement of stresses (especially within lines) and the length or duration of the sounds within syllables. Thus, *duration* as well as *stress* work within the syllables in secondary cadence.

We said that a primary cadence is the number of syllables in the sentence, from its beginning to its end as marked by terminal punctuation. The number of syllables in each line is also immediately evident. Both of these numbers can be determined objectively. The lengths of the speech phrases, however, are somewhat more subjectively determined, because not all interpreters pause at precisely the same places. Sometimes there can be no doubt about the need for a pause, and hence for establishing a cadence—for example, when the poet has inserted a semicolon and you have to pause. More often you make your own decisions about pauses. Be guided by the content (both logical and emotive), by the relationship of phrases and clauses to the terms they modify and to the complete sentence, and by opportunities for conveying variety and contrast within unity and for communicating imagery and tone color. A pause, however slight, breaks the line into speech phrases.

Interestingly, a consideration of the cadences may open up unsuspected possibilities for variety and harmony. Frequently, poets achieve a large part of their rhythm by manipulating the cadences within a strict pattern of scansion. (This is another of the important attributes of successful blank verse.) Tennyson uses cadences most effectively, for instance, in "Ulysses" (Chapter 4). Many of the lines are broken near the middle either by terminal punctuation or by a colon or semicolon. In this manner Tennyson achieves variety without breaking the unity of the iambic pentameter line. Philip Larkin's "Talking in Bed" (Chapter 9) uses such broken lines to suggest some of the tension in the speaker's rocky relationship. A significant pause within a line is called a *caesura.* In other lines, balancing syntax or pointing out a comparative phrase may cause the interpreter to insert a somewhat less distinct pause, which nevertheless interrupts the flow of sound within the line as a unit.

The line-length cadences are probably the most fundamental. Keeping this in mind, look at speech phrases *within* the separate lines, knowing that even an *enjambment line* (a line where the phrase carries over to the following line) has some kind of pause, however unobtrusive, at its end. In extremely long lines (as in Walt Whitman's poems), these speech phrases often provide the surest basis for the rhythm.

We said that Kunitz's "Open the Gates" is an interesting example of carefully controlled variation from traditional metrics. The cadences contribute to unity and harmony as well as to variety and contrast. Look at the patterns we discover simply by counting the syllables and major stresses within lines and speech phrases and noting the sentence lengths: As usual, the *primary cadences* tell us most by their relation to one another. In this poem, the primary cadences are obviously a unifying factor in the first two stanzas. But at the fulcrum everything changes. Shifting so decisively from the established thirty-six syllables to sixteen syllables helps set off the climax.

Looking at the *secondary cadences,* we notice that lines of identical length are used in pairs or in threes, except for the two center lines. These two, neatly bracketed by eight-syllable lines, steady the middle of the poem. The stresses per line are a strong unifying force. The added stress in lines 8 and 10 reinforce the fulcrum and the climax.

	Secondary Cadences				Syllables per Primary Cadence
Line No.	Syllables per line	Stresses per Line	Syllables per Speech Phrase	Stresses per Speech Phrase	
1	10	4	10	4	36
2	10	4	7-3	3-1	
3	8	4	4-1-3	2-1-1	
4	8	4	3-3-2	1-1-2	
5	8	4	1-7	1-3	36
6	11	4	1-7-3	1-2-1	
7	9	4	9	4	
8	8	5	4-4	3-2	FULCRUM
9	8	4	4-4	2-2	16
10	8	5	4-4	2-3	CLIMAX
11	12	4	9-3	3-1	24
12	12	4	2-5-5	1-1-2	

The speech phrases provide needed variety within this unity. They too, however, tend to cluster; three predominate near the opening, varied by units of seven, four, one, and two. The one-and-seven combination is apparent in line 5, and one and seven and three in line 6. The even four-and-four division in lines 8, 9, and 10, mentioned in relation to scansion, helps reinforce the emotional weight of the content.

Why bother to chart a poem? Because this is the simplest way to clarify what you have to work with. A careful analysis of the cadences and stresses in a poem will convince you that conventional poetry can't be read like a nursery rhyme. The discipline inherent in free verse stops us from reading this type of poetry as if it were prose. Free verse, properly written, is probably the most demanding type of poetry to perform, and interpreters who choose it should be prepared to analyze its structure painstakingly. Free verse is *not* verse without structure; rather, the structure of free verse is always uniquely tailored to the poem and often is so carefully crafted that it *appears* invisible. If you follow the clues scrupulously and scrutinize every syllable, your rigorous analysis will greatly increase your artistic ability as well as your appreciation for the poet's artistic achievement.

As is true of what you learn from scansion, what you discover from studying cadence has a direct input into your rehearsal. If, say, you choose to perform "Open the Gates" (by now, you know a great deal about how that poem works), you can embody and evoke this knowledge. Specifically, what rate will you select for the first stanza? Of course, your decisions about where to pause will be guided by what you discover in secondary cadences. Will you simply repeat the same choices in stanza 2? Why not? And, as you approach line 8, how will you negotiate the dangerous phrases in "I brandish the great bone of my death" so that you prepare listeners for "Beat once therewith, and beat no more"? And the last two lines, the longest in the poem—are they rushed to finish the poem off, or paced more deliberately to show the final, appalling sight that confronts the speaker? Possibly—if you are a particularly sensitive reader—you would have intuitively made all the appropriate decisions in performing this poem. Analysis, however, provides you with the certainty of the wisdom of your choices, and in the tumult of anxieties that attends any performance, such certainty is a rock on which interpreters gladly rest.

Clearly, no audience could be expected to grasp fully the subtlety of this rhythmic pattern when the poem is read aloud. Indeed, it would be most unfortunate if you called attention to the pattern. Nevertheless, unless you understand what the poet has done to communicate the total effect, your audience loses.

Rhyme

Rhyme most commonly occurs at the line ends. The lines may contain internal rhymes as well. Unlike rhythm and cadence, rhyme is not an essential element of poetry, but it reinforces rhythm, cadence, pattern, and tone color.

Although corresponding sounds strike the mind's ear in a silent reading, they emerge for complete appreciation only when a poem is read aloud. Like a chime of music, rhyme is satisfying and pleasing to hear; it gives intellectual pleasure through the delights of repetition and anticipation. The reason for rhyme, however, is not to decorate a poem but rather to bind it more closely together. For one thing, rhyme unifies the pattern of sound. Its power doubtless contributes to the continuing popularity of rap music and hip-hop, in which the texts derive much of their potency from the satisfied expectations rhyme creates. Just as in more traditional poetry, rhyme emphasizes the line lengths by creating an expectation of repeated sounds at regular intervals. Experienced poets and rap artists know that rhyme, if used unwisely, can shatter rather than intensify the unity of a poem. Therefore, when they use rhyme, they exhibit great care and ingenuity in handling it. An interpreter who bears down hard on every rhyme makes the physical shape of the poem block out all of its other qualities. Now for some more terms.

Rhyme is the exact correspondence of both final *vowel* and *consonant* sounds (*love–dove*). *Assonance* is the correspondence of *vowel* sounds only, regardless of the final consonant sounds (*place–brave*). There are several kinds of rhyme. In *half rhymes* (*pavement–gravely, river–weather*) only half of a two-syllable word rhymes with another. In *double rhymes*, the two final syllables correspond (*crying–flying, arrayed–afraid*). There are even *triple rhymes* (*din afore–pinafore*). Stephen Sondheim frequently uses the device to suggest the intricate interrelationships of a character's needs, concerns, and problems (see his "Finishing the Hat," at the end of Chapter 8, or if you are interested in how this device works in still an-other poem about Cinderella, see his "On the Steps of the Palace" from *Into the Woods*). There is also *approximate rhyme* or *rhyme by consonance*: most commonly, the final consonant sounds are identical, but the vowel sounds are not (*rock–luck*). Used carefully, rhyme can reinforce tone color.

A rhyme scheme is indicated in prosodic analysis by letters that stand for the terminal rhyme sounds; *a* represents the sound of the first line and of every line corresponding to it; *b* stands for the next terminal sound and its corresponding lines; and so on. Each of the three vil-lanelles at the end of this chapter follows the same rhyme scheme, but look at the first three stanzas of Elizabeth Bishop's "One Art," in which we have marked the rhyme scheme:

The art of losing isn't hard to master;	*a*
so many things seem filled with the intent	*b*
to be lost that their loss is no disaster	*a*
Lose something every day. Accept the fluster	*a*
of lost door keys, the hour badly spent.	*b*
The art of losing isn't hard to master.	*a*
Then practice losing farther, losing faster:	*a*
places, names, and where it was you meant	*b*
to travel. None of these will bring disaster.	*a*

You will see the rhyme scheme is *aba aba aba,* and so forth throughout the poem. Careful readers will note that "fluster" in line 4 does not really rhyme with "master" or "disaster" or "faster," and that it seems to be a *half-rhyme.* This is absolutely correct, but it can also be said that one way to evoke the "flustered" quality of the speaker is to have her get things not quite right; learning to "accept the fluster" may not be so easy as one hopes, or says.

Moreover, a very insistent rhyme can sometimes cause trouble for an interpreter, because the very strict form may seem to obliterate anything that stands in the rhyme's way. A skillful interpreter will work to mitigate the problem by capitalizing on a variety of pauses within the line. If you pay particular attention to *tone color,* some of the internal language can achieve a prominence that challenges the rhyme. And emphasis on *imagery* also adds variety. Look, for example, at Robert Browning's "My Last Duchess" (at the end of this chapter). The poem's rhymed couplets reinforce the ominous restrictiveness that lies beneath the smooth talk of the duke, and they could overpower an audience. Here, however, the poet's skillful use of enjambment encourages the interpreter to focus on sense. It is wise advice; in this poem, sound takes care of itself.

As we have said, the problem of rhyme does not arise in blank verse. But its very absence affects interpreters. On the one hand, you are released from one of the disciplines you often should consider in interpreting poetry; on the other hand, you are deprived of a significant means of communicating structural unity. Therefore, pay particular attention to other elements in the sound pattern of blank verse: alliteration, harsh or euphonious vowel and consonant combinations, the echoing of mood or sense in sound. You can find the surest guide to structural unity in blank verse in the prevalent iambic meter and in the consistent line length.

Writers of free verse may or may not use rhyme. They may use it consistently throughout a poem, but this technique is unusual. Sometimes rhyme appears, if it appears at all, only in brief units of the poem. When these units occur, carefully examine their contribution to content, for the poet will have used rhyme consciously. It will not be part of a conventional pattern but will come out of a subjective decision to use rhyme at that particular point. The sounds of the rhymes and the length of the lines containing the rhymes are important for intensifying certain aspects of the content.

Intention and Performance

Faced with all the complex patterns and diagrams, many students ask—a little dazedly—if poets consciously knew they were doing all of this. "Did they plan all this out?" we hear. Many do know much of it. Some don't know specifically, for example, that an anapest will be better at the end of the line—they just know that it sounds and feels better. Our favorite response is to ask another question: "Does it matter?" Surely the patterns—of sound, of stress, of stanzaic form, of sense— exist in the poem, even if the poet did not specifically set out to create a line rich in assonance and consonance. All the structural devices help the poem become what it wants to be. Do you know where all the joists and girders and electrical wiring are in your own residence? If you were asked to rebuild it precisely, you would certainly want to find out. Faced with performing a poem, you want to know everything you can about its architecture, too.

Performers often are amazed at the intricacies of a successful poem. But poems are not simply structures; rather, structure informs content, and content derives from structure. No single aspect of the structure is the entire work, nor should any part be exhibited for its own sake. In analysis, poems can be astonishing aggregates of interconnected parts. In performance, poems must be whole.

Poetry's condensation provides special challenges to interpreters, and your understanding of the language and structure of poetry is constantly tested in rehearsal and performance. Of course, we do not mean that we are no longer interested in the basic problems of every kind of performance: efficient management of the vocal and physical resources and careful attention to communicating the intellectual, emotional, and aesthetic entirety of the work. But poetry brings more complex uses of sound and sense than do many kinds of narration or drama. The interpreter must be particularly careful not to allow concentration to lapse and the communicative thrust of the performance to fade. Poetry performances in which the interpreter seems chiefly interested in musing over the lines for himself or herself and for the people seated closest are really still in rehearsal.

Analyzing the Rehearsal and the Performance

With the information you have obtained from Chapters 9 and 10, then, and an informed and observant perspective, use the following questions to analyze the performance you gave. As before, any questions you ask of yourself can as well be asked of other performances you see. Keep the poem at the center of your discussion and analysis and for treat it with respect. Remember, it was alive before you met it and will be around long after all of us have gone.

- ◆ Did you let the poet lead the way?

- ◆ Was your audience responsive to what the poet meant and especially to *how* it was meant?

- ◆ Did you use your empathic response fully so that the audience responded empathically as well?

- ◆ Did you carefully preserve the unity of the poem? Did you keep all the other intrinsic factors working fully within it?

- ◆ Was the persona clear? Was the locus clear?

- ◆ Did you take full advantage of all of the sound patterns? Did you use the poem's rhythm, or did it use you? Did you clarify the relationship between the lines and the cadences? Did you demonstrate the interaction of rhyme and tone color?

- ◆ Did you spend more time introducing than performing?

- ◆ Were you able to blend aspects from previous chapters that are applicable to this selection and keep them in their proper relationship to create the "whole" poem?

- Did your audience hear the poem as a totality? Were they primarily interested in and aware of you as performer?

- How did the poem change for you after your analysis? How has it changed for you after your rehearsals and performance?

- What problems still plague you as a performer? What progress have you made in defining them? in solving them? in eliminating them?

For the performances you saw, how did the interpreter suggest the complex language and structure of poetry? Specifically, how did the poem you saw and heard compare with the one you read on the page?

REMEMBER THIS!

Technical discussion can overwhelm beginning students; simply keeping track of new vocabulary can challenge! As you would do with anything new, practice with the terminology and the techniques of analysis for a while before deciding on their usefulness. As you prepare your performance of poetry, keep these concepts in mind, too:

- Prosody helps us understand how poems are made.

- Conventional poems, blank verse, and free verse offer many opportunities for important variations.

- The stanza is the poem's "paragraph of sense" and "paragraph of sound."

- The line serves as construction material of a poem.

- Patterns abound in poetry: in stresses, in syllables, in sounds, in length of line, in rhyme.

- The flow of sound and pause is measured in cadences: complete sentences are primary cadences; speech phrases are secondary cadences, as are individual lines.

Selections for Analysis and Oral Interpretation

Here are three villanelles by three of the most accomplished masters in English. We start with the most recent poem. Notice how the form keeps the speaker on target and how, although she intends it to shield her from an important admission, the truth unintentionally leaks out. Watch that final line!

⑤ One Art

ELIZABETH BISHOP

The art of losing isn't hard to master;
so many things seem filled with the intent
to be lost that their loss is no disaster.

Lose something every day. Accept the fluster
of lost door keys, the hour badly spent.
The art of losing isn't hard to master.

Then practice losing farther, losing faster:
places, and names, and where it was you meant
to travel. None of these will bring disaster.

I lost my mother's watch. And look! my last, or
next-to-last, of three loved houses went.
The art of losing isn't hard to master.

I lost two cities, lovely ones. And, vaster,
some realms I owned, two rivers, a continent.
I miss them, but it wasn't a disaster.

—Even losing you (the joking voice, a gesture
I love) I shan't have lied. It's evident
the art of losing's not too hard to master
though it may look like (*Write* it!) like disaster.

- ◆ Where did the first crack in the speaker's armor appear?
- ◆ Who is the "you" addressed in the last stanza? Was this person there in the first?

This poem precedes Bishop's in date of composition and may have encouraged her to attempt the form. Let Roethke's tight restriction help to keep the cadences from becoming abrupt. Make full use of the remarkable tone color, too, especially the assonance. For Roethke, all of life was a waking toward the sleep of death. Keep that affirmation clear in your concentration.

⑤ The Waking

THEODORE ROETHKE

I wake to sleep, and take my waking slow.
I feel my fate in what I cannot fear.
I learn by going where I have to go.

We think by feeling. What is there to know?
I hear my being dance from ear to ear.
I wake to sleep, and take my waking slow.

Of those so close beside me, which are you?
God bless the Ground! I shall walk softly there,
And learn by going where I have to go.

Light takes the Tree; but who can tell us how?
The lowly worm climbs up a winding stair;
I wake to sleep, and take my waking slow.

Great Nature has another thing to do
To you and me; so take the lively air,
And, lovely, learn by going where to go.

This shaking keeps me steady. I should know.
What falls away is always. And is near.
I wake to sleep, and take my waking slow.
I learn by going where I have to go.

◆ How did you distinguish among the different levels of meaning in
the repeated lines?

*The earliest of these villanelles is probably the most famous. Dylan Thomas
uniquely mastered the condensation of poetic language; here he achieves tur-
bulent poignancy in his plea. For all its emotional intensity, the poem follows
a very logical argument, so make sure we see how the form and the language
serve both the sound and the sense.*

Do Not Go Gentle into That Good Night

DYLAN THOMAS

Do not go gentle into that good night,
Old age should burn and rave at close of day;
Rage, rage against the dying of the light.

Though wise men at their end know dark is right,
Because their words had forked no lightning they
Do not go gentle into that good night.

Good men, the last wave by, crying how bright
Their frail deeds might have danced in a green bay,
Rage, rage against the dying of the light.

Wild men who caught and sang the sun in flight,
And learn, too late, they grieved it on its way,
Do not go gentle into that good night.

Grave men, near death, who see with blinding sight
Blind eyes could blaze like meteors and be gay,
Rage, rage against the dying of the light.

And you, my father, there on the sad height,
Curse, bless, me now with your fierce tears, I pray.
Do not go gentle into that good night.
Rage, rage against the dying of the light.

- ◆ Why does the speaker choose "gentle" rather than "gently"? What does this choice reveal about his internal thought processes?

- ◆ Did you distinguish for your audience among the wise, good, wild, and grave men? How?

In this poem the line-length cadences are not only important for structural rhythm but provide clues to emotional content and connotations. The first five lines are quoted from a famous sermon. Notice how skillfully Eliot moves into his own comment. The quotation should not be set off too obviously from the rest of the stanza. Eliot uses capital letters for spiritual birth and death as opposed to physical birth and death.

Journey of the Magi

T. S. ELIOT

'A cold coming we had of it,
Just the worst time of the year
For a journey, and such a long journey:
The ways deep and the weather sharp,
The very dead of winter.'
And the camels galled, sore-footed, refractory,
Lying down in the melting snow.
There were times we regretted
The summer palaces on slopes, the terraces,
And the silken girls bringing sherbet.
Then the camel men cursing and grumbling
And running away, and wanting their liquor and women,
And the night-fires going out, and the lack of shelters,
And the cities hostile and the towns unfriendly
And the villages dirty and charging high prices:
A hard time we had of it.

At the end we preferred to travel all night,
Sleeping in snatches,
With the voices singing in our ears, saying
That this was all folly.

    Then at dawn we came down to a temperate valley,
Wet, below the snow line, smelling of vegetation;
With a running stream and a water-mill beating the darkness,
And three trees on a low sky,
And an old white horse galloped away in the meadow.
Then we came to a tavern with vine-leaves over the lintel,
Six hands at an open door dicing for pieces of silver,
And feet kicking the empty wine-skins.
But there was no information, and so we continued
And arrived at evening, not a moment too soon
Finding the place; it was (you may say) satisfactory.

    All this was a long time ago, I remember,
And I would do it again, but set down
This set down
This: were we led all that way for
Birth or Death? There was a Birth, certainly,
We had evidence and no doubt. I had seen birth and death,
But had thought they were different; this Birth was
Hard and bitter agony for us, like Death, our death.
We returned to our places, these Kingdoms,
But no longer at ease here, in the old dispensation,
With an alien people clutching their gods.
I should be glad of another death.

◆ Was your persona "glad of another death" as the poem began?
   How did your audience know?

*Here is another and very different poem about the same people. Here, however,
the speaker observes the Magi with mixed emotions. Be sure we see how carefully Glück establishes the scene she wants us to remember.*

The Magi

LOUISE GLÜCK

Toward world's end, through the bare
beginnings of winter, they are traveling again.
How many winters have we seen it happen,
watched the same sign come forward as they pass
cities sprung around this route their gold

engraved on the desert, and yet
held our peace, these
being the Wise, come to see at the accustomed hour
nothing changed: roofs, the barn
blazing in darkness, all they wish to see.

- ◆ How does this speaker's attitude differ from that of the speaker in
  Eliot's poem?

*James Wright's gift for simple eloquence is unmatched among contempo-
rary American poets. Restraint and sincerity characterize the achievement in
this lyric.*

A Blessing

JAMES WRIGHT

Just off the highway to Rochester, Minnesota,
Twilight bounds softly forth on the grass.
And the eyes of those two Indian ponies
Darken with kindness.
They have come gladly out of the willows
To welcome my friend and me.
We step over the barbed wire into the pasture
Where they have been grazing all day, alone.
They ripple tensely, they can hardly contain their happiness
That we have come.
They bow shyly as wet swans. They love each other.
There is no loneliness like theirs.
At home once more,
They begin munching the young tufts of spring in the darkness.
I would like to hold the slenderer one in my arms,
For she has walked over to me
And nuzzled my left hand.
She is black and white,
Her mane falls wild on her forehead,
And the light breeze moves me to caress her long ear
That is delicate as the skin over a girl's wrist.
Suddenly I realize
That if I stepped out of my body I would break
Into blossom.

- ◆ What happened to your body and voice after "wrist" and before
  "Suddenly" (just before the third line from the end of the poem)?
  Why?

The late Melvin Dixon carefully crafted and condensed the experience of en-croaching illness. Patterns abound is this poem, but guard against trying to force the lines to conform. In addition to an understandable fear, the persona shows great courage, and we need to see it all.

Heartbeats

MELVIN DIXON

Work out. Ten laps.
Chin ups. Look good.

Steam room. Dress warm.
Call home. Fresh air.

Eat right. Rest well.
Sweetheart. Safe sex.

Sore throat. Long flu.
Hard nodes. Beware.

Test blood. Count cells.
Reds thin. Whites low.

Dress warm. Eat well.
Short breath. Fatigue.

Night sweats. Dry cough.
Loose stools. Weight loss.

Get mad. Fight back.
Call home. Rest well.

Don't cry. Take charge.
No sex. Eat right.

Call home. Talk slow.
Chin up. No air.

Arms wide. Nodes hard.
Cough dry. Hold on.

Mouth wide. Drink this.
Breathe in. Breathe out.

No air. Breathe in.
Breathe in. No air.

Black out. White rooms.
Head hot. Feet cold.

No work. Eat right.
CAT scan. Chin up.

Breathe in. Breathe out.
No air. No air.

Thin blood. Sore lungs.
Mouth dry. Mind gone.

Six months? Three weeks?
Can't eat. No air.

Today? Tonight?
It waits. For me.

Sweet heart. Don't stop.
Breathe in. Breathe out.

- ◆ How did you demonstrate the *progress* of the disease?

- ◆ Can a performer use his or her own breath support to evoke the breathing problems of the speaker? How?

This poem is a feast of images; each contributes mightily to the flavor and richness of this sensual banquet. Miss no opportunity for tone color.

◉ Who Among You Knows the Essence of Garlic?

GARRETT KAORU HONGO

Can your foreigner's nose smell mullets
roasting in a glaze of brown bean paste
and sprinkled with novas of sea salt?

Can you hear my grandmother
chant the mushroom's sutra?

Can you hear the papayas crying
as they bleed in porcelain plates?

I'm telling you that the bamboo
slips the long pliant shoots
of its myriad soft tongues
into your mouth that is full of oranges.

I'm saying that the silver waterfalls
of bean threads will burst in hot oil
and stain your lips like zinc.

The marbled skin of the blue mackerel
works good for men. The purple oils
from its flesh perfume the tongues of women.

If you swallow them whole, the rice cakes
soaking in a broth of coconut milk and brown sugar
will never leave the bottom of your stomach.

Flukes of giant black mushrooms
leap from their murky tubs
and strangle the toes of young carrots.

Broiling chickens ooze grease,
yellow tears of fat collect
and spatter in the smoking pot.

Soft ripe pears, blushing
on the kitchen window sill,
kneel like plump women

taking a long, luxurious shampoo,
and invite you to bite their hips.

Why not grab basketfuls of steaming noodles,
lush and slick as the hair of a fine lady,
and squeeze?

The shrimps, big as Portuguese thumbs,
stew among cut guavas, red onions,
ginger root, and rosemary in lemon juice,
the palm oil bubbling to the top,
breaking through layers and layers
of shredded coconut and sliced cashews.

Who among you knows the essence
of garlic and black lotus root,
of red and green peppers sizzling
among squads of oysters in the skillet,
of crushed ginger, fresh green onions,
and pale-blue rice wine simmering
in the stomach of a big red fish?

- ◆ How did you separate the distinct flavors and smells?

- ◆ How hungry was your audience when your performance was over?

Be sure you embody the Duke's character. He is moved alternately by guilt and regret, admiration and contempt. And don't ignore the poem's tight structure. Those rhymed couplets are not simply accidental. They suggest some of the restrictions inherent in the Ferrara of the poem.

 ## My Last Duchess

ROBERT BROWNING

Ferrara

That's my last Duchess painted on the wall,
Looking as if she were alive. I call
That piece a wonder, now: Frà Pandolf's hands
Worked busily a day, and there she stands.
Will't please you sit and look at her? I said
"Frà Pandolf" by design, for never read
Strangers like you that pictured countenance,
The depth and passion of its earnest glance,
But to myself they turned (since none puts by
The curtain I have drawn for you, but I)
And seemed as they would ask me, if they durst,

How such a glance came there; so, not the first
Are you to turn and ask thus. Sir, 'twas not
Her husband's presence only, called that spot
Of joy into the Duchess' cheek: perhaps
Frà Pandolf chanced to say, "Her mantle laps
Over my lady's wrist too much," or "Paint
Must never hope to reproduce the faint
Half-flush that dies along her throat": such stuff
Was courtesy, she thought, and cause enough
For calling up that spot of joy. She had
A heart—how shall I say?—too soon made glad,
too easily impressed: she liked whate'er
She looked on, and her looks went everywhere.
Sir, 'twas all one! My favour at her breast,
The dropping of the daylight in the West,
The bough of cherries some officious fool
Broke in the orchard for her, the white mule
She rode with round the terrace—all and each
Would draw from her alike the approving speech.
Or blush, at least. She thanked men,— good! but thanked
Somehow—I know not how—as if she ranked
My gift of a nine-hundred-years-old name
With anybody's gift. Who'd stoop to blame
This sort of trifling? Even had you skill
In speech—(which I have not)—to make your will
Quite clear to such an one, and say, "Just this
Or that in you disgusts me; here you miss,
Or there exceed the mark"—and if she let
Herself be lessoned so, nor plainly set
Her wits to yours, forsooth, and made excuse,
—E'en then would be some stooping; and I choose
Never to stoop. Oh sir, she smiled, no doubt,
Whene'er I passed her; but who passed without
Much the same smile? This grew; I gave commands;
Then all smiles stopped together. There she stands
As if alive. Will't please you rise? We'll meet
The company below, then. I repeat,
The Count your master's known munificence
Is ample warrant that no just pretence
Of mine for dowry will be disallowed;
Though his fair daughter's self, as I avowed
At starting, is my object. Nay, we'll go
Together down, sir. Notice Neptune, though,
Taming a sea-horse, thought a rarity,
Which Claus of Innsbruck cast in bronze for me!

- How did you sketch the world of the Duke's palace?

- How did you keep the Count's emissary present and lively?

This resilient speaker knows herself and admits her shortcomings with sometimes astonishing accuracy. She never feels sorry for herself, either. Can we see her recall her experiences as vividly as she describes Billielou?

The Kilgore Rangerette Whose Life Was Ruined

CYNTHIA MacDONALD

There we were that beautiful line, synchronized as
A row of pistons in an Eldorado, except
There are only eight of them and there were a hundred of us
(Flowers weeded out of flowers, the cream of the crop).
There we were in the Cotton bowl, the world-famous
Kilgore Rangerettes, kicking to "The Eyes of Texas Are Upon You"
And they were. In our white cowhide skirts and white felt hats
And red satin shirts and vests with silver stars and
I kicked with the wrong leg and the heel of
My white patent boot got caught in Marybelle's heel on the right
And we both fell and knocked into
The girls on either side of us who sprawled into
Others and half the line went down
Like a keyboard in a demo derby whacked by an axe.

Maybe I should have known—there had been
Problems of appearances before:

Hugging Grandma too tight after she'd had her surgery.
She held the empty place and cried.
Grandpa said she loves you; be more careful.
He bought me a grey suede bag to keep things in.

Giggling in my Hark the Herald Angels Sing duet,
Infecting my partner, too.
The principal said we ruined the Christmas Concert.
My father gave me a garnet and emerald
Synthastone pin in the shape of a clef.

Having a nosebleed when I was shaking hands with
The head of Pan American who came for dinner.
A drop fell on his tan pants.
My father didn't get promoted
But he said that wasn't why.

My mother gave me a box of linen handkerchiefs
Embroidered Monday, Tuesday, Wednesday . . .

Not only did I have to leave the Rangerettes
I left Kilgore, too, even though my roommate,
Who'd been the Maid of Cotton, told me she still loved me.
My intended said the same and gave me
A satin slip, but I don't know . . .
I felt he shouldn't have a ruined wife.
It was that way with any good job, too.
How could I work in the fine crystal section at Neiman's?
All those long-stemmed goblets. Cascades of glass chimes
Woke me every night. I asked to be transferred to
Sterling and Gems. But the tines, the blades, the facets
Menaced me. I learned you break or are broken.
And then a Texaco receptionist, Jack-In-The-Box waitress . . .
No need to spell the perils out.

They know me in Dallas—the only bag lady—lots in NYC—
But all of them are old and I am not. I saw them
On a Kilgore trip to catch the Rockettes and the Balanchine
Swan Lake. (We all agreed those swans would be
Hissed off the field at any Southwest half-time show.)
It's not a bad life. No one expects grace or precision.

Outdoors scavenging the city's trash—presents for yourself—
You collect what you can, what you want, what you need.
Last night I found a Lilly Daché hat and three foam mats.
Street life has its dangers: cold, jail, insults.
But no humiliation. A year ago I got knocked up.
Rape, yes, but no mutilation.
It wasn't bad. I don't feel much these days.
I keep the baby, Billielou, in my bag, snug
In a nest of rags, a Dallas kangaroo.
If Beebeelou—that's what I call her—wants
To be a Rangerette . . . Well, I don't know . . .
Her fingers curl around my thumb like little tongues.
She'll have to have her chance to kick her boots to the sky,
To slice it with her legs, the perfect blue
Deep in the heart of Texas.

◆ How did you capture the speaker's unique "grace and precision"
of recall and description?

The two long sentences in this poem must not be allowed to become repetitious in their tight syntax. The fulcrum begins in the ninth line and moves slowly to the climax in the last half line. Use the two short cadences in the last line with enough strength to balance the "negative" aspects of the other thirteen lines.

 FROM **Fatal Interview**

EDNA ST. VINCENT MILLAY

Sonnet XXX

Love is not all: it is not meat nor drink
Nor slumber nor a roof against the rain;
Nor yet a floating spar to men that sink
And rise and sink and rise and sink again;
Love can not fill the thickened lung with breath,
Nor clean the blood, nor set the fractured bone;
Yet many a man is making friends with death
Even as I speak, for lack of love alone.
It well may be that in a difficult hour,
Pinned down by pain and moaning for release,
Or nagged by want past resolution's power,
I might be driven to sell your love for peace,
Or trade the memory of this night for food.
It well may be. I do not think I would.

- How did you demonstrate the thought processes of the persona?

- What was happening in the pause between the two sentences in the last line?

Here are a pair of poems about a story we all know, but they are likely to be quite different from the tale you remember. The first—from Anne Sexton's Transformations—*recounts the familiar details in a startling and different way. Be sure to personify fully that contemporary narrator who seems to have done, seen, and heard* everything. *Why is the fulcrum where it is?*

 Cinderella

ANNE SEXTON

You always read about it:
the plumber with twelve children
who wins the Irish Sweepstakes.

From toilets to riches.
That story.

Or the nursemaid,
some luscious sweet from Denmark
who captures the oldest son's heart.
From diapers to Dior.
That story.

Or a milkman who serves the wealthy,
eggs, cream, butter, yogurt, milk,
the white truck like an ambulance
who goes into real estate
and makes a pile.
From homogenized to martinis at lunch.

Or the charwoman
who is on the bus when it cracks up
and collects enough from the insurance.
From mops to Bonwit Teller.
That story.

Once
the wife of a rich man was on her deathbed
and she said to her daughter Cinderella:
Be devout. Be good. Then I will smile
down from heaven in the seam of a cloud.
The man took another wife who had
two daughters, pretty enough
but with hearts like blackjacks.
Cinderella was their maid.
She slept on the sooty hearth each night
and walked around looking like Al Jolson.
Her father brought presents home from town,
jewels and gowns for the other women
but the twig of a tree for Cinderella.
She planted that twig on her mother's grave
and it grew to a tree where a white dove sat.
Whenever she wished for anything the dove
would drop it like an egg upon the ground.
The bird is important, my dears, so heed him.

Next came the ball, as you all know.
It was a marriage market.
The prince was looking for a wife.
All but Cinderella were preparing
and gussying up for the big event.

Cinderella begged to go too.
Her stepmother threw a dish of lentils
into the cinders and said: Pick them
up in an hour and you shall go.
The white dove brought all his friends;
all the warm wings of the fatherland came,
and picked up the lentils in a jiffy.
No, Cinderella, said the stepmother,
you have no clothes and cannot dance.
That's the way with stepmothers.

Cinderella went to the tree at the grave
and cried forth like a gospel singer:
Mama! Mama! My turtledove,
send me to the prince's ball!
The bird dropped down a golden dress
and delicate little gold slippers.
Rather a large package for a simple bird.
So she went. Which is no surprise.
Her stepmother and sisters didn't
recognize her without her cinder face
and the prince took her hand on the spot
and danced with no other the whole day.

As nightfall came she thought she'd better
get home. The prince walked her home
and she disappeared into the pigeon house
and although the prince took an axe and broke
it open she was gone. Back to her cinders.
These events repeated themselves for three days.
However on the third day the prince
covered the palace steps with cobbler's wax
and Cinderella's gold shoe stuck upon it.
Now he would find whom the shoe fit
and find his strange dancing girl for keeps.
He went to their house and the two sisters
were delighted because they had lovely feet.
The eldest went into a room to try the slipper on
but her big toe got in the way so she simply
sliced it off and put on the slipper.
The prince rode away with her until the white dove
told him to look at the blood pouring forth.
That is the way with amputations.
They don't just heal up like a wish.

The other sister cut off her heel
but the blood told as blood will.

The prince was getting tired.
He began to feel like a shoe salesman.
But he gave it one last try.
This time Cinderella fit into the shoe
like a love letter into its envelope.

At the wedding ceremony
the two sisters came to curry favor
and the white dove pecked their eyes out.
Two hollow spots were left
like soup spoons.

Cinderella and the prince
lived, they say, happily ever after,
like two dolls in a museum case
never bothered by diapers or dust,
never arguing over the timing of an egg,
never telling the same story twice,
never getting a middle-age spread,
their darling smiles pasted on for eternity.
Regular Bobbsey Twins.
That story.

◆ Is the narrator's body in the same world as the characters' bodies?
Did your audience see that?

*Now listen to another contemporary Cinderella tell you what happens after
"happily ever after." In Mona van Duyn's "Cinderella's Story" we hear another perspective on the ever-so-familiar details. Here, though, not all of the
happiness keeps on rewarding, and in the final lines Cinderella begins a
poignant quest of her own. This poem and Anne Sexton's display much of the
richness intertextuality affords.*

 ## Cinderella's Story

MONA VAN DUYN

To tell you the truth, the shoe pinched.
I had no way of knowing, you see,
that I was the girl he'd dreamed of.
Imagination had always consoled me,
but I'd tried to use it with care.
My sisters, I'd always thought, were the family

romantics, expecting nice clothes to do the trick
instead of the beholder's transforming eye.
All that dancing I would have to have done,
if it *was* me, had made my feet swollen.
But I didn't know I'd been dancing, I thought him a dreamer.
He had everything—looks, loneliness,
the belief that comforting and love could cure
even an advanced neurosis.
I didn't know whether or not
he was deluded, but I was sure
he was brave. I wanted to have worn the slipper.

And that's all there was to the first transformation,
something that happened so fast I nearly lost it
with one disclaiming murmur, but something
that did happen, that he made me believe.

None of my skills but love was the slightest use
to my husband. Others did well at keeping
the home fires damped or hot.
And so I began to learn the sleeping
senses. I learned wholly to love
the man in the prince, what didn't dance:
bad breath in the morning, sexual clumsiness,
a childlike willingness to let the old queen
dominate. That was easy. And I read a lot.
Snarled in ideas, heading for the unseen,
I heard the wise men snicker when I spoke.
I learned that I had some beauty and, wearing
one gown or another for my husband's sake,
I learned of its very real enhancement.
That was a little harder. I had a ball
before I learned to use what beauty I had
with kindness and honor. That was hardest of all.
Our son was born, and I went to the child
through a clutter of nursemaids to tell him
how it feels to be poor. I started to grow old.
My husband saw everything and was grateful.
Thickening a bit at the waist, he firmed
and stayed, always, faithful.

And that was the second transformation,
slow and solid.
We were happy together.

Everything comes in three's, they say,
and I'm stuck in the third transformation,
flopping like a fish who's out of the life-saving
everyday water. I starve now for a ration
of dreams, I've never learned to live
without dreams. All through the filth and anger
of childhood I ate them like a calming sugar,
my sweet secret. I move through the palace,
gripping its ghostly furniture
till my fingers ache. I guess
that it is real, that I am living,
but what is there left to dream of?
I dream, day and night, of giving.

Prince, soon to be king,
we've made all our lovely exchanges
and my years as your princess are ending.
Couldn't there be, for me,

just one more fairytale?
More fiercely than the silliest clubwoman
in the kingdom, I try to hold onto my looks
because I dream that there was someone
warted, once upon a time,
waiting a kiss to tell him he too
could be beloved. My frog,
my frog, where shall I find you?

- ◆ How did you demonstrate Cinderella's recollections? How did
  your audience see her preparing to reveal her dream?

The long suspended sentence that makes up this poem must be carefully sustained without allowing the variety to break the build. Notice how skillfully the one-line stanzas are used as fulcrum and climax. The poem is full of energy and empathy, especially after the fulcrum. Remember what we have said about poets breaking their lines where they want to achieve subtle effects. Allow Cruz his privilege.

Today Is a Day of Great Joy

VICTOR HERNANDEZ CRUZ

when they stop poems
in the mail & clap
their hands & dance to
them
when women become pregnant
by the side of poems
the strongest sounds making
the river go along

it is a great day

as poems fall down to
movie crowds in restaurants
in bars

when poems start to
knock down walls to
choke politicians
when poems scream &
begin to break the air

that is the time of
true poets that is
the time of greatness

a true poet aiming
poems & watching things
fall to the ground

it is a great day.

◆ How vivid was your persona's desire?

◆ How poignant are the repeated lines?

The single long sentence of the first two stanzas makes the background of the persona remarkably clear. Make full use of the change of style at the fulcrum. Be meticulous about the punctuation and line lengths. Don't slight the faint suggestions of rhyme. Keep the repetitions well within the unity of each stanza as they build to the final single word. Don't overlook the change from "your" to "our" in the last stanza. Although the poem requires superb aesthetic control, it rewards you accordingly.

FROM Horses Make a Landscape Look More Beautiful

ALICE WALKER

for two who
slipped away
almost
entirely:
my "part" Cherokee
great-grandmother
Tallulah
(Grandmama Lula)
on my mother's side
about whom
only one
agreed-upon
thing
is known:
her hair was so long
she could sit on it;

and my white (Anglo-Irish?)
great-great-grandfather
on my father's side;
nameless
(Walker, perhaps?),

whose only remembered act
is that he raped
a child:
my great-great-grandmother,
who bore his son,
my great-grandfather,
when she was eleven.

Rest in peace.
The meaning of your lives
is still
unfolding.

Rest in peace.
In me
the meaning of your lives
is still
unfolding.

Rest in peace, in me.
The meaning of your lives
is still
unfolding.

Rest. In me
the meaning of your lives
is still
unfolding.

Rest. In Peace
in me
the meaning
of our lives
is still
unfolding.

Rest.

- ◆ How did you chart the prayer's progress for your audience?

Bibliography

Dictionaries and Handbooks for the Student

Hirsch, Edward. *How to Read a Poem and Fall in Love with Poetry.* New
York: Harcourt Brace, 1999.

A moving examination of what poetry is and why it matters by a teaching poet committed to sharing his vocation.

Myers, Jack, and Michael Sims. *The Longman Dictionary of Poetic Terms.* New York: Longman, 1989.
A useful source for definitions of structural terms.

Packard, William. *The Poet's Dictionary: A Handbook of Prosody and Poetic Devices.* New York: Harper and Row, 1989.
A handy collection of definitions and examples of poetic structure, devices, and forms.

Poets on Poetry

Heaney, Seamus. *The Redress of Poetry.* New York: Farrar, Straus and Giroux, 1997.
These powerfully written essays on poetry and the role of the poet from a Nobel Prize winner are inspiring and remind us why poetry matters.

Oliver, Mary. *A Poetry Handbook.* New York: Harcourt Brace, 1995.
A congenial and accessible description of poetry's formal components coupled with the poet-author's passion for language and the heart.

Pinsky, Robert. *The Sounds of Poetry: A Brief Guide.* New York: Farrar, Straus & Giroux, 1998.
A poet laureate avoids the technical to celebrate the acoustic artifact of several splendid poems, often in a syllable-by-syllable discussion of their incarnation in sound.

Yeats, William Butler. "Speaking to the Psaltery," "The Theatre," "Modern Poetry," "A General Introduction for My Work," and "An Introduction for My Plays." In *Essays and Introductions.* New York: Macmillan, 1961.
These essays put forth an argument for the importance of reading verse aloud.

Classic Statements on the Study of Poetry

Brooks, Cleanth. *The Well-Wrought Urn.* New York: Harcourt, Brace, and World, 1947.
This classic of poetic criticism argues for poetry as dramatic discourse, in an organic relationship of art and meaning.

Ciardi, John. *How Does a Poem Mean?* Boston: Houghton Mifflin, 1959.
A famous account of the construction of meaning in the reading of poetry; an excellent source book for students and teachers.

Geiger, Don. *The Dramatic Impulse in Modern Poetics.* Baton Rouge: Louisiana State University Press, 1967.
An important text for the oral interpretation of poetry, with special attention to the problem of persona.

Zumthor, Paul. *Oral Poetry: An Introduction.* Translated by Kathryn Murphy-Judy. Minneapolis: University of Minnesota Press, 1990.
The introduction contains a useful theoretical discussion on voice and orality.

PART FIVE

Group
Performance

You must habit yourself to the dazzle of the light and of every moment in your life.

Long have you timidly waded holding a plank by the shore
Now I will you to be a bold swimmer
To jump off in the midst of the sea, rise again, nod to me,
shout, and laughingly dash with your hair.

Walt Whitman
"Song of Myself"

CHAPTER ELEVEN

Group Performance of Literature

Many of the most compelling innovations in performance today arise from the polyvocality that groups discover and evoke in texts.

EXPECT THIS!

Your voice and body are carefully trained. You have performed narration, drama, and poetry—and watched others do the same. Now, you want to collaborate. This chapter explores what happens when solo performers work together. By the end of the chapter, you should be able to:

- List several forms of group performance.
- Report the foundations of group performance.
- Define Readers Theater.
- Describe how Readers Theater features a given text.
- Define Chamber Theater.
- Prepare a Chamber Theater script that dramatizes the point of view of narrative fiction and features the narrator.
- Suggest several possible sources for compiled scripts.
- Select literary, nonliterary, video, and audio "texts" for a compiled script exploring a topic of your choice.
- Cite the challenges and rewards presented by the group performance of concrete poetry and film scripts.
- Understand why directing the group performance of literature requires analysis, patience, planning, and commitment.

Selections Discussed in This Chapter

In explaining some topics, we mention texts that are reprinted either within the chapter itself or at the end of a chapter. Use the guide below for quick reference to acquaint yourself with selections you may not fully recall.

Author	Title	Location
Bernard Malamud	"The Prison"	Chapter 6, page 254
Edward Albee	from *Who's Afraid of Virginia Woolf?*	Chapter 7, page 300
Nathanael West	from *Miss Lonelyhearts*	Chapter 11, page 479
Bertolt Brecht	from *The Caucasian Chalk Circle, Section III*	Chapter 11, page 500
Roger McGough	"40–Love"	Chapter 11, page 503
Mary Ellen Solt	"Forsythia"	Chapter 11, page 504
Reinhard Döhl	"Apfel"	Chapter 11, page 505
David Ray	"Unforgiven"	Chapter 11, page 510
Penelope Gilliatt	from *Sunday Bloody Sunday*	Chapter 11, page 514

CLEARLY, THUS FAR WE HAVE BEEN INTERESTED PRIMARILY IN the solo interpreter. In fact, solo and group performers share common ground, and many of the most compelling innovations in performance today arise from the polyvocality that groups discover and evoke in texts. Obviously, seven performers probing the same work can embody rich contradictions and evoke intriguing intertextualities in ways the solo performer cannot. Groups discover texts for performance in everyday conversations, in ethnographic documents, in oral histories, in texts charged with social change, and in contemporary visions of traditional works. Today, happily, groups successfully tackle everything from a rap version of the *Iliad,* to a compilation of the literature and discourse of the wits of the Algonquin roundtable, to the literature and music of AIDS, to *The Notebooks of Leonardo da Vinci.*

Some form of the group performance of literature has existed since the rhapsodists read plays in relays in ancient Greece. In the past forty years—and particularly in the last two decades—this area of oral interpretation has flourished. Group performance now appears under many different billings. Some more traditional programs offer *Readers Theater* as a generic name for any group performance. *Chamber Theater* refers most often to the staging of any kind of narrative text. *Compiled scripts* are performances that draw their material from the broadest possible range of sources and frequently explore a specific theme, perspective, or relationship among the texts chosen. The phrase *group performance* suffices to describe any event that features more than one performer exploring the ranges of meaning in any given text or texts.

Whatever the name, these innovations in oral interpretation profit from a close collaboration with other performance media—especially contemporary theater. Plays today—as well as films, videos, performance art, music, and the visual arts—freely range through several levels of consciousness. Time stops, advances, recedes. Illusions are frankly admitted, encouraging viewers to remember they are watching a performance. A single character can be performed by several performers, each of whom may embody complementary or contradictory facets of the character. Or one performer may take on several related characters with little outward differentiation. Minimal staging permits easy shifts in scene. The enormous resources of the media—film, audio, video, lighting—can be exploited to illuminate the intricate structure of a single text or the complex interrelationships of several texts.

Such crossbreeding has obliterated whatever line formerly separated "theater performances" and "interp performances" and has encouraged many of the innovative developments that make group performance so attractive. Just as theater events began to feature interpretation's experimental techniques, interpreters discovered that groups could solve literary challenges with theatrical techniques.

The foundations remain the same: a group's analysis and rehearsal begin with, and return to, the embodying of the text. A group performance requires the same kind of technical facility as that needed by an individual performance. The interpreter's respect for the audience's proper function in the creation of the work never changes.

There are dangers, as well: the urge to provide a "good show" might lead interpreters to sacrifice the uncomfortable intricacies of a text. A director/compiler/adapter, eager to prevent the audience from becoming merely complacent observers, might alienate both audience *and* text. Like any other kind of performance we value, group performance should present the text (or texts) in such a manner—through the bodies and voices of performers (and the media)—that the audience can join the ensemble to create an intellectual, emotional, and aesthetic entirety.

Readers Theater

Readers Theater is a performance by a group of interpreters seeking to explore, to embody, and—in special ways—to *feature* a given text. This convention of performance, with a long history rooted in the presentational modes of the ancient Greeks, is used today to explore drama, fiction, nonfiction, and poetry.

There is no recipe for a Readers Theater production any more than there is a recipe for solo performance. Readers Theater—like any group performance of literature—has developed precisely because people have tried different ways to achieve the same goal. Contemporary notions about Readers Theater are flexible and accommodating, and the future for Readers Theater is particularly exciting.

Readers Theater does have certain characteristics and criteria. One of the most obvious conventions of the Greek theater, for example, figures prominently in most Readers Theater: the *presentational,* rather than the representational, reality of the performance. For the Greeks, the actor symbolized the actions of the gods and the great mortals. During the ritual of the performance, the audience believed in the *reenactment* of the story or play, rather than in its immediate illusion of reality. No Greek actually endured the travails of Oedipus; Medea was not meant to be like the woman next door. Telling their stories became the central focus. How beautifully did the dance embody the emotional dilemma of those colossal characters? How richly did the cadences of the verse (with the delicate harmonies of the music) suggest the experiences of those great beings?

If you attend a play about the last days of Abraham Lincoln, your major concern would not be to discover how things turn out. Rather, you would be interested in the character of the man himself. You would, perhaps, admire his efforts, regret his follies, pity his mistakes, understand his limitations, but in the end your attention would focus on *how the story is told* rather than on whether he chooses to attend the theater one night in April 1865. Just as you might be curious about the way a playwright would tell the story of Lincoln, the Greeks were interested in how, say, that young playwright Euripides handled a tale previously told by Aeschylus.

Differences from Familiar Theatrical Conventions

This interest in presentation, in the manner of the telling and hence in the text itself, still primarily influences contemporary experiments in Readers Theater. For one thing, there is no "fourth wall," or illusion of eavesdropping, in Readers Theater. The action is all turned outward because the performers frankly admit that the audience has come to see and hear a text. The performing space is a playing space from which you project the text, not unlike the space you silently describe for yourself when you begin a solo performance.

In the Greek theater this space was called the *orkastra* and was often occupied by the chorus, since they were the ones who interpreted and reflected on the action by commenting about it to the audience. Because the Greek theaters were large and had no sound systems, the actors wore masks with enormous features that not only revealed to even the most distant spectators the inner states of the characters but also projected their voices.

Shakespeare, too, used the stage as a projection space. Many of his characters talk in soliloquy directly to the playgoers, thus allowing them to participate in the characters' inner workings and motivations. Hamlet tells the audience members what he's thinking and, quite openly in front of them, upbraids himself for what he sees as his cowardice.

These presentational conventions have also been used by many modern dramatists, including Sam Shepard and Bertolt Brecht. (See the Singer's interpretation of the internal life of Grusha and Simon in Brecht's *The Caucasian Chalk Circle* at the end of this chapter.) The Readers Theater would open up and project frankly out front a scene that a traditional theatrical convention might play as closed or onstage. When two characters (for example, George and Martha in Edward Albee's *Who's Afraid of Virginia Woolf?*—Chapter 7) talk to each other, traditional staging allows them to play to and with one another. The actor playing George looks directly at the actress playing Martha, perhaps even touching her arm when he delivers her drink. The audience observes them. A line mapping their tension is perpendicular to the sight lines of the audience. George moves toward Martha with a drink, facing her and expecting her to reach for the drink. Compare this with a Readers Theater presentation of the same scene, in which the interpreters performing George and Martha stand several feet apart and "look at" each other out front—that is, each sees the other directly in front, above, and slightly beyond the audience, as shown opposite.

When George approaches Martha, he steps directly toward the audience. Martha sees him approaching as if he were entering from the audience and would reach out there for the drink he carries. Thus, audience members examine the play's multiple levels by sitting literally in the middle of the activity, participating intimately in what is going on between the characters. Recall our earlier analogy to film: the audience sits where a camera would be placed. Furthermore, this form reveals secrets that a staged performance can conceal. When George approaches Martha with the drink, he enables her inebriation, perpetuating her way of life. As she reaches for this sustenance, we sit in center of their partnership, seeing how codependence perpetuated "this sewer of a marriage." The image in front of us—Martha reaching out for help, George offering the alcoholic solution—is an icon of the play itself, foreshadowing what will happen and symbolizing what moves George and Martha. Readers Theater features this element of the text by frankly placing it out front.

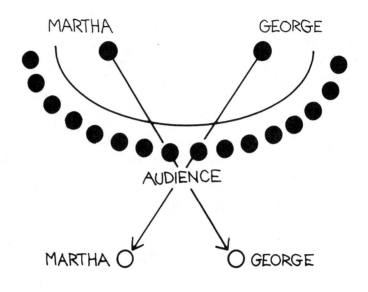

Technical Cautions

Some technical problems arise in this form of performance. George and Martha cannot be so close together on stage that it seems odd for them not to address each other. They cannot enter the same physical relationship that they would display in a staged production, nor can they relate to a background of props and scenery as they might in a staged production. The formality of the convention prohibits such kinds of behavior, even as it allows other kinds. George advances *forward* rather than sideways. If he and Martha were close together, they might legitimately be expected to turn and talk to each other. It's really not so uncommon for us in real life. Think about the last time you had your hair cut. When the barber or stylist asked you about length and shaping, you probably looked at yourself in the mirror, responding to the reflected questioner, who answered your questions by looking at your *reflection*, not at you.

The scene should be projected from a *playing space* or a *performance area* neutral enough to suggest a locale that belongs neither to the audience nor to the characters. For us to accept the convention, the angles of vision need to *intersect*. If George and Martha were to see one another like this

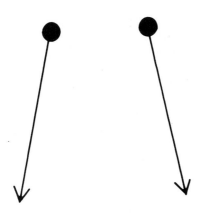

they would not appear to be in the same scene; their angle of vision would not intersect. Moreover, this point of intersection must occur *within the audience,* for there the action clashes. If the intersection of each angle were to occur onstage, as in

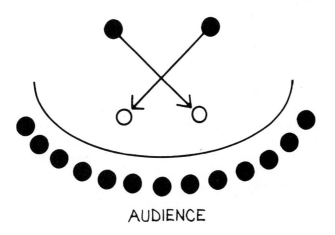

AUDIENCE

it would seem extremely odd for the performers not to turn toward one another and play the scene in that onstage space they both obviously occupy.

For the convention to be accepted, the tension of each character reaching for the other must pierce the "wall" that separates audience from character. Only then can the audience participate in the internal processes of each of the characters.

Readers Theater enables a selection of literature to be presented so that performers—and the audience—share new insights into the text.

Dramatic texts, in particular, richly reward this presentational approach because it so starkly features the interaction of characters. Often two solo interpreters undertake *duo drama* assignments with precisely the challenges of a Readers Theater production. Unless you wish to complete a two-person acting exercise (which can, of course, be useful), work seriously to open up the presentational components of the play you explore. To do this, keep in touch with the literature responsively. In opening up the work, you, too, must remain open.

Chamber Theater

Chamber Theater is a rewarding way for a group to perform narration. Robert Breen, the scholar who was most responsible for the innovation and development of Chamber Theater, defined it as "a technique for dramatizing the point of view of narrative fiction." Remember that in narrative fiction, point of view manifests the relationships between the narrator and the characters and events of the story. Simply discovering the point of view does not solve all performance problems (for either a solo interpreter or a group). It does provide the focus for a group wishing to demonstrate to an audience how a *specific* tale is related by a *specific* narrator. Moreover, Chamber Theater embodies in concrete form the relationships between *that* narrator and *those* characters in *that* setting. Because the action of the tale unfolds with the immediacy of drama, the audience can see and hear the impact of the events on the characters. And because the narrator is retained, the governing central intelligence of the fiction conditions the audience's view of the world. Audience members listen to and watch exactly what—and *only* what—the narrator wants them to hear and see at the same time that they see and hear what the performers embody.

A Chamber Theater production of a novel or a story may boast all of the scenographic resources of a staged production of a play. Costumed performers appear without scripts, may represent one or several characters at one time, and may keep the action onstage rather than placing the action out front, as described above. In all cases, narrators are present and highly visible onstage, *at the center of the action*. Narrators are *not* on the periphery watching the activity, unless they have momentarily stepped aside to let a scene between the characters play uninterrupted. Staged narrators participate in the action, organizing and unifying it, just as they do in the novel. The heart of Chamber Theater remains a careful and intelligent demonstration of the narrator. The narrator governs the selectivity of the story by directing the audience's attention and by conditioning the listeners' responses to the characters and the action.

A Sample Chamber Theater Script

Read the following scene from Nathanael West's *Miss Lonelyhearts*, a novel about a man in his middle thirties who is the author of an advice column in the New York *Post-Dispatch*. He is haunted by his troubled correspondents and plagued by moral and religious doubts. Miss Lonelyhearts (he is never given any other name in the novel) takes Mary Shrike, the wife of his editor, out for dinner. Although they share considerable intimacy, they are not having an affair.

> She came out of the closet wearing a black lace slip and began to fix her hair in front of the dressing table. Miss Lonelyhearts bent down to kiss the back of her neck.
>
> "Now, now," she said, acting kittenish, "you'll muss me."
>
> He took a drink from the whiskey bottle, then made her a highball. When he brought it to her, she gave him a kiss, a little peck of reward.
>
> "Where'll we eat?" she asked. "Let's go where we can dance. I want to be gay."
>
> They took a cab to a place called El Gaucho. When they entered, the orchestra was playing a Cuban rhumba. A waiter dressed as a South-American cowboy led them to a table. Mary immediately went Spanish and her movements became languorous and full of abandon.
>
> But the romantic atmosphere only heightened his feeling of icy fatness. He tried to fight it by telling himself that it was childish. What had happened to his great understanding heart? Guitars, bright shawls, exotic foods, outlandish costumes—all these things were part of the business of dreams. He had learned not to laugh at the advertisements offering to teach writing, cartooning, engineering, to add inches to the biceps and to develop the bust. He should therefore realize that the people who came to El Gaucho were the same as those who wanted to write and live the life of an artist, wanted to be an engineer and wear leather puttees, wanted to develop a grip that would impress the boss, wanted to cushion Raoul's head on their swollen breasts. They were the same people as those who wrote to Miss Lonelyhearts for help.
>
> But his irritation was too profound for him to soothe it in this way. For the time being, dreams left him cold, no matter how humble they were.
>
> "I like this place," Mary said. "It's a little fakey, I know, but it's gay and I so want to be gay."
>
> She thanked him by offering herself in a series of formal, impersonal gestures. She was wearing a tight, shiny dress that was like glass-covered steel and there was something cleanly mechanical in her pantomime.
>
> "Why do you want to be gay?"
>
> "Every one wants to be gay—unless they're sick."
>
> Was he sick? In a great cold wave, the readers of his column crashed over the music, over the bright shawls and picturesque waiters, over her shining body. To save himself, he asked to see the medal. Like a little girl helping an old man to cross the street, she leaned over for him to look into

the neck of her dress. But before he had a chance to see anything, a waiter came up to the table.

"The way to be gay is to make other people gay," Miss Lonelyhearts said. "Sleep with me and I'll be one gay dog."

The defeat in his voice made it easy for her to ignore his request and her mind sagged with his: "I've had a tough time," she said. "From the beginning, I've had a tough time. When I was a child, I saw my mother die. She had cancer of the breast and the pain was terrible. She died leaning over a table."

"Sleep with me," he said.

"No, let's dance."

"I don't want to. Tell me about your mother."

"She died leaning over a table. The pain was so terrible that she climbed out of bed to die."

Mary leaned over to show how her mother had died and he made another attempt to see the medal. He saw that there was a runner on it, but was unable to read the inscription.

"My father was very cruel to her," she continued. "He was a portrait painter, a man of genius, but . . ."

He stopped listening and tried to bring his great understanding heart into action again. Parents are also part of the business of dreams. My father was a Russian prince, my father was a Piute Indian chief, my father was an Australian sheep baron, my father lost all his money in Wall Street, my father was a portrait painter. People like Mary were unable to do without such tales. They told them because they wanted to talk about something besides clothing or business or the movies, because they wanted to talk about something poetic.

When she had finished her story, he said, "You poor kid," and leaned over for another look at the medal. She bent to help him and pulled out the neck of her dress with her fingers. This time he was able to read the inscription: "Awarded by the Boston Latin School for first place in the 100 yd. dash."

It was a small victory, yet it greatly increased his fatigue and he was glad when she suggested leaving.

The first "character" to consider is the narrator, who governs all our responses to Miss Lonelyhearts, the hero of the story. The language of *Miss Lonelyhearts* is often as vivid and brutal as are its characters. The narrator does not spare us from suffering or unpleasantness. His metaphors throughout the novel are blunt, nightmarish, and disturbing, even though they are based on the everyday objects that swarm about the characters. Miss Lonelyhearts receives letters that are "stamped from the dough of suffering with a heart-shaped cookie knife." We see the pathetic, funny, and painfully mundane worlds their writers inhabit. The air in a little park smells "as though it had been artificially heated," and we detect the rancid oil and dense closeness of cheap rooms. The shadow of a lamppost pierced him "like a spear," and "the gray sky looked as if it had been rubbed with a soiled eraser." The narrator exposes how ineffectual Miss Lonelyhearts is in relieving the pain suffered by the people who expect aid from him. Their expectations smudge even the daylight.

So, at the center of this novel is a narrator who speaks strong and vivid poetry. To eliminate such a person from the drama and let only the characters occupy the stage would render only part of the work. The narrator points us carefully into the interior life of Miss Lonelyhearts himself; through the narrator we are privy to the tortured mind and spirit that seek to counsel the troubled world.

Let's get back to the scene itself: "She came out of the closet wearing a black lace slip and began to fix her hair in front of the dressing table." This stage direction describes simply and directly what Mary Shrike is doing, yet the description itself indicates a deliberate move on her part. She is wearing *only* a slip. Why would a woman enter like that? Let us assign the line to the narrator. Try saying that line intending to point up that detail. Perhaps the narrator will even speak to *both* the audience and Miss Lonelyhearts, who needs to know that he is deliberately being tempted by Mary Shrike's display. Perhaps Miss Lonelyhearts does not know quite how to respond. He is, in a sense, impotent and is caught over and over again in the web of other people's problems. Since Miss Lonelyhearts is unsure, let the narrator tell him what to do: the line "Miss Lonelyhearts bent down to kiss the back of her neck" is spoken by the narrator directly to Miss Lonelyhearts so that he knows what to do. The audience will also not miss the closeness of his relationship with Mary.

"Now, now . . . you'll muss me" is obviously Mary's response to the kiss. She is, as you recall, at her dressing table, preening and admiring herself. Since "acting kittenish" is a conscious decision by Mary, as well as another effort to tantalize Miss Lonelyhearts, Mary could take the entire line: " 'Now, now,' she said, acting kittenish, 'you'll muss me.' " Thus, she explores two levels in the performance. Mary is in the scene, reacting and responding on the surface in the public way Miss Lonelyhearts sees. Mary also is inside watching herself, describing her own motivation. The next short paragraph gives another simple stage direction. There might be some value, though, in providing for the audience both the action that is performed by the characters and the narrator's description of it. "When he brought it to her, she gave him a kiss, a little peck of reward." But isn't "a little peck of reward" Miss Lonelyheart's attitude toward the kiss? If we allow him to say so, we can see the part of him that corresponds to the second, interior side of Mary. In revealing these various aspects, the director and adapter of a Chamber Theater production can amplify and expand on the numerous levels of the text, clarifying the author's artistry.

There are further possibilities in the exchanges between Mary and Miss Lonelyhearts. Because scenes in the novel shift fluently from speakeasy to bedroom, from Shrike's apartment to the office or to the little park, even from wakefulness to sleep, the staging requires a mobility that realistic or detailed scenography would prohibit. The space of the novel itself is more psychological than physical in any case. Miss Lonelyhearts moves about his world as through a void, caught here or there by the disturbing troubles of his correspondents. Only a few set pieces and neutral properties are needed to demonstrate the emptiness of Miss Lonelyhearts's world.

Such flexibility itself suggests even further tantalizing possibilities. Throughout the novel we read the letters—full texts of pleas from "Sick-of-it-all" or "Desperate" or "Harold S." or "Broad Shoulders"—but Miss Lonelyhearts actually meets only one of the correspondents during the story. Still, because he doesn't have real bodies for them, his tortured consciousness creates bodies for them out of the real people he encounters every day. He *sees* them everywhere; they have a palpable reality for him. How can he be sure that the woman he passes on the street is not the woman who left her husband because he had contracted tuberculosis and she couldn't stand the smell of death?

Marvelously, Chamber Theater can create these ghosts. The interpreter playing Miss Lonelyhearts confronts *living* letters—real people who pursue him and invade his consciousness at strategic points throughout the action. One may haunt him during the scene with Mary Shrike. The set is minimal, so why not let "Sick-of-it-all" or "Disillusioned-with-Tubercular-Husband" hold Mary's mirror for her? And do you even need an actual glass? Try using just the empty oval mirror frame, so that when Miss Lonelyhearts crosses the room to hand Mary her drink, as he bends over to kiss her neck, he sees into the "mirror," and there, where there ought to be the face of Mary Shrike, he sees the haunting face of one of the correspondents he cannot escape. Staring at that face and thinking, "Will I never be free?" he could hear Mary Shrike's words—echoed by the face in the glass—"Where'll we eat? Let's go where we can dance. I want to be gay."

The novel has begun to become as immediate as a play. Of course, the linear perception of the novel is not lost because the narrator sustains the importance of the progress through the fiction; but in Chamber Theater we see both the question and the answer at the same time. Miss Lonelyhearts is caught vividly between the forces that will destroy him: the decadence and emptiness of Mary Shrike and her world and the pain and privation of the world of "Sick-of-it-all." What an irony it is for Miss Lonelyhearts to seek escape in Mary Shrike's mirror, only to find there the face of the very specter he most wants to avoid!

After Mary says, "I want to be gay," the action speeds up and, as if in a film, we jump to the cab and then to the entrance of El Gaucho. Such a rapid transition requires the stage to be as flexible and dynamic as the screen. There is no scenery to move around, happily. The narrator can cross-fade or dissolve a scene by saying a few words, or by merely walking in front of it. Remember: the narrator controls time. Have the narrator cross down toward the audience, summarizing with the line, "They took a cab to a place called El Gaucho." Mary and Miss Lonelyhearts need do no more than get up and turn arm-in-arm to face what has now become the entrance to the restaurant. If the narrator slips a white towel over an arm and prepares to function as one of the minor service characters, Miss Lonelyhearts himself can observe, after he hears the music, "When they entered, the orchestra was playing a Cuban rhumba." Then the narrator could lead the two characters around the stage and back to the seats at the center, saying, "A waiter dressed as a South-American cowboy led them to a table." Mary, caught up in the atmosphere and again conscious of the effect of her actions, could say, "Mary immediately went Spanish and her movements became languorous and full of abandon."

Mary's narrative comment, spoken about herself, might sound awkward to a beginning performer. Remember that all of the performers on the stage are telling and showing the story to the audience. A slight distancing effect—much like the one created in the Epic Theater of Brecht or in the Japanese Nōh drama—is created when characters are allowed to perceive themselves as participants in a scene. This remove can have aesthetic value as well: it may bring us even closer to the characters, since it reminds us that they lead only fictional lives. And such third-person talk is really not so foreign to everyday lives. Perhaps you have heard a woman cautioning her child, "Mommy doesn't want her little girl to get too near the hot stove."

As Mary plunges into the ambience of El Gaucho, Miss Lonelyhearts becomes troubled and pulls into himself. Although this internalization would be hidden from an audience at a play, the narrator (who has dropped the waiter persona), privy to the workings of Miss Lonelyhearts's heart, reports what an audience needs to know: "But the romantic atmosphere only heightened his feeling of icy fatness." It would be ludicrous to stage this moment with the narrator and characters far apart physically. The closer they are to each other temperamentally, the closer their placement on the stage should be. Together they will share in the same experience. In this way too you can achieve onstage another performance analogue of Nathaniel West's fiction.

Have the narrator speak the line "But the romantic . . . fatness" directly to Miss Lonelyhearts, who, in turn, can respond directly to the narrator with, "He tried to fight it by telling himself that it was childish." This interchange is a good opportunity for Miss Lonelyhearts to remind *himself*—as if he were the narrator, who functions throughout the novel as Miss Lonelyhearts's alter ego. The result becomes a dialogue scene. For the moment the stage becomes Miss Lonelyhearts's mind. Both performers play to each other, listening and responding to each other:

NARRATOR: What had happened to his great understanding heart?

MISS L.:   Guitars, bright shawls, exotic foods, outlandish costumes—all these things were part of the business of dreams.

NARRATOR: He had learned not to laugh at the advertisements offering to teach writing, cartooning, engineering, to add inches to the biceps and to develop the bust.

MISS L.:   He should therefore realize that the people who came to El Gaucho were the same as those who wanted to write and live the life of an artist,

NARRATOR: wanted to be an engineer and wear leather puttees,

MISS L.:   wanted to develop a grip that would impress the boss,

NARRATOR: wanted to cushion Raoul's head on their swollen breasts.

MISS L.:   They were the same people as those who wrote to Miss Lonelyhearts for help.

NARRATOR: But his irritation was too profound for him to soothe it in this way.

MISS L.:   For the time being, dreams left him cold, no matter how humble they were.

Can you see and hear how their dialogue unites them momentarily? Then, in the midst of these revelations, Mary intrudes the external world of the nightclub: "I like this place." Now try to adapt the rest of the scene. When does the narrator step in to advance the action? Is there more internal dialogue? ("Was he sick?") What happens when you get to the paragraph in which suffering voices seem to invade Miss Lonelyhearts's heart with "My father was a Russian prince," "my father was a Piute Indian chief," and so on? Can you use those other specters again?

Each of the narrative forms we examined in Chapter 6—a third-person narrator who is objective, a second-person narrator who addresses a character within the tale, or a first-person narrator who is a character in a story—has its own opportunities for demonstration. Any narration—prose or verse, fiction or nonfiction—can benefit from the scrutiny that Chamber Theater affords.

What Chamber Theater tells us about relationships in narration should not be separated from its entertainment or performance value. Like all forms of interpretation, Chamber Theater should be based on a clear understanding of the mode of presentation, a careful analysis of the text, and a high degree of artistic integrity and flexibility. Chamber Theater does not make plays out of stories. It presents fiction *as it was written,* with the narration as vividly physical as it is focal. Summary, scene, and description all perform their usual functions, and performers physically embody literary style. The transformation of the story thus becomes an endless process of discovery in which all of the skills you have learned contribute to the fullest performance of the text. And, you have the excitement of collaboration!

Group Performance of Compiled Scripts

An increasing interest in the group performance of nonfiction texts prompted experiments to combine fiction and nonfiction in full-length programs. Essays, reportage, memoirs, travel literature, diaries, oral histories, conversation, ethnographic performances, everyday rituals— all offer compelling opportunities for a group using the methods of Chamber Theater or Readers Theater. By supplementing material with slides, film, television, audiotapes, videotapes, or other media, interpreters can exploit contemporary resources to examine the various levels of life in a text.

All the techniques used in Readers Theater and Chamber Theater are flexible enough to be adapted to the performance of such compiled scripts, but the interpreter should keep several key responsibilities in mind. First, the shape of the entire program should reflect the intention of the works involved. Too often the performer can lose sight of the whole when closely engaged with each segment. Second, whatever nonliterary material is used should contribute to the entire program, rather than appear for its own sake. Film and sound effects can enrich, but the goal should be more than a slide show with words. The texts should illuminate each other, and their relationship should be clear to the audience. Third, compiled scripts should be constructed with a clear beginning, middle, and end. Their components should be cohesive, and although they may not be of the same mode or genre, they should still contribute in some apparent way to the progress of the entire program. Combining a series of smaller pieces can lead to either coalescence or diffusion—to a totality that is greater than the sum of the parts, or to simply a string of parts. The possibilities of multimedia presentations are tempting. Remember that it is better to examine a few of the levels of a text clearly and precisely than to examine many levels (or even most of the levels) muddily or incompletely.

Compiled scripts also provide abundant opportunities for performances aimed at social change. Performance can awaken awareness, focus intellectual *and* emotional attention, and engage an audience on several levels simultaneously. Moreover, group performance lends itself well to the embodiment of conflicting positions and contrasting ideas. Thus, texts chosen for performance may differ vehemently in their postures; if this is the case, so much the better. Also, an audience member unaware of some social trouble may confront it directly for the first time. Compiled scripts may encourage audience members to side with one position or another, but they ought not allow people simply to leave with their assumptions unchallenged. Finally, compiled scripts encourage performers to explore the wealth intertextuality brings to any performance event. Compiled scripts reflect not only the personae of the texts chosen for performance but the complex picture of the creator who arranges the texts for performance.

Each performance will restrict your choices and suggest new and sometimes widely different concepts. If the faithful communication of text always remains your guideline, with each selection you will begin an exciting and thoroughly uncharted experiment.

Current interest in nonfiction, journals, letters, diaries, and family and personal narratives as sources for group performance has probably resulted from the flexibility of these texts. To celebrate a particular date, such as the founding of a town or a school, a group of performers could combine audio, visual, or physical representations with selections from several area or national newspapers and magazines, thereby reporting what was happening in the rest of the world at that particular time. A group also could celebrate the variety and impact of a particular publication by presenting selections that represent the publication's characteristic quality or attitude. (Appendix A discusses a production of the *New York Times*.) Groups have commonly celebrated events or anniversaries by combining original documents, diaries, letters, and dispatches with journal accounts that have appeared in various places and relate to the commemorated event.

Such programs offer great opportunities for research, apart from the obvious searches through archives and back issues of serial publications. Consider obtaining oral histories from people who recall the events, who knew the chief agents, or who felt the events' impact directly. Don't stop with "literary" texts. Popular music, art, advertisements, and architecture all can contribute to understanding and embodying a different culture.

If you discover controversy that has faded with time, consider recalling the forces that gave rise to that early debate. It may be that contemporary perspectives on the past raise issues that partisans of the time could not have known about. Consider finding and performing the texts that embody this knowledge. The past unquestionably shapes the present, whether we are conscious of the shaping or not. One of the powers of performance is to body forth the forms of the unsensed influences, to tease out the mix of motives that typically attend any human achievement. In the process you may discover that awareness is the first step to action.

Commercial art often characterizes a time or an event; posters, handbills, advertisements, and catalogs give an excellent impression of what life was like during a particular time. If you select an event in the not-too-distant past, you can also use audio and video recordings. A production about the Chautauqua Institution in New York (see page 532), might feature the advertisements and announcements that heralded the annual opening; typical speeches and performances; photographs or sketches (published and private); songs from original presentations; and descriptions of people who used Chautauqua as a base for their national activities. Through costume, slide, film, sound, and performance, a group can evoke the earnest yet brash attempt to popularize and democratize "culture."

You could use the arsenal of performance techniques to focus action on a major social concern. If, for example, child abuse alarms your group, you could compile a script that presents the problem from a number of perspectives: victim, abuser, unaware siblings, friends who were aware but were unequipped to deal with the social and political structures that either ignored the abuse or permitted it. The texts you choose can be testimony, oral history, personal essays, political documents, video footage, and the like. (We start you on your search for material with David Ray's "Unforgiven," at the end of this chapter.)

Contemporary issues always ensure audience interest, but don't be limited to the topics of today's headlines. For example, comb the works about the American experience in Vietnam. You will find numerous powerful passages for performance in any of the several oral histories of the soldiers who served there (such as Al Santoli's *Everything We Had* or Wallace Terry's *Bloods*); in the histories of the people who made the decisions about involving American personnel (such as Stanley Karnow's *Vietnam*); in the reportage filed on the scene (such as Michael Herr's *Dispatches*); in the attitudes about U.S. involvement offered by an articulate officer (such as Philip Caputo's *A Rumor of War*); or in descriptions of the effects of the war at home (as in C. D. B. Bryan's *Friendly Fire*). Combined with video and film clips from television news reports or press conferences, with newspaper headlines and music of the period, and perhaps with clips from films that examine the experience (such as Francis Ford Coppola's *Apocalypse Now,* or *Platoon, The Deer Hunter,* or *Born on the Fourth of July*) and the testimony of the many Vietnamese who now live in America, any of these sources could be shaped by an interpreter into a stirring and powerful production. Indeed, any major historical event—the Holocaust, the civil rights struggles, or the Depression— offers countless opportunities to examine and understand. Ken Burns's monumental video exploration of the Civil War demonstrates how tellingly image and sound, word and picture can touch the reaches of our national consciousness. Terrible events, when carefully scrutinized, reveal human beings in the very acts of heroism and cowardice that are the stuff of great literature.

The most valuable tools for the director/adapter to use in this form of script composition are imagination and tact. Keep your mind open to possible inclusions. An artfully structured program that allows the greatest flexibility and achieves the maximum impact has at its center substantial literature that is worth performing. Perform the literature as fully as possible, while simultaneously suggesting what the event, time, or publication was like. Chamber Theater techniques work just as well with nonfiction narrative as they do with fiction. Bodies and voices can suggest the nonverbal and visual elements as powerfully as they do in Readers Theater or Chamber Theater productions.

Other Kinds of Literature

Many discoveries occur when a group attempts to perform materials that are not usually associated with performance, such as concrete poetry or film scripts, to name only two. Naturally, these sources should conform to the criteria for selecting performance material, but the new challenges each form creates offer experienced students new ways to understand literature.

Concrete Poetry

Concrete poetry can be defined broadly as a verbal work in which visual, tactile, or iconographic representation carries at least as much weight as any of the denotative and connotative meanings of the words. Sometimes concrete poems are printed in patterns, which themselves tell stories about the "text" of the poem; sometimes they are not reproducible as print on paper but rather appear as pictures or forms or sculpture or even, appropriately enough, castings in concrete. Once again, *form* is tangible, realizable in three dimensions.

When you perform a sonnet, you know that the poem is composed of fourteen lines of iambic pentameter that follow certain formal strictures. All of these elements are parts of the poem's *form*. Your performance corresponds to that form, insofar as your body and your voice are able. Concrete poetry asks you to present your body and voice in a form that corresponds to the form of the work. Because group performance has many more options for the creation of that form, concrete poetry allows groups to experiment with the sounds and attitudes of the work by combining voices and bodies to suggest—in three dimensions—the full size and shape of the poem. Roger McGough's "40–Love," Mary Ellen Solt's "Forsythia," and Reinhard Döhl's "Apfel" (all at the end of this chapter) are enormously challenging and a great deal of fun. Your experience thus far probably will not have prepared you for this kind of experimentation. We encourage you to stretch your understanding of performance. That stretch will permit you to perform more traditional literatures in a much broader world.

Film Scripts

Initially it would seem that performing a film script would come easily to interpreters. Film scripts are, after all, stories put on film. Interpreters perform dialogue all the time. Even a cursory study of well-written scripts, however, indicates how very different a good film is from a play, although the outward similarities of dialogue remain obvious (see the excerpt from Penelope Gilliatt's fine screenplay for *Sunday Bloody Sunday* at the end of this chapter). Rather, a better analogy can be made between fiction and film—that of a narrator and the eye of a camera. If you are particularly impressed by a script, why not perform it by casting a performer or performers as the camera and allowing an interpreter to perform all of the camera directions? The performer would operate much as a narrator would in a work of narrative fiction. Continue the analogy while the camera, in its role as eye, displays carefully to audience members what it wants them to see. Since characters in film exist only insofar as the camera sees or hears them, why not show characters as the camera does? Perhaps the camera could even assist a *character* in performing actions that an audience should see, and then, as it turns its eye to someone else, let the *performer* resume normal behavior. The tension that is created between the illusion of *what the camera shows* and *what is seen after the camera leaves* can demonstrate still another level of the tale.

Directing the Group Performance of Literature

Whatever texts and forms you choose to explore, you will face the usual limitations of time, talent, cooperation, and technical demands. The following discussion will not answer all the questions you are likely to encounter, but it can give you an idea of the kinds of problems that most often plague group performances.

A director's first responsibility is to prepare the text for performance. Allow for innovation during rehearsal, but provide the individual performers with the foundation to begin their explorations. Use the now-familiar touchstones for selecting literature.

Suppose you choose Bernard Malamud's "The Prison" (Chapter 6). Now you begin a series of questions for yourself that does not end until well after the final performance. Do you fully understand everything that is going on in the story? Read it again, and then again, to be sure. Look at other stories by Malamud. How can you cast the story with the available performers? (If yours is a group of eleven nine-year-olds, you probably can't.) Do you have enough time to prepare the story? Will you be able to suggest the atmosphere of the candy store, its inhabitants, and their lives?

Reread the story. What interests you? Do you visualize any particular images that suggest what the audience might see? Have you any vague ideas of how a specific scene or a sentence or even a phrase may sound or look to an audience? Reread the story again. Do you still want to spend all the time and effort on this work? If you are still convinced of your choice at this point, prepare a *working* script.

Next you must solve the issue of permissions. Performance outside of class—whether for public audiences or other classmates, regardless of whether an admission fee is charged—requires permission from the copyright holder. Although the work you select may be in the public domain, even older works (such as the plays of Shakespeare) exist in several different editions, each the product of an editor who is likely to hold the copyright on the work. Rather than risk any legal unpleasantness, write a letter well ahead of time to the publisher(s) of the work(s) you are presenting, stating performance dates and the nature of your production plans for each work you are using. You may wish to enclose a copy of the script you have prepared. Only when you receive the permission of the copyright holder are you legally (and ethically) free to show your work to the public. Because you have chosen Malamud's "The Prison," contact the copyright holder, Farrar, Straus and Giroux, Inc.

Since this story features a narrator who is sympathetic toward the central character, you will use the technique of Chamber Theater for your presentation. Examine the story from the perspectives of the audience and of the director, using the analytical principles we discussed in Chapters 2, 5, and 6 as well as the technical suggestions given earlier in this chapter. Many of your decisions will be adjusted or even discarded when rehearsal comes, and some things that you think ought to work stupendously will have to be changed.

What of the playing space and its configuration? At this point, you should make some firm decisions about the visual statement you expect the performance to make. Typically, this decision will be based on the amount of time and money you budget and on the degree to which crucial action, properties, and scenes must be enacted. Don't waste time, money, and effort trying to dress an army battalion in complete costumes when helmets alone might suffice. Audiences can create finer settings than any designer if given the proper clues. Slides can suggest a Boeing 747 in flight; one period chair can suggest an entire English great house library. The settings and practical stage pieces need to be available soon into the rehearsal period because the longer the performers work with them, the more confident they will appear to the audience.

Several business problems reemerge. Has the publisher responded to your request for permission? If not, write again. Programs, tickets, ushers, advertising, house management, and other similar details can quickly grow into major dilemmas if ignored. Can you count on someone reliable to assist in any of this? Enlist that person now.

You have not even begun to audition potential performers, but you have made tremendous progress toward your goal. Avoid performing and directing simultaneously, because either task is difficult enough alone. When you audition performers for your production, you will doubtless have ideas about how each of the characters should behave. You may have a specific person in mind for a particular part. Allow each auditioning performer sufficient time to make an impression but do not waste that person's—and your own—time. If there is no possible way for the seven-foot-tall basketball player to play a little girl, don't expect him or ask him to try. Generally, you should cast the strongest performer as the narrator because, as you'll recall from Chapter 6, the narrator carries the heaviest burden by being responsible for moving along the action of the story. Be sure that the performers whom you have tentatively selected look and sound appropriate together; unless you wish to achieve some comic or outlandish effect, be sure that they are able to operate as an ensemble. For many directors, casting a production is the most difficult job, but if you have done your homework, you know what you need. Take the time you need to make sure you have what you want, but make the choice as soon as you can.

Now put cast and *working* script together. See what the story does under the close pressure of this group's attention to it. Watch what happens as the performers begin to feel their bodies and their voices. Be patient, attentive, and clear-sighted. Respond to the performers with suggestions. Answer their questions frankly. A performer needs to understand the perspective of the director but also wants room to create. Don't crowd the performers with too many details too soon. They need a little freedom to get used to new ways of walking, talking, seeing, and thinking. Give them time.

Slowly the story will begin to come alive, sometimes through only a sentence or a phrase, in brief moments. Work out a rehearsal schedule that uses each performer's time economically. Does the distribution of lines exactly demonstrate the relationship between narrator and character? Serious and responsible interpreters will begin by asking questions and end by helping. In this process of creating, everyone involved comes to know the story at its fullest.

The production should be on its feet now; scripts should be disappearing at this point. Certain moments should be emerging as clear and stable, but do not allow the story to become glib or easy. Be patient. At this point in rehearsal, no performer wants (or needs) to hear, "Something's wrong with that line. Try it another way." Specify what you expect; be prepared to let the performer work on it, too.

As the performance date approaches, integrate the technical elements as soon as they are available. Sound and film cues should be rehearsed as often as possible to enable the people responsible for their operation to understand how their contribution enhances the entire presentation. Also, the performers have to know what is going on around and behind them so that they can cooperate with it. In performance, people must accommodate machines. It frequently makes sense to rehearse only the technical elements, including lights, tapes, film, and set or property changes. Be sure that every item that must be obtained or action that must be performed is clear and set and ready.

The scenography is ready; the performers are rehearsed; the script probably looks somewhat different from what you originally intended, but somehow more accurate than you imagined. Run-throughs before an audience of sympathetic friends alert performers to how an audience may respond, and where to expect a laugh. Follow each rehearsal with brief discussions with performers and technical people to solve new problems as well as to improve the production.

Each performance ought to be a learning experience for you. Take notes and discover the story under the pressure of performance with an audience. This production probably will not capture everything you know to be in the story, nor will it represent everything this group of people is capable of doing. But you have begun.

Some Concluding Cautions

The suggestions we give are not the only ways to perform these materials or direct group performances. Many difficulties attend the group performance of literature. Everything printed—and even that which is not printed—is fair game for the sensitive, serious, and tactful interpreter. If you have understood and followed the touchstones we presented at the beginning of the book, you will be able to present literature and performances that interest your audiences.

We are convinced that the students who enjoy and learn from solo performance develop richer kinds of knowledge from working in group performances. No one method of performance is always best for all kinds of literature with all casts. Literature responds in different ways to the pressure put on it by different performance techniques, yielding quite diverse and surprising discoveries under each different test. Only the potential rewards are limitless.

Admitting that a group performance differs from a solo performance suggests that the criteria for evaluating the two kinds of performance must be different. This is both true and insufficient. Group performances are made up of individual performers, and many of their responsibilities are not radically different from those we have discussed thus far. Each performer must understand the language of the text; must carefully attend to the tone, color, and imagery of the text; and must be able to be seen and heard without difficulty. In short, each performer must suggest the intellectual, emotional, and aesthetic entirety of that segment of the whole work that is his or her specific charge.

In a group performance, however, each individual executes these responsibilities in concert with other interpreters. All work under the direction of still another interpreter whose general vision and principal concern remains the work as a whole. The audience responds to the contributions of several individuals. Analyzing such performances often requires a preliminary sorting out of responsibilities and an attempt to understand, first of all, what was *conceived* before judging what was *achieved*.

Analyzing the Rehearsal and the Performance

This procedure does not greatly differ from the familiar process of analysis we have examined throughout this book—describing what was seen and heard and comparing that description with the text itself. In analyzing a group performance, however, some special questions arise that can apply to performances of narration, lyric poetry, dramatic prose, or any combination of these types. First, however, be sure that you are familiar with the specific kinds of questions that the efficient management of body and voice bring to mind (see Chapters 3 and 4). If you are unsure about problems in performing narration, consult Chapter 6; if the technique of drama still puzzles you, see Chapter 8; ways to discuss the performance of poetry appear in Chapter 10. These questions all provide the foundation on which we can build some questions for group performance.

- How did the presentational nature of the Readers Theater display the text? Was the literature the center of the production?

- Did the various interpreters vocally and physically demonstrate significantly different aspects of the literature?

- How did the individual performers contribute to the total impression of the event? Did they detract from the aesthetic entirety? How?

- What dimensions of the text(s) seemed most fully demonstrated in performance? What dimensions needed to be clearer? Give specific examples.

- How well did the individual performers project themselves into the audience? Was there sufficient opportunity for the audience to participate in the creation of the work?

- Was the overall concept both clear and responsive to the text(s) performed?

- In a Chamber Theater performance of a story (or stories), was the narrator central or incidental to the action? How was the narrative presence demonstrated in performance? What dimensions were emphasized by the group? What dimensions were ignored or lost?

- Was the distribution of dialogue lines appropriate to the characters? What was demonstrated when the characters spoke narrative lines? Were there clear and apparent reasons in the story?

- How did the scenography clarify and refine the goals of the story? What functions did members of the group serve in making these goals clear during performance?

- How did this adaptation of the story explore dimensions or levels a solo performer could not?

- In a compiled script, did the components individually and collectively advance the progress and intention of the entire program? Did each component clearly and significantly contribute to a newer, fuller understanding of the topic? Was the beginning concise? Did the development cover all the major aspects? Was the climax clearly presented? Did the conclusion permit the audience to understand the full implications of the works and the topic?

- Did nonliterary material clearly serve the texts? Were the media used effectively? How did the media used clarify those dimensions of the work(s) inaccessible to the performers?

- Was there sufficient variety in the selections and modes of performance to sustain the audience's interest? Did the components appropriately contrast tempo, rhythm, attitude, and persona?

- What did you see and hear from the group that you could not have seen and heard from an individual? How did this enrich your understanding and appreciation of the material performed? How did the vividness of collected bodies and voices demonstrate the intentions of the literature?

Obviously, you can develop further questions that respond more accurately to any specific presentation. Remember that as the number of performers increases, the number of potential problems a director can face increases geometrically. The realms of literature open to group performance almost always make the possibility of staging an attractive option. In that "almost" is all of the attraction and danger of the experience.

This chapter's expanded attention to groups may have puzzled you momentarily, but the principles we developed in the prior chapters are still essential here. This chapter asks you to broaden your horizons. As you reflect on what you have discovered, keep these ideas in mind:

- Group performance takes many forms.

- The essential skills of solo performers are all used in group performance.

- Readers Theater explores, embodies, and features a given text.

- Chamber Theater dramatizes the point of narrative fiction.

- Compiled scripts tap all forms of print, visual, and audio resources.

- Concrete poetry and film scripts respond richly to group performance.

- Directing the group performance requires planning, analysis, patience, and commitment.

- The potential rewards of group performance are limited only by the imagination of the performers.

Selections for Analysis and Oral Interpretation

From the Fifth Book of Ovid's The Metamorphoses (*as translated by the American poet Rolfe Humphries*) *comes this tale of an old couple able to stay together even after death. This classic story offers countless opportunities for group performance and intertwines insights on hospitality, relationships, justice, and the rich complexities of age. Imagine ways to make the audience see the changes undergone by the characters. Perhaps dance can clarify the enduring bond they share. Encourage your performers to trust the line length to help in balancing these long sentences.*

 FROM **The Metamorphoses**

OVID

The Story of Baucis and Philemon

An oak-tree stands

Beside a linden, in the Phrygian hills.
There's a low wall around them. I have seen
The place myself; a prince once sent me there
To land ruled by his father. Not far off
A great marsh lies, once habitable land,
But now a playground full of coots and divers.
Jupiter came here, once upon a time,
Disguised as mortal man, and Mercury,
His son, came with him, having laid aside
Both wand and wings. They tried a thousand houses,

Looking for rest; they found a thousand houses
Shut in their face. But one at last received them,
A humble cottage, thatched with straw and reeds.
A good old woman, Baucis, and her husband,
A good old man, Philemon, used to live there.
They had married young, they had grown old together
In the same cottage; they were very poor,
But faced their poverty with cheerful spirit
And made its burden light by not complaining.
It would do you little good to ask for servants
Or masters in that household, for the couple
Were all the house; both gave and followed orders.
So, when the gods came to this little cottage,
Ducking their heads to enter, the old man
Pulled out a rustic bench for them to rest on,
As Baucis spread a homespun cover for it.
And then she poked the ashes around a little,
Still warm from last night's fire, and got them going
With leaves and bark, and blew at them a little,
Without much breath to spare, and added kindling,
The wood split fine, and the dry twigs, made smaller
By breaking them over the knee, and put them under
A copper kettle, and then she took the cabbage
Her man had brought from the well-watered garden,
And stripped the outer leaves off. And Philemon
Reached up, with a forked stick, for the side of bacon,
That hung below the smoky beam, and cut it,
Saved up so long, a fair-sized chunk, and dumped it
In the boiling water. They made conversation
To keep the time from being too long, and brought
A couch with willow frame and feet, and on it
They put a sedge-grass mattress, and above it
Such drapery as they had, and did not use
Except on great occasions. Even so,
It was pretty worn, it had only cost a little
When purchased new, but it went well enough
With a willow couch. And so the gods reclined.
Baucis, her skirts tucked up, was setting the table
With trembling hands. One table-leg was wobbly;
A piece of shell fixed that. She scoured the table,
Made level now, with a handful of green mint,
Put on the olives, black or green, and cherries
Preserved in dregs of wine, endive and radish,
And cottage cheese, and eggs, turned over lightly
In the warm ash, with shells unbroken. The dishes,

Of course, were earthenware, and the mixing-bowl
For wine was the same silver, and the goblets
Were beech, the inside coated with yellow wax.
No time at all, and the warm food was ready,
And wine brought out, of no particular vintage,
And pretty soon they had to clear the table
For the second course: here there were nuts and figs
And dates and plums and apples in wide baskets—
Remember how apples smell?—and purple grapes
Fresh from the vines, and a white honeycomb
As centerpiece, and all around the table
Shone kindly faces, nothing mean or poor
Or skimpy in good will.
                                        The mixing-bowl,
As often as it was drained, kept filling up
All by itself, and the wine was never lower.
And this was strange, and scared them when they saw it.
They raised their hands and prayed, a little shaky—
"Forgive us, please, our lack of preparation,
Our meagre fare!" They had one goose, a guardian,
Watchdog, he might be called, of their estate,
And now decided they had better kill him
To make their offering better. But the goose
Was swift of wing, too swift for slow old people
To catch, and they were weary from the effort,
And could not catch the bird, who fled for refuge,
Or so it seemed, to the presence of the strangers.
"Don't kill him," said the gods, and then continued:
"We are gods, you know: this wicked neighborhood
Will pay as it deserves to; do not worry,
You will not be hurt, but leave the house, come with us,
Both of you, to the mountain-top!" Obeying,
With staff and cane, they made the long climb, slowly
And painfully, and rested, where a bowman
Could reach the top with a long shot, looked down,
Saw water everywhere, only their cottage
Standing above the flood. And while they wondered
And wept a little for their neighbors' trouble,
The house they used to live in, the poor quarters
Small for the two of them, became a temple:
Forked wooden props turned into marble columns;
The thatch grew brighter yellow; the roof was golden;
The doors were gates, most wonderfully carved;
The floor that used to be of earth was marble.

Jupiter, calm and grave, was speaking to them:
"You are good people, worthy of each other,
Good man, good wife—ask us for any favor,
And you shall have it." And they hesitated,
Asked, "Could we talk it over, just a little?"
And talked together, apart, and then Philemon
Spoke for them both: "What we would like to be
Is to be priests of yours, and guard the temple,
And since we have spent our happy years together,
May one hour take us both away; let neither
Outlive the other, that I may never see
The burial of my wife, nor she perform
That office for me." And the prayer was granted.
As long as life was given, they watched the temple,
And one day, as they stood before the portals,
Both very old, talking the old days over,
Each saw the other put forth leaves, Philemon
Watched Baucis changing, Baucis watched Philemon,
And as the foliage spread, they still had time
To say "Farewell, my dear!" and the bark closed over
Sealing their mouths. And even to this day
The peasants in that district show the stranger
The two trees close together, and the union
Of oak and linden in one. The ones who told me
The story, sober ancients, were no liars,
Why should they be? And my own eyes have seen
The garlands people bring there; I brought new ones,
Myself, and said a verse: *The gods look after*
Good people still, and cherishers are cherished.

- What did your audience see when the characters observed the flood? when the characters were transformed?

- What other texts for performance does this tale suggest?

Simon and Grusha pledged themselves to each other before Simon went to war. Then, Grusha rescues the Governor's abandoned infant, Michael, and together they begin an uncertain, event-filled life. And now, of course, Simon returns. Keep the Singer close to the two—and don't forget the river that separates them. Their poignant formality increases the tension in the scene.

FROM **The Caucasian Chalk Circle, Section III**

BERTOLT BRECHT

MICHAEL *runs away. The children run after him.* GRUSHA *laughs, following them, with her eyes. On looking back, she sees* SIMON SHASHAVA *standing on the opposite bank. He wears a shabby uniform.*

GRUSHA: Simon!

SIMON: Is that Grusha Vashnadze?

GRUSHA: Simon!

SIMON (*formally*):   A good morning to the young lady. I hope she is well.

GRUSHA (*getting up gaily and bowing low*):   A good morning to the soldier. God be thanked he has returned in good health.

SIMON: They found better fish, so they didn't eat me, said the haddock.

GRUSHA: Courage, said the kitchen boy. Good luck, said the hero.

SIMON: How are things here? Was the winter bearable? The neighbor considerate?

GRUSHA: The winter was a trifle rough, the neighbor as usual, Simon.

SIMON: May one ask if a certain person still dips her toes in the water when rinsing the linen?

GRUSHA: The answer is no. Because of the eyes in the bushes.

SIMON: The young lady is speaking of soldiers. Here stands a paymaster.

GRUSHA: A job worth twenty piasters?

SIMON: And lodgings.

GRUSHA (*with tears in her eyes*):   Behind the barracks under the date trees.

SIMON: Yes, there. A certain person has kept her eyes open.

GRUSHA: She has, Simon.

SIMON: And has not forgotten? (GRUSHA *shakes her head.*) So the door is still on its hinges as they say? (GRUSHA *looks at him in silence and shakes her head again.*) What's this? Is anything not as it should be?

GRUSHA: Simon Shashava, I can never return to Nuka. Something has happened.

SIMON: What can have happened?

GRUSHA: For one thing, I knocked an Ironshirt down.

SIMON: Grusha Vashnadze must have had her reasons for that.

GRUSHA: Simon Shashava, I am no longer called what I used to be called.

SIMON (*after a pause*):   I do not understand.

GRUSHA: When do women change their names, Simon? Let me explain. Nothing stands between us. Everything is just as it was. You must believe that.

SIMON: Nothing stands between us and yet there's something?

GRUSHA: How can I explain it so fast and with the stream between us? Couldn't you cross the bridge there?

SIMON: Maybe it's no longer necessary.

GRUSHA: It is very necessary. Come over on this side, Simon, Quick!

SIMON: Does the young lady wish to say someone has come too late?

GRUSHA *looks up at him in despair, her face streaming with tears.* SIMON *stares before him. He picks up a piece of wood and starts cutting it.*

SINGER:
So many words are said, so many left unsaid.
The soldier has come.
Where he comes from, he does not say.
Hear what he thought and did not say:
"The battle began, gray at dawn, grew bloody at noon.
The first man fell in front of me, the second behind me, the third at
    my side.
I trod on the first, left the second behind, the third was run through
    by the captain.
One of my brothers died by steel, the other by smoke.
My neck caught fire, my hands froze in my gloves, my toes in my
    socks.
I fed on aspen buds, I drank maple juice, I slept on stone, in water."

SIMON: I see a cap in the grass. Is there a little one already?

GRUSHA: There is, Simon. There's no keeping *that* from you. But please don't worry, it is not mine.

GRUSHA: When the wind once starts to blow, they say, it blows through every cranny. The wife need say no more. (GRUSHA *looks into her lap and is silent.*)

SINGER:
There was yearning but there was no waiting.
The oath is broken. Neither could say why.
Hear what she thought but did not say:
"While you fought in the battle, soldier,
The bloody battle, the bitter battle
I found a helpless infant
I had not the heart to destroy him
I had to care for a creature that was lost
I had to stoop for breadcrumbs on the floor
I had to break myself for that which was not mine
That which was other people's.
Someone must help!

For the little tree needs water
The lamb loses its way when the shepherd is asleep
And its cry is unheard!"

SIMON: Give me back the cross I gave you. Better still, throw it in the stream. (*He turns to go.*)

GRUSHA (*getting up*):   Simon Shashava, don't go away! He isn't mine! He isn't mine! (*She hears the children calling.*) What's the matter, children?

VOICES: Soldiers! And they're taking Michael away!

GRUSHA *stands aghast as two* IRONSHIRTS, *with* MICHAEL *between them, come toward her.*

ONE OF THE IRONSHIRTS: Are you Grusha? (*She nods.*) Is this your child?

GRUSHA: Yes. (SIMON *goes.*) Simon!

IRONSHIRT: We have orders, in the name of the law, to take this child, found in your custody, back to the city. It is suspected that the child is Michael Abashwili, son and heir of the late Governor Georgi Abashwili, and his wife, Natella Abashwili. Here is the document and the seal. (*They lead the* CHILD *away.*)

GRUSHA (*running after them, shouting*):   Leave him here. Please! He's mine!

◆ How did your group underline the physical separation between the characters?

◆ Hadn't your Singer better sing?

The following three poems owe at least as much to their typographic layout as to their words. They require flexible bodies and voices. In Roger McGough's poem, be sure your group physically shows the line separating the couple. Play tennis with the words.

 ## 40—Love

ROGER McGOUGH

middle	aged
couple	playing
ten	nis
when	the
game	ends
and	they
go	home
the	net
will	still
be	be
tween	them

◆ How did your group let the audience see the net and hear the rackets?

Note how the stems of the forsythia in this poem telegraph a kind of code. Can a chorus of voices suggest that sound?

 **Forsythia**

MARY ELLEN SOLT

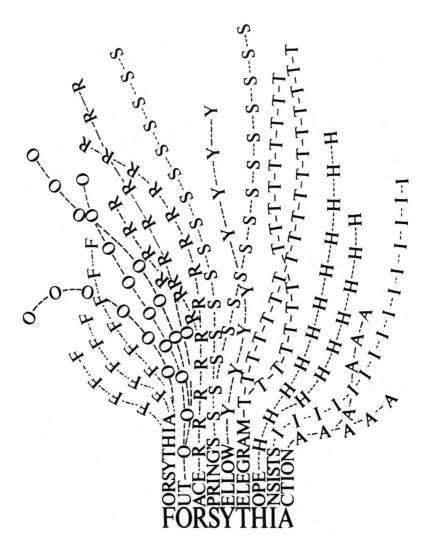

◆ How did your bodies and voices suggest the delicacy of the forsythia? How can this delicacy also "insist action"?

Reinhard Döhl offers an elusive intruder in his apple. Consider the apple as a symbol in Western mythology before you plan your group performance.

Apfel

REINHARD DÖHL

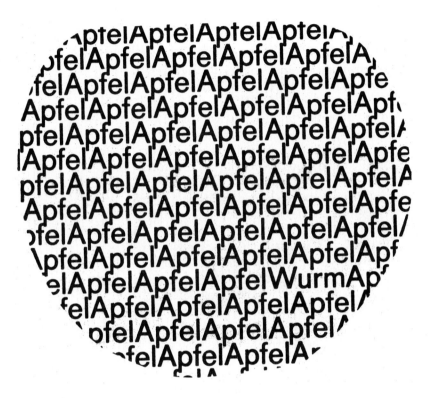

◆ Did your audience meet the surprise visitor the way the silent reader does? How?

Oedipus, king of Thebes, who once answered the riddle of the Sphinx and thus destroyed its power, has been visited by the elders and townsmen, who beg him to deliver them once again from famine and pestilence. He tells them that he has sent his brother-in-law, Creon, to the oracle to find out what he might do to save the state. When Creon returns, he reveals that the oracle has said the curse will not be lifted until the murderer of King Laius, who held the throne before Oedipus, is found and driven from Thebes. Oedipus issues a proclamation that this task should be carried out and sends for the blind prophet Tiresias in the hope that he can help identify the murderer through his powers of divination.

In this scene, Oedipus stands on the steps of his palace, surrounded by citizens,
waiting for the arrival of the revered man. Let the presentational foundation of
Greek theater guide your group: have the performers face the audience directly.

 FROM **Oedipus the King**

SOPHOCLES

(*Enter* TIRESIAS, *led by a* BOY.)

OEDIPUS: You know all things in heaven and earth, Tiresias:
    Things you may speak of openly, and secrets
    Holy and not to be revealed. You know,
    Blind though you are, the plague that ruins Thebes.
    And you, great prophet, you alone can save us.
    Phoebus has sent an answer to our question,
    An answer that the messengers may have told you,
    Saying there is no cure for our condition
    Until we found the killers of King Laius
    And banished them or had them put to death.
    Therefore, Tiresias, do not begrudge your skill
    In the voice of birds or other prophecy,
    But save yourself, save me, save the whole city,
    Save everything that the pestilence defiles.
    We are at your mercy, and man's noblest task
    Is to use all his powers in helping others.
TIRESIAS: How dreadful a thing, how dreadful a thing is wisdom,
    When to be wise is useless! This I knew
    But I forgot, or else I would never have come.
OEDIPUS: What is the matter? Why are you so troubled?
TIRESIAS: Oedipus, let me go home. Then you will bear
    Your burden, and I mine, more easily.
OEDIPUS: Custom entitles us to hear your message.
    By being silent you harm your native land.
TIRESIAS: You do not know when, and when not to speak.
    Silence will save me from the same misfortune.
OEDIPUS: If you can be of help, then all of us
    Kneel and implore you not to turn away.
TIRESIAS: None of you know the truth, but I will never
    Reveal my sorrow—not to call it yours.
OEDIPUS: What are you saying? You know and will not speak?
    You mean to betray us and destroy the city?
TIRESIAS: I refuse to pain you. I refuse to pain myself.
    It is useless to ask me. I tell you nothing.
OEDIPUS: You utter scoundrel! You would enrage a stone!
    Is there no limit to your stubbornness?

TIRESIAS: You blame my anger and forget your own.

OEDIPUS: No one could help being angry when he heard
　　　　How you dishonor and ignore the state.

TIRESIAS: What is to come will come, though I keep silent.

OEDIPUS: If it must come, your duty is to speak.

TIRESIAS: I will say no more. Rage to your heart's content.

OEDIPUS: Rage? Yes, I will rage! I will spare you nothing.
　　　　In the plot against King Laius, I have no doubt
　　　　That you were an accomplice, yes, almost
　　　　The actual killer. If you had not been blind,
　　　　I would have said that you alone were guilty.

TIRESIAS: Then listen to my command! Obey the edict
　　　　That you yourself proclaimed and never speak,
　　　　From this day on, to me or any Theban.
　　　　You are the sinner who pollutes our land.

OEDIPUS: Have you no shame? How do you hope to escape
　　　　the consequence of such an accusation?

TIRESIAS: I have escaped. My strength is the living truth.

OEDIPUS: This is no prophecy. Who taught you this?

TIRESIAS: You did. You forced me to speak against my will.

OEDIPUS: Repeat your slander. Let me learn it better.

TIRESIAS: Are you trying to tempt me into saying more?
　　　　I have spoken already. Have you not understood?

OEDIPUS: No, not entirely. Give your speech again.

TIRESIAS: I say you are the killer, you yourself.

OEDIPUS: Twice the same insult! You will pay for it.

TIRESIAS: Shall I say more to make you still more angry?

OEDIPUS: Say what you want to. It will make no sense.

TIRESIAS: You are living in shame with those most dear to you,
　　　　As yet in ignorance of your dreadful fate.

OEDIPUS: Do you suppose that you can always use
　　　　Language like that and not be punished for it?

TIRESIAS: Yes. I am safe, if truth has any strength.

OEDIPUS: Truth can save anyone excepting you,
　　　　You with no eyes, no hearing, and no brains!

TIRESIAS: Poor fool! You taunt me, but you soon will hear
　　　　The self-same insults heaped upon your head.

OEDIPUS: You live in endless night. What can you do
　　　　To me or anyone else who sees the day?

TIRESIAS: Nothing. I have no hand in your destruction.
　　　　For that, Apollo needs no help from me.

OEDIPUS: Apollo! Is this your trick, or is it Creon's?

TIRESIAS: Creon is guiltless. The evil is in you.

OEDIPUS: How great is the envy roused by wealth, by kingship,
　　　　By the subtle skill that triumphs over others

In life's hard struggle! Creon, who has been
For years my trusted friend, has stealthily
Crept in upon me to seize my power,
The unsought gift the city freely gave me.
Anxious to overthrow me, he has bribed
This scheming mountebank, this fraud, this trickster,
Blind in his art and in everything but money!
Your art of prophecy! When have you shown it?
Not when the watch-dog of the gods was here,
Chanting her riddle. Why did you say nothing,
When you might have saved the city? Yet her puzzle
Could not be solved by the first passer-by.
A prophet's skill was needed, and you proved
That you had no such skill, either in birds
Or any other means the gods have given.
But I came, I, the ignorant Oedipus,
And silenced her. I had no birds to help me.
I used my brains. And it is I you now
Are trying to destroy in the hope of standing
Close beside Creon's throne. You will regret
This zeal of yours to purify the land,
You and your fellow-plotter. You seem old;
Otherwise you would pay for your presumption.

CHORUS: Sir, it appears to us that both of you
Have spoken in anger. Anger serves no purpose.
Rather we should consider in what way
We best can carry out the god's command.

TIRESIAS: King though you are, I have a right to answer
Equal to yours. In that I too am king.
I serve Apollo. I do not acknowledge
You as my lord or Creon as my patron.
You have seen fit to taunt me with my blindness.
Therefore I tell you this: you have your eyesight
And cannot see the sin of your existence,
Cannot see where you live or whom you live with,
Are ignorant of your parents, bring disgrace
Upon your kindred in the world below
And here on earth. And soon the double lash
Of your mother's and father's curse will drive you headlong
Out of the country, blinded, with your cries
Heard everywhere, echoed by every hill
In all Cithaeron. Then you will have learned
The meaning of your marriage, learned in what harbor,
After so fair a voyage, you were shipwrecked.
And other horrors you could never dream of

Will teach you who you are, will drag you down
To the level of your children. Heap your insults
On Creon and my message if you choose to.
Still no one ever will endure the weight
Of greater misery than will fall on you.

OEDIPUS: Am I supposed to endure such talk as this,
Such talk from him? Go, curse you, go! Be quick!

TIRESIAS: Except for your summons I would never have come.

OEDIPUS: And I would never have sent for you so soon
If I had known you would prove to be a fool.

TIRESIAS: Yes. I have proved a fool—in your opinion,
And yet your parents thought that I was wise.

OEDIPUS: What parents? Wait! Who was my father? Tell me!

TIRESIAS: Today you will see your birth and your destruction.

OEDIPUS: You cannot speak unless you speak in riddles!

TIRESIAS: And yet how brilliant you are in solving them!

OEDIPUS: You sneer at me for what has made me great.

TIRESIAS: The same good fortune that has ruined you.

OEDIPUS: If I have saved the city, nothing else matters.

TIRESIAS: In that case I will go. Boy, take me home.

OEDIPUS: Yes, let him take you. Here, you are in the way.
Once you are gone, you will give no further trouble.

TIRESIAS: I will not go before I have said my say,
Indifferent to your black looks. You cannot harm me.
And I say this: the man whom you have sought,
Whom you have threatened, whom you have proclaimed
The killer of King Laius—he is here.
Now thought an alien, he shall prove to be
A native Theban, to his deep dismay.
Now he has eyesight, now his wealth is great;
But he shall make his way to foreign soil
Blinded, in beggary, groping with a stick.
In his own household he shall be shown to be
The father of his children—and their brother,
Son to the woman who bore him—and her husband,
The killer and the bedfellow of his father.
Go and consider this; and if you find
That I have been mistaken, you can say
That I have lost my skill in prophecy.

(*Exeunt* OEDIPUS *and* TIRESIAS.)

   ◆ Did you embody Tiresias's blindness physically?

   ◆ How did you resolve the countless other ironies of this text?

♦ When did your Oedipus get seriously worried? What happened to him during Tiresias's final speech? How did your audience see his discovery reflected in his face and body?

The harrowing experiences that shaped—and still shape—the persona of David Ray's "Unforgiven" raise troubling social issues that group performance can usefully explore. We discussed one way a group performance might include this essay, and here's another. Assign each performer a character and charge all the performers with finding texts—their own or texts by others—that illumine the unique dilemmas each character faces. Thus, Sis and Mom and Lee and Old Lady Spivey would each speak in the narrator's text but at different crucial moments would also speak their own text. In the counterpoint of that interaction, you and your audience could come to understand more completely the sins of omission and commission for which the persona still seeks to atone.

Unforgiven

DAVID RAY

I don't know how far it had gone by the time I left town. I was 15 and my sister, 14 months younger. I knew more about it than I wanted to, and no doubt it was one of the many reasons I lit out West the first chance I got. But there was a lot, too, that I didn't know. I remember our stepfather Lee leering at Sis and teasing her onto his lap from the first evening Mother brought him around, and I remember his nudist magazines stuck deep in the glove compartment of his old DeSoto, behind his pliers and ever-loaded pistol.

Mom and Sis and I have never talked about it, and Lee's name almost never comes up. In fact, after his death it was as if my mother had succeeded in washing him out of her mind. When she finally signed up for Social Security and the clerk asked about her marriages, she left out No. 2. The clerk also informed her that Lee Pape was not his real name; it had been changed for some reason, courtesy of the United States Army. "I assure you, there's no point trying to find out," the man told Mom. "The Government regards all that sort of thing as highly confidential, classified—you've got to protect people's rights to privacy."

Of course, Lee hadn't respected anybody's privacy—Sis's, for example, when he peeked at her while she was taking a bath. Heating the water a teakettle at a time and pouring it into that galvanized tub set on the floor was hard enough work without having to worry about a leering stepfather sneaking up on her.

What it was all building up to, a few months after I left, may have been inevitable. Mom and Sis were both working in the kitchen

of the roadside tavern Lee managed; Sis was obliged to be a waitress after school. Sis said she was fixing hamburgers, about a dozen, the half-buns awaiting the greasy patties. The customers out front were waiting to wash down the burgers and fries with their bottles of Bud and Schlitz.

"I was spreading mustard when he came in the back door with the damn pistol," she told me when I went back for Lee's funeral. It had been my sister's chore, at Mother's insistence, to follow Lee any time he said he was going to get the gun and to talk him out of it or even wrestle the gun away from him. That sort of thing—waving the gun around and threatening suicide—had been going on more and more often before I left. Mom would tell Sis to get the gun from him, and Sis was plucky enough and insulting enough and brave enough to do it.

But this time she refused to argue with Lee. "Go ahead and do it," she told him, sounding as bored and disgusted as a 14-year-old could.

"You think I don't have the guts to do it, don't you?" he answered back. It was all between the two of them. Mother was just a bystander, like the customers who had pushed in through the saloon doors from the front room even before they heard the first shot.

Lee sank to his knees and was about to fire again. Sis said she looked at him a long time, his bloodshot eyes begging her to stop him. "I didn't give a damn," she said. "I had already told myself I wouldn't lift a finger if he waved that damn gun around one more time, and I wasn't about to." I still think it is terrible for a girl to ever have a reason to be so bitter. He pulled the trigger again.

Lee lived 10 days in the hospital, long enough to convince Mom that all was going to be rosy. I guess that's love, that a woman could believe such bilge after what she and her daughter had been through. He would stop drinking and find another job so he wouldn't be around beer all the time. It's hard to believe he could have done so much damage to brain and liver with the 3.2-percent-alcohol beer of Oklahoma, but he was never without a bottle of it, as he stood around the bar, his beer belly pressed against the coolers, his great spatulate hands spread wide on the bar top.

Decades later, Sis and I finally get around to talking a little about that period right after I left her behind. She tells me how mean her junior-high math teacher, Old Lady Spivey, had been to her: "'You don't have your smartie brother to help you out any more,' she'd say. She would rub that in, standing over me and checking every answer. Then she'd slap my hands with her damn ruler and make me cry." At the humiliations recalled, Sis almost wept anew. "I didn't want to give her the satisfaction," she said, "but sometimes I just couldn't keep from crying."

It was the closest Sis had ever got to accusing me of leaving her alone to face the monsters—but mostly the one she didn't mention. I never knew how she survived it.

I guess we all let one another down. Mom seemed helpless to protect her children. She didn't feel like much, I guess, after my stepfather was through with her; she might not have got tied up with him in the first place if she had thought better of herself.

Maybe there was someone like Lee in her childhood, about as surely as there's a sun outside Plato's shadowy cave somewhere—a lot of stuff gets reflected, and that's the only way you finally figure it out.

Driving past the town one time, I turned into the cemetery and had no trouble finding Lee's grave, though I hadn't been there since the day he was buried. Sis wouldn't go to the funeral. The grave was at the far edge of the cemetery, covered with weeds, and the oblong mud that had been shoveled in that day by some of Lee's Elk Club friends had dropped several inches, a permanent recession.

I was going through a period of trying to forgive everybody, so I knelt at the grave and tried to talk to him. I said I forgave him, but by the time I got back to the car I realized I had no right to do that, certainly not on behalf of my sister.

I wish I could tell Sis how much I admire her for the fight she put up. In a better world she would have had more help, someone to protect her.

Instead, I try to show how sympathetic I am about Old Lady Spivey.

I think that helps a bit. And maybe Sis knows as well as I do that had I tried to step between her and our stepfather he'd have blown me away in an instant—an underweight asthmatic runt with the effrontery to stand up to him. But sometimes, maybe pretty often, I still wish I'd stayed in that little Oklahoma town and given it a try.

- ◆ Lee's death is important, but what is the crisis? How did your group shape that scene's conclusion?

- ◆ If you interpolated the characters' own texts, who had the last word?

Certainly the pain and frustration that arises from an inability to help those we love informs many texts. Robin Robertson's poem "After the Overdose" explores a very intimate admission in a very public way. Again, let your group find the echoes of this poem in other poems—or, even more challenging, in popular music or videos. Stage the discourse that results from these multiply related images when they interact.

After the Overdose

ROBIN ROBERTSON

What surprised me most?
Coming home to an open door,
rose petals everywhere, the bed
incongruous with blood?
The paramedic's satchel
left behind in all the rush?

Or you in the hospital,
the crusted corners of your mouth,
the gown they'd put you in?
You never wore short sleeves,
not since you burned a name
into your arm with cigarettes.

Or, finally, that you weren't dead?
That surprised me. That regret.

- ◆ The form of this poem crucially dictates its powerful conclusion. How did your group embody those three primary cadences in the final two lines?

Dr. Daniel Hirsh and Alexis Greville (known in the script as Alex) have shared the affections of young Bob Elkin for some time. Although each knows about the other, they have never met. Alva and Bill Hodson, their daughter Lucy, and Professor Johns are friends of all three of the principals. Pauline Kael called Sunday Bloody Sunday *"a novel written on film," and the precise, literate direction of the camera narrates for us the impact of this segment, the last minutes of the film.*

FROM Sunday Bloody Sunday

PENELOPE GILLIATT

Sunday

Daniel's consulting room and garden. Dawn.
    "Sunday" title on shot.
    DANIEL *is playing Italian language-records, wearing a polo-necked sweater and grey flannels. He opens the French windows.*
    He walks out to his pool and crouches down to look at the goldfish. The sound of the recorded voice comes out into the cold garden. Time passes.

Daniel's stairs. Dawn.
    BOB *is coming quietly down the stairs in a raincoat. He leaves the front door key on the kitchen table.*
    DANIEL *is still crouched by the pool. He has his head bent and the sight of* BOB *going out of the house is not visible to him.*

Street outside Daniel's house. Dawn.
    Long shot of BOB *letting himself out of* DANIEL'S *house.*

Answering service. Early morning.

ANSWERING SERVICE WOMAN: We'll be sorry, Mr. Elkin. But you'll be back, will you? Well, I can't say I blame you. The dollar's where the future is. I'll give that message to Miss Greville, yes. And to Dr. . . . ? Well, very well. (*She unplugs, and smirks a bit and nods to herself, and opens a packet of fruit pastilles.*)

Bob's pad. Sunday morning.

He comes downstairs with rubbish and leaves it outside his front door. A VOICE *from the area yells up.*

VOICE FROM AREA: Rubbish belongs down here, Mr. Elkin. (*He slams the front door behind him and goes away.*)

The Hodsons'. Sunday morning.

ALEX *drives up in her car, looking at the* HODSON FAMILY *having lunch inside the house.* DANIEL *is with the* FAMILY *and* PROFESSOR JOHNS.

ALVA: When are you off to Italy?

DANIEL: The twenty-first, God willing.

ALVA: Are you going with Bob?

DANIEL: I don't think so.

ALVA *makes commiserating sound, checked by* BILL.

BILL: We've always thought we should try to be a bit more grownup ourselves about having holidays on our own. Separately, I mean. Have you ever thought of one of those Scholars' Cruises? Alva nearly went on one.

DANIEL: It isn't what I'd have chosen.

ALVA *makes her own married warning gesture to* BILL *and speaks to* DANIEL, *meaning what she says, in her own way.*

ALVA: I'm terribly sorry.

Sprightly snigger from LUCY. DANIEL *looks at them coldly.*

DANIEL: No need.

There is a view of the scene from the outside of the house, from ALEX*'s point of view, and a long snatch of "Così."* DANIEL *comes out of the house.*

ALEX *gets out of her car and sits on the wing of his. They shake hands, absurdly. He sits down in his own driving seat.*

ALEX: I didn't know you were going to be here. I'm sorry. You know who I am.

DANIEL: Thank you for not coming in. You must have been out here a long time. (*awkward*) Have you had lunch?

ALEX: It's the sort of thing we say, isn't it? (*pause*) I'm ravenous. (*pause*) He's all right, is he?

DANIEL: I think so. (*pause*) This isn't very easy, is it?

She shakes her head.

ALEX: I thought he'd be with you today.

They light cigarettes.

DANIEL: He's gone away, yes?

ALEX: I don't know.

DANIEL: It's all right to tell me.

ALEX: I'm sorry. I only had it from the answering service.

They make wry faces at each other. As she goes up the path to the HODSONS', DANIEL *raises his voice at her.*

DANIEL: You're welcome to them today.

London airport. Sunday afternoon.
    BOB *buys American magazines and walks to the Pan Am counter.*

Alex's studio. Sunday afternoon.
    She comes in and finds an envelope with her name on it facing her on the floor, and a key like the one in her hand wrapped up in a piece of paper with a note: Could you look after the toucan for a bit? The TOUCAN *stares at her from the window sill. She stares it out.*

Daniel's consulting room. Sunday afternoon.
    DANIEL *is in his patient's chair, with his back to camera. His own seat behind the desk is empty because he is managing a Hi-Fi nearer his grasp from this position. The Italian language-record is going.*

RECORD: I prefer my scampi without garlic and my wife would like a steak if the meat is first class.

Record repeats phrase in Italian.

RECORD: Preferisco i miei scampi senz' aglio e mia moglie desidera una bistecca purchè la carne sia buonissima.

Pause for the student to repeat the Italian. DANIEL *says the phrase, in a shorter time than the record allows. Pause.*
    Camera starts to move round very slowly. We see DANIEL's *profile.*

RECORD: You have used the present tense and the conditional. Now we will repeat the phrases in the past tense as if telling a story. "I said that I preferred my scampi without garlic and my wife would have liked a steak provided that the meat was first class."

The record repeats the phrase in Italian. DANIEL *speaks simultaneously with the record.*

RECORD AND DANIEL: Ho detto che volevo i miei scampi senz' aglio e mia moglie avrebbe preferito la bistecca se la carne era buonissima.

RECORD: Molto bene. Arrivederci.

The gramophone switches itself off. By this time the camera movement has brought us to a view of DANIEL *in full face, looking at the book on his knee. It is as if he is the patient now, talking to himself: or to us, it begins to be clear.*

DANIEL: We went to hear "Aida" in the open air and it was not first class but we enjoyed the music and the landscape.

He repeats the phrase in Italian, lifting his head and staring straight at us.

DANIEL: Siamo andati a vedere l'Aida all'aria aperta. Saremmo andati a vedere l'Aida. (*pause*)—Bugger the conditional. (*pause*) When you're at school and want to quit, people say you're going to hate being out in the world. Well, I didn't believe them and I was right. When I was a kid I couldn't wait to be grown up and they said childhood was the best time of my life and it wasn't. Now I want his company and people say, what's half a loaf, you're well shot of him; and I say, I know that, I miss him, that's all. They say he'd never have made me happy and I say, I am happy, apart from missing him. You might throw me a pill or two for my cough. (*pause*) All my life I've been looking for someone courageous and resourceful, not like myself, and he's not it. (*pause*) But something. We were something. You've no right to call me to account. (*pause*) I've only come about my cough.

He, too, stares us out. Fade to black. Full credits.

- ◆ How sympathetic to Daniel was *your* camera?
- ◆ If the narrator also takes the lines of the record, what is the impact on Daniel's last scene? Why?

Bibliography

Readers Theater and Chamber Theater

Breen, Robert S. *Chamber Theater.* Evanston, IL: William Caxton, 1986.
   The foundation study that documents the theory and practice of Breen's approach to the performance of fiction.

Coger, Leslie Irene, and Melvin R. White. *Readers Theatre Handbook: A Dramatic Approach to Literature.* Rev. ed. Glenview, IL: Scott, Foresman, 1973.
   One of the earliest works to describe Readers Theater as a "theater of the mind."

Kleinau, Marion L., and Janet Larsen McHughes. *Theatres for Literature.* Sherman Oaks, CA: Alfred, 1980.

A substantial discussion of Readers Theater, Chamber Theater, and other group performance events.

Long, Beverly Whitaker, Lee Hudson, and Phillis Rienstra Jeffrey. *Group Performance of Literature.* Englewood Cliffs, NJ: Prentice-Hall, 1977.
Theory coupled with a substantial collection of script ideas and analysis.

Maclay, Joanna H. *Readers Theatre: Toward a Grammar of Practice.* New York: Random House, 1971.
An influential study that provides the impetus for the staging of literature.

Yordon, Judy. *Experimental Theatre: Creating and Staging Texts.* Prospect Heights, IL: Waveland Press, 1996.
A lively investigation of experimental group performance opportunities, including ethnographic studies, conversation analysis, and personal narratives.

Concrete Poetry

Hollander, John. *Types of Shape.* 2nd ed. New York: Oxford University Press, 1991.
An accomplished poet discusses contemporary patterned poems.

McHughes, J. L. "The Poses of Space: Prosodic Structures in Concrete Poetry." *Quarterly Journal of Speech* 63, no. 3 (1977): 168–179.
A discussion arguing that space is the axis from which the poem emerges.

Building and Presenting a Program

YOU CAN DERIVE CONSIDERABLE PLEASURE FROM PRESENTING a program or lecture recital to audiences outside the classroom. What follows can also be used for longer class performances or for the increasingly popular reading hours. After all, the techniques used in performance are dictated by the demands of the *material* rather than by the length or circumstances of the presentation.

The difference between a program and a lecture recital is primarily one of proportion and degree. A *program* uses a minimum of transitional material and focuses almost entirely on the literature. A *lecture recital*, by contrast, has a strong central unity and can feature critics' opinions, historical data, and even video and audio clips as transitions. The selections illustrate whatever theme the speaker has chosen. The lecture recital emphasizes evaluation as much as appreciation. You may, of course, perform a range of material, but works with which you disagree deserve the same respect in performance that you bestow on your favorites.

Because the lecture recital appeals to a more specialized audience and is much less practical for the beginning interpreter, in this appendix we build *programs* of varied selections, referring to material in this textbook as well as to selections you can find easily in your library or on the Internet.

Selecting Material

The first consideration in selecting the material you will present is its literary worth. Do not read inferior material because you think your audience will not accept anything more difficult. It is your job to perform the selection so that it does not seem difficult. The second consideration is permission to use the material. Reread the advice about copyright in Chapter 11 if you are in doubt (see page 490).

You might be asked to do a special program for a particular group or occasion. Perhaps the group is following a particular course of study—contemporary theater, the Old Testament, human relations, ecology, or any one of a number of areas of interest—and they want you to add a new dimension or an introductory or concluding unit. The time of year may influence your selection. For a Christmas program, for example, you might want to include both an old favorite (Truman Capote's *A Christmas Memory*) and a less well known piece (say, Ogden Nash's witty "Epstein, Spare That Yule Log"). A spring luncheon could feature Elizabeth Bowen's "The Little Girls." February offers the opportunity to read love poems, love letters, and love scenes from plays. Since February also celebrates the birthdays of two famous Americans, it offers the opportunity to present historical material or patriotic selections. Perhaps a scene from Gore Vidal's *Lincoln* and selections from Walt Whitman's journals and his poem "When Lilacs Last in the Dooryard Bloom'd" could be used in a program on Lincoln. Any topic of human interest can become the focal point of a program. The range of possibilities is limited only by the interpreter's skill and imagination.

Unifying the Program: A Traditional Method

Whatever the occasion, your program should have a unifying theme dictated in part by what you know about your audience and in part by the purpose of the group for whom you are performing. The program itself should demonstrate the intrinsic factors of unity and harmony, variety and contrast, balance and proportion, rhythm of emotional impact, and focus of interest.

Although a unified program is important, often it is more practical to begin planning with what you like to read and can get ready in time. Then, see what thematic unity your preferences offer. For example, suppose you have already prepared for a class Robert Frost's "Wild Grapes." This poem is about many things, all operating within a harmonious unity: the memory of childhood, a young girl and her brother, an experience with nature, wisdom, letting go with the hands but not with the heart, and so on. Any one of these topics could unify your program. Suppose you choose memories of childhood for your program topic. You might wish to include William Stafford's "First Grade," a selection from Amy Tan's *The Joy Luck Club*, Cynthia MacDonald's "The Kilgore Rangerette Whose Life Was Ruined," Corrine Hales's "Power," and Mary Stewart Hammond's "Saving Memory." A black girl's memories fill the the poem "Nikki-Rosa" by Nikki Giovanni and Toni Cade Bambara's story "The Lesson." Or explore the diverse perspectives offered by Maury Yeston's "New Words" and the scene from Lanford Wilson's *Fifth of July*. Although all these works are reprinted in this text, the list of available material is practically endless. The interpreter needs only time and interest.

You might decide to set the theme with Jaques's speech from Shakespeare's *As You Like It*, about man's moving from infancy and childhood to maturity and old age. Why not close with Roethke's "Old Lady's Winter Words" and Tennyson's "Ulysses"? Along the way you might include Peter Cameron's "Homework" and the Roger McGough poem "40–Love," followed by "The Story of Baucis and Philemon" from Ovid's *The Metamorphoses*. Or you could look at three fellows as they enter or leave their teens: Terry Pickens from Studs Terkel's *Working*, the narrator of Lynda Barry's "KEEP OUT! (A Boy's Bedroom)," and Sammy, the narrator of John Updike's "A & P." There are innumerable variations on the theme of youth and age. The readings might have a strongly humorous tone or a rhythm that combines the gently humorous and the deeply moving.

Interesting programs can be arranged around people and places, rural and urban life, regional American literature, descriptive and dramatic writing about foreign places, or the letters, travel accounts, and diaries of famous people.

The works of one particular author may unify a program. Concentrate on the treatment of a theme, such as Shakespeare's kings, or on a method of revealing character, as through Browning's monologues or Ann Beattie's short stories. You could reveal a developmental trend by beginning with an author's early works and concluding with the later ones.

Consider the rhythms of the emotional impact carefully to make the entire performance move smoothly and without monotony. Don't be afraid of variety: use materials from various sources, interspersing them for contrast and illumination. Different texts talk to each other. Often throughout this text, we have juxtaposed works on the same topic (stars, the death of a pet, childhood mischief) to suggest that each work viewed next to another creates special access to the wealth of the texts.

Using Multiple Readers, Different Types of Literature, and Multimedia

Using more than one reader for a program often helps solve the problems of short preparation time and inexperience. Moreover, two or more interpreters add variety and thus increase the program's audience appeal. Refer to "Group Performance of Compiled Scripts" in Chapter 11 (page 485) for some advice on assembling material. There is danger of diffusion when several people simply read whatever they happen to have handy. There must be some central unity. The several readers need to rehearse together so that transitions are clear and the material is arranged to provide variety and contrast, rhythm of emotional impact, and effective use of climactic selections.

Program building with groups provides great opportunities for experimentation. Much literature combines well with dance and music, which can either accompany the reading or be inserted at various places in the program to underscore, sustain, or alter mood. Electronic media strike instant and effective responses in an audience—but be sure to eliminate any potential technical glitches. Visual art can also be used. For example, William Blake and e. e. cummings were both artists of some distinction as well as poets, and some of their drawings and paintings might well be combined with their writings for an interesting program. Hundreds of poems have been written about specific paintings. Why not stage a "gallery" of such poems using slides of the art they illumine?[1] The drawings and prose writings in Gerard Manley Hopkins's *Notebooks* might be combined with his poetry to provide an unusual and enlightening program. Or you could combine Vaslav Nijinsky's intriguing diaries with dance, adding film clips of Rudolf Nureyev or Mikhail Baryshnikov performing some of the ballets that Nijinsky created, and enriching the entire presentation with excerpts from Igor Stravinsky's music, Charles Rosen's essays, and slides of the stage designs.

Staging the *New York Times*

You could stage the *New York Times*. After examining several issues, you understand the newspaper's characteristic attitudes toward advertisements, politics, presentation, and news. Remember, any publication frankly seeks readers. The performance analogue for such frankness is an equally frank frontal placement and focus—bodies and voices creating the presentational equivalent to the newspaper. Such placement frees the bodies and voices to suggest the pictures, drawings, and graphics.

What does the *New York Times* represent? It holds a position as the "paper of record" in the United States, offering preeminent news reporting, widely respected editorials, broadly distributed features, an immediately recognizable logo, a particular style of presentation, and a certain kind of straightforward seriousness, and the newspaper itself is a newsworthy subject not unfamiliar with controversy.

What then, should a performance represent? There is no need to limit oneself to any single issue of the paper. Select from among the finest of the editorials, op-ed articles, obituaries, sports stories, fashion news reports, lifestyle and social information, the television-film-

---

1. Beverly Whitaker Long, University of North Carolina, Chapel Hill, created a powerful program in this manner, with the performers serving as "docents" in front of rear-projected slides of the artworks.

theater-dance-music reviews, the Sunday *New York Times Magazine* articles and crossword puzzles, the book reviews and interviews with authors, the advertisements, the personal columns, and the job offerings. Your selection, of course, will be based on the needs and interests of your audience, so you may wish to slant your presentation toward a particular period or event, so long as you maintain an accurate reflection of the typical components of an issue. Should you include selections from among the many works written about the *Times* (Gay Talese's *The Power and the Glory*, Harrison Salisbury's *Without Fear or Favor*, David Halberstam's *The Powers That Be*, Edwin Diamond's *Behind the Times*)? It all depends on what you intend this performance to demonstrate.

Look at the visual responsibilities. What are the characteristic graphic elements used in the *Times?* How can these be suggested in performance by bodies and voices? Your rehearsals will begin with experimentation, so don't restrict yourself in terms of the visual elements. Sometimes the group can represent the visual elements better than slides or set pieces could.

Consider what could happen with just the front page in a group production. The front page of the *Times* is characterized by several different but related factors. First, the chief stories of the day all begin (but never end) on the front page. On occasion, a feature story or a research story also begins on the front page, but it, too, never ends there. The front page also includes—in extremely small print—one- or two-line advertisements at the bottom of some columns, the weather forecast, and price and publication information. Usually there is one large three- or four-column color photograph, often illustrating the major story of the day. Sometimes, a small chart or a symbol linked to a story that begins elsewhere appears above the fold to the left of center. The most important stories appear in the columns that begin at the top of the page; stories of lesser importance begin below the fold. Several stories about the same event are clustered, usually to the upper right or the upper left. The front page also features variations in print size, from the most prominent headline to the smallest classified advertisement, but the largest print on the page is always the Gothic type masthead—*The New York Times*. (The one, sad exception to this rule was the headline on September 12, 2001.)

How can the bodies and voices of the performers suggest that page? Obviously, if you perform the news stories, you will need to give them all the attention normally given the performance of nonfiction. But since the stories are separate, why not give one story to each performer? When a news figure is quoted, let the performer—or another—characterize the figure as fully as possible, and let the stories continue simultaneously. At first everyone talking at once may seem cacophonous, but the blurt of all the news is one of the distinctive features of the paper's front page. Before the stories begin, the group can suggest the elaborate archaic type of the masthead by singing the words *The New York Times* like a madrigal. Perhaps the large picture could be frozen into space by three or four of the performers, or a slide of the performers in an identical posture could be projected on a screen in back. Although the performers start together with the stories skipping along, they will stop at random, as their contents are continued elsewhere and other new stories take their place. How can you suggest the newer, less important news? Should you whisper those tiny want ads?

Ask yourself—and answer—similar questions for all the parts of the paper you intend to perform. The attitudes of the editorials tend to be dignified, except for an occasional whimsical salute to a change of season, but the attitudes of the letters and op-ed page offer real potential for characterization. Photos can duplicate fashion news, but might not bodies and voices better suggest fashion's attitudes? Try to achieve the peculiar attitude of the recipes: knowledgeable, clear-sighted, with an extraordinarily well-equipped kitchen. Can you convey the intriguing, sometimes cryptic, world that lies behind the terse abbreviations of want ads or personal advertisements? Surely there are several opportunities for characterization among these. Use postures and voice to capture the appeal each advertisement makes. Plan each of the components carefully.

When compiling the parts—putting the paper together, as it were—be careful to watch the amount of time you spend on each "page." Work for balance and continuity by trying to achieve the feeling of the page turning. The arrangement of the pieces depends on changes of tempo in the stories, on the sizes of the advertisements you encounter, on how "thick" a paper you want to present, and on the degree to which you want to embody pictorial elements or to represent them with slides.

Whatever choices you make, the performance should build to a climax—something that the paper never does but that an audience must see. Your decision to perform a newspaper imposes a structure that the paper itself does not necessarily follow, but your performance should convey to the audience all that is involved in reading the *New York Times*.

Other Options

Of course, a newspaper is not the only kind of publication that would benefit from such an effort. Perhaps the most obvious choice among magazines would be *The New Yorker:* its unsurpassed collection of nonfiction, poetry, light fiction, articles, and humor, with renowned cartoons and the unmistakably bemused hauteur of Eustace Tilley, the magazine's monocled symbol, provide a wonderfully varied forum for a performance. Your program might include other works from typical *New Yorker* writers, or passages about the magazine from Brendan Gill's

Here at the New Yorker, or segments from the memoirs and autobiographies of some of its most famous staffers. A collection of *New Yorker* pieces, including Janet Flanner's "Letter from Paris" (collected as *Paris Was Yesterday*), might provide the foundation for another program. Whatever you choose, you should determine the attitude that makes the publication unique, and you should develop the corresponding physical and vocal behaviors.

Programs can respond to important social problems by featuring texts (literary, visual, aural) that lead to action. Consider the anguish and anger surrounding AIDS. Poets, novelists, essayists, painters, composers, choreographers, and playwrights have all contributed to the growing canon of works about AIDS. One of the most powerful of such works is Susan Sontag's "The Way We Live Now." This story, narrated by all the friends of a person with AIDS, can provide the site for interpolating others' works. Indeed, that story prompted a collection of short stories about the AIDS crisis called *The Way We Write Now.* Many other works address the issue from other perspectives: poems such as Michael Lassell's "How to Watch Your Brother Die," Mark Doty's "Tiara," or Melvin Dixon's "Heartbeats"; fiction such as John Weir's *The Irreversible Decline of Eddie Socket* or Paul Monette's *Afterlife;* plays such as William Hoffman's *As Is,* Larry Kramer's polemic *The Normal Heart,* or Tony Kushner's *Angels in America.* When you add the works of historians (Randy Shilts's *And the Band Played On*), essayists, filmmakers, and composers, you encounter a broad array of possibilities from which to construct a program that can enlighten at the same time it empowers.

The important thing to remember is that the performance as a whole should have both unity and variety. It should have an introductory unit, a climax (usually the longest selection and the one that most clearly exemplifies your theme), and a conclusion. When you have selected and arranged your material, look at the whole program and check to see that it includes each of the intrinsic factors. Keep the introduction short. The audience came to hear the program, not a long preamble. Your introductory remarks establish the mood and prepare your audience for what follows. The transitions between selections should allow the listeners a few seconds to complete their emotional response to the preceding selection and should lead them economically into the mood of the one that follows.

Adapting to the Audience

It is impossible to know precisely what interests your audience, unless the group has a special purpose. It is possible, however, to make some generalizations. Gender makes less difference than age, which is probably the most important factor to consider in audience adaptation. In general, a young audience is more open to experimental material and to a wider range of subject matter. An audience of elderly people usually wants to see and hear traditional, familiar material. In a group with a wide age spread, there should be something for everyone, but if you are in doubt about the suitability of a selection for even a segment of the audience, omit it.

Children make a wonderful audience. They like material about people, animals, nature, and anything they can visualize, whether real or imaginary. They like poetry with a clear rhythm and a rhyme. You should choose selections that are short, and you should handle the transitions carefully to connect what the children know with what the literature says. Stories, of course, are great favorites, and children enjoy having the characters made vivid by more explicit vocal and physical characterization than would be appropriate for a mature audience. Find ways for them to participate in the event; in any case, they *will*—and you want to use their enthusiasm. Don't limit yourself to children's literature exclusively. Children are young in experience but they are sensitive and intelligent; they might enjoy the sounds and basic references in Macourek's "Jacob's Chicken," or Lewis Carroll's "Jabberwocky."

Don't diminish your own standards of literary value. There are dozens of ways to write about any subject. Your audience is interested in the substance of your material and in how professionally that material is presented. Second-rate material, even if flawlessly performed, remains second-rate.

Timing

Keep your program within its allotted time. Listeners often become ill at ease and distracted if the program runs long. It is better to leave audience members wishing for more than to risk their sighs of relief and hurried exit.

Time your selections and transitions frequently during your preparation. You are likely to consume more time as you progress. Add at least ten minutes per hour to your early reading time. Audience response and your own increased control of the selections will slow your pace in final performance. If you are sharing a program with other readers or with musicians, find out how much time you have been allotted and stick to it *precisely*.

A program of varied selections is particularly difficult to time, because it may be lengthened by laughter within or applause between selections. This is, of course, a phenomenon no performer wishes to prevent. Nevertheless, enthusiastic applause can add ten minutes or more to a fifty-minute program of fairly short selections. Be sure to consider this in your planning. In general, applause permits the audience to complete their response to what you have just given them. Accept it graciously.

In some instances, applause is inappropriate. If you sense that this is the situation, a moment's pause after each selection and before the next transition can be helpful. Do not prolong the pause so that your audience thinks you are waiting for applause. This sense of timing will develop as your experience increases. Applause might break a mood that you are trying to establish, especially if you are using a number of short selections. In this case, you might indicate in your transition that you will be using a group of short poems that touch on one aspect of your theme. Hold your performance posture and attitude for a brief pause after each piece, and then move directly into the next selection or brief transition. When you finish the group of poems, drop your directness slightly and allow the audience to show its appreciation before you move into the next unit. Your audience will be sensitive to your wishes and will take your cues easily.

Whenever you do a program, remember that in your role of interpreter you *share* a text with your audience. Your art and your technique should serve the material. Planning and preparing a performance takes time and energy. Even so, the experience of sharing good literature with an audience always rewards careful preparation.

A Brief History of Theories of Interpretation

FROM EARLIEST TIMES, THE SPOKEN WORD HAS ATTRACTED audiences and influenced their thinking. The history of public speaking has been traced by numerous authorities, who have shown that its thread has been unbroken from the fourth century BC to the present. The theater enjoys a similarly clear history. Oral interpretation, too, even though its genesis and growth as a distinct art may be less easy to define, has a long lineage of its own.

The art of interpretation probably had its beginnings with the *rhapsodists* of ancient Greece, poets who gathered to read their works in public competition. However, the emergence of interpretation as a field of study in its own right was delayed, because for a long time it was subsumed in oratory and rhetoric. In the eighteenth and nineteenth centuries, actors and ministers were given extensive training in what was, in reality, interpretation. It is enough to sketch the outlines briefly here to note the development of certain theories and to see where we now stand in relation to those theories.

American colleges were already giving some attention to the oral interpretation of literature at the beginning of the nineteenth century. As early as 1806, when John Quincy Adams assumed the chair of Rhetoric and Oratory, Harvard University, which from its founding had carried on the medieval tradition of "declamations" and "disputations," was offering a few courses that included the interpretative approach to literary materials. As the century progressed, more and more colleges offered specific courses in spoken English—courses that carried such titles as "Declamation and Composition," "Declamation," "Elements of Orthoepy and Elocution," or simply "Elocution."

The word *elocutio* (Latin, *eloqui, elocutus,* "to speak out") originally referred to effective literary or oratorical style. Between 1650 and 1750, however, a shift in connotation took place, and the term *elocution* was applied to the manner of oral delivery rather than to the written style of a composition. *Pronuntiatio,* which had meant primarily the management of voice and body, gradually took on our modern meaning of pronunciation as the correct phonation of individual words. These shifts in meaning had taken place by 1750, and the term *elocution* had come to connote a considerable degree of emphasis on delivery. By this time, also, a renewed interest in reading aloud and in oratory had developed, especially in England, where an important group of writer-speakers known as the English Elocutionists had come into being. Outstanding among them were Thomas Sheridan (1719–1788) and John Walker (1732–1807), whose books and lectures had great bearing on the development in America of what we now call interpretation.

Thomas Sheridan, father of the famous dramatist Richard Brinsley Sheridan and himself an actor, published his *Course of Lectures on Elocution* in 1763. This book came out strongly against artificialities and stressed the method of natural conversation in the oral presentation of literature. Sheridan thus became known as the leader of the "natural school." His thesis was that elocution should follow the laws of nature. He held that body and voice are natural phenomena and are therefore subject to the laws of nature. He pointed out that nature gives to the passions and emotions certain tones, looks, and gestures that are perceived through the ear and the eye. Therefore, he contended, the elocutionist should reproduce these tones, looks, and gestures as nearly as possible in presenting literature orally to an audience.

As often happens in the application of a theory, however, Sheridan became trapped in his efforts to be specific, and he began to evolve a system of markings and cues for the discovery and reproduction of these "natural" tones and gestures. By the end of his career, he had become the exponent of a method that, judged by modern standards, was much more mechanical than natural. Nevertheless, the term *natural school* has persisted to the present day.

The other famous eighteenth-century English elocutionist, John Walker, published his *Elements of Elocution* in 1781. He, too, professed to take his cues from nature. However, he could not (or at least did not) resist the urge to set down specific rules and markings for the slightest variations of vocal tempo, inflection, and force, and for the various aspects of gesture. These markings caught the public fancy because they were more concrete than anything that had been offered before. (It is always so much easier to be told exactly how to do something than to put one's own intelligence to work to solve each individual problem as it arises!) Walker must be given credit for stating clearly that these markings were intended as aids toward the satisfactory projection of the material at hand, and perhaps he is not to be held wholly responsible for the fact that future generations placed more emphasis on the markings and other mechanical devices than on the projection of material. Walker and his imitators, then, established what has been called the "mechanical school"—in seeming opposition to Sheridan's natural school. Thus began a schism that occupied minds for 150 years.

Two other names must be mentioned in connection with the English elocutionists of the eighteenth century. Although they were less prolific and influential than were Sheridan and Walker, John Mason (1706–1763) and James Burgh (1714–1775) both wrote books that enjoyed considerable popularity. Mason's *An Essay on Elocution or Pronunciation* (1748), the first book to include the word *elocution* in its title, put heavy emphasis on the "right" management of the voice.

James Burgh was primarily a political philosopher whose interest in speech probably grew out of his political activities. In his book *The Art of Speaking* (1762), he discussed with some vehemence the rules for expressing "the principal Passions and Humors." This volume, which contained an anthology of readings, with the passions and humors carefully documented, was based on the theory that nature had given every passion its proper physical expression and that only by careful attention to the physical features, such as the eye, can the proper passion be projected.

To summarize, the closing years of the eighteenth century saw an increased interest in the use of voice and body in the oral presentation of literature. Sheridan had set up a natural school, purportedly based on the laws of nature; Walker had established a mechanical school, based in fact on the same premises but more preoccupied with markings and charts. It is understandable that the followers of these men tended to emphasize their differences rather than their similarities, and that some degree of confusion and dissension resulted.

In the nineteenth century, two names stand out above all others in the history of interpretation. The first is that of an American, James Rush (1786–1869), a medical doctor turned speech teacher and lecturer. Rush confined himself almost entirely to the study of vocal projection. He believed that the management of the voice is in reality not an art but a science, and he went to great lengths to develop an appropriate vocabulary for that science. Indeed, much of his terminology became standard among teachers of speech. He also went to great lengths in the title of his book, published in 1827: *The Philosophy of the Human Voice: Embracing its Physiological History: Together with a System of Principles by Which Criticism in the Art of Elocution May be Rendered Intelligible, and Instruction, Definite and Comprehensive, to Which Is Added a Brief Analysis of Song and Recitative.*

Rush developed elaborate charts and markings for pitch, force, abruptness, quality, and time. He was convinced that rules could be developed to govern the analysis of vocal technique, although he was careful to point out that the practice of these rules must be accompanied by concentration on the literature being read. This last bit of advice, however, was often forgotten by his more zealous and less discriminating followers; as a result, attention was focused even more sharply on markings and symbols. Nevertheless, Rush's use of appropriate scientific method and vocabulary and his studies of the mechanisms of the human voice were valuable contributions to the field of speech.

The second significant name in nineteenth-century interpretation is François Delsarte (1811–1871). About the time Rush's method was making its way in America, Delsarte was delivering lectures in France on elocution and calisthenics. He left no writings, but so strong was his influence that many of his students recorded his philosophy and system in great detail. The Delsarte system concerned itself entirely with bodily action, and it became an accepted complement to Dr. Rush's treatises on vocal management. Delsarte based his system on a philosophy of the interrelation of the human soul, mind, and body and on a complicated and highly mystical concept of a corresponding triune relationship throughout the entire universe. Despite this philosophical premise, the system became mechanical in the extreme.

Delsarte, like Sheridan, Walker, and Rush, suffered somewhat at the hands of his followers. One example of the perversion of a basically sound but inadequately expressed theory—that gestures must spring from the heart—was the notion that all gestures must start from the breastbone and sweep out in a graceful curve. This misconception persisted for generations. Although Delsarte's system in practice took on mechanical aspects that had some unfortunate results, modern teachers of speech have been greatly influenced by his concept of mind, soul (heart or emotions), and body working together.

Thus, almost simultaneously, Rush in America was setting up a scientific approach to vocal technique and Delsarte in France was teaching a philosophical approach to bodily action. Although both men were originally concerned with the artistic projection of materials, the people they influenced often concentrated on the *application* of techniques rather than on the *reasons* for the techniques. In this way, the mechanical school, well established under the aegis of Walker's disciples, became even more firmly entrenched.

Near the close of the nineteenth century, the natural school received new impetus under the leadership of Samuel Silas Curry (1847–1921). His first book, *The Province of Expression*, published in Boston in 1891, was based on the premise that the mind, to express an idea, must actively hold that idea and thus dictate the appropriate means of expression. This theory he summed up in the admonition "Think the thought!" It is understandable that such a phrase would catch the fancy of those who read his books and heard of his teachings—and equally understandable that it would lead to oversimplification, to the extent that Curry's fundamentally sound theory came to be popularized as "Think the thought and all things else will be added unto you." As a result, many teachers began to assert that the training of voice and body were wholly artificial and mechanical procedures, and that comprehension of thought and active concentration on that thought will alone ensure adequate projection of any material to an audience.

Admittedly, this idea came as a relief to those who had become weary of the exhibitionism that prevailed among the second- and third-generation advocates of the mechanical method. In an attempt to break more completely with the earlier artificialities, teachers even began to shy away from the term *elocution,* with all its connotations, and to adopt instead Curry's term *expression.* Thus, lessons in "elocution" became lessons in "expression."

One of the most interesting and influential teachers in America at the close of the century was Charles Wesley Emerson (1837–1908), founder of the Emerson College of Oratory, now Emerson College in Boston. His *Evolution of Expression* (1905) stressed vocal technique and gymnastics for their therapeutic value as well as for their contribution to the techniques of communicating literature.

By the end of the nineteenth century, then, three distinct groups had emerged. One militantly carried on the traditions of the mechanical school. Another, distrustful of mechanics, relied on the natural method and developed in the direction of "think-the-thought." A third was composed of a few independents who found some values in each camp and attempted to blend the two approaches.

During the same time period, Victorian interest in earnest self-improvement and edification gave rise to emporiums for the dispersal of culture—for example, the Lyceum Movement, and, more prominently, the Chautauqua Institution. The latter was begun in the mid-nineteenth century as a Sunday-school teachers' summer camp and still thrives as a lively cultural center. At its most influential time, Chautauqua established nationwide book clubs and correspondence schools; great readers, speakers, and artists performed on its lecture platforms. Chautauqua was not an isolated phenomenon. From across the country came the call for performers and a full complement of touring guest artists and readers, who covered the country with uplifting readings and speeches, lectures, and programs. Famous readers or lecturers—Charles Dickens and Wendell Phillips, for example—were paid considerable sums for their personal appearances. These professionals catered to the call for living performers. Periodicals and publications like *The Voice* and *Werner's Magazine* carried testimonials for products like voice balm, scripts with appropriate and elaborate markings, annotated transcriptions of how famous performers read famous speeches—all responding to the needs of amateur elocutionists in remote towns and villages.

By the beginning of the twentieth century, a number of colleges were offering courses in elocution or expression, but most students did not include speech in their program of studies unless they were preparing themselves for the ministry, politics, or law. Most of those who wished to do "platform work" as "readers" enrolled in private schools or studios. There they worked under teachers often three or four times removed from the originators of basically sound theories, receiving instruction that, having filtered through several personalities, was strongly flavored by the individual teacher's own taste and understanding.

The first three decades of the twentieth century were the era of the private, highly specialized school or studio of speech. Each had its own staff of teachers, most of whom had been trained by the head of that particular school. Each had its own course of study and its own special emphasis. And each prided itself on its independence and its difference from the others. Consequently, there was no common philosophy or methodology. Each school emphasized its individuality, rather than working with the others toward solidarity and a unity of purpose among all teachers in the field.

Many people who studied at these schools returned to their homes, framed their certificates and hung them on their walls, and opened their own studios, where they taught to the best of their ability what they had learned. Their students, in turn, acquired certificates and went out to spread the gospel as they understood it. Thus, of the thousands of teachers who were conducting classes and giving private lessons, very few had had an opportunity to receive sound training under the great leaders. As a result, the original principles and practices were continually watered down. Not only were teachers often imperfectly prepared, but they worked in comparative isolation, without professional associations and strong university departments to serve as centers for the exchange of ideas. The better informed and more progressive teachers who studied under Curry and his contemporaries grew with the entire educational system to become the outstanding men and women in the field of speech as a whole and in the more specialized area of interpretation. Others, however, continued to teach specific gestures, highly obtrusive vocal technique, and the use of materials of questionable literary merit, thus perpetuating not only the more regrettable excesses and misconceptions in vogue in the early years of the century but also a confusion in terminology and in standards of performance.

An important link between the theorists and teachers of the nineteenth century and the present is *Principles of Vocal Expression* (1897) by William B. Chamberlain (1847–1903) and Solomon H. Clark (1861–1927). This book, acknowledging a deep indebtedness to Curry, stressed the interaction of mind and body and the control of "instincts" by reason. Clark made a more important contribution in his *Interpretation of the Printed Page* (1913), which helped turn the attention of teachers and students from the mechanical techniques to the appreciation and analysis of the literature itself. His concept of "impression" as distinct from and prerequisite to "expression" became the basis of *The Art of Interpretative Speech* by Charles H. Woolbert and Severina E. Nelson, published in 1929.

Another popular book of the early twentieth century was *Natural Drills in Expression with Selections* (1909). The author, Arthur Edward Phillips (1867–1932), reflects much of Chamberlain's interest in paraphrase and tone drills, and the book was used extensively for many years in schools and colleges.

With the advance of the twentieth century, departments of speech grew in stature in colleges and universities and became fully accepted members of the academic family. Speech training, freed from the cultist studio, flourished under the stimulating crosswinds of professional associations and the spur of more commonly shared standards. Ideas were pooled, theories argued, heritages reevaluated. Interpretation emerged from the straitjacket of the "reading" (which was not a reading at all but a virtuoso exhibition of memory and technique) and reoriented itself to the printed page.

The period of the 1940s was one of transition and stabilization. Interest in history and research increased, as described by Mary Margaret Robb in *Oral Interpretation of Literature in American Colleges and Universities* (1947) and as evidenced by the establishment of doctoral programs in the field.

Cornelius Carman Cunningham, Gertrude Johnson, Wayland Maxfield Parrish, Solomon Henry Clark, and Maud May Babcock published texts that had an important effect on the whole area of study. Although these books differ somewhat in emphasis, all firmly insist on the primacy of the literature and the importance of the demands it makes. These authors' ability to come to grips with critical and aesthetic principles and to formulate standards that apply to both analysis and performance contributed mightily to the field at midcentury.

In the 1950s and 1960s, the academic study of interpretation centered on the unique and powerful rewards performance offered the literary study of texts. It followed, then, that during this period several analytical studies of individual texts, authors, and genres influenced the development of theory. These studies all emphasized in some way the unique information obtained through performance. At the same time, other theorists continued to view interpretation from a communication perspective: interpreter derives information from a text and proceeds to communicate this information to an audience. Still another group of theorists—smaller but no less energetic or informed—believed that interpretation was essentially a method for developing the performance techniques of students while exposing them to good literature. Obviously, all of these theories have value. Since its first edition, this book has drawn on aspects of each of them, although we have consistently prized the value of performance as a way of knowing a literary work of art, recognizing that technical skills enhance and refine the act of performance both for audiences and interpreters themselves.

During the 1970s changing ideas about the social responsibilities of literature and changing perspectives on the nature of performance outside the academic establishment began to affect the three prevalent theories of interpretation. Literary study continued to influence interpretation theory, but as literary theory began to reflect the insights obtained through deconstruction, poststructuralism, and the decentering of the *literary* text, contemporary interpretation theory had to confront new concepts of "text." In this respect—and in others— phenomenologists and speech act theorists greatly influenced the philosophical and theoretical foundations of the field.

If the definition of a "text" was expanding, so, too, was the nature, variety, function, and extent of "performance." The pervasive influences of performance in everyday life suggested other modes of research and discourse. Interpreters became interested in the ways that performance could derive from, and contribute to, political and social causes; thus, for example, theory needed to reflect Marxist or feminist perspectives on texts in performance. Interpreters saw more clearly how performance could alter the performer, and thus theory had to recognize the psychological and healing powers of the act of performance. As interpreters looked at their roots, at a heritage of one-person shows, and at monologists such as Ruth Draper, theory needed to account for the ways that popular culture affected the art. Indeed, because performance is central to how we acquire knowledge of cultures, ethnographers contributed their insights to theory. Contributions from such diverse areas of interest (and there are many others, with vigorous adherents and important assistance to offer) obviously changed theory and reshaped the field. New questions were being asked, and traditional answers were being reconsidered. Some of this healthy ferment has been reflected in the emergence of the term *performance studies* as a way to describe the expanded scope of interest.

The last decade of the twentieth century and the beginning of a new century saw scholars studying performance in a number of venues. Not only were the instances of performance in everyday life explored, but popular culture itself became an ally and subject of study. Literature continued to occupy many scholars, but because its forms, shapes, and aspirations changed, so did the nature of its study. Experimental fiction and poetry have always stretched boundaries, and now video and other mediated arts collaborate by discovering new ways to convey the experiences of art. If anything has remained constant, it is the human hunger to feel and respond more deeply and broadly. Precisely this impulse has led performers to devise new ways to embody and evoke new methods of communication.

In the flux of these heady times, we must remember that social consciousness, political awareness, philosophical acumen, anthropological sensitivity, and responsiveness to developing literary theory are not mutually exclusive interests. Each contributes to a fuller understanding of how inclusive "performance" has become in our—indeed, in every— culture. Among the paths to Eden are many graveled walks. Our field rewards any number of avenues, not the least of which remains the performance of literature. Careful scrutiny and thorough analysis of a "text" best permits the interpreter with a flexible, articulate instrument to "perform" that work for and with an audience.

Happily, the different paths of research pursued today are relatively free of the "thou-shalt-nots" that characterized interpretation in the early part of the twentieth century—and that is how it should be. With a mind open to the rich and startling insights offered by aestheticians, literary theorists, linguists, philosophers, ethnographers, folklorists, and performance theorists, today's interpreter realizes that the opportunities offered by performance and text are more numerous, attractive, and empowering now than at any other time in our history.

Bibliography

The following works explore various aspects of the history of oral interpretation (under a number of different names) and propose avenues for future development.

Bahn, Eugene, and Margaret L. Bahn. *A History of Oral Interpretation.* Minneapolis: Burgess, 1970.
A detailed but concise history of orality in the West from 650 BC to the late 1960s.

Dailey, Sheron J., ed. *The Future of Performance Studies: Visions and Revisions.* Annandale, VA: National Communication Association, 1998.
A lively collection of statements, rejoinders, and proposals from forty-two contributors inside and outside the academic community.

Pelias, R. J., and J. VanOosting. "A Paradigm for Performance Studies." *Quarterly Journal of Speech* 73 (1987) 4: 219–31.
One of the earliest and most articulate rationales for naming the field to reflect broadening research interests.

Strine, M. S., B. W. Long, and M. F. HopKins. "Research in Interpretation and Performance Studies: Trends, Issues, Priorities." In *Speech Communication: Essays to Commemorate the 75th Anniversary of the Speech Communication Association,* edited by G. Phillips and J. Wood. Carbondale: Southern Illinois University Press, 1989.
A magisterial discussion of how the development of the field has opened new territory to contemporary researchers, with potent suggestions for the research the field needs.

Taft-Kaufman, J. "Oral Interpretation: Twentieth Century Theory and Practice." In *Speech Communication in the 20th Century*, edited by T. W. Benson. Carbondale: Southern Illinois University Press, 1985.

A readable and clear-headed discussion of the development of oral interpretation in the twentieth century.

Text and Performance Quarterly (formerly *Literature in Performance*)

A journal, sponsored by the National Communication Association, that is "concerned with the whole process from creation to criticism of text through the creation and criticism of performance, together with the history and theory of both ends of the spectrum."

Thompson, D. W., ed. *Performance of Literature in Historical Perspectives.* Lanham, MD: University Press of America, 1983.

The product of eight years of research by six editors and thirty-three prominent scholars, this compendium explores "five continuing concerns of the field of interpretation: namely, language, culture, teaching, theory, and entertainment."

Warren, Dorothy. *The World of Ruth Draper.* Carbondale: Southern Illinois University Press, 1999.

A life of the world-renowned monologist, drawing on correspondence, reviews, interviews, and a long personal association.

Acknowledgments

Ackerman, Diane. "Still Life." Diane Ackerman, a poet and naturalist, is the author of 10 books, the most recent of which are *A Natural History of the Senses* (prose), *Jaguar of Sweet Laughter* (poetry), and *The Moon by Whale Light.*

Albee, Edward. Excerpt from "Act 1-Fun and Games" (pp. 13-19) reprinted with the permission of Scribner, an imprint of Simon & Schuster Adult Publishing Group, from *Who's Afraid of Virginia Woolf?* by Edward Albee. Copyright (c) 1962 by Edward Albee; copyright renewed.

Allison, Jay. "Back at the Ranch" by Jay Allison from *The New York Times Magazine*, 5/27/90. Copyright (c) 1990 by The New York Times Co. Reprinted by permission.

Angelou, Maya. From *I Know Why the Caged Bird Sings*, by Maya Angelou. Copyright (c) 1969 and renewed 1997 by Maya Angelou. Used by permission of Random House, Inc.

Bambara, Toni Cade. "The Lesson," copyright (c) 1972 by Toni Cade Bambara, from *Gorilla, My Love* by Toni Cade Bambara. Used by permission of Random House, Inc.

Baraka, Amiri. *Preface to a Twenty Volume Suicide Note*, by Amiri Baraka. Copyright by Amiri Baraka. Reprinted by permission of Sterling Lord Literistic, Inc.

Barry, Lynda. "Keep Out! (A Boy's Bedroom)," by Lynda Barry, from *Home: American Writers Remember Rooms of Their Own*, by Sharon Sloan Fiffer, copyright (c) 1995 by Lynda Barry. Used by

permission of Pantheon Books, a division of Random House, Inc.

Beattie, Ann. "Snow," by Ann Beattie. Reprinted by permission of International Creative Management, Inc. Copyright (c) 1983 by Ann Beattie. First appeared in *Vanity Fair*.

Bierhorst, John, editor. From "The Night Chant," Navajo Ceremonial Chant, translated by Washington Matthews from *Four Masterworks of American Indian Literature*, edited by John Bierhorst, University of Arizona Press, 1984. Reprinted by permission of John Bierhorst.

Bishop, Elizabeth. "One Art," from *The Complete Poems 1927-1979*, by Elizabeth Bishop. Copyright (c) 1979, 1983 by Alice Helen Methfessel. Reprinted by permission of Farrar, Straus and Giroux, LLC.

Bissinger, H.G. From *Friday Night Lights: A Town, A Team, and A Dream*, by H.G. Bissinger. Copyright by Perseus Books Group. Reproduced with permission of Perseus Books Group in the format Textbook via Copyright Clearance Center.

Bowen, Elizabeth. "The Little Girls," from *Collected Stories of Elizabeth Bowen*, by Elizabeth Bowen, copyright (c) 1981 by Curtis Brown Ltd., Literary Executors of the Estate of Elizabeth Bowen. Reprinted by permission of Alfred A. Knopf, a division of Random House, Inc.

Brecht, Bertolt. From *The Caucasian Chalk Circle*, by Bertolt Brecht. Reprinted by permission of the University of Minnesota Press.

Cameron, Peter. "Homework." Copyright (c) 1984 by Peter Cameron. First appeared in *The New Yorker*. Reprinted by permission of the author.

Capote, Truman. Excerpt from *A Christmas Memory*, by Truman Capote. Copyright (c) 1956 by Truman Capote. Reprinted by permission of Random House, Inc.

Carver, Raymond. "Popular Mechanics," from *What We Talk About When We Talk About Love*, by Raymond Carver. Copyright (c) 1981 by Raymond Carver. Reprinted by permission of Alfred A. Knopf, a division of Random House, Inc.

Chekhov, Anton. Excerpt from "The Three Sisters," from *Chekhov: The Major Plays*, by Anton Chekhov. Translated by Ann Dunnigan. Copyright (c) 1964 by Ann Dunnigan. Used by permission of Dutton Signet, a division of Penguin Group (USA) Inc.

Ciardi, John. "Most Like an Arch This Marriage," from *Collected Poems of John Ciardi*. Copyright 1997 by Edward M. Cifelli. Reprinted by permission of the University of Arkansas Press.

Cleage, Pearl. Excerpted from *Flyin' West and Other Plays*, by Pearl Cleage. Copyright (c) 1999 by the author. Published by Theatre Communications Group. Used by permission.

Clifton, Lucille. "Affirmative Action," by Lucille Clifton. From *The New York Times*, 9/4/95. Copyright (c) 1995 by The New York Times Co. Reprinted with permission.

Coben, Harlan. Harlan Coben, "The Key to My Father," from *The New York Times*, June 15, 2003. Copyright (c) 2003, The New York Times. Reprinted by permission.

Cruz, Victor Hernandez. From *Today Is a Day of Great Joy*, by Victor Hernandez Cruz. Reprinted by permission of the author.

cummings, e.e. "Spring is like a perhaps hand," copyright 1923, 1925, 1951, 1953, (c) 1991 by the Trustees for the e.e. cummings Trust. Copyright (c) 1976 by George James Firmage, from *Complete Poems: 1904-1962*, by E.E. Cummngs, edited by George J. Firmage. Used by permission of Liveright Publishing Corporation.

Dann, John C. Excerpt from *The Revolution Remembered*, edited by John C. Dann. Copyright (c) 1980. Published by The University of Chicago Press

Dickey, James. "The Hospital Window," (c) 1962 by James Dickey. Reprinted from *Drowning With Others* by permission of Wesleyan University Press.

Dickinson, Emily. "I felt a funeral in my brain" is reprinted by permission of the publishers and the Trustees of Amherst College from *The Poems of Emily Dickinson*, Thomas H. Johnson, ed., Cambridge, Mass.: The Belknap Press of Harvard University Press, Copyright (c) 1951, 1955, 1979 by the President and Fellows of Harvard College. Letter from Emily Dickinson to Austin Dickinson, 17 October 1851 is reprinted by permission of the publishers from *The Letters of Emily Dickinson*, Thomas H. Johnson, ed., Cambridge, Mass.: The Belknap Press of Harvard University Press, Copyright (c) 1958, 1986 by the President and Fellows of Harvard College.

Didion, Joan. "The Seacoast of Despair," from *Slouching Towards Bethlehem*, by Joan Didion. Copyright (c) 1966, 1968, renewed 1996 by Joan Didion. Reprinted by permission of Farrar, Straus and Giroux, LLC

Dixon, Melville. "Heartbeats," by Melvin Dixon, from *Poets for Life*, edited by Michael Klein. Copyright (c) 1989. Reprinted by permission of Jane Rotrosen Agency.

Döhl, Reinhard. "Apfel," by Reinhard Döhl. Used by permission of the author.

Eliot, T.S. "Journey of the Magi," from *Collected Poems 1909-1962*, by T.S. Eliot, copyright 1936 by Harcourt, Inc., copyright (c) 1964, 1963 by T.S. Eliot, reprinted by permission of the publisher.

Foer, Jonathan Safran. From *Everything is Illuminated,* by Jonathan Safran Foer. Copyright (c) 2002 by Jonathan Safran Foer. Reprinted by permission of Houghton Mifflin Company. All rights reserved. First appeared in the *New Yorker,* June 18 and 25, 2001.

Frost, Robert. "Desert Places" and "Wild Grapes," from *The Poetry of Robert Frost,* edited by Edward Connery Lathem. Copyright (c) 1923, (c) 1969 by Henry Holt and Co., copyright 1964 by Lesley Frost Ballantine, copyright 1936, 1951 by Robert Frost. Reprinted by permission of Henry Holt and Company, LLC.

Gilbert, Joanne. "Upon Learning that a Junior High School Acquaintance Has Been Nominated for an Academy Award," by Joanne Gilbert. Reprinted by permission of the author.

Gilliat, Penelope. From *Sunday, Bloody Sunday,* by Penelope Gilliatt. Reprinted by permission of the Estate of Penelope Gilliatt.

Giovanni, Nikki. "Nikki Rosa," from *Black Feeling, Black Talk, Black Judgment,* by Nikki Giovanni. Copyright (c) 1968, 1970 by Nikki Giovanni. Reprinted by permission of HarperCollins Publishers Inc.

Glück, Louise. "The Magi," from *The First Four Books of Poems,* by Louise Glück. Copyright 1968, 1971, 1972, 1973, 1974, 1975, 1976, 1977, 1978, 1979, 1980, 1985, 1995 by Louise Glück. Reprinted by permission of HarperCollins Publishers, Inc.

Hales, Corinne. "Power," by Corinne Hales, in *New Voices 1979-1983,* ed. May Swenson. Reprinted by permission of the Academy of American Poets.

Hammond, Mary Stewart. "Saving Memory." Copyright (c) 1989 by Mary Stewart Hammond, from *Out of Canaan,* by Mary Stewart Hammond. Reprinted by permission of W.W. Norton & Company, Inc.

Hayes, Bill. "Flying Finish," by Bill Hayes, from *The New York Times Magazine,* 7/9/95. Copyright (c) 1995 by The New York Times Co. Reprinted with permission.

Heaney, Seamus. "Mid-Term Break," from *Opened Ground: Selected Poems 1966-1996,* by Seamus Heaney. Copyright (c) 1998 by Seamus Heaney. Reprinted by permission of Farrar, Straus and Giroux, LLC

Hongo, Garret Kaoru. "Who Among You Knows the Essence of Garlic?" (c) 1980 by Garrett Kaoru Hongo. Reprinted from *Yellow Light* by permission of Wesleyan University Press.

Howes, Barbara. "On Sleeping Together," by Barbara Howes, from *Collected Poems of Barbara Howes, 1945-1990.* Copyright (c) 1995. Reprinted by permission of University of Arkansas Press.

Hoyt, Helen. "The Sense of Death," by Helen Hoyt, from *The Home Book of Modern Verse,* edited by Burton E. Stevenson. Reprinted by permission of the Trustee for the Burton E. Stevenson Endowment for Children.

Hughes, Langston. "The Negro Speaks of Rivers," from *The Collected Poems of Langston Hughes,* by Langston Hughes. Copyright (c) 1994 by the Estate of Langston Hughes. Used by permission of Alfred A. Knopf, a division of Random House, Inc.

Joans, Ted. "The .38," from *Black Pow-Wow, Jazz Poems,* by Ted Joans. Copyright (c) 1969 by Ted Joans. All rights reserved. Reprinted by permission of the Author's Representative, Gunther Stuhlmann.

Kincaid, Jamaica. "Girl," from *At the Bottom of the River,* by Jamaica Kincaid. Copyright (c) 1983 by Jamaica Kincaid. Reprinted by permission of Farrar, Straus and Giroux, LLC.

Koestenbaum, Phyllis. "Admission of Failure," by Phyllis Koestenbaum. Copyright (c) 1991 by Phyllis Koestenbaum. Published in *Epoch* 40, no. 1 (1991): 19. Also published in *The Best American Poetry* 1992.

Kunitz, Stanley. "Open the Gates," copyright 1944 by Stanley Kunitz, from *The Poems of Stanley Kunitz 1928-1978,* by Stanley Kunitz. Reprinted by permission of W.W. Norton & Company, Inc.

Larkin, Philip. "Talking in Bed," from *Collected Poems,* by Philip Larkin. Copyright (c) 1988, 1989 by the Estate of Philip Larkin. Reprinted by permission of Farrar, Straus and Giroux, LLC.

Lassell, Michael. "How to Watch Your Brother Die," from *Poems for Lost and Unlost Boys,* (c) 1985 by Michael Lassell. Reprinted by permission of the author.

Least Heat Moon, William. From *Blue Highways,* by William Least Heat Moon. Copyright (c) 1982, 1999 by William Least Heat Moon. By permission of Little, Brown and Company, Inc.

Leavitt, David. "The Crane Child," from *The Lost Language of Cranes,* by David Leavitt. Copyright (c) 1986 by David Leavitt. Reprinted by permission of The Wylie Agency, Inc.

Lux, Thomas. "The Voice You Hear When You Read Silently," from *New & Selected Poems, 1975-1995,* by Thomas Lux. Copyright (c) 1997 by Thomas Lux. Reprinted by permission of Houghton Mifflin Company. All rights reserved.

MacDonald, Cynthia. "The Kilgore Rangerette Whose Life Was Ruined," from *(W)holes,* by Cynthia MacDonald. Copyright (c) 1980 by Cynthia MacDonald. Reprinted by permission of Alfred A. Knopf, a division of Random House, Inc.

MacLeish, Archibald. "Ars Poetica," from *Collected Poems 1917-1983,* by Archibald MacLeish. Copyright (c) 1985 by The Estate of Archibald MacLeish. Reprinted by permission of Houghton Mifflin Company. All rights reserved.

Macourek, Milos. "Jacob's Chicken," by Milos Macourek, translated from the Czech by Dagmar Herrmann. Reprinted from the *Prairie Schooner* by permission of the University of Nebraska Press. Copyright (c) 1992 by the University of Nebraska Press

Madgett, Naomi Long. "Her Story" from *Star by Star* by Naomi Long Madgett, Detroit. Harlo, 1965, Evenill, 1970. With permission of the author.

Malamud, Bernard. "The Prison," from *The Magic Barrel,* by Bernard Malamud. Copyright (c) 1950, 1958 and copyright renewed (c) 1977, 1986 by Bernard Malamud. Reprinted by permission of Farrar, Straus and Giroux, LLC.

Matthews, William. "A Night at the Opera," from *Time & Money: New Poems*, by William Matthews. Copyright (c) 1995 by William Matthews. Reprinted by permission of Houghton Mifflin Company. All rights reserved.

McBroom, Amanda. "Dreaming," by Amanda McBroom. (c) 1986 McBroom Music/BMI. All rights reserved.

McGough, Roger. "40-Love," from *After the Merrymaking*, by Roger McGough. Reprinted by permission of PFD on behalf of Roger McGough. (c) 1971, Roger McGough.

Millay, Edna St. Vincent. "Sonnet XXX" of *Fatal Interview*, by Edna St. Vincent Millay. From *Collected Poems*, HarperCollins. Copyright (c) 1931, 1958 by Edna St. Vincent Millay and Norma Millay Ellis. All rights reserved.

Minot, Susan. "Toast," from *4 A.M.*, by Susan Minot, copyright (c) 2002 by Susan Minot. Used by permission of Alfred A. Knopf, a division of Random House, Inc.

Morrison, Toni. Excerpt from *Sula* by Toni Morrison. Reprinted by permission of International Creative Management. Copyright (c) 1973 by Toni Morrison.

Olds, Sharon. "The Race," from *The Father,* by Sharon Olds. Copyright (c) 1992 by Sharon Olds. Used by permission of Alfred A. Knopf, a division of Random House, Inc.

Ovid. "The Story of Baucis and Philomen," from *The Metamorphoses,* by Ovid, translated by Rolfe

Humphries. Copyright (c) 1955. Reprinted by permission of Indiana University Press.

Pinter, Harold. Excerpt from Scene Five, *Betrayal,* by Harold Pinter. Copyright (c) 1978 by H. Pinter Ltd. Used by permission of Grove Press, Inc., and Faber and Faber Ltd.

Ray, David. "Unforgiven," by David Ray. From *The New York Times Magazine,* 8/20/95. Copyright (c) 1995 by The New York Times Co. Reprinted with permission.

Robertson, Robin. "After the Overdose," from *A Painted Field,* copyright (c) 1997 by Robin Robertson, reprinted by permission of Harcourt, Inc.

Roethke, Theodore. "Old Lady's Winter Words," copyright 1952 by Theodore Roethke. "The Waking," copyright 1953 by Theodore Roethke, from *The Collected Poems of Theodore Roethke,* by Theodore Roethke. Used by permission of Doubleday, a division of Random House, Inc.

Roth, Philip. Excerpt from "The Conversion of the Jews." from *Goodbye, Columbus,* by Philip Roth. Copyright (c) 1959, renewed 1987 by Philip Roth. Reprinted by permission of Houghton Mifflin Company. All rights reserved.

Rowling, J.K. Excerpt from *Harry Potter and the Sorcerer's Stone,* by J. K. Rowling, 1997, pp. 81-85. Copyright (c) J.K. Rowling, 1997. Reprinted by permission of Christopher Little Literary Agency.

Santoli, Albert. Excerpt from *Everything We Had,* by Albert Santoli. Copyright (c) 1981 by Albert Santoli and Vietnam Veterans of America. Used by permission of Random House, Inc.

Schlissel, Lillian. From *Women's Diaries of the Westward Journey,* edited by Lillian Schlissel. Reprinted by permission of Gertrude Tortillot Bradley.

Sexton, Anne. "Cinderella," from *Transformations.* Copyright (c) 1971 by Anne Sexton.

Reprinted by permission of Houghton Mifflin Co. All rights reserved. "Ringing the Bells," from *To Bedlam and Part Way Back,* by Anne Sexton. Copyright (c) 1960 by Anne Sexton, renewed 1998 by Linda G. Sexton. Reprinted by permission of Houghton Mifflin Company. All rights reserved.

Shakespeare, William. From *Complete Plays and Poems of William Shakespeare,* edited by William Allan Neilson and Charles Jarvis Hill. Copyright (c) 1942 by Houghton Mifflin Company. Used with permission.

Shepard, Sam. Excerpt from "Curse of the Starving Class," copyright (c) 1976 by Sam Shepard. From *Seven Plays,* by Sam Shepard. Used by permission of Bantam Books, a division of Random House, Inc.

Sherman, Deborah. "Dulce," by Deborah Sherman. Reprinted by permission of the author.

Smiley, Jane. "Confess, Early and Often." Copyright (c) 1995 by The New York Times Company. Reprinted by permission.

Smith, Anna Deavere. "Bad Boy, Anonymous Young Man," "Roslyn Malamud: The Coup," from *Fires in the Mirror,* by Anna Deavere Smith. Copyright (c) 1993 by Anna Deavere Smith. Used by permission of Doubleday, a division of Random House, Inc.

Solt, Mary Ellen. "Forsythia," by Mary Ellen Solt. From *Concrete Poetry: A World View* (1969), Bloomington, Indiana: Indiana University Press. Reprinted by permission of the author.

Sondheim, Stephen. "Finishing the Hat," by Stephen Sondheim. Copyright (c) 1984 and 1987 by Revelation Music Publishing Corp. & Rilting Music, Inc. A Tommy Valando Publication, International Copyright Secured. Made in U.S.A., All Rights Reserved.

Sophocles. *Oedipus the King,* from *Three Theban Plays: Antigone, Oedipus the King, and Oedipus at*

Colonus, by Sophocles, edited by Theodore Howard Banks. Copyright (c) 1956 by Oxford University Press, Inc. Used by permission of Oxford University Press, Inc.

Soyinka, Wole. From *Death and the King's Horseman*, by Wole Soyinka. Copyright (c) 1975 by Wole Soyinka. Used by permission of W.W. Norton & Company, Inc.

Stafford, William. "First Grade," copyright 1987, 1998 by the Estate of William Stafford. Reprinted from *The Way It Is: New & Selected Poems* with the permission of Graywolf Press, Saint Paul, Minnesota.

Stevens, Wallace. "The House Was Quiet and the World Was Calm," from *The Collected Poems of Wallace Stevens*, by Wallace Stevens. Copyright 1954 by Wallace Stevens and renewed 1982 by Holly Stevens. Used by permission of Alfred A. Knopf, a division of Random House, Inc.

Swenson, May. From "To Make a Play," by May Swenson. Used with permission of The Literary Estate of May Swenson.

Swofford, Anthony. From *Jarheads*, by Anthony Swofford. Reprinted with the permission of Scribner, an imprint of Simon & Schuster Adult Publishing Group. Copyright (c) 2003 by Anthony Swofford.

Tan, Amy. "Two Kinds," from *The Joy Luck Club*, by Amy Tan. Copyright (c) 1989 by Amy Tan. Used by permission of G.P. Putnam's Sons, a division of Penguin Group (USA) Inc.

Terkel, Studs. Excerpt from *Working*, by Studs Terkel. Reprinted by permission of Donadio & Olson, Inc. Copyright 1974 by Studs Terkel.

Thomas, Dylan. "Do Not Go Gentle Into That Good Night," by Dylan Thomas. From *The Poems of Dylan Thomas*. Copyright (c) 1952 by Dylan Thomas. Reprinted by permission of New Directions Publishing Corp.

Tierney, Dana. "The Makeup Artist," by Dana Tierney. From *The New York Times*, 8/6/98. Copyright (c) 1998 by the New York Times Co. Reprinted with permission.

Updike, John. "A & P," from *Pigeon Feathers and Other Stories*, by John Updike. Copyright (c) 1962 and renewed 1990 by John Updike. Used by permission of Alfred A. Knopf, a division of Random House, Inc.

Van Duyn, Mona. "Cinderella's Story," from *If It Be Not I*, by Mona Van Duyn. Copyright (c) 1959 by Mona Van Duyn. Used by permission of Alfred A. Knopf, a division of Random House, Inc.

Walker, Alice. Poem from *Horses Make a Landscape Look More Beautiful*, Poems by Alice Walker, copyright (c) 1984 by Alice Walker, reprinted by permission of Harcourt, Inc.

Welty, Eudora. Excerpts from "June Recital," in *The Golden Apples*, copyright 1947 and renewed 1975 by Eudora Welty, reprinted by permission of Harcourt, Inc. Excerpt from *Losing Battles*, by Eudora Welty. Copyright (c) 1970 by Eudora Welty. Used by permission of Random House, Inc.

West, Nathanael. Excerpt by Nathanael West, from *Miss Lonelyhearts & Day of the Locust*. Copyright (c) 1939 by Estate of Nathanael West. Reprinted by permission of New Directions Publishing Corp.

Wilson, Lanford. Excerpt from *5th of July: A Play*, by Lanford Wilson. Copyright (c) 1979 by Lanford Wilson. Reprinted by permission of Hill and Wang, a division of Farrar, Straus and Giroux, LLC.

Wright, James. "A Blessing," from *The Branch Will Not Break*. (c) 1963 by James Wright, Wesleyan University Press. Reprinted by permission of Wesleyan University Press. "Autumn Begins in Martin's Ferry, Ohio." (c) 1971 by James Wright. Reprinted from *Collected Poems* by permission of Wesleyan University Press.

Yeats, W.B. Two lines from "Among School Children" are reprinted with the permission of Scribner, an imprint of Simon & Schuster Adult Publishing Group, from *The Collected Works of W.B. Yeats, Volume 1: The Poems, Revised*, edited by Richard J. Finneran. Copyright (c) 1928 by The Macmillan Company; copyright renewed (c) 1956 by Georgie Yeats. "The Second Coming" is reprinted with the permission of Scribner, an imprint of Simon & Schuster Adult Publishing Group, from *The Collected Works of W.B. Yeats,*

Volume 1: The Poems, Revised, edited by Richard J. Finneran. Copyright (c) 1924 by The Macmillan Company; copyright renewed (c) 1952 by Bertha Georgie Yeats.

Yeston, Maury. "New Words." Words and Music by Maury Yeston. Copyright (c) 1975 Yeston Music Ltd. (BMI). Worldwide Rights for Yeston Music Ltd. Administered by Cherry River Music Co. International Copyright Secured. All Rights Reserved.

Subject Index

A

Abridging works, 248–250, 356–357
Abruptness, 530
Accent, 100
Acting, interpretation *versus*, 10–13, 292–293
Action
  placement of, 35–37, 352–355
  plot and, 241–242, 294, 302
  remembered, 344
Active elements, 306
Adams, John Quincy, 528
Addressing, in narration, 237
Aesthetic components, in analysis, 39–43
Aesthetic distance, 338
Aesthetic entirety, of literature, 10
Affectation, 99
Age of audience, 525–526
Alliteration, 400
Allusions, 31–32, 185, 393–394
Ambiguity, 23, 237
Analogies, 394
Analysis. *See also* Selections, analyzing
  of content, 9
  in interpretation, 20–25
  of rehearsal, 148–150, 250–253, 357–359, 443–444, 493–494
  of structure, 9–10
Anapestic foot, 431
Angle of placement, 352–355
Anthologies, 13
Apostrophe, 395
Approximate rhyme, 441
Argument, performance as, 4
Articulation, 99
Associations, 22, 31–32, 40, 143, 188
Assonance, 186, 400, 441
Asymmetrical balance, 41–42
Attitude, set speech, 339
Audience
  adapting to, 525–526

  analysis and, 57
  children as, 526
  classes as, 59
  dialects and, 101
  inclusion of, 36–37
  interaction of work with, 42
  interpretation and, 6–8, 11
  locus and, 34
  rate of speech and, 97
  for solo drama performance, 292
Audience sense, 93
Auditory imagery, 140
Autistic gesture, 138
Awareness exercises, 146

B

Babcock, Maud May, 534
Balance, 39, 41–42, 46, 50, 52, 54, 143
Balanced construction, 181–182
Balancing sentences, 183–185, 251
Ballads, 386
Barzun, Jacques, 190
Bennett, Arnold, 178
Blank verse, 427, 435, 442
Blogging, 192
Body (human), in interpretation, 133–172
  in drama technique, 344–347
  empathy in, 143–145
  eye contact in, 147–150
  kinesics of, 136–140
  posture of, 136
  rehearsal of, 145–147
  selectivity of, 343
  sense imagery and, 140–143
  technique and, 134–136
Breath control, 88–93
Brecht, Bertolt, 475
Breen, Robert, 478
Brinsley, Richard, 529
Buford, Bill, 232
Burgh, James, 530

C

Cadence, 187, 437–440
Caesura, 438
Central participants, 236
Chamberlain, William K., 533
Chamber Theater, 478–485
Characters
  embodiment of, 336, 343–344
  interplay of, 348–350
  narration and, 242–243, 245–247
  with physical disabilities, 346–347
Chautauqua Institution, 487, 532
Children, as audience, 526
Choreography, 352
Chorus (Greek), 474
Clark, Solomon, Henry, 533–534
Climax, 37–39, 42, 47, 50, 57, 179, 294, 303, 438
Closed situations, 37
Clothes, in drama, 345–346
Clues, in drama, 291, 295
Collaboration, 473
Colloquial speech, 430
Colons, 183
"Commonplace books," 192
Communication, 5, 136
Communication apprehension, 7–8
Communion, 5
Compiled scripts, 485–488
Concentration, 8
Conclusions, 179
Concrete poetry, 488
Condensation, in poetry, 398, 424, 443
"Confessional" school of poetry, 65
Conflict, 241–242, 294
Confrontation, 299
Connectives, 40, 181
Connotative meanings, 31–32, 54, 97, 185, 304
Consonance, 186, 400
Consonants, final, 441

Construction, balanced, 180–182
Contact, physical, 347–348
Content, 8–9, 15
    fulcrum and, 42
    poetic structure and, 442
    of poetry, 383–385
    rhythm of, 43, 57, 187
Contrast, 39–41, 47, 49–50, 52, 54,
    96, 188, 303, 438
Control, 338–339, 342
Controlled relaxation, 138
Conventional types of poetry, 425
Conversational mode, 195
Copyrights, 490
Crisis, 38, 241. *See also* Climax
Criticism, 359
Crossbreeding, in group perfor-
    mance, 473
Cues, 349–350
Cultures, 4, 195
Cunningham, Cornelius Carman,
    534
Curry, Samuel Silas, 531, 533
Cutting, 248–250, 356–357

D
Dactylic foot, 431
Dashes, 183
Declamation, 528
Delsarte, François, 531
Denotative meanings, 31–32, 185,
    304
Denouement, 294
Description, 187–189, 359
Dialect, 100–102
Dialogue, 35, 187, 243–245
Diaphragm, 88
Diaries, 191–193
Dickens, Charles, 532
Diction, 6, 185–186
Dictionary, 31
Differences, 41
Dimeter, 431
Diphthongs, 101
Direct discourse, 244
Directing group performance,
    489–492
Disabilities, performers with, 86,
    346–347
Disbelief, suspended, 290
Discourse, direct and indirect,
    244
Disputation, 528
Distance, aesthetic, 338
Double rhymes, 441

Drama, solo performance of,
    289–332
    acting *versus* interpretation in,
        292–293
    analyzing scenes in, 295–299
    combining elements for, 309–310
    nature of, 290–291
    reason for, 291–292
    rhythm in, 306–307
    scenography in, 308–309
    structural elements in, 9, 294–295
    style in, 307
    working scenes in, 299–306
Drama, technique in, 335–378
    character embodiment and, 336,
        343–344
    character interplay in, 348–350
    cutting and excerpting and,
        356–357
    interpretation and, 337–341
    physical contact in, 347–348
    physical focus and, 350–355
    properties and, 341–342
    reading stand in, 355–356
    rehearsal analysis in, 357–359
    voice and body coordination in,
        344–347
Dramatic lyric, 390
Dramatic monologues, 390
Dramatic narrative, 390
Dramatic poetry, 389–391
Dramatis Personae, 340
Draper, Ruth, 535
Duo drama assignments, 478

E
Eavesdropping, illusion of, 474
Elegy, 388
Elocution studies, 189, 528–531
Emerson, Charles Wesley, 532
Emerson College (Boston), 532
Emotional climax, 38, 42–43, 47
Emotional entirety, of literature,
    8–10
Emotional response, 9, 15, 97, 188
Empathy, 143–145, 188
English Elocutionists, 529
Enjambment, 436, 438
Epic, 387
Essays, 190–191
Ethical responsibilities, 7, 101
Ethnographic performance, 4
Excerpting, 57–60, 248–250, 356–357
Exercises
    awareness, 146

breathing, 89–93
voice, 87–88
Exhalation, 88, 90
Exhibitionism, 532
Experience, sharing, 5
Explicit clues, in drama, 291, 295
Expression studies, 147, 189,
    531–533
Eye contact, 147–150

F
Facial expressions, 147
Factual prose, 189–190
Faulkner, William, 15
Figurative language, 392–398
Figures of speech, 185, 394–396
Film scripts, 489
First-person narrators, 18,
    234–236
Flexibility, vocal, 7
Focus, physical, 350–355
Folktales, 195–197
Foot prosody, 430–431
Force, 530
Forced exhalation, 90
Forster, E. M., 243
Frame, of performance, 340
Free verse, 425, 427–428, 435, 439, 442
Frost, Robert, 427–428
Fulcrum (balance point), 42, 183,
    434, 438

G
Games, drama as, 290
Gender, 344–345, 525–526
Gesture, 137–138, 342
Giovanni, Nikki, 101
Grammatical structure, 182
Graphic elements, 523
Group performance, 471–518
    Chamber Theater as, 478–485
    of compiled scripts, 485–488
    of concrete poetry, 488
    directing, 489–492
    of film scripts, 489
    Readers Theater as, 473–478
    rehearsal analysis for, 493–494
Gustatory imagery, 140

H
Half rhymes, 441
Harmony, 39–40, 47, 49, 52, 54, 186,
    188, 438

Harvard University, 528
Hexameter, 431
Hidden clues, in drama, 291, 295
History of interpretation, 528–537
  elocution studies, 528–531
  expression studies, 531–533
  impression/interpretation studies, 533–534
  performance studies, 534–536
  rhapsodists of ancient Greece, 528

I
Iambic foot, 430
Iambic pentameter, 425, 431
Illusions, 308, 474
Imagery, 140–143, 240, 388, 442
Immediacy, 195
Implicit clues, in drama, 295
Impression/interpretation studies, 533–534
Impressions, 22, 189
Inaction, 302
Incident, 299, 302
Indirect discourse, 244
Individuality, 16, 21–25
Inflection, 96, 343
Inhalation, 88
Insincerity, 99
Intellectual entirety, of literature, 8–10
Intelligibility of speech, 99–100
Intensity, 42, 247, 342
Interaction, 42, 299, 350
Internet, 192
Interpretation, 3–27
  acting *versus*, 10–13, 292–293
  analysis in, 20–25
  audience and, 6–8
  choosing material for, 15–20
  in drama technique, 337–341
  history of, 528–537
  intertextuality and, 14
  of literary works, 8–10
  poetry line lengths and, 435–437
  sources of material for, 13–14
Intertextuality, 14, 31–32
Intrinsic factors, 39–43, 52–55

J
James, Henry, 234
Johnson, Gertrude, 534
Journals, 191–193

K
Kinesics, 136–140
Kinetic imagery, 140
Klang ("ring"), 97

L
Langelier, Kristin, 195
Language, 23, 392–398
Lectern, 355–356
Lecture recital, 519
Letters, 191–193
Lines in poetry, 427, 430–437
  foot prosody in, 430–431
  lengths of, 427, 435–437
  scanning, 431–433
  stress prosody in, 433
  syllabic prosody in, 433–435
Listening, 8
Literary theory, 14
Literary works, 5, 8–10
Locus, 33–34, 40
Logical climax, 38, 42, 50
Lyceum Movement, 532
Lyric poetry, 33, 387–390

M
Make-believe, drama as, 290
Mason, John, 530
Material for interpretation
  choosing, 15–20, 519–520
  different, in one program, 521–522
  sources of, 13–14
McBroom, Amanda, 33
Mechanical school of speech, 532
Melody, 96
Memorization, 8, 339
Mental directness, 95
Mental readiness, 135
Metaphors, 11, 185, 394
Metonymy, 395
Metrical feet, 426
Metrical tale, 386
Mime, 146
Mimed props, 341
Mimetic gestures, 137, 342
Minor climax, 57
Mispronunciation, 99
Mock epic, 387
Modifiers, 180
Molière, 290
Monologues, 307, 390
Monometer, 431
Monotone, 96

Mood, 182
Motif, 51, 61
Motives, 309
Multimedia, 521–522
Multiple readers, 521–522
Muscle tone, 138–139, 188
Musculoskeletal disabilities, 86
Music, 96, 391–392

N
Narration, 11, 18, 32–33, 48, 187, 192, 195, 231–286, 490
  action and plot in, 241–242
  characters and, 242–243, 245–247
  cutting and excerpting for, 248–250
  definition of, 232–233
  dialogue in, 243–245
  dramatic, 390
  point of view and, 233–241
  rehearsal analysis for, 250–253
  setting and, 247–248
Narrative poetry, 385–387
Natural method of speech, 532
Nelson, Severina E., 533
Neurological disabilities, 86
New York Times, staging, 522–524
Nondramatic prose, 177, 197
Nonverbal communication, 136
Novels, 197

O
Obscurity, 23
Observers, 4, 236, 238, 241
O'Connor, Flannery, 101
Odes, 388
Olfactory imagery, 140
Omniscient observers, 238, 241
Onomatopoeia, 400
Open situations, 37
Opposition, 41
Oral histories, 193–194
Oratory, 528
Orkastra (Greek), 474
Outward characteristics, 304

P
Paragraphs, 178–179
Parallelism, 181–182, 251
Parentheses, 183
Parrish, Wayland Maxfield, 534
Passive elements, 306
Passive voice, 48

Patterns, sound, 425, 440
Pause, in speech, 97–99, 435, 438
Pentameter, 431
Performance, 4–6. *See also* Drama,
    solo performance of; Group
    performance; Materials for
    interpretation
  aesthetic components of, 39
  first, 30–31
  frame of, 340
  reading *New York Times* as,
    522–524
  reasons for, 10–13
  study of, 534–536
  unifying, 520–521
Performance anxiety, 7–8, 87, 139–140
Performance arena, 476
Periodic construction, 180
Permissions, 490
Persona, 32–33, 51–52, 57
  action placement and, 35
  audience and, 42
  unity and, 40
Personal essays, 190–191
Personal narrative, 192
Personification, 395
Phillips, Arthur Edward, 534
Phillips, Wendell, 532
Phrasal pauses, 98
Phrases, speech, 182–183
Physical contact, 347–348
Physical disabilities, performers
    with, 86, 346–347
Physical focus, in drama, 350–355
Physical positions, 33
Physical suggestion, 6
Picasso, Pablo, 428
Pitch, of voice, 6, 96–99, 182, 435, 530
Placement of action, 35–37, 352–355
Platform presence, 6
Plays. *See* Drama, solo performance
    of; Group performance
Plot and action, 241–242, 294
Podium, 355–356
Poetry, 381–420
  analysis of, 49–55, 403
  concrete, 488
  "confessional school" of, 65
  content of, 383–385
  dramatic, 389–391
  drama *versus*, 291
  figurative language in, 392–398
  lyric, 33, 387–389
  music as, 391–392
  narrative, 385–387
  structure of, 9–10, 54

syntax of, 398–399
titles of, 402–403
tone color in, 400–402
Poetry, structure of, 54, 423–467
  cadence in, 437–440
  lines in, 430–437
  prosody study in, 425–426
  rehearsal analysis in, 443–444
  rhyme in, 440–443
  stanzas in, 429–430
  verse types in, 426–428
Point of view, 233–241. *See also*
  Narration
Political performance, 4
Popular ballads, 386
Positions, 33
Posture, 136
Presentational skills, 6, 10, 474
Prevailing foot, 427
Primary cadence, 437
Probability, in plays, 294
Programs. *See* Performance
Progression, 32
Projection
  in dialogue, 246
  stage space for, 475–476
  of voice, 93–96
Pronunciation, 99, 432, 528
Properties, 309, 341–342
Proportion, 39, 41–42, 50, 52, 54, 143
Prose, 175–229
  balancing sentences in, 183–185
  description in, 187–189
  diction in, 185–186
  drama *versus*, 291
  factual, 189–190
  folktales as, 195–197
  journals, letters, and diaries as,
    191–193
  nondramatic, 177
  oral histories as, 193–194
  paragraphs in, 178–179
  personal essays as, 190–191
  rhythm in, 187
  sentences in, 179–182
  short stories and novels as, 197
  speech phrases in, 182–183
  storytelling as, 194–195
  tone color in, 186
Prosody
  foot, 430–431
  stress, 433
  study of, 425–426
  syllabic, 433–435
Proximity, 195
Psychological positions, 33

Public speeches, 37
Punctuation, 98, 182–183, 429
Pyrrhic foot, 431

Q
Quality, of voice, 96–99, 343, 530
Quantity, of sounds, 99

R
Range, of voice, 7, 343
Rate of speech, 6, 97–99, 187, 440
Readers, multiple, 521–522. *See also*
  Group performance
Readers Theater, 473–478
Reading stand, 355–356
Recital, lecture, 519
Reenactments, 474
Reflective lyric poetry, 388
Reflexive physical activity, 347
Rehearsal, 8, 11
  analysis of, 148–150, 250–253,
    357–359, 443–444, 493–494
  of body, in interpretation,
    145–147
  cadence and, 439
  intrinsic factors in, 52–55
  of selections, 56–57
Relative stress, 432
Relaxation, 8, 43, 138
Remembered action, theory of, 344
Repetition, 20, 250
Resolution, 294
Responsibilities, of interpreters, 7–8,
    59, 101
Rhapsodists of ancient Greece, 528
Rhetoric, 528
Rhyme, 427, 440–443
Rhyme scheme, 427
Rhythm, 39, 43, 48–49, 52, 55, 57, 63,
    187, 250, 299, 304, 306–307, 343,
    425
Rituals, 4, 290
Robb, Mary Margaret, 534
Rush, James, 530

S
Scansion, 430, 435, 439
Scenes
  analyzing, 295–299
  working, 299–306
Scenography, 308–309, 340, 492
Scripts, 485–489
Secondary cadence, 437–438

Second-person narrators, 236–238
Selections, analyzing, 29–83
    action placement in, 35–37
    aesthetic components in, 39–43
    climax in, 37–39
    denotative and connotative
        meanings in, 31–32
    for first performance, 30–31
    locus in, 33–34
    personas in, 32–33
    poetry example of, 49–55
    story example of, 44–49
    synthesis in, 55–60
Self-disclosure, 299
Self-referencing power, 338
Semicolons, 182–183
Sensation, 50
Sense imagery, 140–143
Sensitivity sessions, 146
Sensory appeals, 396–398
Sentences, 179–185
"Set," 135
Set speech attitude, 339
Shakespeare, William, 427, 475
Shaw, George Bernard, 177
Shepard, Sam, 475
Sheridan, Thomas, 529
Short stories, 197
Silence, 299, 302
Similes, 185, 394
Single dash, 183
Smith, Anna Deavere, 195
Soliloquy, 390
Sondheim, Stephen, 33, 441
Sonnets, 389, 488
Sound, unit of, 429
Sound patterns, in poetry, 425,
    440
Speech, 299
    college departments of, 534
    colloquial, 430
    dialect of, 100–102
    disorders of, 86
    intelligibility of, 99–100
    mechanical school of, 532
    natural method of, 532
    rate of, 6, 97–99, 187, 440
    set, 339
    voice mechanisms and, 530–531
Speech phrases, 182–183
Spelling, 100
Spondee foot, 431
Stage fright, 7–8
Standard American Speech, 100
Stanzas, 398, 425, 440

Stories, analysis of, 44–49
Storytelling, 4, 194–195, 195. *See also*
    Narration
Stress, 187
    in poetry, 431–433, 438
    prosody of, 433
    of voice, 7
Structural components, in analysis,
    30–39
    climax in, 37–39
    denotative and connotative
        meanings in, 31–32
    locus in, 33–34
    personas in, 32–33
    placement of action in, 35–37
Structure
    grammatical, 182
    of literature, 8–10, 15. *See also*
        Selections, analyzing
    parallel, 251
    of poetry. *See* Poetry, structure of
    rhythm in, 187
    in solo performance of drama,
        291, 294–295
Succession, of sentences, 180
Suggestion, 6, 16, 21–23, 25, 97
Suspended disbelief, 290
Syllabication, 432
Syllabic prosody, 432–435
Syllables, 182, 437
Symmetrical balance, 41
Synecdoche, 395
Syntactical distinctions, 179
Syntax, 100, 398–399, 438
Synthesis, 55–60

T
Tactual imagery, 140
Tale, metrical, 386
Technical display, 5
Technical responsibilities, 7–8
Tempo, 182, 250, 306, 343
Tetrameter, 431
Theater. *See* Drama, solo perfor-
    mance of; Group performance
Thematic approach, 519–520
Theory of remembered action, 344
Thermal imagery, 140
Third-person narrators, 11, 238–241,
    243
Thought, unit of, 429
Throwing the voice, 94
Thurber, James, 190
Timbre, 97

Timing programs, 526–527
Titles, of poetry, 402–403
Tone, 97
Tone color, 186, 400–402, 441
Tragedy, 294
Tragic flaws, 11
Transitions, 349–350
Trimeter, 431
Triple rhymes, 441
Trochaic foot, 431
Turning points, 241

U
Unequal balance, 41–42
Unit of sound, 429
Unit of thought, 429
Unity, 39–40, 49, 52–54, 188, 294, 438
Universality, 15, 20–25

V
Value, in parallelism, 181–182
Vantage points, 33
Variety, 39–41, 46, 49, 52, 54, 96, 188,
    303, 438
Verbatim recordings, 244
Villanelles (poetry), 429
Visual imagery, 140
Vocal suggestion, 6
Voice
    breath control and, 88–93
    controlling, 251
    in drama, 344–347
    exercise for, 87–88
    flexibility in, 7
    pitch of, 6, 96–99, 435, 530
    projection of, 93–96, 246
    quality of, 96–99, 530
    range of, 7, 343
    selectivity of, 343
    speech phrases and, 182
    stress of, 7
    throwing, 94
volume of, 6–7, 93–96, 182
Vowels, final, 441

W
Walker, John, 529
Welty, Eudora, 101
Woolbert, Charles, H., 533
Word choice, 100
Word play, 303
Writers, 5

Author and Selection Index

A

Aarne, Antti, *The Types of the Folktale*, 196

"A Blessing" (Wright), 449

Ackerman, Diane, "Still Life," 134, 160

Admission of Failure (Koestenbaum), 171

"Affirmative Action," (Clifton), 162–163

Afterlife (Monette), 525

"After the Overdose" (Robertson), 513–514

Albee, Edward, *Who's Afraid of Virginia Woolf?*, 300–306, 336, 472, 475–476

Allison, Jay, *Back at the Ranch*, 115–118

"Among School Children" (Yeats), 132

An Essay on Elocution or Pronunciation (Mason), 530

Angelou, Maya, *I Know Why the Caged Bird Sings*, 101, 211–213, 232

Angels in America (Kushner), 525

"A Night at the Opera" (Matthews), 103

"Apfel" (Döhl), 472, 488, 505

A&P (Updike), 232, 234, 259–265

Arnold, Matthew, "Dover Beach," 114

As Is (Hoffman), 525

As You Like It (Shakespeare), 170

A Tale of Two Cities (Dickens), 134, 141

Auden, W. H., "Leap Before You Look," 2

"Autumn Begins in Martins Ferry, Ohio" (Wright), 134, 156–157

A Very Rigid Search (Foer), 100, 104–106

B

Back at the Ranch (Allison), 115–118

Bambara, Toni Cade, *The Lesson*, 86, 100, 119–125, 232, 520

Baraka, Imamu Amiri, "Preface to a Twenty Volume Suicide Note," 419–420

Barry, Lynda, *KEEP OUT! (A Boy's Bedroom)*, 176, 224–227

Beattie, Ann, *Snow*, 232, 265–267

"Beowulf," 387

Betrayal, Scene Five (Pinter), 336, 367–373

Bishop, Elizabeth, "One Art," 424, 429, 441, 445

Bissinger, H. G., *Friday Night Lights*, 157–158

Blue Highways (Moon), 126–129

Bowen, Elizabeth, *The Little Girls*, 110–114, 232

Brecht, Bertolt, *The Caucasian Chalk Circle, Section III*, 472, 500–502

Brinsley, Richard, *Course of Lectures on Elocution*, 529

Browning, Robert, "My Last Duchess," 382, 424, 442, 453–455

Burgh, James, *The Art of Speaking*, 530

Burns, Ken, 487

C

Cameron, Peter, *Homework*, 30, 33–34, 57, 68–73

"Canterbury Tales" (Chaucer), 386

Carroll, Lewis, "Jabberwocky," 109–110

Carver, Raymond, *Popular Mechanics*, 176, 232, 272–273

Chamberlain, William B., *Principles of Vocal Expression*, 533

Chaucer, Geoffrey, "Canterbury Tales," 386

Chekhov, Anton, *The Three Sisters*, 294–299, 336

Chopin, Kate, *The Story of an Hour*, 30, 34, 42, 44–46, 58, 133, 231, 250

Christmas Memory (Capote), 64–65

Ciardi, John, "Most Like an Arch This Marriage," 382, 384, 394, 418–419

"Cinderella" (Sexton), 3, 14, 457–460

"Cinderella's Story" (van Duyn), 3, 14, 460–463

Clark, Solomon H., *Interpretation of the Printed Page*, 533

Cleage, Pearl, *Flyin' West*, 327–331

Clifton, Lucille, "Affirmative Action," 162–163

Coben, Harlan, *The Key to My Father*, 275–280

Confess, Early and Often (Smiley), 106–109

Course of Lectures on Elocution (Brinsley), 529

Cruz, Victor Hernandez, "Today Is a Day of Great Joy," 424, 429, 463–464

Cummings, E. E., "Spring is like a perhaps hand," 382, 410

Curry, Samuel Silas, *The Province of Expression*, 531

Cyrano de Bergerac (Rostand), 86, 97–98

D

Dann, John C., *The Revolution Remembered*, 176, 203–205

Death and the King's Horseman (Soyinka), 373–377

de Saint-Exupéry, Antoine, *Wind, Sand, and Stars*, 176

"Desert Places" (Frost), 62

Devotions, XVII (Donne), 176

Dickens, Charles, *A Tale of Two Cities*, 134, 141, 532

Dickey, James, "Hospital Window," 416–418

Dickinson, Emily, 380, "I Felt a Funeral," 3, 17–18, 22–23, 30, 42–43, 49–50; *To Austin Dickinson*, 219–221

Didion, Joan, *The Seacoast of Despair*, 176, 190, 207–210

Dixon, Melvin, "Heartbeats," 424, 450–451, 525

Döhl, Reinhard, "Apfel," 472, 488, 505

Donne, John, *Devotions, XVII*, 176

"Do Not Go Gentle into That Good Night" (Thomas), 422, 424, 429, 446–447

Doty, Mark, "Tiara," 525

"Dover Beach" (Arnold), 114

"Dreaming" (McBroom), 30, 33, 66–67, 381, 386

Dulce (Sherman), 3, 16, 18–20, 23–25, 29, 33–34, 133

E

Elements of Elocution (Walker), 529

Eliot, T. S., "Journey of the Magi," 424, 436, 447–448

Emerson, Charles Wesley, *Evolution of Expression*, 532

"English Prose Style" (Read), 174

Evans, Bergen, *The Natural History of Nonsense*, 176

Everything We Had (Santoli), 176, 194, 205–207

Evolution of Expression (Emerson), 532

F

Fatal Interview (Millay), 389, 424, 457

Fifth of July (Wilson), 311–313, 336, 520

"Finishing the Hat" (Sondheim), 30, 33, 360–361, 382, 391, 424

Finnegans Wake (Joyce), 230

Fires in the Mirror (Smith), 176, 195, 307, 313–320, 336, 340

"First Grade" (Stafford), 419, 520

Flanner, Janet, "Letter from Paris," 525

Flying Finish (Hayes), 134, 152–154

Flyin' West (Cleage), 327–331

Foer, Jonathan Safran, *A Very Rigid Search*, 100, 104–106

"Forsythia" (Solt), 472, 488, 504

"40-Love" (McGough), 472, 488, 503

Freneau, Philip, "The Wild Honeysuckle," 86, 96

Friday Night Lights (Bissinger), 157–158

Frost, Robert, "Desert Places," 62; "The Death of the Hired Man," 386; "Wild Grapes," 382, 392, 407–410, 424, 427

G

Gilbert, Joanne, "Upon Learning That a Junior High School Acquaintance Has Been Nominated for an Academy Award," 30, 37, 74–75, 382, 393

Gill, Brendan, *Here at The New Yorker*, 524–525

Gilliatt, Penelope, *Sunday Bloody Sunday*, 472, 489, 514–517

Giovanni, Nikki, "Nikki-Rosa," 394, 411–412, 520

Girl (Kincaid), 86, 101, 134, 161–162, 176

Glück, Louise, "The Magi," 448–449

Goldsmith, Oliver, *She Stoops to Conquer*, 323–326, 336

"Greenleaf" (O'Connor), 232, 244

Gulliver's Travels (Swift), 176

H

Hales, Corrine, "Power," 404–406, 520

Hammond, Mary Stewart, "Saving Memory," 382, 388, 413–414, 520

Handke, Peter, *Offending the Audience*, 28

Harry Potter and the Sorcerer's Stone (Rowling), 78–81

Hayes, Bill, *Flying Finish*, 134, 152–154

Heaney, Seamus, "Mid-Term Break," 382, 388, 414–415

"Heartbeats" (Dixon), 424, 450–451, 525

Hellman, Lillian, *Pentimento*, 176, 183–184

Henry IV, Part I (Shakespeare), 176, 182

Here at The New Yorker (Gill), 524–525

Her Story (Madgett), 118–119

Hoffman, William, *As Is*, 525

Homer, *Odyssey*, 232, 234

Homework (Cameron), 30, 33–34, 57, 68–73

Hongo, Garrett Kaoru, "Who Among You Knows the Essence of Garlic?", 424, 428, 451–453

Hopkins, Gerard Manley, "The Starlight Night," 62; "The Windhover," 382, 389, 398–399, 402, 406

"Horses Make a Landscape Look More Beautiful" (Walker), 424, 429, 464–465

"Hospital Window, The" (Dickey), 416–418

Howes, Barbara, "On Sleeping Together," 415–416

"How to Watch Your Brother Die" (Lassell), 30, 42, 75–77, 231, 236, 525

Hoyt, Helen, "The Sense of Death," 3, 17, 20–22

Hughes, Langston, "The Negro Speaks of Rivers," 165–166

I

"I Felt a Funeral" (Dickinson), 3, 17–18, 22–23, 42–43, 49–50

"I Hear America Singing" (Whitman), 86, 96

I Know Why the Caged Bird Sings (Angelou), 101, 211–213, 232

Interpretation of the Printed Page (Clark), 533

J

"Jabberwocky" (Carroll), 109–110, 526

Jacob's Chicken (Macourek), 232, 273–275, 526

James, Henry, *The Spoils of Poynton*, 176

Jarheads (Swofford), 168–169, 194

Joans, Ted, *The .38* (Joans), 134

"Journey of the Magi" (Eliot), 424, 436, 447–448

Joyce, James, *Finnegans Wake,* 230
Joy Luck Club (Tan), 200–203, 520
Julius Caesar (Shakespeare), 85, 94
June Recital (Welty), 176, 198–99

K
Keats, John, "Sonnet," 62; "The Eve of St. Agnes," 386; "To Autumn," 382, 395–398, 401–402
KEEP OUT! (A Boy's Bedroom) (Barry), 176, 224–227
Kincaid, Jamaica, *Girl,* 86, 101, 134, 161–162, 176
Koestenbaum, Phyllis, *Admission of Failure,* 171
Kramer, Larry, *The Normal Heart,* 525
Kunitz, Stanley, "Open the Gates," 424, 428, 433–434, 438
Kushner, Tony, *Angels in America,* 525

L
Larkin, Philip, "Talking in Bed," 416, 424, 438
Lassell, Michael, "How to Watch Your Brother Die," 30, 42, 75–77, 231, 236, 525
"Leap Before You Look" (Auden), 2
Leavitt, David, *The Lost Language of Cranes,* 232, 269–272
"Letter from Paris" (Flanner), 525
Look Homeward, Angel (Wolfe), 142
Losing Battles (Welty), 232, 239
Lux, Thomas, "The Voice You Hear When You Read Silently," 129–130

M
Macbeth (Shakespeare), 393
MacDonald, Cynthia, "The Kilgore Rangerette Whose Life Was Ruined," 455–456, 520
Macourek, Milos, *Jacob's Chicken,* 232, 273–275, 526
Madgett, Naomi Long, *Her Story,* 118–119
Malamud, Bernard, *The Prison,* 232, 254–259, 472, 489
Mason, John, *An Essay on Elocution or Pronunciation,* 530
Matthews, Washington, "The Night Chant," 126

Matthews, William, "A Night at the Opera," 103
McBroom, Amanda, "Dreaming," 30, 33, 66–67, 381, 386
McGough, Roger, "40-Love," 472, 488, 503
"Mid-Term Break" (Heaney), 382, 388, 414–415
Millay, Edna St. Vincent, "Sonnet XXX," 389, 424, 457
Milton, John, "Paradise Lost," 387
Minot, Susan, "The Toast," 388, 389, 407
Miss Lonelyhearts (West), 472, 479–485
Monette, Paul, *Afterlife,* 525
Moon, William Least Heat, *Blue Highways,* 126–129
Morrison, Toni, *Sula,* 232, 267–269
"Most Like an Arch This Marriage" (Ciardi), 382, 394, 418–419
"My Last Duchess" (Browning), 382, 424, 442, 453–455

N
Natural Drills in Expression (Phillips), 534
Navajo ceremonial chants, 126
"New Words" (Yeston), 29, 34, 37–38, 381, 391, 520
New York Times, 522–524
"Nikki-Rosa" (Giovanni), 394, 411–412, 520

O
O'Connor, Flannery, "Greenleaf," 232, 244
Odyssey (Homer), 232, 234
Oedipus the King (Sophocles), 506–510
Offending the Audience (Handke), 28
"Old Lady's Winter Words" (Roethke), 134, 166–167, 382, 402
Olds, Sharon, "The Race," 134, 163–165, 382, 394
"Omeros" (Wolcott), 387
"One Art" (Bishop), 424, 429, 441, 445
"On Sleeping Together" (Howes), 415–416
"Open the Gates" (Kunitz), 424, 428, 433–434, 438

Oral Interpretation of Literature in American Colleges and Universities (Robb), 534
Othello (Shakespeare), 320–323, 336, 347
Ovid, "Story of Baucis and Philemon," 382, 390, 496–499

P
"Paradise Lost" (Milton), 387
Pentimento (Hellman), 176, 183–184
Phillips, Arthur Edward, *Natural Drills in Expression,* 534
Phillips, Wendell, 532
Pinter, Harold, *Betrayal, Scene Five,* 336, 367–373
Pope, Alexander, "The Rape of the Lock," 387
Popular Mechanics (Carver), 176, 232, 272–273
Pound, Ezra, 334
"Power" (Hales), 404–406, 520
"Preface to a Twenty Volume Suicide Note" (Baraka), 419–420
Principles of Vocal Expression (Chamberlain), 533
Proust, Marcel, *Within a Budding Grove,* 84

Q
Quite Early One Morning (Thomas), 232, 247

R
Ray, David, *Unforgiven,* 472, 510–513
Read, Herbert, "English Prose Style," 174
"Ringing the Bells" (Sexton), 30, 34, 65–66
Robb, Mary Margaret, *Oral Interpretation of Literature in American Colleges and Universities,* 534
Robertson, Robin, "After the Overdose," 513–514
Roethke, Theodore, "Old Lady's Winter Words," 134, 166–167, 382, 402; "The Waking," 424, 429, 445–446
Romeo and Juliet (Shakespeare), 336, 365–367
Rostand, Edmond, *Cyrano de Bergerac,* 86, 97–98

AUTHOR AND SELECTION INDEX

Roth, Philip, *The Conversion of the Jews*, 280–285

Rowling, J. K., *Harry Potter and the Sorcerer's Stone*, 78–81

Rush, James, *The Philosophy of the Human Voice*, 530

S

Santoli, Al, *Everything We Had*, 176, 194, 205–207

"Saving Memory" (Hammond), 382, 388, 413–414, 520

Schmitt, Gladys, *The Godforgotten*, 176

Seth, Vikram, "The Golden Gate," 386

Sexton, Anne, "Cinderella," 3, 14, 30, 34, 65–66, 457–460

Shakespeare, William, *As You Like It*, 170; *Henry IV, Part I*, 176, 182; *Julius Caesar*, 85, 94; *Macbeth*, 393; *Othello*, 320–323, 336, 347; *Romeo and Juliet*, 336, 365–367; *The Merchant of Venice*, 85, 95

Shepard, Sam, *The Curse of the Starving Class*, 336, 362–364

Sherman, Deborah, *Dulce*, 3, 16, 18–20, 23–25, 29, 33–34, 133

She Stoops to Conquer (Goldsmith), 323–326, 336

Smiley, Jane, *Confess, Early and Often*, 106–109

Smith, Anna Deavere, *Fires in the Mirror*, 176, 195, 307, 313–320, 336, 340

Snow (Beattie), 232, 265–267

Solt, Mary Ellen, "Forsythia," 472, 488, 504

Sondheim, Stephen, "Finishing the Hat," 30, 33, 360–361, 382, 391, 424

"Song of Myself" (Whitman), 470

"Sonnet" (Keats), 62

"Sonnet XXX" (Millay), 389, 424, 457

Sontag, Susan, "The Way We Live Now," 525

Sophocles, *Oedipus the King*, 506–510

Soyinka, Wole, *Death and the King's Horseman*, 373–377

"Spring is like a perhaps hand" (Cummings), 382, 410

Stafford, William, "First Grade," 419, 520

Stevens, Wallace, "The House Was Quiet and the World Was Calm," 411

"Still Life" (Ackerman), 134, 160

"Story of Baucis and Philemon" (Ovid), 382, 390, 496–499

Sula (Morrison), 232, 267–269

Sunday Bloody Sunday (Gilliatt), 472, 489, 514–517

Swenson, Mary, "To Make a Play," 288

Swift, Jonathan, *Gulliver's Travels*, 176

Swofford, Anthony, *Jarheads*, 168–169, 194

T

"Talking in Bed" (Larkin), 416, 424, 438

Tan, Amy, *Joy Luck Club*, 176, 200–203, 520

Tennyson, Alfred, Lord, "Ulysses," 154–156, 382, 390, 424, 438

Terkel, Studs, *Terry Pickens*, 176, 221–224

Terry Pickens (Terkel), 176, 221–224

"The Aeneid," 387

The Art of Interpretative Speech (Woolbert and Nelson), 533

The Art of Speaking (Burgh), 530

The Caucasian Chalk Circle, Section III (Brecht), 472, 500–502

The Common Reader (Woolf), 176, 185

The Conversion of the Jews (Roth), 280–285

The Curse of the Starving Class (Shepard), 336, 362–364

"The Death of the Hired Man" (Frost), 386

"The Eve of St. Agnes" (Keats), 386

The Godforgotten (Schmitt), 176

"The Golden Gate" (Seth), 386

The Golden World (Wolfe), 134, 142

"The House Was Quiet and the World Was Calm" (Stevens), 411

The Irreversible Decline of Eddie Socket (Weir), 525

The Key to My Father (Coben), 275–280

"The Kilgore Rangerette Whose Life Was Ruined" (MacDonald), 455–456, 520

The Lesson (Bambara), 86, 100, 119–125, 232, 520

The Little Girls (Bowen), 110–114, 232

The Lost Language of Cranes (Leavitt), 232, 269–272

"The Magi" (Glück), 448–449

The Makeup Artist (Tierney), 176

The Merchant of Venice (Shakespeare), 85, 95

The Metamorphoses (Ovid), 382, 390, 496–499

The Natural History of Nonsense (Evans), 176

"The Negro Speaks of Rivers" (Hughes), 165–166

The New Yorker, 524–525

"The Night Chant" (Matthews), 126

The Normal Heart (Kramer), 525

The Philosophy of the Human Voice (Rush), 530

The Prison (Malamud), 232, 254–259, 472, 489

The Province of Expression (Curry), 531

"The Race" (Olds), 134, 163–165, 382, 394

"The Rape of the Lock" (Pope), 387

The Revolution Remembered (Dann), 176, 203–205

The Seacoast of Despair (Didion), 176, 190, 207–210

"The Second Coming" (Yeats), 151–152

"The Sense of Death" (Hoyt), 3, 17, 20–22

The Spoils of Poynton (James), 176

"The Starlight Night" (Hopkins), 62

The Story of an Hour (Chopin), 30, 34, 42, 44–46, 58, 133, 231, 250

The .38 (Joans), 134, 159–160

The Three Sisters (Chekhov), 294–299, 336

"The Toast" (Minot), 388, 389, 407

The Types of the Folktale (Aarne and Stith), 196

The Voice, 532

"The Voice You Hear When You Read Silently" (Lux), 129–130

"The Waking" (Roethke), 424, 429, 445–446

"The Way We Live Now" (Sontag), 525

"The Wild Honeysuckle" (Freneau), 86, 96

"The Windhover" (Hopkins), 382, 389, 398–399, 402, 406

Thomas, Dylan, "Do Not Go Gentle into That Good Night," 422, 424, 429, 446–447
Thomas, Dylan, *Quite Early One Morning*, 232, 247
Thompson, Stith, 196
"Tiara" (Doty), 525
Tierney, Dana, *The Makeup Artist*, 176
To Austin Dickinson (Dickinson), 219–221
"To Autumn" (Keats), 382, 395–398, 401–402
"Today Is a Day of Great Joy" (Cruz), 424, 429, 463–464
"To Make a Play" (Swenson), 288
Tortillot, Jane Gould, *Women's Diaries of the Westward Journey*, 176, 191, 213–217

U

"Ulysses" (Tennyson), 154–156, 382, 390, 424, 438
Unforgiven (Ray), 472, 510–513
Updike, John, *A&P*, 232, 234, 259–265
"Upon Learning That a Junior High School Acquaintance Has Been Nominated for an Academy Award" (Gilbert), 30, 37, 74–75, 382, 393

V

van Duyn, Mona, "Cinderella's Story," 3, 14, 460–463

W

Walker, Alice, "Horses Make a Landscape Look More Beautiful," 424, 429, 464–465
Walker, John, *Elements of Elocution*, 529
Weir, John, *The Irreversible Decline of Eddie Socket*, 525
Welty, Eudora, *June Recital*, 176, 198–199; *Losing Battles*, 232, 239
Werner's Magazine, 532
West, Nathaniel, *Miss Lonelyhearts*, 472, 479–485
"When I Heard the Learn'd Astronomer" (Whitman), 30, 41, 61
Whitman, Walt, "I Hear America Singing," 86, 96; "Song of Myself," 470; "When I Heard the Learn'd Astronomer," 30, 41, 61
"Who Among You Knows the Essence of Garlic?" (Hongo), 424, 428, 451–453
Who's Afraid of Virginia Woolf? (Albee), 300–306, 336, 472, 475–476

"Wild Grapes" (Frost), 382, 392, 407–410, 424, 427
Wilson, Lanford, *Fifth of July*, 311–313, 336, 520
Wind, Sand, and Stars (de Saint-Exupéry), 176
Within a Budding Grove (Proust), 84
Wolcott, Derek, "Omeros," 387
Wolfe, Thomas, *The Golden World*, 134, 142
Women's Diaries of the Westward Journey (Tortillot), 176, 191, 213–217
Woolbert, Charles H., *The Art of Interpretative Speech*, 533
Woolf, Virginia, *The Common Reader*, 176, 185
Working (Terkel), 176, 221–224
Wright, James, "A Blessing," 449; "Autumn Begins in Martins Ferry, Ohio," 134, 156–157

Y

Yeats, William Butler, "Among School Children," 132; "The Second Coming," 151–152
Yeston, Maury, "New Words," 29, 34, 37–38, 381, 391, 520